Time Out

Barcelona Guide

Penguin Books

PENGUIN BOOKS

Published by the Penguin Group
Penguin Books Ltd., 27 Wright's Lane, London W8 5TZ, England
Penguin Books USA Inc., 375 Hudson Street, New York, New York 10014, USA
Penguin Books Australia Ltd., Ringwood, Victoria, Australia
Penguin Books Canada Ltd., 10 Alcorn Avenue, Toronto, Ontario, Canada M4V 3B2
Penguin Books (NZ) Ltd., 183–190 Wairau Road, Auckland 10, New Zealand

Penguin Books Ltd., Registered offices: Harmondsworth, Middlesex, England

First published 1996
10 9 8 7 6 5 4 3 2 1

Copyright © Time Out Group Ltd,. 1996
All rights reserved

Colour reprographics by Precise Litho, 34–35 Great Sutton Street, London EC1
Mono reprographics, printed and bound by William Clowes Ltd, Beccles, Suffolk NR34 9QE

Edited and designed by
Time Out Magazine Limited
Universal House
251 Tottenham Court Road
London W1P OAB
Tel: 0171 813 3000
Fax: 0171 813 6001
http://www.timeout.co.uk
E-mail: net@timeout.co.uk

Editorial
Managing Editor Peter Fiennes
Editor Nick Rider
Copy Editors Cath Phillips, Merran White
Researcher Laia Oliver

Design
Art Director Warren Beeby
Art Editor John Oakey
Designers Paul Tansley, Mandy Martin
Picture Editor Catherine Hardcastle

Advertising
Group Advertisement Director Lesley Gill
Sales Director Mark Phillips
Advertisement Sales (London) Alison Gray
Advertisement Sales (Barcelona) Joan Font

Administration
Publisher Tony Elliott
Managing Director Mike Hardwick
Financial Director Kevin Ellis
Marketing Director Gillian Auld
Production Manager Mark Lamond

Features in this guide were written and researched by:
Introduction Nick Rider. **Essential Information** Nick Rider. **Getting Around** Nick Rider. **Accommodation** Anne Heverin. **Barcelona by Season** Matthew Tree. **Sightseeing** Richard Schweid, Nick Rider. **Architecture** Jane Opher, David Howel Evans. **History** Marcy Rudo; *Barcelona red & black* Nick Rider. **Barcelona Today** Conor Murphy. **D-i-Y BCN** Quim Monzó (translated by Matthew Tree). **Barcelona by Area** EM Butterfield; *The creation of the Barri Gòtic* Marcy Rudo. **Restaurants** Matthew Tree. **Cafés & Bars** Suzanne Wales. **Nightlife** William Truini. **Shopping** Anne Heverin. **Services** Vic Aicken. **Art Galleries** Jeffrey Swartz. **Museums** Jeffrey Swartz. **Media** Richard Schweid; *Wonderful world of chat* Nick Rider. **Dance** Richard Schweid. **Film** Richard Schweid. **Music: Classical & Opera** Sarah Lewis. **Music: Rock, Roots & Jazz** Suzanne Wales. **Sport & Fitness** Vic Aicken. **Theatre** Gerald Fannon. **Business** Lisa Gilbert. **Children** Mary Ellen Kerans. **Gay & Lesbian Barcelona** Steven Short, Heather Murray. **Students** Sarah Lewis. **Women's Barcelona** Helen Rowson, Heather Murray. **Trips Out of Town** Matthew Tree. **Survival** Nick Rider. **Further Reading** Nick Rider.

The Editors, writers and publisher would like to thank the following for their invaluable assistance: Maria Luisa Albacar, Mònica Terol and Mònica Colomer of Turisme de Barcelona; Josep Ejarque of the Catalonia Tourist Board; Ricard Blanco, Transports Municipals de Barcelona; Charo Canal, Col.lecció Thyssen-Bornemisza; Inés del Maschio, Museu Nacional d'Art de Catalunya; Angels Pomarol, IMBE, Ajuntament de Barcelona; Marta Muntada, OBC; Iberia Airlines; Hotel Gaudí; Lisa Berger; Elena Blanco; Ignasi Camprodon; Anna-Rosa Cisquella; Isidre Estévez; Josep Maria Flotats; Jordi González; Daniel Martínez; Antonio Narváez; Yolanda Ocón; Pep Planas; Nick Rawlinson; Salvador Rigol; Glòria Sallent; Tom Seix Salvat; Matthew Tree; Neus València; Ethel Rimmer.

Maps by Mapworld. Map on page 290 courtesy of Transports Municipals de Barcelona.

Photography by Arnhel de Serra except for:
pages 1, 35 **Turisme de Barcelona**; page 32 **Ramon Pomarol/IMBE**; pages 45, 47, 54 **Barry J. Holmes**; pages 64, 67, 71, 72, 73, 75, 76 **Arxiu Històric de la Ciutat, Barcelona**; page 74 **Bridgeman Art Library**; page 78 **Hulton Getty**; page 178 **Col.lecció Thyssen-Bornemisza**; pages 180, 181 **Museo Nacional d'Art de Catalunya**; page 187 **Lanònima Imperial Cia de Dansa**; page 194 **Eddie Saeta SA**; pages 243, 248, 253, 257 **Robert Harding Picture Library**; pages 246, 250 **Trip**; page 252 **Spanish Tourist Board**; pictures on pages 174, 191, 199, 201, 212, 213, 215, 244 were supplied by the featured companies/establishments.

Contents

About the Guide

This is the first edition of the *Time Out Barcelona Guide*, one in a series of city guides that includes London, Amsterdam, Paris, New York, Berlin, Prague, Rome, Budapest, Madrid, San Francisco and Brussels. It gives you a complete picture of Barcelona – the endless streetlife of the Rambla, eccentric bars and design bars, food and theatre, smart shops and flea markets, and nightlife from back-street cabarets to the last thing in clubs. We cover in full the masterpieces of Gaudi, the Medieval city and all the many projects undertaken in the 1990s that have become just as much a part of Barcelona's modern identity.

The *Barcelona Guide* is more than a book solely for tourists and casual visitors. We point you towards obscure events and hidden-away shops and venues, explain what goes on at the city's rumbustious *festes* and say how to tackle the bureaucracy if you're thinking of staying here for a while. Written and researched by people who live in the city, this *Guide* offers an informed, personal view: Barcelona as the insiders know it.

CHECKED & CORRECT

All information was checked and correct at press time, but please bear in mind that, as in most cities, things can change, places can close, and owners and managers can change their arrangements at any time. In addition, in Barcelona smaller shops and bars may not keep to precise opening hours, and close earlier or later according to the level of trade. Similarly, the dates of arts festivals and similar events can fluctuate from year to year. Before going anywhere out of your way it's as well to phone first to check times, dates and other details.

LANGUAGE

Barcelona is a bilingual city; however, the majority language is Catalan, and it is the sole language used on street signs, and most maps. We have followed Catalan usage in all addresses and in most sections of this Guide. In many areas, though, Catalan and Spanish are mixed constantly, and the Spanish equivalents can in some cases be very different. Where both versions of a word or phrase can be useful we give both, always with the Catalan first, as in *demà/mañana* (tomorrow). *See also chapter* **Essential Information**.

RIGHT TO REPLY

It should be stressed that the information we give is impartial. No organisation or enterprise has been included in this guide because its owner or manager has advertised in our publications. Their impartiality is one reason why our guides are so successful and well respected. We hope you will enjoy the *Time Out Barcelona Guide* and that it helps you make the most of your stay. But, if you disagree with any of our assessments, let us know; your comments are always welcome. You'll find a reader's reply card with this book.

Prices

The prices listed should be used as guidelines. Fluctuating exchange rates and inflation can cause prices, in shops and restaurants especially, to change rapidly. If prices and services vary wildly in any case from those we've quoted, ask if there's a good reason. If there's not, go elsewhere and, then, please let us know. We try to give the best and most up-to-date advice, so always want to hear if you've been overcharged or badly treated.

Telephones

Telephone numbers in Spain are sometimes changed at relatively short notice for technical or other reasons. In Barcelona, in particular, many numbers beginning with a *2* have been changed to begin with a *4*. If you call a number beginning *2* and can't get through, try again substituting a *4* as first digit. Other changes are less predictable.

Credit Cards

The following abbreviations have been used for credit cards throughout this guide: **AmEx** – American Express; **DC** – Diners Club; **EC** – Eurocard; **JCB** – Japanese credit bank card; **MC** – Mastercard/Access; **TC** – travellers' cheques in any currency; **$TC**, **£TC** – travellers' cheques in US dollars or pounds sterling; **V** – Visa.

> There is an on-line version of this Guide, plus weekly events listings for Barcelona and other international cities, at:
> *http://www.timeout.co.uk*

Introduction

Joan Maragall, the great Catalan poet of the turn of the century, called Barcelona *'la gran encisera'*, 'the great enchantress'. He also wrote, in a rare lapse of manners, *'Barcelona, m'has ben fotut'*, roughly meaning 'Barcelona, you've really fucked me over'. But then, love affairs are like that.

Today, as the poet's grandson, Mayor Pasqual, inaugurates an award-winning bridge here, a gleaming high-tech museum there, all of them surrounded all the while by soaring rhetoric about the role of cities in the new millenium, the new Europe and so on and so forth, it's also sometimes hard to know what to make of Barcelona. Is it really the city over which design professors drool and where planners go on pilgrimages, the model city of the 1990s, the perfect demonstration of the rational application of resources, creativity and daring to solve problems everyone else just puts up with? Or is it just a mini-series starlet addicted to nips and tucks, with a shiny grin moulded in silicone on its face? Could be a bit of both.

An essential particularity of Barcelona is that it has the awareness and ambitions of a capital city of a state without actually being one. Catalans in general, too, are an existential nation: they have far more of an identity and distinctive, creative culture than, say, a fatuous entity like Luxembourg, but many people do not know they exist, which sometimes leads them to a niggling doubt whether they do themselves. Hence the emphasis given in official circles to sometimes-bumptious self-promotion, as if the place was a marketing plan as much as a country, which can bemuse or irritate outsiders. However, even if you find this sort of thing off-putting, you should be aware that this tension and Catalans' self-awareness is also a principal – though not the only – root of the special combination of energy and imagination that is one of the greatest features of the city of Barcelona, one of the reasons so many people come here, and why it is not Luxembourg. This is a city whose inhabitants have felt inspired to create great buildings, great painting, great writing. And most cities in the Anglo-Saxon world would do well if they had one-tenth of Barcelona's civic pride.

Barcelona, as has often been said, is a city that has had to reinvent itself several times. It's also full of quirks and contradictions that, beneath the surface gloss of whichever design project is currently capturing the world's attention, are essential to its fascination. It's a city whose citizens have erected a cult around their own seriousness and

ability to get down to *feina*, work, and yet is also intensely theatrical, laid out like a giant stage between its two great mountains of Montjuïc and Tibidabo, with a dancing fountain at the foot of one and a funfair on top of the other that on summer nights shines out like a giant bauble.

It's an ideally-sized city, small enough to walk around but dense enough to be enormously varied. As well as citizens who like to cultivate their own solidity it has also attracted a long stream of eccentrics from home and abroad, and like any great city is a place of encounters. In the bars of Barcelona, before and since some of them acquired high-design window frames, you might run into someone who said he'd been in Bolivia with Che Guevara, and pulled up his trouser-leg to show you the bullet-holes to prove it, or someone who said he was the Spanish yo-yo champion and had been taken to Japan by a Japanese yo-yo conglomerate, and pulled out the air ticket to prove it, or a woman who worked in a girly bar in the *Barrio Chino* but lived in a flat entirely papered with photos of trees.

For a quick introduction to Barcelona, arrive on 23 June, Midsummer Night's Eve or Sant Joan. Wander through the Medieval thoroughfare of the Carrer Montcada, take in some art and some of the world's most enjoyable bars, and then take in the infinite human fauna on the Rambla. Have a dinner that must include lashings of *all i oli* made with fresh garlic. At night, as the city explodes with fireworks and detonations from end to end and the fountain dances vigorously, join in one of the raves and revels that will be going on, or better still wander through several. Then, as dawn spreads along the streets, wander up through the pines onto Montjuïc to watch the first sun catch the spires of the Medieval city, the glass blocks of the Olympic village, and the flanks of Collserola. It rarely fails to impress. *Nick Rider.*

Essential Information

The basics – changing money, getting informed, avoiding hassles and choosing your language.

Before Arriving

Visas

Visas are not needed by European Union nationals, or by US, Canadian and New Zealand citizens for stays of up to three months. British and all non-EU citizens must have full passports. Citizens of Australia, South Africa and several other countries need visas to enter Spain. They can be obtained from Spanish Consulates in other European countries as well as in the home country.

EU citizens intending to work, study or live permanently in Spain should register with the police within 15 days of arrival to obtain a Residence Card (*carta de residencia*). Non-EU nationals who wish to work or study in Spain for more than three months officially should have the relevant visa before entering the country. For more on living and working in Spain and the bureaucracy involved *see chapter* **Survival**.

Customs

As in other European Union countries EU citizens do not have to declare goods imported into Spain for their personal use, if tax has been paid on them in the country of origin. Customs can still question whether large amounts of any item really are for your own use or are intended for sale, and random checks are also made for drugs. Quantities accepted as being for personal use are:
- up to 800 cigarettes, 400 small cigars, 200 cigars or 1kg of loose tobacco
- 10 litres of spirits (over 22% alcohol), 90 litres of wine (under 22% alcohol) and 110 litres of beer.

For non-EU citizens the following limits apply:
- 200 cigarettes **or** 100 small cigars **or** 50 cigars **or** 250 grams (8.82 ounces) of tobacco
- 1 litre of spirits (over 22% alcohol) and 2 litres of wine or beer (under 22% alcohol)
- 50 grams (1.76 ounces) of perfume

There are no restrictions on the import of cameras, watches or electrical goods, within reasonable limits, and visitors can also carry up to 1 million pesetas in cash. Non-EU residents can also reclaim the Value-Added Tax (IVA) paid on some large purchases when they leave Spain. For details, *see chapter* **Shopping**.

Insurance

EU nationals are entitled to make use of the Spanish state health service, provided they have an E111 form, which in Britain is available from post offices, Health Centres and Social Security offices. This will cover you for emergencies, but using an E111 will involve confronting some of the complexities of Spanish health bureaucracy, and for short-term visitors it is generally simpler to take out private travel insurance before departure, which will also normally cover you for stolen or lost cash or valuables, as well as medical costs. Some non-EU countries have reciprocal health-care agreements with Spain, but, again, for most travellers it will be more convenient to have private travel insurance. For more on health services *see chapter* **Survival: Health**.

Money

The Spanish currency is the *peseta*, the usual abbreviation of which is *ptas* (*pesseta*, *ptes*, in Catalan). There are coins for 1, 5, 10, 25, 50, 100, 200 and 500 pesetas. Confusingly, there are several different kinds of 1, 5, 25, 50 and 200ptas coin, including a range of commemorative editions. A 5-peseta coin is called a *duro*. Notes begin with the green 1,000ptas, and continue through 2,000 (red), 5,000 (brown) and 10,000ptas (blue).

Banks & Foreign Exchange

Banks and savings banks readily accept travellers' cheques (you must have your passport with you), but are less keen to take personal cheques with the Eurocheque guarantee card. Commission rates vary greatly, and it's worth shopping around before changing money; also, given the rates charged by Spanish banks, the least expensive way to obtain money is often through a cash machine with a credit card (*see below*) rather than with travellers' cheques, despite the fee charged by card companies for cash withdrawals. It is always quicker and more trouble-free to change money at major bank offices rather than at local branches.

If you need to have money sent to you, the most convenient method is through American Express or Western Union.

Bank Hours

Banks are normally open 8.30am-2pm, Mon-Fri, and from 1 October to 31 May most branches also open 8.30am-1pm Sat. Hours vary a little between different banks, and some open slightly earlier or later, while several branches stay open until 4-4.30pm one day a week, usually Thursday. Savings Banks (*Caixes d'Estalvis/Cajas de Ahorros*), which offer the same exchange facilities as banks, open 8.30am-2pm Mon-Fri, and from Oct-May also 4.30-7.45pm Thur. They never open on Saturday. Banks and *caixes* are closed on public holidays.

Out-of-Hours Services

Outside normal hours there are bank exchange offices open at the **airport** (Terminals A and B, open 7.15am-10.45pm daily), **Barcelona-Sants** station (open 8am-10pm daily) and the **Estació de França** (open 8.15-10.30am, 7-9pm, Mon-Fri; 8-10.30am, 6-9.30pm, Sat, Sun, holidays). There are also several private bureau de change (*cambio*) offices, mostly in the Rambla, the city centre and Sants station. Some offices in the Rambla are open until midnight, or till 3am during the July-Sept summer season. *Cambio* offices do not charge commission but their exchange rates are notably less favourable than bank rates. At the airport, Sants and outside several banks around or near Plaça Catalunya there are also automatic cash exchange machines which accept notes in major currencies, so long as they are in good condition.

Credit Cards

Major credit and charge cards are very widely accepted in hotels, shops, restaurants and many other services (including Metro ticket machines, and pay-and-display parking machines in the street). You can also use major cards such as MasterCard and Visa to withdraw cash from most bank automatic cash machines, which provide instructions in different languages at the push of a button. Exchange rates and handling fees are often more favourable than with cash or travellers' cheque transactions. Banks also advance cash against a credit card, but prefer you to withdraw the money directly from a cashpoint.
Card Emergencies If you lose a credit or charge card, phone one of the emergency numbers listed below. All lines have English-speaking staff and are open 24 hours daily.
American Express *(card emergencies 91 572 03 03/travellers' cheques freephone 900 99 44 26).*
Diner's Club *(302 14 28/24-hour helpline 91 547 40 00).*
MasterCard/Access/Eurocard/Visa *(315 25 12).*

American Express

Passeig de Gràcia 101 (217 00 70). Metro Diagonal/bus all routes to Passeig de Gràcia. **Open** 9.30am-6pm Mon-Fri; 10am-noon Sat.

Bureau de change, poste restante, card replacement and a travellers' cheque refund service, as well as a cash machine for withdrawals with AmEx cards. Money can be transferred from American Express offices anywhere in the world within 24 hours. Charges must be paid by the sender.

Western Union Money Transfer

Loterías Manuel Martín *La Rambla 41 (412 70 41). Metro Liceu/bus 14, 18, 38, 59, 91.* **Open** 10am-11pm daily.
Western Union offers the quickest, if not the cheapest, means of having money sent from abroad, which should arrive within an hour. Commission is paid by the sender on a sliding scale. This is the most central of the four agents in Barcelona.
Branches: Mail Boxes *C/Pau Claris 89 (454 69 83).* **Open** 9.30am-2pm, 4-8pm Mon-Fri, 9.30-2pm Sat; also Avda Meridiana 316. **Open** 9.30am-1.30pm, 4.30-8.30pm Mon-Sat; **Viajes Itiner** Avda Diagonal 329 (457 25 99). **Open** 9am-2pm, 5-8pm Mon-Fri.

Tourist Information

Both the City council (the *Ajuntament*), and the Catalan regional government (the *Generalitat*) maintain tourist information offices, and the city operates an efficient information service for local citizens that's also useful to visitors. The best information on what's on in music, theatre, sports and so on at any time will be in local papers and listings magazines (*see chapter* **Media**).

Centre d'Informació Plaça Catalunya

Plaça Catalunya. Metro Catalunya/bus all routes to Plaça Catalunya. **Open** 9am-9pm daily.
The main office of the City tourist board *Turisme de Barcelona* is right in the city centre and has a full information service (with good maps), a money exchange desk and a souvenir and book shop. There is also a hotel booking service, which is not available at the smaller offices. City tourist offices do not answer telephone enquiries.
Branch Offices: Barcelona-Sants station *Metro Sants-Estació/bus 27, 43, 44, 109.* **Open** *Oct-May* 8am-8pm Mon-Fri; 8am-2pm Sat, Sun, holidays; *June-Sept* 8am-8pm daily. Closed Christmas & New Year.
Palau de Congressos (Trade Fair office) *Avda Reina Maria Cristina. Metro Espanya/bus all routes to Plaça d'Espanya.* **Open** *during trade fairs only* 10am-8pm daily.

Temporary Offices & 'Red Jackets'

Information Booths are located at: *La Rambla, near Metro Drassanes; Passeig de Gràcia, corner of C/Aragó; Sagrada Familia.* **Open** *April-24 June* 10am-8pm Mon-Sat; *25 June-Sept* 9am-9pm daily.
From Easter to the end of summer *Turisme de Barcelona* also opens up three temporary booths in prominent locations, with the usual maps and information but no accommodation service. From 24 June-end Sept there is also an information office in the **Ajuntament** (City Hall) in Plaça Sant Jaume, open 8.30am-2.30pm Mon-Fri. Lastly, during the same June-Sept period young information officers called 'Red Jackets' in bright red uniforms with big I-for-Information badges roam the Barri Gòtic and other central areas ready to field any question in a heroic variety of languages, 9am-9pm daily.

Oficines d'Informació Turística

Gran Via de les Corts Catalanes 658 (301 74 43). Metro Passeig de Gràcia, Urquinaona/bus all routes to Urquinaona, Pau Claris. **Open** 9am-7pm Mon-Fri; 9am-2pm Sat. Closed public holidays.

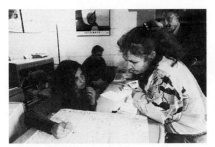

Getting on track at **la Virreina.**

This and the offices at the airport are operated by the Catalan government and do not have quite as complete coverage of Barcelona itself as the City offices – although they still have city maps and other essentials – but have a wider range of information on other parts of Catalonia, and the rest of Spain. **Branches: Airport Terminal A** (478 47 04). **Open** 9.30am-3pm Mon-Sat; **Airport Terminal B** (478 05 65). **Open** 9.30am-8pm Mon-Sat (*mid-June-mid-Sept* 9.30am-8.30pm), 9.30am-3pm Sun, holidays

Centre d'Informació de la Virreina

Palau de la Virreina, La Rambla 99 (301 41 98). Metro Liceu/bus 14, 18, 38, 59, 91. **Open** *Oct-May* 11am-2pm, 5-8pm, *June-Sept* 10am-8pm, Mon-Sat.
Not mainly for visitors but the information office of the City cultural department, with ample information on exhibitions, concerts, theatres and so on and a free monthly listings leaflet *Barcelona: Informació Cultural*. Also the best place to buy tickets for events in the **Grec** summer festival (*see chapter* **Barcelona by Season**), and productions at the **Mercat de les Flors** (*see chapter* **Theatre**) during the rest of the year. In the same building is the **Llibreria de la Virreina** bookshop, with a comprehensive selection of books on Barcelona, some in English-language editions.

010 Phoneline

Open 8am-10pm Mon-Sat.
A City-run information line that's again primarily directed at local citizens, but will answer queries of any and every kind, from public transport details and health service enquiries to concert timings. Calls are accepted in French and English as well as Catalan and Spanish, although you will probably have to wait for an English-speaking operator.

Language

Barcelona is a bilingual city. Around 60 per cent of the population speak Catalan, it is more and more the principal language of public life, and all streets are signposted (and maps printed) exclusively in the language. Other fields are much less straightforward, for there are plenty of Spanish-speakers here too, and Catalan and Castilian Spanish are continually intermixed, with a spectrum of usage between the two. With regard to foreigners, some Catalans will speak to you from the outset in their own language, but in practice most still expect to deal with visitors in Spanish. Any recognition on your part of the Catalan language, though, if only in a few phrases, will always be appreciated, and is an effective ice-breaker. If you

are thinking of staying here for any length of time, it is strongly advisable to learn Catalan, as otherwise you will only be ghettoising yourself.

We have followed current Catalan and local usage in addresses in this Guide (*see* **About the Guide**), but be prepared to meet Castilian-Spanish equivalents that can be substantially different. With other terms, where both forms are equally useful we have given both, always with the Catalan first. For useful phrases in both languages, *see* **Vocabularies**. For more on Barcelona's linguistic soup, *see chapter* **Barcelona Today**.

The Seasons

Barcelona is a coastal city and its weather, while rarely extreme, can often produce surprises, with cold snaps in mid-spring and occasional heavy rains at the height of summer. In general, though, the seasonal pattern is pretty clearly marked.
Spring *Average temperature 15°C (59°F).* The March weather is unpredictable, with bright, sunny days still interspersed with rain or chilly winds, but warm air and clear skies become more consistent from early April. Easter Week is when locals finally cast off their winter coats: café tables rapidly appear around the streets, and May is one of the most enjoyable of all times to be in Barcelona, warm enough to sit out through the night but never oppressive.
Summer *Average temperature 24°C (75°F).* In early summer the weather is delicious, and Barcelona's street life is at its most vibrant. The real heat hits from late-July to mid-August; more of a problem than the actual temperature is the humidity, which can make things very heavy and muggy. In August many locals still escape the city altogether: for the visitor this has the compensation that there is much less traffic, and the part-empty city has an atmosphere all of its own. Many businesses are closed, but recently fewer people have abandoned Barcelona for the whole month, and for those who are still around there are several events such as the *Festa Major* in **Gràcia**. Amid the heat, there may be brief, intense but refreshing thunderstorms.
Autumn *Average temperature 16°C (61°F).* In September the weather is again beautiful, warm and fresh, and ideal for the beginning of the football season and a range of arts events leading up to Barcelona's biggest festival, **La Mercè**. In October the summer visibly 'breaks', sometimes with torrential rain. Pavement tables are mostly taken in by November, although some remain all year.
Winter *Average temperature 11°C (53°F).* It can snow in Barcelona, but the winter weather is more likely to be damp, with snatches of crisp sunshine. One of the busiest times of the year for business and the arts, as well as a series of festivities around **Christmas** and **Carnaval**.

Street Crime

In the 1980s Barcelona won a certain ill-fame as a black spot for petty theft and street crime. Today, following a string of police and social measures, the incidence of street crime is very much less, but it is still advisable to be cautious in certain areas. Violent muggings are now rare, but bag-snatching and pickpocketing still happen, above all in and around the lower Rambla and the Plaça Reial.

Many of these robberies, though, are aimed very directly at the unwary, and could be avoided with

a few simple precautions. Stated bluntly, these suggestions may suggest a certain level of paranoia, but they are really just a question of common sense and need not interfere with your enjoyment of your stay once taken on board:

• When sitting in a café, especially outside, **never** leave your bag on the floor, on the back of a chair, or on a chair where you cannot see it clearly. If in doubt, keep it on your lap.

• Wear shoulder bags pulled round to the front, not at your back. Keep the bag closed and keep a hand on top of it.

• Avoid pulling out large-denomination notes to pay for things, especially in the street late at night; try not to get stuck with large notes when changing money.

• Be aware that street thieves often work in pairs or groups: one may ask you the time, get you into a conversation about football or whatever to distract you while his friend hovers behind you and then grabs your bag. This is often done very crudely so it's not hard to recognise. Ignore any sudden requests to shake your hand, as they will try and pull you toward them. Another variant is the 'chocolate' trick: someone stops you, says you have something on your back and offers to help clean it off. While you are rearranging your things, someone else makes off with your bag. Sometimes they actually will spray chocolate sauce, ketchup or something similar on your back. Either way it is best to ignore them, keep walking and if necessary clean it up later.

For information on what to do if you are a victim of crime or lose your passport, *see chapter* **Survival: Police & Security**.

Reference Points

Electricity

The standard current in Spain is today 220v. A few old buildings still have 125v circuits, though, and it's advisable to check before using electrical equipment in hotels, particularly in older, cheaper places. Plugs are all of the two-round-pin type. The 220v current works fine with British-bought 240v products, with a plug adaptor. They are available locally at **El Corte Inglés** (*see chapter* **Shopping**). With US 110v appliances you will also need a current transformer.

Holidays

On public holidays (*festes/fiestas*) virtually all shops, banks and offices, and many bars and restaurants, are closed. Public transport runs a Sunday service, except on Christmas Day and New Year's Day, and some museums are also open, if for shorter-than-usual hours. Efforts have been made to reduce the impact of public holidays, but when a holiday falls on a Tuesday or Thursday some people still take the intervening day before or after the weekend off as well, in a long weekend called a *pont/puente* (bridge). Few offices close for the whole of Easter Week, but activity diminishes greatly from midday on the Wednesday. For a calendar of the city's festivals, *see chapter* **Barcelona by Season**. The usual official holidays, with some variations each year, include:
New Year's Day (Cap d'Any) 1 January; **Three Kings (Dia de Reis)** 6 January; **Good Friday (Divendres Sant)**; **Easter Monday (Dilluns de Pasqua Florida)**; **May (Labour) Day (Festa del Treball)** 1 May; **Whit Monday (Dilluns de Pasqua Granada)**; **Saint John/Midsummer's Day (Sant Joan)** 24 June; **The Assumption (L'Assumpció)** 15 August; **Catalan National Day (Diada Nacional de Catalunya)** 11 September; **Our Lady of Mercy (La Mercè)** 24 September; **Discovery of America (Día de la Hispanitat)** 12 October; **All Saints' Day (Tots Sants)** 1 November; **Constitution Day (Día de la Constitució)** 6 December; **Immaculate Conception (La Immaculada)** 8 December; **Christmas (Nadal)** 25 December; **Boxing Day (Sant Esteve)** 26 December.

Opening Times

Most shops open 9-10am to 1-1.30pm, 4.30 to 8-9pm, Mon-Sat, although many may stay closed on Saturday afternoons. Markets open earlier, at 7-8am, and except for the central Boqueria market generally close by 3pm. Major stores, shopping centres and a growing number of shops in the city centre are open all day 10am-9pm, Mon-Sat. These larger stores are also allowed to open on a few Sundays and holidays during the year, and every Sunday in the month up to Christmas. The only shops always open on Sundays are the *pastisseries/pastelerías* (cake shops). For other shops open outside normal hours, *see chapter* **Shopping: Out of Hours**.

In business, a growing number of offices work on an 'intensive' schedule of 9am-6pm, Mon-Fri, and stagger their holidays, but many restaurants and shops still close up completely for all or part of August. Most (but not all) museums are open at weekends but close for one day each week, usually Monday or Tuesday. They do not close in summer. For restaurant hours, *see chapter* **Restaurants**.

Queuing

Catalans like other Spaniards have a highly developed queuing culture. In small shops and at market stalls people may not stand in line, but they are generally well aware of when it is their turn. Common practice is to ask when you arrive, to no one in particular, *Qui es l'últim/la última?* ('Who's last?'); see who nods back at you, and follow after them. Say *jo* ('me') to the next person who asks the same question.

Smoking

It's unusual to find non-smoking areas in restaurants or bars – especially cheaper ones –, although smoking bans in cinemas, theatres and on trains are generally respected. Smoking is also banned throughout the Metro and FGC, but many people take this to mean on the trains only, and not the station platforms. For places to buy tobacco, *see chapter* **Shopping**.

Tabacs/Tabacos (Tobacco Shops)

The tobacco shop, also known as an *estanc/estanco* and identified by a brown-and-yellow sign, is a very important Spanish institution. First and foremost, as the name suggests, they supply cigarettes and every other kind of tobacco to the majority of the local population still devoted to the weed, but they are also the main places to buy postage stamps, and the only shops where you can obtain the official money vouchers (*papel de estado*) demanded by Spanish state bureaucracy in all kinds of minor procedures. They also have sweets, postcards and a range of other less usual items.

Time

Local time is one hour ahead of British time, except at the beginning and end of summer. Clocks are changed earlier than in the UK, so that for a while the two usually coincide. For most of the year, though, when it's 6pm in Barcelona, it's 5pm in London, and midday in New York.

Tipping

There are no fixed rules, nor any expectation of a set 10% or more, and many locals tip very little. It is common to leave around 5% for the waiter in a restaurant, up to and rarely ever over 500ptas, and people may also leave something in a bar, maybe part or all of the small change, according to how much they have had and the level of service. It's also usual to tip hotel porters, toilet attendants, in places that have them, and the ushers in the more traditional cinemas. In taxis, the usual tip is around 5%, but more is given for longer journeys, or if the driver has helped with luggage.

Water

Barcelona tap water is perfectly safe and drinkable, but has a rather minerally taste. By preference, most people drink bottled water, and if you ask for water in a restaurant you will automatically be served this unless you specifically request otherwise.

Vocabularies: Spanish...

Note that in Catalonia, still more than in the rest of Spain, this language is generally referred to as *castellano* (Castilian), rather than *español*. Like other Latin languages, it has different familiar and polite forms of the second person (you). Many young people now use the familiar *tú* form most of the time. For foreigners, though, it's always advisable to use the more polite *usted* with people you do not know, and certainly with anyone over forty. In the phrases listed here all verbs are given in the *usted* form. *See also chapter* **Restaurants** for help in making your way through Menus.

Spanish Pronunciation

c, before an i or an e, and **z** are like th in thin
c in all other cases is as in **c**at
g, before an i or an e, and **j** are pronounced with a guttural h-sound that doesn't exist in English – like **ch** in Scottish lo**ch**, but much harder
g in all other cases is as in **g**et
h at the beginning of a word is normally silent
ll is pronounced almost like a **y**
ñ is like **ny** in ca**ny**on
A single **r** at the beginning of a word and **rr** elsewhere are heavily rolled

Useful Expressions

hello *hola*
hello (when answering the phone) *hola, diga*
good morning, good day *buenos días;* **good afternoon, good evening** *buenas tardes;* **good evening** (after dark), **good night** *buenas noches*
goodbye/see you later *adios/hasta luego*
please *por favor*
thank you (very much) *(muchas) gracias*
you're welcome *de nada*
do you speak English? *¿habla inglés?*
I don't speak Spanish *no hablo castellano*
I don't understand *no entiendo*
can you say that to me in Catalan, please? *¿me lo puede decir en Catalán, por favor?*
speak more slowly, please *hable más despacio, por favor*
wait a moment *espere un momento*
Sir/Mr *señor (sr.);* **Madam/Mrs** *señora (sra.);* **Miss** *señorita (srta.)*
excuse me/sorry *perdón*
excuse me please *oiga* (the standard way to attract someone's attention, politely; literally 'hear me')
OK/fine/(or to a waiter) **that's enough** *vale*
how much is it *¿cuánto es?*
where is... *¿dónde está...?*
why? *¿porqué?;* **when?** *¿cuándo?;* **who?** *¿quién?;* **what?** *¿qué?;* **where?** *¿dónde?;* **how?** *¿cómo?*
is/are there any...? *¿hay...?*
very *muy;* **and** *y;* **or** *o;* **with** *con;* **without** *sin*
open *abierto;* **closed** *cerrado*
what time does it open/close? *¿a qué hora abre/cierra?*
I would like... *quiero...* (literally, 'I want')
how many would you like? *¿cuántos quiere?*
good *bueno/a;* **bad** *malo/a;* **well/badly** *bien/mal;* **small** *pequeño/a;* **big** *gran, grande;* **expensive** *caro/a;* **cheap** *barato/a;* **hot** (food, drink) *caliente;* **cold** *frío/a.*
more/less *más/menos;* **more or less** *más o menos*
do you have any change? *¿tiene cambio?*
price *precio;* **free** *gratis;* **discount** *descuento*

bank *banco;* **alquilar** to rent; **(en) alquiler** (for) *rent, rental;* **post office** *correos;* **stamp** *sello;* **postcard** *postal;* **toilet** *los servicios*

Getting Around

airport *aeropuerto;* **railway station** *estación de ferrocarril/estación de RENFE* (Spanish railways)
Metro station *estación de Metro*
entrance *entrada;* **exit** *salida*
car *coche;* **bus** *autobus;* **train** *tren*
a ticket *un billete;* **return** *de ida y vuelta;* **bus stop** *parada de autobus;* **the next stop** *la próxima parada*
excuse me, do you know the way to...? *¿oiga, señor/señora/etc, sabe cómo llegar a...?*
left *izquierda;* **right** *derecha;* **here** *aquí;* **there** *allí;* **straight on** *recto;* **to the end of the street** *al final de la calle;* **as far as** *hasta;* **towards** *hacia*
near *cerca;* **far** *lejos*

Accommodation

do you have a double/single room for tonight/one week? *¿tiene una habitación doble/para una persona para esta noche/una semana?*
we have a reservation *tenemos reserva*
an inside/outside room *una habitación interior/exterior*
with/without bathroom *con/sin baño;* **shower** *ducha;* **double bed** *cama de matrimonio;* **with twin beds** *con dos camas*
breakfast included *desayuno incluido*
lift *ascensor;* **air-conditioning** *aire acondicionado;* **swimming pool** *piscina*

Time

morning *la mañana;* **midday** *mediodía;* **afternoon/evening** *la tarde;* **night** *la noche;* **late night** (roughly 1-6am) *la madrugada*
now *ahora;* **later** *más tarde*
yesterday *ayer;* **today** *hoy;* **tomorrow** *mañana;* **tomorrow morning** *mañana por la mañana*
at what time...? *¿a qué hora...?*
in an hour *en una hora;* **the bus will take 2 hours (to get there)** *el autobus tardará dos horas (en llegar)* **at 2** *a las dos;* **at 8pm** *las ocho de la tarde;* **at 1.30** *a la una y media;* **at 5.15** *a las cinco y cuarto;* **at 22.30** *a veintidos treinta*

Numbers

0 *zero;* **1** *un, uno,una;* **2** *dos;* **3** *tres;* **4** *cuatro;* **5** *cinco;* **6** *seis;* **7** *siete;* **8** *ocho;* **9** *nueve;* **10** *diez;* **11** *once;* **12** *doce;* **13** *trece;* **14** *catorce;* **15** *quince;* **16** *dieciséis;* **17** *diecisiete;* **18** *dieciocho;* **19** *diecinueve;* **20** *veinte;* **21** *veintiuno;* **22** *veintidos;* **30** *treinta;* **40** *cuarenta;* **50** *cincuenta;* **60** *sesenta;* **70** *setenta;* **80** *ochenta;* **90** *noventa;* **100** *cien;* **1,000** *mil;* **1,000,000** *un millón*

Days, Months & Seasons

Monday *lunes;* **Tuesday** *martes;* **Wednesday** *miércoles;* **Thursday** *jueves;* **Friday** *viernes;* **Saturday** *sábado;* **Sunday** *domingo*
January *enero;* **February** *febrero;* **March** *marzo;* **April** *abril;* **May** *mayo;* **June** *junio;* **July** *julio;* **August** *agosto;* **September** *septiembre;* **October** *octubre;* **November** *noviembre;* **December** *diciembre*
Spring *primavera;* **Summer** *verano;* **Autumn/Fall** *otoño;* **Winter** *invierno*

...and Catalan

Catalan is a Latin language that is readily comprehensible with a little knowledge of French or Spanish grammar. The extent to which Catalans expect visitors to speak it varies greatly (*see* **Language**), but it is certainly useful to have some recognition of the language to be able to read signs, understand what's said to you and, especially, pronounce place names correctly. Catalan phonetics are significantly different from those of Spanish, with a wider range of vowels and soft consonants. Catalans often use the familiar (*tu*) rather than the polite (*vosté*) forms of the second person very freely, but, again, for convenience verbs are given below in the polite form. For food and Menu terminology, *see* chapter **Restaurants**.

Catalan pronunciation: some basics

In Catalan, as in French but unlike in Spanish, words are run together, so *si us plau* (please) is more like *sees-plow*.

à at the end of a word (as in Francesc Macià) is an open
a rather like when you say **ah**, but very clipped
ç, and **c** before an i or an e are like a soft **s**, as in **sit**
c in all other cases is as in **cat**
unstressed **e**, in a plural such as cerveses (beers), or Jaume I, is a weak sound like centre or comfortable
g before an i or an e and **j** are pronounced like the **s** in pleasure; **tg** and **tj** are similar to the **dg** in badge
g after an i at the end of a word (Passeig, Puig) is a hard **ch** sound, as in watch
g in all other cases is as in **get**
h at the beginning of a word is normally silent
ll is like the **lli** in million
l.l the 'split double-l', the most unusual feature of Catalan spelling, actually refers to a barely audible difference, a slightly stronger stress on a single **l** sound
o at the end of a word is like the **u** sound in flu
ó at the end of a word is similar to the **o** in tomato
ò is like the **o** in hot
A single **r** beginning a word and **rr** are heavily rolled
r at the end of a word strengthens the previous vowel but is almost silent, so *carrer* (street) sounds like *carr-ay*
s at the beginning and end of words and **ss** between vowels are soft, as in **sit**
A single **s** between two vowels is a **z** sound, as in lazy
x is like the **sh** in shoe, except in the combination **tx**, which is like the **tch** in watch
y after an **n** at the end of a word or in **nys** is not a vowel but adds a nasal stress and a y-sound to the n

Things everyone here knows

please *si us plau;* **very good/great/OK** *molt bé*
hello *hola;* **goodbye** *adéu*
nothing at all/zilch *res de res* (said with both s silent)
price *preu;* **free** *gratuit/de franc;* **change, exchange** *canvi;* **llogar** *to rent;* **(de) lloguer** (for) *rent, rental*
entrance *entrada;* **exit** *sortida*
open *obert;* **closed** *tancat*
up with Barcelona FC *Visca el Barça* (corny as hell, but every foreign footballer who comes here has to say it, and it rarely fails to get you a cheap laugh)

More Expressions

hello (when answering the phone) *hola, digui'm*
good morning, good day *bon dia;* **good afternoon, good evening** *bona tarda;* **good night** *bona nit*
see you later *fins després*
thank you (very much) *(moltes) gràcies*
you're welcome *de res*

Do you speak English? *parla anglés?*
I'm sorry, I don't speak Catalan *ho sento, no parlo català;* **I don't understand** *no entenc*
Can you say it to me in Spanish, please? *m'ho pot dir en castellà, si us plau?*
how do you say that in Catalan? *com se diu això en Català?;* **what's your name?** *com se diu?*
Sir/Mr *senyor (sr.);* **Madam/Mrs** *senyora (sra.);* **Miss** *senyoreta (srta.);* **excuse me/sorry** *perdoni/disculpi*
excuse me please *escolti* (literally 'listen to me')
OK/fine *val/d'acord;* **enough** *prou*
how much is it *quant és?*
why? *perqué?;* **when?** *quan?;* **who?** *qui?;* **what?** *qué?;* **where?** *on?;* **how?** *com?*
is/are there any...? *hi ha...?/n'hi ha de...?*
very *molt;* **and** *i;* **or** *o;* **with** *amb;* **without** *sense*
I would like... *vull...* (literally, 'I want')
how many would you like? *quants en vol?*
good *bo/bona;* **bad** *dolent/a;* **well/badly** *bé/malament;* **small** *petit/a;* **big** *gran;* **expensive** *car/a;* **cheap** *barat/a;* **hot** (food, drink) *calent/a;* **cold** *fred/a*
more *més;* **less** *menys;* **more or less** *més o menys*
toilet *el bany/els serveis/el lavabo*

Getting Around

a ticket *un bitllet;* **return** *d'anada i tornada;* **card expired** (on Metro cards) *títol esgotat*
left *esquerra;* **right** *dreta;* **here** *aquí;* **there** *allí;* **straight on** *recte;* **at the** (street) **corner** *a la cantonada;* **as far as** *fins a;* **towards** *cap a;* **near** *a prop;* **far** *lluny*

Time

In Catalan quarter- and half-hours can be referred to as quarters of the next hour (so, 1.30 is two quarters of 2)
morning *el matí;* **midday** *migdia;* **afternoon** *la tarda;* **evening** *el vespre;* **night** *la nit;* **late night** (roughly 1-6am) *la matinada*
now *ara;* **later** *més tard;* **yesterday** *ahir;* **today** *avui;* **tomorrow** *demà;* **tomorrow morning** *demà pel matí*
at what time...? *a quina hora...?*
in an hour *en una hora;* **the bus will take 2 hours (to get there)** *l'autobús trigarà dues hores (en arribar)* **at 2** *a les dues;* **at 8pm** *les vuit del vespre;* **at 1.30** *a dos quarts de dues/la una i mitja;* **at 5.15** *a un quart de sis/a las cinc i quart;* **at 22.30** *a vint-i-dos-trenta*

Numbers

0 *zero;* **1** *u, un,una;* **2** *dos, dues;* **3** *tres;* **4** *quatre;* **5** *cinc;* **6** *sis;* **7** *set;* **8** *vuit;* **9** *nou;* **10** *deu;* **11** *onze;* **12** *dotze;* **13** *tretze;* **14** *catorze;* **15** *quinze;* **16** *setze;* **17** *disset;* **18** *divuit;* **19** *dinou;* **20** *vint;* **21** *vint-i-u;* **22** *vint-i-dos, vint-i-dues;* **30** *trenta;* **40** *quaranta;* **50** *cinquanta;* **60** *seixanta;* **70** *setanta;* **80** *vuitanta;* **90** *noranta;* **100** *cent;* **1,000** *mil;* **1,000,000** *un milló*

Days, Months & Seasons

Monday *dilluns;* **Tuesday** *dimarts;* **Wednesday** *dimecres;* **Thursday** *dijous;* **Friday** *divendres;* **Saturday** *dissabte;* **Sunday** *diumenge*
January *gener;* **February** *febrer;* **March** *març;* **April** *abril;* **May** *maig;* **June** *juny;* **July** *juliol;* **August** *agost;* **September** *setembre;* **October** *octobre;* **November** *novembre;* **December** *desembre*
Spring *primavera;* **Summer** *estiu;* **Autumn/Fall** *tardor;* **Winter** *hivern*

Getting Around

Barcelona is a walkers' city, but to speed you along there's also public transport that's cheap, efficient and reliable.

Barcelona's distinctive geometry, visible at a glance on any map, makes it easy for newcomers to get their bearings. At its core, running back from the port between Avinguda Paral.lel and the Ciutadella park, is a tight, clearly demarcated lozenge-shaped mass of narrow streets that is old Barcelona, until the last century the entire city, divided through the middle by the great avenue of La Rambla (*Ramblas* in Castilian Spanish).

At the top of the Rambla is the Plaça Catalunya, the city's centre and main hub of the Metro and bus networks. It also marks the beginning of the regular grid of the *Eixample*, the nineteenth-century 'Extension' to the city. Beyond that, there are districts that were once separate villages, such as Sants or Gràcia, the new beach and port areas, and Barcelona's two great mountains, Montjuïc and the Serra de Collserola, with Tibidabo at its centre, towering over the whole city. Equally evident are the great arterial avenues that run for miles through the Eixample, the Gran Via de les Corts Catalanes (better known simply as *Gran Via*), Avinguda Diagonal and Passeig de Gràcia. One oddity of the city is that, because it fits so neatly between Tibidabo and the sea, it is virtually never drawn on maps with north at the top. Due north is actually along the line of Avinguda Meridiana, as the name suggests.

Beneath its hills, Barcelona is a compact city that invites you to explore it on foot. Within the old city, everywhere is in easy walking distance of the main squares. For longer journeys, a fast, safe Metro (underground/subway) system and buses enable you to get to most parts of the city in half an hour or less, during daytime. Metro stations also make handy reference points, and it's useful to familiarise yourself with the Metro map (nearest Metro stations are indicated with most entries in this Guide). Barcelona also offers several special rides, such as the Tibidabo tram; for these, and organised tours, *see chapter* **Sightseeing**.

Despite the efficiency of public transport and the easy availability of taxis, locals show a near-perverse determination to try to get about their city by car, but in general this is the slowest and least convenient way of travelling within Barcelona. More handy in the city traffic is a bike or moped, although a car is naturally much more useful for trips out to the coast and the countryside. For bike and car hire and travel agencies, *see chapter* **Services**. For information on parking and

all aspects of driving, *see chapter* **Survival: Driving in Barcelona**. For transport services outside Barcelona, including Balearic Islands ferries, *see chapter* **Trips Out of Town**. For details of tourist offices, *see chapter* **Essential Information**. **Please note that all transport and taxi fares are subject to revision each January**.

Arriving & Leaving

By Air

Barcelona's **Aeroport del Prat**, rebuilt for 1992, is 12km (7½ miles) south of the city, in Prat de Llobregat. Foreign airlines use Terminal A; Iberia international flights mainly use Terminal B. In both there are tourist information desks, cash machines from which you can obtain Spanish currency with a credit card, and exchange offices (open 7.30am-10.45pm daily). From the airport there are three ways of getting into town: bus, train or taxi. For airport information, call **478 50 00**.

Aerobús

This special bus service is usually the most convenient means of getting to central Barcelona, if also the most expensive after taxis. Buses pick up outside all the terminals, and run to Plaça Catalunya with stops at Plaça d'Espanya and Gran Via. Buses to the airport also pick up at Sants railway station. Buses leave the airport every 15 minutes, 6am-11pm, Mon-Fri (5.30am-10.15pm, in the opposite direction). At weekends and on public holidays, buses run 6am-10.50pm (6am-10.20pm, from Plaça Catalunya). The trip takes about 30 minutes; a single ticket costs 450ptas. Two local buses also run between the airport and Plaça d'Espanya, the **EA** and **EN** (6.20am-2.40am daily; 7am-3.15am, from Plaça d'Espanya). The fare is only 130ptas but the journey can take over an hour.

Airport trains

Getting to the airport station involves a walk that can be laborious with luggage in tow. To find it, walk out of the Terminal buildings to the long bridge (with moving walkway) between Terminals A and B. All trains stop at four stations in Barcelona: Sants, Plaça Catalunya, Arc de Triomf and Clot-Aragó, all of which are also stops on the Metro system. Trains leave Prat at 13 and 43 minutes past each hour, 6.13am-10.43pm, and from Plaça Catalunya at 8 and 38 minutes past the hour, 6.08am-10.08pm, Mon-Fri. At weekends and on public holidays, timings vary slightly but there are still trains every half-hour. The journey takes 30 minutes (20 minutes to/from Sants), and the current fare is 300ptas (345ptas, Sat, Sun, public holidays).

Taxis from the airport

The taxi fare to central Barcelona should be about 2,000ptas, including a 300ptas airport supplement, although fares are slightly higher after 10pm and at weekends (*see below* **Taxis**). There is a minimum charge for trips to/from the airport of 1,500ptas, and also a supplement for larger items of luggage placed in the car boot. It's advisable to ignore any cab drivers who approach you inside the airport; take only the next cab in line at the ranks outside each terminal.

British Airways

Passeig de Gràcia 85 (487 21 12). Metro Diagonal/bus all routes to Passeig de Gràcia. **Open** 9am-5pm Mon-Fri. **Credit** AmEx, DC, JCB, MC, V. *Airport office (379 44 68/baggage enquiries 379 26 12).* **Open** 7am-7pm daily.

Delta Airlines

Passeig de Gràcia 16, 5-B (412 43 33). Metro Catalunya/bus all routes to Plaça Catalunya. **Open** 9am-6pm Mon-Fri. **Credit** AmEx, DC, EC, MC, TC, V.

Iberia

Main sales office, Passeig de Gràcia 30-C/Diputació 258 (24-hour information 412 56 67/international reservations 412 47 48/domestic reservations 412 70 20). Metro Passeig de Gràcia/bus 7, 16, 17, 63. **Open** 9am-6pm Mon-Fri. **Credit** AmEx, DC, MC, TC, V.

TWA

C/Consell de Cent 360, 5° (215 81 88). Metro Passeig de Gràcia/bus 7, 16, 17, 63. **Open** 9am-5pm Mon-Fri. **Credit** AmEx, DC, JCB, MC, $TC, V. *Airport office (379 51 12).* **Open** 8am-2pm daily.

By Bus

Eurolines international coach services (information 490 40 00) from Britain and other European countries stop or terminate in Barcelona at the **Estació d'Autobusos Barcelona-Sants**, alongside Sants railway station and Sants-Estació Metro. **Linebus** international services and most long-distance coaches from other parts of Spain and the Catalan coast and countryside operate from the **Estació d'Autobusos Barcelona-Nord** at C/Alí Bei 80, next to Arc de Triomf station on Metro line 1 (general information 265 65 08; individual companies have their own phone lines). Some coaches stop at both. *See also chapter* **Trips Out of Town**.

By Train

Most Spanish state railways (RENFE) long-distance trains terminate at or pass through the giant **Barcelona-Sants** station. It's a little way from the centre, but has a Metro (Sants-Estació) at the junction of two lines. At Sants there are exchange facilities, a tourist office, a hotel booking office and other services. Some international services from France do not stop in Sants but terminate at the lavishly-restored 1920s **Estació de França**, near Ciutadella park and Barceloneta Metro. On many trains you can choose either station, and many also stop at the central **Passeig de Gràcia** station, which can be the handiest place to get off. *See also chapter* **Trips Out of Town: Getting Started**.

RENFE Information

General information (490 02 02). **Open** 7am-10pm daily. *International information & reservations (490 11 22).* **Open** 8am-8pm Mon-Fri.

Maps

Metro and central area street maps are included at the back of this guide. Tourist offices provide a reasonably detailed free street map, and the City tourist offices (but not the Generalitat office on Gran Via) also have a better map for 200ptas. Metro maps are available free at all Metro stations (ask for '*una Guia del Metro*'); these and free bus maps can also be obtained from the city transport information offices (*see below* **Public Transport**).

Public Transport

The Metro is generally the quickest, cheapest, most reliable and most convenient way of getting around the city, although there are certain 'holes' in the network – places without a well-located Metro station – notably around Plaça Francesc Macià, for which buses are more useful. Metro and local buses are run by the city transport authority (TMB), but one of the underground rail lines (from Plaça Catalunya with branches to Avda Tibidabo and Sarrià/Reina Elisenda) is not part of the Metro, but is run by Catalan government railways, the *Ferrocarrils de la Generalitat de Catalunya* or FGC, which also runs trains out into the surrounding countryside. However, the systems connect.

For information on any aspect of local transport call the city information line (**010**), which has English-speaking operators. For lost property offices and left luggage, *see chapter* **Survival**.

Central TMB Information Office

Main vestibule, Metro Universitat (318 70 74). **Open** 8am-7pm Mon-Fri. **Other offices**: Ronda Sant Pau 43; Vestibule, Metro Sagrada Familia; Vestibule, Metro Sants-Estació. Information, maps and a full range of tickets.

FGC Information

Vestibule, Plaça Catalunya FGC station (205 15 15). **Open** Sept-July 7am-9pm, Aug 8am-8pm, Mon-Fri.

Fares & Tickets: *Targetes*

The basic fare for a single ticket on the Metro, FGC and buses is the same, currently 130ptas, and each trip costs the same

A STROLL THROUGH THE CULTURE OF CATALONIA

Museu Nacional d'Art de Catalunya

Parc de Montjuïc. Tel. 93/423 71 99
Tuesday to Saturday 10.00 a.m. to 7.00 p.m.• Thursay 10.00 a.m. to 9.00 p.m.
• Sundays and bank holidays 10.00 a.m. to 2.30 p.m.

Museu d'Història de Catalunya

Palau de mar. Pç. Pau Vila,1. Tel. 93/225 47 00
Tuesday to Thursday 10.00 a.m. to 7.00 p.m.• Friday and Saturday 10.00 a.m. to 8.00 p.m.
• Sundays and bank holidays 10.00 a.m. to 2.30 p.m.

Museu d'Art Contemporani de Barcelona

Pç. dels Àngels 1. Tel. 93/412 08 10
Tuesday to Friday, 12.00 a.m. to 8.00 p.m.• Saturday, 10.00 a.m. to 8.00 p.m.
• Sundays and bank holidays, 10.00 a.m. to 3.00 p.m.

no matter how far you travel. Unless you plan to make only a very few journeys, however, buying tickets singly will waste your money, and it's much better to buy one of the various kinds of multi-journey tickets or *targetes*. Some can also be shared between a group of people, so long as one unit is cancelled on the card for each person travelling.

Most kinds of *targeta* are valid for Metro and FGC, but note that, whereas you can change Metro lines on the same ticket, if you change onto the FGC (at Plaça Catalunya or Diagonal/Provença) you must pay twice. The outlets at which they can be bought also vary, and they cannot be bought on buses. T2 and T50/30 *targetes*, though, can be bought by credit card through *Servi-Caixa* machines in savings banks (*see chapter* **Services**). The *targetes* currently available are:

T1 Valid for 10 trips on buses, Metro and FGC. It costs 700ptas and is available from Metro/FGC stations, transport offices and over the counter at most savings bank (*Caixa d'Estalvis*) offices.
T2 Valid for 10 trips on Metro and FGC. Available from transport information offices and the ticket desks and automatic machines at Metro/FGC stations, for 680ptas.
T50/30 Gives 50 trips within any 30-day period on Metro and FGC. From transport offices and ticket desks and automatic machines at Metro/FGC stations, for 2,900ptas.
T-Mes Unlimited travel on all three systems for one month, for 4,750ptas. Note, though, that this does mean a calendar month, not 30 days from the date of purchase. With your first monthly card you must obtain an identity card (which requires a photograph), available only at the TMB and FGC offices. In succeeding months you can renew your card at any Metro station.
T-Dia Unlimited travel for one person on Metro, FGC and buses for one day, for 500ptas. Available from larger Metro/FGC stations and transport offices.
3 Dies Unlimited travel for one person on Metro and buses (but **not** the FGC) for three days, for 1,200ptas. Available from the same outlets as the T-Dia.
5 Dies The same, but giving five days travel for 1,800ptas, and again not valid on the FGC.

Metro & FGC

The five Metro lines are identified by a number and a different colour on maps and station signs. At interchanges, lines in a particular direction are indicated by the names of the stations at the end of the line, so you should know which they are when changing between lines. On the FGC, some of the suburban trains that use the line may not stop at every station. The Metro is still being expanded, and during 1997 line 2 (purple line) should be extended to meet line 1 (red line) at Clot.

Boarding the train

At Metro and FGC stations, with a single ticket or a *targeta* from one of the automatic machines, you insert the ticket into the machine at the platform gate, which cancels one unit for each trip, and will reject expired tickets. Tickets are not checked or collected at station exits. Trains run about every 5 minutes during weekdays, and every 7-9 minutes after 9pm and at weekends. The Metro gets very crowded during peak hours (7.30-9.30am, 6-8.30pm), but trains are rarely excessively full at other times.

Metro & FGC Hours

Mon-Thur 5am-11pm
Fri, Sat & days preceding public holidays 5am-1am
Sun 6am-midnight
Public holidays midweek 6am-11pm

Buses

City bus stops are easy to find, and a great many routes originate in or pass through the Plaça Catalunya, Plaça Universitat and/or Plaça Urquinaona. Because of the many one-way streets, especially in the Eixample, buses often do not follow exactly the same route in both directions, but run along parallel streets.

Taking the bus

Most routes run from about 5am-11pm daily (although some, such as the 64, continue until 1am), with buses about every 10-15 minutes on each route. Services are less frequent on Sundays, when a few routes do not operate. You board buses at the front, and get off through the doors at the middle and rear of the bus. Only single tickets can be bought on board. If you have a T1 *targeta*, insert it into the machine to the left of the doors as you board, which automatically clips off one unit. If you change buses you must pay again. With a one- or more-days unlimited travel card, just show it to the driver. On suburban services fares increase on a zone system outside the city limits, and tickets must be bought on board.

Useful routes

22 From Plaça Catalunya to Pedralbes via Passeig de Gràcia, C/Gran de Gràcia or the Via Augusta, the *Tramvia Blau* tram stop, Sarrià and the Pedralbes monastery.
24 From C/Manso, near the Paral.lel, to Carmel via Plaça Universitat, Plaça Catalunya, Passeig de Gràcia, C/Gran de Gràcia or the Via Augusta and the Parc Güell. The best way to get from the city centre to Gaudí's delicious park.
41 From the Vila Olímpica to Plaça Francesc Macià via the Ciutadella, Plaça Urquinaona, Plaça Catalunya, Plaça Universitat and C/Calàbria or C/Viladomat.
45 From Passeig Marítim, by the beach, to Horta via the Barceloneta, Via Laietana, Plaça Urquinaona, Passeig de Sant Joan, Hospital de Sant Pau and the Passeig Maragall.
64 From Barceloneta to Pedralbes via Pla del Palau, Colom, Avda Paral.lel, Ronda Sant Antoni, Plaça Universitat, C/Aribau or C/Muntaner, Sarrià and the Pedralbes monastery.
66 From Plaça Catalunya to Sarrià via Plaça Universitat, C/Aribau or C/Muntaner and Plaça Francesc Macià.

Night Buses

There are 14 *Nitbus* (night bus) routes, numbered N1-N14, which mostly operate between 10.30pm-4.30am nightly, with buses about every 30 minutes. All the N routes originate in or pass through Plaça Catalunya, and some run out into surrounding towns such as Badalona or Castelldefels. Note that standard *targetes* are **not** valid on night buses; instead, you must buy single tickets (145ptas) or the special 10-trip night bus *targeta* (900ptas), both available only on board.

Bus Turístic (Number 100)

Dates Easter-end Oct. **Frequency** *Mar-April, Oct* every 30 min, *May-Sept* every 15 min, 9am-7.40pm daily.
Tickets 1,300ptas per day; 1,800ptas for 2 days; 900ptas 4-12s; free under-4s. **No credit cards.**

The 'tourist bus' is a special service that runs on a circular route beginning in Plaça Catalunya and taking in all the main sights (including the Vila Olímpica and Parc Güell). The full trip takes about two hours, and with one ticket you can get on and off the bus as many times as you like during the same day. You cannot use standard *targetes* on the bus, but must buy tickets on board. All the buses are air-conditioned, adapted for wheelchairs and have guides on board. With the *Bus Turístic* ticket you also get discount vouchers for a wide range of attractions (such as Sagrada Familia, Tibidabo and Fundació Miró), which need not be used the same day.

TombBus

A special shoppers' bus service (the name means 'round trip', nothing to do with graveyards) that runs between Plaça Catalunya and Plaça Pius XII on the Diagonal, roughly 8am-9.30pm Mon-Fri, 9am-9.30pm Sat. Again, *targetes* are not valid on the bus, and single tickets cost 160ptas.

Local Trains

For trips into the suburbs and surrounding towns there are, as well as buses, regional rail lines run by both the FGC and RENFE. The FGC has two stations in Barcelona: **Plaça Catalunya** (the same as for the FGC line within the city), for trains to Sabadell, Terrassa and the small towns immediately beyond Tibidabo, and **Plaça d'Espanya**, for services towards Hospitalet and Montserrat. The centre of the RENFE local network (signposted *Rodalies/Cercanías* at mainline stations) is **Plaça Catalunya**, the main station for lines along the coast and toward the Pyrenees. Several towns are served by both systems. Fares vary according to zones. For more on rail services, *see chapter* **Trips Out of Town: Getting Started.**

Taxis

Barcelona's 11,000 black-and-yellow taxis are among the city's most distinctive symbols, and at most times easy to find. Fares are reasonable.

Taxis can be hailed on the street when they show a green light on the roof, and a sign saying *Lliure/Libre* ('Free') behind the windscreen. There are also taxi ranks at railway and bus stations, the main squares and at several other locations throughout the city. It's a good idea to know the name of the district you are heading for and maybe a local landmark as well as the street name. *See also above* **Arriving & Leaving.**

Fares

Current official fare rates and supplements are shown inside each cab. The minimum fare at time of writing is 285ptas, which is what the meter should register when you first set off. The basic tariff applies 6am-10pm, Mon-Fri; fares increase after the first 1.75km at a rate per kilometre, or on a time rate at slow speeds. At all other times (including mid-week public holidays) the additional rate is higher, although the initial charge remains the same. There are also supplements for each item of luggage larger than 55cm x 35cm

(100ptas), and for animals (125ptas). If you require a taxi to wait, you will be charged 2,100ptas per hour. Note, also, that taxi drivers are not officially required to carry more than 2,000ptas in change, and that very few accept credit cards.

Receipts & Complaints

To obtain a receipt, ask for *'un rebut, si us plau/un recibo, por favor'*. If you have a complaint of any kind about a taxi driver you must insist that the receipt is made out in full, with the time, beginning and end of the journey, details of the fare and the driver's signature. Make a note, too, of the license plate and the taxi number, shown inside and on the rear doors of the cab. Call transport information on *010* to explain your complaint to them, and follow their instructions.

Phone Cabs

All the companies listed below take phone bookings 24 hours daily. Only some operators will speak English, but if you are not at a specific address give the name of a street corner (ie *Provença/Muntaner*), or a street and a bar or restaurant, where you want to wait. You'll be asked your name. Phone cabs start the meter from the moment the call is answered.
Barnataxi *(357 77 55)*; **Fono-Taxi** *(300 11 00)*; **Ràdio Taxi** *(300 38 11)*; **Servi-Taxi** *(330 08 04)*; **Taxi Groc** *(490 22 22)*; **Taxi Miramar** *(433 10 20)*; **Taxi Mòbil** *(358 11 11)*; **Tele-Taxi** *(392 22 22)*.

Cycling

Riding a bike in Barcelona might seem foolhardy, but several cycle routes have been established in recent years, sometimes with special cycle lanes (*Carrils Bici*), particularly around the Ciutadella, the Port, along the Diagonal and from Sants to Montjuïc. *See also chapter* **Sports & Fitness** and, for cycle hire companies, *see chapter* **Services**.

Disabled Travellers

For information on transport facilities for disabled people, call the special phoneline **412 44 44**. For more on facilities in general, *see chapter* **Survival**.

Buses

All buses on the **Aerobús** service from the airport and the **Bus Turístic** are fully accessible to wheelchair users, with low-entry doors, wheelchair points and so on. In addition, similar, fully adapted buses alternate with standard buses on some regular bus routes, currently the **24, 33, 44, 47, 59, 72** and the night buses **N1, N2** and **N3**.

Metro & FGC

Banks of steps and a lack of lifts close off most Metro and FGC stations to wheelchair users, but all stations on line 2 (Paral.lel-Sagrada Família) and the Montjuïc Funicular (*see chapter* **Sightseeing**) have lifts and ramps to provide full access. It is planned to extend these facilities, but at present only some stations on line 1, and Provença and St Gervasi on the FGC, are fully accessible.

Taxis

All taxi drivers are officially required to transport wheelchairs (and guide dogs) for no extra charge, but their cars can be inconveniently small, and in practice the willingness of drivers to cooperate varies widely. Special minibus taxis adapted for wheelchairs can be ordered through **Barnataxi** on 357 77 55; say that you want a *Taxi Amic* when ordering. Fares are the same as for standard cabs, but there are currently only a few such taxis in Barcelona, so call well in advance to get a cab for a specific time.

Accommodation

Five-star glamour, refined elegance, old-world comfort, no-frills functionality or BYO sleeping bags: it's all here.

In looking at the hotel scene in Barcelona it's unavoidable to refer to the 1992 effect. The need for accommodation in the lead-in to the Olympics sparked off a frenetic burst of hotel building and renovation – nearly 30 new hotels have been built in the last decade, mostly in the three- to five-star brackets, and many more have been given a complete facelift. As a result there's now a glut of luxury options, and a wide choice of mid-range hotels with greatly expanded services; at the same time, though, the local authorities closed many of the cheapest *pensions* in the old city, deeming them too run down to be acceptable, and so it is now harder to find a really cheap hotel in Barcelona.

Some foreign (mostly northern) visitors think that Barcelona's post-92 accommodation lacks character, especially the new mid-range hotels with their uniformly abundant marble in reception areas and bathrooms, and abhorrence of fitted carpets. However, marble is cool and clean in a Mediterranean city, and these hotels do guarantee visitors well-equipped comfort at reasonable prices; also, in among the functional business hotels there is still a good selection of more individual places to stay.

In the last century Barcelona's first real hotels were all built along the Rambla, and a large number of hotels can still be found concentrated in the old city, also still the best area for cheaper accommodation. The other main hotel area is the Eixample, where there are several mid-range places and some good-value *hostals*. This is the best area to stay if you need easy vehicle access, preferably in a hotel with its own parking, as on-street parking is both risky and very inconvenient (*see chapter* **Survival: Driving in Barcelona**).

STARS, HOTELS, *HOSTALS* & PRICES

All accommodation in Catalonia is regulated by the regional government, the Generalitat. Formerly, accommodation in Spain included a bewildering mix of *fondas*, *residencias*, *pensions* and hotels. Today, there are officially only two categories, hotels (H) and *hostals* (HS), although many places continue to use the old names, which can be confusing. To be a hotel, star-rated one to five, a place must have bathrooms

The ultra-modern **Hotel Claris**. *See page 17.*

Downtown

Hotel Lloret

Las Ramblas - Pl. Catalunya

Barcelona

HOTEL LLORET located in La Rambla de Canaletes, is a strategic point for your pleasure or bussines travel, next to Plaza Catalunya, and a walk to the subway, close to the railway and just only twenty minutes from the airport. or by train by bus.

Rambla Canaletes, 125 • 08002 Barcelona Teléfonos 317 33 66 • Fax 301 92 83

52 rooms

telephone in rooms

meeting room

heating

breakfast

CREDIT CARD credit card

air conditioning in bedrooms

fire system

laundry

TV in rooms

FAX fax service

safebox

Economical prices • The Best relation Quality-Prices See information in accomodation section

Post-Olympic Palaces

The **Hotel Arts** and **Hotel Claris** are the most spectacular products of Barcelona's frenetic nineties' hotel-building boom. They're also both united by a focus on art and design: contemporary at the Arts, while the Claris takes a bolder tack, marrying ancient artefacts with some very modern design and technology.

Towering 44 storeys above the beach and the Port Olympic, a skyscraper designed by Skidmore, Owings and Merrill, the Arts went through a tortuous process of creation involving many recriminations and several writs as contruction companies pulled out or went bankrupt, and projected completion dates came and went. Although it was planned as part of the Olympic project, it was not until 1994 that owners Ritz-Carlton were able to open for regular business. The eventual result, though, is a quite lavish level of state-of-the-art, trans-continental luxury and service.

The Arts's high-tech metal-and-glass visage conceals a soothing and surprisingly warm interior. Fountains and waterfalls play beside the entrance, and palm-fringed gardens surround a distinctive selection of modern sculptures. The hotel has commissioned works by many contemporary Catalan and Spanish artists, including Ràfols Casamada, Bennassar, and Xavier Corberó, and furniture by Oscar Tusquets, among others, and they are all on view in the public areas. Outside, there is Frank Gehry's giant fish, and the Japanese-owned **Sogo** shopping centre (*see chapter* **Shopping**). Rooms, meanwhile, are equipped with every conceivable mod con. The hotel's greatest advantage, though, is its stunning views of the city and the Mediterranean, above all from the corner rooms. Each of its restaurants and bars also opens onto a terrace overlooking the sea, and the swimming pool is fabulous.

If the Arts looks outwards, one could say that the Claris is inward-looking: discreet, refined,

The ultra-modern **Hotel Claris**.

and unostentatiously luxurious. Here the most traditional touches are on the outside, for it occupies an early-nineteenth-century mansion in the Eixample, the Palau Vedruna. However, only the façade of the palace was retained by star Barcelona architects Bohigas, MacKay and Martorell, who built a completely new, stylishly low-key interior around a striking atrium and small garden, apparently of Zen inspiration, with murmuring fountain. On the roof, there's another beautiful swimming pool.

The hotel's most unique feature, though, stems from the archaeological interests of owner Jordi Clos, who also maintains the private **Museu Egipci** of Egyptian relics (*see chapter* **Museums**). Inside the Claris there are around 350 items from his collections, from Rome, India and Burma as well as Egypt, plus more recent antique furniture and carpets, some of them in a small museum and the rest scattered all around the hotel. Hence, in your room, as well as every kind of modern service, you might find original engravings commissioned for Napoleon in Egypt, or the benevolent gaze of a fifth-century Vedic deity.

For details of both hotels, *see* **Real Luxury**.

Mediterranean city, and these hotels do guarantee visitors well-equipped comfort at reasonable prices; also, in among the functional business hotels there is still a good selection of more individual places to stay.

In the last century Barcelona's first real hotels were all built along the Rambla, and a large number of hotels can still be found concentrated in the old city, also still the best area for cheaper accommodation. The other main hotel area is the Eixample, where there are several mid-range

places and some good-value *hostals*. This is the best area to stay if you need easy vehicle access, preferably in a hotel with its own parking, as on-street parking is both risky and very inconvenient (*see chapter* **Survival: Driving in Barcelona**).

STARS, HOTELS, *HOSTALS* & PRICES

All accommodation in Catalonia is regulated by the regional government, the Generalitat. Formerly, accommodation in Spain included a bewildering mix of *fondas, residencias, pensions*

ɧOTEL
GAUDI

✳ ✳ ✳

Located near las Ramblas and the Gothic Quarter.
Totally refurbished respecting the original architecture.
73 bedrooms, each with a complete bathroom, colour TV, parabolic
antenna, direct telephone line, four channels of piped music and safe.
Fast food cafeteria open from 7am through to 12pm.
Bar, conference hall, social lounge and air conditioning.
Private car park with 63 places in the building itself.

Nou de la Rambla, 12 - 08001 Barcelona
Tel: (93) 317 90 32 - 82
Fax: (93) 412 26 36

*Book yourself into a Modernist landmark: the **Hotel España**. See page 23.*

built around a central patio or air shaft, which can be gloomy. Inside (*interior*) rooms, however, often gain in quietness what they lack in light. For student and youth accommodation booking services, *see chapter* **Students**.

Ultramar Express

Vestibule, Estació de Sants (491 44 63). Metro Sants-Estació/bus 27, 43, 44, 109. **Open** 8am-10pm daily. Closed Christmas Day, New Year, 6 Jan.
When booking you will be required to pay a deposit, which will be incorporated into your final hotel bill, plus a small fee (under 200ptas), and will be given a map and directions.

Real Luxury

Barcelona Hilton

Avda Diagonal 589-591, 08021 (419 22 33/fax 405 25 73/telex 99623). Metro Maria Cristina/bus 6, 7, 33, 34, 66, 67, 68. **Rates** *single* 23,000ptas; *double* 28,000ptas; *suites* 40,000-80,000ptas. **Credit** AmEx, DC, EC, JCB, MC, TC, V.
Opened in 1990, Barcelona's 288-room Hilton was designed by Helio Piñón and Albert Viaplana – architects of the Plaça dels Paisos Catalans in Sants, and lately of Maremagnum (*see chapter* **Sightseeing**), in a minimalist steel-and-glass style. It lacks the range of facilities of some of its competitors, but some of its rooms are a little more intimate. Located in the heart of Barcelona's modern main business area, it concentrates particularly on providing business services.
Hotel services *Air-conditioning. Bar. Business/conference facilities. Car park. Currency exchange. Gym. Interpreters. Laundry. Lifts. Limousine service. Multilingual staff. Non-smoking rooms. Restaurants. Safe. Shops. Terrace. Wheelchair access.* **Room services** *Hairdryer. Minibar. Radio. Room service (24-hours). Rooms (3) adapted for the disabled. Telephone. TV (satellite). Video (in-house).*

Hotel Ambassador

C/Pintor Fortuny 13, 08001 (412 05 30/reservations 318 91 33/fax 302 79 77/telex 99222). Metro Liceu/bus 14, 18, 38, 59, N4, N6. **Rates** *single* 15,900ptas; *double* 19,900ptas. **Credit** AmEx, DC, EC, JCB, MC, TC, V.
Excellently located just off the Rambla, near **Le Meridien** (*see below*), the elegantly modern Ambassador made a name for itself during the Olympics when it was booked up complete by the US basketball team. It was deliberately built on a smaller scale than other hotels at this level, with only 105 rooms. There's also an attractive ground-floor lounge bar, a rooftop pool, an underground car park and prices that make it a real find for a hotel with this kind of facilities.
Hotel services *Air-conditioning. Bar. Car park. Conference facilities.Currency exchange. Gym. Laundry. Lifts. Interpreters. Limousine service. Multilingual staff. Restaurant. Sauna. Swimming pool (outdoors). Ticket agency. Wheelchair access.* **Room services** *Hair dryer. Minibar. Room service (7am-midnight). Rooms (4) adapted for the disabled. Safe. Telephone. TV (satellite). Video.*

Hotel Arts

C/Marina 19-21, 08005 (221 10 00/fax 221 10 70/reservations from UK freephone 0800 234 000/from US freephone 800 241 3333). Metro Ciutadella/bus 36, 41. **Rates** *standard room* 26,000ptas; *suite* 30,000ptas. **Credit** AmEx, DC, EC, JCB, MC, TC, V.
This giant tower with unique beachfront location (first in Europe run by the Ritz-Carlton chain) has all of 455 rooms: on the three top floors is *The Club*, a separate area for guests desiring extra privacy and service. As well as its standard rates, though, the Arts also offers a range of special weekend and other price packages, making a few days' spree in this most opulent symbol of the new Barcelona a possibility even if you don't have the backing of an unlimited expense account. *See also* **Post-Olympic Palaces**.
Hotel services *Air-conditioning. Bar. Beauty salon. Car park. Conference facilities. Currency exchange. Dry cleaning. Fitness centre (gym/sauna/massage). Garden.*

Barcelona's first Grand Hotel

Visitors looking for a taste of history in a Barcelona hotel can find it at the **Hotel Oriente**. It was inaugurated in 1842, incorporating part of a Franciscan monastery built nearly two centuries earlier. Despite many subsequent alterations and overlays that make them hard to recognise, the cloisters and several other parts of the building remain today, and you may notice that some first-floor rooms are a step higher than the corridor, the step having been used originally as a kneeler for night prayer. In the basement there are the remains of a crypt, and the entrance to a vaulted tunnel that once led to the Capuchin monastery on the site now occupied by the Plaça Reial.

The opening of Barcelona's first modern hotel was a great social event. Among the eminent guests was the then US Ambassador to Spain, writer Washington Irving. Such luxury had never been seen. One feature that particularly impressed was the possibility of a rudimentary bath – upon request – consisting of a wooden tub with shower incorporated (requiring a servant to hold the hose). In the 1920s, porcelain baths replaced the wooden tubs, but the old-style facilities are still on show.

Along with Irving, the Oriente has played host to many illustrious travellers, including Hans Christian Anderson, General Grant, who stopped off on a round-the-world trip. and, in 1913, ex-Sultan Muley Hafid of Morocco, who was given to leaning over his balcony at midday to toss basketfuls of coins to passers-by, creating great revelry. Four years later, during the 1917 general strike (*see chapter* **History: The City of the New Century**), the same balcony was used as a platform by politicians trying to calm protestors on the Rambla. Even that didn't create as much commotion as the arrival in 1924 of silent-screen star Mary Pickford, who gave the hotel more publicity than any guest has before or since.

The Oriente was rebuilt again in the 1880s, and then in 1929, coinciding with the International Exhibition, the cloisters were covered to become a ballroom and banquet hall that would host King Alfonso XIII and later cellist Pau Casals. The hotel's proximity to the Liceu made it a favourite with musicians: Toscanini and Maria Callas both stayed here, and so too did many sports stars, while a different kind of glamour was lent by Errol Flynn. It celebrated its 150th anniversary, coincidentally, in 1992, and still provides more characterful accommodation than many of its more recent competitors. For details, *see* **Mid-Range**.

Hairdresser. Interpreters. Laundry. Lifts. Limousine service. Non-smoking floor. Restaurants. Shops. Swimming pool (outdoors). Ticket agency. Wheelchair access. **Room services** CD player. Fax & computer data lines/modem. Minibar. Radio. Refrigerator. Room service (24-hours). Rooms (5) adapted for the disabled. Safe. Telephone. TV (satellite). Video.

Hotel Claris

C/Pau Claris 150, 08009 (487 62 62/fax 215 79 70). Metro Passeig de Gracia /bus 20, 21, 43, 44, 45, N4, N5. **Rates** single 25,500ptas; double 31,850ptas. **Credit** AmEx, DC, EC, JCB, MC, TC, V.
A unique 121-room hotel in the heart of the Eixample, well located for Passeig de Gràcia and the best shopping areas. For lovers of ancient art, modern design, new technology and la dolce vita. See also **Post-Olympic palaces**.
Hotel services Air-conditioning. Bar. Business services. Car park. Childminding service. Conference facilities. Currency exchange. Garden. Interpreters. Lifts. Limousine service. Multilingual staff. Non-smoking floor. Restaurants. Swimming pool (outdoors). Ticket agency. Wheelchair access. **Room services** Hairdryer. Minibar. Radio. Refrigerator. Room service (24-hours). Rooms (4) adapted for the disabled.Safe. Telephone. TV (satellite). Video.

Hotel HUSA-Palace

Gran Via de les Corts Catalanes 668, 08010 (318 52 00/fax 318 01 48/telex 52739). Metro Passeig de Gràcia/bus 7, 18, 47, 50, 54, 56, N1, N9. **Rates** single 32,800ptas; double 43,000ptas-57,000ptas. **Credit** AmEx, DC, EC, JCB, MC, TC, V.
Since 1995, when this hotel was taken over by the HUSA chain – owners of many other Barcelona hotels – the city no longer has a Ritz, even though the name is actually built into the façade. The nineteenth-century ex-Ritz was also extensively renovated in the early nineties, but nevertheless still qualifies as the most elegant hotel in town, offering old-fashioned style its late-coming rivals can only envy. Woody Allen recently occupied the legendary 108 royal suite, also a favourite of Orson Welles and the Duke and Duchess of Windsor, but the old Ritz's most regular celebrity guest was Salvador Dalí, who spent months there at a stretch. The 150 large rooms have luxurious bathrooms, and despite redecoration have kept their classical furnishings and atmosphere. The sumptuous restaurant is open to the public.
Hotel services Air-conditioning. Bar. Business services. Car park. Childminding services. Conference facilities. Currency exchange. Dry cleaning. Interpreters. Laundry. Lifts. Limousine service. Multilingual staff. Non-smoking floor. Restaurants. Ticket agency.
Room services Hair dryer. Minibar. Radio. Refrigerator. Room service (24-hours). Safe. Telephone. TV (satellite).

The **Hotel Oriente**, *a Barcelona original.*

Hotel Le Meridien Barcelona

La Rambla 111, 08002 (318 62 00/fax 301 77 76/telex 54634). Metro Liceu/bus 14, 18, 38, 59, N4, N6. **Rates** *single* 23,000-32,000ptas; *double* 29,000-38,000ptas; *suite* 68,000ptas. **Credit** AmEx, DC, TC, JCB, MC, V.

Part of the French Meridien chain, this 209-room hotel couldn't be more centrally placed and has acquired a certain hip status through its popularity with celebrities and pop stars: Bruce Springsteen, Michael Jackson, the Stones and lately Oasis have all put up here. The restaurant, *Le Patio*, serves Mediterranean cuisine. Again, good 'Winter-Passport' and 'Summer-Passport' rates are available in December-February and July-August.

Hotel services *Air-conditioning. Bar. Business/conference facilities. Car park. Childminding service. Currency exchange. Dry cleaning. Gym. Interpreters. Laundry. Lifts. Limousine service. Multilingual staff. Non-smoking rooms. Restaurant. Safe. Sauna. Valet service. Wheelchair access.* **Room services** *Minibar. Minitel. Radio. Refrigerator. Room service (24-hours). Rooms (4) adapted for the disabled. Telephone. TV (satellite). Video on request.*

Smooth Comfort

Hotel Balmes

C/Mallorca 216, 08008 (451 19 14/fax 451 0049). FGC Provença/bus 7, 16, 17, 20, 21, 43, 54, 58, 64 . **Rates** *single* 12,600ptas; *double* 17,350ptas; *suite* 21,000ptas; **Credit** AmEx, DC, EC, MC, TC, V.

A very pleasant 1990-vintage 100-room hotel in the middle of the Eixample. Rooms are very comfortable: those at the rear get the morning sun and look out onto the garden, solarium and pool, and some ground-floor rooms have their own outside terraces. All-round comfort and service above the norm for this grade of hotel.

Hotel services *Air-conditioning. Bar. Car park. Childminding service. Conference facilities. Currency exchange. Laundry. Lifts. Multilingual staff. Non-smoking rooms. Restaurant. Swimming pool (outdoor).* **Room services** *Hairdryer. Minibar. Refrigerator. Room service (8am-11pm). Safe. Telephone. TV (satellite).*

Hotel Colón

Avda de la Catedral 7, 08002 (301 14 04/fax 317 29 15/telex 52654 COLON-E). Metro Jaume I/ bus 17, 19, 40, 45. **Rates** *single* 13,750-20,000ptas; *double* 20,500ptas; *suites* 32,500-37,000ptas. **Credit** AmEx, DC, EC, MC, TC, V.

This 147-room hotel occupies a prime position opposite the Cathedral, so that from its front rooms you have a matchless view, and can watch the *sardana* dancing on Sundays, and the antique market on Thursdays. The piano bar is a relaxing corner, and there's a good restaurant. The hotel is splendidly furnished, and staff are efficient.

Hotel services *Air-conditioning. Bar. Car park. Childminding service. Conference facilities. Currency exchange. Interpreters. Laundry. Lifts. Limousine service. Masseur. Multilingual staff. Non-smoking rooms. Restaurants. Sauna. Solarium. Swimming pool (outdoor). Whirlpool..* **Room services** *Minibar. Refrigerator. Safe. Telephone. Rooms adapted for the disabled. TV (satellite). Video.*

Hotel Condes de Barcelona

Passeig de Gràcia 75, 08008 (487 37 37/fax 487 14 42/telex 51531). Metro Passeig de Gràcia/bus 7, 20, 21, 22, 24, 43, 44, N7. **Rates** *single* 17,900ptas; *double* 23,300ptas. **Credit** AmEx, DC, EC, MC, V.

The 1891 Hotel Condes was fully renovated in the '80s, and is beautifully floodlit at night. Its marble-floored, pentagonal lobby has retained the features of the original courtyard, right up to the pentagonal skylight, and rooms are decorated in keeping with the overall magnificence of the building, plus

there's a spectacular view from the roof-top terrace. One of Barcelona's more popular hotels, so book well in advance.

Hotel services *Air-conditioning. Bar. Car park. Conference facilities. Dry cleaning. Laundry. Restaurant.* **Room services** *Minibar. Radio. Room service (24-hours). Telephone. TV. Video.*

Hotel Duques de Bergara

C/Bergara 11, 08002 (301 51 51/fax 317 34 42). Metro Universitat/bus all routes to Pl aça Catalunya. **Rates** *single* 13,500ptas; *double* 14,900ptas. **Credit** AmEx, EC, DC, JCB, MC, TC, V.

A luxury hotel created in 1987 from an 1898 Modernist edifice by Gaudi's professor Emili Sala, and located just off Plaça Catalunya. The original style has been kept in hall and stairways, while communal rooms are very modern. The 54 guest rooms are spacious and well furnished, and double rooms often have a small seating area as well. Most rooms are light and look onto the street or a quiet courtyard, but check when booking, as a few rooms are very dark.

Hotel services *Air-conditioning. Bar. Business services. Car park next door. Childminding service. Conference facilities. Currency exchange. Laundry. Lift. Limousine service. Multilingual staff. Non-smoking floor. Restaurant. Safe.* **Room services** *Hairdryer. Minibar. Radio. Room service (24-hours).Telephone. TV (satellite).*

Hotel Regente

Rambla Catalunya 76, 08008 (487 59 89/fax 487 32 27/telex 51939). Metro Passeig de Gràcia/FGC Provença/bus 20, 21, 43, 44, N7. **Rates** *single & double* from 9,500ptas; *during special events, single* 15,400ptas; *double* 19,500ptas. **Credit** AmEx, DC, EC, JCB, MC, TC, V.

Stained-glass decoration in the interior gives this 78-room hotel a distinctive charm, even if the décor is showing its age. The rooftop pool area has stunning views over Montjuic, and makes a perfect place to enjoy the sunset. If you want to stay in the Eixample, the Regente is an excellent choice.

Hotel services *Air-conditioning. Bar. Conference facilities. Currency exchange. Laundry. Lift. Multilingual staff. Restaurant. Swimming pool. Roof terrace.* **Room services** *Hairdryer. Minibar. Radio. Room service (7am-11pm). Safe. Telephone. TV (satellite).*

Hotel Rivoli Ramblas

La Rambla 128, 08002 (302 66 43/reservations 412 09 88/fax 317 50 53/telex 99222 RIVO-E). Metro Catalunya/bus all routes to Plaça Catalunya. **Rates** *(breakfast included) single* 14,000ptas; *double* 16,000ptas. **Credit** AmEx, DC, JCB, MC, TC, V.

And elegant and luxurious hotel rebuilt in the early nineties, the Rivoli is a world apart from the bustle on the Rambla outside, but still just a few minutes walk from Plaça Catalunya. The 90 rooms have interesting colour schemes, and the hotel is a popular stopover for both local business and international visitors.

Hotel services *Air-conditioning. Bar. Business services. Car park. Conference facilities. Currency exchange. Gym. Laundry. Lifts. Limousine service. Multilingual staff. Restaurant. Sauna. Ticket agency. Wheelchair access.* **Room services** *Minibar. Room service (7am-11pm). Safe. Telephone. TV(satellite). Video.*

Park Hotel

Avda Marqués de l'Argentera 11, 08003 (319 60 00/fax 319 45 19/telex 99883). Metro Barceloneta/bus 16, 17, 39, 45, 51. **Rates** *(breakfast included) single* 8,000ptas; *double* 11,000ptas. **Credit** AmEx, DC, JCB, MC, V.

Despite its resemblance to a shabby seaside apartment block,

The **Hotel Ambassador:** *favoured by the American basketball team.*

the Park Hotel, opposite the Estació de França, has been refurbished with style and imagination. Public areas and the 87 rooms are comfortably decorated in pale yellow, and the hotel has kept its neo-art deco turquoise mosaic bar, a place you might go to even if you weren't staying here. Service is friendly, and there are good facilities for disabled visitors. **Hotel services** *Air-conditioning. Bar. Car park. Lounge. Lift. Multilingual staff. Restaurant. Wheelchair access.* **Room services** *Minibar. Radio. Rooms (2) adapted for the disabled. Safe. Telephone. TV (satellite). Video.*

Mid-Range

Hotel España

C/Sant Pau 9-11, 08001 (318 17 58/fax 317 11 34). Metro Liceu/bus 14, 18, 38, 59, N4, N6. **Rates** *single* 5,200ptas; *double* 9,810ptas. **Credit** AmEx, DC, MC, V.
The Hotel España, in the Raval just off the Rambla, is one of the landmarks of Modernist architecture, ranking almost with the **Palau de la Música** in renown. The lower floors were designed by Domènech i Montaner in 1902: the main restaurant, in which a good lunch menu is available, is decorated with floral motifs in tile and elaborate woodwork, while beyond it is a larger dining room, with extravagant murals of river-nymphs by Ramon Casas, also in tiles. In the adjoining bar, there's a huge fireplace by sculptor Eusebi Arnau. After these rooms, the more modern guest rooms can come as a disappointment, but several open onto a bright interior patio. Book well in advance.
Hotel services *Bar. Conference room. Lift. Multilingual staff. Restaurant. TV. Wheelchair access.* **Room services** *Safe. Telephone.*

Hotel Gaudí

C/Nou de la Rambla 12, 08001 (317 90 32/fax 412 26 36). Metro Drassanes/bus 14, 18, 38, 59, N4, N6. **Rates** *single* 7,000ptas; *double* 9,000ptas. **Credit** AmEx, DC, EC, JCB, MC, TC, V.
The Gaudí's great selling point has been its status as the main mid-level hotel in a very central, convenient and much-visited area that's also within the old *Barrio Chino*, its well-equipped rooms contrasting with the shabbiness nearby. Directly opposite Gaudí's **Palau Güell** (*see chapters* **Architecture** *and* **Museums**), it has recently acquired an all-new, Gaudí-inspired reception area, and the 73 rooms rate among the best for this area and price bracket.
Hotel services *Air-conditioning (floors 4-6). Bar. Car park. Conference facilities. Currency exchange. Gym. Laundry. Lift. Limousine service. Multilingual staff. Restaurant. Wheelchair access.* **Room services** *Hair-dryer. Radio. Room service (7am-midnight). Rooms (2) adapted for the disabled. Safe. Telephone. TV (satellite).*

Hotel Internacional

La Rambla 78-80, 08002 (302 25 66/fax 317 61 90). Metro Liceu/bus 14, 18, 38, 59, N4, N6. **Rates** *single* 5,600ptas; *double* 7,600ptas. **Credit** AmEx, DC, EC, MC, V.
An institution on the Rambla, a fabulously elegant establishment built in 1894 but which has been totally refurbished and now offers outstanding quality in a prime, albeit noisy location. With an outside room, you can sit on the balcony and watch the movement on the Rambla come and go, and all 60 rooms have high ceilings and new bathrooms. It's always full, and it's advisable to book a week in advance.
Hotel services *Bar. Currency exchange. Fax. Lift (from first floor). Multilingual staff. Safe (for hire). TV.* **Room services** *Telephone.*

Lapping up the sun on the roof terrace of the **Hotel Arts**.

Hotel Mesón Castilla

C/Valldonzella 5, 08001 (318 21 82/fax 412 40 20). Metro Universitat/bus all routes to Plaça Catalunya. **Rates** *single* 7,500 ptas; *double* 11,150ptas. **Credit** DC, EC, MC, V.
A favourite with British visitors, who enjoy the hearty buffet breakfasts served in the cosy dining room. With an old-world look, the hotel was founded in 1930. In its 55, impeccably clean rooms there is antique, hand-made furniture, and some rear rooms have balconies with views of the nearby **Museu d'Art Contemporani** (*see chapter* **Museums**). Despite the central location, all rooms are quiet. Exceptional service for a two-star hotel.
Hotel services *Air-conditioning. Bar. Car park. Currency exchange. Laundry. Lift. Multilingual staff. Wheelchair access.* **Room services** *Minibar. Room service (7am-midnight). Safe. Telephone. TV.*

Hotel Metropol

C/Ample 31, 08002 (310 51 00/fax 319 12 76). Metro Drassanes/bus 14, 36, 57, 59, 64. **Rates** *single* 9,500ptas; *double* 11,900ptas. **Credit** AmEx, DC, MC, V.
Another nineteenth century hotel that was given a makeover in 1992, although its reception area still has its old charm. Half the 68 rooms look onto C/Ample, which is unusually quiet for a street in the old city, very near the port. The Metropol offers very good weekend deals, and also has reservation agreements with several local restaurants.
Hotel services *Air-conditioning. Conference facilities. Interpreters. Laundry. Lift. Limousine service. Multilingual staff. Wheelchair access.* **Room services** *Minibar. Radio. Refrigerator. Rooms adapted for the disabled. Safe. Telephone. TV (satellite)*

Hotel Onix

C/Llançà 30, 08015 (426 00 87/fax 426 19 81). Metro Espanya/bus 27, 109, 127. **Rates** *single* 10,000ptas; *double* 12,000ptas. **Credit** AmEx, DC, MC, V.
A comfortable hotel in the Plaça d'Espanya area, close to Sants rail station and with easy access to the airport. The quiet outside rooms face the old Arenas bullring on one side, and the **Parc Joan Miró** (*see chapter* **Sightseeing**) on the other. Ideally placed for anyone attending trade fairs or shows at the **Fira** (*see chapter* **Business**) or visiting the other attractions of Montjuïc.
Hotel services *Air-conditioning. Café-bar. Car park. Conference facilities. Laundry. Lifts. Multilingual staff. Swimming pool (outdoor). Ticket agency. Wheelchair access.* **Room services** *Hairdryer. Minibar. Radio. Refrigerator. Room service (7am-10pm). Rooms (2) adapted for the disabled. Safe. Telephone. TV (satellite).*

Hotel Oriente

La Rambla 45-47, 08002 (302 25 58/fax 412 38 19). Metro Drassanes/bus 14, 18, 38, 59, N4, N6. **Rates** *single* 7,500ptas; *double* 12,000ptas. **Credit** AmEx, DC, EC, MC, TC, V.
The most atmospheric hotel in its price bracket. Some of its 142 spacious rooms overlook the Rambla; rooms on the C/Unió side face the site of the currently-under-reconstruction Liceu Opera House, which can make them noisy during work hours. Often good weekend rates and low-season offers. *See also* **Barcelona's first Grand Hotel.**
Hotel services *Bar. Conference facilities. Currency exchange. Laundry. Lift. Limousine service. Multilingual staff. Restaurant.* **Room services** *Minibar. Refrigerator. Room service (24-hours). Safe. Telephone. TV.*

Hotel Principal

C/Junta de Comerç 8, 08001 (318 89 74/fax 412 08 19). Metro Liceu/bus 14, 18, 38, 59, N4, N6. **Rates** *single* 4,000ptas; *double* 7,500ptas. **Credit** AmEx, DC, EC, MC, TC, V.

One of several hotels and *hostals* on this quiet street near the Rambla, the Principal has some distinctive features of its own – notably the ornate furniture in the bedrooms. All 60 rooms have recently-modernised bathrooms. The same management also runs the Hotel Joventut along the street.
Hotel services *Air-conditioning. Bar. Business & conference facilities. Currency exchange. Interpreter. Laundry. Lift. Multilingual staff. TV. Wheelchair access.* **Room services** *Air-conditioning. Minibar. Room service (8am-7pm). Rooms adapted for the disabled. Safe. Telephone.*
Branch: Hotel Joventut C/Junta de Comerç 12 (301 84 99).

Hotel San Agustín

Plaça Sant Agustí 3, 08001 (318 16 58/fax 317 29 28). Metro Liceu/bus 14, 18, 38, 59, N4, N6. **Rates** (breakfast included) *single* 6,800ptas; *double* 8,900ptas. **Credit** AmEx, MC, TC, V.
A traditional hotel that's been going well over 100 years, but underwent yet another '92 refit, with the addition of a new reception area, lifts, modern bathrooms, full air-conditioning and TV's in every room. Some would say it's lost character, but its rooms are comfortable and still have oak-beamed ceilings, and it hasn't lost its most attractive feature, a very pleasant lounge-bar overlooking Plaça Sant Agustí. One of the most attractive, best-value hotels in the area.
Hotel services *Air-conditioning. Bar. Conference facilities. Currency exchange. Laundry. Lift. Multilingual staff. Restaurant. Wheelchair access.* **Room services** *Minibar (some rooms). Radio. Room service (9am-11pm). Rooms (3) adapted for the disabled. Safe. Telephone. TV (satellite).*

Hotel Toledano

La Rambla 138, 08002 (301 08 72/fax 412 31 42). Metro Catalunya/bus all routes to Plaça Catalunya. **Rates** *single* 4,500ptas; *double* 6,900ptas; *triple* 8,600ptas. **Credit** AmEx, DC, MC, V.
Very near to Plaça Catalunya on the upper stretch of the Rambla, the Toledano can be a little noisy, but is certainly convenient. The 28 rooms are basic but have been fitted with bathrooms, and there's a chintzy communal sitting area, complete with caged parrot, looking out over the Rambla.
Hotel services *Lift. Multilingual staff. Safe. Wheelchair access.* **Room services** *Telephone. TV (satellite).*

Budget

Long-established as the favourite place to look for those in search of an inexpensive room in Barcelona is the Plaça Reial, just off the Rambla. Other good areas to find cheap hotels in the old city are the Raval, on the other side of the Rambla, and in La Ribera, near the Estació de França. The Eixample, also, has some rather more tranquil, but still good-value, budget hotels and *hostals*. Note that some budget places do not have someone on the door 24 hours a day, so check when going out.

Hostal Ambos Mundos

Plaça Reial 10, 08002 (318 79 70/fax 412 23 63). Metro Drassanes/bus 14, 18, 38, 59, N4, N6. **Rates** *single* 3,000ptas; *double* 4,000ptas. **Credit** AmEx, MC, V.
One of the most popular of the Plaça Reial *hostals*, above a bar of the same name. The Ambos Mundos' 13 simple, tiled rooms are quite large, and all have baths. Outside rooms have small balconies overlooking the action, and in the cavernous reception area you can relax, play pool or watch TV.
Hotel services *Pool table. Safe. TV.* **Room services** *Telephone.*

Hostal Ciudad Condal

C/Mallorca 255, 08008 (215 10 40). Metro Passeig de Gràcia, FGC Provença/bus 20, 21, 28, 43, 44, N7. **Rates** *single* 3,800-4,000ptas; *double* 5,500-5,800ptas. **Credit** AmEx, MC, V.
A 15-room *hostal* in the Casa Àngel Batlló – a block of three *Modernista* houses with one façade designed by Josep Vilaseca i Casanovas in 1896. Rooms are a little spartan, but the outside rooms have high ceilings and balconies.
Hotel services *Laundry. Multilingual staff. Snack bar.* **Room services** *Radio. Telephone. TV.*

Hostal Jardí

Plaça Sant Josep Oriol 1, 08002 (301 59 00/fax 318 36 64). Metro Liceu/bus 14, 18, 38, 59, N4, N6. **Rates** older rooms *single* 3,800ptas; *double* 5,000-5,500ptas; new rooms *single or double* 6,000ptas; *triples (two people)* 7,000ptas; *(three people)* 8,500ptas. **Credit** AmEx, DC, MC, V.
One of the most popular lower-range hotels in Barcelona, overlooking the quiet, leafy Plaça del Pi in the Barri Gòtic, the Jardí post-renovation has rooms with a different level of facilities, and so varying prices. The fully-renovated outside rooms are more expensive, but still a bargain. All rooms have bathrooms, but the internal rooms are more basic, and the patio can be noisy. Book well in advance.
Hotel services *Lift (from first floor). Safety deposit box. Refreshments available from reception 24-hours daily.* **Room services** *Telephone. TV (some rooms).*

Hostal Lausanne

Avda Portal de l'Àngel 24, 08002. (302 11 39) Metro Plaça Catalunya/bus All routes to Plaça Catalunya. **Rates** *single* 2,000ptas; *double* 3,000ptas; *(with shower)* 3,990ptas; *(with bath)* 4,600ptas. **No credit cards.**
This 17-room, family-run *hostal* is on the first floor of a beautiful old building with a magnificent entrance, and inside there are high ceilings and spacious rooms, some with balconies overlooking the busy pedestrian strip between Plaça Catalunya and the Cathedral. It's clean and bright, with a large sitting room, and the owners are helpful and friendly .
Services *Lift . Multilingual staff. Safe. 24-hour reception.*

Hostal Layetana

Plaça Ramon Berenguer el Gran 2, 08002 (319 20 12). Metro Jaume I/bus 17, 40, 45. **Rates** *single* 2,300ptas; *double* 3,600ptas; *double (with shower)* 5,200ptas. **Credit** MC, V.
A view along the Roman wall and a stunning hall give this *hostal* character. Service is friendly, most of its 20 rooms have been renovated and given bathrooms; the communal bathrooms are well-kept. Noise from Via Laietana is a drawback.
Hotel services *Lift. Multilingual staff. Refreshments available 24 hours. Safe. TV.*

Hostal Noya

La Rambla 133, 1º, 08002 (301 48 31). Metro Catalunya/bus all routes to Plaça Catalunya. **Rates** *single* 1,800ptas; *double* 3,400ptas. **No credit cards.**
This modest *hostal* is in an excellent position on the Rambla, and good value for its location. All 15 rooms have balconies overlooking the crowds, but bathrooms are communal. No breakfast either, but there's a good café-restaurant below.
Hotel services *Safe. Telephone. TV.*

Hostal Orleans

Avda Marquès de l'Argentera 13, 08003 (319 73 82/fax 319 22 19) Metro Barceloneta/bus 14, 39, 51. **Rates** *single (with bath)* 2,500ptas; *double (with shower, one person)* 3,500ptas; *double (with shower, two people)* 5,500ptas; *double (with bath, two people)* 6,500ptas. **Credit** AmEx, DC, MC, V.

Rooms with views at the **Hotel Internacional.**

*It can be cheap, or relatively expensive, but it's always full. The **Hostal Jardí**.*

This family-run *hostal* near the Port and the Ciutadella has 17 good-sized rooms with balconies, most of which look onto a wide but noisy avenue or a quieter side-street. All rooms are spotless, but the upper-floor accommodation is more modern. There are special rates for triple or quadruple occupancy, and weekly rates can be negotiated for all rooms. **Hotel services** *Currency exchange. English-speaking staff. Laundry. Telephone. Vending machine.* **Room services** *TV (satellite).*

Hostal Parisien

La Rambla 114, 08002 (301 62 83). Metro Liceu/bus 14, 18, 38, 59, N4, N6. **Rates** *single* 2,000ptas; *double* 3,500ptas; *double (with shower)* 4,000ptas; *(with bath)* 4,500ptas. **No credit cards**.
A 13-room *hostal* run by a friendly young couple that's a student favourite, with a great mid-Rambla location opposite the Palau Virreina. The rooms are well-kept, and four have en suite bathrooms. The ones overlooking the Rambla are noisy, but atmospheric, while others are darker but quieter. **Hotel services** *Laundry. Lounge. Multilingual staff. Safe. TV (satellite).*

Hostal Plaza

C/Fontanella 18, 08010 (tel/fax 301 01 39). Metro Urquinaona/bus all routes to Plaça Catalunya. **Rates** *single* 2,500-3000ptas; *double* 3,500-5,000ptas. **Credit** AmEx, DC, MC, V.
Run by eager-to-please Hispanic Americans, the Plaza is a fun budget hotel with all-new plumbing and a glut of services for guests – laundry (5kg, 1,000ptas), sitting room with TV, the use of a fridge, freezer and microwave, information on the city and even, they say, discounts at local restaurants and clubs. All 14 rooms have showers and three-speed fans. A change from more traditional Spanish cheap hotels. **Hotel services** *Air-conditioning. Fax. Kitchen facilities (microwave). Laundry. Lift. Multilingual staff. Safe. TV room. Vending machine. Ventilators.* **Room services** *Fan. Radio.*

Hostal Rembrandt

C/Portaferrissa 23, 08002 (tel/fax 318 10 11). Metro Liceu/bus 14, 18, 38, 59, N4, N6. **Rates** *single* 2,500ptas; *(with shower)* 3,000ptas; *double* 3,600ptas; *(with shower)* 4,500ptas. **No credit cards**.

A cheerful 29-room *hostal* centrally located on the main shopping street of the Barri Gòtic. Refurbished a few years ago, it's spotlessly clean, with pleasantly décorated rooms. The foyer opens onto a tiled patio used as an eating or sitting area. Popular with backpackers, and the owners will put up to five people in a room at very reasonable prices. **Hotel services** *Multilingual staff. Safe. TV room.*

Hostal-Residencia Oliva

Passeig de Gràcia 32, 4°, 08007 (488 01 62 & 488 01 62). Metro Passeig de Gràcia/bus 7, 16, 17, 22, 24, 28, N4, N6. **Rates** *single* 3,000ptas; *double* 5,350ptas; *(with bath)* 6,420ptas. **No credit cards**.
A 16-room *hostal* on the top floor of a massive old Eixample apartment block. It's a relaxed, family-run place, and most rooms are light and well-aired: doubles with bathrooms are especially comfortable. Most rooms face Passeig de Gràcia, however, and as there's no double glazing it can be noisy. **Hotel services** *Lift.*

Hostal Rey Don Jaime I

C/Jaume I 11, 08002 (tel/fax 310 62 08). Metro Jaume I/bus 17, 40, 45. **Rates** *single* 3,800ptas; *double* 5,500ptas. **Credit** EC, JCB, MC, TC, V.
Handy for both the Barri Gòtic and La Ribera, but this *hostal* sits on the noisy main artery through the centre of the old city. Basic but clean, the 30 rooms all have balconies and bathrooms, and it's popular with a mostly-young clientèle. **Hotel services** *Currency exchange. Laundry. Lift. Lounge. Multilingual staff. Safe. Ticket agency. 24-hour reception.* **Room services** *Telephone.*

Hostal La Terrassa

C/Junta de Comerç 11, 08001 (302 51 74/fax 301 21 88). Metro Liceu/bus 14, 18, 38, 59, N4, N6. **Rates** (breakfast included) *single* 1,900ptas; *(with bath)* 2,400ptas; *double* 2,950ptas; *(with bath)* 3,400ptas; *triple* 3,800ptas; *(with bath)* 4,500ptas. **Credit** AmEx, DC, MC, $TC, V.
One of the most likeable of Barcelona's cheap *hostals*. Around half the rooms have bathrooms, and the best have balconies overlooking the street or an interior patio, where breakfast is served in summer. The owner also runs Hostal Jardí. **Hotel services** *Dry cleaning. Laundry. Multilingual staff. Safe. Terrace. TV.*

Hostal Victòria

C/Comtal 9, 1° 1a, 08002 (318 07 60/317 45 97). Metro Catalunya/bus all routes to Plaça Catalunya. **Rates** *single* 2,000ptas; *double* 3,000ptas. **No credit cards**.
A spacious 30-room *hostal* in the heart of the old town, and ideal for budget travellers as it has communal cooking and washing facilities. The owner can be a bit authoritarian and the rooms are basic, but they're clean and light, and most have balconies. Also a patio, rare for a one-star *hostal*.
Hotel services *Dining room. Kitchen. Laundry. Lift. Lounge. Terrace. Safe. TV.* **Room services** *Telephone.*

Hostal Windsor

Rambla Catalunya 84, 08008 (215 11 98). Metro Passeig de Gràcia/bus 20, 21, 43, 44, N7. **Rates** *single* 3,700ptas; *double* 6,000ptas. **No credit cards**.
A cheap'n'cheerful way of enjoying the *fin de siècle* splendour of the Eixample, the Windsor occupies a stylish Modernist building in a thriving, well-communicated area. It's small, and can get crowded, so book ahead.
Hotel services *Lift. Multilingual staff. TV. Wheelchair access.* **Room services** *Rooms adapted for the disabled.*

Hosteria Grau

C/Ramelleres 27, 08001 (302 31 30/fax 301 81 35). Metro Catalunya/bus all routes to Plaça Catalunya. **Rates** *single* 2,500-3,000ptas; *double* 5,000-6,000ptas. **Credit** AmEx, DC, EC, V.
On a corner of C/Tallers just a short walk from the Rambla, this pleasant *hostal* is ideal if you're likely to get the munchies: it offers breakfast until noon for 325ptas, either downstairs in their very likeable café (open until 9pm) or in the tiny first-floor sitting room. The rooms are clean and pleasant, but the inside singles are gloomy. In reception, they provide a variety of information on what's on in the city.
Hotel services. *Fax. 24-hour reception.*

Hotel Oasis

Pla del Palau 17, 08003 (319 43 96/fax 310 48 74). Metro Barceloneta/bus 16, 17, 45. **Rates** *single* 4,000ptas; *double* 6,000ptas; *triple* 8,000ptas; *quadruple* 10,000ptas. **Credit** AmEx, DC, EC, MC, $TC, V.
An unusually well-equipped budget hotel conveniently located near Estacio de França and the Port Vell – all rooms have bathrooms and TV. Most are external, with balconies, but can be noisy. Downstairs, the restaurant offers a reasonable menu for 1,000ptas, and there's a café-bar that's open all day.
Hotel services *Bar. Currency exchange. Laundry. Lift (from first floor). Multilingual staff. Restaurant. Safe.* **Room services** *Air-conditioning (some rooms). Safe (some rooms). Telephone. TV (satellite).*

Hotel Peninsular

C/Sant Pau 34-36, 08001 (tel/fax 302 31 38). Metro Liceu/bus 14, 18, 38, 59, N4, N6. **Rates** (breakfast included) *single* 4,655ptas; *double* 5,565ptas. **Credit** EC, MC, TC, V.
Like its grander neighbour the **Oriente** (*see above* **Mid-Range**), the Peninsular was built (in the 1880s) using the remains of a former monastery, and its best feature is its tiled, plant-lined patio. Like other hotels it was modernised in the early nineties, and all 80 rooms are clean and comfortable and have en suite baths or showers. If you want a room with a view, secure one that looks over the courtyard.
Hotel services *Lounge. Safe.* **Room services** *Telephone.*

Hotel Triunfo

Passeig Picasso 22, 08003 (tel/fax 315 08 60) Metro Arc de Triomf/bus 39, 51. **Rates** *single* 4,500ptas; *double* 7,500ptas. **No credit cards**.
The great attraction of this small, intimate hotel is its location, since most of its 15 rooms have balconies overlooking the Ciutadella park and the zoo, and it's also very handy for the rest of La Ribera. All rooms have been recently renovated

and are clean and bright, with good bathrooms. An alternative to more congested areas of the old city.
Hotel services *Air-conditioning. Lift. Safe.* **Room services** *Telephone. TV (satellite).*

Pensión-Hostal Mari-Luz

C/Palau 4, 2° 1a, 08002 (317 34 63). Metro Jaume I/bus 17, 40, 45. **Rates** *per person* 1,300-1,500ptas. **No credit cards**.
A spotlessly clean *hostal* a few streets' walk from the main Plaça Reial-drag, where Mari-Luz takes great care of her lodgers. The patio and staircase of the old building could do with some paint, but it's atmospheric, and affordable. The 18 rooms, five of which have showers, are plain but quiet.
Hotel services *Laundry. Multilingual staff. Refreshments available from reception (24 hours). Safe.*

Pensión Vitoria

C/Palla 8, pral (302 08 34). Metro Liceu/bus 14, 18, 38, 59, N4, N6. **Rates** *single* 1,800ptas; *double* 3,000ptas; *(with bath)* 4,000ptas. **No credit cards**.
Very close to the Plaça del Pi, the Vitoria has 12 clean, light and airy rooms, all with balconies. Ten rooms share one bathroom, while two doubles have en suite showers and toilets. Despite the basic facilities they have a loyal bunch of repeat guests, so book early, especially for private facilities.
Hotel services *Multi-lingual staff.*

Apartment Hotels

Apartment hotels comprise self-contained small flats, with cooking facilities, plus maid service. They are good for slightly longer stays, and usually offer reduced monthly or longer-term rates.

Apartamentos Mur-Mar

La Rambla 34, 08002 (318 27 62/fax 412 50 39). Metro Drassanes/bus 14, 18, 38, 59, N4, N6. **Apartment rates** (per night) *one person* 5,600ptas; *two people* 7,700ptas; *three people* 9,700ptas; *four people* 11,700ptas. **Credit** AmEx, DC, JCB, MC, TC, V.
Near the bottom of the Rambla, these 33 apartments are relatively basic, but still a bargain. Each sleeps up to four, and has a small but well-equipped kitchen, lounge, double bedroom and bathroom. Interior apartments are quiet but dark.
Hotel services *Air-conditioning. Bar. Fax. Laundry. Lift. Multilingual staff. Restaurant. Safe.* **Room services** *Kitchen with refrigerator. Radio. Telephone. TV.*

Apartaments Calàbria

C/Calàbria 129, 08015 (426 42 28/426 74 85/fax 426 76 40). Metro Rocafort/bus 9, 41, 50, 56. **Apartment rates** (per night) *one person* 7,250ptas; *two people* 8,750ptas; *any additional persons* 3,250ptas extra; *(monthly)* 145,000ptas irrespective of number of persons. **Credit** AmEx, MC, V.
An Eixample apartment block, well-placed between the centre and Plaça d'Espanya, recently converted into 72 short-term apartments. While they don't overflow with character, all have good kitchen and bathroom facilities and separate lounge areas, and the reception has efficient office services. Its rates are also more competitive than other *aparthotels* and it needs to be booked well in advance.
Hotel services *Air-conditioning. Car park. Catering service. Fax. Laundry. Lifts. Multi-lingual staff. Photocopier. Wheelchair access.* **Room services** *Safe. Kitchen with refrigerator. Telephone. TV.*

Aparthotel Senator

Via Augusta 167, 08021 (201 14 05/fax 202 00 97). FGC Muntaner/bus 58, 64, N8. **Apartment rates** (per night) *one person* 8,000ptas; *two people* 10,000ptas; *three*

people 12,000ptas; *four people* 13,500ptas; (monthly) *one person* 180,000ptas, plus supplements for double occupancy. **Credit** AmEx, DC, MC, V.
Comfortable, white-walled apartments, fitted out with bamboo furniture and plants, in the Sant Gervasi area of the Zona Alta (*see chapter* **Barcelona by Area**). No restaurant or bar, but the kitchen is fine for preparing light meals.
Hotel services *Air-conditioning. Laundry. Lift. Multilingual staff (some).* **Room services** *Minibar. Radio. Kitchen with refrigerator. Safe. TV.*

Youth Hostels

For student and youth travel and information services that will also make reservations in youth hostels, *see chapter* **Services**.

Albergue Kabul

Plaça Reial 17, 08002 (318 51 90/fax 301 40 34). Metro Drassanes/bus 14, 18, 38, 59, N4, N6. **Open** 24 hours daily. **Rates** *per person* 1,300ptas. **No credit cards.**
A welcoming private youth hostel on the Plaça Reial. There's a reception/TV room with tables, benches and a soft-drinks dispenser; rooms house from two to 12 people, and vary from cramped dormitories with mattresses on the floor to light and airy doubles with views onto the Plaça. No private bathrooms, but the communal showers and toilets are clean.
Hotel services *Billiard table. Kitchen. Laundry. Lift. Multilingual staff. Refreshments available. TV (satellite). Video.*

Albergue Pere Tarrés

C/Numància 149-151, 08029 (410 23 09). Metro Les Corts/bus 15, 43, 59, 63, 67, 68. **Open** 8.30-10am, 4pm-midnight, daily. **Rates** (breakfast included) 1,350ptas per night; sheets extra. **Credit** MC, V
This renovated official hostel has 94 places (four to 10 beds per room) and five shared bathrooms. There's an attractive roof terrace, but regulations are strict: no cigarettes or alcohol in dorms; no eating or drinking outside the dining room. International Youth Hostel (IYHF) cards are required, and you should book ahead in summer.
Hotel services *Car park. Kitchen. Laundry. Multilingual staff. Meals cooked for groups. Patio. Refreshments available. TV lounge.*

Alberg Mare de Déu de Montserrat

Passeig de la Mare de Déu del Coll, 41-51, 08023 (210 51 51/fax 210 07 98). Metro Vallcarca/bus 25, 28, 87. **Open** 7.30am-midnight daily. **Rates** (under 25) *full board* 2,450 ptas; *half-board* 1,975ptas; *b&b* 1,500ptas; (over 25) *full board* 3,350ptas; *half-board* 2,725ptas, *b&b* 2,075ptas. **Credit** V
This giant, 183-bed hostel is some way from the city centre, up the hill at the back of Barcelona in Vallcarca, but far from a Metro station. Guests stay in a pleasant old house surrounded by gardens; rooms house from two to eight people, and there are lots of facilities. IYHF cards required.
Hotel services *Auditorium. Car park. Dining room. Fax & photocopy service. Laundry. Multilingual staff. Refreshments available. Safe. Slide projector. TV/video room. Wheelchair access.* **Room services** *Room adapted for the disabled.*

Hostal de Joves

Passeig Pujades 29, 08018 (tel/fax 300 31 04). Metro Arc de Triomf/bus 40, 41, 42, 141, N6. **Open** 7-10am, 3pm-midnight, daily. **Rates** (breakfast included) *under-25* 1,300ptas; *over-25* 1,500ptas. **No credit cards.**
This hostel, renovated a few years ago, looks out over the Ciutadella. Most of the 68 beds are in non-smoking dormitories, but there are a few double rooms; IYHF cards are needed, and five nights is the maximum length of stay.
Hotel services *Dining room. Kitchen. Laundry. Lockers. Multilingual staff. Refreshments available.*

Campsites

There are 13 campsites within a short radius of Barcelona. For more comprehensive information, get the *Catalunya Campings* brochure from Generalitat tourist offices (*see chapter* **Essential Information**)

Cala Gogó

Carretera de La Platja s/n, 08820 El Prat de Llobregat (379 46 00/fax 379 47 11). Bus 65 from Plaça d'Espanya/by car C-246 to Castelldefels, then Airport exit to Prat beach (7km). **Open** 15 Mar-15 Oct 9am-10pm (reception), 9am-2pm (office), daily. **Rates** *Mar-Jun, Oct* 1,000ptas per plot per night; *with light* 1,300ptas; plus *adults* 390ptas; *children 2-9* 300ptas; *Jun Sept:* 1,400ptas per plot per night; *with light* 1,800ptas; plus *adults* 560ptas; *children 2-9* 420ptas. **Credit** EC, MC, TC, V.
The nearest campsite to the city, large, well-equipped and with capacity for 4,500 people, four miles (7km) to the south near the beach at Prat, but also near the airport. There's a supermarket, restaurant, bar and swimming pool on-site, and campers can fish, play tennis, or use diving facilities.

Camping Albatros

Autovia de Castelldefels, km 15, 08850 Gavà (tel/fax 633 06 95). Bus L95 from Barcelona (Ronda Universitat), stops 250m from the camp entrance/by car C-246 to Gavà (15km). **Open** 1 May-27 Sept 7am-midnight (campsite); 8am-10pm (reception). **Rates** 575ptas per person per night; *under-10s* 400ptas; plus extra charges for cars, motorbikes, caravans, tents & light. **No credit cards.**
An extensive campsite on the beach in Gavà, between the airport and Castelldefels. There's a First Aid centre, shopping, hairdresser, laundry, bar and restaurant on site. You can also hire mobile homes. Nearby is a sports centre with tennis, minigolf and water sports. Videos in English are shown free in the video-cinema, and in July and August there are also free children's entertainments and city excursions.

Masnou

Carretera N-11, km 6393, 08320 El Masnou (tel/fax 555 15 03). Bus CASAS from Passeig Sant Joan/by car N-11 to Masnou (11km)/by train RENFE to Masnou from Plaça Catalunya. **Open** (reception) *Sept-June* 8am-1pm, 2.30-7pm; *June-Sept* 8am-1pm, 2.30pm-8.30pm, daily; (campsite) 8am-midnight daily. **Rates** 610ptas per person per night; *under-10s* 495ptas; plus extra charges for cars, motorbikes, caravans, tents, & light. **No credit cards.**
North of Barcelona, tucked under an attractive range of hills and offering pleasant respite from the city. The site is small, with capacity for only 360 people. Pitch a tent under the trees, or hire a bungalow (3,500ptas per person per day). Showers are included in the price and there's a bar, restaurant, supermarket, kids' playground and swimming pools on site. The nearby beach is sandy, and has diving and sailing facilities.

El Toro Bravo

Autovia de Castelldefels, km 11, 08840 Viladecans (637 34 62/fax 658 80 54). Bus L95 from Barcelona (Ronda Universitat)/by car C-246 to Viladecans (11km). **Open** *mid-June-Aug* 8am-8pm; *Sept-mid-June* 8.30am-7pm. **Rates** *1 Sept-14 June* 550ptas per person per night; *under-9s* 400ptas; *15 June-31 Aug* 600ptas per person per night; *under-9s* 450ptas; plus extra charges for cars, tents, caravans & light. **Credit** AmEx, EC, MC, TC. V.
It's seven miles (10km) from the main road bus stop to the site, but we're assured that lifts are often given to puffed-out campers. Open all year, it has space for 3,500 campers and services that include on-site hairdressers. They also rent out 2-4-berth caravans (3,900-5,800ptas per day) and bungalows (4,450-11,950ptas per day), rates varying according to size and season. The site has lots of shade, swimming pools and tennis courts, and is by the sea.

Barcelona by Season

Giants and fire-spitting dragons are welcome figures at the city's many celebrations.

Every year 141 different festivals take place in Barcelona, ranging from carnival parades and neighbourhood street parties to political commemorations and special food displays. These events are complemented by performing arts festivals, such as the open-air **Festival del Grec** each summer, as well as around 45 international trade shows, some of which attract major crowds.

Many of the city's festivals follow the Catholic calendar of Saints' days and holy days, but only a few are still genuinely religious in any sense. Many have pre-Christian roots, such as **Sant Joan**, or are even relatively modern urban inventions. City and local *festes* are able to draw on a unique body of Catalan folklore and celebration (*see* **Giants, dragons & human towers**). The climax of each *festa* tends to be packed with people, wild and noisy, with barrages of fireworks, but there are also children's parties and other activities in which all ages are catered for. While they may seem based in time-honoured tradition, these festivals happily mix older elements with others a few years old, for the *festa* is as much a product of the modern city as of history. Under Franco, many events were banned, or rendered lifeless. Hence, there was a break in historical continuity, but the *festes* have been revived with creativity as well as a sense of tradition, and are continually evolving. Many are accompanied by seasonal foods, which also continue to be invented. Large quantities of alcohol are put away, but locals' reluctance to show they are drunk means the revelry rarely turns nasty, and everyone can take part all night long.

The most important city events are **Sant Joan**, the **Grec**, **La Mercè**, **Christmas** and the following weeks and Carnival, **Carnestoltes**. The best sources of information on what's on are the city's **Centre d'Informació de la Virreina** on the Rambla and 010 line (*see chapter* **Essential Information**), or the *Festes Populars* department on 481 00 04. Programmes are also listed in the local press. In the listings below public holidays are marked *. For more on children's involvement in *festes*, *see chapter* **Children**, and for music festivals, *see chapters* **Music: Classical & Opera** *and* **Music: Rock, Roots & Jazz**. For festivals outside the city, *see chapter* **Trips Out of Town**.

Spring

Festes de Sant Medir de Gràcia

Gràcia to Sant Cugat and back, usually via Plaça Lesseps, Avda República Argentina & Carretera de l'Arrabassada. Metro Fontana/bus 22, 24, 28. **Information** City information line (010). **Date** 3 March.

A local, increasingly popular celebration held since 1830, in which a procession of riders on horses and mules, with beautifully decorated bridles, leave Gràcia in the morning after parading around Plaça Rius i Taulet with special banners, one for each of the *colles* or groups who organise the event. They head over Collserola by the winding Arrabassada road for the Hermitage of Sant Medir ('saint of the broad beans') near Sant Cugat, where they have a beany lunch. In the afternoon, as they return, they parade down Gran de Gràcia, throwing sweets into the crowd, as they did on the way out.

Setmana Santa

Information City information line (010). **Dates** Easter Week, Mar-April.

Holy Week, most important festival of the year in southern Spain, is of relatively little importance in Barcelona, although outside the city there are more Catalan Easter celebrations (*see chapter* **Trips out of Town**). However, three different groups run by Andalusian migrants do organise southern-style processions: most interesting is the lay procession, celebrated since 1978, known as the *Proceción del Santo Cristo de la Expiración*, which sets off from the Parc de les Bòbiles in Hospitalet de Llobregat (Metro Can Vidalet) at 9pm on Good Friday. In addition, *L'Ou com Balla* (*see below*) is repeated in the Cathedral cloister, which is decorated with flowers and herbs. For most people, though, Easter week is simply a holiday when most of the city closes down – with the notable exception of the pastry shops. Having produced the sweet cakes called *bunyols* every Wednesday and Friday through Lent, they sell their *mones* (chocolate sculptures) for Easter. A run-of-the-mill *mona* will be a rabbit or a figure of whichever cartoon character is the rage that year, but many *pastisseries* also make elaborate set-pieces, including reproductions of famous buildings, people and events. The most spectacular are usually in **Escribà** (*see chapter* **Shopping**).

Sant Jordi

La Rambla, and all over Barcelona. **Date** 23 April.

Saint George, patron saint of Catalonia and a true romantic, slew the dragon and saved the lady, and 23 April has long been celebrated here as a local alternative to Saint Valentine's Day, when men give red roses to women. In 1923, a Barcelona bookseller noticed that the date also coincided with the birthdays of both Shakespeare and Cervantes, and declared it the *Dia del Llibre*, the Day of the Book, obliging women to reply in kind by giving men a book. Since the advent of modernity, however, everybody can give everybody else a book and/or a rose at their discretion, in *el Dia del Llibre i de la Rosa*. As a result, half of total book sales in Catalonia take

Part of the show in the **Festival del Grec.**

place on this day – and the rose industry doesn't do badly either. The best way to see this colourful and civilised festival is to make your way down the Rambla: it's lined with temporary bookstalls, surrounded by packed crowds, and the flower stalls have truly spectacular displays of roses. This is also the only day of the year that the **Generalitat** is fully open to the public, with its own rose display, but the queues to enter are, again, huge (*see chapter* **Sightseeing**).

Feria de Abril
Can Zam, Santa Coloma de Gramenet. Metro Santa Coloma, then special buses from the Metro. **Information** Federación de Entidades Culturales Andaluces en Cataluña (453 60 00).* **Date** end April- early May.
The *Feria*, inspired by the famous month-long fair in Seville, is the main event of the year for Catalonia's Andalusian community, with hundreds of different groups saving up all year to provide food and drink stalls for their members. Non-members, however, can also watch dozens of different live events – all in some to do way with Andaluz culture – including some very authentic flamenco. Continuing for over a week, the fair is enormously popular, and not just with Andalusians, attracting well over a million visitors.

Dia del Treball* (May Day)
Date 1 May.
Demonstrations are organised by the different labour unions, the most popular routes being along Passeig de Gràcia, Passeig de Sant Joan and the Paral.lel. Attendance, massive in the first days of democracy, has fallen in recent years.

Sant Ponç
C/Hospital. Metro Liceu/bus 14, 18, 38, 59, 64, 91. **Date** 11 May.
Sant Ponç is the patron saint of beekeepers and herbalists, and on his day, the Carrer Hospital is packed from end to end with stalls – some of whose owners have travelled from as far away as Extremadura on the Portuguese frontier to take part – selling honey, herbs, very sweet candied fruit, perfumes, sweet wine and other natural products. It's a charming, crowded and very colourful event, and the scents of the great bunches of fresh herbs are exhilarating.

Marató de l'Espectacle
Mercat de les Flors, C/Lleida 59. Metro Espanya/bus 9, 13, 38, 61, 65, 91. **Information** (268 18 68). **Dates** late May.
And perhaps the main event for Barcelona's alternative arts-performance-club-and-much else scene. Over a weekend the **Mercat de les Flors** (*see chapter* **Theatre**) is taken over by any number of comedians, theatre groups, musicians and other creator/performers, including art installations and performance art, who start up and keep going, in a real 'cultural marathon'. With tremendous participation by performers and audience, it's a good showcase for new talents. Things usually start around 8pm, and go on through the night.

Festival Internacional de Poesia de Barcelona
Palau de la Música Catalana. Metro Jaume I/bus 17, 19, 40, 45. **Information** Centre d'Informació de la Virreina & 010. **Date** late May.
A free evening of poetry readings by around a dozen international and Catalan poets, in Barcelona's most *modernista* venue, the Palau de la Música. Previous participants have included Tahar Ben Jelloun, Wole Soyinka and Joan Brossa.

Festa de la Bicicleta
Information Servei d'Informació Esportiva (402 30 00). **Date** a Sunday in May.
Celebrated as the 'Day of the Pedal' before the Civil War broke out in 1936, this festival was revived and modernised by Mayor Pasqual Maragall in 1982, in an effort to encourage local residents to use their cars less. The Mayor – a cycle enthusiast – leads some 15,000 cyclists on a ride around the city, and anyone with a bike can join in. For cycle hire shops, *see chapter* **Services**.

Summer

L'Ou com Balla
Venues *Ateneu Barcelonès, C/Canuda 6; Casa de l'Ardiaca, C/Santa Llúcia 1; Cathedral Cloister; Museu Frederic Marés, Plaça Sant Iu 5. Metro Jaume I/bus 17, 19, 40, 45.* **Dates** Corpus Christi (May or early June) & the following Sunday.
L'Ou com Balla (roughly, 'The Egg that Dances') is a curious custom that traditionally took place only during Corpus Christi, once the most important festival in Barcelona. A previously-emptied eggshell is left to bob on top of the jet from a fountain, in the Cathedral cloister, in the patio of the Casa de l'Ardiaca in front of the Cathedral and in other patios of the Barri Gòtic. This is a very old Barcelona tradition, reported in the sixteenth century. The fountains, wonderfully garlanded with broom and carnations, may represent the model of the cathedral that was carried in the Corpus procession, with the 'canopies' formed by the eggshells over the fountain-tops representing the monstrance held over the model cathedral by attendants. *L'Ou com Balla* can also be seen in the Cathedral cloister in Easter week (*see* **Setmana Santa**).

Trobada Castellera (Meeting of Human-Tower Builders)
Plaça Catalunya. Metro Catalunya/bus all routes to Plaça Catalunya. **Information** 010. **Date** June.
Organised by the *Castellers de Barcelona*, this is a non-competitive display of human-tower building, involving all the existing *casteller* groups in Catalonia (for an explanation fo castells, *see* **Giants, dragons & human towers**).

Sant Joan*
Throughout Barcelona. **Date** night of 23 June.
The night of 23 June, Midsummer Night and, less importantly, the eve of the feast of Saint John the Baptist, is *la Nit del Foc*, the Night of Fire, throughout Catalonia and the Balearics. As the summer solstice, its origins are obviously

pagan, and it's the wildest night of the year, both mad and magical. Days before the event, kids start letting off bangers all over the city, with the noise culminating on the night itself, when the city sounds like a war zone. Bonfires are lit at street junctions, despite Ajuntament attempts to prohibit them, and *cava* is drunk through the night, accompanied by a sweet cake, rather like a pizza base with candied fruit, called a *coca*. If you don't want to celebrate at a disco – expensive and closed-in – join in the more reasonably-priced mass parties organised in the Monumental bull ring, the Tibidabo funfair or the Velòdrom in Horta. Alternatively, walk along the Rambla, lined with *cava* vendors, and watch the small *correfoc* at Plaça Barceloneta; or head for Montjuïc, where there's music for free. At midnight, fireworks erupt into the air at many points around the city, with two huge displays mirroring each other on Montjuïc and Tibidabo. The holiday is actually the day after, the 24th, so there's plenty of time to sleep it off, and a favourite way to end the night of Sant Joan is to watch the sunrise over the sea.

Festival del Grec

Information & tickets Centre d'Informació de la Virreina. **Dates** late June-July.

The Grec is the Barcelona City Council's annual summer arts festival, mainly of theatre, contemporary dance and music, with a strong representation of world music. Many shows, particularly theatre, take place at the Greek-style amphitheatre on Montjuïc, from which the festival gets its name, but performances go on in several other venues, most open-air: the Poble Espanyol, the Mercat de les Flors, the Plaça del Rei – a superb setting for concerts, with the Gothic walls floodlit –the Palau de la Música, in parks, or on the streets. Each year, the Ajuntament tries to spend its budget on a balanced selection of local and international artists, and is always criticised for not having enough of one or the other.

Festa Major de Gràcia

All over district of Gràcia. Metro Fontana/bus 22, 24, 28. **Information** (291 66 00). **Date** ten days, late Aug.

Held every year since the early nineteenth century, Gràcia's *festa major* has now almost outgrown the *barri* itself, and attracts people from all over the city – to an extent that can irritate local residents. A unique feature is the competition between different streets for the best decoration: they are decked out to represent elaborate fantasy scenarios, from desert-island themes to satires or comments on current events. Each street also has its own programme of events, entertainment and dancing, plus an open-air meal in the street for all the neighbours. District-wide events are centred on the Plaça Rius i Taulet, and there's also music nightly in the Plaça de la Revolució, Plaça del Sol and Plaça de la Virreina. The *festa* opens with *gegants* and *castells* in the Plaça Rius i Taulet, and reaches its climax on the last night with the *Correfoc* and fireworks display.

Festa Major de Sants

All over district of Sants. Metro Plaça de Sants; Sants Estació; Plaça del Centre/bus 44, 54, 56, 57, 109. **Date** around 24 Aug.

Sants' *festa major*, once one of the most important in Barcelona, has not had the benefit of the same historical continuity as the Gràcia festival, and had to be revived after the dictatorship. Major events, such as the *correfoc*, are held in the futuristic Parc de l'Espanya Industrial (*see chapter* **Sightseeing**). Other events are centred on the Plaça del Centre, Carrer Sant Antoni and Plaça de la Farga.

Diada Nacional de Catalunya* (Catalan National Day)

All over Barcelona. **Date** 11 September.

On 11 September 1714, Barcelona fell to the Castilian/French army in the War of the Spanish Succession, a national disaster that led to the loss of all Catalan institutions for over 200 years (*see chapter* **History: The Fall & Rise of Barcelona**). This heroic defeat is now commemorated as Catalan National Day. In 1977, the first time it could be celebrated openly in Barcelona after the dictatorship, over a million people took to the streets. It is now a public holiday and has lost its force somewhat, but is still a day for serious national reaffirmation and demonstrations, with thousands of Catalan flags displayed on balconies. At night, independentist demonstrators have confrontations with the police.

La Diadeta de la Barceloneta

All over Barceloneta. Metro Barceloneta/bus 17, 39, 45, 57, 59, 64. **Date** weekend in mid-September.

Held shortly before the Barceloneta has its full *festa major* (*see below*), the *Diadeta* ('little day') is an unusual, very local celebration organised by dozens of *penyes* (local associations), each of which is connected to a different bar or restaurant. The men of these groups, wearing an assortment of traditional regalia, disappear for a day, then come back laden with rabbits and other animals they have supposedly hunted for food, while the rest of the area celebrates their return with a procession of symbols of all the different guilds linked to the fishing industry in this traditional fishermen's district. Little-known among the city's popular festivals, this is one that's well worth a visit.

Mostra dels Vins i Caves de Catalunya

Information INCAVI (487 67 38).

Dates two weeks mid-Sept.

The official showcase for Catalan wines, coinciding with the Mercè. In previous years it's been held in stands along main thoroughfares – the Gran Via or Rambla Catalunya – but in a regrettable step it's likely that in future it will be confined to one of the shopping malls, L'Illa or Maremagnum. Virtually every wine producer in the country sets up their wares, with plenty of opportunity for tastings.

Festes de la Mercè*

All over Barcelona. **Information** Centre d'Informació de la Virreina & (010). **Date** one week around 24 Sept.

Our Lady of Mercy – *Nostra Senyora de la Mercè* – housed in the church of the same name close to the port, joined Santa Eulàlia as one of the city's patrons in 1637, when she saved the city from a plague of locusts; in 1871, her name was given to the whole city's *festa major*, Barcelona's biggest celebration of itself. Official ceremonies include a mass and the reading of a speech of dedication by an invited cultural figure. There's an extensive music programme, including jazz, flamenco, Catalan folk and dance music, and other events, some of them free. Concerts are held in many squares in and around the old city: usually the Plaça Catalunya, Plaça Sant Jaume, Plaça del Rei and Plaça Reial, as well as the Poble Espanyol out on Montjuïc. Another fixture of the modern Mercè are large-scale rock concerts, held at waterside venues such as the Moll de la Fusta. The many associated sports events include the *Cursa de la Mercè* (24 Sept), a fun run with 20,000 participants from Plaça Catalunya to Montjuïc, and swimming competitions across the harbour. As well as this, there's the folkloric element of the *festa*, with *gegants* and *castellers* on the mornings of the first and last days, and Barcelona's biggest *correfoc*, usually on the evening of 23 September, for a grand climax.

Autumn

Festa Major de la Barceloneta

All over district of Barceloneta. Metro Barceloneta/bus 17, 39, 45, 57, 59, 64. **Date** end-Sept-early Oct.

One of the liveliest of the smaller district *festes*. Activities are centred around the Plaça de la Barceloneta and the Plaça de la Font, and a grotesque general, General Bum Bum (Boom Boom), leads a procession of kids round the district firing off a cannon – a tradition dating from 1881. There's dancing on the beach every night.

Tots Sants (All Saints' Day)*

All over Barcelona. **Date** 1 November.
All Saints' Day is the day for remembering the dead, and traditional Barcelonans visit the city's cemeteries to pay their respects. Around this time, roast *moniatos* (sweet potatoes) and chestnuts, traditionally deemed the favourite food of the dead, are sold at street stalls, and *panellets* (cakes of almonds and pine-nuts) at pastry shops. This event has also become increasingly festive, with people holding All Saints' Eve parties at which these traditional foods are washed down with sweet wine s such as *moscatell* or *malvasia*.

Fira del Disc de Col.leccionista (Record Collectors' Fair)

Fira de Barcelona, Avda Reina Maria Cristina (233 20 00). Metro Espanya/bus 9, 13, 38, 51, 53, 61, 65, 91, 109. **Dates** usually first or second weekend Nov.
Organised since 1985 by rock enthusiast and restaurant owner Jordi Tardà (*see* **Port Olímpic** in *chapter* **Restaurants**), this is now the largest fair of its kind in Europe. It takes a different musical theme each year, offers a vast selection of second-hand LPs, 45s, tapes and CDs, and ends with an auction of rock memorabilia that attracts buyers from around the world.

Winter

Fira de Santa Llúcia

Pla de la Seu & Avda de la Catedral. Metro Jaume I/ bus 17, 19, 40, 45. **Dates** usually 8-24 December.
Christmas in Barcelona begins with the Christmas fair in front of the Cathedral, at which accessories are sold – many hand-made– for the nativity scenes that Catalan and Spanish families build up year by year. These include not only the usual Josephs and Marys, but also the exclusively Catalan figure of the *caganer*: a man, sometimes a woman, having a realistically-sculpted crap within spitting distance of the King of Kings. It's by far the most popular figure in the

Giants, dragons & human towers

Festivals in Barcelona are very varied, but have in common a handful of very special popular traditions. Some hark back to pagan revels of ancient epochs, and all are at least four centuries old. Today, scarcely a town in Catalonia is without its dragon association and resident devils, not to mention its giant clubs, tower-builders and *sardana* groups, and all expanding by the year.

Gegants & Capgrossos

The *Gegants* or giants – five-metre-high wood-and-papier-mâché figures, each supported by a person peeping out through a mesh in the skirts – were originally part of the festival of Corpus Christi, instituted by the Church in 1264, partly in order to incorporate popular pre-Christian figures into conventional ritual. There are many theories of their origin, one being that they are based in David and Goliath, but they represent many folkloric characers. In Barcelona two of the most historic giants are the *Gegants del Pi*, kept in the church of Santa Maria del Pi. Equally popular are the *capgrossos* ('fatheads') who accompany the parade of giants, wearing huge papier mâché and wood heads, usually with bizarre fixed smiles. Archetypal leprechaun-like figures, they once represented the Biblical tribes of Sem, Cam and Japhet, but these theatrical set-pieces have long been dropped, and the heads can now look like celebrities or all sorts of other figures. Like the *Correfoc* (see below), and other events in the *festa* these parades are accompanied by special music played on traditional instruments. One of the most skilled makers of them is **El Ingenio** (*see chapter* **Shopping: All kinds of everything**). The festival of Corpus went into decline, but in the meantime the giants and heads had been incorporated into the *festa major* – village or district festival – developed in the nineteenth century. Like other *festa* traditions *gegants* and *capgrossos* have enjoyed a boom in popularity since the 1980s, their numbers increasing tenfold (today, there are 197 in Barcelona alone). *Gegants* and their friends can be seen in every district *festa* as well as at the city-wide **Mercè**.

Dracs, Dimonis & the Correfoc

If you see the giants and fatheads during the day, you can be almost certain that at sunset you will see the *dracs* (dragons) and *dimonis* (devils) come out to play, waving fireworks and scuttling after crowds of screaming spectators. The dragon is a recurrent feature in Catalan folklore, in contrast to the bull-obsession of much of Iberia. The *festa* dragons are big, wood-and-canvas monsters, carried by teams, with fireworks in their snouts; their attendant devils are men and women in demon suits carrying powerful fireworks that spin round on sticks. Their procession is the *Correfoc*, literally 'fire-running', the wild climax of the *festa*, when the dragons spin and swirl through a surging crowd amid a manic atmosphere and clouds of smoke. If you intend to be at the front of the crowd, it's advisable to cover as much of your body as possible, with hoods and handkerchiefs over the mouth, which is how you'll see dedicated fire-runners dressed, even in August. After the dragons have got worn out, the party continues with yet more fireworks, and dancing.

Castells

The formation of *castells* or human towers has become a major spectator sport in Catalonia, with teams training throughout the year. *Castells* possibly have their origins in Medieval prowess games, and in a popular dance of the seventeenth-century, the *moixiganga*. At the end of this dance, men would form a human tower up to six people high. Late, the tower-building began to take precedence over the dancing, and by the last century tower-building clubs, known as *colles*, began to form. In each *castell*, a large group link arms at the bottom to form the base, the *pinya* (pine-cone), with the crowd joining in around them for extra support. Then succeeding layers climb on top of them, the upper levels getting smaller until it comes down to a single small boy or girl who tops the tower off with a wave. There are several distinctive formations of towers: the most difficult are combinations like a *5 of 8* (five people in each level, eight levels) or anything with nine levels. The completion of each level is accompanied by its own music, and there's a tremendous sense of suspense in the final, most precarious stages. Interest in *castells* waned over the last century, until the early 1980s, when a major revival began. Tower formations that hadn't been attempted since the previous heyday of the 1850s have been successfully repeated in competitive *castell* events. And, as in the dragons and other *colles*, *castells* are now entirely open to women and girls. There are now 38 *colles castelleres* around Catalonia, including places that have never before had a tower-building tradition.

The Miracle of Art

Catalan crib, and local artesans compete each year to create new *caganer* designs. As for the origins of Catalans' scatological obsession (especially visible in Christmas traditions), it awaits a full anthropological explanation. At the fair you can also find Christmas trees – a relatively recent foreign import, but well established – and a range of craft work.

Christmas & Sant Esteve* (Boxing Day)

All over Barcelona. **Dates** 25, 26 December.
The centrepiece of Barcelona's Christmas decorations. is an extravagant life-size crib in the Plaça Sant Jaume, surrounded by real palms and live animals. Some people have their main Christmas dinner late on Christmas Eve, as is the custom throughout the rest of Spain, but many Catalans have two large lunches, one on Christmas Day with the family of one parent and another on Boxing Day with the family of the other. Around Christmas children get to expend their energies in a ritual known as the *Caga Tió*, when the kids 'beat the crap' – more incorrigible scatology – out of a wooden log with sticks, and then run into an adjoining room. When they return, they find the log has crapped them out small presents.

Cap d'Any (New Year's Eve)

All over Barcelona. **Date** 31 December.
As they do for **Sant Joan** (*see above*), most discos and music bars charge outrageous entrance fees for New Year parties: cheaper are the mass celebrations around the city, the best of which is at the Monumental bullring. Wherever you are, at twelve – well announced on TV – you will be expected to start stuffing 12 grapes into your mouth, one for every chime of the bell, without stopping until the New Year has been fully rung in (missing a grape brings bad luck for the coming year). Most taxi drivers take the night off and transport stops at 1am, so this is not a good night to travel unless you have access to a car.

The Sardana

The sedate Catalan dance the *sardana* is not limited to seasonal celebrations, since it can be seen throughout the year, but it is also a part of every local *festa*. Its origins are believed to go back to ancient Greece; the name comes from the *ballo sardo* of Sardinia, an island occupied by Catalans for centuries, and the first written reference to it is from 1587. It consists of a moving circle, whose members hold hands and mark a set pattern of paces that shift from left to right and back again. Dancing in the streets doesn't quite give the right idea: it's more like a folk dance invented by mathematicians, as serious dancers have to concentrate to follow the step sequences. The *sardana* was already popular as a folk dance in the Empordà, the coastal area near the French border, before 1800, but was given its modern form in the last century almost single-handedly by a self-taught musician, Pep Ventura. He established the line-up of the traditional *sardana* band, the *cobla*, combining traditional and brass instruments, and gave the dance a definitive musical form, writing 400 scores for it himself. After his death in 1875 other musicians took up the baton, and the *sardana* quickly spread across the country. Charged with symbolic references to unity and equality, it was adopted by nationalists as Catalonia's national dance, and has become one of its best-known symbols.

In Barcelona, *sardanes* are danced every Sunday in front of the Cathedral from about noon to 2pm, and in the Plaça Sant Jaume from 7pm to 9pm. You don't have to be an expert to join in, and anyone wanting to try just has to enter a circle.

Cavalcada dels Reis* (Three Kings' Parade)

Route *Kings normally arrive at Moll de la Fusta, the parade up the Rambla to Plaça Sant Jaume, and continue to Passeig de Gràcia; detailed route changes each year.*
Information City information line (010) or (301 41 98).
Date 5 January.
Epiphany, or the day of the Three Kings (6 January) is marked in most Latin countries, and until the recent advertising of Father Christmas was the time when children, and often adults, received their main presents, only smaller ones having been given on Christmas Day. On 5 January the Kings arrive by sea (from across the harbour) and are formally welcomed by the Mayor. They then parade around the city, with accompanying floats, and throw sweets to children in the crowd. A toy fair is also held on Gran Via (usually 2-6 Jan), which stays open through the night for late present-buyers. And, in case you'd forgotten the scatology, they also sell sugary coal and turd lookalikes made from fig-paste, for kids who have been naughty in the preceding year.

Festa dels Tres Tombs

All over district of Sant Antoni. Metro Sant Antoni/bus 24, 41, 55, 64. **Date** 17 January.
Sant Antoni Abat (Saint Anthony the Abbot) is the patron saint of domestic animals and muleteers. There may no longer be any members of this trade left, but a small procession of horsemen, dressed in tail coats and top hats, still commemorates his day by riding three times (the Tres Tombs or Three Turns) around a route that goes from the Ronda Sant Antoni, through the Plaça Universitat, Pelai and the Plaça Catalunya, down the Rambla and back along Nou de la Rambla. This parade coincides with the *festa major* of the nearby *barri* of Sant Antoni, which continues for a week, complete with *sardanes*, *castellers* and neighbourhood giants.

Carnestoltes (Carnival)

All over Barcelona. **Date** February.
Hugely popular in the first years after its re-legalisation in the 1970s, Barcelona's Carnival suffered a decline in the 1980s from which it has only recently recovered. The main event – a procession from Plaça Catalunya to Colom and back, known as the *Rua* – is as impressive today as ever. During the day, children's fancy-dress carnivals are organised, both by schools and the city's markets, so it's common to see kids being taken to school dressed up as bees or Marie Antoinettes. Carnival parties are put on for older folk later in clubs and bars. The origins of Carnival are in a once-traditional outburst of eating, drinking and fornicating prior to the limitations imposed by Lent. King Carnestoltes – a masked personification of the Carnival spirit – also used to criticise the authorities and reveal hidden scandals, a tradition which has unfortunately died out. The end of Carnival on Ash Wednesday is marked by the *Enterrament de la Sardina*, the Burial of the Sardine, when, yes, a small fish is buried to indicate the start of Lent, usually on Montjuïc. More spectacular than Barcelona's Carnival are those in Vilanova i la Geltrú and Sitges, which benefit from an unbroken tradition and feature wilder parties. A gay parade is now part of the Sitges Carnival (*see chapters* **Gay & Lesbian Barcelona** *and* **Trips Out of Town**).

Barcelona Fashion

Fira de Barcelona, Avda Reina Maria Cristina (information 233 20 00). Metro Espanya/bus 9, 13, 38, 51, 53, 61, 65, 91, 109. **Date** February.
The big event of the year for the rag trade, which as well as the *Gaudí Barcelona* salon for the main autumn and winter collections now includes sections such as *Mediterraneo Jeans* for leisure wear, *Intimoda* for underwear and so on. It's officially trade-only, but attracts over 14,000 visitors, so some members of the public presumably get in. There's a smaller *Gaudí Barcelona* event in September, for the next year's spring and summer collections.

I THINK THEREFORE I AM THEREFORE I AM... CONTEMPORARY

Contemporary Art is about you and me. Neither yesterday nor tomorrow can anyone understand it better than you.

The art of our time

MUSEU D'ART CONTEMPORANI
MAC
BA
BARCELONA

Sightseeing

Gothic wonders, Modernist visions, dramatic urban parks, fairground rides and the beach- and streetlife itself – the choice Barcelona offers is nothing if not varied.

Barcelona is an easy city to explore, compact and with many of its major sights clustered within easy walking distance of each other. Wandering around and soaking up the streetlife, between regular stopovers in bars and cafés is as enjoyable a way of getting to know the city as visiting specific sights, and the best way to absorb quintessential Barcelona. When sites are further afield, the excellent city transport system makes it easy to reach them. For more on the lesser-known attractions and character of the city's districts, *see chapter* **Barcelona by Area**, and for background on architectural styles, *see chapter* **Architecture**.

Hubs of the City

Colom & the Port

At the foot of the Rambla, Columbus, in Catalan **Colom**, points out to sea from atop his column, confusingly enough towards Italy (*see* **Parks & Panoramas**). To his right are the fourteenth-century shipyards or **Drassanes**, now the **Museu Marítim**, and the Balearics ferry terminal. From near the foot of the column, you can cross the harbour and sail to the Port Olímpic on the **Golondrines** (*see* **Rides**). It used to be that, unless you took a *Golondrina*, there was little to do after seeing Colom but turn back up the Rambla, since the port was nothing but a dingy collection of warehouses and rail tracks. No longer, for Barcelona's waterfront, rechristened the **Port Vell** or Old Port, has been transformed forever, mostly since the Olympics. Today, across the inner harbour from Colom there is **Maremagnum**, a complex of chic shops, restaurants and bars at the end of a high-design pedestrian pier. This quay is also the site of an eight-screen moviehouse, an **IMAX** cinema, and the **Aquàrium**. The city-side of this part of the port, to the left of Colom, is bordered by the Passeig de Colom, which runs along the waterfront beside the **Moll de la Fusta** or Wood Quay. This was the first part of the port to be redeveloped, in the mid-eighties, and has a string of pavement bars and restaurants, including Javier Mariscal's **Gambrinus**, topped by a giant fibreglass lobster that has become a new city landmark. As one might expect, these bars are pricey, but the promenade is a cool and pleasant place to mingle and watch the harbour lights on balmy evenings.

There are benches and grassy promenades, too, as you walk toward Roy Lichtenstein's giant mosaic sculpture at the end of the Passeig de Colom. If you carry on round the port to the right, you reach the **marina** and the **Palau de Mar**, a converted warehouse which has the **Museu d'Història de Catalunya**, and a number of water-side restaurants. Alternatively, if you continue along Passeig de Colom you'll come to the central **Post Office**, the **Estació de França**, the **Ciutadella** park and the **Zoo**. Crossing Passeig de Colom here will take you back into the old city and the **La Ribera** area, with its bars and architectural attractions. Across the harbour is the **Barceloneta** district, tradition-

ally the home of the city's fishing families and famed for its fish restaurants, and beyond it, the **Port Olímpic** and the all-revamped beaches (*see* **Barcelona Beach**).

Plaça Catalunya & Passeig de Gràcia

The Plaça Catalunya is the city's centre, and the point at which the old, once-walled city meets the Eixample – the 525 square blocks above it, built as a grid-pattern urban extension (in Catalan, *Eixample*) in the last century (*see chapter* **History: Factories, Barricades & Lyric Poetry**). Most of the *Plaça*'s statues and fountains date from the 1920s, but recently it's been repeatedly dug up and relaid to accommodate new traffic patterns. Surrounded by bank offices, it also houses the main branch of **El Corte Inglés** department store. The Plaça Catalunya is an obvious focal point, in that it's a transport hub: many bus routes stop here; two Metro lines meet; the FGC lines to Tibidabo, Sarrià and the suburbs begin; and it has a main line (RENFE) railway station serving the airport, the coast to the North, the Montseny mountains and the Pyrenees. The *Plaça*'s attractions have also increased thanks to the City's pavement-widening schemes, which have greatly expanded the space available

Columbus wonders which way to go.

The greatest street in the world

It is near-inevitable that one of the first things any visitor to Barcelona does is to stroll along **La Rambla** (or the *Ramblas*, in Castilian), the magnificent mile-long walkway that cuts through the middle of the old city and leads down to the port. Often described as the world's greatest street, it's certainly the definitive pedestrian boulevard. A Catalan writer, Quim Soler, has said of it that it's not Barcelona's main artery, but its main vein, a place where you come to soak up the essence of the city through the eyes.

The *Rambla* is an urban feature unique to Catalonia, and there is one in most Catalan towns. Originally, the Rambla of Barcelona, like most of its smaller equivalents, was a seasonal river bed, running along the western edge of the thriteenth-century city. The name comes from the Arabic word for riverbed, *ramla*. From the Middle Ages to the Baroque era, a great many churches and convents were built beside the Barcelona Rambla, four of which have given their names to sections of it: as one descends from Plaça Catalunya, it is successively re-named Rambla dels Estudis, Rambla de Sant Josep, Rambla dels Caputxins and Rambla de Santa Mònica.

The Rambla also served as the meeting ground for city and country dwellers, for on the far side of these ecclesiastical buildings lay the still scarcely-built up Raval, 'the city outside the walls', and rural Catalonia. This open ground alongside the city wall was a natural place to hold markets. At first, there were probably just individual farm folk selling produce; later, they became more organised. From these beginnings sprang **La Boqueria**, Barcelona's largest market, still on the Rambla today.

La Rambla took on its recognisable, present form roughly between 1770 and 1860. The city wall came down in 1775, and the Rambla was gradually filled in and turned into a boulevard. Seats were available to strollers for rent, and some street lighting provided, as early as 1781. The land to the south-west was soon densely urbanised, as the *barri* of the **Raval**, and the Rambla, no longer on the city's edge, became a wide path through its heart. It used to be said that it was an obligation for every true Barcelona citizen to walk down the Rambla and back at least once a day. Nowadays, many locals are more blasé about the place, and the street has been seriously targeted by the international fast-food industry, but the Rambla, and the people-watching opportunities it provides, remains one of the city's essential attractions.

There are many ways of going along the Rambla, from a saunter to a purposeful stride, but the best way to get a feel for it is, perhaps, complete immobility, best achieved by taking one of the seats flanking the top of the avenue (for which you have to pay a few coins) or, more expensively, by heading for a convenient café. The parade passing before your chair will be diverse and entertaining enough for you to want to sit therefro quite a while. Should you get up and join the flow, one feature of *ramblejant* (strolling the Rambla, a specific verb) that can be surprising is eye contact: people look you in the eye, see what's what, and glance away. It may be personal, or it may not.

As well as having four names, the Rambla is divided into territories: turfs determined by tradition rather than street numbers. The first part – at the top, by Plaça Catalunya – is known as the Rambla de Canaletes, and belongs by unwritten agreement to a group of elderly men who engage perpetually in a *tertulia*, a classic Iberian quasi-conversation, quasi debate about anything from politics to football. On Sunday evenings, especially, they form a sizeable crowd. This part of the Rambla also has the **Font de Canaletes**, the first drinking fountain on your right as you descend. Legend has it that if you drink from it, you'll return to Barcelona – although its water is now no different from that of any tap.

Below this, around the mid-point of the Rambla, there are kiosks divided between those selling fauna and those selling flora. There's a brisk trade in birds of every variety, from hens and pigeons to brilliant macaws and parrots. Keep walking, past the **Poliorama** theatre, and C/Portaferrisa, a fashionable shopping street that leads to the **Cathedral** and the Barri Gòtic, opens on your left.

The boulevard's next section is popularly known as the *Rambla de les Flors*, understandably, because it contains a string of magnificent flower-stalls that stay open well into the night. On the right, still looking downhill, and past the **Virreina** exhibition and information centre, is the great **Boqueria** central market. Continue and you'll reach the **Pla de l'Os**, centre-point of the Rambla, with an entry to the Liceu metro station and a large pavement mosaic created in 1976 by Joan Miró. On the left more streets run off into the Barri Gòtic, past the extraordinary **Bruno Quadros** building (1883), with its oriental umbrellas on the wall and a Chinese dragon protruding over the street. Almost opposite on the right-hand side is the façade of the **Liceu** opera

Part of the endless variety that you can find in Barcelona's largest free theatre.

house, burned down in 1994 and now being feverishly rebuilt. Behind it lies the *Barrio Chino* (*Xino*, in Catalan), 'Chinatown', traditional home of Barcelona's low-life, although now much changed (*see chapter* **Barcelona by Area**). Today, it's one of the city's most multicultural areas, where, Moslem *halal* butcher shops serving North Africans sit alongside *carnisseries* selling every part of the pig to Catalans.

The Rambla de Caputxins section is lined with mostly-expensive cafés. The **Café de l'Opera** (*see chapter* **Cafés & Bars**), opposite the Liceu, is the best, has a wonderful art deco interior and reasonable prices, and is a great favourite with locals and foreigners. Further down on the left are Carrer Ferran, the most direct route to **Plaça Sant Jaume**, and the **Plaça Reial**, with its cafés and budget hotels.

A brief detour along C/Nou de la Rambla to the right will take you to Gaudí's **Palau Güell**, before you hit the stretch of La Rambla that has been a thriving prostitution belt. You may still see the occasional extravagantly-garbed transvestite, but of late the authorities' determined city-sanitisation efforts have greatly reduced the visibility (if not the existence) of street soliciting. Thanks to a new arts centre, university (the Pompeu Fabra) and a

fitness complex, this part of the Rambla now attracts a wider range of people and its sleazy ambience has been substantially diluted, although you should still be wary of pickpockets at all times.

Towards the port, the promenade widens into the Rambla de Santa Mònica, where you'll find the **Museu de Cera** wax museum and, on Sundays, stalls selling bric-a-brac and craftwork of varying quality, alongside a string of fortune-tellers and tarot-readers catering to the incorrigible local interest in all things astrological.

In addition to the fixed sights, you'll see droves of buskers, clowns, living statues, puppeteers, tango dancers, and musicians working the length of the walkway, many of them licensed by the Ajuntament and 'Rambla regulars'. There are the 24-hour newsstands, offering the Spanish and international press and huge quantities of porn. This is where you come to buy a paper late at night or on Sundays, when other newsstands are closed. And finally, there's the hustler with three walnut shells and a pea under one of them, challenging you to bet on the pea's position. Save your money: he never loses.

La Rambla
Metro Catalunya, Liceu, Drassanes/bus 14, 18, 38, 59, 64, 91, N4, N6, N9.

*The pompous dome of the Palau Nacional on **Montjuïc**, from the Poble Espanyol.*

for cafés. A favourite vantage point is the **Café Zurich** (*see chapter* **Cafés & Bars**), slated for closure since the dingy buildings behind it were torn down, but which has been saved for a while at least by a stop imposed by the Catalan government on new construction, and so far stays open.

Stretching away from the square is the **Passeig de Gràcia**, the main artery of the Eixample. Along it are two of Gaudí's greatest works: **La Pedrera** and the **Casa Batlló**, and on either side the long, straight streets are full of lesser-known Modernist gems. The Eixample also contains many of Barcelona's modish shopping haunts. Parallel to Passeig de Gràcia is **Rambla Catalunya**, the *Rambla* of the Eixample, with more cafés, and back on the Passeig itself, halfway up, is Passeig de Gràcia RENFE station, stopping-point for long-distance trains and for services to the beach towns of Castelldefels and Sitges. At the top, the Passeig de Gràcia crosses the great avenue of the **Diagonal**, then narrows to disappear into the old town of **Gràcia**, where there are several small squares with attractive bars. To the left, the Diagonal, the longest single street in Europe, runs away up to Plaça Francesc Macià, the modern business centre of Barcelona and another fashionable shopping area.

Plaça d'Espanya

The Plaça d'Espanya is the main entrance route to the park of **Montjuïc** and the **Palau Nacional**, home of the **Museu Nacional d'Art de Catalunya**. Like the Palau the *plaça* itself was created for Barcelona's last major international jamboree, before 1992, the Exhibition of 1929. Today, most of the original Exhibition area is occupied by the **Fira de Barcelona**, the city's Trade Fair. Montjuïc was also the most important of the Olympic sites for 1992, and is the site of many museums. From Plaça d'Espanya a 61 bus will take you up the hill to the **Olympic Ring**, the **Fundació Miró**, the **funfair** or, nearer the bottom, the **Poble Espanyol**. Giant escalators have also been installed alongside the steps leading to the Palau Nacional, giving easy access to the top of the hill, and another way up is to take the **Funicular** from another side of Montjuïc, by Paral.lel Metro. Not to be missed is a summer evening visit, when the **Font Màgica**, the giant illuminated fountain, midway between Plaça d'Espanya and

the Palau Nacional, dances in changing pastel hues to Tchaikovsky's *Nutcracker Suite*, Abba hits and other favourites while searchlights play over the palace dome. It's a wonderful extravaganza that conquers even cynics (23 June-23 Sept 9-11.30pm; music 10-11pm; Thur-Sun).

The Plaça d'Espanya also contains a railway station, for the FGC line to western Catalonia and **Montserrat**. On the opposite side of the Plaça to Montjuïc, C/Tarragona runs up to Barcelona's main station in Sants. On the right side, facing Sants, is the **Parc de l'Escorxador**, with a spectacular obelisk by Miró (*see* **Parks & Panoramas**).

Plaça de les Glòries

More a hub in potential than reality, although in Ildefons Cerdà's original plan for the Eixample it was intended that it should eventually become the centre of the city. At present an unlovely giant traffic junction, it is however of particular interest if you come into Barcelona by car, for it has a special **Metro-Park** car park that can be recommended as a place to leave your vehicle for the day (*see chapter* **Survival: Driving in Barcelona**). It is the location of the traditional **Els Encants** flea market, and recently has also begun to be redeveloped, with the vast **Barcelona Glòries** shopping mall on one side and two major cultural projects, the **Teatre Nacional** and the **Auditori**, on the other.

The Barri Gòtic & the Old City

Pick up any map of Barcelona and you will see a tightly-packed mass of narrow streets bordered by the Avda Paral.lel, the Ciutadella park, the Plaça Catalunya and the sea. This is the area that fell within the Medieval walls and, until 150 years ago, comprised the entire city. At its heart is the *Barri Gòtic* (Gothic Quarter), a body of interconnecting streets and buildings from Barcelona's Golden Age, within the line of the original Roman city wall. Relics of Medieval Barcelona can be found, though, throughout the old city: next to the **Drassanes** shipyard on Avda Paral.lel a substantial section of the fourteenth-century third city wall still stands. Below we list the most important Medieval monuments of Barcelona, not alphabetically but on the basis of their distance from the core of the *Barri Gòtic*.

Catedral de Barcelona

Pla de la Seu (315 15 54). Metro Liceu, Jaume I/bus 17, 40, 45. **Open** *Cathedral* 8am-1.30pm, 4-7.30pm, Mon-Fri; 8am-1.30pm, 5-7.30pm, Sat, Sun; *cloister* 9am-1.15pm, 4-7pm, daily; *museum* 10am-1pm daily. **Admission** *Cathedral/cloister* free; *choir* 300ptas; *museum* 50ptas. **No credit cards.**

The first cathedral on this site was founded in the sixth century, but the present one dates from between 1298 and 1430, except for its façade, which was finally finished, in a slightly un-Catalan neo-Gothic style, in 1913. In the far right corner of the Cathedral, looking at the façade, is the older and simpler Romanesque chapel of Santa Llúcia. The most striking aspect of the Cathedral is its volume: it has three naves of near-equal height. It contains many images, paintings and sculptures, and an intricately-carved choir built in the 1390s. In the crypt is the alabaster tomb of Santa Eulàlia, local Christian martyr and first patron saint of Barcelona. The cloister, bathed in light filtered through arches, palms and fountains, is the most attractive section of the Cathedral, and an atmospheric retreat from the city. It contains some white geese, for reasons that seem to have been lost in history, although the most common explanation is that they represent the purity of Santa Eulàlia. *See also chapter* **Museums.** *Wheelchair access.*

Plaça del Rei

Metro Liceu, Jaume I/bus 17, 19, 40, 45.
This wholly-preserved Medieval square is flanked on two sides by the **Palau Reial** (Royal Palace), most of it built in the thirteenth and fourteenth centuries for the Catalano-Aragonese 'Count-Kings', and now part of the **Museu d'Història de la Ciutat**. With additions from different periods piled on top of each other, the *Plaça* gives a vivid impression of the nature of life in the Medieval city, particularly since the square, as well as receiving all the traffic of the court, also served as the main flour and fodder market. It has been fairly well-established that Ferdinand and Isabella received Columbus on his return from America either on the palace steps or in the **Saló del Tinell** behind, although some sceptics still place the story in doubt. To the left, looking into the *Plaça*, is the sixteenth-century Viceroys' palace, with its five-tiered watchtower, the **Mirador del Rei Martí.** The square, magnificently floodlit, is used for concerts during the **Grec** festival (*see chapter* **Barcelona by Season**).

Museu d'Història de la Ciutat

C/Veguer 2 (315 11 11/315 30 53). Metro Jaume I/bus 17, 19, 40, 45. **Open** *Oct-June* 10am-2pm, 4-8pm, Tue-Sat; 10am-2pm Sun, public holidays. *July-Sept* 10-8pm Tue-Sat; 10am-2pm Sun, public holidays. **Admission** 500 ptas; 250ptas students, over-65s; free under-16s. **No credit cards.**

Roman Barcino

Medieval Barcelona and all subsequent buildings in the Barri Gòtic were constructed on top of the Roman settlement, founded in 15 BC, and many a local resident has set out to remodel a kitchen or bathroom and turned up a bit of *Barcino*. A good deal of the Roman town still lies undisturbed, but in the last few years the area excavated and opened up to public view has increased enormously.

The original Roman city was small, covering only some 10 hectares. Examples of its perpendicular street plan can be seen in the remarkable remains underneath the **Museu d'Historia de la Ciutat.** Stretching all the way from the museum itself to beneath the Cathedral, this is the largest underground excavation of a Roman site in Europe, and very well-presented, if labelling is only sometimes in English. There are numerous other Roman remains in the area: the museum's excellent pamphlet in English, *Itinerary Through Roman Barcelona*, suggests a two-to-three-hour walk covering the important sites.

Most impressive are the many surviving sections of the Roman defensive wall. It's easy to follow their perimeter by walking, from in front of and facing the Cathedral, left down C/Tapineria, then past the large stretch of wall on Plaça Ramon Berenguer el Gran onto C/Sots-Tinent Navarro, right at the post office onto C/Ample, then right again onto C/Avinyó, C/Banys Nous and C/de la Palla to come back to the Cathedral, where the two drum towers on C/Bisbe Irurita are also of Roman origin, although much altered since.

On C/Sots-Tinent Navarro, turn right to the Plaça dels Traginers, a small, shady *plaça* from which you can gaze on the circular tower that once defended Barcino's eastern corner. From here, if you walk straight on to C/Regomir and turn right, you will come to the **Pati Llimona**. Then, walk west to C/Avinyó, to the Pakistani restaurant at no 19: its rear dining room is a cave-like space incorporating a Roman wall. Further up, across C/Ferran at C/Banys Nous 16 there is a centre for disabled children which has inside it a large piece of Roman wall, with a relief of a pair of legs and feet (phone 318 14 81 to ask for a viewing time). Perhaps most striking of all Barcelona's Roman relics, however, are the four huge columns inside C/Paradis 10, behind the Cathedral, on the site of the Forum and the centre of *Barcino*.

Pati Llimona

C/Regomir 3 (268 47 00). Metro Jaume I/bus 17, 40, 45. **Open** 8am-10pm Mon-Fri; 10am-2pm Sat, Sun; *exhibitions* 10am-2pm, 4-8pm, Mon-Fri; 10am-2pm Sat, Sun. **Admission** free.
This is one of the oldest continually-occupied sites in Barcelona, incorporating part of a round tower that dates from the first Roman settlement, and later Roman baths. The excavated foundations are visible from the street, through large windows. Most of the building above is a fifteenth-century aristocratic residence, imaginatively converted into a social centre in 1988.

Temple of Augustus

C/Paradís 10 (Information Museu d'Història de la Ciutat, 315 11 11). Metro Jaume I/bus 17, 40, 45. **Open** 10am-2pm, 4-8pm, Tue-Sat; 10am-2pm Sun, public holidays. **Admission** free.
The *Centre Excursionista de Catalunya* (a hiking club) contains the largest single Roman relic in the city, four fluted columns with Corinthian capitals from the eastern, rear, corner of the Temple of Augustus, built in the first century BC.

The interest of the City History Museum lies more in the buildings it occupies than in the collections it holds. The basements of the fifteenth-century main building contain excavations of a large area of the Roman city, which extend like a complex cavern under the adjoining square (*see* **Roman Barcino**). Another part consists of several sections of the **Palau Reial**, especially the chapel of **Santa Agata**, and the Great Hall or **Saló del Tinell** – its massive, unadorned arches a classic example of the Catalan Gothic style. The chapel has a fifteenth-century altarpiece by Jaume Huguet, one of the greatest Catalan Medieval paintings. From the upper floors, there is also access to the inside of the city wall, and from the chapel you can climb up the **Mirador del Rei Martí** watchtower. Another section, the Casa Padellàs, houses temporary exhibitions. Like others, the Museum has been recently renovated, and has a well-stocked bookshop and information centre with a range of informative leaflets, many in English. *See also chapter* **Museums**. *Shop.*

Plaça Sant Jaume

Metro Liceu, Jaume I/bus 17, 19, 40, 45.
The main square of the old city and still the administrative centre of modern Barcelona, the Plaça Sant Jaume contains both the City Hall (**Ajuntament**) and the seat of the Catalan regional government (**Palau de la Generalitat**), which stand opposite each other in permanent rivalry. They have not always done so: the square was only opened up in 1823, after which point the present neo-Classical façade was added to the Ajuntament. That of the Generalitat is older, from 1598-1602. The greater part of both buildings, however, was built in the early fifteenth century, and both of their original main entrances give onto the street now called Bisbe Irurita on one side of the Plaça, and Ciutat on the other.

Ajuntament de Barcelona

Plaça Sant Jaume (402 70 00/special visits 402 73 64).
Metro Liceu, Jaume I/bus 17, 19, 40, 45. **Open** *office* 8am-3pm Mon-Fri; *visits* 10am-2pm Sat, Sun. **Admission** free.

Contrasting completely with the main façade, the old C/Ciutat entrance to the City Hall is entirely a work of Catalan Gothic. The centrepiece of the Ajuntament is the fifteenth-century *Saló de Cent* (Hall of One Hundred), site of all major municipal ceremonies. Visitors can see the main rooms at weekends, and you can also admire the *Saló de Cent* at weekly free concerts (*see chapter* **Music: Classical & Opera**). *Wheelchair access.*

Palau de la Generalitat

Plaça Sant Jaume (402 46 17). Metro Liceu, Jaume I/bus 17, 19, 40, 45. **Open** 23 April. **Admission** free.
Like the City Hall, the Generalitat has a Gothic side entrance, with above it a beautiful relief of Saint George, patron saint of Catalonia, made by master carver Pere Johan in 1418. Inside, the finest features are the raised patio, part of which is planted with orange trees, and the magnificent chapel of **Sant Jordi** of 1432-34, the masterpiece of Catalan architect Marc Safont. Unfortunately, the Generalitat is only regularly open to the public on Sant Jordi, 23 April (when queues are huge); at other times, call the information number to inquire if tours are being arranged, or ask at tourist offices.

Santa Maria del Mar

Plaça de Santa Maria (310 23 90). Metro Jaume I/bus 17, 19, 40, 45. **Open** 8.30am-12.30pm, 4.30-8.10pm, daily. **Admission** free.
The Cathedral may attract more attention, but Santa Maria del Mar, known as 'the people's cathedral' because of its traditionally greater popularity, is undoubtedly the city's finest church, the summit of Catalan Gothic. Built remarkably quickly for a Medieval building, between 1329 and 1384, it has an unusual unity of style. Inside, two ranks of slim, perfectly proportioned columns soar up to fan vaults, creating a wonderful atmosphere of space and peace. It's not so much a historical artefact as simply a marvellous building, somehow outside of time. There's also superb stained glass, particularly the great fifteenth-century rose window above the main door. Our ability to appreciate it is helped greatly by

A timeless elegance to contrast with Gaudí: the superb **Santa Maria de Mar.**

the fact that revolutionaries set fire to it in 1936, clearing out the wooden Baroque images that clutter so many Spanish churches, allowing the simplicity of its lines to emerge. *Wheelchair access (side door only).*

Antic Hospital de la Santa Creu

C/Carme 47-C/Hospital 56 (no phone).
Metro Liceu/bus 14, 18, 38, 59, 64, 91. **Open** 9am-8pm Mon-Fri; 9am-2pm Sat.
A hospital was founded on this site in 1024: the present buildings are a combination of a fifteenth-century Gothic core with Baroque and Classical additions. It remained the city's main hospital until 1926, and Gaudí died here.Today it houses Catalonia's main library, an arts school and, in the chapel, an exhibition space (*see chapter* **Art Galleries**).

Sant Pau del Camp

C/Sant Pau 101 (310 23 90).
Metro Paral.lel/bus 20, 36, 57, 64, 91. **Open** 11am-1pm Mon, Wed-Sun. **Admission** free.
Barcelona's oldest church was built in the twelfth century, when the surrounding Raval was just open fields, as part of a monastery. The Romanesque structure has none of the towering grandeur of the Cathedral or Santa Maria del Mar: it is a squat, hulking building, rounded in on itself to give a sense of intimacy and protection to worshippers. On either side of the portal are columns made from material from seventh- and eighth-century buildings. Closed for many years, it recently re-opened to visitors.

Monestir de Pedralbes (Col.lecció Thyssen-Bornemisza)

Baixada del Monestir 9 (280 14 34). FGC Reina Elisenda/bus 22, 63, 64, 75. **Open** 10am-2pm Tue-Sun. **Admission** *Monastery & Col.lecció Thyssen* 500ptas; 325ptas over-65s; *Wed except public holidays* 450ptas; 325ptas over-65s; *Monastery only* 300ptas; 150ptas over-65s; *Wed except public holidays* 225ptas; 150ptas over-65s; *Col.lecció Thyssen only* 300ptas; 175ptas over-65s; *Both sections* free under-16s. **Credit** (shop only) AmEx, MC, V.
Founded in 1326 by Queen Elisenda, wife of Jaume II of Aragon, this monastery still houses a community of 24 nuns. With the installation of the Col.lecció Thyssen-Bornemisza art collection in part of the cloister the rest of the monastery that is on view has also been thoroughly reorganised. A tour through the building now provides a fascinating glimpse of daily life in a Medieval cloister: in addition to the day and

Atop the **Sagrada Família**. *See page 49.*

evening cells, visitors can see the pharmacy, the kitchens, and the huge refectory with its vaulted ceiling. The main attraction, though, is the convent itself, and above all, the magnificent, entirely intact three-storey Gothic cloister. To one side is the tiny chapel of Sant Miquel, covered with striking murals from 1343 by Ferrer Bassa, Catalan painter and student of Giotto. The Thyssen collection occupies a former dormitory on one of the upper floors (*see chapter* **Museums**). *Wheelchair access.*

The Carrer Montcada

It's only a short walk from end to end, but along the Carrer Montcada you'll find no fewer than six palaces from the late Middle Ages. The centre of merchant life in La Ribera in the Catalan Golden Age, this beautiful street, impassable to vehicles, was then the broadest thoroughfare in the district, and its busiest. Its merchant residences conform to a typical style of Mediterranean urban palace – elegant entrance patios with the main rooms on the first floor – and are closely packed together. Most have features from several periods, and in the last thirty years this old street has also become one of the great museum centres of Barcelona. Beginning at C/Princesa and walking down Montcada, the first palace you reach is the **Palau Berenguer d'Aguilar**, home of the **Museu Picasso**, part of which is thirteenth century. The museum also occupies the neighbouring **Palau Castellet**.

Opposite, at no. 12, is one of the finest and largest, the **Palau dels Marquesos de Lió**, now the **Museu Tèxtil**, with a fine café where you can nurse a coffee protected by the palace's fourteenth-century walls. At no. 19 stands the **Palau Meca**, also part of the Picasso. For a drink and a *tapa* it's hard to do better than at no. 22, **El Xampanyet**, which has plied the public with refreshments since 1929. Next door is a relative newcomer, the **Palau Dalmases**, built in the seventeenth century, which now houses a different, eccentric kind of bar (for both, *see chapter* **Cafés & Bars**). Across the street at no. 25 is the fifteenth-century **Palau Cervelló**, now the **Galeria Maeght**. On the left, just before Passeig del Born, is Barcelona's narrowest street, **Carrer de les Mosques** (Street of Flies), not even wide enough for an adult to lie across. If it wasn't closed by barred gates, you could test it for yourself.

Carrer Montcada

Metro Jaume I/bus 17, 19, 40, 45.

TEATRE VICTÒRIA

"A Barcelona stage, open to the world"

BALLET • CONTEMPORARY DANCE
FLAMENCO • OPERA • MUSICAL
PLAY • CONCERTS
CLASSICAL DRAMA
COMEDY • CIRCUS
CABARET

34/3 417 00 60

*Gaudí's friendly dragon greets you at the gates of the **Parc Güell**.*

Gaudí & *Modernisme*

The building of the Eixample was the background to the growth of Catalan Modernism, a very distinctive variant of art nouveau, *Modernisme* gave equal respect to decorative as to fine art, and one result of this is that alongside major works small gems in the style can be found in bars and shops all over Barcelona. Most famous of all Catalan architects of the time, naturally, was Antoni Gaudí (1852-1926); although normally classified as a *Modernista*, he was, in fact, a complete original. For more on Modernism and Gaudí, *see chapter* **Architecture**.

La 'Mansana de la Discòrdia'

Passeig de Gràcia 35-45. Metro Passeig de Gràcia/bus 7, 16, 17, 22, 24, 28.

The 'Block of Discord', between Carrers Consell de Cent and Aragó, is so-called because on it, almost alongside each other, stand buildings by the three greatest figures of Catalan Modernist architecture, all constructed between 1900 and 1907, in wildly clashing styles. At number 35 is Domènech i Muntaner's **Casa Lleó Morera**, a classically *Modernista* building of exuberantly convoluted, decorative forms. Three doors up at number 41 is Puig i Cadafalch's Gothic-influenced **Casa Amatller**; next to that is Gaudí's unclassifiable **Casa Batlló**, rising like a giant fish out of the pavement.

Palau Güell

C/Nou de la Rambla 3-5 (317 39 74).
Metro Liceu/bus 14, 18, 38, 59, 64, 91. **Open** details unavailable at time of writing.
This Medievalist palace was built in 1886-88 as a residence for Gaudí's patron Eusebi Güell, on one of the less prepossessing streets in the Barrio Chino. It was Gaudí's first major commission for Güell, and also one of the first buildings in which he revealed the originality of his ideas. Once past the fortress-like facade, one finds an interior in impeccable condition, with lavish wooden ceilings, dozens of snake-eye stone pillars, and original furniture – like a dressing table whose mirror looks like its about to fall off. The roof terrace is a garden of decorated chimneys, each different. The building used to house the Catalan theatre museum, but this is being relocated; after restoration the Palau will reopen as a purely architectural attraction.

Palau de la Música Catalana

C/Sant Francesc de Paula 2 (268 10 00). Metro Urquinaona/bus 17, 19, 40, 45. **Guided tours** *Oct-May* 3pm Tue & Thur; *June* 3pm Tue-Thur; *July, Sept* 3pm, 3.30pm, 4pm, Mon-Fri. Closed Aug. **Admission** 200ptas. **No credit cards.**
Gaudí may be the best-known of Barcelona's turn-of-the-century architects, but the building that most truly represents the pure *Modernista* style is Domènech i Montaner's 'Palace of Catalan Music'. Built in 1905-8, it's still the most prestigious concert hall in the city. The façade, with its combination of bare brick, busts and mosaic friezes representing Catalan musical traditions alongside the great composers, is impressive enough, but it is surpassed by the building's staggering interior. Decoration erupts everywhere: the ceiling centrepiece is of multi-coloured stained glass; 18 half-mosaic, half-relief figures representing the musical muses appear out of the back of the stage; and on one side, massive Wagnerian carved horses ride out to accompany a bust of Beethoven. The best way to see it is to go to a concert, but guided tours are available (you must call for an appointment). *See also chapter* **Music: Classical & Opera.** *Wheelchair access.*

Parc Güell

C/d'Olot. Bus 24, 25. **Open** *Nov-Feb* 10am-6pm; *Mar, Oct* 10am-7pm; *April, Sept* 10am-8pm; *May-Aug* 10am-9pm.
In 1900, Gaudí's patron Eusebi Güell commissioned him to oversee the design of a garden city development on a hill on the edge of the city, which he envisaged would become a

good i-Deas every month!

fashionable residential area. Gaudi was to design the basic structure and main public areas; the houses were to be designed by other architects. The wealthy families of the time, however, did not appreciate Gaudi's wilder ideas, scarcely any plots were sold, and eventually the estate was taken over by the city as a park. Its most complete part is the entrance, with its Disneylandish gatehouses and the mosaic dragon that's become another of Barcelona's favourite symbols. The park has a wonderfully playful quality, with its twisted pathways and avenues of columns intertwined with the natural structure of the hillside. At the centre is the great esplanade, with an undulating bench covered in *trencadís* broken mosaic – much of it not the work of Gaudi but of his assistant Josep Maria Jujol. Gaudi lived for several years in one of the two houses built on the site (not designed by himself), now the **Casa-Museu Gaudí** (*see* chapter **Museums**). The park stretches beyond the area designed by Gaudi, away into the wooded hillside. *Café-restaurants.*

La Pedrera

Passeig de Gràcia 92 (487 36 13/484 59 80).
Metro Diagonal/bus 7, 16, 17, 22, 24, 28. **Open** 10am-8pm Tue-Sat; 10am-3pm Sun. **Admission** 500ptas.
No credit cards.
The last building Gaudi worked on before succumbing to the Sagrada Familia represents his most radical departure from a recognisably Modernist style. Built entirely on columns and parabolic arches, with no supporting walls, and supposedly without a single straight line or right-angled corner, this curving, globular apartment block, also known as the Casa Milà, contrasts strikingly with the angularity of much of the Eixample. Its revolutionary features were not appreciated by the Milà family – who paid for it – nor by contemporary opinion, which christened it *La Pedrera* ('The Stone Quarry') as a joke. It is now owned by the **Fundació Caixa de Catalunya**, which has beautifully restored the building and uses one floor as a separate exhibition space (*see* chapter **Art Galleries**). With the ticket to the building you can see a permanent exhibition on the architect and Modernism, the *Espai Gaudí*, and go on the informative guided tours (in English as well as Spanish and Catalan), which let you see some of its main features and especially the roof, with its extraordinary semi-abstract sculptures (actually ventilation shafts and chimneys). Note that in winter tours may not continue after dark, even though the exhibition space stays open. *Shop.*

Temple Expiatori de la Sagrada Família

Plaça Sagrada Família-C/Mallorca 401 (455 02 47).
Metro Sagrada Família/bus 19, 33, 34, 43, 50, 51, 54.
Open *Oct-Feb* 9am-6pm; *Mar, Sept* 9am-7pm; *April-Aug* 9am-8pm, daily. **Admission** 750ptas; 500ptas over 65s; free under-10s; group discounts. *Lifts to the spires* 200ptas. **No credit cards**.
Gaudi's masterpiece or monsterpiece, to which he dedicated himself for the last 18 years of his life, often sleeping on the site – although the project had in fact been initiated by another architect, Francisco del Villar, in 1882. Only the crypt, the apse and the four towers of the Façade of the Nativity, along the C/Marina, were completed in his lifetime. Every element in the decoration, much of it carved from life, was conceived by Gaudi as having a precise symbolic meaning, and he was deeply opposed to the idea of anyone appreciating the building outside of its religious context. An essential part of any visit is an attempt to climb the towers beyond the level that can be reached by lift: this gives the remarkable sensation of walking out into space. Few people reach the top. The museum in the crypt contains models and a history of the project and other information on Gaudi (*see chapter* **Museums**). Work on the cathedral was resumed in 1952 by some of Gaudi's assistants, who drew up plans based on some of his sketches and what they remembered of the great man's ideas (he never used detailed plans), and has accel-

erated in the last few years. The new towers of the Façade of the Passion are nearly completed, complete with sculptures by Josep Maria Subirachs that horrified many Gaudi admirers. The second sculptor now working on the building is Japanese, Etsuro Sotoo, who seems to be adhering more faithfully to Gaudi's intentions, with six musicians, adorning the rear of the cathedral, that are flowing and modest. *Museum. Shop.*

The Twentieth Century

Barcelona has often grown chaotically in the last century, as in the 1920s and 1960s; then, since 1979, it has sought to resolve its problems with a vengeance, launching into a burst of urban renovation unequalled in Europe. As well as the major Olympic sites, equally or more attractive are the many parks and squares created through the City's dynamic open-spaces programme: for more on these, *see below* **Parks & Panoramas**, *and chapters* **Barcelona by Area** *and* **Art Galleries**.

Pavelló Barcelona (Pavelló Mies van der Rohe)

Avda Marquès de Comillas (423 40 16). Metro Espanya/bus 9, 13, 38, 61, 65, 91. **Open** 10am-7.30pm Mon-Fri; 11am-6.30pm Sat, Sun, public holidays. **Admission** 300ptas; 250ptas students; free under-18s. **No credit cards**.
The German Pavilion for the 1929 Exhibition, designed by Ludwig Mies van der Rohe, is also home to the Barcelona chair, since copied worldwide in millions of office waiting rooms. It was one of the most important founding monuments of modern rationalist (not to be confused with Modernist) architecture, with a revolutionary use of stone, glass and space. It was demolished after the Exhibition, but in 1986 a replica was built on the same site. Purists may regard it as a synthetic inferior of the original, but the elegance and simplicity of the design are still a striking demonstration of what rationalist architecture could do before it was reduced to production-line clichés.

Nou Camp

Avda Aristides Maillol, access 9 (330 94 11/496 36 00). Metro Collblanc/bus 15, 52, 53, 54, 56, 57, 75.
Open *Nov-Mar* 10am-1pm, 3-6pm, Tue-Fri; 10am-2pm Sat, Sun, public holidays. **Closed** Mon. *April-Oct* 10am-1pm, 3-6pm, Mon-Sat; 10am-2pm public holidays. **Closed** Sun. **Admission** 400ptas; 200ptas students; 150ptas under-13s. **No credit cards**.
The largest football stadium in Europe, the shrine of Barcelona FC. First built in 1954, Nou Camp has been added to since to accommodate more of the club's 100,000-plus members. It also has the club museum, visitors to which can tour the stadium (*see chapters* **Museums** *and* **Sport & Fitness**). *Wheelchair access.*

L'Anella Olímpica (The Olympic Ring)

Avda de l'Estadi. Metro Espanya, or Paral.lel, then Funicular de Montjuïc/bus 61.
Information: *Estadi Olímpic (Catalan 481 00 92/Spanish 481 10 92); Palau Sant Jordi (Catalan 481 01 92/Spanish 481 11 92); Palau d'Esports, C/Lleida (Catalan 481 10 93/Spanish 481 10 93).* Also from Gran Via/Aribau ticket booth (*see chapter* **Services**).
What was the core area for the 1992 Games consists of a compact hub of monumental buildings, in contrasting styles, in the centre of Montjuïc. The main **Estadi Olímpic** – now rather glaringly under-used – although entirely new, was built within the façade of the existing 1929 stadium, by a design team led by Federico Correa and Alfonso Milá. Next

to it is the most original and attractive of the Olympic facilities, Arata Isozaki's **Palau de Sant Jordi** indoor sports hall. Its vast metal roof was built on the ground and raised into place by hydraulic jacks. In the *plaça* in front of the hall, locals gather on Sunday afternoons for family walks and picnics, next to Santiago Calatrava's remarkable bow-like **Telefònica** tower. Further along is the Sports University, designed by Ricard Bofill and Peter Hodgkinson in their neo-Classical style. At the foot of Montjuïc in C/Lleida by the Plaça d'Espanya is another sports hall, the **Palau d'Esports**, built in the sixties but also rebuilt for 1992, and now often used for pop concerts despite its poor acoustics.

Vila Olímpica & Port Olímpic

Metro Ciutadella-Vila Olímpica/bus 36, 41, 71.

Occupying a huge area between the Ciutadella and the old industrial district of Poble Nou, the Olympic Village, which housed the athletes and their entourages in '92, is now a residential district. Those who have acquired the flats in which the Olympic contingents stayed have at their disposal an impressive range of new leisure areas: the Port Olímpic, seafront parks and the newly-created beaches. At the Vila's centre are two 40-storey blocks – the tallest buildings in Spain – one offices, the other, the **Hotel Arts** (*see chapter* **Accommodation**). The entire village has been developed

to an integrated plan, and the project as a whole is spectacular, but the quality of some individual buildings is nondescript and there are signs that corners were cut to get them up in time. Nevertheless, residents of the Olympic Village flats generally pronounce themselves satisfied.

Parks & Panoramas

Barcelona is an intensely urban city, but fortunately, there are quiet, green areas and even near-virgin woodland a short distance from the city centre, and the tireless efforts of the city authorities have also produced a great many new open spaces. Another feature of Barcelona is that people often seem to feel the urge to get above it, on the great vantage points of Montjuïc and Tibidabo.

Montjuïc

Metro Espanya, or Paral.lel then Funicular de Montjuïc/bus 9, 13, 20, 36, 38, 56, 57, 61, 65, 91.
Parks open *Nov-Feb* 10am-6pm; *Mar, Oct* 10am-7pm; *April, Sept* 10am-8pm; *May-Aug* 10am-9pm, daily.

Barcelona beach

Many people have perhaps still not caught on to the fact that Barcelona now qualifies as a beach resort. Just a few years ago, much of the sea frontage north-east of the harbour was an industrial wasteland. However, nothing is

beyond the whit of the city's planners, and one of the key slogans of the whole pre/post-Olympic renewal project has been that it should create a *Barcelona Oberta al Mar*, a 'Barcelona Open to the Sea', or in other words that the city should take on board, and enjoy, the fact that it stands beside the Mediterranean. Beginning in the mid-eighties, the city seafront was transformed beyond recognition: over four kilometres of new beaches were created, with dikes to prevent erosion and thousands of tons of fresh sand, backed by – naturally – stylish parks and palm-lined promenades; special measures were taken to improve water cleanliness; and, as a centrepiece, the **Port Olímpic** marina was built, initially for the Olympic yachting events, although it's since become one of Barcelona's most popular new amenities.

Since the beginning of the nineties Barcelonans have caught on to their new beaches in a big way, and on any summer's day can be found in great numbers along the sand, playing beach volleyball or rollerblading along the prom. The beaches have good, new showers and safety facilities, plus ramps for wheelchair access. On some sunny days, they're positively too successful, and unless you're exceptionally gregarious, it's best to avoid the city beaches on weekends, especially in July.

Sun, sea and sand aren't the only attractions of Barcelona's renovated beachfront, for there's a great, leisurely walk between the beach and Colom. Centrepiece is the **Port Olímpic**, with an endless supply of popular bars and restaurants for when you come off the beach (*see chapter* **Restaurants**). Beyond the marina, looking towards the city, you'll see gleaming in the sunshine Frank Gehry's huge copper *Fish* sculpture in front of the **Hotel Arts** tower and **Sogo** shopping complex, next to which there's a footbridge that will take you past more pleasant, clean beach to Barceloneta.

Beaches of Barceloneta, Nova Icària, Bogatell & La Mar Bella

Metro Ciutadella-Selva de Mar, yellow line/bus 36, 41, 45, 59, 71, 92.

The huge, sprawling mass of Montjuïc, looming over the city from beside the port, is the largest area of open space within Barcelona. It's a world of its own, encompassing a number of quite different areas. It is also the site of all kinds of attractions and amenities: the **Olympic Ring**, the Trade Fair, a string of museums, the **Fundació Miró**, the **Grec** open-air theatre, the **Poble Espanyol**, swimming pools and the **funfair**. On the south side facing the airport, you'll also find Barcelona's largest cemetery. Despite all the activity on Montjuïc, and its proximity to the city centre, it's surprisingly easy to find peaceful, shaded places among the many park areas. From all over the hill, you get great views: they're particularly spectacular by the Palau Nacional, and at Miramar, next to the harbour. At the top sits the castle, best reached by the **Telefèric** (*see* **Rides**), which houses the **Museu Militar**, and has sweeping views north and south. Around the castle and on the south side, Montjuïc is wild and full of isolated corners; however, the authorities plan to change this, and a new botanical garden and more park areas are to be created. *See also chapter* **Barcelona by Area**.

Parc de la Ciutadella

Metro Arc de Triomf, Barceloneta/bus 14, 16, 36, 39, 40, 41, 42, 51. **Open** *Sept April* 8am-8pm; *May-Aug* 8am-9pm, daily.

The 'lungs' and main park of Barcelona, the Ciutadella occupies the site of the Citadel that dominated the city in the eighteenth century. Begun in the 1870s, the park was created as the site of the 1888 Exhibition. Just outside it stands the **Arc de Triomf** (Triumphal Arch) that formed the main entrance to the Exhibition. In the centre of the park is a lake, where boats can be hired (200ptas per person, per half-hour); beside it is the great Cascade or ornamental fountain, on which the young Gaudí worked as assistant to Josep Fontseré, the architect of the park. Although formally laid out, the Ciutadella makes an attractive change from the surrounding streets, and its unusual statues – a life-sized model mammoth – increase its appeal. Surprisingly extensive, the Ciutadella also contains specific attractions: the **Zoo**, the **Museu d'Art Modern**, which shares the surviving buildings of the old Citadel with the Catalan Parliament, two other museums, the **Museu de Geologia** and the **Museu de Zoologia** (neither of great interest, although the latter occupies one of Domènech i Montaner's most important *Modernista* buildings). Not to be missed are the **Umbracle** or greenhouse, also from the 1880s, which has been beautifully restored to provide a mysterious pocket of tropical forest in the city, and the **Hivernacle** or winter garden, which has an interesting bar (*see chapter* **Cafés & Bars**). Outside the Ciutadella bikes can be hired to ride in the park (*see chapter* **Sport & Fitness**).

Parc del Clot

C/Escultor Claperós. Metro Glòries/bus 56, 92. **Open** *Nov-Feb* 10am-6pm; *Mar, Oct* 10am-7pm; *April, Sept* 10am-8pm; *May-Aug* 10am-9pm, daily.

A few streets north of the flea market at Glòries and the Clot metro, this is a park built on three levels full of flowering shrubs, palms and pines. A RENFE warehouse once stood here, and some sections of its curving brick walls still wind through the park.

Parc de la Creueta del Coll

C/Mare de Déu del Coll. Metro Vallcarca/bus 22, 25, 27, 28, 87. **Open** *Nov-Feb* 10am-6pm; *Mar, Oct* 10am-7pm; *April, Sept* 10am-8pm; *May-Aug* 10am-9pm, daily.

A new park created from an old quarry by Josep Martorell and David Mackay in 1987, and considered something of a model for the renovation of disused urban land. At its centre is a large lake with an artificial beach: visitors looking to appreciate the architectural features may find the number of kids enjoying it in summer overwhelming, and it hasn't been very well kept sometimes in the last few years, but it's still

a n attractive park. In winter, the lake is used for boating. Like other new parks in Barcelona, it contains modern sculptures, by Eduardo Chillida and Ellsworth Kelly.

Parc Joan Miró (Parc de l'Escorxador)

Metro Tarragona, Espanya/bus 27, 109, 127.

This park takes up four square city blocks but feels like much more. Built on the site of a slaughterhouse, it's all stubby, leafy *palmera* trees, with lots of paths and benches, full of people engaged in *petanca* matches, jogging, dog-walking and reading. There's a surprising tranquillity to this large dirt space, bordered on the Avda Tarragona side, in Plaça de l'Escorxador, by Miró's 22-foot-high *Dona i Ocell* sculpture, in the pool of water for which it was designed.

Parc del Laberint

C/Germans Desvalls (near Passeig de la Vall d'Hebron). Bus 27, 60, 73, 76, 85. **Open** *Nov-Feb* 10am-6pm; *Mar, Oct* 10am-7pm; *April, Sept* 10am-8pm; *May-Aug* 10am-9pm, daily.

One of Barcelona's most attractive parks is also the most out -of-the-way. It adjoins one of the four main Olympic areas in the Vall d'Hebron. Originally the grounds of an eighteenth-century mansion (long ago demolished), it centres on a rambling, romantic formal garden with a strong element of fantasy and including the maze that gives the park its name. On Saturdays, its secluded corners and ornamental statuary make it extraordinarily popular for wedding photographs, so there's a good chance you'll be greeted by the sight of dozens of white bridal gowns flitting among the pines.

Parc de l'Espanya Industrial & Plaça dels Països Catalans

Metro Sants-Estació/bus 27, 33, 44, 109. **Open** (Espanya Industrial) *Nov-Feb* 10am-6pm; *Mar, Oct* 10am-7pm; *April, Sept* 10am-8pm; *May-Aug* 10am-9pm, daily.

The Espanya Industrial, by Basque architect Luis Peña Ganchegui, is the most post-modern of Barcelona's new parks. A line of 10 peculiar watchtowers, reminiscent of ship superstructures, look out over a boating lake: at night, lit up, they create the impression that some strange warship has managed to dock alongside the Sants railway station. The re is sculpture by Anthony Caro and Andrés Nagel. On the other side of the station is the ferociously modern Plaça dels Països Catalans, created by Helio Piñón and Albert Viaplana in 1983 on a site where, the architects claimed, nothing could be planted due to the amount of industrial detritus in the soil. The square is an open, concreted space, with shelter provided not by trees but by giant steel ramps and canopies, the kind of architecture that you either find totally hostile or consider to have great monumental strength.

Parc de l'Estació del Nord

C/Nàpols-C/Almogàvers. Metro Arc de Triomf/bus 40, 42, 54, 141. **Open** *Nov-Feb* 10am-6pm; *Mar, Oct* 10am-7pm; *April, Sept* 10am-8pm; *May-Aug* 10am-9pm, daily.

Behind the new bus station at Estació de Nord, is a striking three-square-block park, opened in 1991. It's a big, open, grassy crescent with few trees or benches, just flat ceramic forms in turquoise and cobalt, which swoop and curve through the park, accentuating its natural lines: part of a specially-designed earthworks by Beverly Pepper.

Tibidabo

FGC Av Tibidabo/bus 17, 22, 58, 73, N8; then Tramvia Blau and Funicular.

Local dignitaries have customarily taken official visitors to the top of Tibidabo for an overview of Barcelona. The view is certainly magnificent, even with the smog, and the clean air a welcome change from the sometimes murky mix below. Getting there by **Tramvia Blau** and **Funicular** is part of the fun (*see* **Rides**). The square between the two is one of the best places for an *al fresco* drink or meal: try the

Mirablau bar or the restaurant **La Venta** (*see chapters* **Restaurants** *and* **Cafés & Bars**). Past the square, tracks lead along the flanks of the Serra de Collserola, the great ridge of which Tibidabo is the centre, and are great to jog along. At the top of the Funicular is Barcelona's best funfair (*see* **Attractions**), and, for a completely limitless view, the giant needle of the **Torre de Collserola**. Next to it is a church, built in an extravagantly bombastic style and completed in 1940 to atone for Barcelona's revolutionary role in the Spanish Civil War. To the left of it, on the other side of the ridge, there are stunning views over the Vallés plain to the north and, on a good day, Montserrat and the Montseny. Down the hillside are tracks where you can easily lose yourself for an afternoon among near-virgin pinewoods.

Parc d'Atraccions de Montjuïc (Montjuïc Funfair)

Avda Miramar (441 70 24). Metro Paral.lel, then Funicular de Montjuïc/bus 61. **Open** *mid-Sept-23 June* 11.30am-9pm Sat, Sun, public holidays; *24 June-early Sept* 6pm-midnight Tue-Thur; 6pm-1am Fri, Sat; noon-11.15pm Sun. **Admission** *entrance only* 600ptas; *individual rides* approx 300ptas; *pass with unlimited number of rides* 1,800ptas; free under-3s. **No credit cards**.

The newer of the city's two funfairs, this one lacks the period charm of its Tibidabo competitor, but is still packed on

Rides

No-one should leave Barcelona without trying its fun forms of transport, all institutions in the city fabric. One, though, that's currently unavailable is the 1929 **Transbordador** cable car that used to clank its way across the harbour from Miramar on Montjuïc. It was closed for safety reasons in 1995, and seems unlikely to reopen.

Funicular de Montjuïc

Metro Paral.lel – Avgda Miramar (443 08 59). Metro Paral.lel/bus 20, 36, 57, 64. **Open** *Nov-early June*

10.45am-8pm Sat, Sun, public holidays; *June-Sept* 11am-10pm daily; *Oct* 10.45am-8pm daily. Daily service also Christmas, Easter week, public holidays. **Tickets** *single* 185ptas; *return* 325ptas. **No credit cards**. Not much of a sightseeing trip, as for most of its route it runs underground, but this modern Funicular brings you out at a spot on Montjuïc convenient for the park, the **funfair**, the **Fundació Miró** and Miramar, and saves you a walk up the hill. It also connects with the **Telefèric** (*see below*).

Funicular de Tibidabo

Plaça Doctor Andreu – Plaça del Tibidabo (211 79 42). FGC Av Tibidabo/bus 17, 22, 58, 73, N8, then

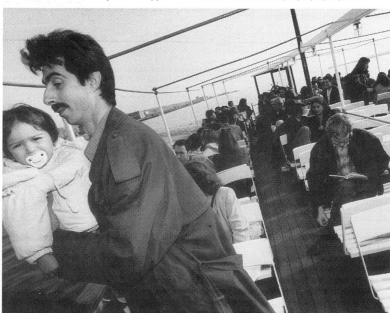

Get some air and take a trip round the bay on the **Golondrines**.

warm nights. It also has an open-air theatre, where Spanish singing stars of the traditional variety exercise their ample lungs each summer. Best way to get there is by **Telefèric** to the top of the funfair, and then walk down (*see* **Rides**).

Parc d'Atraccions de Tibidabo (Tibidabo Funfair)

Parc d'Atraccions del Tibidabo, Plaça del Tibidabo 3-4 (211 79 42). FGC Av Tibidabo/bus 17, 22, 58, 73, N8; then Tramvia Blau and Funicular to park. **Open** *Oct-Mar* noon-7pm Sat, Sun, public holidays; *April, 15-30 Sept* noon-8pm Sat, Sun, public holidays; *May* noon-8pm Wed-Sun; *June, 1-14 Sept* noon-8pm Tue-Sun; *July, Aug* noon-10pm Tue-Sun. **Admission** *entrance only* 400ptas;

200ptas over-65s; free under-5s. *Individual rides* 200-400ptas. *Pass with unlimited number of rides* 1,800ptas; 400ptas under-5s. **Credit** AmEx, DC, MC, V.

The funfair at the top of Tibidabo was first opened in 1901, and some of the rides date from the twenties: the giant model aeroplane that takes you slowly out into space on a revolving arm; the wonderfully silly and unfrightening *Castillo Misterioso* (Haunted Castle); and the **Museu d'Autòmates** (*see chapter* **Museums**). A major effort has been made since the '80s to pep up the park, now dubbed *Tibidabo, la Muntanya Màgica* ('The Magic Mountain'), with dynamic new rides, such as a 'Tunnel of Terror'. Its greatest asset, though, is the soaring view, which adds to the impact of any ride.

Tramvia Blau. **Open** 7.45am-9.45pm daily (trains every 30min Mon-Sat; every 15min Sun). **Tickets** *single* 300ptas; *return* 400ptas; (0ver-65s) *single* 150ptas; *return* 200ptas; free under-3s. **No credit cards.**

The Funicular that takes you from the end of the tramline to the very top of the mountain is part art deco-esque, like much of the funfair. Each train has two halves, one pointing down and one pointing up, and if you secure a good seat at the bottom of the 'down' end, you'll get a panoramic view of the city.

Golondrinas (Swallow boats)

Moll de la Fusta (442 31 06). Metro Drassanes/bus 14, 18, 36, 38, 57, 64.

Drassanes-Breakwater & return (30min): **Departures** *Nov-23 June* every 45min 11am-5pm Mon-Fri; every 25min 11.30am-7pm Sat, Sun. *24 June-Oct* every 25min 11.30am-7.30/8pm daily. Closed late Dec. **Tickets** 415ptas; 225ptas 4-10s; free under-4s.

Drassanes-Port Olímpic & return (2hrs): **Departures** *Nov-23 June* 11am, 1pm, 4.30pm Sat, Sun, public holidays. *24 June-Oct* 11am, 1pm, 4.30pm, 6.30pm, daily. **Tickets** 1,225ptas; 850ptas over-65s, 11-18s; 525ptas 4-10s; free under-4s; group discounts. **Credit** V.

The double-decker 'Swallow boats' take you around the harbour to the end of the breakwater, where you can eat out, take in the sea air, go fishing, or come straight back. More solid, sea-going boats now run on a longer trip round to the **Port Olímpic**.

Horse-drawn Carriages

Portal de la Pau (421 88 04/421 15 49). Metro Drassanes/bus 14, 18, 38, 59, 64, 91. **Services** *Mar-Nov* 9am-9pm daily. **Charges** 4,000ptas per hour; rates negotiable for special parties. **No credit cards.**

If you want the ultimate tourist experience and don't mind looking silly, ask a man for a ride behind his tired old nags. The usual route is up the Rambla from the port and back.

Telefèric de Montjuïc (Montjuïc Cable Cars)

Estació Funicular, Avda Miramar (443 08 59). Metro Paral.lel, then Funicular de Montjuic/bus 61. **Open** *Nov-Mar* 11.30am-2.45pm, 4-7.30pm, Sat, Sun, public holidays; *April-May, mid-Sept-Oct* 11.30am-2.45pm, 4-7.30pm, daily; *June-mid-Sept* 11.30am-9.30pm daily. **Tickets** *single* 375ptas; *return* 575ptas; (under-12s) *return* 425ptas; group discounts. **No credit cards.**

Beginning outside the station of the Funicular, the Montjuïc cable cars run up to the castle at the top, with a

stop at one side of the funfair. The four-seater cars are small and entirely open, so vertigo sufferers won't enjoy it, but all along the route there are superb views over Montjuïc and the port.

Tramvia Blau (Blue Tram)

Avda Tibidabo-Plaça Doctor Andreu (441 29 99). FGC Avda Tibidabo/bus 17, 22, 58, 73, N8. **Services** *mid Sept-22 June* 9.05am-9.35pm Sat, Sun, public holidays; (bus service 7.05am-9.45pm Mon-Fri); *23 June-mid-Sept* 9.05am-9.35pm daily. **Tickets** *single* 185ptas; *return* 325ptas. **No credit cards.**

The Blue Trams, beautiful old machines that have been running since 1902, clank their way along Avda Tibidabo between the FGC station and Plaça Doctor Andreu, passing many large Modernist houses en route. Once there, you can take in the view, have a meal or a drink, or catch the Funicular to the funfair on Tibidabo's peak. Note that there's only a plain bus service on weekdays except in summer.

Vertical Rides: Different Views

Colom (Columbus Monument)

Plaça Portal de la Pau (302 52 24). Metro Drassanes/bus 14, 18, 38, 59, 64, 91. **Open** *end-Sept-Mar* 10am-2pm, 3.30-7pm, Tue-Sat; 10am-7pm Sun, public holidays. *April, May* 10am-2pm, 3.30-8pm, Tue-Sat; 10am-8pm Sun, public holidays. *June-end-Sept* 9am-9pm daily. **Admission** 250ptas; 125ptas over-65s, under-14s; group discounts. **No credit cards.**

Ride to the top of the Columbus column, built for the Universal Exhibition of 1888, for a panoramic view of the old city and the port from within the crown at the explorer's feet. The lift only holds four people plus an attendant at one time, so there may be a sizeable queue.

Torre de Collserola

(211 79 42). FGC Av Tibidabo/bus 17, 22, 58, 73, N8; then Tramvia Blau and Funicular. **Open** 11am-2.30pm, 4-8pm, Mon-Fri; 11am-8pm Sat, Sun, public holidays. **Admission** 500ptas. **No credit cards.**

Norman Foster's 288-metre (800-foot) communications tower, built to take TV signals to the world in 1992, stands atop Collserola like some mutant insect poised to swoop on the city. A glass-walled lift takes you to an observation deck 115m up. On a decent day, it's a staggering bird's-eye view of Barcelona: a couple of times a year, it's clear enough to see Mallorca. There is free transport from the Funicular station to the tower.

Plaza de Toros Monumental

Gran Via de les Corts Catalanes 743 (245 58 04). Metro Monumental/bus 6, 7, 18, 56, 62. **Open** (visits & museum) *April-Sept* 10.30am-2pm, 4-7pm, Mon-Sat; 10.30am-1pm Sun. (Bullfights) *April-June, Sept* 5.30pm Sun; *July-Aug* 6pm Sun. **Admission** *visits & museum* 350ptas; 250ptas under-16s. **No credit cards.**

If you're set on seeing a bullfight, carry on to Madrid or Seville – this archetypally Spanish activity has never had a strong following in Barcelona, and in recent years one of the city's two bullrings has closed down. The other, the Monumental, holds fights every Sunday during the season (*see also chapter* **Museums**).

Ticket office: *C/Muntaner 24 (453 38 21). Metro Universitat/bus all routes to Plaça Universitat.* **Open** *April-Sept* 11am-2pm, 4-8pm, Wed-Sat. Closed public holidays. **No credit cards.**

Poble Espanyol

Avda del Marquès de Comillas (325 78 66). Metro Espanya/bus 9, 13, 38, 61, 65, 91, 109, N1. **Open** *Sept-June* 9am-8pm Mon; 9am-2am Tue-Sat; 9am-midnight Sun. *July, Aug* 9am-8pm Mon; 9am-2am Tue-Thur; 9am-4am Fri, Sat; 9am-midnight Sun. **Admission** 950ptas; 500ptas students, over-65s, 7-14s; free under-7s; group discounts. **Credit** not for admission; some shops only.

As part of the preparations for the 1929 Exhibition, someone had the bright idea of building, in one enclosed area, examples of traditional architecture from every region in Spain. The result was the *Poble Espanyol* or Spanish Village. Inside it, a Castilian square leads to an Andalusian church, then to replicas of village houses from Aragon, and so on. There are bars and restaurants of every kind, including vegetarian, and over 60 shops. Many of its businesses are workshops in which craftspeople hand-make and sell Spanish folk artefacts – ceramics, embroidery, fans; metalwork, candles and so on. Some of the work is quite attractive, some tacky, and prices are generally high.

A few years ago the village was given a facelift, with improved services and the installation of some quality (but expensive) restaurants. With the revamp came the 'Barcelona Experience': a half-hour audio-visual run-through of the city's life and history (with English commentary via headphones). Outside, street performers re-create bits of Catalan and Spanish folklore, and there are special children's shows. The *Poble* has an unmistakeable tourist-trap air, but it does have its fun side, and many of its buildings and squares are genuinely attractive. It also tries hard to promote itself as a night-spot, with karaoke bars, Cuban dinner-and-dancing restaurants, discos and a flamenco show, and dance bands perform regularly in the main square. Attached to the village is the bar that's the *summum bonnum* of Barcelona design-bar-dom, **Torres de Avila** (*see chapter* **Nightlife**). This effort to make the village a happening night venue is not always successful, mainly because the space is so large that it's hard to get it full enough to create an atmosphere.

Tours

The most useful tour facility, and an excellent first introduction to the city, is the special **Bus Turístic** bus service (*see chapter* **Getting Around**). Julià and Pullman offer tours of the classic coach-and-multilingual-guide variety, both covering the same routes, which have changed little in decades. Unfortunately, no-one now offers simpler walking tours in English in Barcelona, and a programme begun by the **Museu d'Història de la Ciutat** in 1992 has since been dropped. However, the museum occasionally organises historical walking tours in Catalan and Spanish, and it's worth enquiring to see what they have available.

Julià Tours

Ronda Universitat 5 (317 64 54). Metro Universitat/bus all routes to Plaça Universitat. **Tours** 9.30am-1pm, 3.30-7pm, daily. **Tickets** approx 4,000ptas. **No credit cards.**

Pullman Tours

Gran Via de les Corts Catalanes 635 (317 12 97/318 02 41). Metro Passeig de Gràcia/bus 7, 18, 50, 54, 56. **Tours** 9.30am-1pm, 3.30-7pm, daily. **Tickets** approx 4,000ptas. **No credit cards.**

All the fun of the fair, and mountain views too: the **Tibidabo** *funfair. See page 53.*

Architecture

Catalan creativity is revealed at its exuberant best in the buildings of Barcelona, from Gaudí's eccentric masterpieces to the modern marvels of 1992.

In Catalonia architecture has always had special importance, appearing as the most appropriate medium – ahead of painting, music or any other artform – through which to express national identity. Periods when architecture flourished have paralleled eras of increased Catalan freedom of action, greater wealth and a reinforcement of collective civic pride.

It's possible to see a clear line of continuity, of recurring characteristics, between generations of Catalan architects. Ideas and attitudes are taken in from abroad, but are assimilated into this strong local culture. There has always been a desire to decorate surfaces, and a constant preoccupation with texture and the use of fine materials and finishes. This is combined with a simplicity of line and a sense of sobriety often seen as distinguishing Catalan character from that of the rest of Spain. Other common elements are references to the traditional architecture of rural Catalonia – the large farmhouses or *masies*, with chalet-type tile roofs, massive stone walls and round-arched doorways, a style maintained by anonymous builders for centuries – and to the strong constructions of Catalan Romanesque and Gothic. There has also long been a close relationship between architects and craftsmen in the production of buildings, especially in the working of metal and wood.

Modern Catalans have a sense of contributing to their architectural heritage in the present day, rather than preserving it as a relic. Contemporary buildings are daringly constructed alongside (or even in) old ones, and this mix of old and new is a major characteristic of many recent architectural projects in Barcelona. At the Casa de la Caritat, for example, architects Viaplana and Piñón have used a dynamic, modern idiom to redesign an old workhouse (the **Centre de Cultura Contemporània**; *see chapter* **Art Galleries**).

It is inevitably only possible here to mention some of the city's notable buildings. There are also several architectural guides available, but some of the handiest (and free) are the informative leaflets on different styles available (in English editions) from Generalitat tourist offices, such as *Discovering Romanesque Art in Catalonia, Routes of Gothic Art in Catalonia* and so on. They cover the whole country, but have sections on Barcelona.

Old Barcelona

The old city of Barcelona, confined within its successive rings of walls, had become by 1850 – and also remains today – one of the densest urban areas in Europe. Open space is at a premium here. Small squares and paved areas feel almost sculpted out of a solid mass of buildings. The Mediterranean sun, which rarely reaches some streets, fills these often modest spaces with light, giving an unequalled sense of drama. The spaces within buildings also sometimes seem hollowed out from the mass of the city fabric. The breathtaking beauty of **Santa Maria del Mar**, or the

Antoni Gaudí

Seen as the genius of the *Modernista* movement, Gaudí was really a one-off, an unclassifiable figure. His work was a product of the social and cultural context of the time, but also of his own unique perception of the world, as well as a typically Catalan indulgence of anything specifically Catalan. Whereas his two great colleagues in Modernism, Domènech and Puig, were both public figures who took an active part in politics and many other fields, Gaudí, after being fairly sociable as a youth, became increasingly eccentric, leading a semi-monastic existence and enclosed in his own obsessions.

Born in Reus in 1852, he qualified as an architect in 1878. His first architectural work was as assistant to Josep Fontseré on the building of the **Parc de la Ciutadella** during the 1870s. The gates and fountain of the park are attributed to

Gaudí's first major work: **Casa Vicens**.

him, and around the same time he also designed the lampposts in the **Plaça Reial**. His first major commission was for the **Casa Vicens** in 1883-8. An orientalist fantasy, it is structurally fairly conventional, but already highlights his early control of the use of surface material in its exuberant neo-Moorish decoration and the superbly elaborate decorative ironwork on the gates. The **Col.legi de les Teresianes** convent school, undertaken a few years later (1888-9), is more restrained still, but the clarity and fluidity of the building, with its simple finishes and use of light, is very appealing.

An event of crucial importance in Gaudí's life occurred in 1878, when he met Eusebi Güell, heir to one of the largest industrial fortunes in Catalonia. Güell had been immediately taken by some of Gaudí's early furniture, and they also discovered they shared many religious ideas, on the socially-redemptive role of architecture and (for Güell) philanthropy. Güell placed such utter confidence in his architect that he was able to work with complete liberty. He produced several buildings for his patron, beginning with the **Palau Güell** (1886-8), a darkly impressive, still-historicist building that established Gaudí's reputation, and including the chapel crypt at **Colònia Güell**, one of his most original, structurally experimental and surprising buildings.

In 1883 Gaudí had first become involved in the design of the temple of the **Sagrada Família**, begun the previous year. He would eventually devote himself entirely to this work. Gaudí was profoundly religious, and an extreme Catholic conservative; part of his obsession with the building was a belief that its completion would help redeem Barcelona from the sins of secularism and the modern era. From 1908 until his death he worked on no other projects, often sleeping on site, a shabby, white-haired hermit, producing visionary ideas that his assistants had to 'interpret' into drawings (on show in the museum alongside). If most of his modern admirers were to meet him they would probably say he was mad, but this strange figure would have an immense effect on Barcelona.

The Sagrada Família became the testing ground for his ideas on structure and form. However, he would see built only the crypt, apse and the nativity façade, with its representation of 30 different species of plants. As Gaudí's work matured, he abandoned historicism and developed free-flowing, sinuous expressionist forms. His boyhood interest in nature began taking over from more architectural references, and what had previously provided decorative motifs became the inspiration for the actual forms of his buildings.

In his greatest years, he combined other commissions with his cathedral. **La Pedrera** or **Casa Milà**, begun in 1905, is the most complete of his projects. Occupying a prominent position on a corner of Passeig de Gràcia, it has an aquatic feel about it: the balconies resemble seaweed, and the undulating façade the sea, or rocks washed by it. The interior patios are painted in dark blues and greens, and the roofscape is like an imaginary landscape inhabited by mysterious figures. The **Casa Batlló**, on the other side of Passeig de Gràcia, was an existing building remodelled by Gaudí in 1905-7, with a roof resembling a reptilian creature perched high above the street. His later work has a dreamlike quality to its decoration, which makes it unique and personal.

Gaudí's fascination with natural forms found full expression in the **Parç Güell**, of 1900-14. Here he blurs the distinction between natural and built form in a series of colonnades winding up the hill. These seemingly informal paths lead to the surprisingly large central terrace projecting over the hall below, a forest of distorted Doric columns planned as the marketplace for Güell's proposed 'garden city'. The benches of the terrace are covered in some of the finest examples of *trencadís* or broken mosaic work, much of it probably due in great part to Gaudí's assistant Josep Maria Jujol, himself a very original *Modernista* architect.

In June 1926, Antoni Gaudí was run over by a tram on the Gran Via. Nobody recognised the down-at-heel old man, and he was taken to a public ward in the old Hospital de Santa Creu in the Raval. When it was discovered who he was, however, Barcelona gave its most famous architect an almost state funeral.

Gaudí in Barcelona

Gaudí left ten buildings in Barcelona. There are buildings by him nearby at the **Colònia Güell** and **Garraf** (*see chapter* **Trips Out of Town**).
Casa Batlló *Passeig de Gràcia 43. Metro Passeig de Gràcia/bus 7, 16, 17, 22, 24, 28. See chapter* **Sightseeing**.
Casa Calvet *C/Casp 48. Metro Urquinaona/bus all routes to Plaça Urquinaona.* An apartment block, apparently quite conventional from the exterior, with a more radical interior.
Casa Vicens *C/Carolines 22. Metro Fontana/bus 22, 24, 25, 28, 31, 32.* Not open to the public, but the exterior is very visible from the street.

Col.legi de les Teresianes *C/Ganduxer 95-105 (212 33 54). FGC Bonanova/bus 14, 16, 70, 74.* **Open** *Sept-June* 11am-1pm Sat. **Admission** free.
Palau Güell *C/Nou de la Rambla 3-5. Metro Liceu/bus 14, 18, 38, 59, 64, 91. See chapter* **Sightseeing**.
Parc Güell *C/d'Olot. Bus 24, 25. See chapter* **Sightseeing**.
Pavellons de la Finca Güell *Avda Pedralbes 7. Metro Palau Reial/bus 7, 74, 75, 114.* Gaudí's spectacular dragon gates can be seen from the street.
La Pedrera *Passeig de Gràcia 92 (487 36 13). Metro Diagonal/bus 7, 22, 24, 28. See chapter* **Sightseeing**.
Temple Expiatori de la Sagrada Família *C/Mallorca 401 (455 02 47). Metro Sagrada Família/bus 19, 33, 34, 43, 50, 51, 54. See chapter* **Sightseeing**.
Torre Bellesguard *C/Bellesguard 16-20. Bus 22, 64, 75.* A more than usually Gothic-looking fantasy house, built in 1900-9.

*The flamboyant entrance to **Parc Güell**.*

scale of the **Saló del Tinell**, contrast greatly with the tightly-packed streets around them. This gives a feeling of luxury to even the simplest square or church, adding to their enchantment.

Roman to Romanesque

The Roman citadel of *Barcino* was founded on the hill of *Mons Taber*, just behind the Cathedral, which to this day remains the religious and civic heart of the city. It left an important legacy in the shape of the fourth-century first city wall, fragments of which are visible at many points around the old city (*see chapter* **Sightseeing**: **Roman Barcino**).

Barcelona's next occupiers, the Visigoths, left little here, although there are the remains of some Visigothic churches nearby in **Terrassa**. When the Catalan state began to form under the Counts of Barcelona from the ninth century, the dominant architecture of this new community was massive, simple Romanesque. Towards the Pyrenees there are hundreds of fine Romanesque buildings, notably at **Ripoll**, **Besalú** and **Sant Pere de Rodes** (*see chapter* **Trips Out of Town**). There is though relatively little in Barcelona. On the right-hand side of the Cathedral, looking at the main façade, is the simple thirteenth-century chapel of **Santa Llúcia**, incorporated into the later building, and in La Ribera there is the currently closed **Capella d'en Marcús**. The greatest Romanesque monument in the city, though, is the beautifully plain church and cloister of **Sant Pau del Camp**, built in the twelfth century as part of a larger monastery.

Catalan Gothic

By the thirteenth and fourteenth centuries, Barcelona was the capital of an empire that dominated the western Mediterranean. Its population grew rapidly, and settlements called *Ravals* or *Vilanoves* grew up outside the Roman walls. This led to the construction of the second set of walls, begun by Jaume I, extending the city west to the Rambla, then just an often-dry riverbed.

This was the background to the great flowering of Catalan Gothic, and the construction of many of Barcelona's most important civic and religious buildings, replacing Romanesque equivalents. The **Cathedral** was begun in 1298, in substitution of an eleventh-century building. Work commenced on the **Ajuntament** (*Casa de la Ciutat*) and **Palau de la Generalitat** (later subject to extensive alteration) in 1372 and 1403, respectively. The **Saló del Tinell**, one of many additions made to the **Palau Reial** since the eleventh century, was built in 1359-62, and the great hall of the **Llotja**, the trading exchange, in 1380-92.

Catalan Gothic has very distinctive characteristics that mark it off clearly from more northern,

classic Gothic. It is simpler, and above all gives much more prominence to solid, plain walls between towers and columns rather than the empty spaces between intricate, leaping buttresses of the great French cathedrals. Buildings thus appear much more massive. In façades, as much emphasis is given to horizontals as to verticals, and the latter and their octagonal towers end in flat roofs, not spires. Decorative intricacies are mainly confined to windows, portals, arches and gargoyles. Many churches have no aisles but only a single nave, the classic example being the beautiful **Santa Maria del Pi** in the Plaça del Pi, built from 1322 to 1453.

This style has provided the historic benchmark for Catalan architecture. It is simple and robust, yet elegant and practical. Original and sophisticated construction techniques were developed: transverse arches supporting timber roofs allowed the spanning of great halls uninterrupted by columns, a system used in the **Saló del Tinell**. The sheer scale of the arches gives a feeling of splendour to the space. The **Drassanes**, built from 1378 to house the royal shipyards (and now the **Museu Marítim**), is really just a very beautiful shed, but the enormous parallel aisles make it one of the most exciting spaces in the city.

La Ribera, also known as the *Vilanova del Mar*, had become the commercial centre of the city, and for its parish church would have the great masterpiece of Catalan Gothic, **Santa Maria del Mar**, built between 1329 and 1384. Its superb proportions are based on a series of squares imposed on one another, with three aisles of, unusually, almost equal height, and the interior is staggering for its austerity and the spareness of the structure.

Leading away from it on one side is the **Carrer Montcada**, where the city's merchants built palaces to show their confidence and wealth. They all conform to a similar design of Mediterranean urban palace, presenting a blank exterior to the street, and with heavy doors opening into a large, imposing patio. A grand external staircase rises on one side, leading to the main rooms on the first floor, which often have elegant open loggias. Several of these palaces now house some of Barcelona's most visited cultural institutions.

Forgotten Centuries

By the end of the fifteenth century, political and economic decline meant there was much less patronage available for building. In the next three centuries, however, a good deal was still built in Barcelona, although rarely in any distinctively Catalan style, so that it is often disregarded.

In the 1550s the **Palau del Lloctinent** was built for the royal viceroys on one side of Plaça del Rei, and in 1596 the present main façade was added to the **Generalitat**, in an Italian

Renaissance style. The Church built lavishly, with Baroque convents and churches along the Rambla of which the **Betlem** from 1680-1729, at the corner of C/Carme, is the most important survivor. Later Baroque churches include **Sant Felip Neri** (1721-52) and **La Mercè** (1765-75).

Another addition after the siege of Barcelona in 1714 was new military architecture, since the city was encased in massive ramparts and fortresses. Examples remain in the **Castell de Montjuïc**, the buildings in the **Ciutadella** – one, curiously, the Catalan parliament – and in the **Barceloneta**.

A more positive late-eighteenth-century alteration was the conversion of the Rambla into an urbanised promenade, which began in 1775 with the demolition of Jaume I's second city wall. Neo-Classical palaces were built alongside: thus, **La Virreina** and the **Palau Moja** (at the corner of Portaferrisa) both date from the 1770s. Another fine eighteenth-century building in a less classical style is the **Gremial dels Velers** (Candlemakers' Guild) at Via Laietana 50, with its two-coloured stucco decoration.

It was not, however, until the closure of the monasteries in the 1820s and 1830s that major rebuilding on the Rambla could begin. Most of the constructions that replaced them were still in international, neo-Classical styles. The site that is now the **Mercat de la Boqueria** was actually first remodelled in 1836-40 as Plaça Sant Josep to a design by Francesc Daniel Molina based on the English Regency style of John Nash, now buried beneath the 1870s market building, although its Doric colonnade can still be detected.

Molina was also responsible for the **Plaça Reial**, begun in 1848. Another fine example of early nineteenth-century building is the collonaded **Porxos d'en Xifré**, the 1836 blocks opposite the Llotja.

The Eixample & the New City

In the 1850s, Barcelona was able to expand both physically – with the long-awaited demolition of the walls – and psychologically, with economic expansion and the cultural reawakening of the Catalan *Renaixença*. The stage was set for it to spread into the great gridiron plan for the **Eixample** of Ildefons Cerdà (*see chapter* **History**: **Factories, Barricades & Lyric Poetry**).

While Cerdà's more visionary ideas were largely lost, the construction of the Eixample did see the refining of a specific type of building: the apartment block, with large flats on the lower *Principal* floor (ie, the first above the ground), often with large glassed-in galleries for the drawing-room. The growth of the area also provided perfect conditions for the emergence of the most famous of Catalan architectural styles, Modernism.

Modernisme

In the second half of the last century, there was uncertainty in the arts and architecture across Europe. This coincided with the vast expansion of cities, dramatic social upheavals and new political pressures, while the introduction of the new materials of iron and steel demanded a new architectural language. As the end of the century approached, the movement known in French and English as art nouveau emerged, encompassing some of these concerns and contradictions.

International interest in Gaudí has often eclipsed the fact that the branch of art nouveau seen in Catalonia, known as *Modernisme* (always confusing, since 'modernism' in English usually refers to twentieth-century functional styles), was quite distinctive in its ideas and its products, and that the style was perhaps more widely accepted in Barcelona than in any other city in Europe.

It developed out of the general renaissance of Catalan culture. Influenced like other forms of art nouveau by Ruskin, William Morris and the Arts and Crafts movement, French Symbolism and other international currents, *Modernisme* was also an indigenous expression that made use of its own Catalan traditions of design and craftwork. *Modernista* architects, as the name indicates, sought to function entirely within the modern world – hence their experimental use of iron and glass – but also to revive and express distinctly Catalan traditions – and so showed enormous interest in the Gothic of the Catalan Golden Age.

Modernisme was also a very wide-ranging and flexible movement. It permitted the coexistence and reinterpretation of Gothic revivalism, floralising and decoration to the point of delirium, a rationalist machine worship and the most advanced and revolutionary expressionism. Catalan Modernism also sought to integrate both fine and decorative arts, and so gave equal weight to furniture-making, glasswork and so on as to painting or architecture.

Modernist architecture was given a decisive boost by the buildings for the Universal Exhibition of 1888, most of which were by Lluís Domènech i Montaner (1850-1923). Most no longer exist, notably the 'International Hotel' on the Moll de la Fusta that was built in under 100 days, but one that remains is the 'Castle of the Three Dragons' in the Ciutadella, built as the exhibition restaurant and now the **Museu de Zoologia**. It already showed many key features of Modernist style: the use of structural ironwork allowed greater freedom in the creation of openings, arches and windows, and plain brick, instead of the stucco previously applied to most buildings in Barcelona, was used in an exuberantly decorative manner. As further decoration, there is an eclectic mix of neo-Moorish and Medieval motifs in terracotta and glazed tiles. Domènech was one of the main Modernist architects who developed the idea of the 'total work', working closely with craftsmen and designers on every aspect of a building – ornament, lighting, window glass. His greatest creations are the **Hospital de Sant Pau**, built as many small 'pavilions' within a garden to avoid the depressing effect of a monolithic hospital, and the **Palau de la Música Catalana**, an extraordinary display of outrageous decoration.

After Domènech – and Gaudí – the third of the trio of leading Modernist architects was Josep Puig i Cadafalch (1867-1957), who showed a strongly neo-Gothic influence in such buildings as his *Casa de les Punxes* ('House of Spikes', officially the **Casa Terrades**) in the Diagonal, combined with many traditional Catalan touches. Although these are the major names of *Modernista* architecture, there were many others. Modernist creativity was at its peak for only about twenty years, from 1888 to 1908, but the amount of work produced, large and small, was extraordinary, and the Eixample contains the greatest concentration of art nouveau in Europe (the Ajuntament's *Quadrat d'Or* book is a good architectural guide). There are also *Modernista* constructions throughout Catalonia.

The Twentieth Century

By the 1900s *Modernisme* had become too extreme for the Barcelona middle class. The new 'proper' style for Catalan architecture was declared to be *Noucentisme*, which stressed the importance of Classical proportions. However, this style failed to produce anything of much note: the main buildings that survive are those of the 1929 Exhibition, which also brought with it some indeterminate monumental architecture, topped by the bizarre neo-Baroque **Palau Nacional**.

The 1929 exhibition also brought to Barcelona, however, by importation, one of the most important buildings of the century: Mies van der Rohe's German Pavilion, the **Pavelló Barcelona**. Even today it appears modern in its challenge to conventional ideas of space, and its impact at the time must have been extraordinary. The famous Barcelona chair was designed for this building, which was rebuilt to its original design in 1986.

The major figure in Catalan architecture during the 1930s was Josep Lluís Sert, who with the architectural collective GATCPAC struggled to introduce the ideas of his friend Le Corbusier and the 'International Style'. Under the Republic he built a tuberculosis sanatorium in C/Torres i Amat, off C/Tallers, and the **Casa Bloc,** a workers' housing project at Passeig Torres i Bages 91-105 in Sant Andreu. In 1937 Sert also built the pavilion for the Spanish Republic at the Paris Exhibition. His most important work, however, came much later, in the magnificent **Fundació Joan Miro**, built in the 1970s after he had spent years in exile in the USA.

Barcelona Builds Apace

The Franco years had an enormous impact on the city: as the economy expanded at breakneck pace in the 1960s, Barcelona received a massive influx of migrants from the south, accompanied by ruthless property speculation and minimal planning controls. The city was thus surrounded by endless high-rise suburbs. Another legacy of the era are some ostentatiously-tall office blocks, especially around Plaça Francesc Macià.

Hence, when the new democratic city administration took over Barcelona at the end of the 1970s, there was a great deal that they could do. Budgets were limited, so it was decided that resources should be concentrated not on buildings as such but the gaps in between, the public spaces. From this beginning, Barcelona has put itself in the forefront of international urban design and won recognition around the world for the success of its approach (*see chapter* **Art Galleries**).

This programme of renewal only accelerated with the award of the 1992 Olympics, which were intended to be stylish and innovative, a decision made clear by the choice of Javier Mariscal's Cobi as official mascot. The three main Olympic sites – Vila Olímpica, Montjuïc and Vall d'Hebron – each have quite different characteristics. The **Vila Olímpica** had the most comprehensive masterplan: it seeks to extend Cerdà's grid down to the seafront, maintaining the continuity of the urban fabric. The village also has its twin skyscrapers, which fail to provide much of a focal point, but with Norman Foster's **Torre de Collserola** provide new emblems for Barcelona's skyline.

The main project in the **Montjuïc** site was the transformation of the 1929 stadium, but alongside it the city also acquired the **Palau Sant Jordi**, with its unusual space-frame roof structure, by Japanese architect Arata Isozaki. The **Vall d'Hebron** area is least successful of the three sites, but the **Velòdrom** by Esteve Bonnell is one of the finest (and earliest) of the sports buildings, built before the Olympic bid in 1984.

Barcelona's eclectic collection of modern architecture has continued to grow since 1992, with Richard Meier's bold white **MACBA**, the transformation of the **Port Vell**, and commercial projects like **L'Illa** shopping mall. The latest major projects are Ricard Bofill's **Teatre Nacional** and alongside it the **Auditori** by Rafael Moneo.

The distinction between architecture, interior design, product design, graphics and even fine art in Barcelona is usually blurred. As with the *Modernistes*, architects today still design everything, including furniture, door handles, streetlights and paving, as complements to their buildings and squares. The shop **BD Ediciones de Diseño** (*see chapter* **Shopping**), in the basement of Casa Thomas, acts as their showcase.

History

Key Events

The Origins

c15 BC *Barcino* founded by Roman soldiers.
Fourth century AD Roman stone city walls built.
415 Barcelona briefly capital of Visigoths under Ataülf.
719 Moslems attack and seize Barcelona.
801 Barcelona taken by Franks, under Louis the Pious.
878 Guifré *el Pilós* become Count of Barcelona.
985 Moslems under Al-Mansur sack Barcelona; Count Borrell II renounces Frankish sovereignty.

The Golden Age

1035-76 Count Ramon Berenguer I of Barcelona extends his possessions into southern France.
1064-68 First Catalan *Usatges* or legal code written.
1137 Count Ramon Berenguer IV marries Petronella of Aragon, uniting the two states in the 'Crown of Aragon'.
1148-49 Lleida and Tortosa taken from the Moslems.
c1160 *Homilies d'Organyà*, first Catalan texts, written.
1213 Battle of Muret: Pere I is killed and virtually all his lands north of the Pyrenees are seized by France.
1229 Jaume I conquers Mallorca, then Ibiza (1235) and Valencia (1238); second city wall built in Barcelona.
1265 *Consell de Cent* (Council of 100), municipal government of Barcelona, established; Ramon Llull devotes himself to thought and writing.
1282 Pere II conquers Sicily.
1298 Gothic Cathedral begun. Population of city c40,000.
1323-4 Conquest of Corsica and Sardinia.
1347-8 Black Death cuts population by half.
1391 Thousands of Jews massacred in Barcelona *Call*.
1401 *Taula de Canvi*, first deposit bank, founded.
1412 Crown of Aragon given to Fernando de Antequera.
1462-1472 Catalan civil war.
1474 First book printed in Catalan, in Valencia.
1479 Ferran II (Ferdinand) inherits Crown of Aragon, and with his wife Isabella unites the Spanish Kingdoms.

The Fall & Rise of Barcelona

1484 Inquisition introduced into Catalonia.
1492 Final expulsion of Jews, and discovery of America.
1516 Charles of Habsburg (Charles V), King of Spain.
1522 Catalans refused permission to trade in America.
1640 Catalan national revolt, the *Guerra dels Segadors*.
1652 Barcelona falls to Spanish army.
1659 Catalan territory of Roussillon is given to France.
1702 War of Spanish Succession begins.
1714 Abandoned by the British and the Dutch, Barcelona falls to Franco-Spanish army after siege.
1715 *Nova Planta* decree abolishes Catalan institutions; new ramparts and citadel built around Barcelona. Population of the city around 33,000.
1775 Paving of the Barcelona Rambla begun.
1808-13 French occupation.

Factories, Barricades & Poetry

1814 Restoration of Ferdinand VII after French defeat.
1824 Building of Carrer Ferran begun on former church land; in 1827, route of the Passeig de Gràcia is laid.
1832 First steam-driven factory in Spain, in Barcelona.

1833 Aribau publishes *Oda a la Pàtria*, beginning of Catalan cultural renaissance. Carlist wars begin.
1836-7 Dissolution of most monasteries in Barcelona.
1839 First workers' associations formed in Barcelona.
1842-4 Barcelona is bombarded for the last time from Montjuïc, to suppress a liberal revolt, the *Jamancia*.
1844 Liceu opera house first opened.
1848 First railway line in Spain, between Barcelona and Mataró. Population of Barcelona (1850) is 175,331.
1854 Demolition of Barcelona city walls begins.
1855 First general strike is violently suppressed.
1859 Cerdà plan for the Barcelona *Eixample* approved.
1868 September: Revolution overthrows Isabel II. November: first anarchist meetings held in Barcelona.
1873 First Spanish Republic.
1874 Bourbon monarchy restored under Alfonso XIII.
1881 First Barcelona department store opens.
1882 Work begins on the Sagrada Família.
1888 Barcelona Universal Exhibition.

The City of the New Century

1892 *Bases de Manresa*, demands for Catalan autonomy.
1897 Gràcia and Sants incorporated into Barcelona.
1898 Spain loses Cuba and Philippines in war with USA.
1899 FC Barcelona founded; first electric trams.
1900 Population of Barcelona 537,354.
1907 Via Laietana cut through old city of Barcelona.
1909 *Setmana Tràgica*, anti-church and anti-army riots.
1910 CNT anarchist workers' union founded.
1919 CNT general strike paralises Barcelona.
1920 Spiral of violence in labour conflicts in Catalonia.
1921 First Barcelona Metro line opened.
1923 Primo de Rivera establishes Dictatorship in Spain.
1929 Barcelona International Exhibition on Montjuïc.
1930 Population 1,005, 565. Fall of Primo de Rivera.
1931 14 April: Second Spanish Republic. Francesc Macià declares Catalan independence, then accepts autonomy.
1934 October: Generalitat attempts revolt against new right-wing government in Madrid, and is then suspended.
1936 February: Popular Front wins Spanish elections; Catalan Generalitat restored. 19 July: military uprising against left-wing government is defeated in Barcelona.
1937 May: fighting within the Republican camp in Barcelona, mainly between anarchists and communists.
1939 26 January: Barcelona taken by Franco's army.

Repression to Style Capital

1951 Barcelona tram strike.
1953 Cooperation treaty between Spain and the USA.
1959 Stabilisation Plan opens up Spanish economy.
1970 Juan Carlos declared Franco's successor.
1975 20 November: Death of Franco.
1977 First democratic general elections in Spain since 1936; provisional Catalan Generalitat re-established.
1979 First local elections in Barcelona won by Socialists.
1980 Generalitat fully re-established under Jordi Pujol.
1982 Pasqual Maragall becomes Mayor; urban spaces programme gains momentum.
1986 Barcelona awarded 1992 Olympic Games.
1990 Population of Barcelona 1,707, 286; of the *Area Metropolitana*, over 3,000,000.
1992 Barcelona Olympics.

The Origins

From Roman Barcino to independent capital, via the Empire of Charlemagne.

It was during the first thousand years in Barcelona's history that the foundations were laid of Catalan identity and language. Multiple invasions between periods of growth and others of decay left the isolated, self-reliant people of the city and surrounding countryside with traditions and characteristics quite distinct from those of other residents of the Iberian peninsula.

The Romans founded Barcelona, in about 15 BC, on the *Mons Taber*, a small hill between two streams with a good view of the Mediterranean, today crowned by the Cathedral. The plain around was sparsely inhabited by the Laetani, an agrarian Celtic-Iberian people known for producing grain and honey and collecting oysters. Known as *Barcino*, the town was much smaller than the capital of Roman *Hispania Citerior, Tarraco* (Tarragona), but had the only harbour, albeit a poor one, between there and Narbonne.

Like virtually every other Roman new town in Europe it was a fortified rectangle with a crossroads at its centre, where the Plaça Sant Jaume is today. It was a decidedly unimportant, provincial town, but nonetheless the rich plain provided it with a produce garden, and the sea gave it an incipient maritime trade. It very early acquired a Jewish community, and was associated with some Christian martyrs, notably Barcelona's first patron saint, Santa Eulàlia. She was supposedly executed at the end of the third century via a series of revolting tortures, including being rolled naked in a sealed barrel full of glass shards down the alley now called Baixada (descent) de Santa Eulàlia.

Even so, Barcelona accepted Christianity shortly afterwards, in 312 AD, together with the rest of the Roman Empire, by then under growing threat of invasion. In the fourth century *Barcino*'s rough defences were replaced with massive stone walls, many sections of which can still be seen today. It was these ramparts that ensured Barcelona's continuity, making it a stronghold much desired by later warlords (for more on relics of Roman Barcelona, *see chapter* **Sightseeing**).

These and other defences did not prevent the Empire's disintegration. In 415, Barcelona briefly became capital of the kingdom of the Visigoths, under their chieftain Ataulf. However, they soon moved on southwards to extend their control over the whole of the Iberian peninsula, and for the next 400 years the town was a neglected backwater.

Busts at **Museu d'Historia de la Ciutat**.

It was in this state when the Moslems swept across the peninsula after 711, crushing Gothic resistance. They made little attempt to settle Catalonia, but much of the Christian population retreated into the Pyrenees, the first Catalan heartland. Then, by the end of the eighth century, the Franks had begun to drive southwards against the Moslems from across the mountains. In 801 Charlemagne's son Louis the Pious took Barcelona and made it a bastion of the *Marca Hispanica* or 'Spanish March', the southern buffer of his father's empire. This gave Catalonia a trans-Pyrenean origin different from that of the other Christian states in Spain; equally, this is one reason that the closest relative of the Catalan language is Provençal, not Castilian.

Loyal Counts were given sections of the Catalan territories to rule, charged in exchange with defending the frontier against the Saracens. At the end of the ninth century, Count Guifré *el Pilós*, 'Wilfred the Hairy' (approx 860-898), succeeded in gaining title to several Catalan counties. He united the area, founded the dynasty of the Counts of Barcelona and created the basis for a future Catalan state, making Barcelona his capital and so setting the seal on the city's future (*see also* **The Golden Age: Wilfred's blood**).

In 985 the great minister of the Caliph of Córdoba, Al-Mansur, attacked and sacked Barcelona. Wilfred's great-grandson Count Borrell II requested aid from his theoretical feudal lord the Frankish king. He received no reply, and so repudiated all Frankish sovereignty over Catalonia. From then on – although the name was not yet in use – Catalonia was effectively independent, and the Counts of Barcelona free to forge its destiny.

The Golden Age

Under its 'Count-Kings' Barcelona won an empire and attained an opulence it has never forgotten.

In the year 1000 Barcelona had a growing population of nearly 6,000, and was witnessing the first glimmerings of mercantile and artisan activity. During the first century of the new millennium Catalonia was consolidated as a political entity, and entered a period of great cultural richness.

The Catalan Counties retained from their Frankish origins a French system of aristocratic feudalism – another difference from the rest of Iberia – but also had a peasantry who were notably independent and resistant to noble demands. During the 1070s the *Usatges*, the 'Usages', were established, the first legal code in Europe to grant commoners equal rights in law against the nobility. Monasteries were endowed throughout Catalonia by the new ruling class, consecrating the influence of a powerful clergy.

This provided the background to the great age of Romanesque art, which saw the building of the great monasteries and churches of northern Catalonia, such as **Sant Pere de Rodes** near Figueres, and the painting of the superb murals now in the **Museu Nacional** on Montjuïc. There

was also a flowering of scholarship, produced by the confluence of Islamic and Carolingian cultures. In Barcelona, shipbuilding, and trading in grain and wine all expanded, and a new trade developed in textiles. The city grew both inside its old Roman walls and outside of them, where *vilanoves* or new towns appeared at Sant Pere and La Ribera.

Catalonia – a name that gained currency, in Latin, in the eleventh century – was also gaining more territory from the Moslems to the south, beyond the Penedès. For a long time, though, the realm of the Counts of Barcelona continued to look just as much to the north, across the Pyrenees, where the Provençal-speaking Languedoc was then the most sophisticated society in western Europe. After 1035, during the reign of the four Counts Ramon Berenguer, large areas of land in what is now southern France were acquired through marriage, or with Arab booty. In 1112, the union of Ramon Berenguer III 'the Great' (1093-1131) with Princess Dolça of Provence extended his authority as far as the Rhone.

A more significant marriage occurred in 1137, when Ramon Berenguer IV (1131-1162) wed

The Catalan Count-Kings' mercenary army terrified the rest of the Mediterranean.

Wilfred's blood

The Catalan flag, the *Quatre Barres* (Four Bars), also called *La Senyera*, is the oldest national flag in Europe. The founder of Catalonia is also credited with the legacy of its flag, and there are many legends surrounding its design of four thick red stripes on a golden background, all of which have served to justify its special status.

In the ninth century, when Count Guifré *el Pilós*, Wilfred the Hairy, was establishing the possessions of the House of Barcelona and so the Catalan nation, he was nevertheless still a vassal of the Frankish Emperor. The story goes that he was called to serve his lord (appropriately, in some versions, Charles the Bald), and was mortally wounded in a battle against the Saracens. In recognition of his heroism, the Emperor dipped his fingers into Wilfred's bloody wounds as he lay dying and traced his fingers down Wilfred's golden shield, creating the four red stripes on the yellow background, the *Quatre Barres*.

Whatever their mythical origin, the *Quatre Barres* first appeared on the Romanesque tomb of Count Ramon Berenguer II in 1082, thus predating the flag of Denmark, its nearest competitor, by a hundred years. What is not known is just why, and in what way, Catalonia's founding patriarch was so hairy. *See also chapter* **The Origins**.

Petronella, heir to the throne of Aragon. This would, in the long term, bind Catalonia into Iberia. The uniting of the two dynasties created a powerful entity known as the 'Crown of Aragon', each element retaining its separate institutions, and ruled by monarchs known as the 'Count-Kings'. Since Aragon was already a kingdom, it was given precedence and its name was often used to refer to the state, but the court language was Catalan and the centre of government remained in Barcelona.

Ramon Berenguer IV also extended Catalan territory to its current frontiers in the Ebro valley. At the beginning of the next century, however, the dynasty lost virtually all of its lands north of the Pyrenees to France, when Count-King Pere I 'the Catholic' was killed at the battle of Muret in 1213. This was a blessing in disguise. The Catalan-Aragonese state would in future be oriented decisively towards the Mediterranean and the south, and was able to embark on two centuries of imperialism equalled in vigour only by Barcelona's burgeoning commercial enterprise.

MEDITERRANEAN EMPIRE

Pere I's successor was the most expansionist of the Count-Kings. Jaume I 'the Conqueror' (1213-1276) abandoned any idea of further adventures in Provence and joined decisively in the campaign against the Moslems to the south, taking Mallorca in 1229, Ibiza in 1235 and then, at much greater cost, Valencia in 1238. He made it another separate kingdom, the third part of the 'Crown of Aragon'.

Barcelona became the centre of an empire extending across the Mediterranean. The city grew tremendously under Jaume I, and in mid-century he ordered the building of a new, second wall, along the line of the Rambla and roughly encircling the area between there and the modern Parc de la Ciutadella, thus bringing La Ribera and the other *vilanoves* within the city. In 1274 he also gave Barcelona a form of representative self-government, the *Consell de Cent* or council of one hundred chosen citizens, an institution that would last for over four hundred years. In Catalonia as a whole royal powers were limited by a parliament, the *Corts*, with a permanent standing committee, known as the *Generalitat*.

Catalan imperialism advanced by conquest and marriage well beyond the Balearic Islands. The Count-Kings commanded a sail-powered fleet, more flexible than oar-driven galleys, and an army of mercenaries, the 'Catalan Companies' (*Almogàvers*). For decades they were led by two great commanders, the fleet by Roger de Llúria and the army by Roger de Flor. The *Almogàvers*, in particular, with their sword-raised battle cry '*Desperta ferro!*' ('Awaken, iron!'), made themselves feared equally by Christians and Moslems, as they travelled the Mediterranean conquering, plundering and enslaving in the name of God and the Crown of Aragon.

In 1282, Pere II 'the Great' annexed Sicily, considered both of strategic importance and an important source of grain. Catalan domination over it would last for nearly 150 years. Shortly afterwards an episode occurred that has been depicted as a great military feat (by Catalan romantic historians) or as utterly discreditable (by many others). In 1302 Roger de Flor and his *Almogàvers* were sent to Greece to assist the Byzantine Emperor against the Turks. Finding he could not pay them adequately, they turned against the Emperor and carved out an independent dukedom for themselves in Athens that would last for eighty years.

The Catalan empire reached its greatest strength under Jaume II 'the Just' (1291-1327). Corsica (1323) and Sardinia (1324) were added to the possessions of the Crown of Aragon, although the latter would never submit to Catalan rule and would be a constant focus of revolt.

MEDIEVAL BARCELONA

Although the Crown of Aragon was often at war with Arab rulers, its capital flourished through commerce with every part of the Mediterranean, Christian and Moslem. Catalan ships also sailed into the Atlantic, to England and Flanders. The Count-Kings and the burghers of Barcelona worked to support this trade. Barcelona boasted a lighthouse as early as 1094, and by the late thirteenth century nearly 130 consulates ringed the Mediterranean, engaged in a complex system of commerce involving spices, coral, grains, slaves, metals, textiles, olive oil, salt fish and leather goods. It was regulated by the first-ever code of maritime law, the *Llibre del Consolat de Mar* (written 1258-72), an example of the Catalans' early tendency to legalism, the influence of which extended far beyond their own territories.

Not surprisingly, this age of power and prestige was also the great era of building in medieval Barcelona. The passion for the Catalan Gothic style reached its peak between the reigns of Jaume the Just and Pere III 'the Ceremonious' (1336-1387). The Count-Kings' imperial conquests may have been ephemeral, but their talent for permanence in building can still be admired today. Between 1290 and 1340 the construction of most of Barcelona's major Gothic buildings was initiated. Religious edifices such as the **Cathedral**, **Santa Maria del Mar** and **Santa Maria del Pí** were matched by civil buildings such as the **Saló de Tinell** and the **Llotja**, the old market and stock-exchange. As a result, Barcelona today contains the most important nucleus of Gothic civil architecture in Europe.

The ships of the Catalan navy were built in the monumental **Drassanes** (shipyards), begun by Pere II and completed under Pere III, in 1378. In 1359, Pere III had also built the third, final city wall, along the line of the modern Paral.lel, Ronda Sant Pau and Ronda Sant Antoni. This gave the 'old city' of Barcelona its definitive shape, although large areas of the Raval, between the second and third walls, would not be built up for centuries.

La Ribera, 'the waterfront', was the centre of trade and industry in fourteenth-century Barcelona. Once unloaded at the beach, wares were taken to the Llotja (the Lodge), the porticoed market place and exchange. Just inland, the Carrer Montcada, built around this time, was the street *par excellence* where newly-enriched merchants could display their wealth in opulent Gothic palaces. All around were the workers of the various craft guilds, grouped in their own streets: Agullers (needle-makers), Espaseria (swordsmiths), Mirallers (mirror-makers) and so on, names that all still survive today.

Women's domains in this Barcelona were initially limited to the monastery or the home, although in 1249 they were given the right to own and inherit property, a necessary measure for the perpetuation of Catalan land rights. Aside from midwives and wet nurses, respected and meticu-lously regulated professions, women were at one time the principal textile workers, involved in all phases of production. However, the guilds barred them, and limited their opportunities for work.

The Catalan 'Golden Age' was not only an era of economic expansion, but also of cultural greatness. Catalonia was one of the first areas in Europe to use its vernacular language, as well as Latin, in written form and as a language of culture. The oldest written texts in Catalan are the *Homílies d'Organyà*, translations from the Bible in the twelfth century. Not only monks, but also the aristocracy seem very early to have attained an unusual level of literacy, and Jaume I wrote his own autobiography, the *Llibre dels Feits* or 'Book of Deeds', dramatically recounting his conquests.

Incipient Catalan literature was given a vital thrust by the unique figure of Ramon Llull (1235-1316). After a debauched youth, he turned to more serious pursuits after a series of religious visions, and became the first man in post-Roman Europe to write philosophy in a vernacular language. Steeped in Arabic and Hebrew writings, he brought together Christian, Islamic, Jewish and classical ideas, and also wrote a vast amount on other subjects – from theories of chivalry to poetry and visionary tales. In doing so, he effectively created Catalan as a literary language. Catalan translations of classical works were also undertaken at this time; troubadours brought legends and tales of courtly love to Barcelona, while chroniclers such as Ramon Muntaner recorded the exploits of Count-Kings and *Almogàvers*. In the very twilight of the Golden Age, in 1490, the Valencian Joanot Martorell published *Tirant Lo Blanc*, the bawdy story considered the first true European novel.

PLAGUE & DECLINE

Barcelona was not, though, necessarily a peaceful and harmonious place during its Golden Age, especially as the fourteenth century wore on. Social unrest was a frequent occurrence, and violence in the streets was common; grain riots, popular uprisings, attacks on Jews and gang warfare were a way of life. A constant struggle took place between two political factions, known as the Biga (roughly representing the most established merchants) and the Busca (roughly composed of smaller tradesmen).

The extraordinary prosperity of the medieval period was not to last. The Count-Kings had over-extended Barcelona's resources, and over-invested in too many far-off Mediterranean ports. By 1400 the effort to maintain their conquests by force, especially Sardinia, had exhausted the spirit as well as the coffers of the Catalan imperialist drive. In the 1340s, the Black Death arrived, and had a devastating impact on Catalonia, killing perhaps 40 per cent of the population. This only intensified the bitterness of social conflicts, between the aristocracy, merchants, peasants and the urban poor.

Jewish Barcelona: The Call

The Jewish ghetto founded in Barcelona in the second century AD within the original Roman city enclosed one of the most well-documented, important medieval Jewish populations in Spain. Under the Visigoths, all Jews were decreed slaves, in 694. Later, the Count-Kings improved their status to that of serf. Heavily taxed with no civil rights, Jews were required to be identifiable at all times by a law of Jaume I of 1243. Men wore a long hooded cape, and women a low-wrapped turban; both were marked by a prominent red-and-yellow button.

The Barcelona *Call* or ghetto was nevertheless highly reputed among other Jews as a very learned, religious community. Its inhabitants were also known for their excellence in several fields: as fine artisans in jewellery and weavers of precious cloth; as fiscal agents and money changers, frequently employed by the Barcelona nobility to negotiate in North Africa; and as doctors, Arabic translators, scholars, and booksellers. Benjamin of Tudela, a twelfth-century rabbi, wrote of the 'wise and learned men among the Jewish community in Barcelona'. Jewish women were unusually well-educated, and enjoyed great prestige as midwives; so highly respected were Jewish women doctors that they attended Catalan Queens – even though this profession was officially outlawed to them – and were well-paid for their services. Catalan nobles often married wealthy Jewish women.

The same laws that imposed specific dress also required that the community be enclosed from dusk to dawn by gates at either end of Carrer del Call, the ghetto's main street, at Sant Honorat and Banys Nous, which bordered the street of bordellos. Today, only street names ending *del Call* denote the remains of the ghetto, but a walk around these silent, winding streets can still turn up its fragments. Its religious centre was on Sant Domènec del Call: the synagogue, several smaller centres of learning, and the kosher slaughter houses. At numbers 3, 5 and 6 medieval windows remain. Arc de Sant Ramon del Call housed the women's school, and

The Jews' mark, a red and yellow button.

at 1, C/Marlet we can still read a twelfth-century Hebrew inscription marking the site of the house of Rabbi Samuel Ha-Sareri.

Although it endured more than a thousand years, the Call was effectively reduced to ashes during the pogrom of 6-8 August 1391. A furious Christian mob, blaming Jews for plagues, economic crisis and anything else on hand, set the ghetto alight and massacred hundreds of its inhabitants. The Call never recovered, until Jews were banned from Barcelona in 1424, a prelude to the final expulsion of all Jews from Spain in 1492.

In 1410 Martí I 'the Humane' died without an heir, bringing to an end the line of Counts of Barcelona unbroken since Guifré *el Pilós*. After much deliberation the Crown of Aragon was passed to a member of a Castilian noble family, the Trastámaras, Fernando de Antequera (1340-1416).

His son, Alfons IV 'the Magnanimous' (1416-1458), undertook one more conquest, of Naples, but the empire was under ever-greater pressure, and Barcelona merchants were unable to compete with Genoese and Venetians. Inside the country, in the 1460s, the effects of war and catastrophic famines led to a collapse into civil war and peasant revolt. The population was depleted to such an extent that Barcelona would not regain the numbers it had had in 1400, 40,000, until the eighteenth century.

The Fall & Rise of Barcelona

Defeated in war, Barcelona fell to its lowest ebb.

In 1469 an important union for Spain initiated a woeful period in Barcelona's history, dubbed by some Catalan historians la Decadència, which would lead to the end of Catalonia as a separate entity. In that year Ferdinand of Aragon (1479-1516) married Isabella of Castile (1476-1506) thus uniting the different Spanish kingdoms, even though they would retain their separate institutions for another two centuries. It was theoretically a union of equals, but it soon became clear that the new monarchy would be decidedly dominated by Castile.

As Catalonia's fortunes had declined, those of Castile had risen. While Catalonia was impoverished and in chaos, Castile was larger, richer, had a much bigger population and was on the crest of a wave of expansion. In 1492 Granada, last Moslem foothold in Spain, was conquered, Isabella decreed the expulsion of all Jews from Castile and Aragon, and Columbus discovered America.

It was Castile's seafaring orientation toward the Atlantic, rather than the Mediterranean, that began a long interval of decline for Catalonia. The discovery of the New World was a disaster for the Catalans: trade shifted decisively away from the Mediterranean, while Catalans were officially prohibited from participating in the exploitation of the new empire until the 1770s. The weight of Castile within the monarchy was greatly increased, and it became the clear seat of government.

In 1516 the Spanish crown passed to the House of Habsburg, in the shape of Ferdinand and Isabella's grandson the Emperor Charles V. His son, Philip II of Spain, established Madrid as the capital of all of his dominions in 1561. Catalonia was managed by appointed Viceroys, the power of its institutions increasingly restricted, with a down-at-heel aristocracy and a meagre cultural life. For this reason, this period left little mark on the city, beyond a few baroque churches and official buildings, many of them since demolished.

THE GREAT DEFEATS

While Castilian Spain went through its 'Golden Century', Catalonia was left more and more on the margins. Worse was to come, however, in the following century, with the two national revolts, both heroic defeats, that have since acquired a central role in Catalan nationalist mythology.

The problem for the Spanish monarchy was that, whereas Castile was an absolute monarchy and so could be taxed at will, in the former Aragonese territories, and especially Catalonia, royal authority kept coming up against a mass of local rights and privileges. As the empire became bogged down in endless wars – against the English, the Dutch, the French – and expenses that not even American gold could satisfy, the Count-Duke of Olivares, the great minister of King Philip IV (1621-1665), resolved to extract more money and troops from the non-Castilian dominions of the crown. The Catalans, however, felt they were taxed quite enough already.

In 1640, a mass of peasants, the 'Reapers', gathered on the Rambla in Barcelona, outside the Porta Ferrisa or 'Iron Gate' in the second wall. They rioted against royal authority, surged into the city and murdered the Viceroy, the Marqués de Santa Coloma. This began the general uprising known as the *Guerra dels Segadors*, the 'Reaper's War'. The authorities of the Generalitat, led by Pau Claris, were fearful of the violence of the poor and, lacking the confidence to declare Catalonia independent, appealed for protection from Louis XIII of France. French rule, however, created another, new set of problems, and the French armies were in any case unable to defend Catalonia adequately. In 1652, a destitute Barcelona capitulated to the equally exhausted army of Philip IV. Then, in 1659, France and Spain signed a treaty by which the

Sant Miquel del Port, in the Barceloneta.

Catalan territory of Roussillon, around Perpignan, was given to France. Afterwards, Philip IV and his ministers were surprisingly magnanimous, allowing the Catalans to retain what was left of their institutions despite their disloyalty. This war, however, provided the Catalan national anthem, *Els Segadors*, 'The Reapers'.

Fifty years later came the second of the great national rebellions, in the War of the Spanish Succession, the last time Catalonia has sought to regain its national freedoms by force. In 1700, Charles II of Spain died without an heir. Castile accepted the grandson of Louis XIV of France, Philip of Anjou, as King Philip V of Spain (1700-1746). However, the alternative candidate, the Archduke Charles of Austria, promised to restore the traditional rights of the former Aragonese territories, and so won their allegiance. He also had the support, against France, of Britain, Holland and Austria. Once again, though, Catalonia backed the wrong horse, and was let down in its choice of foreign allies. In 1713 Britain and the Dutch made a separate peace and withdrew their aid, leaving the Catalans stranded with no possibility of victory. After a 13-month siege in which every able-bodied citizen was called to arms, Barcelona fell to the French and Spanish armies on 11 September 1714.

The most heroic defeat of all, this date marked the most decisive political reverse in Barcelona's history, and is now commemorated as Catalan National Day, the *Diada*. Some of Barcelona's staunchest resisters were buried next to the church of Santa Maria del Mar in the **Fossar de les Moreres** ('The Mulberry Graveyard'), now a memorial (*see chapter* **Barcelona by Area**).

In 1715 Philip V issued his decree of Nova Planta, abolishing all the remaining separate institutions of the territories of the Crown of Aragon and so, in effect, creating 'Spain' as a single, unitary state. Barcelona's own institutions, such as the *Consell de Cent*, were also dismantled, and local authority was vested in the military commander, the Captain-General. Large-scale 'Castilianisation' of the country was initiated, and Castilian replaced the Catalan language in all official documents.

In Barcelona, extra measures were taken to keep the city under firm control. The crumbling medieval walls and the castle on Montjuïc were refurbished with all-new ramparts, and a massive new Citadel (*Ciudadela*) was built on the eastern side of the old city, where the Parc de la Ciutadella is today. To make space for it, thousands of people had to be expelled from La Ribera and forcibly rehoused in the Barceloneta, Barcelona's first planned housing scheme, and unmistakably built by French military engineers. This Citadel became the most hated symbol of what Catalans considered to be a Castilian occupation.

THE CITY BOUNCES BACK

Politically subjugated and without much of a native ruling class after the departure of many of its remaining aristocrats to serve the monarchy in Madrid, Catalonia nevertheless resuscitated in the eighteenth century, thanks to the resilience of its civil society. Catalans continued speaking their language, and went about developing their own, independent commercial initiatives. Barcelona began to grow again, as peasants flowed in from the war-devastated Catalan countryside.

Ironically, the Bourbons, by abolishing all legal differences between Catalonia and the rest of Spain, also removed the earlier restrictions on Catalan trade, especially with the Americas. In 1758, an independent Board of Trade (*Junta de Comerç*) was created in Barcelona to encourage commerce. The strength of the guild system of Barcelona had enabled it to maintain its artisan-oriented industries throughout, and the city revived particularly following the authorization to trade with the Americas by King Charles III in 1778.

Maritime traffic picked up again, and during the last years of the century Barcelona had a booming export trade to the New World in wines and spirits from the newly planted Catalan vineyards, and textiles, wool and silk, especially the hand-stamped cotton calico cloth called *Indianas*. In 1780, a local merchant called Erasme de Gómina opened Barcelona's first true factory, a hand-powered weaving mill in C/Riera Alta with over 800 employees. From 1784 to 1792 Catalan trade with Spanish American colonies quadrupled; Barcelona's population had grown from around 30.000 in 1720 to close to 100.000.

This late-eighteenth-century prosperity was naturally reflected in a new wave of building in the city. A number of neo-Classical mansions appeared, notably on C/Ample and the Rambla. The greatest transformation, though, was made to the Rambla itself. Until the 1770s it was just a dusty, dry river bed, lined on the Raval side mostly with a line of giant religious houses and on the other with Jaume I's second wall, where country people came to sell their produce. In 1775, the Captain General, the Marqués de la Mina, embarked on an ambitious scheme to demolish the wall and turn the Rambla into a paved promenade, work that would continue into the next century. Beyond the Rambla, the previously semi-rural Raval was rapidly becoming densely populated.

Barcelona's economic expansion was briefly interrupted by the French invasion of 1808. Napoleon sought to appeal to Catalans by offering them national recognition within his empire, but, curiously, met with very little response. After six years of turmoil, Barcelona's growing business class would resume their projects in 1814, with the restoration of the Bourbon monarchy in the shape of Ferdinand VII.

Factories, Barricades & Lyric Poetry

As Spain slid into disorder, manufacturers and revolutionaries alike found in Barcelona a new strength and vitality.

The upheaval of the Napoleonic occupation ushered in sixty years of conflict and political disorder in Spain, as new and traditional forces in society – reactionaries, conservatives, reformists and revolutionaries – struggled with each other to establish a viable system of government. Even so, Barcelona was able to embark upon the industrial revolution, Catalonia, with Lombardy, being one of only two areas in southern Europe to do so before the last years of the nineteenth century.

On his restoration, Ferdinand VII (1808-1833) attempted to reinstate the absolute monarchy of his youth and reimpose his authority over Spain's American colonies, and failed to do either. Upon his death his brother Carlos, backed by the most reactionary sectors in the country, claimed the throne. To defend the rights of her daughter, the three-year-old Isabel II (1833-1868), the Regent Queen Maria Cristina was obliged to seek the support of liberals, and so granted a very limited form of constitution. Thus began Spain's Carlist Wars, in which Don Carlos' faction won a considerable following in conservative, rural Catalonia, in part because of their support for traditional, local rights.

THE INDUSTRIAL CITY

While this see-saw struggle went on around the country, in Barcelona a liberal-minded government, freed from subordination to the military, was able to engage in some city planning, opening up the soon-fashionable Carrer Ferran and Plaça Sant Jaume in the 1820s, and later adding the Plaça Reial. A fundamental change came in 1836, when the liberal government in Madrid decreed the Desamortización or disentailment of Spain's monasteries. In Barcelona, where convents and religious houses still took up great sections of the Raval and the Rambla, a huge area was freed for development.

The Rambla took on the appearance it roughly retains today, while the Raval rapidly filled up with tenements and textile mills, built several stories high to maximise space, for this would be the main district for the new industries of a Barcelona still tightly contained within its defensive walls. In 1832 the first steam-driven factory in Spain was built on Carrer Tallers, sparking resistance from the city's hand-spinners and weavers. Catalans who had made fortunes in the colonies invested their profits back home, and the industry developed apace.

Most of their factories, though, were still relatively small, and Catalan manufacturers were very aware that they were at a disadvantage with regard to the industries of Britain and other countries to the north. For decades, their political motto would be not any idea of nationalism but protectionism, as they incessantly demanded of Madrid that the textile markets of Spain and its remaining colonies be sealed against all foreign competition.

Also, they did not have the city to themselves. Not only did the anti-industrial Carlists threaten from the countryside, but Barcelona soon became a centre of radical ideas. Its people were notably rebellious, and liberal, republican and even utopian socialist groups proliferated between sporadic bursts of repression. In 1842 a liberal revolt, the *Jamancia*, took over Barcelona, and barricades went up around the city. This was the last occasion Barcelona was bombarded from the castle on Montjuic, as the army struggled to regain control.

The Catalan language, by this time, had been relegated to secondary status, spoken in every street but rarely written or used in cultured discourse, until in 1833 Bonaventura Carles Aribau published his *Oda a la Pàtria*, a romantic eulogy in Catalan of the country, its language and its past. This one poem is credited with initiating the *Renaixença* or rebirth of Catalan heritage and culture. Its early literature was lyrical and romantic rather than political, but often reflected the underlying energies of a renascent culture. The year 1848 was a high point for Barcelona and Catalonia, with the inauguration

Factories burn in 1851, but Barcelona's push for modernity continued relentlessly.

of the first railway in Spain, between Barcelona and Mataró, and the opening of the Liceu opera house. Improved transport increased Barcelona's contacts with Paris, the mecca for all new ideas, and so augment the city's cosmopolitan patina.

BARCELONA BREAKS ITS BANKS
The ebullient optimism of Barcelona's new middle class was counterpointed by two persistent obstacles: the weakness of the Spanish economy as a whole, and the instability of their own society, reflected in alarming labour relations. No consideration was given to the manpower behind this industrial surge, the underpaid, overworked men, women and children who lived in increasingly appalling conditions in high-rise slums within the cramped city. Epidemics were frequent, and unrest multiplied. In 1855 the first general strike took place in Barcelona. The Captain General, Zapatero, inaugurating a long cycle of conflict, flatly refused to permit any workers' organisations, and bloodily suppressed all resistance.

One solution to some of the city's problems that had almost universal support in Barcelona was the demolition of the city walls, which imposed a stifling restriction on its growth. For years, however, the Spanish state refused to contemplate relinquishing this hold on the city. To find space, larger factories were established in the villages around Barcelona, such as Sants and Poble Nou. In 1854 permission finally came for the demolition of both the hated citadel and the walls, which began with enthusiastic popular participation. Barcelona at last broke out

of the space it had occupied since the fourteenth century and spread outward into its new *Eixample/Ensanche*, the 'Extension'.

The city's expansion was carried out to a plan by Ildefons Cerdà (*see* **Cerdà's great grid**). In 1868, Isabel II, once a symbol of liberalism, was overthrown by a progressive revolt. During the six years of turmoil that followed, power in Madrid would be held by a provisional government, a constitutional monarchy under an Italian prince and then a federal republic. Workers were free to organise, and in November 1868 Giuseppe Fanelli, an Italian emissary of Bakunin, brought the ideas of Anarchism to Madrid and Barcelona, encountering a ready response in Catalonia. In 1870, the first Spanish workers' congress was held in Barcelona. The radical forces, however, were divided between multiple factions. The established classes of society felt increasingly threatened, while Carlist guerrillas reappeared in the countryside, sending refugees streaming into Barcelona. The Republic proclaimed in 1873 was unable to establish its authority, and succumbed to a military coup.

THE YANKEES OF EUROPE
In 1874 the Bourbon dynasty was restored to the Spanish throne, in the shape of Alfonso XII, son of Isabel II. Workers organisations were again suppressed. The prosperous middle classes, however, were ever more confident. The 1870s saw a frenzied boom in stock speculation, called the *Febre d'Or* or 'Gold Fever'. From the 1880s *modernisme*,

related to art nouveau but with Catalan features, became the preferred style of the new district, and provided the perfect expression for the self-confidence, romanticism and impetus of the industrial class. The first modern political Catalanist movement was founded by Valentí Almirall.

Barcelona, though, felt it needed to show the world what it had achieved. In 1885 an exhibition promoter named Eugenio Serrano de Casanova proposed to the Ajuntament the holding of an international exhibition, such as had been held successfully in London, Paris and Vienna. Serrano was actually a dubious character, but by the time this became clear the city fathers had already committed themselves. The 'Universal Exhibition' of 1888 was used as a pretext for the final conversion of the Ciutadella into a park; giant efforts had to be made to get everything ready in time, including the building of an 'International Hotel' to a design by Domènech i Montaner (which had to be demolished immediately after the exhibition) in only 100 days on the present-day Moll de la Fusta, a feat that led the Mayor, Rius i Taulet, to exclaim that 'the Catalan people are the yankee people of Europe'. The first of Barcelona's three efforts to demonstrate that it was more than just a 'second city', the 1888 Exhibition signified both the consecration of the modernist style, and the end of provincial, dowdy Barcelona and its establishment as a modern-day city on the international map.

Cerdà's great grid

Once Barcelona's walls were down, a plan was needed to develop the land beyond them and connect the city with Gràcia and the outlying towns. The Ajuntament held a competition for projects in 1859. They actually preferred one by Antoni Rovira i Trias, for long straight streets radiating fan-like from Plaça Catalunya. Controversially, however, and for reasons that have never been explained, orders came from Madrid that the plan to be adopted was that of another Catalan engineer, Ildefons Cerdà (1815-1875).

Cerdà had surveyed and drawn the city's first accurate plans in 1855. He was also a radical influenced by utopian socialist ideas, concerned with the cramped, unhealthy conditions of workers' housing in the old city. With its love of straight lines and uniform grid, Cerdà's plan is very much related to the visionary ideas of its time, as was the idea of placing two of its main avenues along a geographic parallel and a meridian. His central aim was to alleviate overpopulation problems while fomenting social equality by using quadrangular blocks of a standard size, with strict building controls to ensure that they were built up on only two sides, to a limited height, leaving a garden in between. Each district would be of twenty blocks, containing all community necessities.

In the event, though, this idealised use of urban space was scarcely ever achieved, for the private developers who actually built the Eixample regarded Cerdà's restrictions on their property as pointless interference. Buildings went up to much more than the planned heights, and in practice all the blocks from Plaça Catalunya to the Diagonal have been enclosed, with very few inner gardens withstanding the onslaught of construction.

Ildefons Cerdà, the man with the vision.

The most enduring feature of Cerdà's plan is the *xamfrà*, the bevelled corner of each block. The Ajuntament had disliked the scheme because it seemed to disregard the old centre of the city, and the principal *Modernista* architects railed against the project as a horror. Nevertheless, it served as a showcase for their imaginative feats, and has become an essential part of Barcelona's identity.

The City of the New Century

Utopians and financiers, gamblers, artists and philanthropists, all came together in an extraordinary fifty years.

The 1888 Exhibition left Barcelona huge debts, a new look, and reasons to believe in itself as a paradigm of progress. As the year 1900 approached, in few cities was the new century regarded with greater anticipation than in Barcelona.

The Catalan *Renaixença* continued, and acquired a more political tone. In 1892 the *Bases de Manresa* were drawn up, the first draft plan for Catalan autonomy. Middle-class opinion was becoming more sympathetic to political Catalanism. A decisive moment came in 1898, when the underlying weakness of the Spanish state was abruptly made plain, despite the superficial prosperity of the first years of the Bourbon restoration.

Spain was manoeuvred into a short war with the United States, during which it very quickly lost its remaining empire in Cuba, the Philippines and Puerto Rico. Catalan industrialists were horrified at losing the lucrative Cuban market and swung behind a conservative nationalist movement founded in 1901, the *Lliga Regionalista* or Regionalist League, led by Enric Prat de la Riba and the politician and financier Francesc Cambó. It promised both national revival and a modern, efficient government.

Barcelona continued to grow, fuelling Catalanist optimism. The city incorporated most of the surrounding communities in 1897, reaching a population of over half a million, and in 1907 initiated the 'internal reform' of the old city with the cutting through it of the Via Laietana, intended to allow in more air and so make the streets less unhealthy

Catalan letters were thriving: the *Institut d'Estudis Catalans* (Institute of Catalan Studies) was founded in 1906, and Pompeu Fabra set out to create the first Catalan dictionary. Literature had acquired a new maturity, and in 1905 Victor Català (a pseudonym for Caterina Albert) shocked Catalonia with *Solitud*, a darkly modern novel of a woman's sexual awakening that predated DH Lawrence on the subject. Barcelona had a vibrant artistic community, centred on *modernisme*, whether established, wealthy painters like Rusiñol and Casas or the penniless bohemians who gathered round them, like the young Picasso.

Barcelona's bohemians were also drawn to the increasingly wild nightlife of the Raval. The area had already been known for very down-market entertainments in the 1740s, but cabarets and bars, as well as brothels, gambling houses and other locales, all multiplied at the end of the nineteenth century. Looking back many years later from exile, the writer Lluís Capdevila wrote that one thing he missed about the Barcelona of his youth was that he had never known another city where there were so many places to eat at three in the morning.

Around the cabarets, though, there were also the poorest of the working class, whose conditions had continued to decline. Barcelona had some of the worst overcrowding and highest mortality rates of any city in Europe. Most exploited were the women and children, toiling for a pittance in dark, airless textile factories 15 hours a day. A feminist movement, led by such figures as the writer Dolors Monserdà, undertook philanthropic projects aimed at educating the female masses and improving their lot. Barcelona, however, was more associated internationally with revolutionary politics and violence than with gradual reform.

In 1893 over twenty people were killed in a series of anarchist bombings, the most renowned of them when a bomb was thrown down into the stalls of the Liceu during a performance of William Tell. They were carried out by isolated individuals, but the authorities took the opportunity to carry out a general round-up of anarchists and radicals, several of whom, the 'Martyrs of Montjuïc', were tortured and executed in the castle above

In the Carrer Sant Pau, 1913.

Barcelona. In 1906, a Catalan anarchist tried to assassinate King Alfonso XIII on his wedding day.

Anarchism was then only a minority current among the workers of Barcelona, but in general rebellious attitudes, a growing Republican sentiment and fierce hatred of the Catholic church united the underclasses and predisposed them to take to the barricades with very little provocation. In summer 1909 came the explosive *Setmana Tràgica*, the Tragic Week. It began as a protest against the conscription of troops for the colonial war in Morocco, but degenerated into a general riot and the destruction of churches by excited mobs. Over 100 people were killed. Suspected culprits were summarily executed, as was the anarchist educationalist Francesc Ferrer, accused of 'moral responsibility' even though he had not been in Barcelona at the time.

These events dented the optimism of the Catalanists of the *Lliga*, but they continued with their plans and in 1914 secured from Madrid the *Mancomunitat* or administrative union of the four Catalan provinces, the first joint government in Catalonia in 200 years. Its first President was Prat de la Riba, succeeded in 1917 by the architect Puig i Cadafalch. However, the *Lliga*'s further projects for Catalonia were to be obstructed by a further inflammation of social tensions.

EXPLOSIVE TIMES

Spain's neutrality during World War I gave an extraordinary boost to the Spanish, and especially the Catalan, economy. Exports soared, as Catalan manufacturers made millions supplying uniforms to the French army. The economy was able to diversify, from textiles into engineering, chemicals and other more modern sectors.

Barcelona also became the most amenable place of refuge for anyone in Europe who wished to avoid the war. It acquired an international refugee community, among them avant-garde artists Sonia and Robert Delauney, Francis Picabia, Marie Laurencin and Albert Gleizes, and was also a bolt-hole for all kinds of low-life from around Europe. The life of the Raval below Nou de la Rambla became still more febrile, and shortly afterwards it would be dubbed the *Barrio Chino*, 'Chinatown', definitively identifying it as an area of sin and

Ramon Casas (1866-1932) – **'After the Ball'**.

perdition. Some of the most regular patrons of the lavish new cabarets that opened were industrialists, for a primary manifestation of the war profits was a round of very conspicuous consumption.

This took place against a still more dramatic social background. The war also set off massive inflation, driving people in their thousands from rural Spain into the cities. Barcelona doubled in size in 20 years to become the largest city in Spain, and also the fulcrum of Spanish politics.

Workers' wages, meanwhile, had lost half their real value. The chief channel of protest in Barcelona was the anarchist workers' union the CNT, constituted in 1911, which gained half a million members in Catalonia by 1919. The CNT and the socialist UGT launched a joint general strike in 1917, roughly coordinated with a campaign of the *Lliga* and other liberal politicians for political reform. However, the politicians quickly withdrew at the prospect of serious social unrest. Inflation continued to intensify, and in 1919 Barcelona was paralysed for two months by a CNT general strike over union recognition. Employers refused to recognise the CNT, and the most intransigent hired gunmen to get rid of union leaders, especially a gang organised by an ex-German spy known as the 'Baron de Koening'. Union activists replied in kind, and virtual guerrilla warfare developed between the CNT, the employers and the state. Over 800 people were killed on the city streets in five years.

In 1923, in response both to the chaos in Barcelona and a crisis in the war in Morocco, the Captain-General of Barcelona Miguel Primo de Rivera staged a coup and established a military dictatorship under King Alfonso XIII. The CNT, already exhausted, was suppressed. Conservative Catalanists initially supported the coup, but were rewarded by the abolition of the *Mancomunitat* and a vindictive campaign by the regime against the Catalan language and national symbols.

This, however, achieved the contrary of the desired effect, helping to radicalise and popularise Catalan nationalism. After the terrible struggles of the previous years the 1920s were a time of notable prosperity for many in Barcelona, as a good part of the wealth recently accumulated filtered through the economy. Economic change had increased the numbers of office and shop workers, who were able to enjoy new kinds of leisure like jazz, football and the cinema. The first signs of a tourist industry were seen, and a Catalan journalist named Ferran Agulló had coined the name *Costa Brava* for the coast around Palafrugell.

A prime motor of Barcelona's prosperity during the twenties was the International Exhibition of 1929, the second of the city's great showcase events. It had been proposed by Cambó and Catalan business groups, but Primo de Rivera saw that it could be a propaganda event for his regime. Around or in association with the Exhibition a huge number of

Macià addresses the people.

public works projects were undertaken: the post office, the Estació de França and Barcelona's first Metro line, from Plaça Catalunya to Plaça d'Espanya. Thousands of migrant workers came from southern Spain to build them, many living in decrepit housing or shanties on the city fringes. By 1930, Barcelona was very different from the place it had been in 1910; it had over a million people, and its urban sprawl had crossed into neighbouring towns such as Hospitalet and Santa Coloma.

For the Exhibition, the main architects of the day undertook the redevelopment of Montjuïc and Plaça d'Espanya, in the style of the Catalan neo-classical architectural movement *noucentisme*, an austere aesthetic reaction to the excesses of Modernism. Their work, though, contrasted strikingly with the German **Mies van der Rohe pavilion**, announcing the international trend toward rationalism.

THE REPUBLIC

The Exhibition was a considerable success, but in January 1930 Primo de Rivera resigned, exhausted. The King appointed another soldier, General Berenguer, prime minister with the mission of restoring stability. But the Dictatorship had fatally discredited the old regime, and a protest movement spread across Catalonia against the monarchy. In April 1931 Berenguer called local elections, as a first step toward a restoration of constitutional rule. The outcome was a complete surprise, for republicans were elected in all of Spain's cities. Ecstatic crowds poured into the streets, and Alfonso XIII abdicated. On 14 April 1931, the Second Spanish Republic was proclaimed.

The Republic came in amidst real euphoria. It was especially so in Catalonia, where it was associated with hopes for both social change and national reaffirmation. The clear winner of the elections in the country had been the *Esquerra*

Barcelona red & black

One of Barcelona's many distinctions is that of being the only city in western Europe to have experienced a thoroughgoing social revolution within living memory. Another is that this revolution was to a great extent inspired by anarchists. Anarchism arrived in the city during the 1860s, and attained a greater influence here than anywhere else in the world. Over the next seventy years the Catalan anarchist movement hit the depths and scaled the heights, from crude violence to the highest idealism, from euphoria to defeat.

The individual terrorist attacks of the 1890s were very untypical of Catalan anarchism. Rather, anarchists believed that an entirely self-managed society could be achieved through constant collective organisation, and a pugnacious intransigence before the ruling classes and the law. Anarchists set up cooperatives and workers' societies, schools and social centres, and were among the first to introduce progressive ideas on education and sexuality into Spain.

During the thirties, anarchist housing campaigns ensured that many of the poorest of the poor paid no rent, a feminist group, *Mujeres Libres* (Free Women), gained momentum and a group called the 'Practical Idealists' planned a self-managed health service.

Anarchism gained its greatest strength in the 1910s and 1930s, after the creation of the union confederation the CNT. If the Passeig de Gràcia was the heart of the respectable city, the centre of anarchist Barcelona was the Paral.lel. On a corner of the small Plaça by Paral.lel Metro station a Caixa bank office now occupies the site of the bar *La Tranquilidad*, which as one veteran remembers 'had nothing tranquil about it', a regular meeting place of legendary militants

such as Durruti and Ascaso and frequently raided by the police. Opposite in C/Sant Pau, at number 116, an ornate iron awning still indicates the *Pay-Pay*, another favourite anarchist café, now sealed up and scheduled for demolition. Nearby in Avda Mistral, at number 17, was the base of the *Agrupación Faros*, largest of the anarchist clubs of the thirties, which at one time had over 2,000 members.

During the first months of the Civil War, factories and public services, cinemas, the phone system and food distribution were all collectivised. Some of the collectives, such as public transport, worked very well; others encountered more and more difficulties, especially as the war ground on. Today, this world can seem to be just so many ghosts, less commemorated in modern Barcelona than events of the 1640s. Some groups still keep the flame alive, though, such as the Ateneu del Xino, at C/Robadors 25, and the Ateneu del Poble Sec, at C/Elcano 48.

Republicana, a leftist Catalanist group led by Francesc Macià. A raffish, elderly figure, Macià was one of the first politicians in Spain to win genuine affection from ordinary people. He declared Catalonia independent, but later agreed to accept autonomy within the Spanish Republic.

The Generalitat was re-established as a government that would, potentially, acquire wide powers. All aspects of Catalan culture were then in expansion; for the first (and so far only) time a popular press in Catalan achieved a wide readership. Barcelona was a small but notable centre of the avant-garde. The ADLAN (*Amics de l'Art Nou*, Friends of New Art) group worked to promote art, and the GATCPAC architectural collective sought to bring rationalist architecture to Barcelona in

association with the new authorities. Miró and Dalí had already made their mark in painting.

Prospects were still clouded by social conflicts. The CNT revived, and strikes went on in some industries. By this time the anarchist Confederation was only one of many leftist tendencies in the city – albeit one of the largest – for this was a time of enormous political effervescence. Social conflicts were slightly less intense in Catalonia than in the rest of Spain, in part because the *Esquerra* was able to follow its own reformist agenda. Their achievements in five years were more a matter of potential than realities, but tangible advances were made, particularly in primary education.

In Madrid, the first republican government was a coalition of republicans and socialists led by

Manuel Azaña. Its goal was to modernise Spanish society through classic democratic reforms, but as social tensions intensified the coalition collapsed, and a conservative republican party, with support from the traditional Spanish right, secured power after new elections in 1933. For Catalonia, the prospect of a return to right-wing rule prompted fears that they would immediately abrogate the Generalitat's hard-won powers. On 6 October 1934, while a general strike was launched against the central government in Asturias and some other parts of Spain, Lluís Companys, leader of the Generalitat since the death of Macià the previous year, declared Catalonia a Republic. This, though, turned out to be something of a farce, for the Generalitat had no means of resisting the army, and the 'Republic' was rapidly suppressed.

The Generalitat was suspended, and over the next year fascism seemed to become a real threat as the right called more and more openly for authoritarian rule, and political positions became polarised throughout Spain. In February 1936, however, fresh elections were won by the Popular Front of the left. The Generalitat was reinstated, and in Catalonia the next few months were relatively peaceful, even though tensions were reaching bursting point in the rest of Spain. In July, the 1929 stadium on Montjuïc was to be the site of the Popular Olympics, a left alternative to the main Olympics of that year in Nazi Germany. On the day of their inauguration, however, 18 July, army Generals launched a coup against the Republic and its left-wing governments, expecting no resistance.

WAR AND REVOLUTION

In Barcelona, militants of the unions and leftist parties, on alert for weeks, poured into the streets to oppose the troops in fierce fighting. In the course of 19 July the military were gradually worn down, and finally surrendered in the Hotel Colón on Plaça Catalunya. Opinions have always differed as to who could claim most credit for this remarkable popular victory: workers' militants have claimed it was the 'people in arms' who defeated the army, while others stress the importance of the police having remained loyal to the Generalitat. A likely answer is that they actually encouraged each other.

Tension released, the city was taken over by the revolution. Popular militias of the CNT, different Marxist parties and other left-wing factions were marched off to Aragon, led by figures such as the anarchists Durruti and García Oliver, to continue the fight. The army rising had failed in Spain's major cities but had secured a foothold in Castile, Aragon and the south, although in the heady atmosphere of Barcelona in July 1936 it was often assumed that their resistance could not last long.

Far from the front, Barcelona was the chief centre of the revolution in Republican Spain, the only truly proletarian city. Its middle class avoided the streets, where, as Orwell recorded in his *Homage to Catalonia*, worker's clothing was all there was to be seen. Barcelona became a magnet for leftists from around the world, including writers such as Malraux and Hemingway. Industries and public services were collectivised. Ad-hoc 'control patrols' roamed the streets supposedly checking for suspected right-wing spies and sometimes carrying out summary executions, a practice that would be condemned by many leftist leaders.

Tensions soon arose in the unstable alliance between the various left-wing groups. The Communists, who had extra leverage because the Soviet Union was the only country prepared to give the Spanish Republic arms, demanded the integration of the loosely-organised militias in a conventional army; this was resisted by the anarchists and a radical-Marxist party, the POUM, as a dilution of the revolution. The authority of the Generalitat was for a while inoperative before the workers' militias, but in September 1936 a new government was formed with, remarkably, CNT ministers, who were also represented in the central Republican government. The following months saw continual political infighting between the CNT, the POUM and the Communists, and cooperation broke down completely in May 1937, when Republican and Communist troops seized the telephone building in Plaça Catalunya from a CNT committee, sparking off the confused war-within-the civil-war witnessed by Orwell from the roof of the **Teatre Poliorama**. A temporary agreement was patched up, but shortly afterwards the POUM was banned, and the CNT excluded from power. A new Republican central government was formed under Dr Juan Negrín, a Socialist allied to the Communists.

The war became more of a conventional conflict. This did little, however, to improve the Republic's position, for the Nationalists under General Francisco Franco and their German and Italian allies had been continually gaining ground. Madrid was under siege, and the capital of the Republic was moved to Valencia and then to Barcelona, in November 1937.

Catalonia received thousands of refugees, and food shortages and the lack of armaments ground down morale. Bombing raids were frequent after 1937, reaching a crescendo in the three days of terror caused by Italian bombers in March 1938. The Basque Country and Asturias had already fallen to Franco, and in the same month of March 1938 his troops reached the Mediterranean near Castellón, cutting the main Republican zone in two. The Republic had one last throw, in the Battle of the Ebro in summer 1938, when for months the Popular Army struggled to retake the river. After that, the Republic was exhausted. Barcelona fell to the Francoist army on 26 January 1939. Half a million refugees fled to France, to be interred in barbed-wire camps along the beaches.

Repression to Style Capital in Forty Years

Years of silence, and then Barcelona sets about reinventing itself once again.

In Catalonia the Franco regime was iron-fisted and especially vengeful. Thousands of Catalan republicans and leftists were executed, Generalitat President Lluís Companys among them; exile and deportation were the fate of thousands more. Publishing, teaching and any other public cultural expression in Catalan, including even speaking it in the street, were rigorously prohibited, and every Catalanist monument in the city was dismantled. All independent political activity was suspended: censorship and the secret police were a constant presence, and the resulting atmosphere of fear and suspicion was to mark many who lived through it.

Franco, the man himself.

The entire political and cultural development of the country during the previous century and a half was thus brought to an abrupt halt.

Barcelona was also impoverished, for the city would not regain its standard of living of 1936 until the mid-1950s. Both food and electricity were rationed. Nevertheless, migrants in flight from the still-more brutal poverty of the south continually flowed into Barcelona, occupying precarious shanty towns that spread around Montjuïc and other areas on the city's edge. Reconstruction in post-war Barcelona of the nearly two thousand buildings destroyed by bombing was slow, for the regime built little in Barcelona during its first few years other than monumental showpieces and the vulgarly ornate basilica on top of Tibidabo, completed to expiate Barcelona's 'sinful' role during the war. Later, cheap housing projects, standardised blocks, were undertaken to accommodate some of the city's mushrooming population.

Some underground political movements were able to operate. Anarchist urban guerrillas such as the Sabaté brothers attempted to carry on armed resistance, and March 1951 saw the last gasp of the pre-war labour movement in a general tram strike, the only major strike during the harshest years of the regime, which met with severe repression, but also achieved some of its goals. Clandestine Catalan groups began to make themselves known in small acts of resistance and rebellion, through underground publications or the clandestine performance of a new Catalan play. Some Catalan culture was tolerated: the poet Salvador Espriu promoted a certain resurgence of Catalan literature, and the young Antoni Tàpies held his first solo exhibition in 1949. For a great many people, though, the only remaining public focus of Catalanist sentiment was Barcelona FC, which acquired an extraordinary importance at this time, above all in its bi-annual meetings with the 'team of the regime', Real Madrid.

Years of international isolation and attempted self-sufficiency by the regime, which had also been subject to a UN embargo, came to an end in 1953, when the United States and the Vatican saw to it that this anti-communist state was at least partially readmitted to the western fold. Even a limited opening up to the outside world meant that foreign money began to enter the country, and the regime relaxed some of its control over its population. In 1959 the national *Plan de Estabilización* (Stabilisation Plan), drawn up by Catholic technocrats of the Opus Dei, brought Spain definitively within the western economy, throwing its doors wide open to tourism and foreign investment.

Two years earlier, in 1957, José María de Porcioles was appointed Mayor of Barcelona, a post he would retain until 1973. Porcioles has since been regarded as the personification of the damage inflicted on the city by the regime during its sixties boom, accused of covering it with drab high rises and road schemes without any concern for the context of the city. His most positive contribution to the city was the creation of the Picasso Museum, with a donation from Picasso's Catalan secretary Jaume Sabartès, in 1970.

In the sixties, when money began to flow in from tourism, the city grew chaotically, stretching in every direction, and surrounded by polluting factories. Many valuable historic buildings – especially the grand cafés of the Plaça Catalunya – were torn down to make way for bland modern business blocks, and minimal attention was paid to collective amenities. This still-grey Barcelona received a rare visit from the Beatles, in July 1965.

After the years of repression and the years of development, 1966 marked the beginning of what became known as *tardofranquisme*, 'late francoism'. After making its opening to the outside world, the regime was losing its grip, and youth and student movements began to claim freedoms that had been denied their elders over the previous twenty-five years. Nevertheless, the Franco regime never hesitated to show its strength. Strikes and demonstrations were dealt with savagely, and just months before the Dictator's death the last person to be executed in Spain by the traditional method of the garrote, a Catalan anarchist named Puig Antich, went to his death in Barcelona.

However, the previous year Franco's closest follower, Admiral Carrero Blanco, had been blown into the sky by a bomb planted by the Basque terrorist group ETA, leaving no one to maintain the style of the regime. Change was in the air. The Catalans were getting feisty, agitation grew; they did not have long to wait.

TRANSFORMATION

When Franco died on 20 November 1975, the people of Barcelona took to the streets in celebration, and not a bottle of cava was left in the city by evening. However, no one knew quite what was about to happen. The Bourbon monarchy was restored, under King Juan Carlos, but his attitudes and intentions were not clearly known. In 1976, he appointed a little-known former Francoist bureaucrat, Adolfo Suárez, as prime minister, charged with leading the country to democracy.

The first months and years of Spain's 'transition' were still a difficult period. Nationalist and other demonstrations continued to be repressed by the police with considerable brutality, and ultra-rightist groups threatened less overt violence. However, political parties were legalised, and in June 1977 the first democratic elections since 1936 were held. They were won across Spain by Suárez' own new party, the UCD, and in Catalonia by a mixture of Socialists, Communists and other, nationalist, groups.

It was, again, not clear how Suárez expected to deal with the demands of Catalonia, but very shortly after the elections he surprised everyone by going to visit the President of the Generalitat in exile, a veteran pre-Civil War politician, Josep Tarradellas. His office was the only Republican institution to be so recognised, perhaps because Suárez identified in the old man a fellow conservative. Tarradellas was invited to return as provisional President of a restored Generalitat, and in October 1977 announced his arrival with the simple phrase, *'Ja soc aquí'* ('Here I am!') from the balcony in the Plaça Sant Jaume.

The following year the first free local elections took place, won by the Socialist Party, with Narcís Serra as Mayor. They have retained control of the Barcelona Ajuntament ever since. Led by highly-educated technocrats, they began, gradually at first, to 'recover' the city from its decaying state and remedy the perceived neglect of the previous decades, enlisting the elite of the Catalan intellectual and artistic community in their support. No-one epitomises this more than Oriol Bohigas, the architect and writer who was for long the city's head of culture and chief planning consultant. A rolling programme of urban renewal was initiated, from entirely new schemes like the squares and public sculpture programme (*see chapters* **Sightseeing** *and* **Art Galleries**) to the *'Barcelona, posa't guapa'* campaign, through which hundreds of decaying historic façades were given an overdue facelift.

The year 1980 saw yet another set of elections, to the restored Generalitat, won by Jordi Pujol and his party Convergència i Unió. Again, they have retained the post ever since. Pujol was imprisoned for Catalanist activities in 1960, and set up a bank to provide Catalonia with a stronger financial base. He and his party represent a strain of conservative Catalan nationalism that goes right back to Prat de la Riba. Their highly successful platform includes not only autonomy and vigorous promotion of the arts, design and of course the Catalan language, but also the recuperation of Catalan identity through traditions, folklore, even – fortunately – cuisine. This has often made for an uneasy relationship

If it stands still, design it

At the end of the seventies, the inherent dowdiness of the Franco years was swept away by a new Catalan style for the new Catalonia: postmodern, high-tech, punkish, comic strip, minimalist and tautly fashionable. Innovative designers in all media added a new layer of sleek, chromed shine to a city whose Gothic and Modernista heritage had faded from years of neglect. The design mania that struck the city in the 1980s can be attributed to a recuperation of Barcelona's artistic, artisan and architectural traditions, or to another outbreak of that historically repetitive urge to remake the city in its own, Catalan, image, as occurred in the 1880s in preparation for the Exhibition of 1888. It can be experienced everywhere, in every visual aspect of the city: from shopping arcades to shopping bags, discotheques to door handles, art galleries to ashtrays, no object has escaped the Catalan designer's eye.

The outrageous pre-Olympic reinvention of the city pointed up the all-important distinction between what is considered Spanish taste and what is considered Catalan taste. As ever, rather than turn to the classic red-and-black imagery of Spain, Catalans tended in the 1980s to look to Italy and the USA for their inspiration. Aggressive designers combined a pseudo-Memphis toy look with cartoon-like Mickey Mouse overtones and duped many international taste-makers into believing that that was most representative of Catalan design, when in fact there was often little originality involved in mixing these styles.

Since then, however, the steam appears to have gone out of the movement, which can leave the bewildered spectator with the sensation that it's all been done before, and somewhere else. One alternative to repetitively outré bars, coldly chic restaurants and shopping malls is to take a journey back in time in Catalan design history, which includes Gaudí's organicallly curved objects, Francesc Vidal's heavy lion-headed carved chairs, Gaspar Homar's Modernist whiplash marquetry, or Domènech i Montaner's phantasmagorical fireplaces and ceramics (many of which are in the **Museu d'Art Modern**: *see chapter* **Museums**). There is style-a-plenty in a city which has left no object or environment in its prosaic state.

with the less purely nationalistic view of the Socialist Mayors of Barcelona, first Serra and, since the latter left to join the Madrid government in 1982, Pasqual Maragall. Facing each other across the Plaça St. Jaume, the Generalitat and the Ajuntament are the two constants of Catalan politics. Nevertheless, they needed to work together when Barcelona presented its candidature for the 1992 Olympic Games, which it was duly awarded in 1986. The two entities quickly learnt to sink their differences in the service of a shared grandiose vision of what Barcelona could become.

BOOMTOWN

Not since the preparations for the Universal Exhibition of 1888 had the city seen such a frenzy of construction. Taking advantage of public and private investment, Barcelona planned an entirely new reorientation of itself toward the sea, and would spend over two billion dollars in the process. When Barcelona, like all Spanish cities a byword for urban blight only a few years before, had announced its candidacy it had seemed an outlandish proposal, but gradually the Olympic project emerged as the cornerstone of the Ajuntament's whole project for the new city.

From the Communications Tower on Tibidabo to the complete renovation of the port, Barcelona spent six years *en obres* (under construction). Necessary infrastructure such as new sewer systems and ring roads around the city, housing and hotel construction was complemented by the refurbishment of several areas. The Olympic Village, officially labelled *Nova Icària*, was built by razing abandoned factories along the sea in Poble Nou and replacing them with an entire housing complex, alongside which there are five kilometres of cleaned-up city beaches. Every Catalan designer, architect or artist of talent was recruited to design and construct the new Barcelona, as well as renowned architects and sculptors from abroad.

The Games, the third and grandest of Barcelona's 'special events', were finally held in July-August 1992, and almost to everyone's surprise all the most important buildings were ready. No-one could quite say if they were worth it, but all were agreed they were a great success.

Barcelona Today

Others may regard a new millenium with hesitation, but Barcelona remains cocksure.

Barcelona's port, intended focus of the new city.

Visitors to post-Olympic Barcelona are often surprised to discover that the vast and vastly expensive building projects undertaken in often-frantic preparation for 1992 do not seem to have come to an end, and that massive infrastructural developments are still the order of the day. In fact, the Games, far from representing a conclusion, were rather the end of the beginning of the reinventing of Barcelona. The city that in the 1890s was 'a bourgeois paradise', as Robert Hughes describes it in his book *Barcelona*, and in the 1930s was a symbol of workers' revolution, was still on track to relaunch itself for the world as the model classless, sophisticated, post-modern European city of the new millenium, in which the nasty conflicts of former years would disappear in a welter of design committees and rational planning.

Barcelona's two previous great attempts to cast aside any suggestion of second-city status and show its wares to the world, the great Exhibitions of 1888 and 1929, had given the city opportunities to carry out sizeable urban development projects in and around the Ciutadella and Montjuïc. Juan Antonio Samaranch and the International Olympic Committee then provided a unique opening to work on a city-wide scale. Samaranch, a Catalan, had been elected President of the IOC in 1980 after a rather 'chequered' political career that included a stint as Civil Governor of Barcelona under the Franco regime, but is largely attributed with cajoling the IOC into making the award of the 1992 Games. Consequently he, too, was able to reinvent himself, as a local hero.

Hosting the Games became the perfect excuse to embark upon a programme of urban regeneration on a scale unknown in Europe since the end of World War II. While the planners set to work implementing their vision of Barcelona for 1992 and beyond, the marketing and public relations element began the task of designing, packaging and selling Barcelona as a concept, for the Barcelona-project was never just a matter of bricks and mortar. The result is that seductive, occasionally misleading but astonishingly successful cocktail of impressions and references with which we identify 1990s Barcelona. Picasso, Gaudí, Miró, Tàpies, Tapas, Architecture, Primary Colours, the

Mediterranean, Design, Alternative, Barcelona – *més que mai*, more than ever, as the city council's spectacularly meaningless but characteristically subtle advertising slogan of the 1980s put it.

THE MAN WITH A PLAN

The emergence of Barcelona as an internationally-acknowledged reference point in urban affairs is inextricably linked to the career of Barcelona's almost-maverick Mayor Pascual Maragall. Brought up in a well-heeled and long established Barcelona family, the grandson of revered Catalan poet Joan Maragall, this one-time Harvard lecturer is as much as any one individual responsible for the Barcelona phenomenon. Jacques Delors said about him that 'more businessman than politician, Pascual knows how to take risks'. He represents the Catalan Socialist Party (PSC), but attracts a personal vote that goes well beyond party allegiance, and the image of urban dynamism he presents is curiously apolitical.

Maragall has managed to hold the reins during a period of enormous and volatile change, maintaining and even increasing the socialist majority in the city Ajuntament even as the Catalan Socialists' sister-party in the rest of Spain, the PSOE of Felipe González, was being ravaged by corruption scandals and showing its age after 13 years in national government. With a combination of political savvy, a 'man-of-the-people' approach, an off-centre sense of humour and the added bonus of producing the goods, Maragall has stayed Mayor of Barcelona since 1982, and looks set to continue in office for the foreseeable future.

The Mayor himself has been responsible for a good deal of the rhetoric of the new Barcelona, and appears regularly at international conferences to put forward his idea of what a city should be. He has also taken a lot of people with him, though, and makes great play on the idea of 'citizenship' and of the right of citizens to alter their urban environment. Programmes such as the *'Barcelona, posa't guapa'* ('Barcelona, do yourself up') campaign, encouraging the cleaning and restoration of the façades of old buildings across the city, have relied on considerable public participation.

Today, what he has dubbed 'the second great transformation' is fully under way, and the building programme initiated *after* 1992 has already produced some significant results. Rather than Montjuïc, a major focus has been the Port Vell, the old port, where the Maremagmum complex, with its shops, restaurants and leisure facilities, has already opened its doors, and work has begun on the unfortunately-named World Trade Centre. In the Plaça de les Glòries, which Barcelona's greatest-ever planner Ildefons Cerdà long ago envisaged as the future centre of the city, a vast shopping mall opened in 1995 which received 16 million visitors during its first year in business, much to the

dismay of Barcelona's thousands of traditional small shopkeepers. The following year has seen the completion of the Richard Meier-designed MACBA gallery and museum, centrepiece of the slow regeneration of the old Raval district, work has finally finished on the long-awaited Museu Nacional d'Art de Catalunya on Montjuïc, and not to be outdone the city's semi-private trade fair and exhibition organisation the Fira de Barcelona has completed construction of a 40,000 square metre extension to be known as Montjuïc II.

It goes on. In addition to these projects that can already be seen the city also naturally has other programmes in hand of which the visitor may as yet only catch a glimpse. Forthcoming attractions include two massive development schemes centred on the delta areas of the rivers Llobregat and Besòs which, along with Tibidabo, have traditionally marked the perimeter of the city. The Llobregat project involves the creation of a Logistics Centre and the extension of both port and airport facilities. The Besòs plan includes extending the Avinguda Diagonal through the district of Poble Nou to reach the sea, the building of 5,700 new homes and the regeneration of the polluted and decaying post-industrial wasteland around the mouth of the river.

DREAMS & REALITIES

While Barcelona continues on this frenetic path of convincing a global audience of its unique blend of tradition, style and innovation, many city residents remain unconvinced, ironic spectators enjoying the show but unsure quite how it's going to end. Although most of the Olympic facilities have been turned over to public use, for some the transition has been troubled. The Olympic Stadium, the most emblematic 1992 site, has not been used for a major international sporting event since the Games, and the 'Barcelona Dragons' American football team and the occasional mega-pop concert scarcely justify its existence. The Plaça Catalunya, despite having been dug up many times, has never quite turned out as the imposing city centre the planners have wanted it to be.

Despite a post-Olympic hiccup in 1993 the Catalan economy – possibly in good part because of the relentless self-promotion from the local centres of influence – has stayed relatively buoyant in the mid-nineties, and has avoided the worst effects of the depression that has hit the rest of Spain, especially the south. It remains to be seen, though, what will be the long-term consequences of Barcelona becoming, in the Mayor's phrase, a 'city of services'. Since 1980 the city has lost 138,000 residents to outlying suburban areas. 30,000 left in 1995. Prohibitively expensive property prices in an already densely-populated city centre is the principal cause of this exodus, but other contributory factors include the highest level of direct local taxation in Spain, high water rates,

The Olympic Ring on Montjuïc, embarrassingly underused since 1992.

occasionally unacceptable levels of air and noise pollution, and traffic congestion. The depopulation of some parts of the city is a source of growing concern, and according to one recent report as many as 60 per cent of the flats in some city-centre districts are occupied by single people over the age of 70. Ironically, while the city authorities have worked tirelessly to provide spanking-new community facilities, the real life of some of the communities they are supposed to serve can seem to have been disregarded.

While some move out, others move in. Some of the run-down flats no longer wanted by locals in the Raval and other parts of the old city now house families of North Africans and other non-Spanish immigrants, a relatively new element that has its own particular problems with a majority community that can still be very inward-looking, and equally are the object of blatantly discriminatory treatment by the police. Many other such flats are occupied by the city's large community of young(ish) *guiris*, the modern Spanish and Catalan word for dumb foreigner, meaning, usually, northern Europeans, North Americans and the like who don't mind chronically cold flats and who think it's cool to always hang out in bars with broken chairs.

It's a common phenomenon that the Barcelona tourist authorities attempt to point visitors toward one of their recent creations, a gleaming shopping mall, or a bridge, only for the newcomers to mutter how-interesting and fix their gaze on the city's perennial attractions, Modernist architecture, or the Rambla and the continual life around it. Outsiders, time and again, are drawn to a less tangible Barcelona, to its people's special combination – itself an essential element in all the recent transformation

schemes – of Latin creativity and applied energy, and to a wilder, older, softer Barcelona than the sleek city of Ajuntament propaganda.

FUTURE MODELS

Meanwhile, Mayor Maragall's avowed aim is to convert Barcelona into the 'gateway to Southern Europe' and consolidate its growing importance as a major city in the Mediterranean basin. In all Maragallian rhetoric it's difficult to separate concrete ideas from the emphatic self-belief with which they are expressed, and it has to be questioned how far a city can go on pure promotion, but so far this 'campaign' can claim its successes. The 1995 EUROMED Summit held during Spain's presidency of the European Union set the tone for what many hope may be a future role for the city.

In an increasingly federalised Europe and decentralised Spain, Barcelona would be well placed to become a focus of influence transcending regional and national boundaries, thus overcoming its eternal burden of wanting to act like a full capital city without actually being one. The drive to 'establish' Barcelona has acquired its own momentum, and whatever happens the city and its proud inhabitants are unlikely to pull back from this headlong charge towards their sense of the city's destiny. That self assurance which many foreign visitors find irresistibly attractive in Barcelona often attracts criticism from other parts of Spain. Barcelona casually delights in both responses. American filmmaker Whit Stilman, whose picture *Barcelona* was a story of *guiris* in love, once described the people of the city as 'terrifyingly well-dressed'. In the light of Barcelona's recent development, he could well have been describing the city itself.

The future is another country

When asked his opinion of Canada on a visit in the 1960s, Brendan Behan replied that 'it'll be a great country – when it's finished'. Something similar might be said of 1990s Catalonia. Not since the turbulent years of the 1930s has Catalonia had such a strong international presence, nor played such an ambiguous but influential role within the Spanish political scene. The architect of its international projection and figurehead of mainstream Catalan nationalism is the *Molt Honorable* Jordi Pujol, President of the Generalitat of Catalonia since 1980 and undisputed leader of what former Generalitat President Josep Tarradellas once referred to as the 'nationalists who wear ties'.

The key to Pujol's continued success has been his expert manipulation of the volatile concept of *el fet Català*. A phrase which defies literal translation (also known as *el fet diferencial*, 'the differential fact'), it encompasses everything which distinguishes Catalonia and Catalans from the other identities in what the English-speaking world simplistically envisages as 'Spain'. *El fet diferencial* emphasises the separate nature of Catalan culture and language, and is put forward as evidence of the country's right to increasing forms of self-determination. Many Catalans have a stronger sense of their own identity than a lot of citizens of independent states of the European Union, but still do not have their own stamps, entry in the Eurovision song contest or clear borders as to where their culture begins and another ends, which creates its own set of tensions, practical and psychological. Pujol himself has worked tirelessly to bring an awareness of the separate nature of Catalonia to the outside world as President of the Association of European Regions.

At the same time, it is precisely Pujol's skills as consummate political manipulator which have gained him the unenviable reputation he holds in the rest of Spain. It was Pujol and his Convergència i Unió (CiU) party who kept Felipe González' bedraggled PSOE minority government in power from 1993 to 1996. Opposition leader José Maria Aznar and his Partido Popular (PP) were savagely critical of Pujol's opportunism in demanding greater autonomy for Catalonia in exchange for parliamentary support on key issues. Then, when the PP fell short of an absolute majority in the March 1996 general election, Pujol allowed himself to be wooed by the erstwhile enemy in return for still greater levels of Catalan autonomy, and so Aznar was able to become Prime Minister.

Strikingly, at the most delicate moment in his negotiations with the PP, Pujol announced that Catalonia aspired to a status similar to that of Quebec. The structure of autonomous regions developed in Spain since 1977 gives some local powers to Spanish-speaking regions such as La Rioja and Murcia as well as to 'Historic Nationalities' like the Catalans and Basques. The example of Quebec reinforced Pujol's point that Catalonia had to be regarded as a 'separate society' and not just one more patch on the map.

Since the 1980s, Catalan nationalists have taken a close interest in any new nation-states, particularly in ex-Communist Europe, in a fruitless search for a role model. For a time the Baltic states were the pet neo-nations of many Catalan politicians, but their failure to develop independent economies stopped that. Bosnia was prematurely hailed in Catalonia as a landmark for small nations, but later developments have scarcely made for encouraging parallels.

Quebec, as a highly autonomous entity within a prosperous and politically stable state, offers Catalan nationalists a realistic ideal. The Quebec government enjoys greater political and financial autonomy than the Generalitat, but there are many similarities in the crucial yet controversial area of linguistic reform.

Perhaps the most significant achievement of moderate Catalan nationalism since the restoration of democracy in Spain has been the reimplantation of Catalan as the primary language in public administration and education. This process goes under the somewhat ominous title of 'Linguistic Normalisation'. While not fully emulating the excesses of Quebec language laws, Catalan 'normalisation' has not been without its degree of conflict. Normalisation laws decree that Catalan be the primary language in all public schools. A surprisingly large number of Castilian-speaking parents are happy for this to be so, but a small but vociferous lobby still claims their children's right to non-Catalan education.

A successful Generalitat self-promotion campaign of the early 1990's was a series of TV adverts and billboards proclaiming *'Fem Pais'* ('Let's make a country'). Part of its success lay in its appeal to the solid Catalan work ethic, but it also represented a new political maturity. The reality of the Autonomous Community had been achieved and consolidated. Taken seriously, *'Fem Pais'* expresses a new level of political and national aspiration. The future may indeed be another country.

D-i-Y BCN

Writer Quim Monzó welcomes you to his native city.

Incredible though it may seem to some, there are still tourists who come to Barcelona looking for bullfights and flamenco. What can you do with these people? Stick them on a coach, take them to Lloret de Mar and when you've got them there, under a double-booked sun, have them tried by a People's Court consisting of twelve George Orwells and sentenced to a slow live burial under layers and layers of Coppertone after having been granted a last request of a drink of sangría?

For years, the supposedly 'authentic' Barcelona was the *Xino*: narrow streets, sailors, fat prostitutes, the smell of drains, decadence and prawns fried in garlic. The lascivious writer André Pieyre de Mandiargues made a book of it, *La Marge*, which caused a sensation on the banks of the Seine. Now, for favours rendered, they are going to name a square after him in the very same neighbourhood, and despite the fact that – due to an onset of gentrification and political correctness – the place has even changed its name, from the popular *Xino* to the more historical *El Raval*. One of life's paradoxes, as are the people who see Barcelona as a Mecca of design, sophistication and modernity, all of which form a coating – like glossy Dulux enamel – over a city that until just a short while ago was drooling over the design, sophistication and modernity of Milan, 'the Italian Barcelona'.

More clichés? The Spanish ones. Spaniards tend to praise Barcelona to the skies. For example, by claiming it's the second-most important city in Spain, something which for many Catalans is an insult. If they're feeling in a good mood, Spaniards will drive home the point by adding that it is also Spain's most European city; if, on the other hand, they happened to get out of the wrong side of bed that day, they'll tell you it's a money-grubbing provincial dump. Then again, the promotional brochures of the Catalan Government will pitch you a completely different story, namely, that Barcelona is the capital of a nation, Catalonia, which is fighting to regain its true identity. It, too, is a lie: Catalans are not about to regain anything except their innate fondness for fawning and kowtowing. More commonplace images? Gaudí, for example. For many tourists, Barcelona *is* Gaudí, which is no bad thing in that it helps make up for the fact that – before the arrival en masse of Nikon-bedecked Japanese – most Barcelonans were happy to get on with their lives in blissful ignorance of Gaudí's existence. They certainly know

about him now, but still stare at the Japanese gathered around the Sagrada Família with the mistrust of an EU inspector observing a herd of mad cows. For football fans, I suppose, Barcelona must be the home of FC Barcelona, whose museum, actually, setting aside clichés about design, is the most visited one in the city, leaving Picasso, Modernism and Romanesque art all behind it. Then there's your sunlight, your supposedly-Gothic Quarter, the Rambla, the tapas and the Olé, olé, olé, olé!

Tourism and futility can't help but go hand in hand. Here and everywhere else. The Barcelonans, too, when they travel, are dedicated followers of clichés. They head for London, Nairobi or Prague to check that the clichés and prejudices that they had of London, Nairobi or Prague before they left home correspond to the reality. If everything is as they expected, they head home satisfied, with a plate showing the faces of Charles and Diana, an ebony statuette or a pair of Bohemian glass jars. If London, Nairobi or Prague don't fit in with their preconceived clichés and prejudices, they feel they've been had, and go home claiming that London, Nairobi or Prague are of no interest whatsoever. For all of these reasons, don't let Barcelonans get at you for your clichés. The Barcelonans themselves, if they happened to turn up in Barcelona, would be as much on the lookout for bullfights, flamenco, Gaudí, Latin lovers, design, tapas, sunlight or paella, as anyone else. So sod them.

Quim Monzó is the best-known writer in Barcelona (and Catalonia) today, his sardonic wit seen on TV and in satirical articles as well as in novels and short stories. His last collection of stories, The Why of it All, sold 160,000 copies in Catalan alone, has been translated into several languages and was made into a film in 1995.

Barcelona by Area

Barcelona
by Area

From the Medieval alleys of the old city to twentieth-century avenues and the quiet streets of former villages, Barcelona's districts are full of quirks and distinctive character.

A quieter-than-usual day in the **Plaça Reial**.

Barcelona's history, like that of most cities, can be traced in the lineaments of her streets and buildings. Spectacular bursts of activity interspersed with years of apparent stagnation have left behind clearly identifiable *barris/barrios* (districts) within the city. Despite all the transformations of the twentieth century, most of them still have a visibly individual character.

The twisting streets of the Barri Gòtic grew inside the Roman fortifications, within which the city remained for hundreds of years. Then, as Barcelona grew wealthy in the early Middle Ages, new communities developed north and east of the Roman perimeter. These areas, La Mercè, La Ribera and Sant Pere, were brought within the city with the building of the second wall, in the thirteenth century, and one of them, La Ribera, became the most dynamic part of the medieval city.

The area to the south of this second wall, on the other side of the dusty river bed later to become the Rambla, was the Raval, the 'city outside the walls', and the site of institutions and trades too large or too unpleasant, to be allowed inside the main city. It was enclosed within the third city wall built in the fourteenth century, even though a great deal of it still consisted of farmland, in large part because it was reckoned that this would aid the city to survive a siege.

Barcelona grew little between 1450 and 1800. The old walls remained standing, and when industry developed in the early nineteenth century it had to do so inside them, and mostly in the Raval.

Factories also appeared in the small towns on the surrounding plain, such as Gràcia, Sants, and Sant Andreu. In the 1850s authorisation was finally given for the walls to be broken down, and for Barcelona to extend across the plain, following the gridiron plan of Ildefons Cerdà. The new Eixample rapidly spread to connect Barcelona to the outlying towns, which were incorporated into the city at the turn of the century. Barcelona's last administrative extension was in 1921, when it absorbed the villages of Sarrià and Pedralbes.

Since then other surrounding municipalities, such as L'Hospitalet de Llobregat and Santa Coloma de Gramenet, have managed to remain independent of Barcelona, even though during this century they and the city have increasingly become parts of one, single urbanised whole, and are united in a rather amorphous entity called the *Area Metropolitana* for matters of mutual concern. For decades, the mountain chain to the north west of Barcelona restricted further expansion in that direction, but with the latest building boom even this has been undermined, and a tunnel through Collserola now connects the city to towns like Sant Cugat, a short drive away (*see chapter* **Trips Out of Town: Around the City**).

Barcelona's *barris* may be resilient, but in the last 17 years, as the city has undergone a transformation of its physical features more radical than perhaps any other city in western Europe, their identities and characters have also been altered, pushed and pulled in different directions. One of the central themes of the authorities' renewal schemes has been to raise the standing of neglected outer districts by giving them open spaces, sculptures and central monuments, much appreciated by some residents and half-ignored by others. Barcelona has entered the post-industrial age, and most of its remaining factories are now in the **Zona Franca**, the vast industrial estate between Montjuïc and the airport. In the city, old factories that still had not moved out have been encouraged to, while the shells of those that had have become open spaces, sports centres, civic centres, education centres and discos, all of which has helped property prices to rocket. The Olympic project accelerated these changes, but did not initiate them. The ultimate aim, in the words of Mayor Maragall, has been 'for Barcelona to become a city of services'. Time will tell if it does.

Barri Gòtic

In the first century BC Roman soldiers established a colony on a small hill called the *Mons Taber*, the precise centre of which is marked by a round millstone set into the paving of the Carrer Paradis, between the Cathedral and the Plaça Sant Jaume. The real centre of the Roman city, however, was a road crossing, occupying one part of the modern Plaça Sant Jaume. Large sections of the fourth-century Roman wall can still be seen, particularly

The creation of the Barri Gòtic

The concept of the *Barri Gòtic* or Gothic Quarter of Barcelona was invented in the 1920s, and the name coined during the preparations for the International Exhibition of 1929. It was recognised that the area had highly exploitable tourist potential; another motivation was a desire to raise the standing of the city's Gothic architecture, as a link with Catalonia's Medieval Golden Age.

It was not that a 'Gothic Quarter' didn't exist, for the city had had Gothic buildings quietly gathering dust for centuries. In order to make them into the Barri Gòtic, however, restorers and renovators worked hard to enhance their Gothicness, in changes that have contributed notably to the special charm of these squares and winding streets.This had begun even before the twenties. The Cathedral, built 500 years previously, had until the late nineteenth century a rather plain, only part-finished façade. A wealthy banker, Manuel Girona, subsidised the addition of a façade with a more 'Gothic' look, completed in 1913.

One of the most-photographed features of the Barri Gòtic is the 'bridge of sighs' that crosses Carrer Bisbe from the Generalitat. It was actually built by architect Joan Rubió i Bellver purely for added Gothic drama, and inaugurated in the spring of 1928. Don't forget to look up underneath it to see the skull of death peering down. Another wonderful Barri Gòtic invention is the seemingly ancient Plaça Sant Felip Neri and its Antique Shoe Museum (**Museu del Calçat**). Entered though an authentic gothic arch, the square has a stone fountain in the centre and a timeless silence. But fifty years ago the twelfth-century Shoemakers' Guild building was taken stone by stone from its original site, blocking the view in front of the Cathedral, and reconstructed here to help create this atmosphere. It forms an angle with another reconstructed Gothic building, the Coppersmiths' Guild, while the church and convent across the way are from the baroque period, with a façade with real Civil War shrapnel damage.

in front of the Cathedral and along the Carrer Tapineria, albeit with many additions from later periods, and other relics of Roman *Barcino* can be found in many places around the *barri* (for more on Roman Barcelona, *see chapter* **Sightseeing**).

When Barcelona began to revive under the Catalan Counts, its social and political core remained where it had been under the Romans. As a result it became the site of what is today one of the most complete surviving ensembles of Medieval buildings – from churches to guildhouses to private residences – in Europe, even though the concept of it as a 'Gothic Quarter' is a fairly recent invention, and was introduced with a certain amount of cosmetic surgery (*see* **The creation of the Barri Gòtic**).

The Gothic **Cathedral** is the third one built on the same site; the first was in the sixth century. Many buildings around here represent history written in stone, and deserve a visit. In C/Santa Llúcia, right in front of the Cathedral, is the **Ca de l'Ardiaca**, which houses the city archives, with a curious sculpture of swallows and a tortoise by the *Modernista* architect Domènech i Montaner in the letterbox, said to symbolise the contrast between the swiftness of truth and 'the law's delay'. On the other side of the Cathedral in Plaça Sant Iu is the **Museu Frederic Marés**, with a café in its courtyard that's one of the best places in the city for relaxing on a hot day, the thick surrounding stone having a wonderfully cooling effect.

Alongside the cathedral the Catalan monarchs built the various sections of the Royal Palace, clustered around the **Plaça del Rei**. Most of the buildings of the palace now form part of the **Museu d'Història de la Ciutat**. Even after Catalonia lost its indigenous monarchy in the fifteenth century, this complex was still the seat of the Viceroys who governed the country. Civil administration, meanwhile, was centred in the nearby **Generalitat** and **Ajuntament**, which then faced onto the Carrers Bisbe and Ciutat. Apart from their historic buildings and official institutions, the Barri Gòtic-proper and the other areas between the Rambla and the Via Laietana are known today for a series of popular squares, of which Plaça Reial is the most important, their bars and restaurants and the variety of their shops, from the oldest in Barcelona to the glitzy modern arcades on Portaferrisa.

The narrow streets bounded by Banys Nous, Call and Bisbe once housed a rich Jewish **Call** or ghetto (*see chapter* **History: The Golden Age**). Today it is best known for its antique shops. To walk around this area is to delight in what is perhaps the most satisfying and peaceful sector of the Barri Gòtic. In the centre of the Call is the beautiful little square of Sant Felip Neri, with a fine baroque church that sometimes hosts concerts of classical music and a soothing fountain in the centre. On C/Banys Nous, the old **Portalón** bodega

actually does cheap meals in an area where not much else is now cheap.

Close by are the leafily attractive **Plaça del Pi** and **Plaça Sant Josep Oriol**, where painters exhibit their work in the open air at weekends. Throughout the area there are many good bars. The **C/Portaferrisa** is one of the city's most popular shopping streets, with some of its more street-trendy shops in places such as the **Gralla Hall** mini-mall. The district, though, also contains many of Barcelona's most idiosyncratic shops, including its oldest, the candle shop **Cereria Subirà**.

Despite the expansion of Barcelona into the Eixample, the old centre has remained a major centre of cultural, social and political life throughout this century. In a narrow street off Portal de l'Angel, C/Montsió, is the famous **Quatre Gats** café, legendary turn-of-the-century haunt of Picasso and other artists and bohemians. C/Petritxol, one of the most charming streets of the Barri Gòtic, contains as well as several *Granges* offering coffee and cakes the **Sala Parés**, the city's oldest art gallery, where Rusiñol, Casas and the young Picasso all exhibited.

The area between C/Ferran and the port, properly called La Mercè, has a different atmosphere from the centre of the Barri Gòtic, shabbier and with much less prosperous shops. Its heart is the **Plaça Reial**, known for its cheap hotels and also a favourite spot for a drink or an outdoor meal, provided you don't mind the occasional drunk. Another nineteenth-century addition, built in 1848, it has the *Tres Gràcies* fountain in the centre and lampposts designed by the young Gaudi. The Plaça has had a dangerous reputation in the past, and the atmosphere can still be heavy at times, but permanent policing now keeps things reasonably under control. It has also been made safer by its revival in popularity, reflected in the opening or renovation of restaurants such as **Les Quinze Nits** and clubs such as the **Jamboree**. The **Glaciar** bar, in one corner, remains a perennial favourite with foreigners. On Sunday mornings a coin and stamp market is held here.

Although it can seem hard to imagine today, the streets further towards the port, particularly the Carrer Ample, were until the building of the Eixample the most fashionable in the city. Here too is the Church of the **Mercè**, home of Barcelona's patron Virgin, where thanks are still offered for sporting triumphs. The surrounding area, however, has been becoming steadily more depressed and run down for most of this century. The local authorities, as everywhere, have been making vigorous efforts to change this situation, opening up new squares such as the one in front

Streetlife in **La Ribera**. *See page 92.*

The Arc de Triomf, near the Ciutadella park.

of the Mercè and another on C/Escudellers, which they have named **Plaça George Orwell**. Another tactic is the siting of parts of the Universitat Pompeu Fabra on the lower Rambla, using the students as guinea pigs in urban renewal. Flats in this and other run-down areas of the old city are also popular with young foreigners, who don't object to their state as much as local families do.

Beyond C/Ample and the Mercè you soon emerge out of narrow alleys onto the wide Passeig de Colom facing the port, where shipping offices and ships' chandlers still recall the dockside atmosphere of former decades, even though the quay opposite has been comprehensively transformed into the **Moll de la Fusta**. Monolithic in the centre of the Passeig is the army headquarters, the **Capitanía General**, with a façade that has the distinction of being the one construction in Barcelona directly attributable to the Dictatorship of Primo de Rivera.

Sant Pere & La Ribera

The *barris* contained within the second, thirteenth-century city wall are divided in two by the long, straight Via Laietana. On the right, lokking from the sea, and towards Plaça Urquinaona lies the district of **Sant Pere**, originally centred around the

monastery of Sant Pere de les Puelles, which still stands, if greatly altered, in Plaça de Sant Pere. This has been a centre of textile production since the thirteenth century, and to this day streets like Sant Pere Més Baix and Sant Pere Més Alt are full of textile wholesalers. On Sant Pere Més Alt is the district's most notable monument, the **Palau de la Música Catalana**. Towards the Ciutadella, on the other side of the district, is another pleasant square, the **Plaça Sant Agustí Vell**. This area is in the process of being renovated, with whole blocks being razed to the ground, although Ajuntament plans to demolish the Santa Caterina market in the centre of the *barri* have (so far) been resisted.

The name of the area below Sant Pere, **La Ribera** (the waterfront), recalls the time before permanent quays were built, when the shoreline reached much further inland. One of the most attractive of all the districts of the old city, it has however fallen victim to two historic acts of urban vandalism. The first took place after the 1714 siege, when the victors razed one whole corner of the Ribera in order to construct the fortress of the **Ciutadella**. The second occurred when the strangely-characterless Via Laietana was cut through the *barri* in the 1900s, in accordance with the then-fashionable theory of 'ventilating' insanitary city districts by driving wide avenues through them.

During the city's Golden Age, from the thirteenth century, La Ribera was both the favourite residential area of Barcelona's merchant élite and the main centre of commerce and trade. The main street is still the **Carrer Montcada**, with its extraordinary succession of palaces and the **Museu Picasso**. In 1148 land ceded to Guillem Ramon de Montcada became the site for the construction of this street, where the opulence of the merchant-princes of the time is still very visible. The streets around Montcada were filled with workshops supplying anything that the merchant owners might need, and these trades are still commemorated in the names of many of the streets.

On the corner of Montcada and C/Assaonadors is a small Romanesque chapel, the **Capella d'en Marcús**, which unfortunately always seems to be under restoration and, for the moment, still cannot be visited. It was paid for in the twelfth century by one Bernat Marcús, who is said to have organised the first postal service in Europe. It was from this chapel, then outside the city wall, that his riders set off for the north, and it also provided a refuge for them and other travellers who arrived after the city gates had closed for the night. The C/Carders, close by, is a continuation from C/Llibreteria of the Roman road that led eventually to Rome, and was for centuries the main road out of Barcelona to the north. Like many other parts of the old city, this area now has a declining and ageing population, as young people move out to newer and more problem-free

Montjuic: the favourite mountain

Whether the name means mountain of the Jews or the mountain of Jupiter, this hill of 200 hectares overlooking the city signifies for foreigners the venue for the 1929 Exhibition and the 1992 Olympics. For the city's inhabitants it means much more. It's not a district, for hardly anyone lives there, but it is a delightful place for a stroll.

According to one legend of the origins of Barcelona, it was founded by Hercules and populated by the crew of the ninth ship (*Barca nona*) that went with him on his labours. Hercules then sat on Montjuïc to admire his creation. But it also has other associations. The **Castell de Montjuïc** at the top of the **Teleférico**, originally built in the seventeenth century, became with the Ciutadella one of the symbols of the suppression of Catalan liberties after 1714, and radicals were imprisoned and executed here. A place of fear, the castle was not handed over to the city by the army until 1960, since when it has housed the **Museu Militar**.

At the same time the rest of Montjuïc, wild and empty, was the city's favourite park, and when Barcelona was still confined in its walls people used to climb the hill to spend a day in the country. The military refused to allow much building on the mountain until well into this century, and it was not until the 1920s, during the run-up to the 1929 Exhibition, that Montjuïc was landscaped.

Below the castle, on the steep side of Montjuïc nearest the port, are the **Jardins Costa i Llobera** which abound in exotic plants such as a Mexican cactus popularly known as '*el seient de la sogra*', mother-in-law's seat. Not far above, on the Montjuïc road, Avda Miramar, are the **Jardins del Mirador**, from where there is a spectacular view over the harbour. Carry on the road, past the **Parc d'Atraccions**, one of Barcelona's two permanent funfairs, and you will reach the **Jardins Cinto Verdaguer**, with a beautiful pond, bridge, flowers and a great view. The Avda Miramar continues to the municipal swimming pool, spectacularly rebuilt for the 1992 diving events, the Escola del Bosc, suitably surrounded by pines, and then the **Fundació Miró**.

If you continue straight on you will come to the **Anella Olímpica**, but if on the other hand you turn right down the hill you will come upon a veritable orgy of Monumentalist and Noucentista architecture from 1929, palaces or museums or both, culminating in the ineffable **Poble Espanyol**. Carles Buïgas' water-and-light spectacular the **Font Màgica** near Plaça d'Espanya, however corny, never fails to round off a memorable walk.

housing. The district now has a significant immigrant population, from North Africa and elsewhere.

From C/Carders, C/Montcada leads across Carrer Princesa to the centre of the Ribera, the **Passeig del Born**. Its name originally meant 'joust' or 'list', and in the Middle Ages and many centuries thereafter this was the centre for the city's festivals, processions, tournaments, carnivals and the burning of heretics by the Inquisition. At one end of the square is the old **Born** market, a magnificent 1870s wrought-iron structure that used to be Barcelona's main wholesale food market and the centre of the commercial life of the district. It closed in the 1970s, when the market was transfered to the all-modern **Mercabarna** on the other side of Montjuïc. The building was saved from demolition, but since then no one has ever quite decided what to do with it.

At the other end of the Passeig from the market stands the summit of Catalan Gothic, the magnificent church of **Santa Maria del Mar**. On one side of it a rather ugly new square was opened in 1989 on the site where it is believed the last defenders of the city were executed after the fall of Barcelona to the Spanish army in 1714'. Called the **Fossar de les Moreres**, the 'Mulberry Graveyard', the square is emphatically inscribed with patriotic poetry, and nationalist demonstrations converge here on Catalan National Day, 11 September.

The closure of the Born led to a certain decline in the area, but it has survived as the home of an old-established community, who have kept going as communities like this tend to do in Barcelona, and thanks to its inherent attractions for both tourism and nightlife.

It has many good bars, from the **Local** in C/Ases and the irreplacable traditional **Xampanyet** in Montcada for daytime drinking to night-venues such as **Penúltimo** in the Passeig, and also excellent restaurants. In the eighties it also began to develop as a centre for contemporary art. The promised boom has not quite been sustained, but it is one of the focuses of Barcelona's alternative art scene, with venues such as **Metrònom** and **La Santa**.

From the Passeig and Santa Maria, tiny streets lead through sometimes precarious-looking, centuries-old arches to the main avenue along the harbourside and another symbol of the Ribera, the **Llotja** (Exchange). Its outer shell is a neo-Classical building added in the eighteenth century, but its core is a superb 1380's Gothic hall which, until the Barcelona exchange moved to Passeig de Gràcia in 1994, was the oldest continuously-functioning stock exchange in Europe. It also once housed the *Consolat del Mar*, the Sea Consulate, established to arbitrate in commercial disputes throughout the Mediterranean, and since then has equally accommodated a Customs Post and a School of Fine Arts, where Picasso and many other artists studied.

Unfortunately it can be visited only if you happen to attend a function organised through its owners, the Chamber of Commerce (*see chapter* **Business**).

The Raval

This is the name currently used for the area bounded by the Rambla, Paral.lel, Ronda Sant Pau and Ronda Sant Antoni, although it has been referred to by many different names in the past. 'Raval' is a revival of its original Medieval name, referring to the part of the city outside the walls. The trades and institutions then confined here were those too dangerous or noxious to be allowed inside the city, such as brickmaking, slaughtering or tanning, or the huge old **Hospital de la Santa Creu**, which served the city from the fifteenth century until it finally closed in 1926. Other institutions located here were those that demanded too much space, such as the line of monasteries that once ran down one side of the Rambla. In the corner of the Raval next to the sea were the **Drassanes** or shipyards, now the **Museu Marítim**.

On the Paral.lel, near the port, a large section still stands of Barcelona's third wall, which brought the Raval within the city in the fourteenth century. However, Barcelona largely stagnated during the following centuries, and in 1800 much of the Raval had still not been built up, but consisted of small market gardens that supplied the city. A trace of this earlier Raval can be still seen in the name of one of the most beautiful pockets of peace in the *barri*, the ancient Romanesque church of **Sant Pau del Camp** (St Paul in the Field). Hence, when industry began to develop, it was in this area that most land was available. A great deal more land also came into use when liberal governments dissolved the monasteries in 1836, especially in the area around one of the great hubs of the district, the **Boqueria** market, built on the site of the former convent of Sant Josep.

Barcelona's first industry, mainly textile mills, thus had to grow within the cramped confines of the still-walled Raval, making use of every particle of space. Some of the strange, barrack-like factories from that time can still be seen, particularly in the narrow streets around C/Riereta. The workers from the factories lived alongside them, often in appalling conditions.

Then known to most people as the *Quinto* or Fifth District, this was the district where the dangerous classes of society hung out, and became the great centre of revolutionary Barcelona, a perennial breeding ground for anarchist and other radical groups. Conspiracies galore were hatched here, riots and revolts began on innumerable occasions and whole streets became no-go areas for the police after dark. In 1923, gunmen in the pay of employers murdered the great CNT leader Salvador Seguí on the corner of C/Cadena and C/Sant Rafael.

The other aspect of the area (or of that part of it between C/Sant Pau and the port) that achieved notoriety was its situation as a centre of low-life and the sex industry, with high-class brothels for the rich and cheap dives for the poor in the so-called *Barrio Chino* (*Xino*, in Catalan) or Chinatown. This label was given to the area (which had no Chinese connections) in the twenties by a local journalist, Francesc Madrid, after he saw a film about vice in San Francisco's Chinatown, and swiftly caught on. Barcelona had always had an underworld, centred in the Raval, but it really took off during World War I, when the city became the favourite refuge for people of no fixed means from all over Europe. The two elements of the district, workers and drifters, co-existed side by side, and its narrow streets were crowded 24 hours a day with people coming and going, buying and selling.

Here people on the run from the police found it easy to live clandestinely. The decadent life of the *Barrio Chino* has often been romanticised, particularly by foreign writers like Jean Genet. Its heyday was in the twenties and thirties, but it managed to survive to a certain extent under Franco. Hundreds of bars and cheap hostals lined streets like Nou de la Rambla, catering to a floating population.

Today, however, the whole district has changed enormously. It still has an industrial flavour, but its surviving industry consists of small, old-fashioned workshops in trades like printing, furniture repair or building supplies. The Hospital now houses cultural and academic institutions. Radical politics has failed to revive under the new democracy. The biggest change has been in the *Barrio Chino*, which has been a prime target of the Ajuntament's urban renewal schemes.

Serious problems began for the *Chino* at the end of the seventies, with the arrival of heroin. The area's old, semi-tolerated petty criminality suddenly became much more threatening, affecting both the morale of Barcelona residents and the tourist trade. The authorities set about dealing with the problem with their customary clean-sweep approach. Since 1988 most of the area's cheapest *hostals* have been closed, and whole blocks associated with drug dealers or prostitution have been demolished to make way for new squares. The people displaced were often transferred to newer flats on the outskirts of town, out of sight and so perhaps out of mind. Another element in what the authorities aptly call the *esponjament* (mopping up) of the Raval has been gentrification, with the construction of a students' residence, a new police station and office blocks on the razed sites. Some of the changes have been undeniably for the best, but their cumulative effect has been to rip the heart out of one of the more unique parts of the city, and to leave it looking rather empty. Another, unpredicted change in the

The day starts on **C/Nou de la Rambla.**

Raval, however, has been the recent appearance of a sizeable Moslem community, mostly of Maghrebi immigrants, who have taken over flats no longer wanted by Spaniards.

The main thoroughfare of the lower Raval, **C/Nou de la Rambla**, today has only a fraction of its earlier animation, but retains a surreal selection of shops – theatrical costumiers where strippers could buy all the sequins they could ever need, alongside fashion shops that bizarrely specialise in bridal wear. It also contains a peculiar addition from the 1880s, the **Palau Güell**, built by Gaudí for Eusebi Güell. It was an extremely eccentric decision by Güell to have his new residence located in what was already a deeply unfashionable area, and he often had trouble persuading dinner guests to take up his invitations. It is the upper Raval, towards Plaça Catalunya, that has been the site of the largest-scale official projects for the rejuvenation of the area, with the building of the giant cultural complex that includes both Richard Meier's **Museu d'Art Contemporani (MACBA)** and the **Centre de Cultura Contemporània (CCCB)**, in what was once the *Casa de la Caritat* or workhouse.

As well as acquiring a completely new association with sophisticated culture, parts of the old district have enjoyed a new lease of life thanks to their bars having been rediscovered as places for slightly grungy socialising. The **London Bar** on C/Nou de la Rambla and the **Marsella** on C/Sant Pau are both forever popular with the local foreign community. For a relaxing drink the open-air bars on Plaça Vicenç Martorell are unbeatable, and new bars have appeared, such as the Irish **Quiet Man** on C/Marqués de Barberà.

Barceloneta

The triangular district known as Barceloneta ('Little Barcelona'), the part of the city between the harbour and the sea, was the product of an early example of authoritarian town planning, and had a traumatic birth. When after 1714 a large section of the Ribera (*see above*) was razed to the ground to make way for the new Citadel, the people thus displaced lived for many years in makeshift shelters on the beach, until in the 1750s the authorities decided to rehouse them in line with a plan drawn up by a French army engineer, Prosper Verboom.

The new district was built on land reclaimed from the sea. The street plan of Barceloneta, with long, straight narrow blocks, reveals its military origins. The houses were initially of only one storey, but subsequently second, third and fourth storeys were permitted. In the nineteenth century this became the dockers' and the fishermen's district, and many other industries also set up here.

The massive road and rail barrier that has cut Barceloneta off from the rest of the city for most of the last hundred years helped the area retain a very distinctive atmosphere and identity. The local **Festa Major** is a riot of colour, with streets covered with paper garlands (*see chapter* **Barcelona by Season**). Barceloneta has also traditionally been Barcelona's gateway to the beach. Until quite recently this was of interest only to a few devotees. Some may cavil at the water quality even today, but since the comprehensive reconstruction and cleansing of the city's beaches they have become much more pleasant. Consequently Barceloneta has become still more crowded on summer weekends as the throngs thread their way through its streets on their way to the Port Olimpic and the beaches of Poble Nou.

Barceloneta has also been long associated with another pleasure, in its fine fish and seafood restaurants. There are any number of them in the district, but among the best are **Can Ros** and **Can Ramonet**. Away from the beach and the city Barceloneta leads into the Passeig de l'Escullera, the long road along the breakwater at the end of which is another restaurant and the landing point of the **Golondrinas** trip boats.

A famous feature of the Barceloneta was that it used to be possible to combine the district's two pleasures, in the traditional paella and seafood

Exploring Collserola

It's a much-repeated local cliché to say that Barcelona, until the Ajuntament decided to build it a beach, lived with its back to the sea, but it's at best only half-true. One is on steadier ground, though, in saying that despite the hiking vogue of the last century, the city has cold-shouldered the Collserola mountain chain to its north and west, with the exception of Tibidabo.

Tibidabo is at the centre of the Collserola, with its funfair, bars, restaurants and fabulous views, especially from the huge **Torre de Collserola** to one side. The name Tibidabo comes from the Latin for 'to thee I shall give', the words used by the Devil during his temptation of Christ. The 6,550-hectares of the Serra de Collserola proper, however, are more easily reached by FGC trains on the Terrassa-Sabadell line from Plaça Catalunya, getting off at **Baixador de Vallvidrera** station. A 10-minute walk into the woods along the Carretera de l'Església leads to the **Centre d'Informacio** (280 35 52), where some information about the mountain range is available in English.

The very helpful Information Centre also has an exhibition area and bar. There are five suggested itineraries, ranging from a walk of a mere 20 minutes to an excursion to the Serra d'en Cardona of over two hours. Other, longer hikes have also been signposted. The great thing however is to explore for oneself, because the Collserola is a wonderful natural reserve. Walking is easy, as the paths and climbs are well maintained. You occasionally comes upon abandoned *masies*, traditional Catalan farmhouses. Picnic spaces are clearly indicated, although it is strictly forbidden to light fires following a devastating conflagration in summer 1994.

Holm oak and pines predominate among the trees, squirrels and rabbits are everywhere, and the scents and colours of herbs and wild flowers are exhilarating. A Collserola trip can be rounded off by a visit to the quiet hill town of **Vallvidrera**, where an old bar in the main *plaça*, Can Trampa, will provide rest and refreshment for the weary traveller. From there, a ride down a funicular takes you to Peu de Funicular station, from where the FGC will return you to Plaça Catalunya.

restaurants that lined the beach. These rather basic *chiringuitos* were closed down by city edict in 1991, but have (slightly) revived in smarter form. One of the most ambitious aspects of the city's recent schemes has been the opening up of the old port as a leisure area. With regard to the Barceloneta, this has meant in effect re-orienting the area through 180°, from looking out to sea to overlooking the port. So, some former *chiringuito*-owners have been encouraged to reopen – together with all-new restaurants – on the *barri*'s main harbourside thoroughfare, the **Passeig Joan de Borbó**, and in the converted warehouse the **Palau de Mar**, while other old dock buildings have been torn down to open up an entirely new view of the harbour and Montjuïc.

The Paral.lel & Poble Sec

If you stand by the old city walls at Santa Madrona and look across the broad street towards Montjuïc, you will see a *barri* lining the side of the hill. The street is the **Avinguda Paral.lel**, a curious name that derives from the fact that it coincides exactly with 41° 44' latitude north, one of Ildefons Cerdà's more unusual conceits. The barri is Poble Sec. The avenue was the prime centre of Barcelona nightlife – often called its 'Montmartre' – in the early decades of this century, full of theatres, night clubs and music halls. A statue on the corner with C/Nou de la Rambla commemorates Raquel Meller, a legendary star of the street who went on to equal celebrity around the world. She stands just outside the live-porn show the **Bagdad**, a curious combination of modern sex show with some of the aura of the old *Barrio Chino*. Most of the Paral.lel's cabarets have disappeared, but the precarious survival of the **Arnau** – now used more as a theatre than a traditional music hall – and of the most celebrated, **El Molino** (the 'Moulin Rouge' up to 1939), attests to that past.

The name **Poble Sec** means 'dry village', fitting testimony to the fact that as late as 1894 this *barri* of poor workers celebrated with dancing the installation of the area's first street fountain, which still stands, in C/Margarit. By 1914 some 5,000 people lived in shanties up where the *barri* meets Montjuïc, 'in complete promiscuity of sexes, vices and diseases', according to the Mayor of the time. During the *Setmana Tràgica* in 1909, more religious buildings were burnt down here, despite its small size, than in any other part of the city (*see chapter* **History: The City of the New Century**).

On the stretch of the Paral.lel opposite the city walls three tall chimneys stand incongruously in the middle of modern office blocks. They are all that remains of the Anglo-Canadian electricity company known locally as *La Canadenca*, ('The Canadian'), which was the centre of the great general strike of 1919. Beside the chimneys an open space has been created, the **Parc de les Tres Xemeneies**, now popular with rollerbladers (*see* **Of chimneys and squares**).

Today Poble Sec remains a friendly working class *barri* of quiet, relaxed streets and squares. It has plenty of cheap bars, most of whose clientèle are football-crazy, and a number of reasonable restaurants such as **La Tomaquera** or **La Bodegueta**. Towards the Paral.lel there are some distinguished Modernist-era buildings, which local legend has maintained were built for *artistas* from the cabarets by rich protectors. At C/Tapioles 12, there is a beautiful, extremely narrow wooden Modernist door with typically writhing ironwork above it, while at C/Elkano, 4, don't miss *La Casa de les Rajoles*, with a very unusual white mosaic façade that gives an impression of weightlessness. As you penetrate further into the *barri* the streets grow steeper, some becoming narrow lanes of steps that eventually provide a superb view of the city.

The Eixample

A fateful decision was taken in the 1850s when, after Barcelona was finally given permission to expand beyond its Medieval walls, the plan chosen (by the government in Madrid) was the regular gridiron of Ildefons Cerdà. Opinion in Barcelona was much more favourable to the fan-shaped design of the municipal architect Antoni Rovira i Trias, which can be seen at the foot of a sculpture of the man in Plaça Rovira i Trias, in Gràcia (*see also chapter* **History: Factories, Barricades & Lyric Poetry**).

With time, though, the 'Extension' (*Eixample/Ensanche*) has become as much – if not more – of a distinctive feature of Barcelona as the Medieval city. The more utopian features of the plan, though – building on only two sides of each block, and gardens in the middle of each block – have largely been forgotten. Today, most of the interior courtyards are occupied by car parks, workshops and shopping centres. The garden around the **Torre de les Aigües** water tower at C/Llúria 56 is one of the only courtyards in the *barri* where one can get a glimpse of how attractive and humane Cerdà's plan could have been.

The Eixample was built between 1860 and 1920, mostly after 1890. The train to Sarrià from the centre then went overground up C/Balmes, effectively cutting the new *barri* in two, and was not set underground until the 1920s.

The *Dreta* (right – to the right of Balmes looking uphill) of the Eixample contains most of the more distinguished architecture, professional offices, banks, museums and the main shopping avenues. The *Esquerra* (left – to the left of Balmes) was built slightly later, and is more residential and even working class in places. Together they have formed the centre of Catalan middle-class life for most of the last hundred years. To newcomers unused to such straight lines they can be disorientating, but they form a very special urban environment with an atmosphere all of its own.

The Dreta

The great avenue of the Passeig de Gràcia is the centre of the district. It is famous for its architectural masterpieces, built as elegant residences, such as the **Mansana de la Discòrdia**, with buildings by Gaudí, Puig i Cadafalch and Domènech i Montaner, and Gaudí's **La Pedrera**. The Passeig and the parallel Rambla Catalunya are fashionable shopping streets, a centre for both stylish arcades like **Bulevard Rosa** and design emporia like **Vinçon**. Window shopping for art is concentrated close by in C/Consell de Cent between Balmes and Rambla Catalunya, and nearby is one of the most impressive of all Barcelona's art spaces, the **Fundació Tàpies**.

The cafés on Rambla Catalunya are pleasant, but pricey, and a favourite meeting place for affluent local residents on summer evenings. Cheaper possibilities for a stopover on a walk around the area are **La Bodegueta** and the **Velódromo**. This part of the Eixample is also the place to find many of the most famed eighties' design bars and clubs, some of which, though, have been sliding down the pinnacle of fashion for a few years. Particularly notable from a design point of view are **Nick Havanna**, **Velvet** and **Zsa Zsa**, all near the corner of Balmes and Rosselló.

As well as the most renowned Modernist buildings, the streets around Passeig de Gràcia are also full of other extraordinary examples of work from that time, whether whole buildings or shopfronts and hallways. Since the end of the eighties the section of the Eixample between C/Muntaner and C/Roger de Flor has been labelled the *Quadrat d'Or* or 'Golden Square' of Modernism, and plaques have been placed on 150 protected buildings that are considered of special merit. A guidebook to them is available, in English, from the **Llibreria de la Virreina** (*see chapter* **Essential Information**) and other bookshops.

Particularly of note are the hallway and exuberant overall decoration of the **Casa Comalat**, designed by Salvador Valeri in 1906 (Avda Diagonal 442 and Còrsega 316) and the wonderful façade of the **Casa Societat Torres Germans** (C/París 180-182), by Jaume Torres i Grau, from 1905 (neither are open to visitors but can be viewed from the street). On Avda Diagonal are two of the most characteristic buildings of Puig i Cadafalch, the **Casa Vidal Quadras** (number 373), now the **Museu de la Música**, and the **Casa Terrades** (416-420), an extraordinary neo-Gothic fantasy with pointed towers that have gained it the alternative name of *Casa de les Punxes* ('House of

Spikes'). As an alternative to pure architecture, not far away – in the block on the corner of C/València and C/Bruc – there is a small market designed by Rovira i Trias, the **Mercat de la Concepció**, known as the Barcelona market with flower stalls outside that normally remain open 24 hours a day.

The outer Eixample to the north of the Diagonal is mainly a residential area, for the most part built after 1910, but with some striking Modernist buildings such as Puig i Cadafalch's 1901 **Casa Macaya**, now the cultural centre of the **Fundació la Caixa**. The area is dominated, though, by the towering mass of the **Sagrada Família**. Not far away is another great Modernist project, Domènech i Montaner's **Hospital de la Santa Creu i Sant Pau**, begun in 1902 as a long-overdue replacement for the old hospital in the Raval (*see above*), but not completed until 1930. It and Gaudí's creation stand at opposite ends of Avda Gaudi, made into a pleasant walkway in 1985.

The Esquerra

This side of the Eixample quickly became the new area for some activities of the city that the middle classes did not want to see on their doorsteps. A huge slaughterhouse was built in the extreme left of the area, and was only knocked down and replaced by the **Parc Joan Miró** in 1979. The functional **Hospital Clínic** was sited on two blocks between C/Còrsega and C/Provença, and further out still on C/Entença is the city's 1905 **Modelo** prison. There are two great markets, the **Ninot**, just below the hospital, and the **Mercat de Sant Antoni**, designed by Rovira i Trias and touching onto the Raval, which is taken over by a great **second-hand book market** every Sunday morning. This is also an area for academic institutions, from the enormous **Escola Industrial** technical school on C/Comte d'Urgell to the central University on **Plaça Universitat**, set up in 1842.

Beyond the hospital and the Escola Industrial the outer Eixample contains no great sights or monuments, but leads up to the **Plaça Francesc Macià**, developed since the sixties as the centre of the new business district and of the more expensive shopping areas, and the main crossroads of affluent Barcelona. Beyond the office blocks and smart cafés of the Plaça itself lie the fashionable business and residential areas of the Zona Alta.

Gràcia

'Gràcia – independència' and even *'Freedom for Gràcia'* can occasionally be seen on t-shirts here. This isn't a demand for the *barri* to become perhaps the smallest state in the world but a half-serious petition to be separated from Barcelona, to which it was annexed in 1897 amid widespread protests. Fiercely protective of their own identity,

*Take a leisurely coffee in the **Plaça del Sol**; or just run around it shouting your head off.*

Graciencs quite naturally still refer to outsiders as *'barcelonins'*, as if they did not really belong here.

Little more than a village in 1820 with about 2,500 inhabitants, Gràcia had become the ninth-largest city in Spain by 1897. when it had 61,000 by 1897. It also was known as a radical centre, of Catalanism, republicanism, anarchism and to a certain extent, feminism. Place names such as Mercat de la Llibertat, Plaça de la Revolució and Carrer Fraternitat tell their own story.

As you enter the district, and the rigid blocks of Cerdà's grid give way to narrow streets arranged haphazardly, the change in atmosphere is striking: Many streets consist of small, two-storey buildings, and a series of attractive small squares provide space to pause and talk. The most important of them are the **Plaça Rius i Taulet**, site of the pre-1897 town hall and a magnificent clock tower designed by Rovira i Trias, the **Plaça Virreina**, the peaceful and relaxing **Plaça Rovira i Trias**, with an appealing bronze statue of this great-but-unappreciated architect himself; and the **Plaça del Sol**. It acquired a new one in 1993, not elegant but unpretentious and designed for kids, the **Plaça John Lennon**.

Gràcia contains one of Gaudí's earliest and most fascinating works, the **Casa Vicens** of 1883-88, hidden away in C/Carolines. And of course the most visited place in the whole municipal district is his **Parc Güell**, above Plaça Lesseps on the other side of the busy Travessera de Dalt. *Modernisme* is also represented by Domènech's **Can Fuster** (1908-11)

at C/Gran de Gràcia, 2-4, and above all by the work of Francesc Berenguer, Gaudí's assistant, who designed the **Mercat de la Llibertat**.

Gràcia's independent attitude is also reflected in a strong attachment to traditions like the **Festa Major**, the biggest in Barcelona, which for a few days in August makes the *barri* a centre for the whole city (*see chapter* **Barcelona by Season**). The district contains many small factories and workshops, and also has a sizeable Catalan-speaking Gypsy community. Gràcia is also home to a large number of students, and to a substantial creative community – photographers, actors, designers – who contribute much to its atmosphere.

Coffee in Plaça del Sol is a relaxing alternative to busier places in the centre of the city, though the area is at its best after dark. The **Café del Sol** itself is an old favourite but the streets below contain many more. A few years ago, Gràcia also had its turn as the most in-vogue area for night-time wandering – becoming known as *Gràcia divina* – and acquired an additional crop of bars, although the centre of fashion has now moved on, towards the Eixample and lately back to the old city.

The educated nature of local residents is seen in the number of cultural venues in the district, such as the **Centre Artesà Tradicionarius** for folk music and dance, and theatres such as the **Teixidors-Teatreneu**, the **Regina** children's theatre and especially the **Teatre Lliure**. There are also two of the most enterprising cinemas in the city, the **Verdi** and **Verdi Park**.

Sants

The official municipal district of Sants, meaning 'Saints', includes three *barris*, Sants proper, La Bordeta and Hostafrancs. When Barcelona's gates shut at 9pm every night, hostels, inns and smithies grew up around the city to cater for latecomers. Such was the origin of Sants, but by the 1850s it had also become a major industrial centre.

Centred around an old Roman road called for centuries *Camí d'Espanya* ('the Road to Spain') and now C/Creu Coberta, by 1850 Sants had already become the site for the *Espanya Industrial*, one of the largest textile factories in Catalonia. It was also a centre of labour militancy. In 1855 the first general strike in Catalonia broke out here, and the CNT held one of its major Congresses in Sants in 1918. By then it had become integrated into Barcelona, in 1897.

Today Sants remains like Gràcia one of the areas of Barcelona with the strongest sense of its own character and identity, but practically all of these industrial centres have disappeared. The 5-hectare **Espanya Industrial** site, long disused as a factory, became a park in 1985 after pressure by neighbourhood associations had forced its owners to sell it to the city instead of building flats there as they had wished. One of the 1980s Barcelona parks most liked by the public, it has a lovely lake where boats can be hired, a giant statue of Neptune and Andrés Nagel's *Gran Drac de Sant Jordi*, a huge dragon for kids to play on. Other factories have become workshops, libraries and schools.

The **Estació de Sants**, alongside the park, now dominates the *barri*. In front of it is the **Plaça dels Països Catalans**, a square of granite and grim metal as much loathed by local residents as it is admired by design critics. On the other, southern, side of the station are the more appealing *Places* of **Sants** and Peiró. In the latter the first-ever Catalan film was shot, *'Baralla en un café'* ('Cafe Brawl'), in 1898. Near the Plaça de Sants is a complex called **Les Cotxeres**, an old tram depot converted into a multi-functional community and arts centre. From there, C/Creu Coberta runs into Plaça d'Espanya, where C/Tarragona, to the left, sharply marks the end of Sants and the beginning of the Eixample. This street has changed beyond recognition thanks to pre- and post-Olympic projects, with a line of high-rise towers that have led it to be dubbed the 'little Manhattan' of Barcelona.

The Zona Alta & Les Corts

The *Zona Alta* (literally 'Upper Zone', or simply Uptown) is the name collectively given to a series of districts – among them Sant Gervasi, Sarrià, Pedralbes, Putxet – that fan out across the area above the Diagonal and to the left of Gràcia on the map. They are 'upper' both literally, in that they are at a higher elevation than most of the city and so enjoy cleaner air, and in social standing, as these are now the most expensive residential areas of Barcelona. In the Zona Alta the streets are cleaner, quieter and have markedly fewer small shops than in other areas of the city.

This is the home of the *pijos* and *pijas*, the city's pampered and priviliged upper-middle class youth, who throng the area's many bars and cafés. As well as luxury apartment blocks it is common to see large, individual houses with gardens, many of which have been turned into elegant restaurants and bars. **Tres Torres** and **Partycular** are good examples. These areas have plenty of discreetly distinguished buildings, but few major sights other than the **Museu-Monestir de Pedralbes**, now home of the Barcelona branch of the **Museu Thyssen**. However, the centre of **Sarrià** and the area of **Pedralbes** around the monastery still retain an appreciable flavour of what were quite sleepy country towns until well into this century.

The Zona Alta does have dotted around it several works by Gaudí. From Pedralbes, a residential zone for the very wealthy, a walk down the wide green Avda de Pedralbes leads to a wonderful gate house and gates by Gaudí, the **Pavellons de la Finca Güell** at no 15, with a bizarre wrought-iron dragon. In the garden of the **Palau de Pedralbes** on Avda Diagonal, a former residence of the Güell family, there is a delightful Gaudí fountain, and, back on the other side of the Zona Alta off the Plaça Bonanova, near Tibidabo FGC station, is the remarkable, Gothic-influenced house the **Torre Figueres**, or **Bellesguard**.

The Palau de Pedralbes also contains two interesting museums, the **Museu de Ceràmica** and **Museu de les Arts Decoratives**. Around it, on either side of the Diagonal, is the **Zona Universitària**, chosen as the area for the expansion of Barcelona's main university in the fifties. Some 100,000 students pass through it every day, but this doesn't make its buildings any less bleak and impersonal.

From there, turn back along the Diagonal toward Plaça Maria Cristina and Plaça Francesc Macià and you will enter the fastest-growing business district of modern Barcelona. It is equally a fast-growing shopping area, with several stores and fashion malls, and especially the 'horizontal skyscraper', **L'Illa**, where nostalgic British ex-pats can often be spotted in the Marks & Spencer shopping for crumpets. The Illa also houses the re-launched trendy club **Bikini**.

Close to Plaça Francesc Macià itself there is a small, popular park, the **Turó Parc**, and a clutch of art galleries, around Plaça Sant Gregori. On the right-hand side of Turó Parc on the map is **Sant Gervasi**. This area has had its moment of glory as the most fashionable night-time meeting-point in Barcelona, especially the streets around the junction of C/Marià Cubí and C/Santaló, site of bars and clubs such as **Mas i Mas** and **Universal**. The revival of the old city has taken the crowds away a little, which can mean that at least it's easier to get in. Also in Sant Gervasi, but closer to Gràcia, is one of the great survivors of the Barcelona club scene, the **Otto Zutz**.

Les Corts

The rural origin of this *barri* can still be heard in the name, 'The Farmsheds', although there rarely seems much that's rustic in it any more. In amongst its apartment blocks, though, there is the area around **Plaça del Carme**, the surviving core of the old village of Les Corts, annexed to Barcelona in 1867, which can still evoke the atmosphere of an entirely different era. For most Barcelona residents, Les Corts means **Fútbol Club Barcelona**, whose sports complex takes up a great deal of the district's available space. Curiously, the area around the stadium becomes the haunt of prostitutes and transvestites, and cruising drivers, when darkness falls.

Poble Nou, Clot, Sagrera

These three districts, north of the old city along the coast, once formed part of one, quite large independent municipality, **Sant Martí de Provençals**. Originally a farming and fishing community, it was, like Sants, one of the areas chosen by manufacturers as they sought to expand,

and became the centre of heavy industry of Barcelona, disputing with Sabadell the title of *la Manchester Catalana*.

This brought the usual problems – child labour, diseases, overcrowding, noise, smells, smoke – and the usual responses: cooperatives, newspapers, unions, strikes and other conflicts. On Cerdà's maps part of Sant Martí is labelled *Icària*, because groups inspired by the French utopian socialist Etienne Cabet had established themselves there. In 1897 it was, like Sants and Gràcia, absorbed into Barcelona. Sant Martí then split into three *barris*, Poble Nou, Clot and La Sagrera.

Poble Nou contained the greater part of Sant Martí's industry, and so continued to be a centre of radicalism and conflict. As a result it would pay dearly after 1939. Francoist troops carried out executions every night in the *Camp de la Bota*, on the very northern edge of the city by the sea, where a sombre monument to the victims now stands. Then, in the sixties, the *barri* began to change its character. Entire factories folded, moved to the Zona Franca or got out of the city altogether. The departure of the most historical, Can Girona, in 1992 marked the end of an epoch.

Today Poble Nou has become a laboratory for post-industrial experiments. The old factories have become schools, civic centres, workshop centres, art studios, open spaces for public use. One entire section is now the Vila Olímpica. From a hive of dirty industry it has become one of the city's gateways to the beach, through the recovery of two

Of chimneys and squares

Off the Paral.lel, in Gràcia, in the Raval, in the Vila Olímpica, near the Mercat Sant Antoni... they stand singly or in twos or threes all over the city. Often with a thick cement base, these brown-brick chimneys narrow very gradually as they rise to heights of 30-40 metres on the sites of old factories. The factories have closed, but the authorities have preserved the chimneys as mute monuments to Barcelona's earlier frenetic industrial activity.

The workshops beneath these chimneys were centres of a political life in which generations of Barcelona's people were involved, and the Ajuntament has also sought to give acknowledgement to some of the most important participants in these struggles, all now conveniently distant in time, in the equally mute monuments of urban place names. There is a **Plaça Karl Marx** in Nou Barris, although Bakunin would have been more appropriate for this city. The

Raval has its **Plaça Salvador Seguí**, after the great anarchosyndicalist leader murdered nearby in 1923, while **Plaça Angel Pestaña** in Nou Barris and **Plaça Joan Peiró** in Sants honour other leading figures of the CNT. Of foreigners, **George Orwell** has a square, or rather a triangle, named after him at the end of C/Escudellers. Andreu Nin, the leader of the POUM organisation with which Orwell took part in the Civil War, and murdered by the Communists, is recalled by an almost-illegible plaque on La Rambla 128, the last place he was seen alive, and the **Passeig d'Andreu Nin** in Nou Barris. Finally, the greatest Barcelona revolutionary of them all, **Buenaventura Durruti**, is commemorated by a small *plaça* at the foot of Montjuïc, not far from where he was buried. It's reasonable to suppose that all of these people would have been appalled to see the tidy way in which their names are remembered.

beaches, the **Mar Bella** and **Bogatell**. In the middle of it there are still parts of the old Poble Nou, and even earlier Sant Martí: the lovely tree-lined **Rambla del Poble Nou** compares favourably with the one in the city centre, while the area around **Plaça Prim** has kept its own village atmosphere. Some old factory buildings have been recycled as clubs and music venues, the best known **Zeleste**. And Poble Nou still has – looking distinctly odd amid some of the recent developments – Barcelona's oldest cemetery, the **Cementiri de l'Est**, with some extraordinary nineteenth-century graveyard sculptures, especially *El bes de la mort* (the Kiss of Death).

Clot and **La Sagrera**, both small *barris*, experienced much the same history as Poble Nou. **Clot** boasts one of the most intimate and friendly of Barcelona's food markets in the **Plaça Font i Sagué** and the **Parc del Clot**, an old railway station-site transformed with a very effective waterfall design. Next to the giant roundabout of **Plaça de les Glòries** is Barcelona's flea market, **Els Encants**. In Cerdà's original plan for the expansion of Barcelona this *plaça* was earmarked to be the future city centre. This remains very unlikely, but this rather nondescript junction has acquired an enormous mall, the **Barcelona Glòries** centre, and is the site for the future **Teatre Nacional de Catalunya** and the **Auditori de Música**, two giant cultural institutions to be surrounded by a 17-hectare green space. In La Sagrera, meanwhile, the huge Pegaso truck factory has been recycled into a school and the **Parc Pegaso**, with a boating lake, and the area has one of the finest pieces of recent architecture in Barcelona, the **Pont de Calatrava** linking it to Poble Nou via C/Bac de Roda, about the only new building to be popularly known by the name of its architect, Santiago Calatrava.

The Vila Olímpica

In 1986 Barcelona was elected Olympic City for 1992, and the whole population seemed to pour into the streets to celebrate. Then the job began of preparing to build what would soon be called the city's last *barri*. It had often been said that Barcelona turned its back to the sea, and these industrial barriers had effectively cut off the citizens from their abandoned, refuse-strewn beaches. Now the plan was to open out.

Not since Cerdà or Gaudí has anyone had such an impact on the physiognomy of Barcelona as the architects Oriol Bohigas, Josep Martorell and longtime resident Scot David Mackay, who, together with Albert Puigdomènech, were entrusted with the overall design of the *barri*. It was officially named *Nova Icària* to recall the utopian socialist community that briefly existed in this area in the last century, but this name has never really stuck. As well as a range of services some 2,000 apartments were

built, which it was hoped would provide cheap accommodation after the Games, although harsh economic facts have since dictated otherwise.

Cerdà's original concept for the Eixample was taken as an inspiration, with semi-open blocks built around services and garden areas. Every stop had to be pulled out to get the project completed for July 1992, however, and the final effect of the *Vila* is bleak, although the waterway parallel to C/Moscou and the red brick of **Plaça Tirant lo Blanc** go some way to softening the harshness. The gateway buildings to the *barri*, all glass and stone, create a forbidding impression; there are few corner shops or cafés; not many people stroll; the spiky metal pergolas on the Avda Icària look like a grim parody of trees, and even the jokey sculpture in the **Parc de Carles I**, *David i Goliat*, leaves one with the uncomfortable feeling that this is one world in which the Goliaths usually slay the Davids. The whole effect is of a cold, very un-Mediterranean suburb, but as in many such suburbs its open spaces are colonised by cyclists and rollerbladers at weekends. Most successful part of the Vila is the **Port Olímpic**, an entire leisure harbour built up from scratch since 1988, pleasant for walking, and now packed every weekend night in summer.

Horta-Guinardó

The area north of Gràcia, above and to the right of it on the map, is made up of contrasting *barris*, traditionally of rich and poor, the former in valleys and the latter on hillsides. Until the building of the **Túnel de la Rovira**, which begins near the Plaça d'Alfons el Savi, many of these areas were relatively isolated from the city.

Joined to Gràcia by the long Avda Mare de Déu de Montserrat, **Guinardó** above all means two big parks for the visitor. One, the **Parc de les Aigües**, contains a fun sculpture of a buried submarine by Josep Maria Riera, and Barcelona's most eccentrically beautiful municipal district headquarters, the **Casa de les Altures**, a remarkably light neo-Arabic fantasy first built for the city water company in 1890. The other, the **Parc del Guinardó**, is one of the city's older parks, opened in 1920. The *barri* of **El Carmel** has its own **Parc del Carmel**, but also the extraordinary **Parc de la Creueta del Coll**, an old quarry turned into an open-air swimming pool. Escalators have been installed in some of the district's (very) steep streets to make climbing easier.

Incorporated into Barcelona in 1904, the aptly-named **Horta**, 'Market Garden', has managed to retain many rural features, and in particular some very well-preserved *masies* or traditional Catalan large farmhouses. The medieval **Can Cortada**, in C/Campoamor, shows at a glance that these patriarchal houses also served as fortresses, while **Can Mariner** in C/d'Horta is said to date back to 1050.

Towering sculpture in the Olympic Village.

Another is now a great restaurant, **Can Travi Nou**. Horta's abundant water supply once made it the great laundry centre for respectable Barcelona, with a whole community of *bugaderes* or washerwomen, as the open-air stone tanks along the lovely C/Aiguafreda attest.

The **Vall d'Hebron** was one of the city's four main venues for Olympic events, and so has inherited centres for tennis, volleyball, archery and cycling, at the **Velòdrom**. Near the Olympic area is one of Barcelona's most popular street sculptures, Claes Oldenburg's *Matches*. For many city residents, though, the Vall d'Hebron means two things, the magnificent **Parc del Laberint** from 1791, and the **Ciutat Sanitària**, the largest hospital in the city.

Sant Andreu & Nou Barris

Leaving Barcelona along the Meridiana, the traveller has the districts of Sant Andreu on the right, and Nou Barris to the left. Originally a smuggling centre thanks to its strategic position with regard to Barcelona, **Sant Andreu** like Sant Martí and Sants was one of the three industrial and working class hubs of the city. Much altered by mass inward migration and road schemes in the sixties, the district has seen three recent renovations, although it's only fair to add that they have been criticised as window dressing. On Passeig Torres i Bages, at

nos 91-105, the **Casa Bloc**, the Rationalist building that was one of the main contributions of the Republican era to Barcelona, is being restored. Just off the Meridiana a lovely wine press has been installed in **Plaça d'en Xandri**, and in **Plaça Mossèn Clapés** a beautiful ivy-covered modern pergola provides relief from the sun.

Nou Barris (Nine Neighbourhoods), on the western side of the Meridiana, has an entirely different make-up. In the 1940s and '50s, when the flow of migration into the city was at its height, ramshackle settlements were built here, often by the residents themselves, and in the '60s they were followed by tower blocks. Recently parks and monuments have been provided to make it more humane, such as the sports complex **Can Dragó**, with the biggest public swimming pool in Barcelona. It remains, though, the poorest area in the city.

The Outer Limits

As well as Barcelona proper, the *Area Metropolitana* is made up of a ring of smaller towns. Until this century, all were still rural, but beginning in the 1920s, they have acquired industrial estates and large migrant populations from the rest of Spain, and in some cases become dormitory towns for Barcelona.

North of Barcelona, on the other side of the Besós river, **Badalona** is the third largest city in Catalonia, and famous above all for its basketball team, **Joventut**, which has won the European Basketball Cup, something that its FC Barcelona has still not managed. Its neighbour, **Santa Coloma de Gramenet**, has a large Andalusian population and organises the **Feria de Abril**, a 10-day *fiesta* held around the end of April (*see chapter* **Barcelona by Season**). It is the most popular *festa* in Catalonia, said to be visited by three million people, which might be an Andalusian exaggeration.

On some cars in the city, beside the Barcelona number plate, you will occasionally sees the sticker '*L'H*'. This defiant assertion of identity is a reminder that **L'Hospitalet de Llobregat**, just beyond Sants to the south west, is the second city of Catalonia, even though it is completely integrated into Barcelona's transport network. With a large Andalusian-born population, it is also Catalonia's great centre for flamenco. There are several flamenco *peñas*, or clubs, among them the **A.C.A.**, C/Clavells 2-4, (437 55 02), for dancing, and the **Tertulia Flamenca**, C/Calderon de la Barca 12 (437 20 44), which runs classes in flamenco guitar. Equally, Hospitalet has plenty of bars and restaurants with Andalusian specialities – one of the best is **Andalucía Chiquita**, Avda Isabel la Catòlica 89 (438 12 67). In summer, the pedestrian area around C/Severo Ochoa becomes a huge outdoor café, offering tapas of all types (including snails in camomile!) at much more reasonable prices than in Barcelona.

On the Town

Restaurants

Superb seafood, stout country grills and bargain lunches, flavours from subtle spices to strong fresh garlic... they're all there in Barcelona's restaurants.

The first Barcelona Restaurateurs' Guild claims to have been founded in 1455, and hostelries with rough menus have been documented as early as 1600. By 1840, when Barcelona's first restaurant guide was published, the city had become one of the capitals best supplied with eating houses in Europe. A century and a half later, the Olympic Games brought more confidence, more cash, more business people, more tourists – and left the city with more restaurants than ever before.

Most of them, naturally enough, serve Catalan food in all its many variations (*see* **The Catalan Menu**). Contrary to what foreigners often assume, there is no such thing as a generic 'Spanish national' cuisine, once you get away from a few universal basics such as potato omelette and grilled hake. In Barcelona, as well as Catalan restaurants, there are many others – often cheap – that serve the mainly seafood-based cooking of Galicia in north-west Spain, plus a few dozen that offer the food of the Basque Country, Castile, Andalusia, and other Spanish regions. Foreign restaurants have also multiplied in recent years, to add Brazilian, Indonesian, Mexican, Japanese, Pakistani, Syrian and other cuisines to the Chinese fare that has been around for decades (*see below* **International**). Non-meat eaters fare less well, but there are nevertheless some decent vegetarian restaurants to choose from (*see below* **Vegetarian**).

All in all, Barcelona is a wonderful city for dining. As the local proverb puts it, with characteristic earthiness: '*Menja bé, caga fort i riu-te de la mort*', translatable as 'Eat well, shit hard, and laugh in the face of death'. *Bon profit*.

As well as the restaurants listed here, many of the city's bars also provide some kind of food, from snacks to full meals, so for more places to eat, *see* chapter **Cafés & Bars**. For restaurants welcoming a gay clientèle, *see* chapter **Gay & Lesbian Barcelona**. For places to satisfy a hunger in the small hours, *see* chapter **Nightlife**.

Restaurant Customs

When to set your clock, and book Catalans eat late. Lunchtime is at what they call 'midday', around 2pm. In the evening you won't get a full meal before 8.30pm in most places; 9/9.30pm is the average time for dinner. It's always a good idea to book in restaurants from mid-range upwards, and in every kind of restaurant on Fridays and Saturdays.
Children Most restaurants welcome children, but few have specific children's menus, and they're not often seen in top-flight dining rooms (*see also chapter* **Children**).
Prices, tips & taxes The lunch-time *menu del dia* set meal is one of Barcelona's great bargains, with plenty of places offering three courses for around 1,000ptas. It's best to make this your main meal if you want to eat cheaply. Evening prices will usually be higher, although some restaurants now offer a *menu* for dinner as well. There is no percentage rule for tipping: it's common in mid- or upper-range restaurants to leave around 200-300ptas – rarely over 500ptas – but many locals leave no tip at all, or just a nominal 25ptas. Bills include 7% IVA tax (VAT), which is usually, but not always, incorporated into the prices shown on the menu.
Sundays & holidays Despite recent greater flexibility in

Two trips out

A reasonably short journey by road or rail will take you to two of the most impressive restaurants in Catalonia. For transport information, *see chapter* **Trips Out of Town**.

Fonda Europa

C/Anselm Clavé 1, Granollers (870 03 12). By car A7 or N-152(35km)/by train RENFE to Granollers. **Lunch served** 1-4pm, **dinner served** 9-11.30pm, daily. **Average** 4,000ptas. **Credit** AmEx, DC, JCB, MC, V.
First opened in 1714, this inn-restaurant serves very traditional Catalan food such as pork *a la llauna, cap i pota* (tripe, cheeks, and trotters), and cod with *sam-faina*, plus desserts like *codonyat* (quince jelly) with cottage cheese. A cart-driver's breakfast (smoked herring, wine and toasted *pa amb tomàquet*) is served on market-day mornings (Thursdays).
Booking essential.

El Racó de Can Fabes

C/Sant Joan 6, Sant Celoni (867 28 51/38/61). By car A7 or C-251(60km)/by train RENFE to Sant Celoni. **Lunch served** 1.30-3.30pm Tue-Sun. **Dinner served** 8.30-10.30pm Tue-Sat. Closed 30 Jan-13 Feb, 26 June-10 July. **Average** 8,000ptas. **Credit** AmEx, DC, MC, TC, V.
In a small town at the foot of the Montseny mountains, the Racó now has a third Michelin star – one of only two restaurants so distinguished in Spain –, and Santi Santamaria is acclaimed as the greatest of all Catalan chefs. Current specialities include scallop salad, cold vegetable stew with truffles, and a magnificent Mediterranean seafood grill. Desserts and cheeses are equally superb. A true gourmet experience.
Air-conditioning. Booking essential.

*If you want to make sure of a table at **Gaig**, you really must book. Honest. See page 109.*

opening times, there are still relatively few places open on Sunday evenings, and those that are often get very full. Also, many restaurants still close for all or part of August; we've listed annual closing dates where possible, but it's a good idea to phone first to avoid a wasted journey.

*The average prices listed are based on the average cost of a starter, a main course and dessert, **without** drink. Set menus, however, do often include beer, wine or water.*

Top of the Range

Agut d'Avignon

C/Trinitat 3 (302 60 34). Metro Liceu/bus 14, 18, 38, 59, 91, N4, N6. **Lunch served** 1-3.30pm, **dinner served** 9-11.30pm, daily. **Average** 5,000ptas. **Set lunch** 3,000ptas. **Credit** AmEx, DC, EC, JCB, MC, TC, V.
Down a small alleyway, one of Barcelona's finest restaurants offers comfort and service that bely the shabbiness of much of the surrounding area. The menu is based on classic Catalan dishes (excellent *farcellets de col*, stuffed cabbage leaves), others from various Spanish regions, such as Castilian roasts, and some creations of their own, like wild boar with strawberry sauce, duck with figs or oyster soup. *Air-conditioning. Booking advisable.*

Beltxenea

C/Mallorca 275 (215 30 24). Metro Diagonal or Passeig de Gràcia/bus 7, 20, 21, 22, 24, 28, 43, 544. **Lunch served** 2-4.30pm Mon-Fri. **Dinner served** 9-11.30pm Mon-Sat. Closed holidays, Easter week, Aug, Christmas.

Average 8,000ptas. **Gourmet menu** 6,900ptas (includes aperitif). **Credit** AmEx, DC, V.
The foremost outpost of new Basque cuisine in Barcelona. In a first-floor Eixample flat with a pretty interior garden, it's very discreet, so much so that a small brass plaque is the only sign of the restaurant's existence on the street. As in all Basque cooking, the basis is seafood: specialities include a melon and lobster salad and *tronc de lluç Ondarroa* (hake). *Air-conditioning. Booking advisable. Garden terrace.*

Botafumeiro

C/Gran de Gràcia 81 (218 42 30). Metro Fontana/bus 22, 24, 28, N4, N6. **Open** 1pm-1am daily. Closed last three weeks Aug. **Average** 7,000ptas. **Gourmet menu** 5,000ptas. **Credit** AmEx, DC, EC, JCB, MC, TC, V.
This spacious restaurant specialises in the best of Galician food, which means, above all, quality seafood. The lobster, langoustines, scallops, oysters and other shellfish, all selected by chef-proprietor Moncho Neiras, are unbeatable, and it stays open late. There are also two singers, one with guitar, playing only if you want them to, or so they claim. *Air-conditioning. Booking advisable.*

Ca l'Isidre

C/Les Flors 12 (441 11 39/442 57 20). Metro Paral.lel/bus 20, 36, 57, 64, 91, N4, N6. **Lunch served** 1.30-3.30pm, **dinner served** 8.30-11pm, Mon-Sat. Closed holidays, Easter, Aug. **Average** 6,500ptas. **Credit** AmEx, MC, TC, V.
A small family-run restaurant near the Paral.lel that receives regular visits from King Juan Carlos. Chef César

BARCELONA

Estevet: *one-time haunt of Gary Lineker and Maradona, but still popular. See page 111.*

Pastor's regular dishes include artichoke hearts stuffed with wild mushrooms and duck liver, and loin of lamb broiled English-style. Desserts are made by the daughter of the family, master *pastissera* Núria Gironès. English and French are spoken.
Air-conditioning. Booking essential. Vegetarian dishes.

Escuela de Hostalería Arnadí – Restaurant Hofmann
C/Argenteria 74-78 (319 58 89). Metro Jaume I/bus 17, 40, 45. **Lunch served** 1.30-3.30pm, **dinner served** 9-11.30pm, Mon-Fri. Closed Aug. **Average** 6,000ptas. **Credit** AmEx, DC, MC, V.
Mey Hofmann (master pastrycook, Cordon Bleu chef, interior designer and Red Cross nurse) opened this unusual restaurant in 1991, as a showcase for the best students from her catering school. Menus feature creative dishes based on a range of Mediterranean influences, and ingredients are selected with immense care; bread (ten different kinds) is baked twice daily on the premises. Highly recommended.
Air-conditioning. Booking essential. Vegetarian dishes on request.

Gaig
Passeig Maragall 402 (429 10 17). Metro Vilapicina/bus 19, 45, N5. **Lunch served** 1.30-4pm, **dinner served** 9pm-11pm, Tue-Sun. Closed holidays, Easter, Aug. **Average** 7,000ptas. **Gourmet menu** 4,950ptas. **Credit** AmEx, DC, MC, V.
Founded in 1869 as a café for cart drivers, this famous restaurant has been in the Gaig family for four generations. Specialities include *arròs de colomí amb ceps* (young pigeon in rice with wild mushrooms), fish stew with prawns and *espardenyes* (a rare, squid-like crustacean), and stuffed pigs' trotters. A favourite dessert is the *pecat de xocolata* ('chocolate sin', a thick mousse). The wine cellar is a sight in itself.
Air-conditioning. Booking essential. Disabled: access. Tables outdoors (June-Sept). Vegetarian dishes.

Jaume de Provença
C/Provença 88 (430 00 29). Metro Entença/bus 41, 43, 544. **Lunch served** 1-4pm Tue-Sun. **Dinner served** 9-11.30pm Tue-Sat. Closed Easter, Aug. **Average** 8,000ptas. **Gourmet menu** 7,000ptas. **Credit** AmEx, DC, JCB, MC, V.
This small restaurant tucked away in the Eixample is nevertheless one of the most prestigious in Barcelona. Its reputation is due to the quality and originality of the cuisine of chef Jaume Bargués. Menus are a mixture of traditional Catalan recipes and ideas of his own, such as crab lasagne, rabbit with foie-gras and truffles, and salad of wild mushrooms with prawns and clams. Again, a superlative wine list.
Air-conditioning. Booking essential.

Passadís del Pep
Pla del Palau 2 (310 10 21). Metro Jaume I/bus 14, 16, 17, 36, 40, 45, 51, 57, 59, 64. **Lunch served** 1.30-3.30pm, **dinner served** 9-11.30pm, Mon-Sat. Closed holidays. **Average** 8,500ptas (includes drink). **Credit** AmEx, DC, MC, V.
An eccentric restaurant that's impossible to find unless you know where to look (go down the long, unmarked corridor next door to a Caixa office). There is no menu, just some of the best seafood in Barcelona, with a superb, first-course buffet, and *cava* included in the price. *Fideus amb llamàntol* (noodles with lobster) is recommended. For a cheaper alternative, try **Cal Pep** (*see below* **Seafood**), run by the same family.
Air-conditioning. Booking advisable.

Roig Robí
C/Sèneca 20 (218 92 22/217 97 38). Metro Diagonal/bus 16, 17, 22, 24, 27, 28, 33, 34. **Lunch served** 1.30-4pm Mon-Fri. **Dinner served** 9-11.30pm Mon-Sat. Closed holidays, third week Aug. **Average** 6,000ptas. **Gourmet menu** 5,000ptas. **Credit** AmEx, DC, MC, TC, V.
Roig Robí is run by self-taught chef Mercè Navarro and two of her children, an unusual set-up for a top restaurant with leading politicians, writers and artists among its regular customers, including Antoni Tàpies, who designed the menu.

Can Travi Nou – *in Barcelona, not the backwoods of Catalonia.*

Specialities include an *amanida de foie*, lobster with rice, and Palamós prawns with crispy leeks and garlic sauce.
Air conditioning. Booking advisable. Garden terrace. Vegetarian dishes on request.

Tragaluz

Passatge Concepció 5 (487 06 21). Metro Diagonal/bus 7, 16, 17, 22, 24, 28, N4, N6. **Lunch served** 1.30-4pm daily. **Dinner served** 8.30pm-midnight Mon-Wed, Sun; 8.30pm-1am Thur-Sat. **Average** *restaurant* 5,000ptas; *Kusiyaki Bar* 1,500ptas. **Credit** AmEx, DC, MC, V.
Opened in 1990, this Mariscal-decorated restaurant has a top floor and roof converted into a wonderfully airy glass-covered dining room, and a fashionably eclectic menu that might include quails with soya and asparagus, or a fine *carpaccio*. Downstairs, what used to be a kind of McDonalds for yuppies was transformed in early 1996 into a Kusiyaki Bar – a Japanese tavern with an open grill, serving Japanese rice and noodle dishes and small *kusiyaki* roast kebabs.
Air-conditioning. Bookings accepted in main restaurant only. Vegetarian dishes.

Catalan

Agut

C/Gignàs 16 (315 17 09). Metro Jaume I/bus 17, 40, 45. **Lunch served** 1.30-4pm, **dinner served** 9pm-midnight, daily. Closed Christmas Day, New Year's Eve. **Average** 3,000ptas. **Set menus** 1,500ptas, 1,800ptas, Mon-Fri. **Credit** EC, JCB, MC, TC, V.
Agut is known throughout Barcelona for its appetising traditional Catalan food, and, despite being located in a narrow street near the port, all kinds of people make the pilgrimage to its doors. Applauded for its cannelloni, steak with *rocafort* cheese, and home-made profiteroles, among other dishes.
Air-conditioning. Book dinner.

El Cafetí

C/Hospital 99, end of passage (329 24 19). Metro Liceu/bus 14, 18, 38, 59, N4, N6, NS. **Lunch served** 1.30-3.30pm Tue-Sun. **Dinner served** 8.30-11.30pm Tue-Sat. Closed Easter, Aug. **Average** 2,500ptas. **Set lunch** 950ptas Tue-Sat. **Credit** DC, MC, V.
This small restaurant at the end of an alleyway has perfected a series of Catalano-French dishes over the last 15 years, and built up a regular local clientèle. Specialities include house paté, several cod dishes, goulash, and a range of home-made desserts. The staff speak English, French and German.
Air-conditioning. Vegetarian dishes.

Can Culleretes

C/Quintana 5 (317 30 22). Metro Liceu/bus 14, 18, 38, 59, 91, N4, N6, NS. **Lunch served** 1.30-4pm Tue-Sun. **Dinner served** 9-11pm Tue-Sat. Closed 1-21 July. **Average** 3,000ptas. **Set lunch** 1,600ptas Tue-Fri. **Set menu** 2,000ptas. **Pica-Pica seafood menu** 3,500ptas. **Credit** AmEx, DC, MC, V.
The oldest restaurant in Barcelona, founded 1786, with a rambling interior covered in old photos of local celebrities. The lengthy main menu includes rich traditional dishes such as *civet de porc senglar* (wild boar stew) and *cuixa d'oca amb pomes* (goose leg with apples), and the new seafood menu is highly recommended. House policy is to undercharge for the wine, and there are good Raïmats at 650ptas and vintage Riojas for 1,300ptas. Go early to avoid queuing.

Can Travi Nou

End of C/Jorge Manrique (428 03 01). Metro Horta/bus 45, 85, 102. **Lunch served** 1.30-4pm daily. **Dinner served** 8.30-11.30pm Mon-Sat. **Average** 4,000ptas. **Credit** AmEx, DC, MC, TC, V.
Occupying a huge, beautiful old *masia* or traditional Catalan farmhouse, with garden, on a hill above Horta, this feels more like a country- than a city restaurant. The food is traditional Catalan, with speciality *mar i muntanya* dishes such as *sípia amb mandonguilles* and *cueta de rap amb all torrat* (monkfish tail with toasted garlic). Difficult to reach by public transport, so it's best to take a cab, but worth finding.
Booking advisable. Tables outdoors (garden, Easter-Sept).

Los Caracoles

C/Escudellers 14 (302 31 85). Metro Liceu/bus 14, 18, 38, 59, 91, N4, N6, NS. **Open** 1pm-midnight daily. **Average** 3,500ptas. **Credit** AmEx, DC, JCB, MC, V.
One of the best-known restaurants in town, with its chickens roasting on spits outside, the Caracoles appears in almost every guidebook, and is consequently packed with tourists, and even a few locals. Dishes include seafood, roast suckling pig (*lechón*) and paellas. Better, cheaper food, can be found elsewhere.
Booking essential for dinner.

Egipte

C/Jerusalem 3 (317 74 80). Metro Liceu/bus 14, 18, 38, 59, 91, N4, N6, NS. **Lunch served** 1-4pm, **dinner served** 8-11.30pm, daily. **Average** 3,000ptas. **Set lunch** 950ptas Mon-Sat. **Set menus** 1,500ptas, 2,000ptas, 2,500ptas. **Credit** AmEx, DC, MC, TC, V.
A great Barcelona favourite of 17 years standing, so much so that it can seem too popular for its own good on busy nights. The Egipte has four storeys of attractively aged décor and two more branches nearby with the same name, the same easy-going atmosphere and the same menu, offering a choice of 30 dishes for each course, including an excellent *parillada de carn* (mixed grill) and a good *paella*.
Air-conditioning.
Branches: C/Jerusalem 12 (301 62 08); La Rambla 79 (317 95 45).

Estevet

C/Valldonzella 46 (302 41 86). Metro Universitat/bus all routes to Plaça Universitat. **Lunch served** 1-4pm, **dinner served** 9-11.30pm, Mon-Sat. Closed holidays & 5-20 Aug. **Average** 3,000ptas. **Set lunch** 1,200ptas Mon-Fri. **Credit** AmEx, DC, MC, TC, V.
One of the oldest restaurants in the city, run for the last 46 years by Jordi Suñé (who speaks English). It's worth coming here as much for the atmosphere – with some striking paintings, and photos of celebs such as Maradona and Gary Lineker – as for the food, which is good but limited in choice and not over-generous, although the langoustines, grilled asparagus and filet Café de Paris are all recommended.

El Glop

C/Sant Lluís 24 (213 70 58). Metro Joanic/bus 21, 39, 55, N4. **Lunch served** 1-4pm Tue-Sun. **Dinner served** 8pm-1am Tue-Sat. **Average** 2,500ptas. **Credit** MC, V.
El Glop (The Sip') is a long-established success story, serving char-grilled meat and seasonal vegetables at very reasonable prices. Specialities include snails cooked *a la llauna* and *xoriço al vi* (chorizo in wine). One of few restaurants in Barcelona to serve the strong, low-priced *vi de Gandesa*, a good table wine from western Catalonia. It's often very crowded, but the more spacious **Nou Glop** is nearby.
Air-conditioning. Book weekends.
Branches: El Glop Jardi C/Albert Llanas 2 (218 21 43); El Nou Glop C/Montmany 49, torre (219 70 59).

Madrid-Barcelona

C/Aragó 282 (215 70 26). Metro Passeig de Gràcia/bus 7, 22, 24, 28, 39, 45. **Lunch served** 2-4pm, **dinner served** 8.30-11pm, Mon-Sat. Closed holidays. **Average** 3,000ptas. **Set lunch** 1,600ptas. **Credit** AmEx, DC, MC, V.
A café/restaurant in 1940s station café, from the days when an open rail line ran straight through central Barcelona. Food is prepared on a coal-fired range, giving anything cooked *a la brasa* a special flavour, and the place has a lot of charm.
Air-conditioning. Booking advisable.

Not the engine room of a runaway train, but the blazing kitchens of **Los Caracoles**. See p111.

Els Ocellets

*Ronda Sant Pau 55 (441 10 46). Metro Sant Antoni/bus
20, 64, 91, N4, N6.* **Lunch served** 1.30-4pm Tue-Sun.
Dinner served 8.30-11.30pm Tue-Sat. **Average**
2,500ptas. **Set lunch** 950ptas. **Credit** AmEx, DC, MC, V.
This comfortable restaurant and its older, slightly more picturesque parent **Can Lluís**, a little way up a narrow street
across the Ronda Sant Pau, share the same menu and the
same popularity, but lately the Ocellets has had the edge in
cooking. Try the spicy *romescada*, the *esqueixada* or the *filet
de vedella al cabrales* (veal fillet with a powerful goat's cheese
sauce). Bookings are only taken for large groups, so get there
early to avoid queueing. Menu prices do not include IVA.
Air-conditioning at Els Ocellets.
Branch: Can Lluís C/de la Cera 49 (441 11 87).

La Parra

*C/Joanot Martorell 3 (332 51 34). Metro Hostafrancs/bus
52, 53, 56, 57, N2.* **Lunch served** 2-5pm Sat-Sun.
Dinner served 6pm-midnight Mon-Fri; 8pm-midnight
Sat, Sun. **Average** 3,000ptas. **Credit** MC, V.
Another great outlet for stout Catalan country cooking *a la
brasa* within the city asphalt. You enter this 180-year old ex-
coaching inn past a giant wood-fired grill, and the menu
offers one of the best *escalivades* in town and hefty portions
of leg of lamb, rabbit, pork, beefsteaks and spare ribs, served
on wooden slabs with freshly made *all i oli*. Other specialities include roast duck and an unbeatable *orada a la sal* (gilt-
head bream baked in salt), and from November to March
there are also *calçots*, specially-cultivated spring onions from
around the town of Valls (*see* **The Catalan Menu**). Well-
priced wines, and several rare *orujos* (fierce Galician spirits)
as digestifs, but they trenchantly refuse to serve Coca-Cola.
Air-conditioning. Booking advisable. Tables outdoors.

Les Quinze Nits

*Plaça Reial 6 (317 30 75). Metro Liceu/bus 14, 18, 38,
59, 91, N4, N6, NS.* **Lunch served** 1-3.30pm, **dinner
served** 8.30-11/11.30pm, daily. **Average** 2,000ptas. **Set
menu** 950ptas Mon-Fri. **Credit** AmEx, DC, EC, MC, V.

This small chain has caused something of a sensation in
the Barcelona restaurant world by offering a combination
of sophisticated, imaginative modern Catalan food in
light, elegant surroundings at prices significantly lower
than the norm at this level, and, in two cases, in formerly
down-at-heel locations in Plaça Reial and C/Escudellers
where nobody thought a restaurant like this could work.
Defying the doubters, they've been hugely successful.
They all share similar menus. Try the *civet de conill* (rabbit stew), *parillada de peix* (seafood mixed grill) or the suc-
culent *arròs negre*. Also part of the formula is that no
bookings are taken, and the lengthy queues can get annoy-
ing, but this can favour foreigners who often want to eat
earlier than locals do.
Air-conditioning. Tables outdoors (Quinze Nits only).
Branches: La Fonda C/Escudellers 10 (301 75 15);
Hostal de Rita C/Aragó 279 (487 33 60); **L'Hostalet de
la Mamasita** Avda Sarrià (321 92 96).

Senyor Parellada

*C/Argenteria 37 (310 50 94). Metro Jaume I/bus 17, 40,
45.* **Lunch served** 1-3.30pm, **dinner served** 9-11pm,
Mon-Sat. Closed holidays. **Average** 3,000ptas. **Credit**
AmEx, DC, JCB, MC, V.
The atmosphere is relaxed, and the décor a stylish combination of modern touches with the centuries-old walls of a
stone building in La Ribera. As well as the pillared main
dining room, there are attractive rooms upstairs.
Specialities include thyme soup, cod with honey and cin-
namon ice-cream with *crema catalana* and delicious modern variations on Catalan standards such as *escalivada*.
Service is courteous, and it's a place where it's easy to settle in for several hours.
Air-conditioning. Book dinner.

There's plenty to ponder on the menu at
Les Quinze Nits.

The Catalan Menu

Catalan cuisine is not just a list of regional dishes, but a whole system of cooking clearly distinguishable from its neighbours in France and the rest of Spain. Much use is made of four basic elements: included in all kinds of dishes are the *sofregit*, chopped tomato and onion lightly fried together in olive oil; *samfaina*, a mixture of onion, peppers, ripe tomatoes, aubergines and garlic similar to ratatouille, used as an ingredient and an accompaniment; and, most distinctive of all, the *picada*, a variable combination of ingredients mixed in a mortar, perhaps garlic, parsley, saffron, ham, bread and especially crushed nuts, and used for thickening and seasoning. Lastly, there's *all i oli*, garlic mayonnaise, best of all when made fresh just with wild garlic pounded together with olive oil (and, occasionally, an egg yolk), and served on the side with both meats and seafood.

Grilled meat (with *all i oli*) features strongly in traditional Catalan country cooking, especially lamb, pork, sausages and rabbit, and usually prepared on an open charcoal grill (*a la brasa*). There's also a unique vegetarian variant, *escalivada*, consisting of aubergines, red peppers and onions grilled almost black, then peeled and cut into strips. Catalan cuisine is very varied, though, and is not afraid to mix flavours, such as meat, fruit and nuts. Casserole-like dishes, cooked in a broad earthenware bowl called a *cassola*, include fairly conventional things such as chicken with *samfaina*, but also surprises such as the *mar i muntanya* ('sea and mountain') dishes from the Empordà region around Figueres, mixing together meat and seafood surf-and-turf style in subtle combinations such as a stew of prawns, chicken and wild mushrooms, or pork with crayfish. The many fish and seafood dishes also include several made with the big frying pan called a *paella*. The world-famous rice *paella* originally hails from Valencia, but the range of similar Catalan variants includes *arròs negre* ('black rice', cooked in squid ink), and *fideuà*, with noodles instead of rice.

Other important features of Catalan cuisine are its rich variety of salads, and some other interesting vegetable-based dishes, such as the beautifully simple *espinacs a la catalana*. Cannelloni (*canelons*), introduced from Italy in the last century, are, surprisingly, another standard, and used in sufficiently distinctive ways (with no tomatoes in the sauce) to count as a real local speciality. Catalan cooking, moreover, has not stood still, and many Barcelona restaurants

now present inventive modern-Catalan food, incorporating a range of international influences, and lighter, more subtle ingredients. For a note on local wines, *see chapter* **Shopping**; for an explanation of types of coffees and other drinks, *see chapter* **Cafés & Bars**.

Words and phrases below are given in Catalan, Spanish and English, respectively.

Useful basic terminology

una cullera	*una cuchara*	a spoon
una forquilla	*un tenedor*	a fork
un ganivet	*un cuchillo*	a knife
una ampolla de	*una botella de*	a bottle of
una altra	*otra*	another
més	*más*	more
pa	*pan*	bread
sal	*sal*	salt
pebre	*pimienta*	pepper
amanida	*ensalada*	salad
truita	*tortilla*	omelette
la nota	*la cuenta*	the bill
un cendrer	*un cenicero*	an ashtray

vi negre/rosat/blanc
vino tinto/rosado/blanco
red/rosé/white wine

bon profit	*aproveche*	enjoy your meal
sóc vegetarià/ana	*Soy vegetariano/a*	I'm a vegetarian
sóc diabètic/a	*Soy diabético/a*	I'm a diabetic

Cooking terms

a la brasa	*a la brasa*	charcoal-grilled
a la graella/	*a la plancha*	grilled on a hot metal plate
planxa		

a la romana	*a la romana*	fried in batter
al forn	*al horno*	baked
al vapor	*al vapor*	steamed
fregit	*frito*	fried
rostit	*asado*	roast
ben fet	*bien hecho*	well-done
a punt	*medio hecho*	medium
poc fet	*poco hecho*	rare

Catalan specialities

amanida catalana/*ensalada catalana* mixed salad with a selection of cold meats
bacallà a la llauna/*bacalao 'a la llauna'* salt cod baked in garlic, tomato, paprika and wine
botifarra/*butifarra* Catalan sausage: variants include *botifarra negre*, blood sausage, and blanca, mixed with egg
botifarra amb mongetes/*butifarra con judías* sausage with haricot beans
calçots a specially sweet and flavoursome variety of spring onion (scallion), available only from November to spring, and eaten char-grilled, on its own except for *romesco* sauce
conill amb cargols/*conejo con caracoles* rabbit with snails
crema catalana cinnamon-flavoured custard dessert with burnt sugar topping, similar to crème brûlée
escalivada/*escalibada* grilled and peeled peppers, onions and aubergine
escudella thick winter stew of meat and vegetables
espinacs a la catalana/*espinacas a la catalana* spinach quick-fried in olive oil with garlic, raisins and pine kernels
esqueixada summer salad of marinated salt cod with onions, olives and tomato
fideuà/*fideuá* paella made with noodles
pa amb tomàquet/*pan con tomate* bread prepared with tomato, oil and salt (see p118)
peus de porc/*pies de cerdo* pigs' trotters
romesco a spicy sauce from the coast south of Barcelona, made with crushed almonds and hazlenuts, tomatoes, oil and a special type of red pepper (the *nyora*)
sarsuela/*zarzuela* fish and seafood stew
sipia amb mandonguilles/*sepia con albóndigas* cuttlefish with meatballs
suquet de peix/*suquet de pescado* fish and potato soup
torrades/*tostadas* toasted *pa amb tomàquet*

Carn i aviram/Carne y aves/Meat & Poultry

ànec	*pato*	duck
bou	*buey*	beef
cabrit	*cabrito*	kid
conill	*conejo*	rabbit
faisà	*faisán*	pheasant
fetge	*higado*	liver
llebre	*liebre*	gare
llom	*lomo*	loin of pork
llengua	*lengua*	tongue
perdiu	*perdiz*	partridge
pernil	*jamón serrano*	dry-cured ham
pernil dolç	*jamón york*	cooked ham
pollastre	*pollo*	chicken
porc	*cerdo*	pork
porc senglar	*jabalí*	wild boar
ronyons	*riñones*	kidneys
vedella	*ternera*	veal
xai/be	*cordero*	lamb

Peix i marisc/Pescado y marisco/Fish & Seafood

anxoves	*anchoas*	anchovies
bacallà	*bacalao*	salt cod
besuc	*besugo*	sea bream
calamarsos	*calamares*	squid
cloïsses	*almejas*	clams
cranc	*cangrejo*	crab
escamarlans	*cigalas*	crayfish
escopinyes	*berberechos*	cockles
gambes	*gambas*	prawns
llagosta	*langosta*	spiny lobster
llagostins	*langostinos*	langoustines
llenguado	*lenguado*	sole
llobarro	*lubina*	sea bass
lluç	*merluza*	hake
musclos	*mejillones*	mussels
pop	*pulpo*	octopus
rap	*rape*	monkfish
salmó	*salmón*	salmon
sardines	*sardinas*	sardines
sipia	*sepia*	cuttlefish
tonyina	*atún*	tuna
truita	*trucha*	trout

Verdures/Legumbres/Vegetables

all	*ajo*	garlic
alvocat	*aguacate*	avocado
bolets	*setas*	wild mushrooms
ceba	*cebolla*	onion
cigrons	*garbanzos*	chickpeas
col	*col*	cabbage
enciam	*lechuga*	lettuce
endivies	*endivias*	chicory
espinacs	*espinacas*	spinach
faves	*habas*	broad beans
mongetes blanques	*judías blancas*	haricot beans
mongetes verdes	*judiasverdes*	French beans
pastanagues	*zanahorias*	carrots
patates	*patatas*	potatoes
pebrots	*pimientos*	peppers
pèsols	*guisantes*	peas
tomàquets	*tomates*	tomatoes
xampinyons	*champiñones*	mushrooms

Postres/Postres/Desserts

flam	*flan*	crème caramel
formatge	*queso*	cheese
gelat	*helado*	ice-cream
iogur	*yogur*	yoghurt
mel i mató	*miel y mató*	cottage cheese with honey
pastís	*pastel*	cake
postre de músic	*postre de músico*	mixed nuts and raisins with glass of moscatel
tarta	*tarta*	tart

Fruita/Fruta/Fruit

figues	*higos*	figs
maduixes	*fresas*	strawberries
pera	*pear*	pear
plàtan	*plátano*	banana
poma	*manzana*	apple
préssec	*melocotón*	peach
raïm	*uvas*	grapes
taronja	*naranja*	orange

Time Out

International Agenda

The best weekly entertainment listings from around the world

Amsterdam Berlin London Madrid New York Paris Prague
Every Wednesday in *Time Out*
Every Friday in *El Pais*
http://www.timeout.co.uk

Set Portes

Passeig Isabel II 14 (319 29 50). Metro Barceloneta/bus all routes to Passeig de Colom. **Meals served** 1pm-1am daily. **Average** 3,500ptas. **Credit** AmEx, DC, MC, V.
Founded in 1836 and a historic institution in itself, the huge 'Seven Doors' is another restaurant that's on every tourist list and so regularly packed with foreigners, and yet also manages to serve good *paella* and fish dishes. The speciality is *paella de peix*: for maximum flavour ask for the shells to be left on the seafood. Despite the frilly fittings and the piano player, prices are generally reasonable. Bookings are taken only for meals between 1.30-2.30pm and 8-9.30pm; even so, especially on Sunday evenings, expect long queues.
Air-conditioning. Booking advisable when possible.

TickTackToe

C/Roger de Llúria 40 (318 99 47). Metro Urquinaona/ bus 7, 18, 39, 45, 47, 56, N1, N2, N3, N9. **Lunch served** 1.30-4pm, **dinner served** 8.30pm-midnight, Mon-Sat. **Bar open** 8am-3am Mon-Sat. Closed holidays. **Average** *restaurant* 4,500ptas. **Set lunch** 1,700ptas Mon-Fri. **Credit** AmEx, DC, MC, V.
A creation of the design bar era, a rather self-conscious space combining a café and tapas bar at the front, a restaurant in the centre and two snooker tables and a style bar at the back. Despite the gimmickry, the seasonal menu is good quality, and includes asparagus with crab and smoked salmon, veal fillet with cream, and wild strawberries.
Air-conditioning. Book midday & weekends.

La Tomaquera

C/Margarit 58 (no phone). Metro Paral.lel/bus 20, 36, 57, 64, N4, N6. **Lunch served** 2-4.30pm Tue-Sun. **Dinner served** 8.30-11.30pm Tue-Sat, Closed eves of holidays, Easter, Aug, Christmas Day. **Average** 2,000ptas. **No credit cards.**
Despite owner Manel's refusal to have a phone or go into local listings guides, people from all over town visit this very enjoyable Poble Sec restaurant, above all for its specialities: *caracoles* (snails) and *a la brasa* meat, with fabulous *all i oli*. In quality, quantity and preparation the meat is simply the best in the city, and there are also fine salads and desserts.

La Venta

Plaça Dr Andreu (212 64 55). FGC Avda Tibidabo/bus 17, 22, 58, 73, 85, N8, then Tramvia Blau. **Lunch served** 1.30-3.30pm, **dinner served** 9-11.30pm, Mon-Sat. **Average** 5,000ptas.
At the foot of the funicular on Tibidabo, La Venta has an outside terrace that's a lovely place to enjoy a meal in the fresh mountain air. It's also attractive indoors, and in winter a glass conservatory maintains the open-air atmosphere. Regular favourites on the sophisticated, imaginative menu include sea urchins au gratin and cod tail with vegetables, plus some interesting desserts. Service is friendly and efficient.
Booking essential. Tables outdoors (Easter-Oct).

Pica-pica & Llesqueries

It's possible to be here for some time before the realisation hits you that the famous Spanish *tapa* is not actually very prominent in local eating habits. There are some very good tapas bars in Barcelona (*see chapter* **Cafés & Bars**), but thicker on the ground is the genuine local equivalent — places that serve *pica-pica*, more substantial assortments of cheeses, patés, cold meats, anchovies and so on, with slices (*llesques*) of toasted tomato bread (*see* **Pa amb tomàquet**). A place that specialises in *pa-amb-t* with a variety of toppings is called

a *llesqueria*. Restaurants providing food *a la brasa* (*see above* **Catalan**) also generally offer the same dishes, as first courses or on their own. This can be a cheap or an expensive way of eating, according to the status of the main ingredients.

La Bodegueta

C/Blai 47 (442 08 46). Metro Poble Sec/bus 20, 57, 64, N4, N6. **Open** May-Sept 8.30am-1am daily; Oct-Apr 8.30am-1am Tue-Sun. Closed late Aug. **Average** 2,500ptas. **Credit** AmEx, DC, MC, V.
A pleasant local *llesqueria* with great *escalivada* with anchovies and *bacallà amb samfaina*. Very good house wine, fast service and reasonable prices.
Booking essential weekends.

Cafè del Centre

C/Girona 69 (488 11 01). Metro Girona/bus 19, 50, 51, 56, N1, N3, N4, N5. **Open** 8am-2.30am Mon-Sat. **Dinner served** 8.30pm-1.30am. **Average** 2,000ptas. **Credit** MC, V.
This turn-of-the-century marble and wood bar offers fine Catalan cheeses (try the Maó), patés, cold meats, smoked herring and salmon, and a range of ten different salads, until the small hours. Live and untacky piano music on Thur, Fri and Sat nights. A genuine local bar that's well worth a visit.

Flash Flash

C/La Granada del Penedès 25 (237 09 90). FGC Gràcia/ bus 16, 17, 27, N4, N6. **Lunch served** 1.30-5pm, **dinner served** 8.30pm-1.30am, daily. Closed Christmas. **Average** 3,000ptas. **Credit** AmEx, DC, JCB, MC, V.
Not a *llesqueria* but a *sandwicheria*: 1960s through and through, perhaps the first-ever Barcelona design bar, all white with silhouettes of Twiggy-esque models along the walls. House speciality is *tortilla*, with several varieties, and there are also good burgers and sandwiches.
Air-conditioning. Vegetarian dishes.

Pla de la Garsa

C/Assaonadors 13 (315 24 13). Metro Jaume I/bus 17, 40, 45. **Lunch served** 1-4 pm Mon-Sat. **Dinner served** 8pm-1am daily. Closed New Year's Eve. **Average** 2,500ptas. **Set lunch** 1,300ptas. **Credit** AmEx, MC, V.
Antique dealer Ignasi Soler has transformed a sixteenth-century stables and dairy near the Picasso museum into a beautiful restaurant serving high-quality cheeses, patés and cold meats, and an excellent, good-value set menu at midday.

Qu Qu (Quasi Queviures)

Passeig de Gràcia 24 (317 45 12). Metro Passeig de Gràcia/bus all routes to Passeig de Gràcia. **Meals served** 8.30am-1am Mon-Thur, Sun; 8.30am-2am Fri, Sat. **Average** 1,500ptas. **Credit** AmEx, MC, V.
One of a crop of new-style snack restaurants recently opened up on Passeig de Gràcia, the *Qu Qu* is well ahead of the rest, offering a wide range of high-quality food such as salads, cheeses and Catalan charcuterie including *llonganisses, bull, secallona, somaia* and other kinds difficult to find in Barcelona. The deli counter sells the same food to take out.
Tables outdoors (Easter-Oct).

Around Spain

Amaya

La Rambla 20-24 (302 10 37). Metro Liceu/bus 14, 18, 38, 59, 91, N4, N6, NS. **Lunch served** 1-4.30pm, **dinner served** 8.30-11.30pm, daily. **Average** 3,500ptas. **Set lunch** 2,000ptas (two courses). **Set menus** 3,800-6,300ptas. **Credit** AmEx, DC, JCB, MC, TC, V.
A large Basque restaurant traditionally popular with actors, writers, opera singers and politicians. Basque specialities

Pa amb tomàquet: The great invention

According to the head chef of the **Set Portes** (*see review under* **Catalan**), *pa amb tomàquet* (bread with tomato, *pan con tomate* in Castilian) is made as follows: 'Rub the open side of a very ripe tomato, cut in half, against the surface of the bread, so that the tomato pulp is evenly spread over the bread. Add salt and a drop of oil.' Once the slices of bread have been toasted, they're called *torrades*. All very simple, but this basic invention has become one of the most universally appreciated creations of Catalan cooking, with a mystique all of its own.

Although tomatoes first appeared in Catalonia in the sixteenth century, they didn't become well known until the eighteenth, but their application to bread soon seems to have become widespread, and the first written reference appeared in 1884. Leopold Pomés – author, not, it should be said, entirely seriously, of the definitive *Theory and Practice of Bread with Tomato* (1984) – claims *pa amb tomàquet* was invented by a local painter who wanted to combine the colours of the sunset on an edible base, but it most probably originated as a way of using up yesterday's bread.

The 'secret' is that the tomatoes have to be good, and *very* ripe. Both sweet and savoury, tomato bread is delicious with just about anything, but goes especially well with strong hams, cold meats, anchovies and cheeses. For Catalans it's an immediate, strong symbol of home, especially, perhaps, because it's perversely ignored in the rest of Iberia.

---

include *angulas* (elvers, baby eels), *Lubina* (sea bass) and *Besugo* (sea bream). The extensive wine list includes Txakoli, a good, light, dry Basque white wine. IVA is not included in the prices. Livelier at lunchtime than in the evenings.
Air-conditioning.

El Asador de Burgos
C/Bruc 118. (207 31 60). Metro Verdaguer/bus 20, 21, 39, 45, 47. **Lunch served** 1-4pm Mon-Sat. **Dinner served** 9-11pm Mon-Thur; 9-11.30pm Fri-Sat. **Average** 4,500ptas. **Credit** AmEx, DC, MC, V.
Castilian food is for confirmed carnivores, with only a very little vegetable relief. First courses at this restaurant include *morcilla* blood sausage, roast *chorizo*, sliced marinated pork, and baby peppers. Typical main courses are roast lamb, roast piglet, grilled ribs of lamb, and a veal steak that looks like it could kick sand in the face of the standard entrecôte served elsewhere. Booking is essential, as the roasts are prepared fresh three hours in advance, in a traditional tiled oven.
Air-conditioning. Disabled: access; toilets.

Casa Lorca
C/Laforja 8. (218 16 40). FGC Gràcia/bus 16, 17, 27. **Meals served** 1pm-2am daily. **Average** 2,500ptas. **Set lunch** 1,000ptas. **Set dinner** 1,200ptas. **Credit** AmEx, DC, EC, JCB, MC, TC, V.
With 68 dishes on its main menu, Casa Lorca mixes purely Andalusian food – fish or chickpeas *a la andaluza*, or, in summer, soups like *gazpacho* and *ajoblanco* (cold white garlic soup) – with more Catalan-orientated cannelloni, pigs' trotters or *pa amb tomàquet* with cheese or ham.
Air-conditioning.

Hermanos Tomas
C/Pare Pérez de Pulgar 1, at end of Avda Meridiana (345 71 48). Bus 62, 96, 97, N3. **Lunch served** 1-4pm, **dinner served** 9-11pm, Tue-Thur; 9-11.30pm Fri, Sat. Closed holidays. **Average** 3,000ptas. **Credit** DC, MC, V.
A quality restaurant, on the very edge of the city in La Trinitat, in few guidebooks but with a large local clientèle.

The specialities are from Soria in Castile: *cordero asado* (roast lamb with Sorian herbs) is highly recommended, and try the egg custard dessert, *yemas de almazán*: you won't get it anywhere else in Barcelona.

Seafood

Bar Mundial
Plaça Sant Agustí Vell 1 (319 90 56). Metro Arc de Triomf/bus 17, 39, 40, 45, 51. **Bar open** 9am-11pm Mon, Wed-Sat; 9am 5pm Sun. **Meals served** 1.30-11pm Mon, Wed-Sat; 1.30-5pm Sun. Closed 15-30 Aug (phone to check). **Average** 2,500ptas. **No credit cards.**
A small, unpretentious bar-restaurant in La Ribera specialising in freshly cooked seafood, mainly plain grilled. A single *parrillada* (a platter of assorted grilled seafood) is ample for two and costs just 2,200ptas. The fish soup is also recommended. The place, if not the kitchen, stays open late – until the manager promises, the last customer leaves.
Air-conditioning. Book dinner.

Cal Pep
Plaça de les Olles 8 (315 49 37). Metro Jaume I/bus 14, 17, 40, 45. **Lunch served** 1-4.30pm Tue-Sat. **Dinner served** 8pm-midnight Mon-Sat. Closed holidays. **Average** *bar* 2,500ptas; *restaurant* 5,000ptas. **Credit** AmEx, DC, MC, V.
There are more seats at the bar than in the restaurant, a brick-lined room decorated with a boar's head and antique cash registers. At the less expensive bar, Pep himself grills most of the exceptional fish and seafood while keeping up a constant stream of chat. He also runs the costlier **Passadís del Pep** (*see above* **Top of the Range**).
Air-conditioning. Booking essential for restaurant.

Can Ramonet
C/Maquinista 1 (319 30 64). Metro Barceloneta/bus 17, 39, 45, 57, 59, 64. **Meals served** 10am-4pm, 8-11.30pm, daily. Closed second week Aug-first week Sept. **Average** 4,000ptas. **Credit** AmEx, DC, MC, V.

Reportedly the oldest building in Barceloneta, opened as a tavern in 1763, and run since 1956 by the Ballarín family. A spectacular display of fresh seafood greets you at the entrance, and if you're not sure what anything is called you can just point to it. Eat *tapas* at the bar, or larger *raciòns* at one of the tables, perhaps lobster with clams, cod with *romesco*, serrano ham or some of the best anchovies in town.
Air-conditioning. Booking advisable.

Can Ros

C/Almirall Aixada 7 (221 45 79). Metro Barceloneta/bus 17, 39, 45, 57, 59, 64. **Lunch served** 1-5pm, **dinner served** 8pm-midnight, Mon, Tue, Thur-Sun. **Average** 2,500ptas. **Set lunch** 975ptas. **Gourmet menu** 1,600ptas. **Credit** AmEx, V.
The best value in Barceloneta, efficient and unpretentious. A good way to order is to pick a mixture of mussels, clams, *peixets* (whitebait in batter), salted prawns and so on, while waiting for the main course, which can take up to 40 minutes for *paella* or *arròs negre*.
Air-conditioning. Book weekends.
Branch: La Marsalada C/Joan de Borbó 58 (221 21 27).

Els Pescadors

Plaça Prim 1 (225 20 18). Metro Poble Nou/bus 36, 71, 141, N6. **Lunch served** 1-3.45pm, **dinner served** 8pm-midnight, daily. Closed Easter week, Christmas, New Year. **Average** 5,000ptas. **Credit** AmEx, DC, MC, TC, V.
A very attractive restaurant in a small old square back from the beach area, with a beautiful outside terrace. The specialities are refined versions of Catalan fish and seafood dishes, and the oven-cooked fish specials, using the pick of the same day's catch from ports along the coast to the north, are superb. Vegetarian options include a subtle *amanida d'herbes de marge* (watercress salad) and vegetables in batter with *romesco* sauce.
Air-conditioning. Booking essential. Tables outdoors (April-Oct).

El Salmonete

Space 108, Centre Maremagnum, Moll d'Espanya (225 81 43). Metro Drassanes/bus 14, 18, 36, 57, 59, 64. **Lunch served** 1-5pm, **dinner served** 8pm-midnight, daily. **Average** 3,500ptas. **Credit** AmEx, MC, V.
Once one of the best-known of the traditional beach restaurants in Barceloneta, the Salmonete has been resurrected inside the giant **Maremagnum** complex in the middle of the port (*see chapters* **Sightseeing** *and* **Shopping**). Specialities include a range of different *paellas* and *suquet de peix*, and it offers a spectacular, panoramic harbour view.
Air-conditioning. Tables outdoors (balcony).

International

Alsham

C/Mallorca 202 (451 72 89). Metro Diagonal or Passeig de Gràcia/bus 20, 21, 43, 44. **Lunch served** 1-4pm, **dinner served** 8pm-midnight, Mon-Sat. **Average** 3,000ptas. **Credit** MC, V.
The first Syrian restaurant to open in Barcelona and still the best, the Alsham specialises in a variety of kebabs, as well as *makluba* (rice with meat, aubergines and pine nuts). All desserts are also authentically Syrian, as is the coffee.
Air-conditioning. Book weekends. Vegetarian dishes.

La Bella Napoli

C/Margarit 14 (442 50 46). Metro Poble Sec or Paral.lel/bus 20, 57, 64, N4, N6. **Lunch served** 1.30-4pm, **dinner served** 8pm-midnight, Tue-Sun. Closed midday last three weeks in Aug. **Average** *pizza* 1,500ptas; *à la carte* 3,000ptas. **Credit** V.

For many, the best pizzas in Barcelona (ask for the owner's own invention, *pizza primavera*). Other delights include *arancino* (rice, ham, peas and parmesan) and *berenjena a la parmigiana* (aubergine, mozzarella, *ragú* and parmesan).
Air-conditioning.
Branch: C/Villaroel 101 (454 70 56).

Bunga Raya

C/Assaonadors 7 (319 31 69). Metro Jaume I/bus 17, 40, 45. **Dinner served** 8pm-1am Tue-Sun. Closed Sept (usually). **Average** 2,500ptas. **Set dinner** 1,795ptas. **No credit cards.**
The set dinner at this Malaysian-Indonesian restaurant, a single-plate *rijstaffel*, is especially good value. It's a bit cramped, and the service could be quicker, but you can't have everything. English is spoken.
Book Fri, Sat. Vegetarian dishes.

Cantina Mexicana I & II

C/Encarnació 51 (210 68 05) & C/Torrent de les Flors 53 (213 10 18). Metro Joanic/bus 39, 21. **Lunch served** 1-4pm Mon-Sat. **Dinner served** 8pm-12.30am Tue-Sun. Closed Easter week, part of Aug (phone to check). **Average** 2,500ptas. **Credit** MC, V.
Both Cantinas, very close to each other on a street corner, offer the same food – *enchiladas, machaca, guacamole, frijoles* – but number II, in Torrent de les Flors, has a larger, more comfortable space with twice the number of tables. Ingredients are imported from Mexico, and their dishes are much more authentic than standard Tex-Mex.
Air-conditioning. Book weekends. Vegetarian dishes.
Branch: Cantina Mexicana C/Encarnació 51 (210 68 05).

Conducta Ejemplar – El Rodizio

C/Consell de Cent 403 (265 51 12). Metro Girona/bus 6, 19, 50, 51, 55, N1, N4, N5. **Lunch served** 1-4 pm Mon-Sat. **Dinner served** 8.30pm-midnight Mon-Thur; 8.30pm-1am Fri, Sat. **Set lunch** 950ptas. **Lunch buffet** 1,800ptas Mon-Fri; 2,300ptas Sat. **Evening buffet** 2,300 ptas. **Credit** MC, V.
An original: one of very few places in Barcelona to offer a *rodizio*, a Brazilian meat buffet. Eat as much as you like from a good hot and cold buffet, followed by 12 different types of meat including Castilian sausage, rib steak, turkey, leg of lamb, Brazilian-cut beef, veal and marinated pork. Vegetarians beware.
Air-conditioning. Disabled: access; toilets.

Den

C/Quintana 4 (302 49 69). Metro Liceu/bus 14, 18, 38, 59, 91, N4, N6, NS. **Lunch served** 1.30-4pm, **dinner served** 8.30-11.30pm, daily. **Average** 1,500ptas. **Set lunch** 900ptas. **Set menus** 1,500-1,800ptas. **No credit cards.**
A small restaurant with a full-time Japanese chef who prepares *sushi, sashimi, tempura* and a variety of rice dishes and soups. The fixed price menus include the original speciality, *yakiniku*: meat barbecued by diners themselves at gas grills installed at the tables. Prices do not include IVA.
Air-conditioning.

Fu Li Yuan

C/Viladomat 73 (325 10 48). Metro Sant Antoni/bus 13, 41, 55, 91, 141. **Lunch served** noon-4.30pm, **dinner served** 8pm-midnight, daily. **Average** 1,500ptas. **Set lunches** 795ptas, 995ptas, Mon-Fri. **Gourmet menu** 1,200ptas. **Credit** MC, V.
One of the few good budget Chinese restaurants, which also serves a number of dishes, such as Beijing duck, that are normally only found on the menus of its more upmarket competitors. Popular with locals, and service is friendly and fast.
Air-conditioning.

*Service is spookily swift at **L'Hortet**.*

El Ombú

C/València 329 (457 00 11). Metro Verdaguer/bus 19, 43, 44, 45. **Lunch served** 1-3.15pm, **dinner served** 8.30-11.15pm, Mon-Sat. Closed Christmas Eve, New Year's Day. **Average** 3,000ptas. **Set lunch** 1,290ptas Mon-Fri. **Credit** AmEx, DC, EC, MC, $TC, V.
Argentinian food at reasonable prices – *empanadillas criollas*, *matambre* (a kind of Scotch egg slice), maize soup and Argentinian cuts of beef such as excellent *churrasco* steaks. Desserts include pancakes with *dulce de leche* (sweet, milky toffee). Tango singers and guitarists often play at weekends. *Air-conditioning.*

Shalimar

C/Carme 71 (329 34 96). Metro Sant Antoni/bus 24, 64, 91, N4, N6. **Lunch served** 1- 4pm Mon, Wed-Sun. **Dinner served** 8-11.30pm daily. **Average** 2,500ptas. **Credit** MC, V.
One of the best mid-price Pakistani restaurants in town, the Shalimar serves a selection of South Asian standards, with good tandoori dishes, in unpretentious surroundings. *Air-conditioning.*

Vegetarian

Visitors ordering 'vegetarian' sandwiches should not be surprised to find that they include ham or tuna, and that bean or lentil stews often contain meat stock, so check when ordering (ask *¿lleva tocino?* to see if it's made with pork fat). A handful of real vegetarian restaurants are dotted around the city, but life is far, far tougher, for vegans. Indian or South East Asian restaurants usually offer a decent vegetarian selection.

Biocenter

C/Pintor Fortuny 22 (302 35 67). Metro Liceu/bus 14, 18, 38, 59, 91, N4, N6, NS. **Meals served** 9am-11pm Mon-Sat. Closed holidays. **Average** 1,500ptas. **Set menu** 1,075ptas. **No credit cards**.
Has recently moved to new premises, across the road from the health food shop of the same name whose backroom it used to occupy. Wide range of salads and a filling set menu, and vegans are catered for. Beer is the only alcohol served.

La Buena Tierra

C/Encarnació 56. (219 82 13). Metro Joanic/bus 21, 39, 55, N4. **Lunch served** 1-4pm, **dinner served** 8pm-midnight, Mon-Sat. **Average** 2,000ptas. **Set lunch** 900ptas Mon-Fri. **Credit** AmEx, MC, V.
Under new management since 1995, this pleasant restaurant in a little old house in Gràcia, with a pretty garden at the back, has some of the best vegetarian food in town. Specialities include *canelons de bosc* (cannelloni with wild mushrooms), vol-au-vent with cream of asparagus, and refreshing *gazpacho* and melon soups in the summer.
English spoken. Tables outdoors (garden).

Govinda

Plaça Vila de Madrid 4-5 (318 77 29). Metro Catalunya/bus all routes to Plaça Catalunya. **Lunch served** 1-4pm daily. **Dinner served** 8.30-11.45pm, Tue-Sat. Closed holiday evenings. **Average** 2,500ptas. **Set lunch** 1,200ptas. **Credit** AmEx, DC, MC, V.

Waterside eating: The Port & Port Olímpic

Until 1992, one of the time-honoured ways of eating in Barcelona was to sample a *paella* at one of a string of fairly basic seafood restaurants actually on the beach in the Barceloneta. The city's Olympic revamp and EU regulations did away with them, but one of the foremost themes of Barcelona's great reconstruction has been to 'open up the city to the sea', and so create new places where you can dine *al fresco* with a seafront view.

Within the **Port Vell** or old port, by Plaça Pau Vila, Barceloneta Metro and the new marina at the very eastern end of the port, is the newly-restored **Palau de Mar**, lined with restaurants with outside tables such as **Llevataps** (221 24 33) and the **Merendero de la Mari** (221 31 41). Most present similar mainly-seafood menus, and are relatively expensive, but on a warm evening you get in return a superb view of the city back across the harbour. Behind the Palau, the Barceloneta may have lost its beach-front *paella*-bars, but still has the city's largest concentration of good seafood restaurants (*see under* **Seafood**).

Carry on through Barceloneta and you'll eventually come to the **Port Olímpic**, most attractive of the Olympic areas and most successful in establishing a post-games life for itself, above all on summer weekends (*see also chapter* **Sightseeing**). It's big, modern, and surrounded by the parasoled terraces of some 200 bars and restaurants. Some are very overpriced; however, it's also by the sea, busy, smells of freshly-cooked fish, democratic – with fast-food chains vying for space with luxury restaurants – and open late, with plenty of places serving food until 2am. It can even have some of the atmosphere of the old Barceloneta beach.

There's a wide range of fast food on offer,

from Mexican through Japanese, and for a more expensive kind of burger there's also, just outside the Port by Frank Gehry's golden fish, the local satellite of **Planet Hollywood** (221 11 11). It's fish restaurants, though, which predominate, to the extent that a quick wander around the Port leaves the first-time visitor hopelessly spoilt for choice. For cheap seafood, try the **Rey de la Gamba** (221 00 12), a restaurant with several branches in Barceloneta. As the name suggests, *gambas a la plancha* (grilled prawns) is the speciality. **Tinglado Moncho's** (221 83 83) is pricier but serves only fresh seafood, and almost certainly offers the best value in the area; it's usually packed and booking is advisable. More up-market is **La Galerna** (221 27 74; average 3,500ptas), while nearby **La Barca de Salamanca** (221 18 37) offers top-range food for around 5,000ptas a head. Leaving the Port, a longish walk along the beach-side boardwalk will take you to the **Catamaran** (221 01 75), a good-quality, low-priced fish restaurant where you can choose between self-service and (more expensive) table service.

Last but not least, the Port Olímpic is also the site of a bizarre one-off, the **Tardà Rock Cafè Museu** (221 39 93), a home-grown competitor to Planet Hollywood. Jordi Tardà is a Catalan rock enthusiast with his own radio programme, the owner of the largest personal rock record collection in the Mediterranean area, organiser of Europe's most important second-hand record fair and a friend of Keith Richards. His restaurant-museum serves a variety of Mexican, Catalan and Brit-American food at very reasonable prices, served in the company of Brian May's shoes, guitars signed by Kurt Cobain and Bruce Springsteen and other memorabilia. A change from the fish and parasols.

Indian vegetarian restaurant in a quiet, attractive square near the Rambla. An excellent salad bar, home-made bread, a choice of hot dishes and home-made desserts make up a lunch menu of outstanding value. No alcohol or coffee. *Air-conditioning.*

L'Hortet
C/Pintor Fortuny 32 (317 61 89). Metro Liceu/bus 14, 18, 38, 59, 91. **Lunch served** 1-4pm daily. Closed holidays. **Set menu** 800ptas Mon-Fri; 1,100ptas Sat, Sun. **No credit cards.**
Only open at lunchtime, this homey little place is one of the more imaginative of the vegetarian restaurants, offering a different set menu every day. Cheap, too. No alcohol.

L'Illa de Gràcia
C/Sant Domènec 19. (238 02 29). Metro Fontana/bus 22, 24, 28. **Lunch served** 1-4pm Tue-Fri; 2-4pm Sat, Sun. **Dinner served** 9pm-midnight Tue-Sun. Closed Easter week, late Aug. **Average** 1,500ptas. **Set lunch** 750ptas. **Credit** DC, MC, V.
A highly unusual place, at least for northern European sensibilities: while serving strictly vegetarian food, L'Illa allows smoking and serves beer, wine and coffee. Specialities include *crep illa de Gràcia* (pancake with mushrooms, cream, and pepper), and home-made cakes. Prices are very reasonable, with the most expensive dish on the menu at just 675ptas, and they're also open on public holidays. *Air-conditioning from 1997.*

Self Naturista

C/Santa Anna 11-17 (318 23 88/318 26 84). Metro Catalunya/bus all routes to Plaça Catalunya. **Meals served** 11.30am-10pm Mon-Sat. Closed holidays. **Average** 1,000ptas. **Set menu** 845ptas. **No credit cards.**

The best-known vegetarian restaurant in Barcelona looks like a college self-service canteen, only cleaner. The good-value set menu includes stews and soups, most made without dairy products, and Catalan dishes such as *escalivada*, plus special local ingredients such as wild mushrooms, when in season. Popular, so long queues for lunch. *Air-conditioning.*

Budget

Bar Muy Buenas

C/Carme 63 (442 50 53). Metro Liceu/bus 14, 18, 38, 59, 91, N4, N6, NS. **Lunch served** 1-4pm Mon-Sat. **Average** 1,000ptas. **Set lunch** 800ptas. **No credit cards.**

Famous in the 1960s as a haunt of struggling writers, the Muy Buenas, near the Rambla, serves low-priced home cooking (steak and chips and similar), at midday only, without charging extra for its priceless *modernista* wood décor.

Bar-Restaurante Romesco

C/Arc de Sant Agusti 4 (318 93 81). Metro Liceu/bus 14, 18, 38, 59, 91, N4, N6, NS. **Meals served** 1pm-midnight Mon-Sat. **Average** 1,000ptas. **No credit cards.**

Even closer to the Rambla, and nearly always full, the Romesco is enshrined as a favourite with young foreigners, but also many locals too. House speciality is *frijoles*, a Spanish-Caribbean dish of black beans, mince, rice and fried banana, a bargain at just over 500ptas. Noisy and convivial, this is one of the city's best cheap eating houses.

Café de la Ribera

Plaça de les Olles 6 (319 50 72). Metro Jaume I/bus 14, 16, 17, 39, 40, 45, 51, 57, 60. **Open** *Apr-Oct* 8am-10pm Mon-Sat; *Nov-March* 8am-5pm, Mon-Sat. **Lunch served** 1-4.30pm Mon-Sat. **Set menu** 975ptas. **No credit cards.**

Dishes at this popular and crowded restaurant include *revueltos de espinaca* (scrambled eggs with spinach), veal with *cabrales* goat's cheese, and fish soup. There's only a set menu, changed daily and available only for lunch, although from spring to autumn there's also a terrace service, with salads, pizzas and fresh juices all day. *Air-conditioning. Tables outdoors (April-Oct). Vegetarian dishes.*

La Fragua

C/Cadena 15 (442 80 97). Metro Liceu/bus 14, 18, 38, 59, 91, N4, N6, NS. **Meals served** 8pm-1am Tue-Sun. Closed holidays. **Average** 1,500ptas. **No credit cards.**

This large bar-restaurant – still part-owned by the CNT anarchist trade union – has a barn-like atmosphere, with a paved stone floor and high ceiling. The food is simple, with dishes such as grilled rabbit with *all i oli*, grilled fish and salads.

Marcelino 2000

C/Consell de Cent 236 (453 10 72). Metro Universitat or Urgell/bus 54, 58, 64, 66, N3, N8. **Meals served** 1-5pm, 8pm-midnight, Mon-Sat. Closed two weeks Aug (dates vary). **Average** 1,500ptas. **Set lunch** 1,000ptas. **Credit** AmEx, MC, V.

The *Bodegas Marcelino* are a chain of 17 bar-restaurants found across the Eixample, with a straightforward Galician-oriented menu of first-course stews, soups and salads, and mainly meat and seafood grills. The best way to find others is to visit one and pick up a napkin, which gives a full list. *Air-conditioning.*

Mercè Vins

C/Amargós 1 (302 60 56). Metro Urquinaona/bus 17, 19, 40, 45. **Breakfast served** 8am-noon Sat. **Lunch served** 1.30-4pm Mon-Fri. **Dinner served** 8-11pm Wed, Fri. Closed holidays. **Set lunch** 1,075ptas. **No credit cards.**

Well-known for excellent Catalan home cooking, Mercè Vins offers short set menus (no à la carte) with dishes such as *llom amb ametlles i prunes* (pork with almonds and prunes) or *estofat* (beef stew). Tiny, and always packed, and note the individual opening times. In the evenings, there's a *llesqueria* service only (*see above* Pica-pica & Llesqueries). *Air-conditioning.*

La Monyos

C/Hospital 93 (441 11 10). Metro Liceu/bus 14, 18, 38, 59, 91, N4, N6, NS. **Open** 8.30am-11pm daily. **Lunch served** 1-5pm, **dinner served** 8-11pm daily. **Average** 1,000ptas. **Set menu** 790ptas. **No credit cards.**

A neighbourhood institution in himself, Paco Poliés renovated his narrow bar-restaurant in 1993. Now serving simple dishes, some of them from his native region of Lleida, he also has a regular set menu, which is available midday or in the evening.

Restaurante Económico – Borrás

Plaça Sant Agusti Vell 13 (319 64 94). Metro Arc de Triomf/bus 17, 39, 40, 45, 51. **Meals served** 12.30-4.30pm Mon-Fri. Closed most holidays & Aug. **Average** 1,100ptas. **Set lunch** 900ptas. **No credit cards.**

A pretty restaurant looking onto a quiet square. The good set lunch always has around nine first courses and ten second courses, including *fideuà*, baked potatoes, macaroni and *arroz a la Cubana*, rice with tomato sauce, a fried egg – and a fried banana, if you ask for one.

Restaurante Xironda Orense

C/Roig 19 (442 30 91). Metro Liceu/bus 14, 18, 38, 59, 91, N4, N6, NS. **Lunch served** 1-4pm, **dinner served** 8.30pm-2am, Mon-Sat. **Average** 900ptas. **No credit cards.**

Walk past the narrow crowded bar to the narrow crowded dining room where you can choose from a decent variety of salads and mainly meat-based Galician dishes served in surprisingly generous quantities. A Catalan salad costs 350ptas, and a plate of lamb chops just 500ptas. There is no set menu.

Rodrigo

C/Argenteria 67 (310 30 20). Metro Jaume I/bus 17, 40, 45. **Lunch served** 8am-5pm Mon-Wed, Fri-Sun. **Dinner served** 8.30pm-1am Mon, Tue, Fri-Sun. **Average** 1,000ptas. **Set lunch** 975ptas; 1,150ptas Sun, holidays. **No credit cards.**

Home cooking and bargain prices attract huge crowds to Rodrigo's jumble of tables, especially on Sundays. Full meals are not served in the evening, but there is a wide choice of hot and cold sandwiches. Note the unusual closing days.

Los Toreros

C/Xuclà 3-5 (318 23 25). Metro Catalunya/bus 14, 18, 38, 59, 91. **Lunch served** 1-4pm daily. **Dinner served** 8pm-midnight Tue-Sat. Closed two weeks Aug. **Average** 1,100ptas. **Set lunch** 800ptas. **Set dinner** 900ptas. **No credit cards.**

Long-established low-price restaurant serving *ternera* and chips, potato tortilla, salads and other standards. Lovers of all-Spanish stereotypes will find the walls satisfyingly plastered with framed bullfight photos.

Cafés & Bars

Places to stop for a beer, chocolate and cakes, cava and anchovies or fresh lemon through crushed ice – the variety is endless.

Barcelona has bars or cafés on every second street, and of every kind: old-fashioned *bodegas* with wine served from the barrel, trendy 'designer' spots proferring imported beers, neighbourhood bars where you can get a drink and a sandwich and watch the world go by, tranquil *granges* for afternoon coffee and creamy cakes, and some that are beyond any classification. There are bars with history, bars-with-a-view, bars with music and bars with a twist (Irish pubs, internet cafés, archery bars). Lately, it has acquired a string of Italian-ish coffee shops, and for the true tourists among us, there are even celebrity-packed cafés straight outta Hollywood.

Tapas are not generally as varied as in some other parts of Spain, but great examples can be found, and most bars offer food of some kind, from sandwiches to a full lunch menu. The following can only be a selection of the cafés and other drinking-holes around the city. As difficult as categorisation of them is the distinction between places you might visit during the day or evening to talk over a drink or a coffee, and places you'd call in at as part of a night on the town. For more bars that are more clearly oriented to night-time socialising, *see chapter* **Nightlife**, and for some more bar-restaurants, *see chapter* **Restaurants**.

Opening times, especially in older, more traditional cafés, can be variable (many close earlier or later at night, according to trade), and those given below should be taken as guidelines rather than fixed hours. Also, except where indicated the bars listed do not accept **credit cards**.

Barri Gòtic

L'Ascensor

C/Bellafila 3 (310 53 47). Metro Jaume I/bus 17, 40, 45. **Open** 6pm-3am daily.
An old wooden *ascensor* (lift) provides the entrance to this laid-back, unstuffy bar near the Ajuntament. Inside there's always an up-for-it, friendly crowd.

Bar Celta

C/Mercè 16 (315 00 06). Metro Drassanes/bus 14, 18, 38, 59, 64, 91. **Open** 10am-1am Mon-Sat; 10am-midnight Sun.
One of the best of the string of *tascas* (traditional bars, popular for an old-fashioned, weekend night drinks-and-tapas crawl) on C/Mercè, near the port, this Galician bar is also one of the few places left that doesn't warm its tapas by microwave. Huge trays of (mainly) seafood line the bar. Particularly recommended are the *patatas bravas* and *rabas* (deep-fried chunks of squid), washed down with Galician white wine served, as is traditional, in white ceramic cups.

Boadas

C/Tallers 1 (318 95 92). Metro Catalunya/bus all routes to Plaça Catalunya. **Open** noon-2am Mon-Thu; noon-3am Fri-Sat.
One of Barcelona's institutions, a genuine 1933 art deco cocktail bar opened by Miguel Boadas after he learnt the trade in the famed Floridita Bar in Havana. It's now run by his daughter. Boadas' barmen can mix a huge variety of cocktails, and the wooden-lined walls are strung with mementos from their most famous patrons – including a sketch or two by Miró.

Cafè de l'Opera

La Rambla 74 (317 75 85/302 41 80). Metro Liceu/bus 14, 18, 38, 59, 64, 91, N4, N6, N9. **Open** 8am-2am Mon-Thur; 8am-2.45am Fri-Sun.
Equally an institution, the last real nineteenth-century grand café in the city, and by far the best of the terrace-cafés on the Rambla. With genuine Modernist-era décor, the Opera continues to be enormously popular, with a contentedly mixed clientèle – locals, foreigners, a large gay contingent and anyone else. An unbeatable place to watch the Rambla go by. *Tables outdoors (April-Oct).*

Café Zurich

Plaça Catalunya 1 (317 65 38). Metro Catalunya/bus all routes to Plaça Catalunya. **Open** *Nov-Apr* 7.30am-11pm Mon-Fri; 7.30am-midnight Sat; 11am-10pm Sun; *May-Oct* 7.30am-12.30am Mon Sat; 11am-10pm Sun; open until midnight eves of public holidays.
The gateway to the Eixample, or to the old city? Depends which way you're going. Almost nobody spends a stretch in Barcelona without at some time muttering 'Meet me at the Zurich'. Strategically placed at the top of the Rambla, the Zurich's outside terrace makes it prime people-watching territory. The Zurich doesn't quite fit into the Barcelona planners' ideal for the Plaça Catalunya, and they've been threatening to knock it down for years, but it's still standing, and rapidly making its way into the urban history books. *Tables outdoors (all year).*

Mesón del Café

C/Llibreteria 16 (315 07 54). Metro Jaume I/bus 17, 40, 45. **Open** 7am-11pm Mon-Sat.
A charming hole-in-the-wall café that's regularly packed. It's reckoned to have the best coffee in town, served by some of the city's most fast-moving waiters.

La Palma

C/Palma de Sant Just 7 (315 06 56). Metro Jaume I/bus 17, 40, 45. **Open** 7.30am-3.30pm, 7-10.30pm, Mon-Sat; *Oct-May only* noon-3pm, 7-10.30pm Sun.
One of the better *bodegas*, with wine from the barrel and great *torrades* of hams and cheeses. Décor is suitably well-aged.

La Plata

C/Mercè 28 (315 10 09). Metro Drassanes/bus 14, 18, 38, 59, 64, 91. **Open** 9am-11pm Mon-Sat.
The most charming of the C/Mercè *tascas* (*see* **Bar Celta**), this ceramic-lined bar serves only deep-fried whitebait, tomato and onion salads, anchovies and wines from the barrel. Its hours are erratic (they tend to pull the shutters down when the night crowds pour in).

El Portalón

C/Banys Nous 20 (302 11 87). Metro Liceu/bus 14, 18, 38, 59, 91. **Open** 9.30am-midnight Mon-Sat.
Probably the best example of a traditional Barcelona *bodega*, opened in the 1860s, this cavernous barrel-lined bar has kept its rustic charm despite recent renovation. Fine-value food and wine are served from a long wooden bar onto simple old marble tables, while regulars chat and play dominoes.

Els Quatre Gats

C/Montsió 3-bis (302 41 40). Metro Catalunya/bus all routes to Plaça Catalunya. **Open** 8am-2am Mon-Sat; 6pm-2am Sun. **Credit** AmEx, DC, JCB, MC, V.
Not so much an institution as a monument. In 1897 a figure-about-town called Pere Romeu opened this café in a *Modernista* building by Puig i Cadafalch, and for the next few years it was the great meeting-point of Bohemian Barcelona. Major Modernist artists such as Rusiñol and Casas painted pictures especially for it, and the menu illustration was one of Picasso's first adult works. It closed in 1903, and then was used for decades as a textile warehouse, until in the early eighties it was finally restored and reopened, with reproductions by contemporary artists of the original paintings. Under the current management, installed in 1991, it's much more smart than bohemian, but it's an attractive place for a coffee, with good if pricey tapas. In the room at the back, where Pere Romeu presented performances and puppet shows, is the restaurant, which has the extra attraction that the full menu is available throughout the opening times. There's a good set lunch menu for 1,500ptas.

Les Tapes

Plaça Regomir 4 (302 48 40). Metro Jaume I/bus 17, 40, 45. **Open** 9am-11pm Mon-Sat (may be June-Sept).
The sign 'We rip off drunks and tourists' above the bar shouldn't worry you, for this place specially welcomes English-speakers. Run by Santi, who worked in Birmingham as a chef, and his English wife, Les Tapes has English football on TV on Saturday afternoons, shelves of English books to browse through and a noticeboard for foreigners looking for contacts, rooms, jobs and the like. They also do the occasional special dish, such as roast pork or a curry.

La Ribera

Bar Hivernacle

Parc de la Ciutadella (268 01 77). Metro Arc de Triomf/bus 39, 40, 41, 42, 51. **Open** 10am-10pm daily.
A bar inside the beautiful iron-and-glass *Hivernacle*, or greenhouse, of the Ciutadella park, built by Josep Amargós in 1884. With three parts (one shaded room, one unshaded room and a terrace), it hosts exhibitions and occasional jazz and classical concerts, and as well as plants around the bar there's a display of tropical plants in one of the rooms alongside.
Tables outdoors (all year).

Cafè del Born Nou

Plaça Comercial 10 (268 32 72). Metro Barceloneta/bus 14, 16, 17, 39, 45, 51. **Open** 9am-midnight Mon; 9am-2.30am Tue-Fri; 9.30am-2.30am Sat; 9.30am-10pm Sun.
Big, airy cafe opposite the old Born market. With a soothing interior and music, interesting food selection and the odd exhibition from a local artist this new café makes one of the most relaxing places in the area to enjoy a coffee or two.
Tables outdoors (May-Sep).

Euskal Etxea

C/Montcada 1-3 (310 21 85). Metro Jaume I/bus 17, 40, 45. **Open** *restaurant* 1-3.30pm, 9-11.30pm; *bar* 10.30am-midnight, Tue-Sun. **Credit** AmEx, MC, V.

Catalonia may not be famous for its tapas but the Basque Country certainly is, and this bar has the best Basque tapas in Barcelona, with a mouth-watering array of small *pinchos* (anything from chunks of tuna and pickles to delicately deep-fried crab claws, and complicated mixed tapas) that make their grand entrance from kitchen to bar at midday and at 7pm. Get there early for the best selection and be prepared to stand up.
Branch: Txakolín C/Marquès de l'Argentera 19 (268 17 81).

Gimlet

C/Rec 24 (310 10 27). Metro Jaume I/bus 14, 16, 17, 39, 45, 51. **Open** *Oct-June* 7pm-2.30am Mon-Thur, Sun; 7pm-3am Fri, Sat; *July-Sept* 8pm-2.30am Mon-Thur, Sun; 8pm-3am Fri, Sat.
If James Bond ever made it to BCN, you can be sure he'd end up here. It's a classy but comfortable cocktail bar, with white-jacketed waiters exuding an unflappable efficiency.

Palau Dalmases

C/Montcada 20 (310 06 73). Metro Jaume I/bus 17, 40, 45. **Open** 8pm-2am Tue-Sat; 4-11pm Sun. **Credit** AmEx, V.
Not a bar, they say, but a 'Baroque Space', in the ground floor – the former stables – of one of the most beautiful courtyard palaces of the C/Montcada, the seventeenth-century Palau Dalmases. Its promoters aim to provide an 'aesthetic experience' that will 'satisfy all the five senses': the walls are adorned with period paintings, the ornate furniture and semi-religious accoutrements are to match, spectacular displays of fresh flowers, fruit and aromatic herbs give it the look of an Italian still life, and suitably Baroque music plays gently in the background. Fresh fruit drinks are provided as well as alcohol, and there are occasional music recitals. Deeply eccentric, decadent, a tad pretentious, but soothing to ear, nose and eye, and worth the elevated prices.
Tables outdoors (May-Oct).

Tèxtil Café

C/Montcada 12-14 (268 25 98). Metro Jaume I/bus 17, 40, 45. **Open** 10am-midnight, *July, Aug* 10am-1am, Tue-Sun. **Credit** AmEx, MC, V.
Another special bar on C/Montcada, in the courtyard of the fourteenth-century Palau dels Marquesos de Llió, now the **Museu Tèxtil** (*see chapter* **Museums**). Very popular, and a great place to stopover while sightseeing. *See also chapter* **Gay & Lesbian Barcelona**.

El Xampanyet

C/Montcada 22 (319 70 03). Metro Jaume I/bus 17, 40, 45. **Open** noon-4pm, 6.30-11pm Tue-Sat; noon-4pm Sun. **Credit** V.
One of the eternal attractions of C/Montcada. It's lined with coloured tiles, barrels and antique curio, has a few marble tables, and there are three specialities: anchovies, cider and 'champagne' (truth to say, a pretty plain *cava*), served by the glass or bottle. Other good tapas are available, too. Owner Sr Esteve and his family are unfailingly welcoming, and it's one of the best places in which to while away an afternoon. Note that the opening times can vary unpredictably.

Raval

See also the **Bar Marsella** and **London Bar**, in *chapter* **Nightlife**.

Bar Almirall

C/Joaquim Costa 33 (no phone). Metro Universitat/bus 24, 41, 55, 64, 91, N4, N6. **Open** 7pm-2.30am daily.
Opened in 1860, this has the distinction of being the oldest continuously-functioning bar in the city, and still has its elegant wooden early-Modernist decor, albeit now

House rules

Basic etiquette

The civilised and rarely-abused system of pay-as-you-leave is the norm in Barcelona bars, except in very busy night-time bars and some outdoor terraces, such as those in the Plaça Reial, where you will often be asked to pay as soon as drinks are served. If you're having trouble getting a waiter's attention, a loud but polite *Oiga* (literally, 'hear me'), or, if you're trying your Catalan, *Escolti*, should do the trick. As in restaurants tipping is entirely discretionary, but it's common to leave something if you've had table service, and food as well as a drink. Most people just round up the bill to the nearest 100ptas, or leave some of the change. Some people also leave a few coins (rarely over 25ptas) even when served at the bar, more an old-fashioned courtesy than a real tip.

In most local and more traditional bars paper napkins (*servilletas*), olive pips, toothpicks, cigarette butts and other disposables are customarily dropped on the floor, but this is not done in smarter places. Check what local patrons are doing and follow suit. One other point is that Spaniards as a whole are the biggest consumers of low-alcohol drinks in the world (a curious fact for you). Catalans, in particular, do not drink to get drunk, and it's not unusual for people to sit on a drink for an hour or more.

Coffee & Tea

A large, milky coffee is a *cafè amb llet* (in Catalan) or *café con leche* (in Spanish), which locals generally only have with breakfast, although you can order it at any time of day. After mid-morning people are more likely to have a small coffee with a dash of milk, a *tallat* (Catalan)/*cortado* (Spanish), or a black espresso (*cafè sol/café solo*). A *café americano* is a *solo* diluted with twice the normal amount of water, and a *carajillo* is a *solo* with a shot of spirits. If you just ask for a *carajillo* it will normally be with brandy (*carajillo de coñac*), but you can also order a *carajillo de ron* (rum), whisky or whatever takes your fancy. Decaffeinated coffee (*descafeinado*) is widely available, but if you don't want just instant decaf with hot milk, ask for it *de màquina* (espresso).

Tea, except in cafés that specialise in it, is a bit of a dead loss, but herbal teas, *infusiones*, are always available. Very popular are *menta* (mint) or *manzanilla* (camomile).

Beer

The Damm beer company reigns supreme in Catalonia. Their most popular product is *Estrella*, a good, standard lager. *Voll-Damm* is a stronger, heavier brew, and interesting, but not that widely distributed, is their dark beer *Bock-Damm*. Also a common brand, but well behind in local sales, is San Miguel. Bottled beers can be ordered in *medianas* (the standard bottle, at ⅓ litre) or smaller *quintos* (¼ litre). Bars that have draught beer serve it in *cañas* (about the same as a *mediana*) or *jarras* (about ½ a litre). Imported beers are becoming increasingly available (especially Guinness) but they are considerably more expensive than local brands.

Wines, spirits & other drinks

All bars stock a basic red (*negro* or *tinto*), white (*blanco*) or rosé (*rosado*). If a red wine is a bit on the acid side, try it with lemonade (*gaseosa*). Except in bars that specialise in wines, good wines tend to be expensive, and the selection limited: for a wider choice, go to a *bodega*. Most bars also stock popular brands of *cava*, but 'champagne bars' will have more varieties, and traditional specialists such

as the **Xampanyet** and **Can Paixano** have their own cheaper 'house' brands.

Spirit mixes such as a *gin-tonic, vodka-tónica* or a *cuba-libre* (white rum and coke) are very popular for nighttime social drinking. Both Catalonia and Andalusia produce high-quality brandies, more full-bodied than French brandies but still subtle – of Catalan brandies, Torres 5 and Torres 10 are two of the best. Fruit-flavoured schnapps drinks are also popular here. Drunk icy-cold, in peach, lemon or apple varieties, a schnapps is a pleasant way to finish a meal.

Non-alcoholic drinks

Popular alternatives to alcohol are the Campari-like but booze-free *Bitter Kas*, and tonic water (*una tónica*), just with ice and lemon. Mineral water is *aigua/agua mineral*: ask for it *amb gas/con gas* (fizzy), or *sense gas/sin gas* (still).

Food

Most bars have some kind of *bocadillos*, hefty, crusty bread rolls filled with *llom/lomo* (pork), *jamón serrano*, potato tortilla, tuna, cheese and other ingredients; some bars use long, thin rolls called *flautes*. When you order a *bocadillo* the waiter will usually check that you want it *amb tomàquet?* or *con tomate?*, spread with tomato Catalan-style (*see chapter* **Restaurants**). A *sandwich* is made with white sliced bread, and a *bikini* is a toasted ham and cheese sandwich.

Most Barcelona tapas bars offer a fairly standard choice, although some, such as the Basque **Euskal Etxea**, have a wider range. Some Catalan bars have a *llesqueria*-type selection (again, *see chapter* **Restaurants**). The following are some of the most common tapas varieties (in Spanish only). **Albóndigas** meatballs; **Anchoas** salted anchovies; **Berberechos** cockles; **Boquerones** pickled fresh anchovies; **Chipirones en su tinta** small squid cooked in their ink; **Croquetas (de pollo, de bacalao, etc.)** croquettes (with chicken, salt-cod, etc.); **Empanadas** large flat pie, usually with tuna filling; **Empanadillas (de atún)** small fried pastries, usually with tuna filling; **Ensaladilla Rusa** mixed 'Russian' salad; **Gambas al ajillo** prawns fried with garlic; **Habas a la Catalana** broad beans, onions and *botifarra* blood sausage cooked in white wine; **Mejillones** mussels; **Olivas** olives; **Patatas bravas** deep-fried potatoes with hot pepper sauce; **Pincho moruno** peppered pork brochette; **Pulpo a la gallega** octopus with paprika and olive oil.

Bar Hivernacle: *one of the world's grander greenhouses. See page 124.*

Look at that! Novelty bars

Since the Barcelona design-bar phenomenon designed itself into its own navel, the next progression has been towards 'novelty' bars, as bar owners struggle to give their punters something new to look at, play with, or both. **La Bolsa** ('The Stock Exchange', suitably enough in the top part of town near Plaça Macià) offers Wall-Street wannabees amongst you the chance to 'play the market', as drink prices, shown on computer-screens, fluctuate according to a drink's popularity on the night. Put your money on a rum and black and you may make a killing. Techno-buffs will be relieved to know that BCN has joined the **Internet** café craze with two venues, on Gran Via and in Maremagnum. Anyone who believes in the fairies might prefer **El Bosc de les Fades** ('The Fairy Forest') in the courtyard of the wax museum on the Rambla, a Brothers Grimm-grotto with fake trees, toadstools and other twee touches.

If eating in a submarine complete with simulated under-water effects takes your fancy, try the Steven Spielberg-sponsored venture **Dive!**, installed like several ultra-new bars at Maremagnum. And, taking the English idea of pub darts a step further, **L'Arquer** on Gran Via offers four archery ranges, plus instruction from the reigning Catalan champion. Finally, although regretfully full details were not available at time of writing, style victims will be entranced by the opening of Naomi, Claudia and Elle's first **Fashion Café** outside the US, in a prime site at Passeig de Gràcia 56, opposite Gaudí's Casa Batlló.

Locations

L'Arquer *Gran Via de les Corts Catalanes 454 (423 99 08). Metro Rocafort/bus 9, 41, 50, 56, N1, N2.* **Open** 1pm-3am daily.
La Bolsa *C/Tuset 17 (414 70 63). FGC Gràcia/bus 6, 7, 15, 16, 17, 27, 33, 34, 58, 64, N8.* **Open** 8pm-2.30am Mon-Fri; 5.30pm-3pm Sat, Sun.
El Bosc de Les Fades *Passatge de la Banca, La Rambla 4-6 (317 26 49). Metro Drassanes/bus 14, 18, 38, 59, 64, 91.* **Open** 9am-11pm daily.
El Cafè de Internet *Gran Via de les Corts Catalanes 656 (412 19 15). Metro Passeig de Gràcia/bus 7, 18, 39, 45, 50, 54, 56, N1, N9.* **Open** 10am-midnight Mon-Thur; 10am-2am Fri, Sat; 4-10pm Sun.
Dive! *Maremagnum, Moll d'Espanya (225 81 58). Metro Drassanes/bus 14, 18, 36, 57, 59, 64, N4, N6, N9.* **Open** 1-5pm, 8pm-12.30am, daily.
Insòlit Internet Bar/Cafè *Maremagnum Moll d'Espanya (225 81 78). Metro Drassanes/bus 14, 18, 36, 57, 59, 64, N4, N6, N9.* **Open** noon-11pm Mon-Thur, Sun; noon-5am Fri, Sat.

---

charmingly unkempt. It's no ageing relic, but fashionable in a laid-back way. Old travel posters and knick-knacks line the walls, and the vintage sofas and armchairs that fill the large room are great for settling into with groups of friends.

Bar Kasparo

Plaça Vicenç Martorell 4 (302 20 72). Metro Catalunya/bus all routes to Plaça Catalunya. **Open** 9am-midnight daily. Sometimes closed Jan.
A small bar in the arcades of one of the city's more peaceful squares, taken over (and renovated) by three Australian sisters who offer more varied fare instead of basic tapas. The terrace is a great spot for sitting out on a sunny day. *Tables outdoors.*

Bar Pastís

C/Santa Mònica 4 (318 79 80). Metro Drassanes/bus 14, 18, 38, 59, 64, 91, N4, N6, N9. **Open** 7.30am-2.30am Mon-Thur; 7.30pm-3.30am Fri-Sat.
Down a tiny alley off the bottom end of the Rambla, this is another of Barcelona's 'bar-institutions'. It was opened in the forties by Quimet and Carme, a Catalan couple who'd lived in Marseilles, and the pictures around the walls were painted by Quimet himself, apparently always when drunk. They began the tradition of playing exclusively French music, and serving only *pastis*, and the bar became a favourite of boxers, French sailors, *Barrio Chino*-types and the Franco-era intelligentsia. Quimet died in 1963, and for years the bar became more eccentric still, as his wife made it a monument to his memory. Under the present management the drinks menu has expanded, but you're still unlikely to hear any music from south of the Pyrenees except for the occasional

live acoustic gig. Small, dark, quirky, and, with Piaf or Georges Moustaki in the background, a unique atmosphere.

L'Ovella Negra

C/Sitges 5 (317 10 87). Metro Catalunya/bus all routes to Plaça Catalunya. **Open** 9am-2am Mon-Wed; 9am-2.30am Thu; 9am-3am Fri; 5pm-3am Sat; 5pm-2.30am Sun.
Terracotta-tiled bar with long wooden tables and an open kitchen that serves fuelling-type standards such as grilled meat with *pa amb tomàquet*. Rock music, pool tables, video games and cheap alcohol make it a regular pre-partying stop off point for young people, particularly on Saturday nights.

Raval

C/Doctor Dou 19 (302 41 33). Metro Catalunya/bus all routes to Plaça Catalunya. **Open** 8pm-2.30am Mon-Thur; 8pm-3am Fri, Sat.
Well-known as a post-performance watering-hole for the theatrical set, Raval has a broad clientèle who appreciate its elegant design, comfy sofas and late (often spontaneous) opening hours. A perfect place for a late-night chat.

Barceloneta

Can Paixano

C/Reina Cristina 7 (310 08 39). Metro Barceloneta/bus 14, 36, 39, 57, 59, 64. **Open** 9am-10.30pm Mon-Sat.
A hole-in-the-wall bar, cavernous inside, in one of the streets down by the port packed with cheap electrical shops – not actually in Barceloneta proper – and serving very drinkable no-label *cava* and an enormous range of toasted *bocadillos*. Usually packed with workers during the day,

Terrazas with a view

As well as helping you to quench a thirst, Barcelona's shaded outdoor café *terrazas* are naturally great places in which to write a postcard, read a book or just join in the great Mediterranean sport of people-watching. Many also offer ideal vantage points for taking in the scenery to your absolute content without wearing out your feet.

In the last few years several of Barcelona's older museums have realised that their stone courtyards make ideal locations for cafés. One such is the **Tèxtil Cafè** (*see* **La Ribera**); another is the delightful **Cafè d'Estiu** ('Summer Café', as it's only open part of the year) in the leafy Gothic courtyard of the **Museu Frederic Marès**, alongside the Cathedral. Both have a tranquility that makes it easy to forget you're in the middle of the city. Also in the Barri Gòtic is **L'Antiquari** in the Plaça del Rei, with a few tables with an excellent view of one of the area's finest Medieval squares, while across in La Ribera the café/restaurant **Vascelum** is the perfect place from which to contemplate the majestic counterposition of verticals and plain space in the façade of Santa Maria del Mar. On a different note, in the Plaça Reial the **Glaciar** is a perennially hip spot from which to observe the *plaça*'s melting-pot of street life, and in the more peaceful Plaça Sant Josep Oriol the **Bar del Pi** offers a front-row seat for the art market and the jazz and classical buskers that appear there, along with excellent, if a bit pricey, tapas.

From the tables of **Gambrinus** on the Moll de la Fusta, meanwhile, it's possible to admire one of the most characteristically whimsical products of the '80s Barcelona design boom, Javier Mariscal's giant fibreglass prawn on top of the bar, which he designed with Alfredo Arribas. There are good, if again a tad expensive, tapas, and you can also survey the scene around the port. To open the view up, though, the best places are on the mountains that overlook the city. The oddly little-known **Miramar** on Montjuïc, at the end of the road from the Fundació Miró past the funfair, offers a sweeping vista over the port and the Mediterranean. The most breathtaking panorama of all, though, is the one from the **Mirablau**, at the top of the tram line on Tibidabo. It has both an outside terrace and giant floor-to-ceiling windows, seemingly suspended in space, from where you can admire Barcelona laid out below you by day and by night.

Locations

L'Antiquari de la Plaça del Rei *C/Veguer 13 (310 04 35). Metro Liceu, Jaume I/bus 17, 40, 45.* **Open** 9.30am-2am Tue-Thur, Sun; 9.30am-3am Fri, Sat.
Bar del Pi *Plaça Sant Josep Oriol 1 (302 21 23). Metro Liceu/bus 14, 18, 38, 59, 64, 91* **Open** 9am-11pm Mon-Fri; 9.30am-10.30pm Sat; 10am-3pm, 5-10pm, Sun..
Cafè D'Estiu *Museu F. Marès, Plaça de Sant Iu 5 (310 30 14). Metro Liceu, Jaume I/bus 17, 40, 45.* **Open** *Easter-Sept* 10am-10pm Tue-Sun.
Gambrinus *Moll de la Fusta (310 55 77). Metro Drassanes/bus 14, 36, 57, 59, 64.* **Open** 11am-1am Mon, Tue, Thur-Sun.
Glaciar *Plaça Reial 3 (302 11 63). Metro Liceu/bus 14, 18, 38, 59, 64, 91* **Open** 4pm-2.15am Mon-Fri; 4pm-2.45am Sat; 9am-2.15am Sun..
Mirablau *Plaça Doctor Andreu (418 58 79). FGC Tibidabo/bus 17, 22, 58, 73, N8, then Tramvia Blau.* **Open** 11am-4.30am Mon-Thur, Sun; 11am-5am Fri, Sat.
Miramar *Avda Miramar (442 31 00). Metro Paral.lel, then Funicular de Montjuïc/bus 61.* **Open** 10am-3am Mon, Tue, Thur-Sun. Closed Nov.
Vascelum *Plaça Santa Maria del Mar (319 01 67). Metro Jaume I/bus 17, 40, 45.* **Open** 9am-1am Tue-Sun.

---

and young foreigners at weekends. No surprise, for it's about the cheapest place in town to eat and drink seriously at the same time.

Jai-ca

C/Ginebra 13 (319 50 02). Metro Barceloneta/bus 17, 39, 45, 57, 59, 64. **Open** 10am-midnight daily. **Credit** V.
High-quality, no-nonsense Basque tapas bar in the heart of the Barceloneta specialising in fried and grilled seafood. Its pavement tables are a great place for a Sunday aperitif. *Tables outdoors (May-Oct).*

El Vaso del Oro

C/Balboa 6 (319 30 98). Metro Barceloneta/bus 17, 39, 45, 57, 59, 64. **Open** 8.30am-midnight daily.
A very narrow *cerveceria* (beer-bar), one of few in Barcelona that makes its own (excellent) brew. Don't go expecting a table (there aren't any). There is, though, a long, often crowded bar that will test your dexterity as you try not to elbow your neighbour's *patatas bravas*. Tapas-lovers' heaven.

Cerveceria Jazz

C/Margarit 43 (443 05 60). Metro Paral.lel/bus 20, 57, 64, N4, N6. **Open** 6pm-2am Mon-Sat.
German and Belgian beers, a long wooden bar and a rustic-meets-Baroque interior make this one of the more original bars in the area. The sandwiches are great – from a standard 'club' to *frankfurt a la cerveza* (frankfurt in beer) – and the music (varied jazz) never so loud as to inhibit conversation.

Taverna Noray

C/Concordia 42 (442 50 00). Metro Poble Sec/bus 20, 57, 64, N4, N6. **Open** 7pm-2am Mon-Thu & Sun; 7pm-3am Fri-Sat;
Eccentric neighbourhood 'bohemian' bar, crammed with old photos of musicians and film-stars, chandeliers, fish tanks, clocks and anything else you'd find in a mad granny's attic. Its small front terrace gets lively during the summer, inducing

the odd angry neighbour to throw things onto it – the response from the nonchalant owner being a bemused shrug. *Tables outdoors (end May-Oct).*

The Eixample

See **Zona Alta** for **Mas i Mas/Mas i Mas Cafè**, & *chapter* **Restaurants** for **Madrid-Barcelona**.

La Barcelonina de Vins i Esperits
C/València 304 (215 70 83). Metro Passeig de Gràcia/bus 7, 22, 24, 28, N4, N6. **Open** 8am-2.30am Mon-Fri; 7pm-2.30am Sat, Sun, public holidays. **Credit** AmEx, DC, MC, V.
A smart Eixample variant on the *bodega*, with over 500 wines in stock, many displayed in a long wooden cabinet along one wall. To go with them, there's *llesqueria*-type food and toasted *pa amb tomàquet.*

Bar Pastrano
Passeig de Gràcia 63 (no phone). Metro Passeig de Gràcia/bus 20, 21, 43, 44, N7. **Open** 6.30am-1am Mon-Thur; 6.30pm-2am Fri, Sat.

A charming 'don't blink or you'll miss it' basement bar lined with boxing and bullfighting paraphernalia, frequented by local workers and young students at the weekend. It has a limited selection of tapas and great *bocadillos.*

La Bodegueta
Rambla de Catalunya 100 (215 48 94). FGC Provença/bus 20, 21, 43, 44, N7. **Open** 8am-2am Mon-Sat; 6.30 pm-2am Sun;
A straightforward *bodega*-bar slap in the middle of chic-dom. Old wooden barrels line the walls and small marble tables add a classy-intimate feel. There's a great choice of tapas at reasonable prices, and a good set lunch menu for 1,150 ptas.
Tables outdoors (May-Oct).

Bracafè
C/Casp 2 (no phone). Metro Catalunya/bus all routes to Plaça Catalunya. **Open** 7am-midnight daily.
A popular café patronised by Passeig de Gràcia shoppers, known for its Brazilian coffee which has made it onto the 'best in Barcelona' list. It has a shaded outside terrace from which to survey the crowds while you enjoy the brew.
Tables outdoors (all year).

The wonderful **Xampanyet.** *See page 124.*

La Gran Bodega

C/València 193 (453 10 53). Metro Universitat; Passeig de Gràcia/bus 20, 21, 43, 44. **Open** *7am-1am daily.* **Credit** *MC, V.*

Bustling tapas bar, a first stop-off for students and office workers before a night out. Adventurous tourists acquaint themselves here with the *porrón* (the Catalan drinking jug that has you pour the wine down your throat through a long glass spout). It takes several goes to master the art – but it´s fun trying.
Tables outdoors (May-end Sept).

Laie Llibreria Cafè

C/Pau Claris 85 (302 73 10). Metro Catalunya/bus all routes to Plaça Catalunya. **Open** *café 9am-1am, bookshop 10am-9pm, Mon-Sat. Closed public holidays.* **Credit** *AmEx, DC, MC, V.*

Barcelona's bookshop-café, an enormously succesful concept. The upstairs café has its own entrance (and hours), but is popular with a literary set, and anyone looking for a comfortable bar in which to sit and read. It has great cakes and coffees, a selection of magazines for browsing and a good lunch menu, for 1,650ptas. There are a few outside tables on the patio of its Eixample block, and live jazz some evenings. *See also chapters* **Shopping** *and* **Women's Barcelona**. *Tables outdoors (May-Oct).*

Velòdromo

C/Muntaner 213 (430 51 98). Metro Hospital Clínic/bus 6, 7, 15, 33, 34, 58, 64, N8. **Open** *6am-1.30am Mon-Thu; 6am-2.30am Fri-Sat.*

A much-loved two-storey art deco bar from 1933 that attracts a complete mix of people, from office workers during the day to a younger crowd at night. Billiard tables, long leather sofas and an upper balcony give it a real 'café society' feel. A great place to go with a group, or just to write a letter alone in one of its many comfortable corners.

Gràcia

Bar Canigó

C/Verdi 2 (213 30 49). Metro Fontana/bus 22, 24, 28, 39, N4, N6. **Open** *9am-midnight Mon-Fri, Sun.*

One of the last old-style *bodega*-bars in Gràcia that hasn't been thoughtlessly modernised, with a wooden bar and tables, and old mirrors on the walls. No tapas, but great *bocadillos* and *flautas*. Other attractions include a pool table, and the outside tables look out onto the recently-renovated, wonderfully named Plaça de la Revolució.
Tables outdoors (April-Sept).

Cafè del Sol

Plaça del Sol 16 (415 56 63). Metro Fontana/bus 22, 24, 28, N4, N6. **Open** *1pm-2am Mon-Thur, Sun; 1pm-2.30 am Fri-Sat.*

The Plaça del Sol is lined with bars with tables outside, but this remains the most popular. A great place to spend a summer evening, watching the parade of jugglers, fire-eaters and musicians that turn the *plaça* into an impromptu stage.
Tables outdoors (all year).

Cakes & summer coolers

If you feel like something sweet and satisfying rather than a straight drink, head for a *granja*, of which there are many around the city. Most serve alcohol, but that's not the point of going there. Instead, they specialise in coffee, cakes, pastries, dairy products and such things as *suizos* (thick hot chocolate topped by a mountain of whipped cream) and *batidos* (milkshakes). Built to satisfy Catalans' traditional sweet tooth, they're especially popular for afternoon call-ins while shopping.

Some of the best are in C/Petritxol, between Plaça del Pi and C/Portaferrisa. The **Granja Dulcinea** boasts traditional wooden fittings and white-jacketed waiters who cater swiftly for the Saturday evening crowds. **La Pallaresa** nearby has a more antiseptic sixties look, but its *suizos* are rated among the best. In a narrow street on the Raval side of the Rambla, the **Granja M. Viader** has done a roaring trade since 1870. They have an off-sales counter where you can buy fresh cream, milk and cheeses, including the ricotta-like Catalan speciality *mató*. If you're in the Eixample, try the sixties institution **Granja Camps**.

These things can seem pretty heavy in the summer heat, but then other drinks are available. *Orxateries/Horchaterías* serve *Orxata* (Spanish *horchata*), a delicious, milky drink made by crushing a nut called a *chufa*. It may not be appreciated on first tasting, but once you're used to it it's wonderfully refreshing on a hot day. *Orxata* curdles quickly once made, and so has to be bought fresh from a specialised *Orxateria*. They also sell home-made ice-creams and *granissats/granizados* (fruit or coffee drinks drunk through crushed ice). Two fine *horchaterías* very close to one another share the same name, although they rigorously deny any connection: the **Orxatería-Gelateria Sirvent** has outside tables that are a fine place to sit out late, while **Horchatería Sirvent** has none – but on summer nights, crowds of people drink standing around the door. Poble Nou boasts the famous **El Tío Che**, open since 1912, and the only place in town that still does a malt-flavoured *granizado*.

Locations

Granja Camps *Rambla Catalunya 113 (215 10 09). Metro Diagonal, FGC Provença/bus 22, 24, 28.* **Open** *7.15am-9pm Mon-Sat.*
Granja Dulcinea *C/Petritxol 2 (no phone). Metro Liceu/bus 14, 18, 38, 59, 64, 91.* **Open** *9am-1pm, 4.30-9pm, daily.*
Granja La Pallaresa *Calle Petrixol 11 (302 20 36). Metro Liceu/bus 14, 18, 38, 59, 64, 91.* **Open** *9am-1pm, 4-9pm, daily.*
Granja M. Viader *C/Xuclà 4-6 (318 34 86). Metro Liceu/bus 14, 18, 38, 59, 64, 91.* **Open** *5-8.30pm Mon; 9am-2pm, 5-8.30pm, Tue-Sat.*

Casa Quimet

Rambla del Prat 9 (227 87 81). Metro Fontana/bus 16, 17, 22, 24, 28, N4, N6. **Open** 6.15pm-2am Tue-Sun, & Mon if public holiday. Closed Feb, Aug.

Strange but true. Also known as the 'guitar bar', Casa Quimet is just that: over two hundred guitars line the walls and ceiling of this faded old bar, and you're welcome to grab one and join in the ongoing 'jam session'. You might be able to distinguish a song, or you might just hear a lot of people playing and singing at once, and you can also wear one of their stock of silly hats. The drink range is more limited. Don't expect a friendly chat with the owner, for his detachment is legendary, and adds one more surreal touch to the place.

Mediterrani

C/Ramon i Cajal 9 (284 06 51). Metro Fontana/bus 21, 22, 24, 28, N4, N8. **Open** 8pm-2.30am Mon-Thur, Sun; 8pm-3am Fri, Sat.

A sophisticated but comfortable cocktail bar with soft sofas and plenty of tables. The *caipirinhas* (Brazilian *cachaça* rum and lime) are potent, the Italian panini sandwiches are delicious, and well-mixed jazz-y music completes the ambience.

El Roble

C/Lluis Antúnez 7 (218 73 87). Metro Diagonal/bus 16, 17, 22, 24, 25, 28, N4, N6. **Open** 7am-1am Mon-Sat.

Large, bright, old-style tapas bar, with a great selection of fresh seafood tapas and a wide range of tortillas. One of the better places to eat tapas in Barcelona, and often bustling.

Salambó

C/Torrijos 51 (218 69 66). Metro Joanic/bus 21, 39, N4. **Open** noon-2.30am Mon-Thu; noon-3am Fri-Sun. **Credit** MC, V.

An elegant two-storey café, opened only in 1992 but which deliberately echoes the large literary cafés of the 1930s, with plenty of tables, billiard tables and an unusual selection of fragrant teas, sandwiches and salads. Extremely popular, especially with the crowds from the Verdi cinemas. *Tables outdoors (May-Oct).*

Sol Solet

Plaça del Sol 13 (217 44 40). Metro Fontana/bus 22, 24, 28, N4, N8. **Open** 7pm-3am daily. Closed late Aug.

The only bar with 'wholefood' tapas – tabouleh, guacamole, feta and tomato salads, and a selection of tortillas – and so a Godsend for vegetarians. Marble tables, wood-lined walls and intimate lighting add to its appeal. Tapas are all 250ptas. *Tables outdoors (all year).*

Virreina Bar

Plaça de la Virreina 1 (237 98 80). Metro Fontana/bus 22, 24, 28, N4, N6. **Open** noon-2.30am daily.

Friendly bar/meeting place on one of the smaller Gràcia squares with outside tables that fill up quickly on hot summer nights. Known for a good range of imported beers, such as Mexican Desperado and Belgian Chimay, made by monks. *Tables outdoors (all year).*

Sup on chocolate and cream at the **Granja Dulcinea**.

Horchatería Sirvent *C/Parlament 56 (441 27 20). Metro Poble Sec/bus 20, 24, 64, 91, N4, N6.* **Open** *Easter-mid Oct* 10am-1.30am daily.
Orxateria-Gelateria Sirvent *Ronda Sant Pau 3 (441 76 16). Metro Paral.lel/bus 20, 36, 57, 64, 91, N4, N6.* **Open** *Easter-mid-Oct* 9am-2.30am daily.

El Tío Che *Rambla del Poble Nou 44-46 (309 18 72). Metro Poble Nou/bus 36, 71, 92, 141, N6.* **Open** *Oct-May* 9am-2pm, 5-9pm Mon, Tue, Thur-Sun. *May-mid-Oct* 9/10am-1am Mon-Thur, Sun; 9/10am-3am Fri-Sat. Closing times for all the above places vary as the summer season progresses.

Celtic mists

Catalans have long had a soft spot for all things Celtic, and post-Olympics this has been reflected in a blossoming of Irish pubs in the city, helped by the entirely-disinterested support of the Guinness corporation. Patronised, curiously, as much by locals as foreigners – despite Catalan reservations about the idea of a night's drinking – they have had a quiet impact on Barcelona's fickle bar scene.

First to arrive was **Kitty O'Shea's**, at the upper end of town off Avda Sarrià, a branch of the Paris-based Irish pub chain that pulls in the crowds with excellent food – try Dublin coddle and deep-fried brie – along with a huge screen for showing rugby internationals. A little further into town, in the Eixample near Plaça Francesc Macià, is **Flann O'Brien's**, which on the other hand shows English league football. Perhaps most popular of all is Seamus Farrell's **The Quiet Man**, ideally located (for a bar) in the old *Barrio Chino*, and which looks like it's been lifted lock, stock and Guinness barrel from the streets of Dublin, as indeed parts of it may have been. It has some of the best live Irish music of any of the pubs.

Even the Maremagnum centre has got in on the act, and now houses the interestingly-named **Irish Winds**, with the novelty of being an Irish pub with an outside *terraza*. And Barcelona's first Scottish pub **The Clansman**, in a tiny street in La Ribera near Santa Maria del Mar, is wetting eager whistles with Gillespie's Scottish Stout and Newcastle Brown Ale, proving that the city's thirst for things Celtic hasn't been quenched just yet.

Locations

The Clansman *C/Vigatans 13 (319 71 69). Metro Jaume I/bus 17, 40, 45.* **Open** 7pm-3am Tue-Fri, Sun; 4pm-3am Sat.

Flann O'Brien's *C/Casanova 264 (201 16 06). Bus 6, 7,14, 15, 33, 34, 59, 66, N8.* **Open** 6pm-2am Mon-Thur, Sun; 6pm-3am Fri, Sat.

Kitty O'Shea's *C/Nau Santa Maria 5 (280 36 75). Metro Maria Cristina/bus 6, 33, 33, 66, N8.* **Open** 11am-2.30am Mon-Thur; 11am-3pm Fri; noon-3pm Sat; noon-2.30am Sun.

Irish Winds *Maremagnum, Moll d'Espanya (225 81 87). Metro Drassanes/bus 14, 18, 36, 57, 59, 64, N4, N6, N9.* **Open** 11am-4am Mon-Thur, Sun; 11am-6am Fri, Sat.

The Quiet Man *C/Marquès de Barberà 11 (412 12 19). Metro Liceu/bus 14, 18, 38, 59, 64, 91, N4, N6, N9.* **Open** 6pm-2am Mon-Thur, Sun; 6pm-3am Fri, Sat.

Zona Alta

Bar Tomás
C/Major de Sarrià 49 (203 10 77). FGC Sarria/bus 34, 66, 94. **Open** 8am-10pm Mon, Tue, Thur-Sun.
It's not easy to maintain a reputation for serving 'the best *patatas bravas* in the city', but this bar in the old village of Sarrià manages to do just that. Students flock here not only for the *bravas* but also for *empanadilla de atún* and great anchovies.

Casa Fernández
C/Santaló 46 (201 93 08). FGC Muntaner/bus 14, 58, 64, N8. **Open** *restaurant* 1pm-1.30am Mon-Thur, Sun; 1pm-2am Fri-Sat; *bar* 12.30pm-2.30am Mon-Thur, Sun; 12.30pm-3am Fri-Sat; **Credit** AmEx, DC, MC, V.
An elegant variation on the tapas bar, and a regular stop-off on the fashionable bar circuit around C/Santaló, Casa Fernández serves a fine array of tapas, desserts and home-made soups, and their (very good) own-brand beer as well as imported beers. A rather expensive full restaurant menu is also available: particularly good are the meats and steaks.
Tables outdoors (May-Oct).

Mas i Mas
C/Marià Cubí 199 (209 45 02). FGC Muntaner/bus 14, 58, 64, N8. **Open** 7.30pm-2.30am Mon-Thur, Sun; 7.30pm-3am Fri, Sat.
The Mas brothers have made a splash with their string of music/club venues (**La Boîte**, **Jamboree**: *see chapters* **Nightlife** *and* **Music: Rock, Roots & Jazz**). They began with this tapas bar-café, also in the C/Santaló route, an ever-green favourite with the young uptown set. Defying the slightly pretentious image, the tapas are actually very good, and not particularly expensive. In the Eixample, on C/Còrsega near the junction of Passeig de Gràcia and Diagonal, the Mases have a similarly-stylish café-restaurant with fine tapas and a good, fair-value lunch menu.
Branch: Mas i Mas Café C/Còrsega 300 (237 57 31).

Vila Olímpica/Port Olímpic

The Port Olímpic has bars one after the other (*see also chapter* **Restaurants**), but worth singling out are:

Cafè & Cafè
Moll del Mistral 30 (221 00 19). Metro Ciutadella/bus 36. **Open** noon-2/3am Mon, Wed-Sun; open Tue if public holiday.
Relaxed coffee house/cocktail bar in the Port Olímpic with a mind-boggling range of coffees to choose from. Particularly good is the 'Royal', sweetened with cane sugar.
Tables outdoors (all year).

Planet Hollywood
C/Marina 19-21 (221 11 11). Metro Ciutadella/bus 41. **Open** 1pm-1am daily. **Credit** AmEx, DC, EC, JCB, MC, TC, V.
You know the score: cocktails with names like 'The Terminator' and 'Die Harder', plus salads, burgers, pizzas. Packed at weekends (walkie-talkied doormen say who gets in), but fun enough, if only for checking out which Hollywood paraphernalia they've got. Full meals cost about 3,000ptas.
Tables outdoors (April-Oct).

Nightlife

It's all here, from elegant design bars to Latin dance-halls, salsa spots to techno-fuelled all-night mega-parties. BYO energy and prepare to party – late and hard.

The true glamour of showbiz lives on at **El Cangrejo**. *See page 142.*

Nighttime Barcelona seems perennially on the brink of becoming an enormous citywide celebration. The reason for this is simple: the people in this city like to go out, they like to go out in a crowd, and they like to go out late. Combine this with the fact that Barcelona has become one of the most popular holiday spots in Europe, and what you get is a city that's going to be terrific fun after dark.

Waterfront cafés that stay open until 5am, elegant design bars, clubs galore and the occasional radical warehouse party are all part of the mix. Many of the places have been around for years, but the nocturnal terrain has also changed a lot since the pivotal summer of '92 and, as with any vibrant city, keeps on evolving. The scene now encompasses huge new entertainment zones that have opened up in the old port (Maremagnum) and the **Port Olímpic**. With no sleeping neighbours to worry about, these areas, especially in summer, are packed with gleeful revellers until dawn.

Shifts in geography aside, Barcelona's night crowd has long had a fad-conscious element, and now, more than ever, it is receptive to the latest global trends. At present, this means that the hippest new nightspots are firmly in the hands (and sounds) of an instantly recognisable international techno-clan. Well-versed DJs of the genre, who play one place one night and another the next, are a relatively new addition, and bring more sophistication and variety to the scene.

The techno crowd may be the biggest, but the city has plenty more places in which you can find almost anything you desire, from salsa joints, funk and soul clubs, cocktail bars and hip young hangouts to after-hours clubs in the open air.

Barcelona's old city, the *Ciutat Vella*, is in a state of renewal and sometimes, at night, alongside the crowds of foreigners and neighbourhood locals, you'll spot a group of wealthy uptowners – a class that is slowly but surely overcoming its near-in-the-bone avoidance of the inner urban area. The

Plaça Reial is always full of activity and any night of the week you'll find something going on in the clubs and bars there. The nearby district of the Ribera – around the Passeig del Born – continues to be popular, with elegant cocktail bars, techno hangouts and local bars all within a stone's throw of one another.

The no-man's land of the Eixample is worth a visit, to check out its famous, although now somewhat passé designer bars or to visit some rejuvenated clubs. The area near the Plaça Francesc Macia and the Carrer Santaló has a slew of bars and clubs that cater to a young, affluent crowd. In Gràcia, above the Eixample, the atmosphere is more relaxed: its many bars are mostly full of neighbourhood regulars. The two principal squares, Plaça del Sol and Plaça Ruis i Taulet, are good places from which to orient yourself before exploring the area.

Many of Barcelona's wealthy live on or near Tibidabo – the funfair-topped mountain overlooking the city – and the bars and clubs in this area, some with magnificent panoramas, cater to an affluent clientele. Another area of interest is Poble Nou, near the Vila Olímpica, which has its own nightspots and which, like many of the *barris* that make up the city, is very much party to its own scene.

Obviously bars and clubs open and close all the time, so look out for flyers, and check the local press (*see chapter* **Media**). Below is a sample of what to expect as you make the journey through to the end of night.

Unless otherwise stated, **admission** *is free to the places listed and they do not accept* **credit cards**.

Mostly Bars

Andy Capp

C/Bonavista 13 (no phone). Metro Diagonal/bus 6, 15, 22, 24, 28, 33, 34. **Open** 6pm-2.30am Mon-Thur, Sun; 6pm-3am Fri, Sat.
A shabby and amiable rock'n' roll bar named after Reg Smythe's hero. A picture of Andy covers one wall, a graffiti-like mural another. There's no dance space, but there is music, ranging from mainstream rock and reggae to occasional heavy metal. The crowd of regulars are a similar mix of old hippies, students and aspiring rock musicians. The moreish *bocadillos* are another attraction.

Ciutat Vella

C/San Rafael 11 (442 5358). Metro Liceu/bus 14, 18, 38, 59, N4, N6. **Open** 6pm-3am daily. **Credit** V.
A friendly little bar buried deep in the back streets of the Barrio Chino, Ciutat Vella is a regular hangout for resident foreigners and a mixed alternative crowd. There are regular art exhibitions and, on Thursday nights, Irish music shows.

Distrito Marítimo

Moll de la Fusta (221 55 61). Metro Drassanes/bus 14, 36. **Open** noon-4.30am Tue-Sat; 11am-4.30am Sun.
Committed funseekers of BCN clubland like to start their evenings at this modern outdoor bar overlooking the old port. Get here on a Friday or Saturday around 1am and the place is jammed to the walls. Inside the plate-glass-windowed bar, it's all steamy tightness, but outside you can walk around the good-sized terrace in the mild night air, and watch the lights reflected in the water of the harbour. The music is strictly techno/dance and the place serves as a kind of departure lounge and hello-there point for those boarding the local line of the international techno express – the next stop being nearby **Polyester** (*see below* **Clubs**). Distrito Marítimo is also the only outdoor night-bar along the Passeig de Colom that's open year-round.

Eldorado Bar Musical

Plaça del Sol 4 (237 36 96). Metro Fontana/bus 22, 24, 28, N4, N6. **Open** café 6-10pm daily; bar 10pm-2.30am Mon-Thur, Sun; 10pm-3am Fri, Sat; terrace 6pm-2.30am Mon-Thur, Sun; 6pm-3am Fri, Sat.
A noisy and welcoming music, dance and billiards bar, across the Plaça from the Cafe del Sol. Like the other bars on the square, it's popular with a wide variety of ages and types. The walls are painted with near-obligatory figures from comics, while videos flash on the screens next to the bar, though they're not linked to the music, which is mostly mainstream rock. On one side is a billiard table; on the other, the pocket-sized dance floor.

La Fira

C/Provença 171 (323 72 71). Metro Hospital Clínic, FGC Provença/bus 14, 59, 63, 67, 68. **Open** 10pm-3am Tue-Thur; 7pm-4.30am Fri, Sat; 6pm-1am Sun.
A large, airy space that calls itself a 'bar museum' and could claim to be the wackiest museum in town. It's furnished entirely with old fairground equipment: dodgem cars, waltzers, swings and so on provide the seating, and the bars and food stands are designed like stalls. Next to the entrance is a corridor of distorting mirrors, and there's an area full of automata, some of which are rare, and most of which still work. On top of all that, it's also one of the livelier of Barcelona's more extravagant bars. There's no dance space, although people do occasionally twitch a little among the milling crowds.

Fist Bar

C/Almogàvers 122/Pamplona 88 (309 12 04). Metro Marina/bus 6, 40, 42, 141, N6. **Open** 11pm-5am Fri, Sat. **Admission** disco 600-800ptas (includes one drink).
Located in what used to be the private lounge of **Zeleste** (*see chapter* **Music: Rock, Roots & Jazz**), Fist Bar is long and spacious, with plenty of room to dance, and is one of the stops on the ever-more popular 'rotating DJ' circuit. Thursday nights it's reggae-dub; Fridays, it's electronic avant-garde with elements of techno and jungle; and on Saturdays, it's pure electronic dance. Being somewhat out of the centre of things, the bar depends mainly on people in the know and walk-ins from Zeleste. The bar may move in the not-so-distant future, but you can always keep in touch through the management's web address: *http://www.intercom.es/discordia/*, which can also fill you in on many other aspects of Barcelona's club/music scene.

Flat Cat

C/Teodora Lamadrid 52 (417 65 78). FGC Tibidabo/bus 17. **Open** 10pm-3am Tue-Sun. Closed Aug.
A pair of excellent English DJs and a French partner have made this bar into one of the coolest around. Despite being hidden on a quiet street up on Tibidabo, the trio have managed to attract a crowd that consists not only of the beautiful, weathy people of the upscale neighbourhood, but an eclectic mix of trendy *cognoscenti* as well. Why would you travel half-way up the mountain unless you were into the music – a well-mixed blend of house, techno, underground and whatever else the DJ is in the mood to play? There's no real room to dance, so the clientèle come here to talk, chill-out and maybe wiggle a bit. The trio plan to open a dance club in the near future, to give them more room. DJ Jeremy Norris and 'Pussy Power' also put on house-techno parties at Otto Zutz (*see below* **Clubs**).

Gorlero Club

Avda Diagonal 442.(415 46 35). Metro Diagonal/bus 6, 15, 33, 34. **Open** 7pm-3am Mon-Thur, Sun; 7pm-3.30am Fri, Sat.

Until recently known as the Si Si Si, this place was one of the first design bars, and very fashionable in its time, although of late it has fallen out of favour. The design and lighting are striking, even if the atmosphere can be cold, except late on Saturdays, when it fills up. Fewer people make it more attractive as a place to drink, play pool or listen to the excellent selection of (mostly) jazz, acid jazz and soul music.

Kentucky

C/Arc del Teatre 11 (318 28 78). Metro Drassanes/bus 14, 18, 38, 59, 91. **Open** 7pm-3am Mon-Sat.

An old red light 'American' bar left over from the '60s and '70s, when Barcelona was a major port of call for US Navy ships. The bar looks unchanged since then (it still sports photos of battleships) – a long, narrow space with an old juke-box, which has a surprisingly large selection of music. The Kentucky is popular among an eclectic assortment of foreigners, Raval locals and slumming uptowners.

Al Limón Negro

C/Escudellers Blancs 3 (no phone). Metro Liceu/bus 14, 18, 38, 59, N4, N6. **Open** 10pm-2.30am Mon-Thur, Sun; 10pm-3am Fri, Sat.

World music, contemporary art and pastel orange paint on 100-year-old walls give this bar a cheerful, modern ambience. On a narrow street behind the Plaça Reial, it calls itself a 'multi-bar' and hosts occasional live music and theatre along with exhibitions. The crowd is a mix of foreigners, local artists and the local intelligentsia.

London Bar

C/Nou de la Rambla 34 (318 52 61). Metro Drassanes/bus 14, 18, 38, 59, N4, N6, N9. **Open** 7pm-4am Tue-Sun. **Credit** MC, V.

The London, with its old 1910 bar and long wall mirrors, doesn't look much like an English pub but is reminiscent of England in the sense that people tend to arrive and then stay for the rest of the evening. Once a soporific hangout for Catalan hippies, it was taken over at the start of the nineties by a livelier management who have managed to keep it popular among young expat residents and a mixed bunch of party-minded natives. There are regular jazz concerts, for which there's no entrance fee but drink prices are raised accordingly (*see chapter* **Music: Rock, Roots & Jazz**).

Malpaso

C/Rauric 20 (no phone). Metro Liceu/bus 14, 18, 38, 59, N4, N6. **Open** 9pm-2.30am Mon-Thur, Sun; 9pm-3am Fri, Sat, eves of public holidays.

Down a back alley of the Plaça Reial, you'll find this busy little bar, replete with the tastest alternative rock sounds and a hip young crowd. As you sip your on-tap Carlsberg, check out the small model train that runs the length of the glass-covered bar counter and marvel....

Marsella

C/Sant Pau 65 (no phone). **Open** 9pm-2.30am Mon-Thur; 5pm-3.30am Fri-Sun.

An authentic survivor of the *Barrio Chino's* colourful, rapidly disappearing past, the Marsella is a spacious, well-loved bar that's been in the same family for five generations. Dusty untapped 100-year-old bottles sit in tall glass cabinets (it's still possible to buy locally-made absinthe, or *absenta*, here), large old mirrors line the walls, and a motley selection of chandeliers loom over the invariably cheerful clientèle. It's one of the institutions for the Barcelona expat crowd, and also hosts a big gay crowd. The bar gets pretty crowded after midnight on weekends, so it's a good idea to come a bit earlier if you want to secure a comfortable spot at one of the fine old wooden tables.

Miami Bar

C/Assaonadors 25 (319 25 92). Metro Jaume I/bus 17, 39, 40, 45, 51. **Open** 10pm-2.30am Mon, Wed, Thur, Sun; 10pm-3am Fri, Sat.

A hip hideaway on a quiet street near C/Princesa. Painted lizards on a reflecting sheet-metal ceiling look down on the otherwise untouched, decidedly relaxed décor of this one-time girlie bar. The place is owned and run by a young English DJ and his Spanish wife, and the excellent selection of music ranges from soul and funk rare grooves with heavy doses of reggae, to dance/house and drums and bass. Gets crowded on Fridays after midnight with reggae dub parties hosted by DJ Tim of Pushfire.

Mojito Bar

Maremagnum, Moll d'Espanya (225 80 14). **Open** noon-3.30am Mon-Thur, Sun; noon-4.30am Fri, Sat. **Credit** V.

Stroll at night across the wooden walkway of the ultra-new Rambla de Mar with the yachts in the old port bobbing in the breeze and you'll hear the happy sounds of salsa emanating from the Maremagnum leisure palace. Welcome to the Mojito, thatched palm-leaf hut and all, fast becoming a spot to be for a well-dressed crowd of Latin-American-music lovers. Free dance classes (with as many as 100 people on the floor at times) are given every night except Sunday.

Network

Avda Diagonal 616 (201 72 38). Bus 6, 7, 15, 27, 33, 34, 63, 67, 68. **Open** *breakfast* 10am-1pm Mon-Fri; *lunch* 1-4pm daily; *dinner* 8pm-2am Mon-Thur, Sun; 8pm-3am Fri, Sat; *tapas* 7-9pm Mon-Sat. **Set menus** *lunch* 1,200ptas Mon-Fri; *lunch & dinner* 2,500ptas Mon-Fri. **Credit** AmEx, MC, V.

A classic of Barcelona's design-bar circuit, this striking high-tech bar/restaurant obviously owes a lot to *Blade Runner*. From the street, there's little to see: the large underground main space is entered via a spiral staircase. Below, taking the 1950s idea of individual juke-boxes a stage further, designers Eduard Samsó and Alfredo Arribas have installed video monitors on every table, while in the centre, a long, metallic bar continues the harsh aesthetic. Below that there's a third level, with pool tables. In the smartest part of town near Plaça Macià, it attracts a young, yuppyish clientele, and is still a place to be seen. The 'international' food, though – Mexican, Japanese, Italian – is often disappointing.

Nick Havanna

C/Rosselló 208 (215 65 91). Metro Diagonal/FGC Provença/bus 22, 24, 28, N4, N6. **Open** 11pm-4am Mon-Thur, Sun; 11pm-5am Fri, Sat. **Admission** free Mon-Thur, Sun; 1,100ptas (including one drink) Fri, Sat, nights before public holidays. **Credit** MC, V.

Waiters from a post-modern fantasy, a bank of 30 TV screens, bar stools like super-modern saddles, a huge pendulum swinging over the dance floor and the famous toilets are just some of the features of this cavernous space, designed in 1987 by Eduard Samsó and another BCN eighties classic. Nowadays, on weekends after 1am it's packed with a conventional-looking crowd, there's little room to dance and the DJ seems to be in the throes of an identity crisis, playing everything from Spanish rock to techno. But during the week it's a spacious, even friendly place, despite all that design.

El Otro

C/Valencia 166 (323 67 59). Metro Hospital Clínic/bus 20, 21, 43, 44, 63. **Open** 10.30am-3am daily; closed Aug.

A lively place in the midst of the Eixample, El Otro, unlike some design bars, feels genuinely relaxed, and is regularly packed with a chatty young crowd. In shape, it's much the same as a great many Eixample bars: a long bar along one side of the room with – if you can get to it through the crush – a small dance floor at the end. Enquire here about warehouse parties put on by the Colectiva del Caracol (*see* **Warehouse Parties**).

Smiling happy people get into the groove in **Penúltimo**.

Partycular

Avda Tibidabo 61 (211 62 61). No Metro or bus access.
Open 7pm-3am Tue-Sun; *tables outdoors* June-Sept.
Credit AmEx, MC, V.
Although it's pleasant all year round, Partycular really comes into its own in the summer. Located in an enormous house on the hill leading up to Tibidabo (and some way from the nearest public transport, the FGC at Av Tibidabo, although it can be a pleasant uphill walk), it has rambling gardens sprinkled with bars that look across to the lights of the funfair. It has lots of space, beautiful people to look at, areas to dance in, tables to chat at and dark corners to be romantic in. When the weather gets colder, the simple grandeur of the rooms inside make it a good place for an after-dinner drink.

Penúltimo

Passeig de Born 19 (no phone). Metro Jaume I/bus 14, 17, 36, 40, 45, 57, 59, 64. **Open** 7pm-3am daily.
'Cleopatra's milkbar' might be a better name for this dance bar in the heart of the Born, with its bizarre hodge-podge of kitsch and modern design. Soul and funk dance parties are thrown by a creative team of young women, and occasional contests are held, with prizes for best dancer and best (or most outrageously) dressed. The festive atmosphere is catchy, the crowd are a happily eclectic mix and the place on a good night is an oasis of pure funky fun. Look for fliers announcing their parties in local bars.

Rosebud

C/Adria Margarit 27 (418 88 85). No Metro or bus access. **Open** 7pm-4am Mon-Thur, Sun; 7pm-5am Fri, Sat; *tables outdoors* all year. **Admission** usually free.
Credit MC, V.
Built on the way up to Tibidabo, in front of the Museu de la Ciència, this huge two-level bar is rather out of the centre of things. The garden and pond area have views over Barcelona that make it worth a visit, though, even if the ultra-modern décor is slightly characterless. At weekends, it's jammed, and though there's no dance floor as such, punters shuffle along with a fairly standard club mix as far as space allows.

Se7 i Se7

C/de la Rosa 3 (317 88 75). Metro Liceu/bus 14, 18, 38, 59, 64, 91, N1, N4, N6. **Open** *depending on performance* 10pm-4.30am Tue-Thur, Sun; 10pm-5am Fri, Sat.
A clean, well-lit basement bar with arched brick ceilings and contemporary art from local artists on the walls. The music tends to be louder, rockier and more alternative the later it gets. There's a big room in the back where flamenco, improvised rock, alternative theatre, dance, cabaret and any other styles of performance might turn up.

Sidecar

C/Heures 4-6 (302 15 86). Metro Liceu/bus 14, 18, 38, 59, N4, N6. **Open** 10pm-2.30am Tue-Thur; 10pm-3am Fri, Sat.
In one corner of the Plaça Reial, but less seedy than some places around the area, this bar has been here for years. Early evening, it's a quiet place to play pool or read comics (hanging up behind the bar upstairs). Later on it gets much livelier, mostly with a young student crowd, and it can be difficult to move on the basement dance floor, let alone see the various bits of memorabilia, such as an old petrol pump and yes, a sidecar. There's a terrace bar in the Plaça in the summer.

Snooker Club Barcelona

C/Roger de Lluria 42 (317 97 60). Metro Passeig de Gràcia/bus 7, 18, 39, 45, 47, 56, N1, N9. **Open** 6pm-3am Mon-Thur; 6pm-4am Fri, Sat; 6pm-2am Sun.
Admission free; *snooker tables* 1,000ptas per hour.
Credit MC, V.
Built around a novel concept, the designer billiard hall, this large and impressive space was one of the of the first products of the Barcelona design-bar boom, and has won numerous awards. The bar areas, in rag-rolled peach and silver grey with arched roof and broad expanses of space between bar and tables, are striking. The tranquility of the place is appreciated by the predominantly thirtysomething clientèle. Recently, American pool tables have been installed, along with Spanish *carambala* tables, but snooker remains the centre of attraction. *See also chapter* **Sports & Fitness**.

Texaco

C/Pere IV 164 (309 92 64). Metro Llacuna/bus 6, 40, 42, N6. **Open** 10pm-3am Thur-Sat.

An authentic piece of hard-driving rock 'n' roll America, miraculously transplanted to the increasingly popular *barri* of Poble Nou. The walls of this long, narrow bar are littered with imagery of those ubiquitous American archetypes the cowboy, the biker and the rocker. You can even get American-style percolated coffee. There's a small stage at the back where rock bands sometimes play, but with or without the live acts, the place gets crowded at the weekends.

Torres de Avila

Avda Marquès de Comillas s/n Poble Espanyol (424 93 09). Metro Espanyol/bus 13, 61. **Open** *music bar* 7pm-12.30am Thur-Sun; *disco* 1am-7am Fri, Sat. **Admission** 500-1000ptas. **Credit** (bar only) V.

The summit of Mariscalism, the ultimate product of the Barcelona design-bar phenomenon. There are actually seven bars inside this building, constructed inside the main entrance to the Poble Espanyol (*see chapter* **Sightseeing**). The entrance is a copy of one of the gates to the medieval walled city of Avila – hence the name. The main theme of the design, by Javier Mariscal and architect Alfredo Arribas, was day and night, and the whole edifice is full of symbols. One of the towers represents the sun; the other, the moon. As you enter a series of interlocking spaces, cameras flash at you, while in the central bar, a film of an eye blinks continuously from the ceiling and is reflected in glass at your feet. Only the best materials were used in the construction and fittings, and the whole thing cost over three million pounds; whatever you say, the result is beautiful, at times magical. It has been more of a monument than a bar, where people just came to stare, but the once-stiff drink prices have lately been lowered to a more moderate 600 ptas (beer) and 1,000ptas (spirits), and on weekend nights, it now functions as a trance-techno disco. When the rooftop terrace bars open in summer, it's a stunning city vantage point. In July and August, it may also be open on Tuesdays and Wednesdays.

Tres Torres

Via Augusta 300 (205 16 08). FGC Tres Torres/bus 66, 94. **Open** 5pm-3am daily. **Credit** V.

As you go up the hill towards Tibidabo, you also go upmarket. Tres Torres is quite a long way up, and its garden is a favourite summer drinking spot with Barcelona's more affluent citizens. It's worth a visit to see the building, built at the end of the last century as a private house. Cocktails can be taken in a beautiful shady courtyard, with a sandwich stand and a large palm tree, on a small upstairs terrace, or in one of several elegantly decorated rooms. Recently, in a relatively successful attempt to attract a younger clientèle, live blues and jazz acts have been introduced on Thursday nights.

Universal

C/Maria Cubi, 182 bis-184 (201 46 58). FGC Muntaner/bus 14, 58, 64, N8. **Open** 10pm-4am Mon-Sat.

Divided into two floors, Universal has two distinct atmospheres. Downstairs, the music is loud, the decor dark, and away from the bar there's plenty of space for dancing. Upstairs is a light, high-ceilinged bar-room, big enough to seat diners and quiet enough for conversation. The crowd is not the wide cross-section of characters it once was: today, it tends towards a happy, homogenous suburbia. As such, the place gets packed at weekends.

Velvet

C/Balmes 161 (217 67 14). FGC Provença/bus 7, 16, 17. **Open** 8pm-5am Mon-Thur, Sun; 8pm-6.30am Fri, Sat.

A design bar with a 1950s theme that features a larger-than-usual dance floor, dramatic toilets, deafening, naff music and bar staff sporting the shortest skirts and widest epaulettes in town. The affluent young and very young things who fill the place are far less dramatic than the surroundings.

Zsa Zsa

C/Rosselló 156 (453 85 66). FGC Provença/bus 14, 54, 58, 59, 63, 64, 66, N3, N8. **Open** 7pm-3am Mon-Thur, Sun; 7pm-3.30am Fri, Sat. **Credit** V.

Another chic and elegant design bar patronised mainly by an older, middle-class and conventional bunch, who go to talk, and to sample the sophisticated range of drinks (including the house speciality, fresh fruit shakes). The style is eclectic: Oriental carpets on one wall face a continuous mirror on the other, with a steel-and-glass bar in between. The particular innovation of designers Dani Freixes and Vicente Miranda is the lighting, which changes continuously and with great subtlety so that the mirrored wall at times appears completely black and at other times is a blaze of colour. As in all the best design bars, the toilets are impressive. Bar staff are greatly appreciated by regulars for their cocktail skills.

Clubs

Antilla Cosmopolita

C/Muntaner 244 (200 77 14). Bus 6, 7, 15, 33, 34, 58, 64, N8. **Open** *'salsoteca'* 11pm-6am Fri, Sat, nights before public holidays. **Admission** 1,500ptas, including one drink; members free.

A relaxed and friendly mid-sized salsa club that has a regular programme of live acts (*see chapter* **Music: Rock, Roots & Jazz**). Its location, just above Diagonal, ensures a healthy mix of people, including real-life Latin lovers in white suits and uptown girls in short, swirly skirts. Although there are tables and chairs where you can take a breather, most of the space is taken up by the dance-floor, as it should be.

Banana Factory

C/Fusina, corner of Passeig Picasso (no phone). **Open** (sporadically) 10pm-3am Fri-Sat. **Admission** varies.

A pair of young alternative entrepreneurs have turned this one-time banana warehouse into a multi-space where anything from art exhibitions and theatre to music gigs and DJ-led dance parties can take place. Three storeys tall, it's still pretty much like a warehouse inside, but with some handy additions such as 50-pus ropes hanging from the basement -bar ceiling that the punters are wont to swing on as they drink. The Factory is a good place to get information about warehouse parties and other alternative events (*see* **Warehouse Parties**). Though one of Barcelona's more stable alternative venues, they're forever threatened with closure, but if they're not at this site they will probably have moved on somewhere else, so it's worth checking out.

Bikini

C/Deu i Mata 105 (322 00 05). Metro Les Corts/bus 15, 43, 59. **Open** *Cockteleria/dry* 7pm-4.30am Mon-Wed; 7pm-5am Thur; 7pm-6am Fri, Sat; *Rock* 11.30pm-5am Mon-Thur; 11.30pm-6am Fri, Sat; *Salsa* same as Rock room, Mon-Sat; 11.30pm-4.30am Sun. **Admission** 1,000ptas (Mon-Thur, Sun); 1,200ptas (Fri, Sat). **Credit** AmEx, V.

If there were such a thing as a state discotheque, it would probably be like Bikini. Its vaguely institutional can be explained through its past. Dating from the mid-1950s, the original Bikini called itself a 'multi-space' and had a number of different *salas* (rooms) for night-time concerts and activities. After becoming the fervent focus of late-night, late-1980s revelry, it closed up when the grounds of the club were sold and a huge mall, **L'Illa**, was constructed on the site. Six years later, a new Bikini has been opened by the same management in an underground space within the mall complex. True to its origins, the club still offers three distinct public spaces (*see chapter* **Music: Rock, Roots & Jazz**): a rock/disco club; a Latin American/*salsa* room; and a cocktail lounge, but rather than charmingly cranky the new décor has a much colder look to it. The new Bikini is popular, though, with a mixed, middle-of-the road clientèle.

Pleasure port

No area in Barcelona has more bars per square metre than the **Port Olímpic**. From Easter week until October, the 50 or so bars and restaurants that line the lower level of the port are utterly packed: after 11pm, the pocket-sized dance bars pump up the music and by 1am, most of the restaurants have converted into dance spaces as well. Midsummer, it can take a good hour to push your way from one end of the strip to the other. Almost all the Port Olimpic bars are similarly small, and differences in decor are minimal. Every bar has a sizeable outdoor *terrassa*. The music runs from Spanish techno to *salsa* to rock to popular disco, and the same bar that played salsa at 1am may play techno at 2am – it depends what the milling crowd is into. Because it's some way from the centre, most people who start a night out at the Port Olimpic end up staying there, moving from one bar to another until closing time at 5am. A few bars, such as **Panini**, **Mar i Cel**, and **Els Argonautes** are slightly bigger – and so less packed – than the rest, and **Salsa Art Bar** plays only salsa, but generally, since they're all so close to each other and venues change so often, you're best off walking along the strip and choosing for yourself. *See also chapter* **Restaurants**.

La Boîte

Avda Diagonal 477 (419 59 50). Bus 6, 7, 15, 27, 33, 34, 63, 67, 68, N8. **Open** 11pm-5.30am Mon-Thur, Sun; 11pm-6am Fri, Sat. **Admission** 1,200-3,000ptas (incl one drink).
One of a handful of clubs uptown that pulls in people from across the city, owned by the Mas brothers of the **Jamboree**, and also a music venue. They work hard to create a good ambience: the long bar hugs the curved walls, and mirrored columns make the space more intimate than expected. The resident DJ plays mainly soul, funk and old Motown favourites, and the smallish dance floor can get very crowded at weekends. *See chapter* **Music: Rock, Roots & Jazz**.

Club Apolo

C/Nou de la Rambla 113 (441 40 01/442 51 83). Metro Paral.lel/bus 36, 57, 64, 91, N4, N6. **Open** midnight-6am Thur, Fri. **Admission** 1,000ptas (incl one drink).
This elegant old ballroom has changed hands and scenes many times over the years, but has always managed to draw a crowd. The most recent management has put it to good use with a programme of dance parties and concerts, four nights a week. Thursdays, there are house/techno/Goa parties that can get off to a very late (2am) start; Fridays, the scene is more varied, with trip-hop, jungle, Brit-pop and techno. The crowd on these nights is young and up for it. Saturdays and Sundays, the club changes course completely: with salsa drawing an authentically ethnic crowd. It also hosts live concerts (*see chapter* **Music: Rock, Roots & Jazz**)

Jamboree

Plaça Reial 17 (301 75 64). Metro Liceu/bus 14, 18, 38, 59, N4, N6, N9. **Open** 8.30pm-4.30am Mon-Thur, Sun; 8.30pm-5am Fri, Sat. **Admission** *disco* free.
Live acts here end around 1am and the club Jamboree, famed for playing black soul and dance music, begins. At the centre of things in Plaça Reial, this subterranean brick vault is hugely popular, so the floor gets very cramped. Total gridlock is averted by a steady stream of people going upstairs (for free) to **Tarantos**, where they can chill to Latin and Spanish music. *See chapter* **Music: Roots, Rock & Jazz**.

Jimmy'z

Hotel Princesa Sofia, Plaça Pius XII 4 (414 63 62). Metro Maria Cristina/bus 7, 67, 68, 74, 75. **Open** 11pm-4am Mon-Wed; 11pm-5am Thur-Sat. **Admission** 1,000ptas (includes one drink); dress smart. **Credit** V.
In the palatial bowels of highrise Hotel Princesa Sofia, the decor of Jimmy'z is, well, what you'd expect in a big, expensive hotel. Like many larger discos in town, it has four different areas, including an 'ethnic' room where salsa is played; a big central dance floor with lowest-common-denominator techno; and a private lounge, where you need to know Jimmy in person to get in. The clientèle is a young, monied crowd. Thursday nights, there are gala dinners in the 'ethnic' room.

Karma

Plaça Reial 10 (302 56 80). Metro Liceu/bus 14, 18, 38, 59, N4, N6. **Open** 11.30pm-4.30am, *bar* 8.30pm-2.30am, Tue-Sun. **Admission** free-1,000ptas (incl one drink).
Right on the Plaça Reial and with a guard-boys at the door, Karma is impossible to miss. It has a long history of serving not only the tourists who find their way down, but a good cross-section of locals, too. Intense competition from other clubs nearby has lowered the attendance lately, but this underground bomb-shelter of a club remains crammed at weekends. The doormen let you walk right in if they like the looks of you; if not, you pay. Music is mainstream rock.

KGB

C/Alegre de Dalt 55 (210 59 06). Metro Alfons X, Joanic/bus 21, 25, 39. **Open** midnight to morning Wed-Sun. **Admission** (midnight-3am) 500ptas plus one drink; (from 3am) 1,000ptas plus one drink.
The best time to go to this stark, industrial-style warehouse is 2am or later. The crowd are a lively alternative bunch. Despite its residential Gràcia location, KGB stays open late enough to attract hard-core insomniacs: by 5am, the place is thick and thumping. The drill-hammer techno gets harder and faster the later it gets. Frenetic live concerts are held here sometimes, and international DJs pass through, too.

Limbo

C/Beethoven 15 (414 54 61). Bus 6, 7, 33, 34, 63, 66, 67, 68. **Open** midnight-5am Thur; midnight-6am Fri, Sat. **Admission** 1,000ptas (incl one drink). **Credit** AmEx, MC, V.
A tasteful, beautifully proportioned club with a large round dance floor partially ringed by bars. Currently, the music is purely soul, Afro-dance and funk, and the mainly young and sophisticated clientele are right into dance mode. Upstairs is a comfortable lounge where an older crowd hangs out.

Luz de Gas

C/Muntaner 246 (209 77 11/209 73 85). Bus 6, 7, 15, 33, 34, 58, 64, N8. **Open** 11pm (*disco* 2am)-4.30/5.30am daily. **Admission** 1,200-1500ptas (incl one drink). **Credit** AmEx, DC, MC, V.
Elegant red velvet with a touch of kitsch sets the tone for this live venue (*see chapter* **Music: Rock, Roots & Jazz**), which doubles as a disco after 2am. Very popular with an uptown, middle-of-the-road clientèle that congregates *en masse* at the door, eagerly pays the cover charge, then boogies the night away in the sweaty, dense interior.

New York

C/Escudellers 5 (318 87 30). Metro Drassanes/bus 14, 18, 38, 59, N4, N6. **Open** midnight-4.30am Thur-Sat, eves of public holidays. **Admission** (midnight-2am) 500ptas incl one non-alcoholic drink; (2am-close) 1,000ptas incl one alcoholic drink.

Students and teenagers thrash it out to the sounds of Britpop and other contemporary rock in this ex-sex club, which metamorphosed overnight into a hangout for Barcelona's home-grown version of Generation X. It's big, with a mezzanine above the dance floor and red couches that, like the rest of the decor, date from the club's licentious origins in the late 1970s, but with no air-conditioning the atmosphere becomes a sweaty soup. **Panams**, at La Rambla 27, is a similar sex-club venue (which still has a live show) that hosts similar club nights.

Nitsa

Plaça Joan Llongueres 1-3 (458 62 50). Bus 6, 7, 33, 34, 63, 66, 67, 68. **Open** midnight-6am Thur-Sat. **Admission** 800-1,500ptas (incl one drink).

A dark, mid-sized basement that is home (and close to home) for Barcelona's uptown technoverts. The young e-driven crowd has fun on the large, revolving steel dance-floor, then goes upstairs to the lounge/bar to chill-out to salsa. Known for attracting name international DJs of the techno genre. *See also chapter* **Music: Roots, Rock & Jazz**).

Otto Zutz Club

C/Lincoln 15 (238 07 22). FGC Gràcia/bus 16, 17, 25, 27, 127. **Open** 11pm-6am Tue-Sat. **Admission** 1,500-2,000ptas. **Credit** AmEx, DC, MC, V.

A landmark among the city's nocturnal offerings, the Otto offers three levels of hard-edged but elegant warehouse decor, with galleries looking down onto the dance floor. Though in times past it was unquestionably the hottest club in town, it has lost its trendy cachet lately and is moving inexorably towards the mainstream. On an average weekend night, the place fills up with wannabes and people wearing expensive label clothing, and door policy tends to be snooty. Even so, on a night when a good DJ is visiting (keep an eye out for 'Pussy Power' parties, for instance), the spacious club is a great place to dance. There's also live music, usually jazz, most nights of the week (*see chapter* **Music: Rock, Roots & Jazz**).

Polyester

Estació de França, Avda Marquès de l'Argentera (no phone). Metro Barceloneta/bus 17, 39, 45, 57, 59, 64. **Open** 1.30am-any time Fri, Sat, nights before public holidays. **Admission** 1,000ptas, including one drink.

Flagship of the ultra-trendy VOTS club promoters group, Polyester has become *the* place to be for crowds of clubbies caught up in the intricacies of international techno-thump.

Outdoor fun-fests

Come warm weather, there's nothing the vast majority of Barcelona natives like more than to spend an evening in the open air, drinking cool drinks, strolling, dancing, chatting, or just plain observing one another. Conscious of their clients' desire to be outside, the city's bar and club owners have progressively opened up more and more *terrassas* (outdoor bars), primarily at the Maremagnum and the Port Olímpic, but also in the old city, around the Plaça Reial and the Rambla.

The culmination of the outdoor bar boom, however, are the *carpas*: gigantic summer bar-and-dance parties held under circus-like tents. Occupying areas as vast as 15,000 square metres, they're like huge night-time amusement parks. You pay an entrance fee (which includes a drink) and from there, you can visit any one of the 20 or so well-known clubs that have spaces set up within the area. The crowd is mainly young, energetic clubbers, although the events are big enough to draw a cross-section of the populace. Inside, you can dance to salsa, soul, funk, and the omnipresent techno. They usually function Thursday to Saturday, from June to August. *See also* **The Port Olímpic**.

Les Carpes de Cornellà

C/Tirso de Molina/Avda de la Fama, Fira de Cornellà area, Cornellà de Llobregat (322 03 26/fax 419 76 25). FGC Almeda. **Open** June-Aug 10pm-4.30am Thur-Sat; 9pm-3am Sun. **Admission** 1,000ptas (includes one drink).

On the outskirts of greater Barcelona in the unappreciated dormitory suburb of Cornellà de Llobregat, Les Carpes de Cornellà not only has its own posse of participating clubs – about 15 in total – but also lists Bunjee-jumping, live concerts, human fussball games and pocket bike race courses among its attractions. Should you need to sit for a while, it also has an outdoor cinema.

Firestiu

Plaça de l'Univers, Fira de Barcelona area, Palau 4 (322 03 26/fax 419 76 25). Metro Espanya/bus 9, 38, 51, 53, 65, 91. **Open** June-Aug 10pm-4.30am Thur-Sat. **Admission** 1,000ptas (includes one drink).

In one of the Trade Fair (*Fira*) areas near Plaça d'Espanya, Firestiu is probably the largest of the *carpas*. Participating clubs include Up and Down, La Boite, Antilla Cosmopolita (*see above* **Clubs**) and 15 or so others. And of course, there are other things to do – bunjee-jumping, mini-golf, live music and karaoke are all part of the programme.

Gran Terrassa d'America

Avda Muntanyans (no phone). Metro Espanya/bus 61. **Open** check press for details.

Not really a *carpa* but a summertime stage and open-air club behind Poble Espanyol on Montjuïc that opens up each year and is distinguished by the fact that only Latin American and African music is played – ideal music for a hot night. Live bands play till dawn.

Torre Melina

Camí de la Torre Melina & C/Oviedo, off Diagonal next to Hotel Juan Carlos I (414 63 62). Metro Zona Universitària/bus 7, 67, 68, 74, 75. **Open** June-early Oct 10pm-5am Mon-Sat. **Admission** 1,000ptas (includes one drink). **Credit** V.

Classiest of the *carpas*, in a very smart part of town by the Polo Club. Participating clubs include the Yabba Dabba and Jimmy'z (*see* **Clubs**), among others.

Hugely popular, too, with gays and anyone wanting to be right in at the heart of the night-time scene. Located in the huge basement of the Estació de França, this subterranean zoo consists of three spaces, a very large cement dance-floor (which, by 3am, is packed), a medium-sized cement dance-floor, and a smaller lounge area in which cement is not as visible. In the lounge, the orgiastic thumping gives way to lighter-weight disco hits from decades past, but you'll have trouble squeezing through the door. When you leave, don't forget to stop in at the station's serene café/bar (*see below* **Late & Early Eating**). *See also chapter* **Gay & Lesbian Barcelona**.

Salsa Latina

C/Bori i Fontesta 25 (209 88 24). Bus 6, 7, 33, 34, 64, 66, 67, 68. **Open** midnight-6am daily. **Admission** 1,500ptas men, 1,200ptas women (includes one drink).
The music is hot and jumping salsa – swinging hips and fance footwork are here in abundance – but the decor's far from exotic: apart from a few parrots painted on the walls and some cane chairs, there's been little attempt to create a Latin feel. The crowd are very mixed and markedly different from that of the more sophisticated nightspots round the corner in Carrer Beethoven.

La Tierra

C/Aribau 230 (200 35 53). FGC Provença/bus 6, 7, 15, 27, 33, 34, 58, 64, N8. **Open** 11pm-6am Fri, Sat. **Admission** usually 1,500ptas (includes one drink). **Credit** V.
Well-located just above Diagonal, La Tierra has a long history of attracting a varied (though largely uptown) clientèle.The low ceiling, dim lights and long curved bar help create the right atmosphere for unwinding, and the people get right into it on the good-sized dance floor, mainly to funk and popular dance tunes. There are also weekly live acts (*see chapter* **Music: Roots, Rock & Jazz**).

Up and Down

C/Numància 179 (280 29 22/). Metro Maria Cristina/bus 63, 67, 68. **Open** (restaurant) 10pm-3am Tue-Sat; (Up) midnight-5am Tue-Sat; (Down) 6pm-5am Fri, Sat. **Admission** (Up) 2,000ptas, (Down) 1,000ptas, both including one drink. **Credit** AmEx, DC, MC, V.
Barcelona's classic disco for wealthy socialites and their entourages, Up and Down consists of two levels, the 'Up' stairs, where an older crowd congregates for dinner and dancing to live bands; and the 'Down' stairs, where their well-dressed offspring dance to popular disco tunes. It used to be notably snooty and claim to be members-only, but now just *anyone* can get in.

Veneno

C/València 140 (454 07 07). Metro Hospital Clínic/bus 43, 44. **Open** midnight-4.30am Mon-Thur; midnight-5am Fri, Sat. **Admission** 700ptas (includes one drink).
Bigger than a music/dance bar but smaller than most clubs, Veneno is the perfect place to go dancing with a group of friends. Like a number of places invogue since Barcelona rediscovered its louche side, the place began life in the sex industry, as a brothel, and the well-worn but comfortable fittings (red velvet armchairs, dim lighting) help sustain its intimate atmosphere.

Yabba Dabba Club

C/Avenir 63 (989 50 69 25). FGC Muntaner/bus 14, 58, 64, N8. **Open** 11pm-3am Thur-Sat.
Small, pulsing with life, and filled with an active, unpretentious crowd, this place has a bizarre rather than an elegant design. Strange statues and enormous candelabra add a Gothic touch to the sort-of-ancient Egyptian decor, and the walls look like they could well use some paint. The tiny dance floor, ringed with coloured neon tubes, throbs to an enjoyable mix of dance music. Sweaty in the summer, but lots of atmosphere if you're in the right mood.

The legendary **Otto Zutz** *has been attracting an increasingly mixed crowd. See page 139.*

Warehouse parties

At the opposite end of the spectrum from the commercial uniformity of, say, Port Olímpic, you'll find Barcelona's colourful and vibrant warehouse parties. Extremely popular, but not always easy to track down, these events turn up in re-vamped industrial spaces around the city once or twice a month. No one group organises them, nor is there a set scene that defines them: it's more like a bunch of active-minded people all had the same idea at about the same time: open up an abandoned factory or warehouse, turn it into a place where people can create, and then, throw parties. These usually include some combination (or all) of original theatre pieces, dance, circus acts, art exhibitions, live music, home-cooked food, home-made films, DJs of all persuasions, all-night dancing... and so on.

A few of the warehouses – **El Submari**, for example – are more established than the others, and legally call themselves 'cultural associations', which gives them the right to hold gatherings with a nominal entry fee that makes every party-goer a member. Other places, such as **Les Nau** or **La Cine**, are squats, and have a less certain future. There's also a group like **La Colectiva del Caracol** (the snail collective), who don't work out of a fixed location, but stage parties nomad-fashion in different venues.

Obviously, you won't find listings of these parties in newspapers: you learn about them through word of mouth, fliers in shops and bars, and free papers such as *Mondo Sonoro* and *A Barna*. Or you can call them, when they have phones. Entry usually costs between 300 and 500ptas, and food and drink are cheap. They often start early, around 9pm, and go until 2am, if there are neighbours to worry about, or until the next morning, if there aren't. Attendances of 200 to 600 are usual. This sort of event obviously blends in to Barcelona's alternative arts scene (*see chapter* **Art Galleries**). Barcelona also has

a select but growing number of semi-legal, clandestine bars. They obviously can't be listed here, but one with a tad more visible existence is the **Marx Bar** near Plaça Reial. To find it, ask around the hipper bars on the plaça, but note that it's a fairly heavy underground scene, and not everyone's cup of hemlock.

La Cine
Via Laietana, corner of C/Manresa (no phone). Metro Jaume I/bus 17, 40, 45.
A recent squat in a large, abandoned cinema on the edge of La Ribera on Via Laietana. Weekly parties are held here with live bands and house/techno DJs.

La Colectiva del Caracol
No fixed address (451 76 45, ask for Wagner).
Pioneers of the underground warehouse party, La Colectiva stage events that make for a genuinely enriching night out: parties that are visual marathons might include painting and sculpture exhibitions, theatre, film, slide projections, second-hand clothing stands, food from around the world, and DJs who play everything from Brazilian funk to Arabic techno. There are a number of 'nests' in which you can catch up with La Colectiva, including **El Otro** (*see* **Bars**), **Mestizo** (*see chapter* **Music: Rock, Roots & Jazz**), and Etno Musica on C/Pintor Fortuny 33.

Les Nau
C/Alegre de Dalt 52 (no phone). Metro Joanic/bus 21, 39, N4.
A squat in a former textile factory in Gràcia, where a range of activities and workshops happen, including theatre, dance, music, art, photography, circus and tai-chi, and parties with performances, music and food; they go from around 9pm until 2am.

El Submari
C/Fernando Poo 22 (225 46 49/fax 319 26 37). Metro Poble Nou/bus 92.
This huge place in Poble Nou used to be a shoe factory; now, as a 'cultural association', it houses a warren of studios in which people sculpt, paint, make furniture, hold theatre workshops, make music and mount exhibitions. The parties at El Submari are eclectic and ultra-successful. In the future, they plan to hold 'Cool Sessions' with live acoustic music, slide shows, exhibitions, poetry readings, etcetera....

After-hours

On/Off
Camí de la Fuxarda, behind Poble Espanyol (423 96 40). Metro Espanya/bus 13, 61. **Open** 4am-8.30am, Fri, Sat. *July, August only* 5.30pm-8.30am Wed-Sun. **Admission** 1,000ptas, includes one drink.
It's Sunday morning and half the flock should be in church while the other half's in hedonistic revelry at On/Off, a large basilica-like after-hours club that opens up in one of the service buildings somewhere behind the Poble Espanyol. Yet another manifestation of the trendy VOTS group, On/Off doesn't really get going until about 6am, when the crowds start arriving (the sight of a couple of hundred zombied

night-owls queuing up to get in and blinking in the dawn light is worth the visit in itself. Once inside, the club is spacious and modern, with gigantic twin screens projecting swirling psychedelia that interfaces nicely with the blasting house/techno mix.

Roxi
C/Torrent de l'Olla 141 (no phone). Metro Fontana/bus 39. **Open** 7pm-2.30am Mon-Thur, Sun; 7pm-3am Fri, Sat.
In the heart of Gràcia, Roxi is a clean, mercifully dimly-lit after hours bar that opens (semi-officially) on weekend mornings for early-birds and up-all-nighters. There's a pool table in the back, a well-stocked bar, and very good *bocadillos* to replenish lost nutrients and alleviate the munchies; on Thursday nights, you can toss a coin to win a drink.

La Terraza

Camí de la Fuxarda, behind Poble Espanyol (423 12 85).
Metro Espanya/bus 13, 61. **Open** 11pm-9am Wed-Sun.
Admission 1,000ptas, including one drink.
Located in the semi-open air Sotaventa disco (entrance next
to the On/Off) this is a spacious, outdoor after-hours club
that functions in the warmer, more touristed months –
although be prepared for it to be under a different name, for
the management changes each season. The best time to
arrive is around 7am, to enjoy a dawn dance in the cool, elegant garden setting.

Cabaret & Dance Halls

Bodega Bohèmia

Lancaster 2 (302 50 61). Metro Drassanes/bus 14, 18,
38, 59, 91. **Open** 10.30pm-4am Mon-Thur; 5-8.30pm,
10.30pm-4am, Fri-Sun. **Admission** free, but with one
compulsory drink (min 1,000ptas).
An experience lifted from a David Lynch film, the Bodega
Bohèmia is stranger than fiction. To a tiny audience, or even
to nobody at all, Catalan cabaret stars of yesteryear run
through their repertoire, accompanied by an out-of-tune
piano. At times it can be heartbreaking, but rather than let
it affect you, sit back and enjoy what's good, laugh with the
worst, and talk during the stand-up comics.

El Cangrejo

C/Monserrat 9 (301 85 75). Metro Drassanes/bus 14, 18,
38, 59, N4, N6. **Open** 7pm-3am Mon-Wed; 11pm-3am
Thur; 11pm-3.30am Fri, Sat.
Deep in the heart of the *Barrio Chino*, El Cangrejo (The Crab)
is pure sleaze, a leftover from the neighbourhood's days of
fame as a district of forbidden fruits. People come here to be
entertained by an over-the-top troupe of drag queens doing
Liza Minelli and melodramatic Spanish numbers, but the
ageing (like, 70-year-old) camp barmen are as strange as anything you see on the small stage. The clientèle runs from local
devotees who know all the performers to tourists trying out
the Barrio Chino experience. Andaluz tiling, yards of glit-
tering tin-foil and seafood imagery make up the décor, and
an old woman sits in silence by the door and may be the one
who keeps track of the number of drinks you have; take note,
because, while there's no cover charge, drink prices are hefty.

Cibeles

C/Corsega 36 (457 38 77). Metro Diagonal/bus 6, 15,
20, 21, 33, 34, 45, 47. **Open** 11.30pm-5am Thur, Fri; 6-
9.30pm, 11.30pm-5am, Sat; 6-9.30pm Sun. **Admission**
(includes one drink) *Thur* 1,000ptas (women), 1,200ptas
(men); *Fri* 1,500ptas; *Sat afternoon, Sun* 800ptas
(women), 900ptas (men); *Sat night* 1,500ptas.
Built in the 1940s and revamped in the '80s, Cibeles is a large
galleried dance-hall similar to La Paloma (*see above*), but
without the Rococo decoration. It's usually packed with a
good-humoured crowd that gets younger as the evening goes
on, and the resident orchestra play everything from foxtrots
to cha-cha-cha, mambo and rock'n'roll. With bars both
upstairs and in the main hall, and soft bench seats round the
gallery that are ideal for romantic *tête-à-têtes*, the mood
becomes infectious and it's hard not to have a good time.

El Molino

Vila i Vila 99 (441 63 83/329 88 54). Metro Paral.lel/bus
20, 36, 57, 64, 91, N4, N6. **Performances** 6pm, 11pm
Tue-Fri; 6pm, 10.30pm, 1.15am Sat; 6pm Sun.
Admission 1,500ptas-3,500ptas. **Credit** MC, V.
An institution in Barcelona, the brightly-lit Molino (wind-
mill) stages bawdy revues that can make for an entertaining
night out, even if you don't understand a word of Spanish.
The humour is broad and lewd, beyond-Benny Hill-style.
Popular with the hen parties that frequent the upper boxes
are the bored-looking but outrageously camp dancers who

come out at regular intervals to shake a leg. Downstairs, the
seats are hard, and if you're anywhere near the aisle you
might be picked out by the comedians for some audience participation. During the interval, photos are taken of everyone,
and at the end you're offered the chance to buy an El Molino
plate with your face on it.

La Paloma

C/Tigre 27 (301 68 97). Metro Universitat/bus 24, 41,
55, 64, 91, N4. **Open** 6-9.30pm, 11.30pm-5am, Thur-Sat;
6-9.30pm Sun, evenings before public holidays.
Admission *Thur, Fri afternoons* 300ptas (women),
500ptas (men); *Sat afternoon, Sun* 500ptas (women),
600ptas (men); *Sat night* 800ptas.
An enormously wide mix of people frequents this magnificent 1902 dance hall, where trendy clubbers mix it up with
pensioners, many of them seriously practised dancers who
might have been coming here for years. The band gives you
a chance to try anything from cha-cha to jive, passing
through *tango, paso doble* and even flamenco-ish *Sevillanas*.
Anyone who likes kitsch will fall in love with the exuberant
galleried interior, and the atmosphere virtually ensures a hot
night out. Go in a group, grab a table and order a bottle of
cava to get things going.

Late & Early Eating

Bar-Kiosko Pinocho

Stand 67-68, Mercat de la Boqueria (317 17 31). Metro
Liceu/bus 14, 18, 38, 59, 64, 91, N4, N6, N9. **Open**
6.30am-3/4pm Mon-Sat.
A bar-stall inside the Boqueria market that's a popular
breakfast spot for night-birds on their way home, with anything from a coffee to Catalan home-cooking. During the day,
it's also good for lunch, if not as cheap as it looks.

Café Arnau

Avda Paral.lel 62 (329 99 24). Metro Paral.lel/bus 36,
57, 64, 91, N4, N6. **Open** 10am-3am Mon, Tue, Thur-
Sun.
Right beside the Teatro Arnau and close to many bars and
clubs, this café-restaurant stays open all night, every night,
closing for just a few hours. You can order from a fairly standard Spanish menu, or a selection of pastries. After the 'official' closing time, don't be put off by the closed metal
shutters; you get in by ringing the bell beside the metal door.

Churreria Aguilar

Escorial 1 (219 35 53). Metro Joanic/bus 21, 39, 55.
Open 11am-3pm, 4-10pm Mon-Thur, Sun; 11am-8am Fri,
Sat, days before bank holidays.
A small *churreria* in Gràcia that caters for the late-night
crowd. Snacks and hot chocolate are served to revellers doing
the rounds. Opening times are more than usually erratic.

Granja de Gavà

C/Joaquin Costa 37 (317 58 83). Metro Universitat/bus
24, 41, 55, 64, 91, N4, N6. **Open** *Sept-June* 8am-8pm
Mon-Thur; *July, Aug* 8am-8pm, Sun. A clean, well-run, Modernist *granja* (milk bar) in the old city;
here, you can get hot chocolate, fruit juices, sandwiches and,
of course, coffee, from very early on weekends.

Midnight Express

Estació de França, Avda Marqués de l'Argentera (310 14
78). Metro Barceloneta/bus 17, 39, 45, 57, 59, 64. **Open**
6.45am-9pm Mon-Fri; 7am-9pm Sat, Sun.
The grand and early-opening bar in the Estació de França
is a great breakfast favourite for night revellers (especially,
naturally, with those turning out of **Polyester** down below).
It offers good pastries and sandwiches amid elegant, well-
restored neo-Classical décor that comfortably allows your
eyes and ears to regain their bearings.

Shopping & Services

The beer from Spain

Shopping

From mega-malls to markets, elegant designer outlets to quirky old speciality shops - Barcelona has an eclectic retail style that's all its own.

Visit the highly original **Insòlit**, *for one-off works by Juma and Mun.*

Tradition and innovation are the two elements that best characterise Barcelona's shopping scene. Seemingly contradictory, these characteristics so far coexist harmoniously in the city – which may be the secret of its success. Barcelona now has only one real department store, the **Corte Inglés**. The major retail boom of the past few years has been in large mixed spaces, first fashion malls or *galeries*, such as the **Bulevard Rosa**, and, then, most recently, in the arrival of full-scale, giant shopping malls.

The many small, individual, often downright quirky shops that are one of the glories of Barcelona have been struggling on for years – a capacity for survival is one of their distinct characteristics –, but have, thus far at least, also managed to coexist alongside this new huge expansion in retail space. The largest concentration of traditional shops, particularly specialists in such things as feathers, cigars or rope, are in the old city. Most

prestige fashion stores are to be found on Passeig de Gràcia, Rambla Catalunya and around Diagonal and Plaça Francesc Macià, although there are some trendy fashion outlets in the old city as well, especially around Portaferrisa.

Most shops close in the afternoon from about 1.30pm to 4.30pm, although 'large spaces' are allowed to stay open through the day, and on some Sundays (*see chapter* **Essential Information**). On Saturdays, many shops open only in the morning; on public holidays, practically everything is closed. The Ajuntament has also announced a plan for late closing one day a week in the area described as the 'Shopping Line', which starts at the bottom of the Rambla in Maremagnum and includes the Rambla, Passeig de Gràcia, Rambla Catalunya and Avda Diagonal as far as the Corte Inglés. Shops in this 'line' will remain open at midday and close at 10pm on Thursdays.

Out-of-hours

Drugstore David and **Vip's** are both multi-purpose stores offering a variety of things you might need late at night or on Sundays, with supermarkets, bookstores, newsstands, clothing shops and gift outlets, as well as restaurants and cafés.

Depaso
C/Muntaner 14 (454 58 46) Metro Universitat/bus all routes to Plaça Universitat. **Open** 6am-2.30am Mon-Thur; 6am-3am Fri-Sun. **Credit** EC, MC, V.
A general stores for non-sleepers or those in dire straits. Browse through records and newspapers; do the week's food shopping; pick up gifts for friends.... There are several smaller branches dotted around the city, attached to petrol stations.

Drugstore David
C/Tuset 19-21 (200 47 30). FCG Gràcia/bus 6, 7, 15, 16, 17, 27, 33, 34, 58,64. **Open** 7.30am-3am Mon-Sat; 7.30am-midnight Sun. **Credit** AmEx, DC, MC, V.

This pioneer in out-of-hour stores has been more than holding its own since the early 1970s. It incorporates a tobacconist, bookshop, restaurant, foodstore, delicatessen and wine shop.

7-11
Plaça Urquinaona (318 88 63). Metro Urquinaona/bus all routes to Plaça Urquinaona. **Open** 7am-3am daily. **Credit** MC, V.
This familiar international franchise currently has around 50 branches around Barcelona, many of them at petrol stations. This branch is the most central. Note that there are occasional problems with their link with MasterCard.

Vip's
Rambla de Catalunya 7-9 (317 48 05). Metro Catalunya/bus all routes to Plaça.Catalunya. **Open** 8am-2am Mon-Thur; 8am-3am Fri; 9am-3am Sat-Sun. **Credit** AmEx, DC, $TC, V, $.
Vip's house a restaurant, a supermarket, a fairly good bookshop, including some books in English, a newsstand and a toy-gift section.
Branch: C/Comte de Borrell 308.

Sales & Tax refunds
Sales run from the second week in January to the end of February, and during July and August. VAT (IVA) depends on the classification of the product – 7% on food, 16% on items classified as luxury – but note that in many larger stores non-European residents can request a Tax-Free cheque on purchases of more than 15,000ptas, which can be cashed at the airport to reclaim VAT charges. Stores within the scheme have a 'Tax-Free' sticker by their doors.

One-Stop

El Corte Inglés
Plaça Catalunya 14 (302 12 12). Metro Catalunya/bus all routes to Plaça Catalunya. **Open** 10am-9.30pm Mon-Sat. **Credit** AmEx, DC, MC, V.
The bulldozer of retailing in the whole of Spain, with a department-store monopoly since it swallowed up its only competitor, Galerias Preciados, in 1995. Incredibly, the former Galerias store in Portal de l'Angel has to date just been closed up and left to gather dust, and it's not certain if it will reopen as a general department store (considering it's only a stone's throw from the main Plaça Catalunya Corte Inglés) or if departments will be split between the two stores. Not only does El Corte Inglés provide all the goods you might expect to find in a department store, but you can also have keys cut, shoes re-heeled, hair and beauty treatments carried out and meals or snacks in the rooftop café. The air-conditioning also offers respite from a hot August day. Should there be anything you can't find in the main stores (and you have a car), the company also has a giant hypermarket, **Hipercor**, in Sagrera on the north side of the city.
Branches: Avda Diagonal 617-619 (419 28 28); Avda Diagonal 471-473 (419 20 20); **Hipercor** Avda Meridiana 350-358 (346 38 11).

*The striking **Ici et Là**. See page 149.*

Antiques

The streets around C/de la Palla, in the Barri Gòtic, are crowded with small antique shops. Their stock ranges from seventeenth-century furniture and religious artefacts to collections of old electrical goods and specialist books. Antiques are also found around C/Consell de Cent and C/Dos de Maig in the Eixample, and there are some less expensive shops near **Els Encants** (*see* **Markets**).

L'Arca de l'Àvia
C/Banys Nous 20 (302 15 98). Metro Liceu/bus 14, 18, 38, 59, 91. **Open** 10.30am-2pm, 5-8pm, Mon-Fri. **Credit** AmEx, DC, EC, MC, TC, V.
The antique cottons, linens and silks at this shop are always beautifully displayed. Unfortunately, they're not cheap, but the patchwork eiderdowns, dresses (from 20,000ptas) and antique beaded bags (from 18,000ptas) are lovely to look at.

Bulevard dels Antiquaris
Passeig de Gràcia 55 (215 44 99). Metro Passeig de Gràcia/bus all routes to Passeig de Gràcia. **Open** 9.30am-1.30pm, 4.30-8.30pm, Sept-May, Mon-Sat; *early June-early Sept,* Mon-Fri.
Beside **Bulevard Rosa** (*see* **Fashion**), this complex houses 73 antique shops under one roof, from fine paintings to ivory, religious artefacts and porcelain dolls. In **Turn of the Century**, you can find miniature musical instruments from the '30s, old jewellery and furniture for dolls' houses.

Born Subastas
C/Bonaire 5 (268 34 55) Metro Barceloneta, Jaume I/bus 14, 16, 17, 39, 45, 51, 64. **Open** 10am-2pm, 5-8pm, Mon-Sat; 11am-2pm Sun. **Credit** AmEx, MC, V.
Near the Born, this auction house (with antiques sales every other week) is a great place to browse. There's a bit of everything, and prices are reasonable. English is spoken.

Galuchat

C/València 261 (487 58 55). Metro Passeig de Gràcia/bus all routes to Passeig de Gràcia. **Open** 11am-2.30pm, 5-9pm, Mon-Sat. **Credit** AmEx, DC, MC, V.

A shop after Pedro Almodóvar's own heart, filled with kitsch furniture and curiosities. Prices can vary from 800ptas for a '40s metal-and-glass cup, to 145,000ptas for a '50s armchair.

Bookshops

General

Crisol

C/Consell de Cent 341 (215 31 21). Metro Passeig de Gràcia/bus 22, 24, 28, N4, N6. **Open** 10am-10pm Mon-Sat. **Credit** AmEx, DC, MC, V.

A bookshop with a bit of everything from gifts to records, along with a book-finding service, Crisol has well-stocked English-language, foreign press and record sections, too, and the basement photography department has high-standard cameras and equipment. Sections of the Rambla Catalunya branch, including the newsstand, stay open till 1am.
Branch: Rambla Catalunya 81 (215 27 20).

Laie Llibreria Café

C/Pau Claris 85 (302 73 10). Metro Urquinaona/bus all routes to Plaça Urquinaona. **Open** *bookshop* 10am-9pm Mon-Sat; *café* 9am-1am Mon-Sat. **Credit** AmEx, DC, MC,V.

An international, arts-based bookshop-café in which the stock is organised by theme rather than language, the staff are extremely helpful, and the selection of books is imaginative. Upstairs is the splendid and relaxing café/restaurant. *See chapters* **Cafés & Bars** *and* **Women's Barcelona**.

Llibreria Francesa

Passeig de Gràcia 91 (215 14 17). Metro Diagonal/bus 7, 16, 17, 22, 24, 28, N4, N6. **Open** 9.30am-2.30pm, 4-8.30pm, Mon-Fri; 9.30am-2pm, 5-8.30pm, Sat. **Credit** AmEx, MC, V.

A long-established bookshop with Catalan, Spanish, French and English books and a wide selection of travel books.

Comics Shops

Continuarà

Via Laietana 29 (310 43 52). Metro Jaume I/bus 17, 19, 40, 45. **Open** 10.30am-9pm Mon-Sat. **Credit** AmEx, MC, V.

Modern comics, postcards and gimmicky presents. Second-hand comics are on sale in the basement, which has its own opening hours: 10.30am-3pm and 4.30-9pm.

Norma Comics

Passeig de Sant Joan 9 (245 45 26). Metro Arc de Triomf/bus 19, 39, 40, 41, 42, 55, 141. **Open** 10.30am-2pm, Mon, Tue, Thur-Sat; 5-8.30pm Wed. **Credit** AmEx, MC, V.

The largest comic shop in Barcelona, with one floor dedicated to European and American comics, another for Japanese Manga and role-playing games, and special sections for Star Wars and Star Trek, model kits, etcetera. Next door, Norma has opened **Tintin Barcelona**, geared exclusively to the boy and related paraphernalia. Norma also runs an art gallery, showing original drawings of Prince Valiant by Harold Foster and selling prints.

English-Language Bookshops

BCN Books

C/Aragó 277 (487 31 23). Metro Passeig de Gràcia/bus all routes to Passeig de Gràcia. **Open** Sept-May 9am-2pm,

4-8pm, Mon-Fri; 10am-2pm Sat; *June-Sept* 9am-2pm, 4-8pm, Mon-Fri. **Credit** AmEx, V.

Everything from computer instruction books and teaching materials to the latest best-sellers. There is also a large selection of language dictionaries and reference books.

Come In

C/Provença 203 (453 12 04). Metro Hospital Clínic, FGC Provença/bus 14, 21, 59. **Open** 9.30am-2pm, 4.30-8pm, Mon-Sat. Closed Aug. **Credit** MC, V.

Barcelona's largest English bookshop, with a selection that includes teaching books and general material, from Chaucer to Joan Collins. Check the noticeboard if you're looking for Spanish or Catalan classes, or private English classes.

English Bookshop

C/Entença 63 (425 44 66) Bus 9, 27, 41, 50, 56, 109, 127. **Open** 9am-1.30pm, 4-8pm, Mon-Fri; 10am-1.30pm Sat; *July, Aug* 9am-1.30pm, 4-8pm, Mon-Fri. **Credit** V.

A wide variety of themes and titles, and, as with most foreign language selections, educational aids for teacher and student. However, if all you want is a book for beach or train, then the paperback section should see you through.

Second-Hand & Rare Books

Angel Batlle

C/Palla 23 (301 58 84). Metro Liceu/bus 14, 18, 38, 59, 91. **Open** 9am-1.30pm, 4-7.30pm, Mon-Fri. **No credit cards.**

Despite the second-hand paperbacks in the window, this is a time-honoured antiquarian bookshop. Inside, as well as books, there's an enormous and diverse collection of prints: English foxhunting scenes, nineteenth-century fashion plates, botanical studies of Catalan wildlife, colourful old maps, and much more. Prints cost from 1,500ptas.

Travel Specialists

Altaïr

C/Balmes 69-71 (454 29 66). Metro Passeig de Gràcia, FGC Provença/bus 7, 16, 17, 20, 21, 43. **Open** 10am-1.30pm, 4-8pm, Mon-Sat. **Credit** AmEx, DC, MC, V.

A world travel bookstore that also publishes an excellent travel magazine of the same name, in Spanish. Books are classified by country-or region rather than by language. There's an excellent selection on Catalonia and Spain, as well as sections on anthropology, photography, world music, guide-books, dictionaries and maps.

Llibreria Quera

C/Petritxol 2 (318 07 43). Metro Liceu/bus 14, 18, 38, 59, 91. **Open** 9.30am-1.30pm, 4.30-8pm, Mon-Sat. **No credit cards.**

For anyone planning a trip to the Pyrenees or the Catalan countryside, this is the ideal place to find walking maps of every part of the country. Staff also have information on mountaineering and all kinds of outward-bound adventures.

Children

Clothes

Generally, children's clothes are expensive in Spain. Some adult chains, such as **Zara** (*see* **Fashion**), also have imaginative children's lines.

Cache Cache

Passeig de Gràcia 62 (215 40 07). Metro Passeig. de Gràcia/Bus 7, 16, 17, 22, 24, 28. **Open** 10am-8.30pm Mon-Sat. **Credit** V.

*There are stacks of books and a whole heap of prints at **Angel Batlle**.*

Cache Cache design and make everyday, casual clothing in natural fibres – mostly cotton – for children aged from nought to 12. They have 20 shops throughout Barcelona.

Prénatal
Gran Via de les Corts Catalanes 611 (302 05 25). Metro Passeig de Gràcia/bus 7, 16, 17, 22, 24, 50, 54, 56. **Open** 10am-8pm Mon-Sat. **Credit** AmEx, DC, MC, V.
French-owned chain with everything from clothes for the pregnant mum to clothes for kids up to about eight years old. Prams and pushchairs, cots, feeding bottles and toys are sold, too, and all are made from quality materials. There are several branches around Barcelona, including a Barri Gòtic one in **Galeries Maldà**, off Plaça del Pi (302 10 95).

Toys

Joguines Monforte
Plaça Sant Josep Oriol 3 (318 22 85). Metro Liceu/bus 14, 18, 38, 59, 91. **Open** 9.30am-1.30pm, 4-8pm, Mon-Sat. **Credit** AmEx, DC, MC, V.
A traditional toy shop that's one of the oldest in Barcelona. The owner, who took over from her father, tells how she once got rid of 'all those old, dusty toys in the back room', only to find them some time later in nearby antique shops at premium prices.

Xalar
Baixada de la Llibreteria 4 (315 04 58). Metro Jaume I/bus 17, 40, 45. **Open** 10am-2pm, 4.30-8.30pm, Mon-Sat. **Credit** AmEx, DC, MC, V.
Xalar holds its own against the electronic invasion in the toy world by specialising in traditional wooden and educational toys, as well as dolls' houses and miniatures. The owner loves toys, and it shows.

Cosmetics & Perfumes

Catalans spend a bundle on cosmetics, facial treatments and hand care. *Perfumeries* are to be found on just about every street in Barcelona, and, of course, in the **Corte Inglés**.

Perfumeria Anna de Lis
Rambla Catalunya 61 (487 61 13). Metro Passeig de Gràcia/bus 7, 16, 17, 22, 24, 28. **Open** 9.30am-8pm Mon-Fri, 10am-2pm Sat. **Credit** AmEx, DC, MC, V.
A traditional cosmetics shop that stocks well-known brands of creams and potions, numerous perfumes, and make-up.
Branch: C/Aribau 54 (454 19 00).

Regia
Passeig de Gràcia 39 (216 01 21). Metro Passseig de Gràcia/bus 7, 16, 17, 22, 24, 28. **Open** 10am-8pm Mon-Sat. **Credit** AmEx, DC, EC, JCB, MC, TC, V.
Since 1928, Regia has been serving a very select Barcelona clientèle at its main shop and beauty salon. They stock over 60 types of scent alone, plus all the best beauty potions. It's a world apart, in which every detail is attended to. For those interested in nostalgic nose trips, there's also the **Museu del Perfum** at the rear of the shop (*see chapter* **Museums**).

Design & Household

Aspectos
C/Rec 28. (319 52 85). Metro Jaume I/bus 14, 19, 39, 51. **Open** 4.30-8pm Mon; 10.30am-2pm, 4.30-8pm, Tue-Fri; 10.30am-2pm Sat. Closed Aug. **Credit** V.
Opened in 1991 by Camilla Hamm, this shop houses the work of well-known designers such as Mendini, Grawunder, Kima,

Garouste-Bonetti, Carolyne Quartermain, Lowenstein, Forasetti and Eckhart, as well as serving as a showcase for young unknowns. It also runs periodic exhibitions of design work.

BD Ediciones de Diseño S.A.
C/Mallorca 291 (458 69 09). Metro Passeig de Gràcia/bus 20, 21, 39, 43, 44, 45, 47. **Open** 10am-2pm, 4-8pm, Mon-Fri; 10am-2pm, 4.30-8pm, Sat. **Credit** AmEx, DC, MC, V.
BD stocks an impressive array of (reproduction) furniture by design gurus such as Mackintosh and Gaudí, as well as more contemporary designers – Ricard Bofill, Mariscal, Oscar Tusquets and the Memphis group. Exclusive designs by Alessi, Wittman, Celcotti and Owo are also on display in this magnificent modernist house, the Casa Thomas, by Domènech i Montaner. Well worth wandering round for inspiration, even if you can't afford so much as a chairleg.

Dos i Una
C/Rosselló 275 (217 70 32). Metro Diagonal/bus 7, 16, 17, 22, 24, 28. **Open** 10.30am-2pm, 4.30-8pm, Mon-Fri; 10.30am-2pm, 5-8pm, Sat. **Credit** AmEx, DC, JCB, MC, V.
The first design shop to open in Barcelona and an early

patron of Mariscal, Dos i Una has now grown up (it'll be 20 in 1997) and turned into a high-class gift shop, peddling design crockery, embroidered cacti, wacky lamps and accessories, plus postcards, earrings, shirts and T-shirts.

Dou Deu
C/Doctor Dou 10 (301 29 40). Metro Catalunya/bus all routes to Plaça Catalunya. **Open** 10am-2pm, 4.30-8.30pm, Tue-Sat. Closed Aug. **Credit** AmEx, DC, MC, V.
Wonderful shop, associated with the **Galeria Carles Poy** next door (*see chapter* **Art Galleries**), that sells only individual, artist-made objects – but still usable, from T-shirts to watches and glassware, and at surprisingly reasonable prices. The stable of artists includes both very familiar names such as Mariscal and Toni Miró and the less exposed such as Imma Jansana and Nina Pawlowsky.

Ici et Là
Plaça Santa Maria del Mar 2 (268 11 67). Metro Jaume I/bus 17, 40, 45. **Open** noon-2.30pm, 4-8.30pm, Mon; 10.30am-2.30pm, 4-8.30pm, Tue-Sat. **Credit** MC, V.
The brainchild of three women – two French, one Spanish – who believe that original furniture and accessories shouldn't be limited to the well-heeled. They offer a range of

All kinds of everything

Until recently, shops in Barcelona kept themselves to one trade, and sought to know it well.

Almacenes del Pilar
C/Boqueria 43 (317 79 84). Metro Liceu/bus 14, 18, 38, 59, 91. **Open** 10am-1.30pm, 4.30-8pm, Mon-Sat. **Credit** AmEx, MC, V.
This quaint old shop exhibits *Mantones de Manila* (fringed, embroidered silk shawls) in its window, and inside there are more shawls, *mantillas* and a huge selection of the materials used in the traditional costumes of all the regions of Spain. Note the fantastic brocades used in the Valencian outfits.

Casa Calicó
Plaça de les Olles 9 (319 18 18). Metro Barceloneta/bus 14, 16, 17, 45, 51. **Open** 9.30am-1.30pm, 4.30-7.30pm, Mon-Fri; 9am-2pm Sat. **Credit** DC, V.
All types of lines, nets, hooks and bait are available. Fishing nets and baskets can be repaired here, too

Casa Moreli
C/Banys Nous 13 (no phone). Metro Liceu/bus 14, 18, 38, 59, 91. **Open** 5.30-8pm Mon-Fri. Closed Aug. **No credit cards.**
A shop devoted to feathers. They are wrapped carefully in tissue paper and stored in white cardboard boxes stacked up high around the room. There are some rather dusty but beautifully-made feather masks in the window; inside, old ladies try to flog their mangy goose feathers to Sra Moreli.

Cereria Subirà
Baixada de Llibreteria 7 (315 26 06). Metro Jaume I/bus 17, 40, 45. **Open** 9am-1.30pm, 4-7.30pm, Mon-Fri; 9am-1.30pm Sat. **Credit** AmEx, JCB, MC, V.
The oldest shop in Barcelona, opened in 1761 as a ladies' fashion store, and now a candle shop. Apart from the extraordinary range of candles, it's worth a visit for the original décor alone, with steps swirling down from the gallery, and two black maidens holding up torch-shaped lights at the foot of the stairs.

Feltres Serra
C/Argenteria 78 (319 39 00). Metro Jaume I/bus 17, 40, 45. **Open** 9am-1.30pm, 4-8pm, Mon-Fri. Closed Aug. **Credit** MC, V.
A shop that's been selling nothing but felt since 1795. On the ground floor there are over 120 different shades of elegantly displayed material, which can be bought in small squares for school projects, or by the metre for card tables.

El Ingenio
C/Rauric 6 (317 71 38). Metro Liceu/bus 14, 18, 38, 59, 91. **Open** 10am-1.30pm, 4.15-8pm, Mon-Fri; 10am-1pm Sat. **Credit** AmEx, MC, V.
Ingenio lives up to its name with a truly ingenious collection of paper, cardboard, feather and papier mâché masks and party accessories. There are some wonderful fancy-dress outfits, carnival clothes, poppers, decorations, puppets, tricks and jokes to choose from, and stick-on Dalí moustaches are 200ptas each, and can be twisted into exactly the right shape.

Solingen Paris-Barcelona (Ganiveteria Roca S.A.)
Plaça del Pi 3 (302 12 41 & 412 53 49). Metro Liceu/bus 14, 18, 38, 59, 91. **Open** 9.45am-1.30pm, 4.15-8pm, Mon-Fri; 10am-2pm, 5-8pm Sat; Closed 15-20 days Aug. **Credit** AmEx, DC, MC, V.
Every cutting instrument under the sun is available here. Knives and scissors of all shapes and sizes, including every kind of camping knife, are wrapped in green felt and brought forth for inspection by sombre salesmen. Seriously wierd.

Sombrereria Obach
C/Call 2 (318 40 94). Metro Liceu/bus 14, 18, 38, 59, 91. **Open** 9.30am-1.30pm, 4-8pm, Mon-Sat. **Credit** MC, V.
Hat's of all varieties are for sale in Sr Obach's traditional establishment, from nylon pom-poms through top-quality felt berets to formal headgear for men and women.

contemporary creations and exotic craftwork (which they find themselves in world markets, avoiding middle-men), at deliberately-reasonable prices. It's full of wacky and interesting ethnic objects, in line with their multicultural philosophy.

Insòlit

Avda Diagonal 353 (207 49 19). Metro Verdaguer/bus 6, 15, 33, 34. **Open** 10am-2pm, 4.30-8pm, Mon-Sat. **Credit** AmEx, DC, MC, V.

One of the few shops of its kind to stock entirely original work, and owners Juma and Mun's witty, innovative designs are sold only through this outlet (except for some trays made for Axis in Paris). For 20,000ptas, you can pick up a star-shaped table in wood and iron, and there is also tableware, wonderfully bizarre lamps and colourful kitsch furniture. There are a few examples of other people's work, too.

Pilma

Avda Diagonal 403 (416 13 99). Metro Diagonal/bus 6, 7, 15, 16, 17, 27, 33, 34, 127. **Open** 10am-2pm, 4.30-8.30pm, Mon-Sat. **Credit** AmEx, DC, MC, V.

Furniture and household accessories by a number of top Spanish and international designers. The furniture is on the pricey side, but your budget may stretch to fun articles such as a colourful acrylic dinner set (the glasses cost 300 ptas; water jugs 950ptas).

Branch: C/València 1 (226 06 76).

Vinçon

Passeig de Gràcia 96 (215 60 50). Metro Diagonal/bus 7, 16, 17, 22, 24, 28. **Open** 10am-2pm, 4.30-8.30pm, Mon-Sat. **Credit** AmEx, JCB, V.

Barcelona's most renowned design palace, with everything for the home and all kinds of smaller accessories. If you find the shop's stock of superbly extravagant furniture a tad expensive, browse through the lighting, kitchen, bathroom and fabric departments for something more affordable. It often feels, though, that as Vinçon has got bigger and bigger the stock has become less innovative. In December, the shop becomes host to the annual **Hipermerc'art**, a supermarket-style 'art shop' selling paintings en masse: here, astute buyers can pick up original works by young artists for as little as 9,000ptas a pop. Art and architecture buffs will also be tickled to know that Vinçon's upper floor is the former apartment of Santiago Rusiñol, one of the greatest *Modernista* artists.

The venerable **Cereria Subirà**.

Designers

Another very fashionable design store is **Armand Basi**, in **Maremagnum** (*see* **Mega-malls**).

Adolfo Domínguez

Passeig de Gràcia 32 (487 36 87). Metro Passeig de Gràcia/bus 7, 16, 17, 22, 24, 28. **Open** 10am-8pm Mon-Sat. **Credit** AmEx, DC, MC, V.

One of the foremost figures in Spanish fashion, Adolfo Dominguez, from Galicia in northwest Spain, deserves his reputation as a designer of well-made, timeless clothes. A Dominguez suit (for men or women) will set you back around 80,000ptas. The large shop is split into two levels, one for each sex.

Branches: Passeig de Gràcia 89 (215 13 39); Diagonal 490 (416 17 16); C/Pau Casals 5 (414 11 77).

Groc

Rambla Catalunya 100 (215 01 80). Metro Diagonal, FGC Provença/bus 7, 16, 17, 20, 21, 43, 44. **Open** 10am-2pm, 4.30-8.30pm, Mon-Sat. **Credit** AmEx, DC, JCB, MC, V.

The place to find men's and women's clothing by the best

Mega-malls

Barcelona was slow to catch on to the everything-under-one-roof concept – even though the drive to create more fashion malls (*see* **Fashion**) has gone on unabated since 1980 – but has certainly caught up since 1992 with, characteristically, some of the largest malls you'll see, at either end of the Diagonal. Still more giant *centres comercials* are in the pipeline, in the Vila Olímpica and elsewhere. What long-term effect this will have on shopping in Barcelona is another question.

Barcelona Glòries

Avda Diagonal 280 (486 04 04). Metro Glòries/bus 56, 92, N2. **Open** 10am-10pm Mon-Sat.

The largest shopping centre in Spain, a drive-in mall with over 200 shops, including international names such as C&A and Dr Marten's, and a positively Californian look to it. Located by the Plaça de les Glòries, near **Els Encants** flea market (*see* **Markets**), built around an open-air plaza with bars and restaurants, and also has a multiplex cinema (not VO). The mall has several good coffee shops, as well as fine stores specialising in Spanish ham – *jamón serrano* or *jamón ibérico*. For cut-price produce and every other food, there's also the **Continente** hypermarket.

L'Illa

Avda Diagonal 545-557 (444 00 00). Metro Maria Cristina/bus 6, 7, 33, 34, 63, 66, 67, 68. **Open** 9am-9.30pm Mon-Sat.

Thanks to its location in the business centre, on the upper Diagonal, L'Illa attracts an up-market clientèle. It has many trendy-ish fashion shops, and a **Caprabo** supermarket, as well as the only **Marks & Spencers** in Barcelona to date. The novelty of M&S has created quite a stir, and there are now plans to open a larger branch in Plaça Catalunya. Don't miss the **Decathlon** sportswear specialists.

Maremagnum

Moll d'Espanya (225 81 00). Metro Barceloneta/bus 14, 17, 36, 39, 40, 45, 57, 59, 64. **Open** 11am 11pm daily.

Maremagnum, an all-round leisure complex, with restaurants, games, cinemas and night clubs, as much as a shopping mall, is unique because of its port of Barcelona locale, because of its having been designed by two of the lead-architects of Barcelona, Viaplana and Piñon, and because the main access to it is a bridge linking it with the Rambla. The giant mirror-wall above the main entrance makes for a spectacular visual effect. You can get a whiff of sea air while browsing in designer gift shop **D-Barcelona**, or in **Corbata**, which only sells ties, and one of Barcelona's

Visit **Maremagnum** by-the-sea.

most in-vogue current designers, **Armand Basi**, has an outlet here for his youth-oriented leisurewear. **Colomer** make beautiful silver jewellery, and football fans will get a kick out of **La Botiga del Barça**, with every possible kind of football-related merchandise.

Sogo Barcelona-Vila Olímpica

C/Marina 19-21 (221 32 21). Metro Ciutadella-Vila Olímpica/bus 41, 45, 59, 71. **Open** 11.30am-8pm Mon-Fri; 11.30am-9pm Sat.

The Japanese Sogo organisation runs this high-quality centre next to the **Port Olímpic**, with their own store as well as other prestige boutiques including Mikimoto, Sonia Rykiel, Genny Way, Givenchy, Céline and Christian Dior. In their 'souvenir' section, you'll find items with price tags of over 1,000,000ptas, but browsing is free....

known Catalan designer, Toni Miró. His clothes are designed with flair and always beautifully made in irresistible materials. Shoes by Miró and jewellery by Chelo Sastre also feature in the stock.
Branch: C/Muntaner 385 (202 30 77).

Teresa Ramallal

C/Mestre Nicolau 17 (201 39 98). Bus 6, 7, 33, 34, 63, 66, 67, 68. **Open** 4.30-8.30pm Mon; 10.30am-2.30pm, 4.30-8.30pm, Tue-Sat. **Credit** AmEx, DC, JCB, MC, V.
Teresa Ramallal, who opened her own shop nearly a decade ago, designs clothes primarily for the young, professional woman. She also designs a range of beautiful wedding dresses, as well as smart shoes. Prices start at around 13,000ptas.

Designer Bargains

Contribuciones

C/Riera de Sant Miquel 30 (238 18 88). Metro Diagonal/bus 6, 7, 15, 22, 24, 27, 28, 33, 34, 127. **Open** 11am-2pm, 5-9pm, Mon-Sat. **Credit** AmEx, DC, V.
Labels vary depending on what's available, and there is a tendency to stock the previous year's collections, but everything in this spacious fashion store is sold at half-price. The shop's in-house designer, Miguel de Otos, creates a wonderful range of reasonably-priced silks.

Preu Bo

C/Comtal 22 (318 03 31). Metro Urquinaona/bus 17, 19, 40, 45. **Open** 10.30am-8.30pm Mon-Fri; 10.30am-2.30pm, 4.30-8.30pm Sat. **Credit** AmEx, DC, MC, V.
Preu Bo translates as 'good price', and considering that they stock designer clothes, prices are great, with up to 65% off marked prices for end-of-lines by Roberto Verinno, Jordi Cuesta, Purificación García, Joaquim Verdú, María Encarnación and C'ést Comme Ça. The three outlets are all attractive, especially Balmes, and staff are very friendly.
Branches: C/Balmes 308 (414 44 57); C/Craywinckel 5 (418 81 74).

Taxi Moda

Passeig de Gràcia 26 (passatge) (318 20 70). Metro Passeig de Gràcia/bus 7, 16, 17, 22, 24, 28. **No credit cards.**
A large shop on two floors (one for women, one for men), this has cut-price Italian designer fashion. Styles and labels vary greatly, from Ferré, Versace Sport, Versus by Versace, Gigli and Ermenegildo Zegna to Leonard of Paris. The store gives additional discounts in January and August.

Fashion Malls

Galeries of individual small shops have sprouted apace since the early eighties, some occupying the interiors of whole Eixample blocks, and they are the most popular places for fashion browsing.

La Avenida

Rambla de Catalunya 121 (no phone). Metro Diagonal/FGC Provença/bus 6, 7, 15, 16, 17, 22, 24, 28, 33, 34. **Open** 10.30am-2pm, 4.30-8.30pm, Mon-Sat.
Similar to the better known Bulevard Rosa, La Avenida is a luxury arcade built around a tiny garden with a waterfall and a lounge-bar area. Shop till you drop.

Bulevard Rosa

Passeig de Gràcia 55 (309 06 50). Metro Passeig de Gràcia/bus.all routes to Passeig de Gràcia. **Open** 10.30am-8.30pm Mon-Sat.
A major '80s success story, this arcade began the *galeria* boom and has attracted some of the most interesting designers of clothes, shoes and jewellery. It has more than 100

*Get your credit card ready at **Gralla Hall.***

shops, including luxury men´s underwear outlet **Oltre Intimo**. It's popular with fairly well-heeled browsers, and the Diagonal branch is classier still.
Branch: Avda Diagonal 474 (309 06 50).

Gralla Hall

C/Portaferrisa 25 (412 32 72). Metro Plaça Catalunya/bus 14, 18, 38, 59, 91. **Open** 10.30am-2pm, 4.30-8.30pm, Mon-Sat.
In the middle of the shopping area near Portal de l'Àngel, the Gralla Hall arcade spreads through the interior of an 1850s mansion, with a bar in the middle, and is one of Barcelona trendsters favourite places to look for clubwear and similar styles. For young, albeit expensive fashion, the **Fantasy Shop** (412 22 83) is worth a look, while **Duo** (412 45 31) will suit shoppers with more traditional tastes, and as well as fashion there are shops selling jewellery, shoes and records.

El Mercadillo

C/Portaferrisa 17 (no phone). MetroPlaça Catalunya/bus 14, 18, 38, 59, 91. **Open** 11am-8.30pm Mon-Fri; 11am-9pm Sat.
It's hard to miss the entrance to the Mercadillo, Barcelona's grungier fashion mall – as well as the neon strip lights scattered around this former palace, there is a life-sized fibreglass camel. Clothes includes PVC jackets, tartan trousers, Gothic jewellery, tie-dyed jeans, lacy bodices, suede thigh-length boots and nylon bomber jackets. The wonderful rear bar opens onto an old terrace, and stained-glass windows separate customers from the bustle within.

High Street Shops

Mango

Passeig de Gràcia 26 (passatge) (215 75 30). Metro Passeig de Gràcia/bus 7, 16, 17, 22, 24, 28. **Open** 10.15am-8.30pm Mon-Sat. **Credit** AmEx, DC, EC, JCB, MC, V.
With over 80 branches in Spain, and price tags in francs and dollars as well as pesetas, Mango is a high street store with international appeal. Prices are not cheap compared to its foreign equivalents (the UK's Jigsaw or Warehouse), but the fabrics used are good-quality and the clothes are well made.
Branches: C/Mar 44 (384 23 53); C/Portaferrisa 16 (302 08 47); Avda Portal de l'Àngel 4 (317 69 85).

Zara

C/Pelai 58 (301 09 78). Metro Catalunya/bus all routes to Plaça Catalunya. **Open** 10am-9pm Mon-Sat. **Credit** AmEx, DC, MC, V.
A high street store with over 100 branches throughout Spain

and Portugal, and others in Paris and New York. Whatever top designers produce each season, Zara copies at a fraction of the price. They also offer no-nonsense clothes for men, women and children at very reasonable prices.
Branches: Avda Portal de l'Àngel 24 (317 65 86); C/València 245 (488 29 49).

Second-Hand Clothes

There isn´t much of a second-hand clothes culture in Barcelona. Your best bet may be **Els Encants** market, where a number of different stalls specialise in different types of clothes: old Levi's jeans; leather jackets and coats from the '70s; fancy '40s dresses....

Humana

Travessera de Gràcia 85 (573 12 10). FCG Gràcia/bus 16, 17, 27, 127. **Open** 9.30am 1.30pm, 4-8pm, Mon-Sat. **No credit cards.**
Good quality clothes for men and women. They usually have a fair choice of silk shirts at about 2,000ptas; denim shirts are around 1,000ptas. Profits go towards aiding Third World countries. They have several more branches around the city.

Usa 2

C/Verdi 9 (217 75 63). Metro Fontana/bus 39. **Open** *Sept-July* 10am-2pm, 5-8.30pm, Mon-Sat; *Aug* from 11am. **Credit** AmEx, MC, V.
Near Plaça del Sol in Gràcia, USA 2 are the veterans of the Barcelona second-hand clothes business. They sell mainly jeans and leather jackets.

Fashion Accessories

Jewellery

Hipòtesi

Rambla Catalunya 105 (215 02 98). FGC Provença/bus 7, 16, 17, 20, 21, 43, 44. **Open** 5-8.30pm Mon; 10am-1.30pm, 5-8.30pm, Tue-Sat. **Credit** AmEx, DC, MC,V.
A wonderful place in which to contemplate original work by Spanish and foreign designers of gold and silver jewellery and striking costume pieces.

Joaquín Berao

C/Rosselló 277 (218 61 87). Metro Diagonal/bus 7, 16, 17, 22, 24, 28. **Open** 10.30am-2pm, 4.30-8pm, Mon-Fri; 11am-2pm, 4.30-8pm Sat. **Credit** AmEx, DC, MC,V.
One of the most avant-garde jewellery designers in Barcelona, Joaquión Berao works with titanium and aged bronze as well as gold and silver. He's certainly not cheap, but he is good. Berao also has shops in Milan and Tokyo.

Joier Gemmòleg Villegas

C/Comtal 18 (318 60 94). Metro Plaça Catalunya/bus 17, 19, 40, 45. **Open** 10am-1.30pm, 5-8pm, Mon-Sat. **Credit** AmEx, DC, JCB, MC, V.
A tiny establishment in which the owner's daughter creates beautiful silver earrings from her own designs, which sell from 4,500ptas. She also makes silver jewellery inspired by Picasso, Miro or Dali, for about 11,000ptas.

Leather & Luggage

A clutch of relatively inexpensive shops along C/Ferran sell leather bags, cases, belts and purses. Leather goods can also be found in most shoe shops, as well as in the department stores.

Calpa

C/Ferran 53/Call 22 (318 40 30). Metro Liceu, Jaume I/bus 14, 18, 38, 59, 91. **Open** 10am-1.30pm, 5-8pm, Mon-Sat. **Credit** AmEx, DC, JCB, MC, V.
Bags to suit every taste can be found at Calpa. Weekend bags cost from 3,000ptas for a lightweight nylon carry-all, to 30,000ptas for a beautifully-finished leather and suede case.
Branch: C/Pl 5 (412 58 22).

Casa Antich S.C.P.

C/Consolat del Mar 27-31 (310 43 91) Metro Jaume I/bus 17, 40, 45. **Open** 9am-8pm Mon-Sat. **Credit** AmEx, DC, MC, V.
A huge family-owned shop that stocks an enormous range of bags, briefcases, suitcases and enormous metal trunks, one of a clutch of similar shops located in this part of La Ribera for centuries. If they haven´t got what you want, they'll make it for you. Prices are very reasonable.

Loewe

Passeig de Gràcia 35 (216 04 00). Metro Passeig de Gràcia/bus 7, 16, 17, 22, 24, 28. **Open** 9.30am-2pm, 4.30-8pm, Mon-Sat. **Credit** AmEx, DC, JCB, MC, TC, V. Foreign currency accepted.
Loewe, one of the most celebrated leather-goods companies in the world, is housed in Domènech i Montaner's modernist Lleó Morera building, and earned widespread condemnation in the sixties when they insensitively modernised the façade. Recently, they have been obliged to restore it. Inside there are high-priced bags and suitcases of superb quality.
Branches: Avda Diagonal 570 (200 09 20); C/Johann Sebastian Bach 8 (202 31 50).

Lingerie & Underwear

Casa Ciutad

Avda Portal de l'Angel 14 (317 04 33). Metro Catalunya/bus all routes to Plaça Catalunya. **Open** 10am-8.30pm Mon-Fri; 10.30am-2.30pm, 4.30-9pm, Sat. **Credit** AmEx, MC, V.
This charming shop opened in 1892, and today still sells some of the prettiest women's underwear you can find, as well as a large range of toiletry accessories, combs and brushes. A bit quaint, but attractive. Note that opening times are variable, and on some Saturdays it may also stay open at midday.

Santacana

Rambla Catalunya 90 (215 04 21). Metro Diagonal, FGC Provença/bus 20, 21, 22, 24, 28, 43, 44. **Open** *Oct-May* 10am-2pm, 4.30-8pm, *May-Sept* 10am-2pm, 4.30-8.30pm, Mon-Sat. **Credit** AmEx, DC, MC, V.
This well-established shop sells their own exclusive underwear in beautiful silks and satins, as well as stocking designs by Risk and La Perla – a luxurious set of silk pyjamas can cost 23,000ptas, and matching dressing-gown 24,000ptas. They also have a large selection of swimsuits and bikinis.
Branches: Rambla Catalunya 94 (215 04 81); Via Augusta 180 (209 00 00).

Shoes

Noel Barcelona

C/Pelai 46 (317 86 38). Metro Plaça Catalunya/bus all routes to Plaça Catalunya. **Open** 9.45am-2pm, 4.30-8.30pm, Mon-Fri; 9.45am-8.30pm Sat. **Credit** AmEx, MC, V.
Funky, trendy shoes in bright colours with spiky heels; knee-high red (or, if you prefer, green, or silver).boots with platform soles – Noel Barcelona's footwear is not for the shy. A branch on C/València has closed down: the neighbourhood, apparently, is too tame for their goods.

There are flower stalls in abundance on the Rambla.

Tascón

Passeig.de Gràcia 64 (487 90 84). Metro Passeig de Gràcia/bus 7, 16, 17, 22, 24, 28. **Open** 10.30am-2pm, 4.30-8.30pm, Mon-Sat. **Credit** AmEx, DC, EC, JCB, MC, TC, V.
Top quality casual and sports shoes for both sexes, and some sports clothes. Attractive shops with friendly service.
Branch: Bulevard Rosa, Passeig de Gràcia 55 (215 74 31)..

T-40

Rambla Catalunya 68 (487 09 49). Metro Passeig de Gràcia/bus 7, 16, 17, 22, 24, 28. **Open** 10.30am-2pm, 4.30-8.30pm, Mon-Sat. **Credit** AmEx, DC, JCB, MC, V.
Pilar Martin Gordillo designs a very feminine range of shoes in all shapes and colours, and collaborates regularly in fashion shows with designers such as Roberto Verinno and Jordi Cuesta. If you want a design in a different material or colour, she can do it for you. Prices range from 8,000 to 13,000ptas.
Branch: La Avenida, Rambla Catalunya 121 (217 29 09)

Tony Mora

Passeig de Gràcia 33 (487 65 64) Metro Passeig de Gràcia /bus 7, 16, 17, 22, 24, 28. **Open** 10.30am-2pm, 5-8.30pm, Mon-Sat. **Credit** AmEx, DC, EC, MC, $TC, V.
Nothing but boots – ankle-high or knee-high numbers; cowboy boots with an urban look, some in snakeskin; and classic Spanish *campera* boots.

Traditional Shoes

The traditional Catalan shoe (*espardenyes/alpargatas*) is a type of espadrille with ribbons attached. Originally worn by country people, it's now used as leisurewear, and by those performing the *Sardana* – Catalunya's national dance.

Calzados E Solé

C/Ample 7 (301 69 84). Metro Drassanes/bus 14, 36, 57, 59, 64. **Open** 9.30am-1.30pm, 4.30-8pm, Mon-Fri; 9.30am-1.30pm, 5-8pm, Sat. **Credit** AmEx, DC, JCB, MC, V.
Solé sells hand-made shoes, and they come in huge sizes (up to 50). Styles range from cowboy boots to sports shoes, from sandals to mountain boots to furry sheepskin slippers. Boots range in price from 5,500ptas. to 16,000ptas.

La Manual Alpargatera

C/Avinyó 7 (301 01 72). Metro Liceu/bus 14, 18, 38, 59, 91. **Open** 9.30am-1.30pm, 4.30-8pm, Mon-Sat. **Credit** AmEx, DC, JCB, MC, V.
They've been in business since 1910: today, Senor Tasies continues the tradition of individually made espadrilles. He is an expert on this style of footwear, knowing everything from the types of hemp or jute used for the sole to the hundreds of traditional variations in colour and style. And his expertise doesn't go unnoticed: faithful regulars include Michael Douglas, Jack Nicholson and the Pope. Espadrilles can be made to order: your template is stored for future orders. Prices range from 600ptas. to 6,000ptas.

Florists

Flower and plant shops can be found all over Barcelona, and many offer the world-wide Interflora delivery service. As well as the numerous flower stalls on the Rambla, there are some very decent stalls at the **Mercat de la Concepció** (corner of C/València and C/Bruc) that stay open all night.

Food markets

There are over 40 food markets in Barcelona, and every *barri* has its own. La Boqueria off the Rambla is deservedly the most famous, but there are others worth visiting: **Santa Caterina**, off Via Laietana near the Cathedral, has some of the best prices; **Sant Antoni**, near the Paral.lel, has a clothes market around the fringes and food stands in the middle; and the **Mercat de la Llibertat** in Gràcia has a local village atmosphere. The **Mercat del Ninot** in C/Mallorca, at the junction with C/Casanova has everything you could possibly think of, while the **Mercat de la Concepció** at València/Bruc is famous for its flowers.

Markets open early – from 8am – and close at 2pm or 3pm, depending on the stalls. Monday is not the best day to go, as stocks are low. Be prepared to queue at the stalls (*see chapter* **Essential Information**)

La Boqueria (Mercat de Sant Josep)

La Rambla 91 (318 25 84). Metro Liceu/bus 14, 18, 38, 59, 91. **Open** 8am-8pm Mon-Sat. **No credit cards.**
One of the greatest markets in the world, and certainly the most attractive and comprehensive in Barcelona. The Boqueria is always full of tourists, locals and gourmands. Even amid all the bustle, it's possible to appreciate the orderliness of its structure: fruit and vegetables around the edge, meat and chicken kept apart, and fish and seafood stalls in the centre, arranged in a circle. Enter through the main gates, set slightly back from the Rambla, amid great colourful heaps of red peppers, cucumbers and fruit. Don't buy here, though: the stalls by the entrance are noticeably more expensive than those further inside. They do, however, offer delights such as *palmitos* (palm roots), *higos chumbos* (Indian fig) or *caña dulce* (sugar cane sticks). J Colomines (stall 477), on the right-hand side of the entrance, specialises in fresh herbs, tropical fruit and African food. It's one of the few places selling fresh coriander, tarragon, basil, ginger, limes and okra throughout the year. At the back of the market, there's a stall that's a monument in itself, the one of Llorenç Petras (stall 866), with herbs and an extraordinary variety of wild woodland mushrooms: *tofunes*, *rabassols*, *cuirenys* or *ous de reig*, varieties that are virtually unknown outside the Catalan Pyrenees. On the way, admire the glistening meat and fish stalls, kept firmly in order by perfectly made-up ladies in spotless white overalls. Nothing is wasted: heads, toes and tripe are all laid out on marble slabs. Or stop at one of the many cheese stalls offering selections of the 81 types of Spanish cheeses that have a *denominación de origen*: try the pungent *cabrales*, the dry *mahón* from Menorca, or the delicious *garrotxa*, a Catalan cheese made from goats' milk, not to mention the many delicious *Manchegos* of lambs' milk. Specialised stalls selling over 40 different varieties of olives are dotted all over the market.

This lady knows everything there is to know about chopping fish.

Arte Japones

C/Tamarit 168, baixos (442 64 85). Metro Sant Antoni/bus 24, 41, 55, 64, 91. **Open** *Oct-June* 9am-8.15pm daily; *July-Sept* 9am-8.15pm Tue-Sun. **Credit** V.
Near the Sant Antoni market, this shop offers more than the traditional bunch of roses or gladioli – from bonsai to bouquets of exotic origin, it's all blooming here. Has an Interflora connection and a local delivery service.

Food

Chocolate, Cakes & Bread

Escribà Pastisseries

Gran Via de les Corts Catalanes 546 (454 75 35). Metro Urgell/bus 9, 14, 50, 56. **Open** 8am-9pm, Mon-Sun. **Credit** V.
A traditional chocolate shop, famous for its victories in the Easter cake competition (*see chapter* **Barcelona by Season**). Every year, larger and more ambitious creations are produced, such as the huge chocolate woman who languished in the shop for several months. Antoni Escribà, the author of these extravaganzas and champion *pastisser* of Barcelona, is a local celebrity. Escribà's most delectable cakes are the *rambla*, made from biscuit, truffle and chocolate (250ptas). The Rambla branch is installed in the Antigua Casa Figueras, and has a beautiful mosaic façade.
Branch: La Rambla 83 (301 60 27).

Forn de Pa Sant Jordi

C/Llibreteria 8 (310 40 16). Metro Jaume I/bus 17, 40, 45. **Open** 7am-8pm, Mon-Sat. **No credit cards.**
There's nearly always a queue outside the Sant Jordi bread shop – testimony to the delicious cakes on sale inside. The bread is good, and the *xuxos/chuchos* (cream doughnuts) are particularly tasty, but the speciality is *tortellet de cabell d'angel*, a pastry filled with 'angel's hair' (spun candied fruit).

La Mallorquina

Plaça de les Olles 7 (319 38 83). Metro Barceloneta/bus 16, 17, 45. **Open** 8am-2pm, 5-8.30pm, Mon-Sat; 8am-3pm Sun. Closed August. **No credit cards.**
The smell of baking *carquinyolis* (a Catalan biscuit made with almonds) slams you as you walk past La Mallorquina. The chocolate croissants are also worth tucking into.

Pastisseria Maurí

Rambla Catalunya 102 (215 10 20/09 98). Metro Diagonal, FGC Provença/bus 7, 16, 17, 22, 24, 28. **Open** 9am-9pm Mon-Sat; 9am-3pm, 5-9pm, Sun, public holidays; Closed Sun afternoon, Jul-Aug. **Credit** MC, V.
Granja Mauri opened in 1885 as a grocery specialising in cakes, and the elaborate painted ceiling is a relic from that time. Enjoy delicate sandwiches or lunch in the tea room; or take away a ready-to-eat meal from what remains of the grocery store. The nearby branch sells home-made chocolates.
Branch: Rambla Catalunya 103 (215 81 46).

Food Specialities

At its best, Spanish dry-cured ham (*jamón serrano*) is superior to much Parma ham; ham shops offer other meats such as *chorizo*, *salchichón*, the Catalan *botifarra* and spicy Mallorcan *sobresada*. The quality of *jamón* varies; expect to pay up to 14,000ptas a kilo for the best, traditionally-cured *Jabugo* ham. All cheese shops in Spain have the classic *Manchego* – *seco* (or even *seco añejo*) for fans of strong, dry cheeses, *semi* or *tierno* if you want something milder – but it's easy to find more unusual varieties.

Cafés el Magnífico

C/Argenteria 64 (319 60 81). Metro Jaume I/bus 17, 40, 45. **Open** *Oct-June* 8.30am-1.30pm, 4-7.30pm, Mon-Fri; 9.30am-1.30pm Sat; *July-Sept* closed Sat. **No credit cards.**
Since 1919, the Sans family has imported, prepared and blended coffees from around the world. Prices vary from 1,200ptas per kilo for a simple blend, to 12,000ptas per kilo for the especially smooth Jamaican coffee. They also stock over 150 cases of tea, including blends from Formosa, Nepal, India, Sri Lanka, China, Japan, Taiwan and Sikkim.

Casa Gispert

C/Sombrerers 23 (319 75 35). Metro Jaume I/bus 17, 40, 45. **Open** *Oct-May* 8.30am-1pm, 3.30-7pm, Mon-Fri; 10am-2pm, 5-8pm, Sat; *June-Sept* closed Sat pm. **No credit cards.**
Founded in the 1850s, Casa Gispert is a wholesale outlet famous for its top-quality nuts, dried fruit and coffee. Both nuts and coffee (there are two blends, sold under the trade name of Sabor) are roasted on-site in the magnificent original wood-burning stove. A kilo (the minimum order) of Iranian pistachios costs 900ptas. Delve into enormous baskets of almonds and hazelnuts, still warm from the oven.

Formatgeria Cirera

C/Cera 45 (441 07 59). Metro Sant Antoni/bus 20, 64, 91. **Open** 9am-2pm, 5-8.30pm, Mon-Fri; 9am-2pm Sat. **No credit cards.**
As well as a range of home-made cheesecakes – most suitable for diabetics – this shop has a great selection of Spanish cheeses including some from small dairies in Valladolid, a good *Manchego*, *Felix Seco*, and powerful *Cabrales* goats' cheese from Asturias. There is also fine *sobresada* from Mallorca, and patés, hams and *cavas* from all over Spain.

Hermano Gràcia

Ronda Sant Pau 39 (no phone). Metro Paral.lel/bus 20, 36, 57, 64, 91. **Open** 8am-2.30pm, 5-8.30pm, Mon-Sat. **No credit cards.**
One of the few old ham shops that is just a shop, with no bar, Hermano Gràcia stocks an impressive selection of hams, sausages and cheeses, and often has a queue to match.

Jamón Jamón

C/Mestre Nicolau 4 (209 41 03). Bus 6, 7, 33, 34, 66, 67, 68. **Open** 8am-midnight Mon-Sat. **Credit** AmEx, DC, MC, V.
Nothing but the best quality *jabugo* ham. Buy half a kilo, or invest in a whole leg. Like many of these places, Jamón Jamón combines shop with café, and upstairs a restaurant of sorts offers *pa amb tomàquet*, ham and cheese, and wine.

Mantequerías Puig

C/Xuclà 21 (318 12 84). Metro Catalunya/bus all routes to Plaça Catalunya. **Open** 8.30am-2pm, 4.30-8pm, Mon-Fri; 8.30am-2pm Sat. **No credit cards.**
As well as serving the public, this traditional cheese shop supplies many local hotels and restaurants. If you don't see what you want, ask: there are dozens more cheeses out back.

Mel Viadiu

C/Comtal 20 (317 04 23). Metro Urquinaona/bus17, 19, 40, 45. **Open** *Oct-May* 9am-2pm, 4.30-8pm, Mon-Fri; 9am-2pm, 5-8.30pm Sat; *June-Sept* 9am-2pm, 5-8.30pm, Mon-Sat. **Credit** AmEx, DC, MC, V.
Specialists in local honey – practically every product in the shop is made with honey from the Caldes de Montbui, just outside Barcelona. Try their honey sweets to soothe the throat, and a large fridge holds pots of pure royal jelly. Mr Viadiu, who exports honey to Fortnum & Mason, also stocks an array of jams and foreign cereals.
Branch: La Mielerie de Viadiu C/Creu Coberta 85 (431 65 11).

You can pick up the most unlikely bargains at **Els Encants**. *See page 160.*

General Stores

Colmado Murrià

C/Roger de Llúria 85 (215 57 89). Metro Passeig de Gràcia/bus 43, 44. **Open** 9am-2pm, 5-9pm, Mon-Sat. **Credit** AmEx, DC, MC, V.
Two blocks away from Passeig de Gràcia you'll find this beautiful *Modernista* shop, with tiled decoration designed by Ramon Casas, stocking a wonderful range of foodstuffs and over 300 wines, including their own Cava Murrià.

Colmado Quílez

Rambla Catalunya 63 (215 23 56 & 215 87 85). Metro Passeig de Gràcia/bus 7, 16, 17, 22, 24, 28. **Open** 9am-2pm, 4.30-8.30pm, Mon-Fri; 9am-2pm Sat (Oct-Dec 9am-2pm, 4.30-8.30pm, Sat).* **Credit** AmEx, MC, V.
A classic in its own right: the walls of this store are lined with cans and bottles from all over the world, there are huge quantities of hams and cheeses, and the *bodega* stocks every type of alcohol: saké, six types of schnapps, a wall of whiskies, and *cava* from over 55 *bodegas*, including one, Cava La Fuente, which is sold exclusively in this shop. The store's excellent own-brand coffee, Cafe Quílez, is imported from Colombia – and they grind it for you on the spot.

Health Foods

La Botiga del Sol

C/Xiquets de Valls 9 (415 55 30). Metro Fontana/bus 22, 24, 28. **Open** 9am-2pm, 4-9pm, Mon-Sat.* **Credit** MC, V.
One of the better health food shops in Barcelona: La Botiga del Sol stocks general groceries as well as quiches, cakes and spring rolls.

Macrobiotic Zen

C/Muntaner 12 (454 60 23). Metro Universitat/bus 9, 14, 24, 41, 50, 55, 56, 64, 91, 141. **Open** 9am-8pm Mon-Fri (Aug: 9am-2pm, 5-8pm, Mon-Fri). **No credit cards.**
All kinds of cheeses suitable for macrobiotic, diabetic and vegetarian diets, and a self-service canteen in the back. Free cooking classes in Spanish, 6-8pm Monday and Friday.

Supermarkets

Caprabo is a small chain with at least one branch in every district. With a car, the hypermarkets of **Glòries** and **Hipercor** (*see* **One-stop**) become accessible; Pryca hypermarkets are near the north and southern exits to Barcelona on the ring road.

Roca Autoservei

C/Canuda 26 (318 14 46 & 302 27 52). Metro Plaça Catalunya/bus 14, 18, 38, 59. **Open** 8.30am-2pm, 5-8.30pm, Mon-Sat. **Credit** MC, V.
A standard local supermarket, but central, with a good stock of cheeses and cold-cuts, wine, fruit and veg.

Gifts & Crafts

Ceràmica Villegas

C/Comtal 31 (317 53 30).Metro Urquinaona/bus 17, 19, 40, 45. **Open** 9.30am-1.30pm, 5-8.30pm, Mon-Fri; 10am-2pm, 5-8.30pm, Sat. **Credit** AmEx, DC, MC, V.
World-wide distributors of ceramics. The three-floor building houses a wide selection, from one-off or limited-series art pieces to more popular rustic styles. There's a small selection of antique water jugs and ceramic jewellery, too.

Coses de Casa

C/del Pi 5 (317 07 29). Metro Liceu/bus 14, 18, 38, 59, 91. **Open** 9.45am-1.30pm, 4.30-8pm, Mon-Fri; 10am-2pm, 5-8.30pm, Sat. **Credit** AmEx, MC, V.
The rolls of beautiful woven fabric for sale at Coses de Casa are traditional Mallorcan work, of Moorish influence. Cushions and bedcovers abound, and curtains or cushions can be made to order by the staff.
Branch: Plaça Sant Josep Oriol 5 (302 73 28).

2 Bis

C/Bisbe Irurita 2 bis (315 09 54). Metro Jaume I/bus 17, 40, 45. **Open** 10am-2pm, 4.30-8.30pm, Mon-Fri; 10am-2pm, 5-8.30pm Sat. **Credit** AmEx, DC, MC, V.

Wine & similar pleasures

The prime Catalan wine-producing area, the Penedés, produces good reds, whites and rosés: the large-scale Torres and René Barbier labels are reliable, and Bach whites have a great dry tang. The most famous of Spanish wines, Rioja, can be found everywhere, but quality is quite variable. Red Cune is always good, and can cost as little as 550ptas. In recent years Ribera del Duero has been more highly regarded than Rioja for its reds.

Catalan *cava*, sparkling wine, also hails from the Penedès. *Caves* are labelled, according to quality and sweetness, *Brut Nature*, *Brut*, *Seco* and *Semi-Seco*, the latter of which can be not *seco* at all but very sweet, and is the cheapest. Prices range from 500ptas upwards, but expect to pay around 900ptas for a decent *Brut*. For more on Catalan wine regions, *see chapter* **Trips Out of Town**.

El Celler de Gèlida

C/Vallespir 65 (339 26 41). Metro Plaça del Centre/bus 54. **Open** 9am-2pm, 5-8.30pm, Mon-Fri; 9.30am-2.30pm, 5-8.30pm, Sat. Closed Aug. **Credit** AmEx, DC, MC, V.
A little way off the beaten track in Sants, but this large modern cellar has a stock of over 3,000 labels, and an unbeatable selection of Catalan wines. The staff are knowledgeable, and advise many restaurants on their lists.

Lafuente

C/Johann Sebastian Bach 20 (201 25 21). FGC Bonanova/bus 14. **Open** 9am-2pm, 4.30-8.30pm, Mon-Fri; 9am-2pm Sat. **Credit** V.
A smart wine store with another huge selection, covering wines, *cavas* and spirits. A good choice of non-Spanish wines.

Vila Viniteca

C/Agullers 7-9 (310 19 56/268 32 27). Metro Jaume I/bus 17, 40, 45. **Open** 8am-3pm, 5-9pm, Mon-Sat. **Credit** AmEx, DC, MC, V.
Joaquim Vila continues the work of his grandfather, who opened this shop in 1932. From the outside it looks like a

normal grocery store, but inside, there's an enormous selection of wine and *cava*, all explained in a monthly Vila Viniteca broadsheet.

Vins i Caves La Catedral

Plaça de Ramon Berenguer el Gran 1 (319 07 27). Metro Jaume I/bus 17, 40, 45. **Open** 10.30am-2.30pm, 4.30-8.30pm, Mon-Fri; 10.45am-2.30pm, 5.30-8.45pm Sat. **Credit** AmEx, DC, JCB, MC, V.
A good supply of wines from all over Spain, and a particularly good choice of Catalan wines and *cavas*.

Quirky objects for everyone – toys, both for children and adults, tin aeroplanes, life-sized Tintin and other cartoon characters, and lots of other items in wood, paper and papier mâché. A great place to explore, with an upper floor that's almost as packed as the main shop.

Galeria d'Arquitectura en Miniatura (Gault Mini Arquitectura)

C/Boters 8 (412 27 07). Metro Liceu/bus 14, 18, 38, 59, 91. **Open** 4-8pm Mon; 10am-2pm, 4-8pm, Tue-Sat. **Credit** AmEx, MC, V.
Jean-Pierre and Dominique Gault create unique architectural miniatures: each house is an original work of art, sculpted by hand, and no moulds are used. They have recreated Venice, Paris, London and Barcelona as well as many other cities, and the houses can be purchased individually. Less expensive, mass-produced pieces are also sold in the shop.

Germanes García

C/Banys Nous 15 (318 66 46). Metro Liceu/14, 18, 38, 59, 91, 100. **Open** 4.30-7.30pm Mon; 9.30am-1.30pm, 4.30-7.30pm, Tue-Sat. **Credit** V.
There is no name on the shop-front but it's impossible to miss this wickerwork outlet from the number of baskets hanging in the entrance. Inside, browse among wickerware of every description – from fruit baskets at 800ptas to laundry hampers for 3,500ptas. Much of the furniture, which includes screens and chests of drawers, is made in the workshop.

Kitsch

Placeta de Montcada 10 (319 57 68). Metro Jaume I/bus 16, 17, 45. **Open** 11am-3pm, 5-8pm, Oct-Easter Tue-Sat, Easter-Sept Mon-Sat. **Credit** AmEx, MC, V.
Guadalupe Bayona, sister of the twins Pili & Mili, a comedy duo popular in Spanish films of the sixties, combines

being a lawyer with a passion for making objects in papier mâché. Most of her creations are inspired by paintings, by Klimt, Botero, Dali or Picasso, but she also recreates famous living personalities: Mayor Maragall bought the image of himself. *La Rocio*, a life-sized lady in flamenco dress who presides at the entrance, is the symbol of the shop. Prices range from 3,000ptas, up to 100,000ptas, if you wish to be immortalised.

México Lindo
Gran Via de les Corts Catalanes 632 (301 14 36). Metro Passeig de Gràcia/bus 7, 16, 17, 22, 2, 28, 48, 50, 54, 56. **Open** 10am-2pm, 3-8.30pm, Mon-Sat. **Credit** MC, V.
A world apart from the standard pre-Columbian craft shops you'll find sprinkled round Barcelona – the Mexican Purepecha Indian artwork exhibited in this shop will take your breath away. You'll either love it or hate it, but you can't ignore the fantastic, hand-made, lacquered chairs in shocking pink or green, with floral or solar designs in contrasting colours. Also beautifully carved wooden furniture, jewellery, papier maché clowns, *sarape* rugs and ceramics.

Populart
C/Montcada 22 (310 78 49). Metro Jaume I/bus 17, 40, 45. **Open** 11am-3pm, 5-8pm, Tue-Sat; 11am-3pmMon & Sun. **Credit** AmEx, DC, JCB, MC, V.

Make every day a shopping day.

A colourful gift shop very near the Picasso Museum (and **Kitsch**, *above*) filled with brightly painted papier-mâché figurines, including a model of Columbus made from scraps of comics (11,000ptas). Here, you can also buy silver-coated Gaudi door handles for 8,000ptas a pair, and gorgeous antique ceramic pieces.

Markets: Flea, Art & Antique

Art Market
Plaça Sant Josep Oriol (291 61 00). Metro Liceu/bus 14, 18, 38, 59, 91. **Open** (first weekend of every month) 10am-10pm Fri-Sat; 10am-3pm Sun. **No credit cards.**
It's fun to sit on the terrace of one of the local bars in this Barri Gòtic *plaça* and watch the artists crouch under sunshades as they try to sell their paintings, even if the work fails to impress. Music from buskers adds to the scene.

Book & Coin Market
Mercat de Sant Antoni, C/Comte d'Urgell 1 (423 42 87). Metro Sant Antoni/bus 20, 24, 41, 55, 64, 141. **Open** 9am-2pm (approx) Sun. **No credit cards.**
This Sunday morning second-hand book market is an institution in Barcelona and at times can get very crowded. Rummage through boxes of dusty tomes and old magazines, as well as video games, and admire the collections of old coins. If it becomes too much, look for a table at the nearby bar Els Tres Tombs and watch the bargain hunters pass by.

Gothic Quarter Antique Market
Avda de la Catedral 6 (291 61 00). Metro Metro Jaume I/bus 17, 19, 40, 45 . **Open** *Jan-Nov* 10am-10pm Thur. **No credit cards.**
Bric-a-brac and antique stalls are spread attractively in front of the Cathedral every week. Few bargains, but it's always enjoyable to rummage through the lovingly displayed religious artefacts, pipes, watches, lace hankies and old telephones. Before Christmas, it transfers to the Plaça del Pi.
Branch: Plaça del Pi. **Open** *Dec* 10am-10pm daily.

Els Encants – Flea Market
C/Dos de Maig, cnr C/Consell de Cent (246 30 30). Metro Glòries/bus 62, 92. **Open** *Oct-May* 8am-7pm; *June-Sept* 7am-8pm, Mon, Wed, Fri, Sat. **No credit cards.**
Despite modernisation all around it, Els Encants (also known as the *Mercat de Bellcaire*) remains the most authentic of flea markets – from its fringes, where old men lay out battered shoes and toys on cloths on the ground, to the centre, where a persistent shopper can snaffle up enough bargains to furnish a whole flat. Here, you'll find old earthenware jugs and country furniture from La Mancha, second-hand clothes, mostly from the '60s, some good new clothes and textiles, and loads and loads of fascinating junk. If possible, avoid Saturdays, as it can get very crowded, and watch out for short-changing, and for pickpockets. Although, officially, it's open in the afternoons, many stalls pack up at midday. For the best bargains, get there first thing in the morning.

Stamp & Coin Market
Plaça Reial (no phone). Metro Liceu/bus 14, 18, 38, 59, 91. **Open** 9am-2pm (approx) Sun. **No credit cards.**
A market for enthusiasts, this somewhat incongruous gathering blends surprisingly well with the sometimes unsalubrious goings-on in Plaça Reial. Having inspected the coins, stamps and rocks, you can take an *aperitif* in the sun and watch the experts poring over each other's collections.

Coffee? Cava? Cold cuts? **Colmado Quilez** *is at your service. See page 158.*

Records & Music

Discos Castelló

C/Tallers 3 (318 20 41). Metro Catalunya/bus all routes to Plaça Catalunya. **Open** 10am-2pm, 4.30-8pm, Mon-Sat. **Credit** MC, V.

Discos Castelló is a chain of small shops, all with a slightly different emphasis. This one specialises in classical music. The others – all nearby – sell more pop, and the Nou de la Rambla branch has a big selection of ethnic music and flamenco. The staff are very knowledgeable and go out of their way to help.

Branches: C/Nou de la Rambla 15 (302 42 36); C/Sant Pau 2 (302 23 95); C/Tallers 7 (302 59 46); C/Tallers 79 (301 35 75).

Jazz Collectors

Passatge Forasté 4 bis (212 7478). FGC Tibidabo/bus 17, 22, 73. **Open** 10.30am-2pm, 4.30-8.15pm, Mon-Fri; 11am-2pm Sat. **Credit** V.

Make the pilgrimage up to Jazz Collectors, known all over Spain for its eclectic collection ranging from be-bop to swing. Enthusiasts from abroad come here to find deleted American and Japanese jazz records which can cost up to 150,000ptas.

Musical Emporium

La Rambla 129 (317 63 38). Metro Catalunya/bus all routes to Plaça Catalunya. **Open** 4.15-7.30pm Mon; 9.30am-1.30pm, 4.15-7.30pm, Tue-Sat. **Credit** AmEx, MC, V.

A small shop – despite the grandiose name – that crams in an enormous range of stringed instruments. They also sell plenty of sheet music and a comprehensive selection of music books.

Virgin Megastore

Passeig de Gràcia 16 (412 44 77). FGC Provença/bus 7, 16, 17, 22, 24, 28, 48, 50, 54, 56. **Open** 10am-9pm Mon-Thu; 10am-11pm Fri-Sat. **Credit** AmEx, DC, MC, V.

The arrival of Virgin in Barcelona was received with as much excitement as you would expect from a visit by a rock star. Tour buses from Girona and other towns invaded Barcelona for the inauguration. The three-floor megastore seems to be living up to expectations, with all kinds of Spanish and international music, and a healthy stock of videos in English.

Tobacco & Cigars

L'Estanc de Laietana

Via Laietana 4 (310 10 34). Metro Jaume I/bus 17, 40, 45. **Open** 8.30am-2pm, 4-8pm, Mon-Fri; 9am-2pm Sat. **Credit** (for gifts only, not for cigarettes.) MC, V.

The busiest and most famous of the tobacco shops in Barcelona is run with zest and enthusiasm by Senor Porta. One hundred brands of cigarettes and 100 types of rolling tobacco are on sale. He has built an underground cellar at sea level to store his clients' cigars, so that they're kept at exactly the right humidity and temperature.

Gimeno

Passeig de Gràcia 101 (237 20 78). Metro Diagonal/bus 7, 16, 17, 22, 24, 28. **Open** 10am-2pm, 4-8.30pm, Mon-Sat. **Credit** AmEx, DC, JCB, MC, V.

Packed with Catalans having their lighters repaired, Gimeno specialises in anything and everything to do with smoking. The wooden walls are lined with hundreds of pipes and lighters. There's also an interesting collection of ornate walking sticks.

Services

**From old-fashioned cobblers to new-wave cleaners, the city's range
of services is getting faster and better all the time.**

In many respects Barcelona no longer fits the
clichéd preconception that Spain has a *mañana*
mentality. In the last few years the city has
changed radically, especially in the area of all-day
service. Small, family-owned businesses still com-
monly take the long afternoon lunch, but large
stores and supermarkets have helped foster the
idea of fast, efficient service for basic needs. Many
of Barcelona's proliferating shopping malls also
contain fast-service dry cleaners, shoe repairers,
opticians and other franchise-style businesses. The
quaint and the old still exist, however, so that
Barcelona now offers a very wide customer choice.

Vanguard: *look before you reverse.*

Body & Hair Care

Several private gyms offer weekly rates for short-
term visitors. *See chapter* **Sport & Fitness**.

Beauty Treatments

L'Estudi

*C/Casp 12 (tel & fax 317 28 41). Metro Catalunya/bus all
routes to Plaça Catalunya.* **Open** 9am-9pm Mon-Fri (may
vary in summer). **No credit cards**.
A wide range of facilities including sauna and whirlpool.
Short-term visitors are catered for: 6,000ptas a week gives
unlimited access to all equipment. Some staff speak English.

Instituto Francis

*Ronda de Sant Pere 18 (317 78 08). Metro
Catalunya/bus all routes to Plaça Catalunya.* **Open** 9am-
8pm Mon-Fri; 9am-4pm Sat (may vary in summer).
Credit DC, MC, V.
If you want the full works, the Francis has eight floors dedicated to making you look and feel better. Make-up and
makeovers are on the first floor, and you can work your way
up through hairdressing, waxing, facials, slimming and mas-
sages.The top floor has 'medical treatments', from teeth
whitening to wrinkle removing. Not cheap, but a real treat.

Hairdressers

Extensions

*C/Verdi 29 (237 90 37). Metro Fontana/bus 22, 24, 28,
39.* **Open** 10am-7pm Tue-Sat. **No credit cards**.
The latest in hair styling, from a cropped sides to curls,
waves and braids. Children are welcome. Wash, cut and
blow-dry costs 2,000ptas for men, 3,000 ptas for women; speciality cuts and styles are more expensive.

Llongueras

*C/Balmes 162 (218 61 50). Metro Diagonal/FGC
Provença/bus 7, 16, 17.* **Open** 9.30am-6.30pm Mon-Sat;
July, Aug 9.30am-6.30pm Mon-Fri; 9.30am-2pm Sat.
Credit AmEx, DC, V.

One of the best known hairdressing chains in Spain, with
more than a dozen branches in Barcelona. Next to the Balmes
shop there is a hairdressing school where prices are a lot
cheaper. It's best to visit in person to make an appointment
at either the salon or the school, rather than call.

La Pelu

*C/Argenteria 70-72 (310 48 07). Metro Jaume I/bus 17,
40, 45.* **Open** 9.30am-7pm Mon-Wed; 9.30am-9pm Thur,
Fri; 10am-7pm Sat. **Credit** AmEx, DC, MC, V.
Fun hairdressers with groovy cuts for men (from 2,500ptas,
wash and cut), women (from 3,900ptas) and children. On the
night of the full moon each month they also reopen from
11pm-2am, with magic and other entertainments to keep up
the atmosphere while you have your midnight trim. These
sessions are very popular.

Peluquería Vicente

*C/Tallers 11 (no phone). Metro Catalunya/bus all routes
to Plaça Catalunya.* **Open** 9am-1pm, 4-8pm, Mon-Fri;
9am-1pm Sat. **No credit cards**.
For a no-nonsense short-back-and-sides or a crewcut, try this
small barber's shop. If you're feeling specially adventurous,
have what is one of the closest shaves in the world.

Car, Bike & Skate Hire

Cars & Motorcycles

Car hire is relatively expensive here, but price structures vary widely, and with a little effort you can
probably find what you need. You must be 21 and
have had a driving licence for at least a year, and
you will need a credit card for the deposit, or have
to leave a large amount in cash. Check whether the
16% IVA (VAT) is included in the price. For other
aspects of driving here, *see chapter* **Survival**.

Hertz

*C/Tuset 10 (217 80 76/fax 237 29 20). Bus 6, 7, 15, 16,
17, 27, 33, 34.* **Open** 8am-2pm, 4-7pm, Mon-Fri; 9am-
1pm Sat. **Credit** AmEx, DC, JCB, MC, V.

Hiring a small car will set you back 9,000ptas per day, 49,486ptas per week or 19,261ptas for the weekend (including tax, insurance and unlimited mileage). With the major international agencies you can often get a better deal if you book from your home country before arriving in Barcelona. **Branch:** Airport (370 57 52). **Open** 7am-midnight daily.

Sprint
Avda Roma 15, baixos (322 90 12/fax 321 71 16).
Metro Tarragona or Entença/bus 27, 109. **Open** 9am-2pm, 4-8pm, Mon-Fri. **Credit** AmEx, DC, MC, V.
Small car rental for weekends (pick-up Fri, return Mon am) for 20,000ptas including unlimited mileage, insurance, IVA. Seven-days with unlimited mileage costs 6,000ptas a day plus IVA and insurance (around another 2,000ptas).

Vanguard
C/Londres 31 (439 38 80/322 79 51/fax 410 82 71). Bus 15, 27, 41, 54, 59. **Open** 8am-2pm, 4-8pm, Mon-Fri; 9am-1pm Sat, Sun. **Credit** AmEx, DC, MC, V.
Good weekend deals (pick-up at 4pm Fri, return 9am Mon) on almost all ranges of car: a Seat Panda, for example, costs 14,000ptas including IVA, insurance and unlimited mileage. Vanguard is also the best place to rent scooters and motorcycles. All-inclusive weekend rates include 6,500ptas for a Vespino moped and 23,000ptas for a Yamaha 600.

Cycles & Rollerblades

Many locals now make use of Barcelona's cycle-only lanes for fun at weekends, but few use bikes as their everyday means of transport.
Renting The rental shops listed here are all near the Ciutadella park and the port, or the Olympic port and the beach, the most popular areas for weekend cycling, although still within easy striking range of the old city. There are more shops, with different kinds of bikes including *Bicicar* four-wheelers with side-by-side seats. Many, especially near the beach, also rent out rollerblades to satisfy a booming demand. One tip: If you have any ID-card with your photo on it, take it with you to leave as a deposit, as you may prefer not to leave your passport. Also, be sure to get a good lock, as bike theft is increasingly common.

Los Filicletos
Passeig Picasso 40 (319 78 85) Bus 14, 39, 51. **Open** 11am-2pm, 5-8pm, Mon-Fri; 10am-3pm, 5-8pm, Sat, Sun, holidays (may close later in summer). **No credit cards**.
Rent a bike by the hour or day at this shop by the Ciutadella, a favourite, central spot for gentle cycling. A regular street bike costs 450ptas an hour, 2,000ptas per day, while a tandem is 1,000ptas an hour and a mountain bike 600ptas an hour. Daily rates for tandems and MTBs are by negotiation.

Icària Esports
Avda Icària 180 (221 17 78). Bus 41,71. **Open** *Oct-Mar* 4.30-11pm Mon-Sat; 10.30am-11pm Sun, holidays; *Apr-Sept* 10.30am-11pm daily. **No credit cards**.
A mountain bike at this Vila Olímpica shop will cost you 750ptas per hour, 2,000ptas for a half-day and 3,000ptas for a full day. You can also rent street bikes and tandems, and rollerblades with pads and other equipment for 650ptas per hour. Opening hours vary during the winter, so ring to check.

...al punt de trobada
C/Badajoz 24 (225 05 85). Metro Llacuna/bus 36, 41. **Open** 9.15am-10pm daily. **No credit cards**.
Also near the Vila Olímpica and the beach: mountain bikes cost 250ptas per hour, 1,500ptas per half-day and 2,500ptas for a whole day. If you already have a bike, they will provide a secure parking space for 50ptas per hour, 250ptas a day. Rollerblades are available for 500ptas per hour, 1,500ptas for a half-day, with additional discounts on weekdays.

Clothes & Accessories

A wide range of services, including shoe repair and key-cutting, are also available at **El Corte Inglés** department store (*see chapter* **Shopping**).

Cleaning & Repairs

One-hour cleaning and laundry facilities are a growth industry in Barcelona, with prices often lower than those of older neighbourhood dry cleaners. There are still plenty of the latter around, though, and also many of the old, street-corner repairers that make it possible to have virtually any article of clothing altered or restored. Look for any shop offering '*Arreglos*' or '*Brodats/Bordados*'.

5 a Sec
L'Illa Shopping Centre, Avda Diagonal 557 (444 00 34). Bus 6, 7, 33, 63, 66, 67, 68. **Open** 9am-9pm Mon-Sat. **No credit cards**.
With five branches around Barcelona, and plans for more, 5 a Sec is an efficient, modern dry cleaners offering a 1-hour service. Prices range from 300ptas for a shirt or blouse to 500ptas for a jacket and 700ptas for a man's or woman's suit.

Jaimar
C/Numància 91-93 (322 78 04). Metro Plaça del Centre/bus 15, 59. **Open** 9am-1pm, 4-8pm, Mon-Fri. **No credit cards**.
A traditional repair shop that will take up, take apart, or put back together almost any piece of clothing, in virtually any material from wool to leather.

Qualitat Servei
C/Amargós 10 (318 31 47). Metro Urquinaona/bus 17, 19, 40, 45. **Open** 8am-8pm Mon-Sat. **No credit cards**.
Near the Barri Gòtic, this shop will wash and iron or dry clean clothes and deliver them to you within 24 hours; however, there is no pick-up service. Also minor repairs.

Dress & Costume Hire

Menkes
Gran Via de les Corts Catalanes 642 & 646 (412 11 38/318 86-47). Metro Passeig de Gràcia/bus 7, 18, 50 54, 56. **Open** 9.30am-1.30pm, 4.30-7.45pm, Mon-Fri; 10am-1.30pm, 5-8pm Saat. **Credit** AmEx, DC, JCB, MC, TC, V.
Kit yourself out for Carnaval or that special *festa* at this magnificent theatrical costumiers and costume hire store. No. 646 is for sales, with a vast selection of ballet shoes (also made to measure); no. 642 has over 800 sumptuous designs available for rental, for children and adults, from the inevitable Catalan peasant and Flamenco outfits to chicken suits and, should you really want to make a splash, Brazilian Carnival queen regalia worthy of Carmen Miranda herself. Any design can also be made to order. Also jokes, false noses and other silly things, and dinner jackets for the more discreet.

Moss Bros
Galeries David, C/Tuset 19-21 (209 69 48). Bus 6, 7, 15, 16, 17, 27, 33, 34. **Open** 10am-2pm, 4.30-8.30pm, Mon-Fri; 10am-1pm Sat (may be closed July & Aug). **No credit cards**.
Now in Barcelona, Moss Bros offers a complete men's formal outfit for 8,000ptas (7,000ptas without shoes). Also a wide range of women's wear, from cocktail dresses to ball-gowns. Fittings must be at least five days in advance of the hire date.

Shoe Repair

Mr Minit
Centre Comercial Glòries, Avda Diagonal 280 (tel & fax 486 03 52). Metro Glòries/bus 56. **Open** 10am-10pm Mon-Sat. **Credit** V.
On-the-spot shoe repairs and key cutting: soles and heels cost 1,575ptas, heels only cost 670ptas. A Yale-style key will set you back a mere 150ptas. As well as this branch, they have another in **L'Illa** shopping centre (*see chapter* **Shopping**) and a growing number of smaller outlets around the city.

Rápido Salvadó
C/Amargós 2 (no phone). Metro Urquinaona/bus 17, 19, 40, 45. **Open** 9am-1.30pm, 4.30-7.30pm, Mon-Fri. Closed last week in June, first three weeks in Aug. **No credit cards**.
A traditional cobbler, typical of the small, tiny shops found in every older neighbourhood, where shoes are mended with nails and thread rather than glue. If this is too far away, ask at your hotel for a *Rápido* nearer you. You will pay more and wait longer than at the chain repairers, but if you have any favourite shoes in need of work, it can be worth the search.

Food Delivery

There are few places specifically offering take-away meals or food delivery, except for an ever-expanding multitude of pizzerias. However, many restaurants will provide a takeaway service if you make an arrangement in advance.

Pizza World
C/Diputació 329 (487 85 85). Metro Girona/bus 7, 18, 47, 50, 54, 56, 62, N1, N2, N3. **Open** 1-4pm, 7pm-midnight, Mon-Fri; 1pm-midnight Sat, Sun, holidays. **No credit cards**.
Probably the handiest pizza delivery service, with 16 branches throughout the city. This one is in the central Eixample; open from 7-11pm, daily, phone the special line 902 30 53 05 to find out which is your nearest branch. You will be asked the address where you are staying, and will then be told the number of the right branch; you then have to ring it yourself. At other times, call any branch and ask the same question. Deliveries to your door are made until midnight.

Opticians

Grand Optical
Lower level, Centre Comercial Glòries, Avda Diagonal 280 (486 02 77/fax 486 05 52). Metro Glòries/bus 56. **Open** 10am-10pm Mon-Sat. **Credit** V.
If you lose or break your glasses in Barcelona you can now have them replaced or repaired while you wait. Grand Optical can give you an eye-test and a new pair of glasses in two hours. If you have your prescription with you, then an hour will do. English-speaking staff are on hand and prices for the simplest lenses are about 4,000ptas (excluding frames). For bi-focals, graduated or more exotic lenses, expect to pay up to 26,000ptas.

Optipolis
Rambla de Catalunya 75 (215 29 39/fax 215 61 46). Metro Passeig de Gràcia/bus all routes to Passeig de Gràcia. **Open** 10am-8.30pm Mon-Sat. **Credit** AmEx, DC, MC, V.
The same speed, type and price of service as Grand Optical, but closer to the centre of the city. English-speaking staff.
Branch: Centre Comercial Glòries, Avda Diagonal 280 (486 04 28).

For mega-concerts, try **Bulevard Rosa**.

Photocopying & Faxing

A great many local *papereries* (stationers) have photocopiers, and also fax machines.

Central Fotocopia
C/Pelai 1, pral (412 75 36/fax 412 71 59). Metro Universitat/bus all routes to Plaça Universitat. **Open** 9am-2.30pm, 4-8pm, Mon-Fri. **No credit cards**.
A good-value specialist photocopiers much-used by students from the nearby University, with some of the best rates in town for large numbers of copies. Long queues, too, during term time. Also a fax sending and receiving service.

Copisteria Miracle
C/Dr Joaquim Pou 2 (317 12 26/fax 412 18 12). Metro Urquinaona/bus 17, 19, 40, 45. **Open** 9am-1.30pm, 4-7.30pm, Mon-Sat. **Credit** MC, V.
The best in the city for high-quality copying of all kinds, including reproduction of plans and graphics, at reasonable prices. Again, queues are long. This is the most central of the branches: the others do not close at midday.
Branches: C/Rector Ubach 10 (200 85 44/fax 209 17 82; Passeig Sant Joan 57 (265 52 94/fax 265 30 70; C/Aragó 368 (265 63 49/fax 265 93 73).

Photographic

Film developing is expensive in Spain, and unless you need the pictures immediately you might prefer to wait until you get home.

Arpi Foto Video
La Rambla 38-40 (301 74 04/fax 317 95 73). Metro Drassanes/bus 14, 18, 38, 59, 91. **Open** 9.30am-1.30pm, 4.30-8pm, Mon-Sat. **Credit** AmEx, DC, MC, V.
A giant specialist camera store with a wide range of professional-standard cameras and accessories and a good basic

repair department. Service has improved in the past couple of years but can still seem snail-like at times; however, they do know what they are doing. The stock ranges from throw-away happy-snappers all the way up to studio Hasselblads.

Fotoprix
C/Pelai 6 (318 20 36/information 451 10 43/fax 302 13 11). Metro Universitat/bus all routes to Plaça Universitat. **Open** 9.30am-2pm, 4.30-8.30pm, Mon-Fri; 10am-2pm, 4.30-8.30pm, Sat. **Credit** V.
A chain with over 100 branches throughout the city offering one-hour film developing, photocopying and, in many branches, fax services. One-hour developing costs 44ptas per exposure (you pay only for what comes out).

Ticket Agents

Tickets for a wide range of events, concerts and so on are now sold through savings banks (*see* **Caixes don't only have cash**). Otherwise, the best place to get tickets in advance is from the venues themselves. Concert tickets for smaller venues may be sold through record shops (*see* chapter **Shopping**); look out for details on posters. The bullring has its own city-centre ticket office (*see* chapter **Sightseeing**); football tickets are available only from the clubs themselves.

Bulevard Rosa Ticket Desk
Unit 65, street level, Bulevard Rosa, Passeig de Gràcia 53. Metro Passeig de Gràcia/bus all routes to Passeig de Gràcia. **Open** 10am-8.30pm Mon-Sat. **No credit cards**.
Within the Bulevard Rosa shopping centre, this desk has concert and some theatre tickets.

Taquilles Gran Via/Aribau
Plaça Universitat, at corner of Gran Via and C/Aribau (no phone). Metro Universitat/bus all routes to Plaça Universitat. **Open** 10am-1pm, 4.30-7.30pm, Mon-Sat. **No credit cards**.
This booth in one corner of Plaça Universitat has tickets to large-scale pop concerts in any of the local sports arenas, and also American Football games and other events in the Olympic buildings (stadium, Palau Sant Jordi, Velòdrom).

Travel Services

Travel agents have become more competitive here, and it pays to shop around to find good deals.

Nouvelles Frontières
C/Balmes 8 (318 69 98/fax 302 71 58). Metro Universitat/FGC Plaça Catalunya/bus all routes to Plaça Catalunya. **Open** 9.30am-7.30pm Mon-Fri; 10am-6pm Sat. **Credit** AmEx, V.
A no-nonsense agency with very competitive prices, sometimes offering savings of over 10,000ptas on European flights compared to many larger agencies.

Viajes Ecuador
C/Ecuador 7 (322 26 96/fax 410 83 31). Metro Entença or Sants-Estació/bus 15, 54, 59. **Open** 9am-1.30pm, 4-7.30pm, Mon-Fri; 9.45am-1.30pm Sat. **Credit** AmEx, DC, MC, V.
A large, well-equipped agency with offices throughout Spain and helpful staff, some of whom speak English.

Viatges Wasteels
Inside vestibule, Plaça Catalunya RENFE station (301 18 81). Metro Catalunya/bus all routes to Plaça Catalunya. **Open** 8.30am-8.30pm Mon-Fri; 10am-1pm Sat. **Credit** DC, MC, V.

Wasteels offers discount fares on national and (especially) international rail tickets, and many flights, for students and under-25s. An ISIC student card or similar youth document (Euro 26) is required for flight discounts; for international trains a passport (to check your age) is sufficient. Students over 25 are not eligible for rail discounts within Spain.
Branch: Estació de Sants (490 39 29).

Car-sharing/Hitch-hiking

Barnastop
C/Sant Ramon 29 (443 06 32). Metro Liceu/bus 14, 18, 38, 59, 91. **Open** 11am-2pm, 5-8pm, Mon-Fri; 11am-2pm Sat. **No credit cards**.
An agency that puts prospective travellers in touch with drivers going the same way, providing the cheapest means of making any long-distance trip. Passengers are charged 2,000ptas for international destinations, regardless of the distance, and 1,000ptas within Spain; drivers are paid 4ptas/km outside Spain, and 3ptas/km for domestic trips. The most frequent destinations are in France and Holland, but if you're going anywhere else it's worth calling; you might be in luck.

Caixes don't only have cash

Catalonia's savings banks (*Caixes d'Estalvis*) are among its most characteristic institutions, involved in many other fields as well as loans and deposit accounts. Lately, in keeping with Catalans' love of all things modern, they have embraced electronics in a big way to expand into new services, including ticket sales. No booking fee is charged by either Caixa. To find out the tickets currently being sold by each one, check at any branch, or in listings magazines (*see* chapter **Media**).

La Caixa
Next to the cash machines at many branches of the biggest of them all, the Caixa de Pensions, better known simply as *La Caixa*, you will find a machine called a *Servi-Caixa*, through which you can with a Caixa account or a credit card obtain T2 and T50/30 travel cards, local information and tickets to a wide range of attractions and events, including **Port Aventura** and the **Liceu** season, 24 hours a day. You can also order tickets by freephone (**902 33 22 11**).

Caixa de Catalunya
Central Ticket Desk. *Avinguda Catedral branch (no phone).* **Open** 6-10pm Mon-Wed, Fri; 4-10pm Thur, Sat; 3-6pm Sun.
La Caixa's eternal competitor sells tickets for many theatres (never the same ones as the *Servi-Caixa*) over the counter at all its branches. You can reserve tickets by phone with a credit card through their *Tel-Entrades* line (**310 12 12**, open 8am-1am daily); you then collect them at the venue. Also, you can get tickets half-price by buying them (cash only) within three hours of a performance at the Caixa de Catalunya ticket desk at their Avinguda Catedral branch, right opposite the Cathedral.

96 Exhibitions:
Contemporary Barcelona

Maquettes of antiquity

97 Exhibitions:
Pessoa's Lisbons

Barcelona - Madrid

Centre de Cultura Contemporània de Barcelona
Montalegre , 5
Telephone: 34 3 4120781/82

Galleries & Museums

Art Galleries

Picasso, Miró, Dalí, Gaudí – with such inspiring examples, it's no wonder that the Catalan art scene continues to flourish...

Barcelona's rivalry with Madrid in just about everything extends to the visual arts, although the virtues and deficiencies of each city's artistic assets are recognised, however begrugingly, by most natives of both cities. Madrid's museums contain some of the world's finest collections of historic painting. Barcelona can lay claim to a much richer architectural heritage, and can boast links with some of the most illustrious names in twentieth-century art. Even though Picasso came to Barcelona as a teenager, Miró left to set up his studio in Mallorca, and Dalí was driven more by the maddening winds of his native Figueres than by any Barcelonan breeze, all these artists, together with Gaudí, testify to the vitality of Catalan visual culture in the first decades of this century.

Barcelona was a minor hot spot of the early twentieth-century avant-garde, with a liberal bourgeoisie willing to tolerate and even back the ideas of artists and architects. This vitality was brought to a dead halt by the Franco dictatorship. Only a few internationally-relevant artists emerged in the interminable *posguerra*, the post-Civil War period, the best-known of them the painter Antoni Tàpies. Others, such as conceptual artists Francesc Torres and Antoni Muntadas (who made the leap to the international arena, moving to New York), rose to prominence in the final years of the Franco regime.

When Spain returned to democracy in the late seventies, the paltry state of the artistic panorama that remained – a few decent commercial galleries and the memory of a glorious past – convinced many that the city needed to reassert its place as an art capital, and that the main thing required to do this was self-promotion. Barcelona galleries and collectors, old and new, duly set about favouring purely Catalan artists. In Madrid, meanwhile, the all-embracing spirit of the early eighties' *movida*, helped by factors like the ARCO art fair, fostered the growth of a more open, cosmopolitan art scene.

Today, Barcelona has won back a good part of the lost ground. Dealers and collectors have finally begun to break the bonds of nationalistic sentiment when it comes to showing and buying art. More importantly, Barcelona's numerous public galleries and private foundations, many of which have hefty budgets, have ensured that international art has an impressive presence in the city. The opening of the **Museu d'Art Contemporani** (**MACBA**) in 1995 has also sparked a new-found optimism in Catalonia's cultural community (*see chapter* **Museums**).

ADVENTURES IN ART

With so many big institutions patronising contemporary art, the Catalan art scene could have become 'top-heavy'. Fortunately, post-Olympic Barcelona has also been inundated with fresh alternative projects, many run by artists themselves. New spaces, short-term art projects and cultural festivals have sprouted up all over the city. And, while abstract gestural painting and austere minimalist sculpture still predominate in commercial galleries, younger artists defer less to Catalan artistic traditions. Finding what's on offer in this alternative art world can be difficult, but thanks to it, Barcelona has a much more varied and enjoyable art scene (*see* **Art alternatives**).

There is no definitive guide to Barcelona galleries and artistic activities. Listings appear in the *Guia de Ocio* and some newspapers but are not always comprehensive (*see chapter* **Media**). It can be just as easy to go to a gallery district and do the rounds. Almost all galleries are closed on Mondays. Show openings typically take place at around 8pm on Tuesdays and Thursdays, and galleries in a district often coordinate openings to draw a bigger crowd. Curious visitors will also find that most gallery-owners are happy to show their 'backroom' art collections on request.

Public Spaces & Foundations

Many museums, particularly the **Fundació Miró** and the **MACBA**, also host temporary exhibitions. For these, *see chapter* **Museums**.

La Capella (Capella de l'Antic Hospital de la Santa Creu)

C/Hospital 56 (442 71 71). Metro Liceu/bus 14, 18, 38, 59, 91. **Open** *noon-8pm Tue-Sat (hours may be extended in summer).* **Closed Mon.** **Admission** *free.*
Administered by the Ajuntament, this exhibiting space is modelled on the **Sala Montcada** of 'la Caixa' and the Espai 13 of the **Fundació Miró** (*see chapter* **Museums**), with curators seeking out younger artists to create new work. The impressive Gothic building, with its stone walls and high arches, was once the chapel of the medieval hospital alongside it, and the choir balcony and small side chapels add character to the space. As well as exhibiting Spanish artists, the gallery displays work from Barcelona art schools and exchanges exhibits with several foreign non-profit galleries.

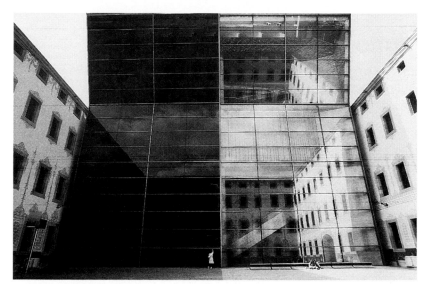

*The **Centre de Cultura Contemporània de Barcelona**. Just say CCCB.*

Centre d'Art Santa Mònica

La Rambla 7 (412 12 72). Metro Drassanes/bus 14, 18, 38, 59, 91. **Open** *11am-2pm, 5-8pm, Mon-Sat; 11am-3pm Sun.* **Admission** *normally free.*

In the 1980s the Catalan government undertook the complete renovation of this seventeenth-century church, formerly part of a monastery, as a centre for contemporary art. The polemical result, by Maremagnum-architects Viaplana and Piñon, is hard enough for installation artists to work with and almost unusable when it comes to showing paintings (observe the extravagant lower cloister, or the ridiculously narrow corridors that pass for galleries on the upper floors). Still, it has played host to some of the best contemporary shows of the past decade, including work by Joseph Beuys, photographer Hannah Collins, General Idea, and Catalans Francesc Torres and Antoni Muntadas. It might soon be forced to close or cut back on programming, as the new **MACBA**, besides absorbing a good part of the Generalitat's art budget, has taken over the Centre's *raison d'etre.* *Wheelchair access.*

Centre de Cultura Contemporània de Barcelona (CCCB)

C/Montalegre 5 (412 07 81/82). Metro Liceu/bus 14, 18, 38, 59, 91. **Open** *11am-2pm, 4-8pm, Tue-Sat; 10am-3pm Sun, public holidays.* **Closed Mon.** **Admission** *Mon, Tue, Thur-Sun* 500ptas one exhibition; 750ptas combined ticket two or more exhibitions. Free *under-16s. Wed, & students, over-65s on all days* 300ptas one exhibition; 500ptas combined ticket two or more exhibitions. Free *under-16s.* **No credit cards.**

This lavishly-equipped centre, with the adjacent **MACBA** making up a duo of recent major cultural projects in the Raval, occupies part of the *Casa de la Caritat*, built in the last century on the former site of a medieval monastery as the city's main workhouse. The massive façade and equally impressive courtyard remain from the 1802 building, but beginning in 1988 the rest was rebuilt wholesale (by Viaplana and Piñon) to transform it into this 'multi-disciplinary, multi-functional' cultural centre. Its guiding focus is on cities in all

their aspects, an idea close to Mayor Maragall's heart. The CCCB offers very solid exhibitions on twentieth-century art, architecture and other themes and a whole gamut of other activites, including a festival of video art (every 18 months), an alternative cinema festival (late Feb), the **Sonar** music festival in June, dance performances, concerts, film screenings and inter-disciplinary courses in urban studies (*see also* **Art alternatives** *and chapter* **Music: Rock, Roots & Jazz**). Many of its art shows effectively fill the gap left by the lack of a Barcelona museum dedicated to international art of the early twentieth century. Visitors, though, are obliged to descend a ramp on one side of the courtyard, pass underneath it through a long hall, pay, and then take escalators up to the galleries – a circuitous route that shows off the architecture while for some reason associating 'contemporary culture' with long, vacuous preludes.
Bookshop. Café. Wheelchair access.

Col.legi d'Aparelladors i Arquitectes Tècnics de Barcelona

C/Bon Pastor 5 (209 82 99). Bus 6, 7, 15, 27, 33, 34, 58, 64, N8. **Open** *10am-2pm, 4-8pm, Mon-Fri. Closed August.* **Admission** *free.*

This professional body for surveyors has a well-run gallery showing all kinds of work by designers, architects and urban planners. Contemporary artists and photographers often also exhibit work on related – architectural or urban – themes. *Wheelchair access.*

Col.legi d'Arquitectes

Plaça Nova 5 (301 50 00). Metro Jaume I/bus 17, 19, 40, 45. **Open** *10am-9pm, Mon-Fri; 10am-2pm Sat.* **Admission** *free.*

The Catalan College of Architects, almost opposite the cathedral, uses this interesting gallery to show all kinds of photography and maquettes related to twentieth-century architecture. The murals on the façade of the building were designed by Picasso in the fifties, but carried out by other artists since at that time he was not able to enter Spain. *Wheelchair access.*

Antoni Tàpies

Time Out designer, Paul Tansley, pays tribute.

Antoni Tàpies has been the most prominent artist in Catalonia for half a century, winning world-wide acclaim. Barcelona has played a very important role in his work. Tàpies' art can be enjoyed simply for its aesthetic qualities, but when it is better understood the viewer also becomes aware of his use of symbolism, and through it of the impact the city has had upon him as an artist.

He began painting in the 1940s after the Civil War, but it was during the 1950s that he developed his own distinctive methods. While abstract artists explored the use of colour and form, Tàpies experimented with texture in the pieces known as his 'Matter paintings' with a technique combining varnish and marble dust to create vast surfaces resembling the decaying walls of the old city. It is this inventive use of materials that has allowed him to create such original art. Incorporated into his paintings and sculptures are real objects from everyday life such as scissors, socks, and other items of clothing: other elements include bold graphic symbols such as his initials, or the red and yellow of the Catalan flag.

One of the most pleasurable aspects of Tàpies' art is the confidence and spontaneity of the marks that he makes. His work has a great simplicity, and his huge canvases seem to be effortlessly put together, in works that have to be seen face-to-face for their full impact to be appreciated.

Fundació Antoni Tàpies

C/Aragó 255 (487 03 15). Metro Passeig de Gracia/bus 7, 16, 17, 22, 24, 28. **Open** 11am-8pm Tue-Sun; 11am-3pm, Sundays in Aug. **Closed Mon. Admission** 500ptas; 250ptas students; free under-10s, over-65s. **No credit cards.**

Antoni Tàpies is arguably Catalonia's best-known living artist, and his foundation in the heart of the Eixample is a must-see, although not for the obvious reasons. Tàpies had the good sense to do more than simply create a shrine to himself: he set up a foundation, with solid public programming, a specialist library and a beautifully-appointed gallery. It is housed in an early *Modernista* building, a renovated former publishing house built in the 1880s by Domènech i Muntaner, and the main space, including the labyrinthine basement, is set aside for international contemporary art. Opened in 1990, it presents some of the best exhibitions in the city: thematic shows (the idea of the museum, the *Fluxus* movement) alternate with retrospectives of artists such as Louise Bourgeois or Hans Haacke. A selection of his own paintings and sculptures, can be seen on the upper floor. The incredible winding tube sculpture on the roof, titled *Núvol i Cadira (Cloud and Chair)*, reflects his fascination with Eastern mysticism. The library contains one of Europe's best collections of books on oriental art. *See also* **Antoni Tàpies**.
Library (restricted access). Wheelchair access.

Fundació 'la Caixa'

Centre Cultural de la Fundació 'la Caixa', Passeig de Sant Joan 108 (458 89 07/458 18 01). Metro Verdaguer/bus 15, 20, 21, 45, 47, 55. **Open** 11am-8pm Tue-Sat; 11am-3pm Sun, public holidays. **Closed Mon. Admission** *Tue-Fri, Sun* 300ptas; 175ptas students, over-65s. *Sat* free. **No credit cards.**

All Spain's *Caixes (Cajas*, in Spanish), or savings banks, are obliged to spend part of their earnings on social and cultural activities. The foundation set up by the largest, the Caixa de Pensions or just 'la Caixa', has since the 1980s built up one of the most important collections of international contemporary art in Spain. More recently the foundation has been shifting its focus towards fields such as ethnology and cultural heritage, but it still produces some of the best art exhibits in Barcelona. The main centre is located in the Palau Macaya, a magnificent *Modernista* building designed by Puig i Cadafalch in 1901, which creatively mixes Moorish and Gothic styles. Recently expanded, the centre usually offers two exhibits, one always of photography. The same building also houses the **Mediateca** open-access music and arts library (*see chapter* **Students**), and an excellent arts bookshop. The foundation also runs one of Barcelona's most reputable spaces for more daring contemporary art, the **Sala Montcada**, opposite the Picasso Museum. Curators invite-merging Spaniards and high-riding foreigners yet to be seen in Barcelona to create new work especially for the gallery. *Bookshop. Café.*
Branch: Sala Montcada C/Montcada 14 (310 06 99).

Fundació Caixa de Catalunya

Passeig de Gràcia 92 (484 59 79). Metro Diagonal/bus 20, 21, 22, 24, 28, 43, 44. **Open** 10am-2pm, 4-8pm, Tue-Sat; 10am-2pm Sun. **Closed Mon. Admission** 300ptas; free before noon and all day Sat. **Credit** (shop only) MC, V.

This *Caixa* foundation has the advantage of owning Gaudí's masterpiece the Casa Milà (**La Pedrera**, *see chapter* **Sightseeing**) although for legal reasons they are not able to use the entire building as a cultural centre. Access to the gallery space is via the spectacular main entrance and stone staircase. The gallery itself is an excellent example of a Gaudí interior: the plaster reliefs in the ceiling recall the building's marine-life themes, and none of the walls are straight. Shows mainly feature high-quality international twentieth-century art and modern Barcelona artists, along with less innovative exhibits brought in from abroad or from private collections. *Wheelchair access.*

Palau de la Virreina

*La Rambla 99 (301 77 75) Metro Liceu/bus 14, 18, 38,
59, 91.* **Open** 11am-8.30pm Tue-Sat; 11am-3pm Sun.
Closed Mon. Admission 500ptas; 300ptas under-16s.
No credit cards.
The Palau de la Virreina takes its name from the wife of a
Viceroy of Peru, who lived there after it was built in the
1770s. The beautiful upstairs rooms still have some original
wall and ceiling painting, although it cannot always be seen.
It is now the Ajuntament's main exhibition space, hosting
shows that vary from selections from the city collection to
travelling international exhibits. The lower floor is used principally to show the work of mid-career Catalan artists, especially those connected with the 1970s conceptual art
movement, and the exhibitions are only sometimes worth
the entry fee. The courtyard is used for installations. Within
the building is the city's cultural information centre, and
bookshop (*see chapter* **Essential Information**).
Wheelchair access.

Off-Barcelona

Tecla Sala Centre Cultural

*Avda Josep Tarradellas 44, Hospitalet de Llobregat
(338 57 71). Metro Torrassa/bus L12 from Plaça
Maria Cristina.* **Open** 4-7pm, Mon; 10am-1pm, 4-7pm,
Tue-Fri; 11am-2pm, Sat-Sun; may be closed Aug.
Admission free.
The magnetism of Barcelona tends to mean that all suburban artistic endeavours are condemned to relative obscu-
rity. In Hospitalet, actually Catalonia's second city and still
on the Metro system, the Tecla Sala has been trying for
years to make a dent in the cultural scene. Belying the problems it faces in attracting a public, this converted factory
is the most spacious and attractive gallery space in the met-
ropolitan area. Recently reorganised, it's now in a position
to present top-level Spanish artists and important travelling exhibits, along with dance, theatre and a number of
other cultural activities.

Art alternatives

Perhaps the oddest aspect of the Barcelona art
scene before the '92 Olympics was the lack of
independent initiative on the part of artists, who
tended to let public bodies and private dealers
set the artistic agenda. While creators elsewhere
struggled to establish alternative spaces and
structures in the 1960s, Spain's history had
made such innovations impossible. Then, in the
1980s, the speculative international market, with
its search for saleable stars straight out of art
school, and the official patronage available in
pre-Olympic Barcelona, seduced many artists
into an aggressive quest for commercial success.

A new type of politicised art activism has
emerged since 1992 and Spain's economic slump.
Some of these initiatives imitate 1970s models
(art parties, performance art, open studios), but
the content is generally high-quality. Many projects – from magazines to new media festivals to
shows – are driven forward by foreigners.

The result is a high number of art activities,
many well-organised and/or with institutional
backing, others short-term and poorly presented.
One venue to welcome this is the **CCCB** (*see*
Public Spaces & Foundations), which hosts
an international multi-media festival, the **Mostra
de Video Independent**, and the **Sonar** new
music festival each June, which also goes on in
bars and clubs (*see* **Music: Rock, Roots & Jazz**).
Another event is the **Marató de l'Espectacle**
performance jamboree in May/June (*see chapter*
Barcelona by Season).

On a smaller scale there is a string of places that
stage shows, art parties, installations and other
events: bars such as **Pastís** and the **Cafè del Sol**,
or nighttime venues such as **Se7 i Se7** or the
Apolo. This kind of thing blends into the wilder

Barcelona nightlife, and there are also semi-legal,
or one-off venues that come and go. The best way
to find out what's happening is to check out some
of the more established venues. One reasonably
permanent place is the **Banana Factory**, despite
legal difficulties. *See chapter* **Nightlife**.

L'Angelot

*C/Correu Vell 10, baixos 3 (345 05 25). Metro Jaume
I/bus 17, 40, 45.* **Open** 5-8pm Tue-Fri.
Run by video specialist Claudia Gianetti and her artist
husband Thomas Nölle, this is a small gallery in the Barri
Gòtic specialising in video art, photography and new
technologies. It's only open when there's something on,
so call ahead.
Wheelchair access.

Centro Cultural La Santa

*C/Guillem 3 (268 11 56). Metro Jaume I/bus 14, 39,
51.* **Open** 5.30-8.30pm Tue, Thur.
In a ramshackle old workshop just off the Born, this is the
'showcase' for an association with an international membership of over 100 artists. As much a part of the exhibit
is the place itself, with a kitsch/surreal décor of post-
Gaudiesque mirrors and tiles. There are also extravagant
chairs, jewellery and other items for sale. The Tuesday
and Thursday events have a party atmosphere; it may be
open at other times, but it's best to check first.

Studio Meyetta

*C/Jupi 4 (319 52 17/310 03 82). Metro Jaume I/bus
17, 40, 45.* **Open** 4-7pm Mon-Fri.
Architect Mirko Meyetta and former gallerist Benet Costa
do small shows of first-rate artists' work. Exhibits can be
viewed on opening night, or afterwards by appointment.
Wheelchair access.

Tallers Oberts (Open Studios)

Information *C/Milans 5, pral. (268 28 33).*
An open studio project held each June in the old city. Over
100 artists receive visitors during set hours. A guide is
published, and there's an Information Point with artist
dossiers. Studios, many in spectacular converted industrial buildings, can be visited year round by appointment.
A similar event is organised in the Poble Nou.

Barcelona has several recognised gallery areas, with a few other venues in other parts of the city. The C/Consell de Cent and the Barri Gòtic are the most long-established gallery locations, but in recent years new gallery clusters have developed in the Raval and around the Born, in La Ribera.

Uptown & Gràcia

There is no defined gallery district in the city's *Zona Alta*, although a few good spaces are dotted around the areas above and below Diagonal. Gràcia has few galleries, in spite of the many artworks gracing the walls of its bars. A new space in the area is **Galeria Metropolitana de Barcelona**, C/Torrijos 44 (384 31 83). Below Diagonal, another gallery is **Galeria María José Castellví**, C/París 213 (415 04 17).

Galeria Alejandro Sales

C/Julián Romea 16 (415 65 33). FGC Gràcia/bus 16, 17, 22, 24, 27, 28, 127. **Open** 11am-1.30pm, 4-8pm, Tue-Sat. Closed Aug.
Alejandro Sales is one of the city's most successful young art dealers. As well as hosting impeccable shows by name artists in his main space, he has 'Backspace', where young Spanish and foreign artists can present small-scale exhibitions – often installations – with little commercial pressure.

Galeria Àngels de la Mota

C/Goya 5 (415 12 36). Metro Fontana/bus 22, 24, 28. **Open** 5.30-8.30pm Tue-Sat. Closed Aug.
This small, out-of-the-way Gràcia gallery is worth taking a look at: De la Mota shows the work of some of Barcelona's more interesting mid-career sculptors (Joan Rom, Jordi Canudas) and photographers (Montserrat Soto, Joan Fontcuberta), plus exhibits by French artists. Feel free to check out the work in the adjoining office/storeroom.

Galeria Antoni Estrany

Passatge Mercader 18 (215 70 51). FGC Provença/bus 7, 16, 17. **Open** 10.30am-1.30pm, 4.30-8.30pm, Mon-Sat. Closed Aug.
Antoni Estrany is a dealer with an important collection of twentieth-century art, although he shows only parts of it in this cavernous, iron-columned basement. He also exhibits Spanish neo-conceptualists such as Pep Agut and the often-impenetrable José Maldonado, sculptors such as Antoni Abad, and foreign artists such as Thomas Grunfeld. A good place for serious collectors who want to consult an expert.

Galeria Carles Poy. *See page 174.*

Galeria Fernando Alcolea

Plaça Sant Gregori Taumaturg 7 (209 27 79). FGC Bonanova/bus 6, 7, 33, 34, 63, 66, 67, 68. **Open** 10am-2pm, 5-8pm, Mon-Sat. Closed Aug.
Although his space is now also a furniture and design showroom, Fernando Alcolea continues to show the work of fine young Spanish painters such as Ramon Roig and Lorenzo Valverde, as well as that of visiting American painters. *Wheelchair access.*

Galeria H20

C/Verdi 152 (415 18 01). Bus 24, 31, 32, 74, N6. **Open** 10.30am-1pm, 5.30-8pm, Tue-Fri; 11am-1pm, Sat. Closed July-Aug.
A space run by industrial designers that occupies the main floor and charming rear garden of a small Gràcia house. They regularly show design, photography, architectural projects and contemporary art. Exhibition hours can be irregular.

Around C/Consell de Cent

Barcelona's most prestigious gallery district. Some have closed in recent years, and those taking their places are not quite of the same calibre.

Galeria Carles Taché

C/Consell de Cent 290 (487 88 36). Metro Passeig de Gràcia/bus 7, 16, 17, 63. **Open** 10am-2pm, 4-8.30pm, Tue-Sat. Closed Aug. **Credit** V.
Taché is one of the only dealers to show exclusively Spanish artists. He has the good fortune to represent some of the best, including Tàpies, installation artist Jordi Benito and Jordi Colomer, as well as senior painter Eduardo Arroyo. Steep prices. *Wheelchair access.*

Galeria Joan Prats

Rambla Catalunya 54 (216 02 84). Metro Passeig de Gràcia/bus 7, 16, 17. **Open** 10.30am-1.30pm, 5-8.30pm, Tue-Sat. Closed Aug. **Credit** V.
This gallery has its origins in an encounter in the 1920s between Joan Prats, son of a prestigious hatmaker, and Joan Miró. The only remnant of the original business is the name and the hat motifs on the facade – Prats' collection of Miró works is on show at the **Fundació Miró**. *'La Prats'* represents senior Catalan painters such as Ràfols Casamada and Hernández Pijoan, presenting individual shows in a winding interior designed by architect Josep Lluis Sert. They also show important mid-career artists, including painter Ferran Garcia Sevilla, the idiosyncratic Perejaume and photographer Hannah Collins. A wide selection of prints by internationally-renowned artists can be viewed and bought at the **Artgràfic-Joan Prats** space, a block away
Branch: Artgràfic-Joan Prats C/Balmes 54 (488 13 98).

Galeria Senda

C/Consell de Cent 292 (487 67 59). Metro Passeig de Gràcia/bus 7, 16, 17, 63. **Open** 11am-2pm, 5-8.30pm, Tue-Sat. Closed Aug. **Credit** MC, V.
In this new upstairs space, dealer Carles Duran shows international painting (mostly by German and Dutch artists), and exhibits and sells work on paper by blue-chip artists like Peter Halley. Duran's previous gallery, the **Espai Passatge**, is used for installations and lower-profile projects.
Branch: Espai Passatge Passatge Mercader 4 (216 09 49).

The upper Raval/MACBA area

With the opening of Richard Meier's luminous white MACBA building galleries have sprouted up all around the upper Raval, in anticipation of an art boom. Some are new, others have moved in

Sculpture in the street

Lichtenstein in the street.

At the end of the seventies the new, democratic Socialist administration of Barcelona set out with a will to renovate their long-neglected city, to an extent that few citizens then realised. Beginning before the '92 Olympics were even a vague project, they embarked, in particular, on a remarkably ambitious programme to develop new public space in the city, with nearly 100 new squares and parks.

Typified by hard surfaces and creatively-designed benches and lampposts, these squares were also conceived to incorporate public sculptures commissioned by the city, in the largest programme of its kind in the world. Artists were offered a modest, flat fee, with costs born by the Ajuntament, and scores of major Spanish and international artists, including Joan Miró, Antoni Tàpies, Eduardo Chillida, Richard Serra, Roy Lichtenstein, Jannis Kounellis and Rebecca Horn, among others, responded. Their works are distributed across the whole of Barcelona, for one of the aims of the open spaces programme was to decentralise the city. A special effort was made to establish visual landmarks in working-class neighbourhoods, what one of the prime movers of the scheme, architect Oriol Bohigas, called 'monuments on the periphery'. The result

is truly impressive – if now stylistically a bit dated, as the initiative was halted in 1993.

Many of the squares could be described as 'sculptures' in their own right. One of the first to be completed is one of the most polemical, Albert Viaplana and Helio Piñon's 1983 **Plaça dels Països Catalans** in front of Sants station. Heavily criticised for its lack of greenery and excessive use of stone and metal, it's impressive nonetheless for its flowing lines and risky design. The same architects have also created the recent **Rambla de Mar**, the footbridge and decking that leads to their **Maremagnum** shopping-and-leisure pier. The graduated sloping of the wooden boardwalk down to the rail-less edge imitates a sandy shore, an innovative 'installation' near-inconceivable in countries where local administrations fear civil suits for accidents in public places. Also worth seeing are Santiago Calatrava's **Bac de Roda** bridge and **Telefònica** tower on Montjuïc, Norman Foster's **Torre de Collserola**, and the overdone deconstructionist sun-shields on Via Icària in the Vila Olímpica by Enric Miralles and Carme Pinós. For these, and park hours, *see chapters* **Sightseeing** *and* **Barcelona by Area**.

Sculptures around the city

Barceloneta & Port Vell *Metro Barceloneta, Drassanes/bus 14, 17, 18, 36, 57, 59, 64.* Sculptures related to harbour themes by Rebecca Horn (Barceloneta beach), Jannis Kounellis (C/Almirall Cervera) and Lothar Baumgarten (the names of the winds of the Catalan coast, set into the paving of Passeig Joan de Borbó). Roy Lichtenstein's unmissable *Barcelona Head* is on Passeig de Colom, across from the post office.

Parc de la Creueta del Coll *Metro Penitents/bus 19, 25, 28.* Sculptures by Ellsworth Kelly and Eduardo Chillida.

Parc de l'Espanya Industrial *Metro Sants-Estació/bus 43, 44, 109.* Sculptures by Anthony Caro, Pablo Palazuelo and others.

Parc de l'Estació del Nord *Metro Arc de Triomf/bus 40, 42, 141.* Large landcape sculptures by Beverly Pepper.

Plaça de la Palmera *Metro La Pau/bus 33, 40, 43, 44.* Richard Serra's *Wall*, a brilliantly conceived double curving wall, divides this square, a former factory site.

Vall d'Hebron *Metro Montbau/bus 27, 60, 73, 85, 173.* Near the former Olympic tennis site are works by Susanna Solano and Claes Oldenburg (his giant *Matches*). Joan Brossa's *Visual Poem* stands near the Horta Velodrome.

Via Júlia *Metro Roquetes/bus 11, 32, 50, 51, 76, 81.* Sculptures by Sergi Aguilar and Jaume Plensa.

Vila Olímpica *Metro Ciutadella-Vila Olímpica/bus 36, 41, 45, 49, 71.* Sculptures including Frank Gehry's *Fish* (at the Hotel Arts) and *The Kite* by Antoni Llena (Parc de les Cascades).

from elsewhere, and the quality of only a few of them is proven. Also worth checking out are **Galeria dels Àngels**, C/Àngels 16 (412 54 54); New York-based **B.A.I.**, C/Ferlandina 25, baixos (no phone); and **Caligrama**, C/Ferlandina 59 (443 14 45), which specialises in works on paper.

Galeria Carles Poy

C/Doctor Dou 10 (412 59 45). Metro Catalunya/bus all routes to Plaça Catalunya. **Open** 11am-2pm, 5-8pm, Tue-Sat. Closed Aug. **Credit** AmEx, DC, EC, MC, TC, V.
Since Poy first opened in the Gothic Quarter in the eighties he has been one of the city's most refreshing young dealers. He has no problem in showing Madrid artists, and has even brought in top-level Canadians. The great shop next door, **Dou Deu**, sells artist-made objects (*see chapter* **Shopping**).

Galeria Ferran Cano

Plaça dels Àngels 4 (310 15 48). Metro Catalunya/bus all routes to Plaça Catalunya. **Open** 5-8pm Tue-Fri; 11am-2pm Sat. **No credit cards**.
One of the most successful dealers in Spain, Mallorca-based Ferran Cano has opened a small gallery on the square facing the MACBA. He shows a tremendous number of different artists, often young, commercially viable painters.

Barri Gòtic

The Gothic Quarter has held its own in spite of the fuss made over the MACBA across the Rambla. On Carrers Petrixol and Portaferrisa you'll mostly find figurative painting, Palla and Banys Nous are the home of historic painting, antiques and book dealers, below Plaça Sant Jaume is mainly for contemporary art. Also interesting are **Galeria Pergamon**, C/Duc de la Victòria 12 (318 06 35); **Galeria Tres Punts**, C/Avinyó 27 (315 03 57); and **L'Angelot** and **Studio Meyetta** (*see* **Art alternatives**).

Antonio de Barnola

C/Palau 4 (412 22 14). Metro Liceu, Jaume I/bus 14, 17, 18, 38, 40, 45, 59, 91. **Open** 5-9pm Tue-Fri; noon-2pm, 5-9pm Sat; *July* 5-9pm Tue-Sat. Closed Aug. **Credit** AmEx, MC, TC, V.
This handsome gallery, opened in 1990, presents impeccable shows of the best of Spanish contemporary art. Dozens of artists, including young Catalan sculptors Lluis Hortalà and Begoña Montalbán, have passed through the space, which also shows work related to architecture and design. Barnola also runs a small space way up the hill in Sarrià. *Wheelchair access.*
Branch: Estudio Sarrià C/l'Avió Plus Ultra 12 (203 13 87).

Sala d'Art Artur Ramon

C/Palla 23 (302 59 70). Metro Liceu, Jaume I/bus 14, 17, 18, 38, 40, 45, 59, 91. **Open** 5-8pm Mon; 10am-1.30pm, 5-8pm, Tue-Sat; 11am-2pm Sun. Closed Aug & some Saturdays June-Sept. **No credit cards**.
The best of the local dealers in historic art, Artur Ramon is a real expert in putting together intelligent exhibits of Catalan and European painters and thematic shows (from Chinese snuff bottles to Catalan ceramics), spending years searching through private collections. His gallery/shop is on a street brimming with antique furniture and book dealers.

Sala Parés

C/Petrixol 5 (318 70 08). Metro Liceu/bus 14, 18, 38, 59, 91. **Open** 10.30am-2pm, 4.30-8.30pm, Mon-Sat; 11am-2pm Sun. Closed Sun, June-Sept, and two weeks Aug. **Credit** AmEx, V.

The Sala Parés opened in 1840 and is owned by a branch of Mayor Pasqual Maragall's family. It promoted *Modernista* painters at the turn of the century (Rusiñol, Mir, Nonell), and it was here that Picasso had his first one-man show. Now renovated, the gallery specialises in figurative painting. Across the street, the associated **Galeria Trama** offers more contemporary work, such as the popular Perico Pastor. **Branch: Galeria Trama** C/Petrixol 8, (317 48 77).

La Ribera & the Born

The Born district was a great beneficiary of the eighties art boom, but the last few years have seen the closure of many galleries. However, the proximity of the **Museu Picasso**, and the reopening of **Metrònom**, have assured the district's continuity. Also innovative are the cooperative **Artual**, C/Rec 20 (319 99 75), **Tristan Barberà**, C/Fusina 11 (319 46 69), which specialises in limited-edition prints, and **La Santa** (*see* **Art alternatives**).

Galeria Berini

Plaça Comercial 3 (310 54 43). Metro Jaume I/bus 14, 39, 51. **Open** *Sept-June* 10.30am-2pm, 5-8.30pm, Tue-Sat; *July* closed Sat. Closed Aug. **No credit cards**.
Dealer Toni Berini owns one of the few prestige Born galleries to have survived the recession and the fanfare surrounding the MACBA. She showcases the work of sculptors and painters from Spain and the United States, and also specialises in fine Latin American figurative painters. *Wheelchair access.*

Galeria Maeght

C/Montcada, 25 (310 42 45). Metro Jaume I/bus 17, 40, 45. **Open** 10am-2pm, 4-8pm, Tue-Sat. **Credit** AmEx, DC, MC, V
The Paris-based Maeght gallery opened this extraordinary art space in the mid-seventies. In a Renaissance palace on Carrer Montcada with a lovely courtyard and a noble staircase, the gallery shows hot Spanish and European painters and sculptors and has the work of many first-class artists in its holdings. The gallery also promotes prints and books produced by France-based Editions Maeght. *Wheelchair access.*

Metrònom

C/Fusina 9, 08003 (268 42 98). Metro Jaume I/bus 39, 51. **Open** 10am-2pm, 4.30-8.30pm, Tue-Sat. Closed July-Aug.
Run by collector Rafael Tous, this was Barcelona's most vital art space in the eighties. After closing briefly, it has now reopened, although its original impetus has been lost. Beneath a glorious *belle epoque* domed ceiling, Tous organises shows of photography, contemporary art and experimental music. It also has a small bookstore. Works are not normally for sale. *Bookshop. Wheelchair access.*

Museums

Like so much else, Barcelona's museums have been through many changes, and can offer acknowledged masterpieces, unfamiliar treasures and some fascinating oddities.

Barcelona has many fascinating, high quality museums, but only a few that can really be considered world-class. The primary reason is historical: while state capitals like London, Paris, or Madrid have had responsibility for creating representative national collections, Barcelona, denied such political status, has pieced its museums together by other means. The fruit of private initiative and individual energies, Barcelona's museums tend to be more partial than comprehensive, more idiosyncratic than conventional, full of innumerable wonderful objects, but with only a handful of recognised masterworks.

Barcelona awoke late to the pleasures of museum culture. Its first museum – now the **Museu de Geologia** – was set up around the time of the 1888 Universal Exhibition, and many more were born following the 1929 Exhibition on Montjuïc. Only since the most recent restoration of the Catalan government, the Generalitat, in 1980 has there been a drive to create 'national' museums, with the aim of representing present-day and historical art

(**MACBA** and the **MNAC** respectively), Catalan history (the **Museu d'Història de Catalunya**), or Catalonia's scientific legacy, in the **Museu Nacional de la Ciencia i la Tècnica**, in Terrassa (*see chapter* **Trips Out of Town**).

Apart from the odd official project, the richness of Barcelona's museums is largely, then, the result of an impressive level of individual effort, especially in the early part of this century. Scientists and academics gathered material for research purposes (as in the older science museums). Wealthy specialised collectors like Rocamora (in the **Museu Tèxtil**) and Plandiura (in the original **Museu Nacional d'Art de Catalunya**) accumulated fine art and objects for pure pleasure, later ceding them to public collections. Equally, artists such as Picasso and Miró, late in life, favoured the city with legacies of their work, while the sculptor Frederic Marès was given an entire building not to show his own work but to display an incredible collection of historical sculpture and other oddities (the **Museu Frederic Marès**). In most

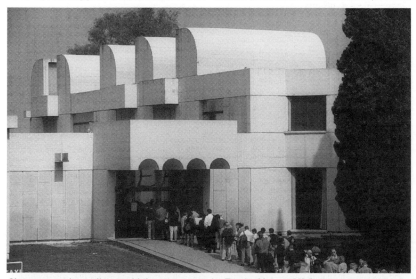

Choose your day well to avoid the queues at the **Fundació Joan Miró**. *See page 177.*

cases these holdings have passed into public ownership, and especially to the City of Barcelona.

Barcelona has had the good sense to house its collections in the best of the city's architecture, from the city history museum (**Museu d'Història de la Ciutat**), literally within the ruins of the Roman city, to the **Museu Picasso** in its Gothic palace and the **Museu Marítim** in the inspiring Medieval shipyard of the Drassanes. Purpose-built and equally impressive are Josep Lluís Sert's impeccable **Fundació Miró**, and the luminous **MACBA** museum of contemporary art, designed by Richard Meier. Visitors often find the settings of many museums sufficient compensation for other limitations they might have.

In contrast to these more spectacular examples, there's a great selection of private, small museums hidden away in the oddest of places, like the **Museu d'Autòmates** on Tibidabo, the **Museu del Perfum** with its 5,000 scent bottles, the **Museu Egipci** with some of its collection in a luxury hotel, or the **Museu del Calçat**, the shoe museum.

TIMES & INFORMATION

Most museums, and virtually all public ones, are closed on Mondays. They are open, with Sunday hours, on most public holidays, but there are some holidays when virtually all museums close, namely: New Year's Day; 6 January; 1 May; 24 June; Christmas Day; 26 December. When it comes to getting a hold on what is being shown, most labelling is exclusively in Catalan, or sometimes in Catalan and Spanish. Most museums, however, have made an effort to provide some explanations in English, whether free brochures or translations which can be consulted while touring the galleries. Some museums offer occasional guided tours, but, again, they are rarely in English.

The Picasso Museum

When his father José Ruiz was hired to teach at a Barcelona art school in 1895, 14-year old Pablo Ruiz Picasso was a budding artist whose drawings suggested a firm academic training. By the time of his definitive move to Paris in 1904 he had already painted his greatest Blue Period works, and was on his way to becoming the most acclaimed artist of the century. Barcelona's Picasso museum is testimony to these vital formative years, spent in the company of Catalonia's nascent avant-garde.

The main part of the museum is in one of the finest of the Medieval courtyard-palaces on Carrer Montcada, the mostly fifteenth-century Palau Berenguer d'Aguilar, with a courtyard almost certainly by Marc Safont, architect of the patios of the Generalitat. In one of the upstairs rooms there is a thirteenth-century painted ceiling depicting the conquest of Mallorca, discovered during restoration work. The museum arose out of a donation to the city by one of Picasso's oldest Catalan friends, Jaume Sabartès. Since it first opened in 1963, it has expanded to incorporate two adjacent mansions, the later but also impressive Palaus Meca and Castellet, and the City of Barcelon plans to make yet further additions, over several years. All to show as much of the collection of over 3,000 paintings and other work as possible, complemented by temporary shows on modern masters and themes, which the museum now has space to exhibit.

Two things stand out in the museum. The seamless presentation of Picasso's development from 1890 to 1904, from schoolboy doodlings – he was a constant, and very skilful, doodler – to art school copies to intense innovations in blue, is unbeatable. Then, in a flash, one jumps to a gallery of mature Cubist paintings from 1917, and completes the hopscotch with a leap to oils from the late fifties, based on Velázquez' famous *Las Meninas* in the Prado in Madrid. This veritable *vistus interruptus* leaves the visitor itchy for more. The culmination of Picasso's early genius in the first Cubist paintings (1907 and after) is completely absent.

There's no choice but to accept the collection's gaps as twists of history, and enjoy its strengths. After some wonderful ceramics – donated by his widow Jacqueline, a relatively recent addition – the chronological galleries begin in 1890, when Picasso still lived in his native Málaga, copying pigeons like his father (who painted them incessantly). Already at the age of nine his skill in drawing was extraordinary. After the portraits of old people and sailors in La Coruña (around 1895), the family came to Barcelona, living in the old city. The work from Picasso's student years includes portraits of family members, life drawings, and landscapes, including some of Barceloneta beach. Pressured by his father to attract patrons, he did some large realist paintings, one of which, *Science and Charity* (1897), won a prize in Madrid. Only in the late 1890s did he begin to sign his nightlife scenes and caricatures with Picasso, his mother's last name. There are fascinating sketches of Barcelona 'decadents', letters-in-cartoons sent on his first trip to Paris,

Major Figures

Casa-Museu Gaudí
*Parc Güell, Carretera del Carmel (284 64 46). Bus 24,
25.* **Open** *Oct-Mar* 10am-2pm, 4-6pm, Mon-Fri, Sun;
April-Sept 10am-2pm, 4-7pm, Mon-Fri; 10am-2pm, 4-6pm,
Sun. **Closed** Sat. **Admission** 250ptas; group discounts.
No credit cards.

One of few buildings actually completed in the **Parc Güell**,
this modest house was designed by Gaudí's colleague and
childhood friend Francesc Berenguer. Gaudí himself lived
here from 1906 to 1926, although in his final years he often
slept in the workshop at the Sagrada Família. The interior
retains an appropriately simple atmosphere, with examples
of the beautiful and outlandish furniture designed by Gaudí
and disciples such as Josep Maria Jujol. Also on show are
memorabilia of Gaudí and his collaborators, and drawings
and plans for some of his wilder, unfinished projects.

Fundació Joan Miró
*Plaça Neptú, Parc de Montjuïc (329 19 08). Metro
Paral.lel, then Funicular de Montjuïc/bus 61.* **Open** *Oct-
June* 11am-7pm Tue, Wed, Fri, Sat; 11am-9.30pm Thur;
10.30am-2.30pm Sun, public holidays. *July-Sept* 10am-
8pm Tue, Wed, Fri, Sat; 10am-9.30pm Thur; 10am-2.30pm
Sun, public holidays. **Admission** 600ptas; 300ptas
students, over-65s; group discounts. **Credit** (bookshop
only) AmEx, MC, V.

Joan Miró created the foundation that bears his name in 1971,
and it opened to the public in 1975. Designed by his friend
Josep Lluís Sert, it is one of the world's great contemporary
art museums: white walls, rustic tile floors, open airy galleries, and a beautiful system of roof arches to let in natural
light. Expanded in the eighties, it houses a collection of over
200 paintings, 150 sculptures, all of Miró's graphic work, and
some 5,000 drawings. This occupies half of the exhibition
space, while the rest is for temporary shows. The basement
Espai 13 shows young contemporary artists. The permanent
collection begins with large paintings from Miró's late period, giving an idea of his trademark use of primary colours
and simplified forms of stars, moon and women. There is
also a huge tapestry. On the way to the sculpture gallery is
the reconstructed Alexander Calder's *Mercury Fountain*,
originally built for the Spanish Republic's pavilion at the
1937 Paris Exhibition. There are some of Miró's bronze
sculptures, made with great technical virtuosity, such as

Picasso's legacy to Barcelona occupies an impressive Gothic pile.

and his menu cover from **Els Quatre Gats**.

As he gained in artistic independence, his
taste for marginal types intensified, with perversely beautiful paintings like *Margot* and *La
Nana* (1901). The intense Blue Period is well represented by *El Loco* (1904) and *Dead Woman*
(1903), among many others. The chronology is
broken with the oils from 1917 – the last extended period Picasso spent in Barcelona –, including one titled *Passeig de Colom*, before you arrive
at the *Meninas* and another series done in

Cannes in 1957. Finally, there are some impressive limited-edition lithographs and lino cuts.

Museu Picasso
*C/Montcada 15-19 (319 63 10). Metro Jaume I/bus 17,
40, 45.* **Open** 10am-8pm Tue-Sat; 10am-3pm Sun.
Admission *museum only* 500ptas; 250ptas students,
over-65s; *temporary exhibitions* 500ptas; 250ptas
students, over-65s; *combined ticket museum &
temporary exhibitions* 750ptas; 375ptas students, over-
65s. *Museum & temporary exhibitions* free under-16s.
Credit (shop only) MC, V.
Café-restaurant. Library. Shop.

Portrait of a woman aged 57 *(1539), by Hans Muelich, from the* **Col.lecció Thyssen**.

Man and Woman in the Night (1969). His transition from youth to maturity is seen in donations from his wife, Pilar Juncosa, and his dealer, Joan Prats. The *Sala Joan Prats* shows Miro as a cubist (*Street in Pedralbes*, 1917), naive (*Portrait of a Young Girl*, 1919), or surrealist, culminating in the ominous *Man and Woman in Front of a Pile of Excrements* (1935). From the *Sala Pilar Juncosa* upstairs a ramp leads to newer paintings. Larger and simpler in form, many use thick black lines, like *Catalan Peasant by Moonlight* (1968). The large

Sunbird (1968) sculpture is of Carrara marble, and more sculpture is found on the roof terrace, with a fine view of the city. Another gallery has an excellent selection of drawings. The collection ends with works by twentieth-century masters – Moore, Leger, Balthus, Ernst, Oldenburg – donated to the foundation. The Miró hosts many other activities, especially in contemporary music (*see chapter* **Music: Classical & Opera**) and has a good research library.

Bookshop. Café-restaurant. Children's theatre weekends

Oct-May. Concerts. Guided tours (12.30pm Sat, Sun). Library. Wheelchair access.

Museu del Temple Expiatori de la Sagrada Família

C/Mallorca 401 (455 02 47). Metro Sagrada Família/bus 19, 33, 34, 43, 44, 48, 50, 51. **Open** *Oct-Feb* 9am-6pm, *Mar, Sept* 9am-7pm, *April-Aug* 9am-8pm, daily. **Admission** 750ptas; 500ptas over-65s; free under-10s; group discounts. *Lifts to the spires* 200ptas. **No credit cards.**

The crypt of the Sagrada Família is a museum dedicated to Gaudí's interminable cathedral itself. Perhaps the most fascinating discovery is that Gaudí's drawings for the project were largely creative expressions of his ideas, rather than detailed plans that could be followed. Photos trace the long history of building the temple, while models and decorative details bring the construction process closer to visitors. There are also Gaudí creations and images from other buildings. *See also chapter* **Sightseeing**.

Shop. Wheelchair access (some areas).

Art Museums

Col.lecció Thyssen-Bornemisza – Monestir de Pedralbes

Baixada del Monestir 9 (280 14 34). FGC Reina Elisenda/bus 22, 63, 64, 75. **Open** 10am-2pm Tue-Sun. **Admission** *Monastery & Col.lecció Thyssen* 500ptas; 325ptas over-65s. *Wed except public holidays* 450ptas; 325ptas over-65s. *Monastery only* 300ptas; 150ptas over-65s. *Wed except public holidays* 225ptas; 150ptas over-65s. *Col.lecció Thyssen only* 300ptas; 175ptas over-65s. *Both sections* free under-16s. **Credit** (shop only) AmEx, MC, V.

The Pedralbes Monastery was a fascinating place to visit even before the Thyssen Collection moved in, and together they make Medieval religious life all the more vivid. Much the greater part of Baron Hans-Heinrich von Thyssen-Bornemisza's collection, definitively acquired for Spain in

1993, is in the Museo Thyssen in Madrid, but the 90 works exhibited in Barcelona have been chosen to harmonise with the setting, with religious themes such as the Virgin predominant. Occupying a former nuns' dormitory on one side of the convent's magnificent cloister, the collection focuses especially on Italian painting from the thirteenth to the seventeenth century – an important influence on Catalan painting – and the European Baroque. There is one true masterpiece, Fra Angelico's *Madonna of Humility*, painted in Florence in the 1430's, and other fine works include a small *Nativity* (c. 1325) by Taddeo Gaddi, a softly coloured *Madonna and Child* by Titian (1545). German painting, as in the whole of the Baron's collection, is well-represented, with a series of saints by Lucas Cranach the Older, some fine portraits and other works, and there is a Rubens *Virgin with Child* from 1618. Spanish Baroque works include a Velázquez portrait of Mariana of Austria, Queen of Spain (1655-57). Still a convent of the 'Poor Clares', the monastery with its enormous three-floor Gothic cloister is one of the best-preserved in Europe. In one of the day cells there are extraordinary mural paintings attributed to the Catalan master Ferrer Bassa (1346), influenced by the school of Siena. It's also possible to visit the chapter house and many other parts of the convent. *See also chapter* **Sightseeing**.

Shop. Wheelchair access.

Museu d'Art Contemporani de Barcelona (MACBA)

Plaça dels Àngels 1 (412 08 10). Metro Catalunya/bus all routes to Plaça Catalunya. **Open** noon-8pm Tue-Fri; 10am-8pm Sat; 10am-3pm Sun, public holidays. **Admission** 600ptas; 400ptas students, over-65s, groups; free under-7s. *Wed only* 300ptas; 200ptas students, over-65s, groups. **No credit cards.**

This pristine white building, set smack in the middle of the old Raval, is more than a museum: it is the shiniest symbol of Barcelona's ongoing project to revitalise the district with culture. While all around it the city is tearing down large tracts of old working-class housing, speculators begin to pounce on what's left, and Richard Meier's Museum of

The last word in Barcelona museums? The bright white ramps of **MACBA.**

The MNAC

In the late eighties work began on creating the **Museu Nacional d'Art de Catalunya**, the 'National Museum of Catalan Art' or MNAC, which is intended to bring together work from every era of the country's rich vi-sual heritage in one, comprehensive museum, housed in the giant Palau Nacional on Montjuïc. This project still has years to run, but, since the reopening of the early-Medieval collections on Montjuïc at the end of 1995 some of its main elements are at last taking shape. Already on view – albeit not in the same place – are the collections from perhaps the two most distinctive periods of Catalan art, very distant in time: the Romanesque paintings, in the main museum on Montjuïc, with a magnificent collection that is the finest in the world, and *Modernisme*, or Catalan art nouveau, in the **Museu d'Art Modern** in the Ciutadella.

THE MAIN MNAC

In the first decades of this century a handful of art historians realised that scores of solitary churches in the Pyrenees were falling into ruin, and with them the extraordinary Romanesque mural paintings that adorned their interiors. While entire chunks of some religious buildings were being 'saved' by private collectors to be set up elsewhere (as in The Cloisters in New York), in Catalonia the laborious task was begun of removing murals intact from church apses and remounting them on new supports. The MNAC is the world's most outstanding haven for this rare legacy, now shown in a new installation opened in December 1995.

The MNAC occupies the **Palau Nacional**, on its regal perch on Montjuïc. Although it may look like the Baroque palace of some absolute monarch, and has become an irremovable part of the Barcelona skyline, it was built only as a 'temporary pavilion' for the 1929 Exhibition. If that clash of times and styles does not make it enough of a pastiche, then its ongoing renovation under architect Gae Aulenti, famous for the Musée D'Orsay in Paris, is bound to provide the finishing post-modern touch. At its heart is the **Sala Oval**, a truly vast great hall which is used for occasional public and corporate events.

Some proud locals call the MNAC the 'Catalan Louvre', but its only resemblance with the Parisian museum is in square feet of galleries.Where the collection really stands out – the Romanesque murals – neither the Louvre nor any other museum can compare. The rest of its stocks, which run from the Gothic period up to the 1930's, do not stand up against the world's

The giant Crist de Taüll.

top art collections. This does not matter overmuch, since for the moment only a fraction of these holdings can be seen. The Gothic section, with Catalan masters like Bernat Martorell and Jaume Huguet, is scheduled to open during 1997, but as yet no dates have been set for the later periods, the Renaissance, Baroque, or the eighteenth century. Only samples can sometimes be viewed in the temporary exhibitions gallery. For now, those interested in tracing the history of Catalan art must make a leap in time and in space, to the **Museu d'Art Modern** (*see below*).

None of which, though, takes anything away from the undisputed star of the MNAC, the Romanesque, a style long disdained as rough and primitive, lacking the perspective and masterly technique of Renaissance art. Curiously enough, if the Romanesque is now admired it is partly due to the avant-garde, with their search for abstract forms and eagerness to shake up classical harmony. Whatever our reasons for enjoying it today, the Catalan Romanesque was developed in other times and for quite other motives. As Christendom pushed southward into the Iberian peninsula, small churches were founded along the way, serving as beacons for beleaguered villagers. Inside, unsophisticated depictions of the *Pantocrator* (Christ in Majesty), the Virgin, Biblical stories and the sufferings of the saints served to instruct believers in the basics of the faith, turning the church walls into a picture book.

The result, though, is a series of images of extraordinary, timeless power. The murals have been on view previously, but due to the protracted renovation of the Palau they have been closed up, and unfairly forgotten, for years. The new display is divided into twenty-one sections, in a loose chronological order, with the murals arranged as they would have been in their original churches. For each group there is a photo and model of the original church, and a map of its location. A guidebook is available in English.

One of the greatest highlights is the tremendous *Crist de Taüll*, from the twelfth-century church of Sant Climent de Taüll in the valley of Boí in the Pallars Sobirà, in section five. The massive figure of the *Pantocrator* holds a book with the words *Ego Sum Lux Mundi*, 'I am the Light of the World'. On the left, near a smaller apse, there is a figure of a monk, meditating. Section seven reveals another treasure, from the nearby church of Santa Maria de Taüll, with an apse of the Epiphany and Three Kings and a wall on the *Last Judgement*, packed with images of demons and the unrighteous being tossed into the flames. On many murals original 'grafitti' has been preserved, scratchings – probably by monks – of animals, crosses and labyrinths.

There are dramatic angels, strange creatures with wings covered in eyes, and also sculptures and carvings, from expressionless early figures of the Virgin and Child to more tender later images. After 1200 (section 13) greater fluidity and sophistication is also evident in painting, so that bodies, faces and gestures vary more between figures, and eyes seem more alive. In the same section is the 'Beam of the Passion', a decidedly anti-Semitic image. The last section, 21, has the only non-Catalan murals, from Sigena in Aragon, a remarkable mix of thirteenth-century influences from Sicilian mosaics to English illuminated manuscripts.

Museu Nacional d'Art de Catalunya

Palau Nacional, Parc de Montjuïc (423 71 99). Metro Espanya/bus 13, 55, 61. **Open** 10am-7pm Tue, Wed, Fri, Sat; 10am-9pm Thur; 10am-2.30pm Sun, holidays. **Admission** *main exhibit* 500ptas; *temporary exhibitions* 300-500ptas; *combined ticket* 600-700ptas; discounts for students, over-65s, under-18s, groups. **No credit cards**.
Café. Shop. Wheelchair access.

Museu d'Art Modern

Parc de la Ciutadella (310 63 08/319 57 28). Metro Arc de Triomf, Barceloneta/bus 14, 39, 40, 41, 42, 51, 141. **Open** 10am-7.30pm Tue-Sat; 10am-2.30pm Sun, public holidays. **Admission** 400ptas; 200ptas students, over-65s, under-18s; free under-7s. **Credit** (shop only) V.

This museum, which rather unsatisfactorily shares one of the eighteenth-century Citadel buildings in the Parc de la Ciutadella with the Catalan Parliament, should not be confused with museums that go by similar names in other countries. Its theme is not contemporary art, but Catalan art from the early nineteenth century to the 1930's. It is therefore the great showcase for the great burst of creativity – other than in architecture – associated with Catalan Modernism. It is now administratively part of the MNAC, and the plan is to incorporate it whole hog into the Palau Nacional, but this won't happen for a good many years. The museum galleries begin with the Romantic painter Marià Fortuny, whose liking for exoticism and ostentation led to the *Odalisque* (1861) and the telling *La Vicaria* (1870). The realism of the Olot school is followed by the impressionist-influenced work of the main *Modernista* painters, Ramon Casas and Santiago Rusiñol. Casas' beloved image of himself and *Quatre-Gats*-owner Pere Romeu riding tandem gives a fine idea of the vibrant spirit of the close of the century (*see chapter* **History: The City of the New Century**), and there is a large collection of drawings and graphic work. Modernism always sought not to discriminate between fine and decorative arts, and a major attraction of the museum is its superb selection of furniture and decorative objects from the period – in wood, glass, and metal – indicating as much as the movement's painting and architecture the creative freedom and new-found wealth of the moment. There is masterful work by Gaudí and Puig i Cadafalch, and exquisite marquetry tables, and other pieces by the great designer and furniture-maker Gaspar Homar. In painting, the collection carries on with the dark, intense Gypsy portraits by Isidre Nonell, who influenced Picasso, the blurry, lavishly-coloured landscapes of Joaquim Mir, and the eerie tones of Josep de Togores. Dalí is represented by two paintings, one a 1925 portrait of his father, and two avant-garde sculptors from the thirties, Julio Gonzalez and Pau Gargallo, point to the roots of abstract sculpture with work such as Gonzalez' welded head ('*The Tunnel*'), from 1932-33. There is also a gallery for temporary exhibits.
Shop. Wheelchair access.

A Modernist Sofa, by Gaspar Homar.

The fine home of the **Museu de la Música**.

Contemporary Art, opened in November 1995 and known to all as MACBA, stands out on its own, as if fallen from the sky. Meier has associated the whiteness of his MACBA with Mediterranean light and sensibility, although this does not explain why he has used the same white in Frankfurt, Des Moines, Iowa and The Hague City Hall as well. Like many of his buildings, the MACBA has a perky geometry: horizontal sun screens break the glass façade; the entrance, marked by a jutting balcony, is like a constructivist puzzle. Most Barcelonans concede the building a certain attraction, but not all are happy about its symbolic value, while those that are – especially architects – seem to care little about more essential things, such as what can be found inside. Like the Raval's other major cultural acquistion, the neighbouring **CCCB** (*see chapter* **Art Galleries**), the MACBA has a lot of excess space, with an entrance hall, lobby, interminable hallways, long ramps, all eventually leading to the shows, which are hidden away behind free-standing walls. The museum has decided always to show a part of its hard-won permanent collection, under the rather provisonal label 'Holdings for a Collection', in combination with temporary exhibits. Since the MNAC is supposed to go up to the Civil War, the MACBA begins with the forties, although earlier work by Paul Klee, Alexander Calder and Catalan sculptor Leandre Cristòfol can be seen. The work from the forties to the sixties is mostly painting, with Spanish artists of the *art informel* style (Millares, Tàpies, Guinovart), a sister movement to abstract expressionism. Holdings from the last 25 years feature more international artists, with Rauschenberg, Beuys, Anselm Kiefer, Mario Merz, Christian Boltanski and photographer Hannah Collins complementing a Spanish collection that includes a thorough review of Catalan painting (Ràfols Casamada, Xavier Grau, Miquel Barceló) and Spanish sculpture (Miquel Navarro, Susana Solano, Sergi Aguilar), with fine Basque abstract work (Jorge Oteiza). The collection is still a bit thin, though, and an expected cession

of works from other collections has fallen through. Temporary shows are a real mixed bag, from small solo shows and collaborations with other museums to exhibits of collections the museum is considering acquiring. Future projects include shows on 1970's feminism, Situationism, and Kandinsky, not exactly a post-war figure. Those who have been waiting for a contemporary art museum in Barcelona literally for decades have given the project the benefit of the doubt, even though its programming thus far has been unspectacular.
Café-restaurant. Library. Shop. Wheelchair access.

Museu de la Catedral

Catedral de Barcelona, Pla de la Seu (310 25 80). Metro Jaume I/bus 17, 19, 40, 45. **Open** 10am-1pm daily. **Admission** 50ptas. **No credit cards.**
The small Cathedral museum, in the seventeenth-century Chapter House, has a collection of religious painting and sculpture with works by the Gothic masters Jaume Huguet, Bernat Martorell and Bartolomé Bermejo, this latter with a stirring *Pietat* (1490). Access is from the cloister.
Shop.

Museu Diocesà (Diocesan Museum)

Edifici de la Pia Almoina, Pla de la Seu (315 22 13). Metro Jaume I/bus 17, 19, 40, 45. **Open** 11am-2pm, 5-8pm, Tue-Sat; 11am-2pm Sun. Closed sometimes Aug. **Admission** 200ptas. **No credit cards.**
The Museu Diocesà is in the Pia Almoina, a former alms house near the Cathedral. This oddly-shaped complex, stuck onto a fragment of the Roman wall, consists of two buildings, one Gothic, the other Renaissance. The Renaissance section, with an impressive covered roof terrace, is still being renovated, and a permanent display has yet to be installed. For now one can see a group of Gothic Virgins on the top floor, although you must pass through temporary exhibits that are sometimes of religious art, but as often include modern work with little relation to the place. When finished it will show religious art from the Middle Ages to this century, taken mostly from parish churches around Barcelona. One of its treasures is the Romanesque mural painting from Sant Salvador de Polinyà, and there is also Gothic work by Bernat Martorell and Baroque painting by Antoni Viladomat.
Shop.

Museu Frederic Marès

Plaça Sant Iu 5-6 (310 58 00). Metro Jaume I/bus 17, 19, 40, 45. **Open** 10am-5pm Tue-Sat; 10am-2pm Sun, public holidays. **Admission** 300ptas; 150ptas over-65s, under-16s; group discounts. **No credit cards.**
The son of a custom's agent in Port Bou on the French border, Frederic Marès spent the 97 years of his life sculpting (his work is found all over Barcelona) and collecting every imaginable type of object. His museum, which the city created for him in the forties, contains his personal collection of religious sculpture, and the stunning 'Sentimental Museum'. The hundreds of sculpted virgins, crucifixions and saints on the first two floors (the lower Romanesque, the upper Gothic, Renaissance and Baroque) testify to an obsessive interest in the history of his own profession. Quantity reigns over quality, although there is work by the odd master (such as Alejo de Vahia, Room 21). Marès even collected clothing for saints. The final floor houses the 'Sentimental Museum', with everything from keys to playing cards to carpenters' tools to Havana cigar labels, pocket watches, early Daguerrotypes, Torah pointers... Especially beautiful is the *Sala Femenina*, in a room once part of the Medieval Royal Palace: fans, sewing scissors, nutcrackers, and perfume flasks give a charming image of bourgeois nineteenth-century taste. From mid-spring to autumn there is a great café in the museum's beautiful Medieval courtyard (*see chapter* **Cafés & Bars**).
Café (Easter-Sept). Shop.

Decorative & Performing Arts

Museu de Ceràmica/
Museu de les Arts Decoratives

Palau Reial, Avda Diagonal 686 (Museu de Ceràmica 280 16 21/34 21/Museu de les Arts Decoratives 280 54 24). Metro Palau Reial/bus 7, 67, 68, 74, 75. **Open** 10am-3pm Tue-Sun. **Admission** *ticket for both museums* 500ptas; 250ptas students, over-65s, under-18s. **No credit cards.**

The Palau Reial on the Diagonal was originally one of the residences of the family of Gaudi's patron Eusebi Güell. It became a 'royal palace' and was significantly extended in the 1920s, when it was ceded to King Alfonso XIII. The gardens are original, and in one corner there's the famous iron gate Gaudi built for Güell. It now houses these two museums, which are run separately, although they can both be entered on the one ticket. The **Ceramic Museum** has a collection exclusively of Spanish ceramics, organised by regional styles, which vary sharply. Especially beautiful are the Medieval dishes, mostly for everyday use, particularly those from around Valencia. Catalan holdings include two wonderful tile murals from the early eighteenth century: *La xocolatada* depicts chocolate-drinking at a garden party, while the other gives a graphic image of a chaotic Baroque bullfight. A recently-added section is dedicated to the famous Valencian manufacturer Alcora, which from 1727 to 1895 supplied the tastes of the world's aristocracies. Upstairs there is a fine collection of twentieth-century ceramics: highlights include the refined simplicity of Catalan master Josep Llorens Artigas, and excellent work by Picasso and Miró. The **Decorative Arts Museum** occupies the opposite wing of the building. The palace's original painted walls provide a handsome setting for furniture and decorative objects from the Middle Ages onward, with styles presented chronologi-

In the **Museu Tèxtil i de la Indumentària.**

cally from the Gothic through to Romanticism and Catalan Modernism, ending with art deco. Quality is high, although not a lot is shown at any one time, even though the museum has large, first-class holdings of decorative clocks, Catalan glasswork and other items. Visitors can look down into the impressive oval 'throne room', with its sumptuous decoration. A second section is dedicated to Catalan industrial design in the twentieth century, in a gesture to Barcelona's ambitious design community. Key works from the fifties and sixties include Antoni Bonet's BKF chair, and designs by Barba Corsini and André Ricard. Recent design is represented by Oscar Tusquets and Javier Mariscal's 'duplex stool'. In a building in the gardens there is a collection of carriages, which for the time being cannot be visited.
Shop. Wheelchair access.

Museu d'Història del Calçat
(Shoe Museum)

Plaça Sant Felip Neri 5 (301 54 33). Metro Liceu, Jaume I/bus 17, 19, 40, 45. **Open** 11am-2pm Sun. **Admission** 200ptas; 100ptas over-65s; free under-7s; group discounts. **No credit cards.**

The Shoe Museum is in the building of the old Medieval shoemakers' guild, located on one of the city's most enigmatic squares, although hard as this may be to believe it has not always been there (*see chapter* **Barcelona by Area: The creation of the Barri Gòtic**). There are two rooms of shoes, although the only genuinely historical ones are from the eighteenth century onwards. The rest are reproductions, covering styles since Roman times, and there's a selection of cobbler's tools. Shoes worn by the famous include pairs donated by cellist Pau Casals and the celebrated Catalan clown Charlie Rivel. There are also seamless shoes, exquisitely embroidered ladies' slippers, and the enormous shoe for the Columbus statue at the foot (where else) of the Rambla.

Museu de la Música

Avda Diagonal 373 (416 11 57). Metro Verdaguer/bus 6, 15, 33, 34, 55. **Open** 10am-2pm Tue-Sun. **Admission** 300ptas; 150ptas over-65s, under-25s; free under-16s. **No credit cards.**

The museum occupies the beautiful Modernist Casa Vidal-Quadras, completed by Puig i Cadafalch on the basis of an existing building in 1902. Its collection compares the European musical tradition with parallel examples of drums, flutes, string or plucked instruments from other continents: there's a very good collection of Andalusian guitars, as well as German Baroque violas and harpsichords. The museum also testifies to a thriving instrument industry in Barcelona since the eighteenth century. Displays end with music boxes, hand organs, and early phonographs. Plans are to move the collection when the new auditorium at Glòries is finally finished (*see chapter* **Music: Classical & Opera**).
Shop. Wheelchair access.

Museu Tèxtil i de la Indumentària
(Textile & Fashion Museum)

C/Montcada 12-14 (310 45 16/319 76 03). Metro Jaume I/bus 17, 40, 45. **Open** 10am-5pm Tue-Sat; 10am-2pm Sun. **Admission** 300ptas; 150ptas students; group discounts. **No credit cards.**

Even if clothing is not your thing, the sight of café tables is bound to draw you into the handsome courtyard of this Medieval palace, just across from the Picasso museum. The museum occupies two side-by-side buildings, the Palau Nadal and the Palau dels Marquesos de Lió; the latter still retains some of its thirteenth-century wooden ceilings. It brings together items from a number of collections, including Medieval Hispano-Arab textiles and the city's lace and embroidery collection. The real highlight is the collection of historical clothing – from Baroque to twentieth century – that Manuel Rocamora donated in the 1960's, one of the finest of its kind. The museum has also received donations from Spanish designer Cristóbal Balenciaga, famous for pill box

hats and the 1958 'baby doll' dress, just the thing for break-fast at Tiffany's. The main floor has galleries for temporary shows, including contemporary textile art.
Café-restaurant. Shop.

Historical & Archeological

Museu d'Arqueologia de Catalunya
Passeig de Santa Madrona 39-41 (423 21 49/423 56 01). Metro Espanya/bus 55. **Open** 9.30am-1.30am, 3.30-7pm, Tue-Sat; 9.30am-2pm Sun. Closed public holidays. **Admission** Tue-Sat 200ptas; free students, over-65s, under-16s. Sun free. **No credit cards**.
In the Decorative Arts Palace built for the 1929 Exhibition on Montjuïc, this is one of the city's better scientific muse-ums, and the art deco centre section has recently been attrac-tively renovated. With pieces mostly from digs in Catalonia and the Balearics, the museum begins in the Paleolithic peri-od, and moves on through subsequent eras, including relics of Greek, Punic, Roman, and Visigoth colonisers, taking us right up to the early Middle Ages. There are fascinating objects related to early metallurgy, along with models of Neolithic and Iron Age burial sites. A few galleries are ded-icated to the Mallorcan Talaiotic culture, and the Carthaginian presence in the Balearics is recalled by lovely terracotta godesses and very beautiful jewellery, pulled from a huge dig on Ibiza. A large gallery is dedicated to Empúries, a source of extensive holdings (for Empúries itself, *see chap-ter* **Trips Out of Town**: **Beaches**). Roman work includes original floor mosaics (curators argue they are better pre-served when walked upon), and a reconstructed Pompeyan palace room. The centre section has quality Greek and Roman pieces, including a sarcophagus showing the rape of Proserpine, and an enormous Byzantine marble capital. Upstairs there are funerary stiles and fine mosaics, one of a woman wearing a grotesque comic mask. For some reason an enormous statue of a sexually-charged Priapus cannot be visited up close (it was formerly hidden from view com-pletely, and they are still unsure what to do with it).
Library. Shop. Wheelchair access.

Museu Egipci (Egyptian Museum)
Rambla Catalunya 57-59 (488 01 88). Metro Passeig de Gràcia/bus 7, 16, 17, 22, 24, 28. **Open** 10am-2pm, 4-8pm, Mon-Sat; 10am-2pm Sun. **Admission** 700ptas; 500ptas students, over-65s, under-15s.
Credit (shop only) MC, V.
This small private museum is run by the *Fundació Arqueològica Clos*, whose founder Jordi Clos owns a chain of hotels that includes the nearby **Hotel Claris**, where part of the collection is also on view (*see chapter* **Accommodation**). Clos has collected Egyptian artifacts since a young man, and his foundation is reputable enough to do official digs in Egypt. Finds from these digs stay in Egypt, but he also buys pieces from auctions and museums. Most of the objects, from pre-dynastic ceramics (3,500 BC) to a sarcophagi from the 'decadent' Ptolemaic period (third century BC), are related to burial rites. A small ancient-empire carved goods carrier, a lower-epoch mummy and a funerary mask are among the most important works, and there are also recreations of tombs, beautiful examples of ornamentation, statues, and impressive x-rays of mummified animals. The guide book-let has a rather unintelligible English translation.
Shop. Library.

Museu d'Historia de Catalunya
Palau de Mar, Plaça Pau Vila 3 (225 47 00). Metro Barceloneta/bus 17, 36, 39, 40, 45, 57, 59, 64. **Open** 10am-7pm Tue-Thur; 10am-8pm Fri, Sat; 10am-2.30pm Sun, public holidays. **Admission** 500ptas; 250ptas students, over-65s; group discounts. **No credit cards**.
Barcelona's newest museum, opened in 1996 in the **Palau de Mar** by the old port. The relative paucity of collection-

able objects has led critics to call it a theme park, but the visually dynamic displays offer a fairly complete overview of the history of Catalonia from pre-history to the restora-tion of the Generalitat in the eighties. To get the point across all kinds of different materials are used, in state-of-the-art museum fashion – texts, photos, real objects, reproductions, videos, animated models and re-creations of domestic scenes. There are some hands-on exhibits, such as a water mill and medieval armour. The museum follows Catalan history through eight sections on two floors, with names lies 'Roots', 'Birth of a Nation' (the consolidation of Catalonia in the Middle Ages, unfortunately downplaying the contributions – and persecution – of Muslims and Jews) and so on, coming into the contemporary era with the 'The Electric Years', including the Civil War, and 'Undoing and New Beginnings' on life under Franco and the restoration of democracy. Despite being a Generalitat project, the museum manages not to be entirely Catalanist-gung-ho. It is labelled in Catalan, but a guidebook is available in English. The *Mediateca* on the top floor has photos, texts and videos on screen and can be consulted in English. Don't miss the restaurant terrace with its unrepeatable view.
Café. Mediateca.

Museu d'Història de la Ciutat
Plaça del Rei (315 11 11/315 30 53). Metro Jaume I/bus 17, 19, 40, 45. **Open** *Oct-June* 10am-2pm, 4-8pm, Tue-Sat; 10am-2pm Sun, public holidays. *July-Sept* 10am-8pm Tue-Sat; 10am-2pm Sun, public holidays. **Admission** 500ptas; 250ptas students, over-65s; free under-16s.
No credit cards.
The City History Museum had a chance beginning: when the Medieval Casa Padellàs was being transferred to this site in 1931, remains of the Roman city of *Barcino* were discovered while digging the new foundations. These ruins can now be visited, along with successive underground extensions that cover a huge portion of the Roman city. There are also many relics found in these excavations of Roman Barcelona, but the attention of most people is usually taken by the muse-um's buildings: many parts of the Medieval royal palace, the Santa Agata chapel, the Rei Martí tower and the superb four-teenth-century Saló del Tinell banqueting hall. The Casa Padellàs itself has recently been renovated to hold long term exhibitions. The museum is also a good place to find infor-mation on visits to other Roman ruins (look for the *Barcino Barcelona* brochure). *See also chapter* **Sightseeing**.
Shop.

Museu Marítim
Avda de les Drassanes (318 32 45/301 18 31). Metro Drassanes/bus 14, 18, 38, 59, 64, 91. **Open** 10am-7pm Tue-Sun. **Admission** *museum & 'Great Sea Adventure' exhibit* 800ptas; 400ptas over-65s, under-16s; *museum only* 500ptas; 150ptas students, over-65s; free under-16s.
No credit cards.
The oft-stated remark that Barcelona has lived with its back to the sea is belied by the building this museum occupies, the impressive *Drassanes* or Medieval shipyards. Since a recent facelift and the addition of new 'temporary' exhibits (which will remain in place for years), the museum has become one of the most popular in the city. The highlight of any visit is the full-scale reproduction of the Royal Galley that was the flagship of Don Juan de Austria at the battle of Lepanto against the Turks in 1571. This battle and the sub-sequent history of Barcelona's port are now presented in 'The Great Sea Adventure', a series of modern, unashamedly audi-ence-pleasing historical simulations accompanied by head-phone commentaries (also in English). Visitors gets caught in a storm in a nineteenth-century trader, take a steamer to Buenos Aires, and go underwater with the *Ictineo*, the first submarine built by Catalan inventor Narcis Monturiol. Another exhibit, 'Catalunya and Ultramar', deals with Catalan trading and commerce with the New World, includ-ing surprising (for self-critical) documentation of slave trad-

ing. The museum has a prolific collection of paintings which allow you to see how the port of Barcelona has changed, as well as real traditional fishing craft, pleasure boats, fishing paraphernalia, explanations of boat-building techniques and a section on mapmaking and navigation. A complete visit takes at least an hour and a half.
Café-restaurant. Library. Shop.

Museu Militar
Castell de Montjuïc, Parc de Montjuïc (329 86 13). Metro Paral.lel, then Funicular and Teleféric de Montjuïc. **Open** 9.30am-8pm Tue-Sun. **Admission** 200ptas; group discounts. **No credit cards.**
The military museum occupies the eighteenth-century castle that overlooks the city from the top of Montjuïc. Inside, surprisingly, there is a collection of some 23,000 lead soldiers from the 1920s: as well as such playful items, there are relics of real war such as weaponry, armour and uniforms from the seventeenth century up to the Spanish Civil War. Used to bombard the city in former centuries and as a prison and execution site after the Civil War (a monument to Catalan president Lluís Companys, executed here in 1940, is found in the moat), the castle has strongly repressive associations, and is the only place in Barcelona where you can still find a statue of Franco. Most people go up there purely for the view.
Bar. Shop. Library.

Science & Natural History

Museu de la Ciència
C/Teodor Roviralta 55-C/Cister 64 (212 60 50). FGC Tibidabo, then Tramvia Blau/bus 17, 22, 73. **Open** 10am-8pm Tue-Sun. **Admission** 500ptas; *additional exhibits* 250ptas extra; 350ptas students; *additional exhibits* 200ptas extra; free under-7s; *additional exhibits* 200ptas. Group discounts. **Credit** (shop only) V.
Barcelona's Science Museum – in a slightly out-of-the-way, but attractive site on Tibidabo – is private, run by the cultural foundation of the ever-active 'la Caixa' savings bank. Oriented especially at children and young people, it is designed to teach basic scientific principles in the most engaging way possible. Fortunately, the quality of the displays and exhibitions is such that there's plenty to interest visitors of all ages. The permanent section uses lively interactive apparatus and hands-on displays to explain optics, wave motions, perception, mechanics, computer technology, the solar system – there's a planetarium – and other topics. There's also a special section for very small children. Temporary presentations last at least a year: a top-notch exhibit titled 'Hurricane, 1724: Navigators and Shipwrecks on the Mercury Route', based around the recovery of two Spanish galleons sunk off Santo Domingo, opened in 1996. It deals with everything from Spanish maritime activity of the time to the underwater techniques used to recover the objects on board. *See also chapter* **Children**.
Café.

Museu Etnològic
Passeig de Santa Madrona (424 68 07). Metro Espanya/bus 55. **Open** 10am-5pm Tue-Sat; 10am-2pm Sun, public holidays. **Admission** 300ptas; 150ptas students, over-65s; free under-16s; group discounts. **No credit cards.**
Extensive holdings from non-European cultures, totalling over 25,000 pieces, are shown in the Ethnology Museum on Montjuïc on a rotating basis. Shows change every two or three years, and are designed to give an idea of different cultures and not just display objects out of context. The museum is especially strong in certain areas: Pre-Colombian ceramics from Ecuador and Peru, Afghan carpets, religious sculptures from India and Nepal, Japanese pottery, and Australian aboriginal bark painting.
Shop. Library.

Museu de Geologia
Parc de la Ciutadella, Passeig Picasso (319 68 95/310 42 99). Metro Arc de Triomf/bus 14, 39, 40, 41, 42, 51, 141. **Open** 10am-2pm Tue-Sun. **Admission** 300ptas; free students, over-65s, under-16s. **No credit cards.**
Once known as the Museu Martorell, the oldest museum in Barcelona was opened in 1882 in this very building to house the extensive private collections of Francesc Martorell. His historical and archeological holdings have since been integrated into other museums, and what's left is a wide-ranging display of different minerals, all painstakingly classified, together with explanations of the formation of various geological phenomena in different parts of Catalonia. The museum also has a collection of over 300,000 fossils.
Library. Shop.

Museu de Zoologia
Parc de la Ciutadella, Passeig Picasso (319 69 12). Metro Arc de Triomf/bus 14, 39, 40, 41, 42, 51, 141. **Open** 10am-2pm Tue-Sun. **Admission** 300ptas; 150ptas students, over-65s; free under-16s. **No credit cards.**
Another of the city's older museums in the Ciutadella, the Zoology Museum occupies the much-loved 'Castle of the Three Dragons', built by Domènech i Muntaner as the Café Restaurant for the 1888 Universal Exhibition. The upper floor has a collection of dissected animals displayed just as they were at the turn of the century, and downstairs there's a Whale Room with, yes, a whale skeleton, along with other vertebrates. Musty and too small for modern purposes, the museum is redeemed by occasional good temporary shows, often on conservation themes.

The **Museu d'Arqueologia de Catalunya.**

Galeria Olímpica

*Estadi Olímpic, Parc de Montjuïc (426 06 60). Metro
Paral.lel, then Funicular de Montjuïc/bus 61.* **Open** *Oct-
May* 10am-1pm, 4-6pm, Tue-Fri; 10am-2pm Sat, Sun,
public holidays. *June-Sept* 10am-2pm, 4-8pm, Tue-Sat;
10am-2pm Sun, public holidays. **Admission** 375ptas;
325ptas students; 150ptas over-65s, under-12s; group
discounts. **Credit** AmEx, MC, V.

Barcelona's great event of 1992 deserves a better monument
than this, for it has little of the kind of thing real sports fans
want to see. Would it really be so difficult to get 1,500 metre-
winner Fermín Cacho's shoes, a Magic Johnson Dream Team
kit, or the swimsuit of some gold-medal Australian crawler?
The small space is chock-full of photos and video fragments,
but the large video library is open only to researchers, a
shame for anyone who'd like to relive their favourite event.
There's a lot of peripheral paraphernalia: a huge inflatable
COBI mascot, a recreation of an Olympic Village room,
designer volleyball holders. The best part is a section of costumes, props and scenery – some by theatre group la Fura
dels Baus – from the opening and closing ceremonies.
Library. Shop.

Museu d'Autòmates del Tibidabo (Automata Museum)

*Parc d'Attraccions del Tibidabo (211 79 42). FGC Av
Tibidabo/bus 17, 22, 73: then Tramvia Blau and
Funicular de Tibidabo.* **Open** as funfair (*see chapter*
Sightseeing). **Admission** 200ptas plus funfair entry.

The first Baroque automata belonged to the mechanical
age, operating without the constant intervention of external energy, so this collection of electrified toys from the
early twentieth century are really automata only in name.
Still, the Automata Museum inside the funfair on Tibidabo
contains some of the finest examples of coin-operated fairground machines in the world. Still in working order, some
date as far back as 1909. The entertaining scenarios include
a 1924 mechanic's workshop and the saucy *La Monyos*
(1913) – named after a real woman who cruised the Rambla
– who claps her hands, shakes her shoulders and winks,
her pigtails flying. Best of all is the depiction of hell (*El
Infierno*): look through a small glass hole into a fireball and,
to the sound of roaring flames, repentant maidens slide
slowly into the pit prodded by naked devils. Admission is
expensive if you don't tour the amusement park too.

Museu de Carrosses Fúnebres (Hearse Museum)

*C/Sancho de Avila 2 (484 17 20/484 17 21). Metro
Marina/bus 6, 40, 42, 141.* **Open** 10am-1pm, 4-6pm,
Mon-Fri; 10am-1pm Sat. **Admission** free.

For obvious reasons this is one museum that doesn't receive
many school trips. A shame, because apart from the lurid
fascination of looking at history from such a quirky angle,
this extraordinary collection of funeral memorabilia is highly evocative of eighteenth- and nineteenth-century Barcelona,
when the death of a wealthy man brought as many people
into the streets as a *festa*. The carriages vary from delicately ornate white hearses reserved for virgins and children, to
a windowless black felt mourning carriage which trans-
ported the unfortunate 'second wife' (lover) only as far as the
cemetery gates. Horses and funeral officials dressed in costume complete the scene and, as witness to the end of the
horse-drawn era, there is the American car used to bury
Generalitat President Francesc Macià in 1933.
Café

Museu del FC Barcelona

*Nou Camp, Avda Arístides Maillol, access 9 (330 94 11).
Metro Collblanc/bus 15, 52, 53, 54, 56, 57, 75.* **Open**
Nov-Mar 10am-1pm, 3-6pm, Tue-Fri; 10am-2pm Sat, Sun,

public holidays. **Closed** Mon. *April-Oct* 10am-1pm, 3-
6pm, Mon-Sat; 10am-2pm public holidays. **Closed Sun.**
Admission 400ptas; 200ptas students; 150ptas under-
13s. **No credit cards.**

No self-respecting footy fan would give this one a miss,
vying with the august Picasso as the city's most-visited
museum, even though those less than fanatical about the
game might dismiss it as nothing more than an overblown
collection of cups and trophies. Those on view include the
European Cup-Winners' Cups of 1979, 1982 and 1989, and
the club's greatest treasure, the 1992 European Cup, won at
Wembley against Sampdoria. Anything goes in the collection, even the display of old entrance tickets and a ref's whis-
tle. In the upper section of the museum there are cabinets of
assorted gifts and artistic pieces – the club still sponsors a
regular art show – some of which make the tackiest of gift
shops look sophisticated. A visit to the museum also enables
you to get a look at the cavernous Nou Camp stadium, and
even the ice rink. Like *Barça*, the museum has plans to
expand further in future.
Wheelchair access.

Museu del Perfum

*Passeig de Gràcia 39 (215 72 38). Metro Passeig de
Gràcia/bus 7, 16, 17, 22, 24, 28.* **Open** 11am-1.30pm, 5-
7.30pm, Mon-Fri; 11am-1.30pm Sat. **Admission** free.

Thousands of people walk past the **Regia** perfumery (*see
chapter* **Shopping**) every day without realising that the
'*Museu del Perfum*' sign is no promotional gimmick.
Entering through a narrow corridor at the back one comes
into a room full of 5,000 scent bottles, from pre-dynasty
Egypt to the present. The museum began when Ramon
Planas moved his shop to this location in 1960, and began
gathering what is now one of the world's finest collections.
A thousand bottles trace the period before bottles were
labelled, including Egyptian, Greek, Roman and Baroque
examples. The rest are shown by brands; examples from the
last century onwards of Guerlain, Dior and 4711, limited-edition bottles such as a Dali creation for Schiaparelli, and
prized flasks by 1920s designer René Lalique for the Coty
Cyclamen. The aromas of other lands – India, Turkey, Iran,
even countries in the former Soviet Union – can also be seen,
if not sniffed.

Museu Taurí de la Monumental (Bullfighting Museum)

*Gran Via de les Corts Catalanes 749 (245 58 03/232 71
58). Metro Monumental/bus 7, 18, 56, 62.* **Open** *April
Sept* 10.30am-2pm, 4-7pm, Mon-Sat; 10.30am-1pm Sun.
Closed most public holidays. **Admission** 350ptas;
250ptas under-16s. **No credit cards.**

Attached to Barcelona's one remaining bullring and only
open during the season, the museum has photos of *toreros*,
fancy costumes and other bullfighting memorabilia. The
corrida has fallen seriously out of favour in Catalonia,
helped in its slide by government antagonism, and nowadays the Monumental ring only fills to capacity for large-
scale summer pop concerts.
Library.

Museu Verdaguer

*Vil.la Joana, Carretera de les Planes, Vallvidrera (204 78
05). By train FGC from Plaça Catalunya to Baixador de
Vallvidrera.* **Open** 10am-2pm Tue-Sun. **Admission** free.

Jacint Verdaguer (1845-1902) was the most famous poet of
the nineteenth-century Catalan *Renaixença*. His neo-roman-
tic poetry, often on nature themes, was enormously popular, and despite the fact that he was a priest thousands of
people in anti-clerical Barcelona lined the streets for his
funeral. There's not much to see in the house where he spent
his last days – a sparse collection of his belongings – but,
an old farmhouse set in the hills of Vallvidrera, it's an attractive place with enticing views on a clear day.
Shop. Library.

Arts & Entertainment

Media

Where to find movie listings, heart-rending tabloid TV or the latest glamour gossip – our guide to the press, TV and radio.

The media world in Barcelona has been marked, more than most, by change. Most print and broadcast media have either been created or totally transformed over the last twenty years. In the press, things have now settled down to some extent, and the big guns of the local newspaper world – *El País*, *El Periódico* and *La Vanguardia* – have established their niches in local life, but other projects continue to be noticeably volatile.

In TV, meanwhile, change continues apace. Spaniards watch more television per capita than any other population in Europe – except for the incorrigible couch potatoes of Britain – and viewing figures in Catalonia are higher than anywhere else in the country. In the last few years, they have had a steadily-increasing number of channels to zap to. In the early eighties, the monopoly of TVE was broken by the arrival of separate channels for the autonomous regions, the first of them Catalan TV3, inaugurated in 1983. Then, private channels arrived in 1989, along with a proliferation of home satellite dishes to bring in TV from all over Europe. Now, the world of the small screen is to be further revolutionised with the coming of cable television, authorised in December 1995.

Another notable feature of the media in Catalonia in the past few years has been the expansion in Catalan-language broadcasting, helped by substantial subsidies from the Generalitat government. Bidding head-to-head for mass audiences with Spanish media, Catalan TV and especially radio have won healthy audiences. This success, however, contrasts rather glaringly with the continuing insecurity of the print media in Catalan.

The Press

All the main dailies are locally-produced – there is no real Spanish 'national' press – and there are no true mass popular papers. In contrast to the rather limited range of papers, the giant newsstands on the Rambla offer a vast and eclectic range of magazines – design magazines, porn, business weeklies, and the inimitable gossip mags (*see* **Wonderful World of Chat**) – which, unlike dailies, are the same from one end of the Spanish state to the other. Barcelona has also long been a major centre of creativity in the comic world. For comic shops, *see chapter* **Shopping**.

Newspapers

Avui

The Avui was launched in 1976 as the first Catalan-language newspaper published openly for forty years, and its appearance was heralded as a great national event. However, it soon established a reputation for stuffiness and failed to win more than a limited readership. A recent redesign has made it much more lively, but its position remains extremely shaky, and some say its days are numbered. In politics, it is strongly loyal to the Generalitat and its President, Jordi Pujol.

Eco

The latest Spanish-language entry in the morning newspaper sweepstakes, *Eco* hopes to be Barcelona's first successful popular tabloid. It uses the familiar formula successful in Britain and Germany, with a focus on what's happening locally, in an easy-to-read format. The price of 50ptas is much less than for other dailies, which may win readers, and it sold out during its first weeks on sale, but previous attempts to launch downmarket papers in Spain have always been dogged by an inability to sustain reader interest.

El Mundo de Catalunya

In Madrid, *El Mundo* is the main rival of *El País*, and won its reputation through its relentless exposure of the scandals of the previous Socialist government of Felipe González. It remains to be seen whether it will sustain such a critical stance under the Aznar government. In 1995 it began publishing a separate Catalan edition, but, again, it's still to be seen if there's a market in Barcelona for another daily, and also whether the Madrid paper's tendency to Castilian-Spanish chauvinism will alienate or attract readers.

El País

Spain's premier daily, and the only one that could claim to be a national newspaper, although to succeed in Barcelona it has a substantially different, Catalan edition. Also founded in 1976, *El País* has been one of the great success stories of modern Spain, and has better international coverage than any other paper. With the Friday edition comes the *Tentaciones* supplement, with arts features and listings, while Saturdays' includes the *Babelia* literature and arts section. In Spanish, with some Catalan arts features. Politically, it has been sympathetic to the Socialists, and critical of the Pujol administration in Catalonia.

El Periódico de Catalunya

The closest of the local papers to a tabloid in appearance, with big headlines, colour and lots of photos, it has built up a healthy readership, but in content and style is still more erudite and wordy than a true mass tabloid would allow itself to be. In politics, more or less leftish and sympathetic to the Socialists. It is in Spanish, with some features in Catalan, and from July to September has a double page with headline stories and the weather forecast in English, French and Italian.

Sport & El Mundo Deportivo

Two competing papers entirely devoted to sports. The place to catch up with the agonies and ecstasies of Barcelona FC, which usually take up at least half their pages. Highlights are the vox-pops, when punters-in-the-street have their say on last weekend's game plan.

Barcelona Metro

A free monthly magazine launched in summer 1996, mainly aimed at English-speaking BCN residents, with sections on what's going on in film, music, the arts, nightlife and business, plus features on aspects of local life. Given the previous lack of this kind of publication here, it'll be interesting to see if it succeeds.

Catatonic

Quarterly with stories and features more or less to do with Barcelona, on sale in some English-language bookshops.

Listings Magazines

The weekly supplements of *El País* (*Tentaciones*) and *La Vanguardia* (*Vang*) are good extra sources of information, and there are several fairly ephemeral free magazines that can help add to the sometimes-limited scope of the *Guía del Ocio*. For titles, *see chapter* **Music: Rock, Roots & Jazz**.

Guía del Ocio

Published weekly, on Thursdays, with basic what's-on information. Good for cinema and theatre details, but its music coverage often has considerable gaps.

TV & Radio

TV

Today it's possible to receive seven conventional channels in Barcelona, as well as the subscription channel Canal Plus (usually written Canal +). The coming of private TV led to a breakneck scramble for audiences in the early nineties, with the main channels going straight for the mass market with a heavy diet of game shows (offering the largest prizes in Europe), chat, soaps and heart-tugging true-life dramas in 'reality shows'. Another characteristic of Spanish TV is that programmes are unusually long, rambling on for well over an hour, perhaps an indication that locals use it more as wallpaper than as something to watch.

All channels, privately-owned or not, carry advertising. Films make up a high proportion of programming and some are shown in the original language with subtitles, particularly on **TVE 2** and **Canal +**. With the right type of set it's also possible to see otherwise-dubbed films and other programmes in the original language on TV3.

TVE 1 (La Primera)

The state television's flagship network has lost a quarter of its audience to private channels, but is still the ratings leader. In Catalonia it's mostly in Spanish, with a few programmes in Catalan. They still score big ratings successes, as, for instance, with the spectacularly successful reality-based *¿Quién Sabe Donde?*, featuring missing-persons cases from across Spain, a remarkable window into the real world of Spaniards, with star host Paco Lobatón.

TVE 2 (La 2)

TVE's second channel shows slightly more intellectual programming than TVE 1 with, particularly at weekends, sports. In Barcelona nearly half its programmes are in Catalan. Recently it has formed an alliance with the pan-European *Artes* channel, bringing some fine documentaries to Spain.

La Vanguardia

Top-selling paper in Catalonia throughout living memory, *La Vanguardia* is the only one that can rival *El País* in resources and coverage. Founded in 1881, it is the only Barcelona paper to have survived since the Franco years (and beyond); it has done so by revamping itself in the late eighties with a complete redesign that has won several international awards. It's now a lively, imaginative paper, with a trendy youth supplement on Fridays, *Vang*, that carries handy special offers. Politically, *La V* has always been conservative and is now generally sympathetic to the Pujol government, but one of the ways that it has survived so long is by never committing itself too strongly to any position. Very good for listings (*Cartelera*), especially for events in Catalonia outside Barcelona. Again, some Catalan-language features.

Classified Ads

The best newspaper for general classified ads is *La Vanguardia*, especially the Sunday edition. There are three specialised classified ad magazines: *Primeramà*, published Tuesdays and Thursdays (321 40 40), carries general ads, as does *Los Clasificados* (906 306 160), every Wednesday, which also has a large job ad section. *Mercat Laboral*, published Friday (321 65 56), is dedicated solidly to job ads. Placing adverts in all three magazines is free.

English-Language Press

The best places to find international newspapers are the kiosks on the Rambla and Passeig de Gràcia, where British papers can usually be found the same day. For more specialised press, try **Crisol** and the **Laie Llibreria-Cafè** (*see chapters* **Shopping** *and* **Cafés & Bars**).

Wonderful world of chat

In March 1996 Rocío Carrasco, 18-year old pregnant daughter of superstar of the traditional Spanish showbiz world, singer Rocío Jurado, married her boyfriend, a Guardia Civil, on the family estate near Jerez in Andalusia. Thing was, the whole event was live on TV, open coach with four white horses and all, and pictures of the rather blank-faced couple covered every kiosk in the country. *Rocíito* herself had never done anything much, apart from get up the duff, but she was known to millions as her entire life had been recorded in *¡Hola!, Lecturas, Semana, Pronto* and *Diez Minutos* – Spain's indestructible gossip magazines.

Spain has a cult of celebrity to rival that in the US, and the mags are its vital channels. What's more, the incorrigible passion for gossip is evidently un-sated, for the same stories can now also be followed on TV in such spots as *¡Qué Me Dices!* (Antena 3, 3.05pm weekdays) and *Corazón, Corazón* (TVE1, 2.30pm weekends). The cast of characters of the *prensa del corazón* ('heart press') includes international celeb-meat such as Claudia

Schiffer, Hollywood stars and the Windsor family, but pride of place is usually won by Spain's home-grown attention-grabbers: singers, Julio Iglesias, bullfighters, TV weathergirls, and some favourite faces who never seem to do much *except* appear in the magazines. The gossip mags have sailed regardless through all the transformations of post-1970s Spain. Moreover, as the regions have moved apart, knowing just who all these people are and being able to comment on their doings (even if you don't really want to) could be one of few things, like the peseta and the potato tortilla, that unites Spain and brings it together.

The gossip biz has also been one of Spain's successful export industries, through the triumphal expansion of *¡Hola!* into Britain with *Hello!* Readers who wish to enter into this wonderful world of fluff and passport to Spanish life might like to try to answer this short test while they're here. a) Who is Carmina Ordóñez? b) How many times has she been married? c) How many of them were bullfighters? and d) Why is she always in the mags?

TV3

Set up by the Generalitat, this all-Catalan-language channel has won healthy audiences with programmes such as the laid-back, a little self-consciously groovy early evening chat show *Bonic Vespre*, amid more routinely conventional material. Original, Catalan-language soap operas have also proven extremely popular, but the channel also produces the occasional quality documentary. One of the main channels for live football, on Saturday nights, and European Barça games on Wednesdays. Programmes shown dubbed on TV3 can be seen in English on sets with a NICAM stereo system.

Canal 33

Opened in 1989 as a second Catalan-language complement to TV3, showing slightly more 'quality' programming, and sports. Its programme *60 Minuts* airs excellent documentaries from around the world.

Antena 3

The first and now the most successful of the private channels, its programmes (the same throughout Spain, and so all in Spanish) are a fairly bland mix of game shows, endless chat, and some good-quality films.

Tele 5

Tele 5 started off as the pace-setter in the ratings war, grabbing itself an audience with a non-stop stream of prizes, soaps and entertainment extravaganzas, but recently the formula seems to have paled, and the channel has become a bit more sober. However, ratings have remained flat.

Canal +

Associated with the similar French channel, Canal + is only available to subscribers, but many hotels now receive it, as well as cafés and bars. Primarily a movie and sports channel, showing recent, quality films, often undubbed, it also has fairly good news slots, international documentaries,

music, and comedy. Recently they have been trying to grab exclusive rights to live football matches, encroaching on the preserves of free networks, and so conquering new subscribers. Canal+ shows US ABC News daily, at 8.05am. This is not codified, and so accessible to non-subscribers.

Barcelona Televisió (Channel 39)

Launched in late 1994, the Barcelona Ajuntament's local public-access channel. It's on-air daily, 6pm-1am, and material runs from concerts and theatre to talk, sports and general information. It relies heavily on work-experience students from university media-studies courses, but even so its 8pm newscast has gained considerable respect. At times when it is not on air, there is a continuous stream of public-service announcements scrolling on-screen.

Radio

Good music stations are **Catalunya Música** (101.5 FM), mainly for classical music, with some jazz, while a newer and interesting format is offered by **Ràdio Associació de Catalunya** (105 FM) with a mix that includes rock, jazz, world music and r'n'b. There's also a good crop of more-or-less stable youth/underground stations, if you can find them on your dial: ones to try for include **Radio Contrabanda** (91.3 FM), which has an English-language slot at 6pm on Saturdays; **Ciutat Vella** (106.8 FM), for multi-varied music; and **Ràdio Pica** (91.8 FM) for a bit of everything.

The **BBC World Service** can be picked up on 15070, 12095, 9410 and 6195 KHz Short Wave at different times of the day.

Dance

Despite problems of finance and facilities, dance in Barcelona is one of the most buoyant of the city's arts.

Catalonia – and especially, naturally enough, Barcelona – is acknowledged as the most vibrant centre for contemporary dance in Spain. There are no large, institutional companies presiding over the scene, but the city is the base for a wide and diverse range of small- to medium-sized groups producing exciting original work.

This situation emerged out of the cultural exuberance of late-seventies Barcelona, when the opening up of Spanish and Catalan society encouraged new departures in all the arts, amid a powerful atmosphere of enthusiasm and fresh ideas. The freedom to experiment was especially evident in dance in Barcelona, where there had never really been any recognised dance groups other than folk ensembles, nor even a classical ballet school. Unhindered by any set tradition, young dancers were free to try anything and everything new. In addition, many dancers such as Cesc Gelabert or Angels Margarit who had studied and worked abroad returned to lend their refined skills to the development of a Catalan dance movement.

Twenty years on, despite the growing international recognition of Catalan dance groups, enthusiasm continues to be an essential element in keeping the dance scene going. The number of venues that feature dance in their programmes has increased, but there is no dedicated dance theatre, and the dance world still suffers from a lack of consistent funding, schools and of any central location where dancers can study, practice and perform. The official Institut del Teatre dance school plays a major role, but apart from that only a few private schools carry on the work of nurturing a continuous line of serious contemporary dancers. In the eighties the most admired of modern Catalan dancers, Cesc Gelabert, opened his own school, La Fàbrica, which quickly became the most important dance location in the city. However, internal tensions and Gelabert's desire to return to pure choreography led to its closure.

What sponsorship is available for dance tends to go into performances, with little left over for development, and the more established groups find it hard to prevent talented young stars from going abroad to further their careers. In some cases, this concentration on performance over preparation can result in well dressed but hurried pieces with an undernourished content; nevertheless, in Barcelona's dance programme it's still

Danat Dansa *in action. See page 192.*

possible to come across fine, inventive performances in which the power of imagination makes the lack of resources seem a minor consideration.

OTHER DANCE: BALLET & FLAMENCO

If contemporary dance, for all its problems, has become an integral part of the local arts scene, opportunities to see other kinds of dance (except folk dancing, for which *see chapter* **Barcelona by Season**) are relatively few. Barcelona still does not have a classical ballet school, nor is there much likelihood of there being a ballet company in the city until the reconstruction of the **Liceu** is completed. In the meantime, the itinerant Liceu programme does occasionally feature visiting companies, at the **Teatre Victòria** (*see chapter* **Music: Classical & Opera**).

As for that most Spanish of dance forms, flamenco, it's not often that the best of the genre can be seen here. There has always been a clutch of nightclubs around Barcelona presenting flamenco shows mostly for tourists, with professional but second-rate performers. Most recently, however, and very surprisingly, flamenco has actually become a little fashionable in Barcelona, and venues such as **Tarantos** have spruced up their décor and, more importantly, their programmes, with the addition of first-rank performers. As yet, this trend for flamenco has had more effect in music and singing than dance, and by and large the best dancers will still be found in other parts of Spain, but you may be lucky and arrive when a really top-flight artist is in town. For venues, *see chapter* **Music: Rock, Roots & Jazz**.

Information

The *Associació dels Profesionals de Dansa de Catalunya*, at Via Laietana 52, pral, 12 (268.24.73), serves as a clearing-house for the various companies, and has information about who is doing what in Barcelona dance at any time. For more immediate programme information, check the *Guía del Ocio*, and also the free monthly *Barcelona en Música*, available in record shops and at venues. It and leaflets for public theatres such as **L'Espai** are also available at **La Virreina** information centre in the Rambla (*see chapter* **Essential Information**).

Dance Groups

Other groups worth looking out for include **Búbulus**, **Satsumas**, **Increpación Danza**, **Hamilton/Renalias**, and Marta Rovira's excellent **Trànsit** company.

Danat Dansa

A company that has continued to experiment ever since they first performed in 1985. Choreography is by Sabine Dahrendorf, from Germany, and Alfonso Ordóñez, from León, in collaboration with a permanent group of five dancers, and their works are based on culture and customs from across Spain. The extensive research behind each piece, and the varied backgrounds of the directors, ensure works with complex content and an original, dynamic language. Recent work includes the acclaimed *Jinete de peces sobre la ciudad* and *El Cielo*, which toured Spain for most of 1996.

Gelabert-Azzopardi Companyia de Dansa

Cesc Gelabert travelled to the USA in the early seventies to study architecture, but then changed to dance, at the Cunningham School in New York. He returned to become the most influential figure in Catalan contemporary dance, helping develop a particular style concentrating more on form than emotion. Later he started working with Lydia Azzopardi, previously at The Place in London, who contributed a more sophisticated level of traditional dance knowledge. In 1990, Gelabert stopped teaching to concentrate on choreography. In the past few years, the company has travelled to Germany, Belgium and France, but they frequently perform in the **Teatre Lliure**. Their double bill of *Sed* and *Armand Dust II*, combining complex historical and philosophical themes, filled the place in the spring of 1996.

Lanònima Imperial Companyia de Dansa

Choreographed by Juan Carlos Garcia, who previously danced with Cesc Gelabert, Lanònima gains much from the time he also spent with Galotta in France and Cunningham in America. Since he founded the company in 1986 he has used his extensive training to develop a rich and very physical language with some philosophical content. At its best, as with the recent *Moving Landscape*, it's exhilarating.

Mal Pelo

Two well-respected dancers, Pep Ramis and Maria Múñoz, formed this company in 1989. Its name means 'bad hair', and also implies a certain rebellious spirit. They have performed across Europe and in the US, where they received excellent reviews for pieces such as *Dol*, performed in Philadelphia and New York in 1995. Their choreography is an attempt to combine abstract dance with a strong storyline, and their latest piece, *La Calle del Imaginero*, explores the idea of a street as communal physical space.

Mudances

Angels Margarit has been gaining in stature as a choreographer over the last decade, producing highly structured, complex work. The group features two male dancers and four women, and has had considerable international success, beginning in 1991 with the piece *Atzavara*. In 1993 the company received the city's Barcelona prize, and in 1994 and 1995 they toured *Corol.la*, a solo piece featuring Margarit, internationally. In late 1996 they will unveil *Arbre de Te*, a work for six dancers, with a world première in Hamburg. Any piece by this company is worth seeing.

Ramon Oller

Never afraid to be criticised as lowbrow, Ramon Oller brings folk and popular influences into his choreography. His work lacks the complexity of other Catalan groups, but is no less enjoyable for that. He has a wide following in the city, and choreographed *Romeo and Juliet* for the Grec festival in 1996.

Roseland Musical

A company formed in 1983 by Marta Almirall to bring exciting, original dance to children. Storylines and choreography are all original, and over the years they have gained an international reputation, touring widely. Their work combines theatre, dance and music, and the latest piece, *Cara, Calla*, is a reflection on the eyes, ears, nose and mouth using seven dancers and special effects of sounds, smells and lights.

Venues

Barcelona has no venue with a consistent dance programme, apart from the Generalitat's **L'Espai**, but several that include dance in with theatre and/or music menus. Dance performances regularly feature at the **Mercat de les Flors**, and the **Teatre Lliure**, the Institut de Teatre's **Teatre Adrià Gual**, and the **Teatre de l'Eixample** all host dance companies with greater or lesser frequency (for all, *see chapter* **Theatre**). There is a regular Monday-night dance season at the **Casa Elizalde** (*see chapter* **Music: Classical & Opera**), and an eclectic range of dance shows can also be caught at the **Centre de Cultura Contemporània** (*see chapter* **Art Galleries**).

There are also some more small-scale, fringe dance events. *La Porta* collective, which won the *Premi Ciutat de Barcelona d'Arts Escèniques* award in 1995, offers dance nights every couple of months at the **Sala Beckett** (*see chapter* **Theatre**), in which choreographers and dancers present short pieces and excerpts from work in progress; small groups also sometimes perform in the **Se7 i Se7** bar (*see chapter* **Nightlife**).

L'Espai

Travessera de Gràcia 63 (414 31 33). FGC Gràcia/bus 27, 58, 64 127. **Box office** 6.30-10pm Tue-Sat; 5-7pm Sun. **Performances** *Sept/Oct-June* 10pm Thur-Sat, 7pm Sun. Tickets 1,000-1,500ptas. **No credit cards.**
Set up by the regional government, this venue's full title is *L'Espai de Dansa i Música de la Generalitat de Catalunya*. Hence it's still not entirely for dance, but combines a regular dance programme with contemporary and other musics of various kinds. The companies presented are nearly always contemporary and generally of a good standard, although in the dance world the complaint is made that there's still no venue that welcomes the most experimental companies.

Film

Catalans are dedicated filmgoers, and thanks to Barcelona's VO cinema boom there's plenty of opportunity to catch non-conventional screen fare.

This is a city of film-lovers, where queues for the latest Hollywood blockbuster stretch around the block. In fact, against the grain of the pattern seen in most other European countries, moviegoing has been increasing in popularity. A string of new cinemas has opened in recent years, including multiplexes such as the eight-screen **Maremagnum** centre in the port, and another 15-screen centre is planned for the Vila Olímpica. Alongside Maremagnum is the latest technological toy in the movie world, a giant-format **IMAX** cinema with a screen supposedly seven storeys high.

Most first-run films are dubbed into Castilian Spanish, or sometimes Catalan. Fortunately, though, there are also many people in the city who want to see independent films in the language in which they were made, with Castilian subtitles, and there's been a great increase in the numbers of cinemas showing films in this format. There are currently about 25 screens regularly showing films undubbed, and more are on the way, but even so, get there early for the 10.30pm show at weekends, as there's bound to be a long queue.

The biggest audiences may be for Hollywood movies, but Spanish and Catalan films also have a strong following in Barcelona. One consequence of the current boom in cinema-going in Spain has been to give new encouragement to domestic production. The quirky melodramas of Pedro Almodóvar have been an international cult phenomenon, and director Fernando Trueba's *Belle Epoque* won the 1993 Oscar for Best Foreign Film. Very popular at home have been the post-Almodovarian comedies of Alex de la Iglesia, such as the 1995 *El Día de la Bestia*, and the wacky work of the group La Cuadrilla, whose black comedy *Matías, Juez de Línea* is a tragic tale of a football linesman who blew a decision against Spain and won the hatred of the entire country.

With the exception of Almodóvar's films, though, Spain has had no real international box-office hit-makers, and production overall is still less than in the sixties and seventies. The central government provides large subsidies in an effort to maintain Spain's film industry, however, and the recent expansion in production may be an indication that this effort is at last bearing some fruit.

If only a handful of Spanish films has had international success, Almodóvar has helped to export

Renoir Les Corts. *See page 195.*

Spanish acting talent, in the shape of Hollywood heart-throb Antonio Banderas. Apart from Almodóvar, the best-known Spanish director is still probably Carlos Saura. In 1994 he released the glorious *¡Flamenco!*, two hours of performances by Spain's top Flamenco dancers and musicians.

CATALAN FILM-MAKING

In the first part of this century, Barcelona itself was also a major film centre. In the sixties, though, Madrid began to exert ever more influence, and today it is unquestionably the centre of Spain's film industry. The Catalan government offers its own subsidies to Catalan-language productions, on condition that the film has to be shown in Catalan, inside Catalonia. However, this incentive hasn't been able to halt Barcelona's slow decline as a production centre for Spanish-language films.

Fortunately, Barcelona's failure to bolster its film production industry has not dampened individual talent. Several recent Catalan films have been shown internationally, and one feature of them is that some have been made all or partly in English. One such to watch out for is director Marta Balletbó-Coll's funny and delightful lesbian romance *Costa Brava (Family Album)*, well-received at festivals in London and San Francisco; another is Isabel Coixet's *Coses que no et vaig dir mai (Things I Never Told You)*, filmed in Oregon.

Not in English but also interesting were two films released in 1994, the hugely successful *El perquè de tot plegat (What It's All About)*, from stories by Quim Monzó and starring Almodóvar regular Rossy de Palma, and *La Teta i la Lluna (The Tit*

Isabel Coixet's 'Things I Never Told You'.

and the Moon), the latest offering from Catalan director Bigas Luna, whose torrid, hormone-packed Spanish-language melodramas *Jamón, Jamón (Ham, Ham)* and *Huevos de Oro (Golden Balls)* caused a certain international stir. Producer Joan Antoni González is currently preparing *La Ciutat dels Prodigis*, an adaptation of Eduardo Mendoza's great Spanish-language Barcelona novel *La Ciudad de los Prodigios (City of Marvels).*

FILMS IN VO

Independent movies are almost always shown undubbed, and it is also more common for Hollywood releases to be shown in English on at least one screen in the city. Films shown undubbed with Spanish subtitles are called *versió original* or VO films, and identified by the letters VO. We give details of specialised VO cinemas below. Barcelona's official film theatre, the **Filmoteca**, shows varied programmes virtually always in VO.

Tickets & Times

Current programme details can be found in the *Guia del Ocio* and all daily papers (*see chapter* **Media**). Like most things in Barcelona, film-going mainly happens later than in more northerly countries, and the most popular sessions are those that start around 10.30pm; real 'late' shows are after midnight on Fridays and Saturdays. There are good VO weekend late shows at the **Casablanca**, **Renoir**, and **Verdi** (*see below*). Of non-VO cinemas, the **Club Capitol**, **Glòries**, **Savoy** and **Lauren** also have late shows.

All cinemas have a cheap day – *el dia del espectador* – on Monday or Wednesday. Few take phone reservations, but getting a ticket is rarely a problem except on weekend evenings. For information on children's film, *see chapter* **Children**.

Mega-Screen Movies

IMAX Port Vell

Moll d'Espanya (902 33 22 11). Metro Barceloneta/bus 14, 17, 36, 40, 45, 57, 59, 64. **Open** *box office* 30 mins before first performance, until 1am. Reservations and sales in advance until one hour before performance time. **Tickets** *Mon-Thu* before 3pm 850ptas; 3-8pm 1,300ptas; after 8pm 1,500ptas. *Fri-Sun* before 3pm 1,000ptas; 3-8pm 1,300ptas; after 8pm 1,500ptas. **Credit** MC, V.
During its first year of operation the IMAX cinema on the Moll d'Espanya in the Port Vell drew some 900,000 spectators. How many will come back again for more 'large format' cinema is an open question. It offers a choice of mega-formats, with films both on a wrap-around, dome-like OMNIMAX screen and on a towering flat IMAX screen in 3-D, with polarised glasses for each customer. Trouble is, there aren't many films made for these screens, and there's only so much interest in nature films like *The Serengeti* or even the IMAX chestnut *The Rolling Stones live at the Max*. A feature film has now been made for the IMAX, an aviation adventure called *Wings of Courage* with Tom Hulce, but the vast costs and uncertain rewards are likely to discourage large-scale production. IMAX tickets can be bought in advance with a credit card through *Servi-Caixa* machines and by phone on 902 33 22 11 (*see chapter* **Services**). *Group discounts before 8pm. Wheelchair access.*

VO Cinemas

Alexis

Rambla Catalunya 90 (215 05 06). Metro Passeig de Gràcia, FGC Provença/bus 7, 16, 20, 21, 22, 24, 28, 43, 44, N4, N6, N7. **Open** *box office* 4-11pm daily. **Tickets** 500 ptas Mon; 675ptas Tue-Fri; 700ptas Sat, Sun, public holidays). Reservations taken on day of performance. **Credit** AmEx, MC, V.
The only one of the screens in the large Alexandra cinema to show VO films, housed in a grand nineteenth-century building with marble floors and columns. *Air-conditioning. Bar/café.*

Arkadin

Travessera de Gràcia 103 (405.22.22) Metro Diagonal, FGC Gracia/bus 22, 24, 28, N4, N6. **Open** *box office* 15 minutes before first performance. **Tickets** 675ptas Mon, Tue, Thur, Fri; 550ptas Wed; 700ptas Sat, Sun, public holidays. **No credit cards.**
This small two-screen near the Via Augusta has been open for about 20 years, and occasionally shows VO films. It's a little shabby and has a cramped feeling to it, with reasonable sightlines and ageing seats. *Air-conditioning.*

Capsa

C/Pau Claris 134 (215 73 93). Metro Passeig de Gràcia/bus 39, 45, N4, N6. **Open** *box office* 15 minutes before first performance. **Tickets** 675ptas Mon, Tue, Thur, Fri; 500ptas Wed; 700ptas Sat, Sun, public holidays. **No credit cards.**
An extremely comfortable cinema, with an attractive bar alongside. The seats are tilted back, giving a clear view of the screen, and the technical quality of the equipment is high. *Air-conditioning. Bar/café.*

Casablanca

Passeig de Gràcia 115 (218 43 45). Metro Diagonal/bus 6, 7, 15, 27, 33, 34, 127, N4, N6. **Open** *box office* from 4pm. **Late shows** 12.30am Fri, Sat and eves before public holidays. **Tickets** 500 ptas Mon; 675ptas Tue-Fri; 700ptas Sat, Sun, public holidays. **No credit cards.**
Two-screen art cinema showing non-mainstream US and

European films. The bar has decent food and the late shows, with a programme of revivals, are extremely popular. *Air-conditioning. Bar/café.*

Cine-Teatre de l'Eixample

C/Aragó 140 (451 34 62). Metro Urgell/bus 14, 20, 59. **Open** *box office* varies according to screening times. Closed Mon. **Tickets** 300ptas Tue; 675ptas Wed-Sun; 800ptas 12.30am shows Thur. **No credit cards.**
The Eixample is usually a fairly serious place with a mixed programme of live drama, dance and original films, often in Catalan, but has taken up the internationally-favourite idea of showing *The Rocky Horror Picture Show* late-night once a week, in English, every Thursday. Go prepared.

Club Doré

Gran Via de les Corts Catalanes 567 (454 56 26). Metro Urgell/bus 9, 50, 54. **Open** *box office* 4.30-11pm daily. **Tickets** 675ptas Mon, Tue, Thu, Fri; 550ptas Wed; 700ptas Sat, Sun, public holidays). **No credit cards.**
The most recent addition to the VO roster, until 1994 a run-down cinema showing children's films in Spanish. It was bought and entirely renovated by the same group that owns the **Rex**, and has two ample, comfortable screens with excellent sound. It's usually the one upstairs that screens in VO. *Air-conditioning. Wheelchair access.*

Maldà

C/del Pi 5 (317 85 29). Metro Liceu/bus 14, 18, 38, 59, 91, N4, N6, N5. **Open** *box office* 4-10 pm daily. **Tickets** 450ptas Mon; 625ptas Tue-Fri; 650ptas Sat, Sun, public holidays. **No credit cards.**
The only movie house to show a double-bill, repertory programme in VO, with a programme that changes each week and often features very interesting film combinations. Just inside the Galeries Maldà shopping arcade near Plaça del Pi, it's also the only cinema housed in an eighteenth century palace, with an imposing staircase for its entrance. *Air-conditioning.*

Renoir Les Corts

C/Eugeni d'Ors 12 (490 43 05). Metro Les Corts/bus 15, 43, 59, 70, 72, N3. **Open** *box office* 3.45-11pm Mon-Thur, Sun; 3.45-11pm, midnight-1am Fri, Sat. **Late shows** from 12.30am Fri, Sat and eves before public holidays. **Tickets** 500ptas Mon; 675ptas Tue-Fri; 700ptas Sat, Sun, public holidays. **No credit cards.**
In a nondescript street a short walk from the Les Corts Metro, this new six-screen opened in late 1995 and shows exclusively VO films, with usually at least two in English, and a separate programme for late shows. The auditoriums are well-sized and comfortable, and the sound system excellent. *Air-conditioning.*

Rex

Gran Via de les Corts Catalanes 463 (423 10 60). Metro Rocafort/bus 9, 50, 56, N1, N2. **Open** *box office* 15 minutes before performance times. **Tickets** 675ptas Mon, Tue, Thur, Fri; 550ptas Wed; 700ptas Sat, Sun, public holidays. **No credit cards.**
A one-screen cinema on the Gran Via that's the largest venue showing VO films. Housed in an unattractive sixties building, it's quite comfortable and has a big screen. *Air-conditioning. Bar/café. Wheelchair access.*

Verdi

C/Verdi 32 (237 05 16). Metro Fontana/bus 39. **Open** *box office* 15 minutes before performance times. **Late shows** 12.45am Fri, Sat and eves before public holidays. **Tickets** 500ptas Mon; 675ptas Tue-Fri; 700ptas Sat, Sun, public holidays. **No credit cards.**
The Verdi cinemas in Gràcia are the great success story of Barcelona's VO film houses. In 1992, the Verdi had three screens; in 1993, it added two more, and then in 1995 they

opened the four-screen Verdi Park on the street behind. They're popular as meeting-places as well as just movie-houses, and on many weekend nights all nine *salas* are packed. Regular revivals of classics are shown alongside contemporary international releases, and there's a separate programme for the late shows. Children's films, usually dubbed, are screened on Sunday mornings and during the first session on Saturday afternoons (*see chapter* **Children**). *Air-conditioning. Bar. Wheelchair access (Sala 1).*

Verdi Park

C/Torrijos 49 (217 88 23). Metro Fontana/bus 39. **Open** *box office* 15 minutes before performance times. **Tickets** 500ptas Mon; 675ptas Tue-Fri; 700ptas Sat, Sun, public holidays. **No credit cards.**
The latest addition to the Verdi complex. The smaller of the four *salas* are a little cramped, but the seats are comfortable and there is no sound bleed from their neighbours. *Air-conditioning. Wheelchair access.*

The Filmoteca

Filmoteca de la Generalitat de Catalunya

Cinema Aquitania, Avda Sarrià 31-33 (410 75 90). Metro Hospital Clínic/bus 15, 27, 41, 54, 59, 66, N3. **Open** *box office* 30 mins before performance. **Performances** 5pm, 7.30pm, 10pm; *June-mid-Sept only* 5.30pm, 7.30pm, 10pm, daily. Closed public holidays & Aug. **Tickets** 400ptas; 300ptas students and over-65s; 2,500ptas block ticket for 10 films **No credit cards.**
The official Filmoteca shows a continually-changing programme of three films each day, nearly always in VO, generally in short seasons on specific themes, countries or directors. In the past, it has been a virtual school for aspiring directors and producers, at one time providing the only opportunity in the city to see classics from other countries. A children's programme is shown at 5pm on Sundays.

Events

Attempts to revive the Film Festival held in Barcelona in the eighties have so far come to nothing, but another event to look out for is the successful Women's Film Festival at the **Filmoteca** each June (*see chapter* **Women's Barcelona**).

Festival Internacional de Cinema Fantàstic de Sitges (Sitges International Festival of Fantastic Cinema)

C/Rosselló 257, 3er-E, 08029 Barcelona (415-39 38/fax 237 65 21). Train RENFE to Sitges. **Dates** first Friday to second Saturday of October.
This festival held every October will be 30 years old in 1997. Unlike most film festivals, it began small and has grown in stature. Designed for both the film and TV industry and the general public, it features all kinds of cinema loosely classed as 'fantastic', from science fiction to horror movies. World premières rub shoulders with classics like *Star Trek* and *Dracula*. In 1994, the Spanish movie *Justino: Un Asesino de la Tercera Edad (Justino: An Elderly Killer),* by La Cuadrilla, shared the best film award with *71 Fragments Of An Accidental Chronology* by Austria's Michael Henke; *Citizen X,* by Chris Gerolmo of the US was the winner in 1995. It's a week of non-stop, nail-biting tension, and the drama doesn't end with the show, as many restaurants and bars join in the spirit of the thing and stay open through the night. *See chapter* **Trips Out of Town** for details of how to get to Sitges, and where to stay and eat once you're there.

Music: Classical & Opera

Barcelona has devoted music-lovers, great singers and an orchestra that's going places, even though its one great concert hall may be about to burst at the seams.

A catastrophe, or just a disaster with a silver lining? In January 1994, when a chance spark from a welder's torch sent the **Liceu** opera house up in smoke in just a few hours, Barcelona went into a state of shock. Presiding over the Rambla since 1847, and rebuilt after an earlier fire in 1861, the Liceu was one of the most venerable cultural institutions in a city that is always creating new ones. It was also a musty old theatre with utterly inadequate backstage facilities, and the inadequacies of which had been discussed for years.

Work began remarkably quickly on building a new Liceu, retaining the old façade – which had survived the fire – but with entirely new, expanded design and rehearsal spaces. The result will thus be that Barcelona will acquire a world-class modern opera house behind the old shell. The current line is that the Liceu will reopen in 1998; the date may be open to question, but in Barcelona these projects tend to get finished sooner or later.

Despite a very old-world elitist image that often put off wider audiences – many of Barcelona's grander families held 'private boxes', which are not going to be replaced in the new opera house – the Liceu had a central position in the musical world because of the particularly strong choral and operatic tradition in Catalonia. Catalans love song, and have produced many great singers, from tenor Francesc Viñas at the turn of the century to Victoria de los Ángeles and today's stars Jaume Aragall, Montserrat Caballé and José (known here as Josep) Carreras. Choral societies have been a Catalan institution since the last century, and the most established – such as as the **Orfeó Català** and Coral Sant Jordi – are of international standing. Indeed, such is the strength of the Catalan tradition in singing that not only the Liceu but also Barcelona's other great musical venue, the **Palau de la Música Catalana**, was built as a choral and operatic, rather than orchestral, concert hall.

ORCHESTRAS & SCHOOLS

The Catalan musical tradition is by no means limited to singing, for the country has also been home to many distinguished musicians in other fields: the immense figure of cellist Pablo (again, always known here as Pau) Casals, pianist Alicia de Larrocha, and composers Robert Gerhard, Eduard Toldrà and Xavier Montsalvatge. Barcelona's orchestras, however, have never enjoyed the same prestige as its singers.

Today, Barcelona has two official orchestras, the Liceu orchestra and the cumbersomely-named **Orquestra Simfònica de Barcelona i Nacional de Catalunya**, formerly the *Orquestra Ciutat de Barcelona* and more easily referred to as the **OBC**. Both are considered competent, but neither has been critically acclaimed away from home. Barcelona's music-lovers are generally happy with the range of artists performing here, but in the past they have often been thinking of the many international outfits who visit rather than home-grown ones. The city's lack of a world-class orchestra has long been a sensitive point, but things are finally set to improve. A two-year period during which the OBC was without a director ended with the appointment of American conductor Lawrence Foster, in permanent residence from 1996. Evidently, a major part of his brief will be to produce a Barcelona-based symphony orchestra with an international reputation.

The absence of an adequate musical infrastructure is one area of particular concern to the city's musicians. They are irked by the authorities' willingness to spend vast amounts on grand events, while paying much less attention to musical education, or the provision of rehearsal and performance spaces. As far as venues are concerned, an apparently impossible burden of activity is now born by the Palau de la Música. Nevertheless, this is one more field in which the Barcelona authorities have a project in hand, the new **Auditori** at the Plaça de les Glòries. This box-like building will contain two ample modern concert halls and abundant rehearsal and ancillary space, and be a new permanent home for the OBC, the Barcelona Conservatory and even the **Museu de la Música** (*see chapter* **Museums**). However, it has been dogged by delays and is less advanced than its equally ambitious neighbour the **Teatre Nacional** (*see chapter* **Theatre**), and is unlikely to see any performances until at least 1998.

Whatever its problems in institutions and hardware, Barcelona nevertheless has a large and enthusiastic audience for classical music, and concert-going is a very popular activity. The city is also the base for a dynamic contemporary music scene. There are several ensembles active in the field, and interesting composers include Joan Guinjoan, Albert Guinovart and the eccentric Carles Santos. The most regular venues for contemporary concerts are the **Fundació Miró** and **Teatre Lliure**, but there are performances fairly frequently at the **Casa Elizalde** and **L'Espai** (*see chapter* **Dance**), and even **Nick Havanna** (*see chapter* **Nightlife**) has hosted concerts.

Programmes & tickets

The *Guia del Ocio* has thin coverage of classical music, and the best sources of information, apart from the programme leaflets of individual venues, are the leaflet *Informatiu Musical* and monthly magazine *Barcelona in Música*, both free from tourist offices and many record shops. Procedures for buying tickets in advance vary. At smaller venues tickets are often available only from the box office, but, as with theatres, tickets for several venues are sold through savings banks (*see chapter* **Services**). Tickets handled by 'la Caixa' can be bought with a credit card from the *Servi-Caixa* machines at the bank's branches, or booked by phone with a card on freephone 902 33 22 11; tickets handled by the Caixa de Catalunya can be bought over the counter at any of its branches or by phone with a credit card on 310 12 12.

The procedure for obtaining tickets for performances at the **Palau de la Música** also varies. Tickets for the **OBC** season are obtainable only from the Palau box office (or by post from the Orchestra's office); many are sold in the form of *Abonaments* or season tickets for the whole year, and season ticket holders have priority when booking, so the number of seats on open sale can be low. Note, though, that many concert series are organised by independent agencies, especially **Ibercàmera** and **Euroconcert**, who are responsible above all for bringing big international names to the city. Tickets for these series, and for the **Liceu** season, are available through *Servi-Caixa*. For all concerts at the Palau, though, demand is very high, and it's advisable to obtain tickets as promptly as possible.

Concert Promoters

Euroconcert *Rambla Catalunya 10, 2° 4ª (318 51 58). Metro Catalunya/bus all routes to Plaça Catalunya.* **Open** 9.30am-1.30pm, 4-7pm, Mon-Thur; 9.30am-1.30pm Fri.
Ibercàmera *Gran Via de les Corts Catalanes 636, 1° 2ª (317 90 50/reservations 301 69 43). Metro Passeig de Gràcia/bus 7, 16, 17, 22, 24, 28, 50, 54, 56.* **Open** 10am-2pm, 3-6pm, Mon-Fri.

Orchestras & Ensembles

Orfeó Català

Information *Palau de la Música, C/Sant Francesc de Paula 2 (268 10 00).*
The Orfeó is a national institution as well as a choir, and such were its status and wealth at the turn of the century that it was able to commission the building of the Palau de la Música. It has undergone radical change since 1985, when the average age of its members was over 60, and programmes very unadventurous. Today, the quality of the

choir has greatly improved, and current director Jordi Casas is considered one of the leading figures in choral music in Europe. The Orfeó's repertoire is the great choral classics. The choir spends most of its time in Catalonia and Spain, but occasionally performs abroad, recently in Berlin.

Orquestra de Cadaqués

Information *C/Arcs 8 (302 27 22).*
Created in 1988, this is the brainchild of conductor Edmon Colomer and the **Festival de Cadaqués**. It is really Catalan in name only, however, as it's made up of 40 musicians from around the world. The players are mostly young, and many of them are British. Its Catalan members include the player-composers Josep Soler and Joan Guinjoan, who perform as soloists and as part of the orchestra. It is not a full-time occupation for its members, but tours several times each year, as well as playing in Barcelona and at the festivals in Cadaqués itself, where Sir Neville Marriner is a regular conductor, and at Perelada (*see* **Festivals**).

Orquestra de Cambra Teatre Lliure

Information *see* **Teatre Lliure**.
This well-regarded chamber orchestra is based at the Teatre Lliure, and like the venue has a strong interest in contemporary music. Directed by Josep Pons, the orchestra has a commission to make two recordings a year for Harmonia Mundi, which so far have included works by Isaac Albéniz, Josep Soler, Luis de Pablo and Joan Albert Amargós. They also sometimes perform at the Auditori de 'la Caixa'.

Orquestra Simfònica de Barcelona i Nacional de Catalunya (OBC)

Information & postal bookings *OBC, Via Laietana 41, pral, 08003 (317 10 96).*
This orchestra was founded as the *Orquesta Municipal de Barcelona* in 1944, and later became the *Orquestra Ciutat de Barcelona*. Its present laborious official title is a giveaway that it is now supported, in a rare moment of collaboration, by both the Barcelona Ajuntament and the Generalitat, who have come together with a clear commitment to establish it as a front-rank international orchestra. As part of this, despite its standing engagements at the Palau, the orchestra will tour more frequently, and in 1997 will travel to Paris and to other parts of Spain. Its recently-installed musical director is American, Lawrence Foster, with the German Franz-Paul Decker as principal visiting conductor. As the old *Ciutat de Barcelona* orchestra it was often accused of complacency and of relying too much on the loyalty of the Palau season-ticket holders, and Decker himself had a confrontation with the orchestra's members during a spell as its director in the eighties when he suggested that one quick way to improve it would be to introduce some foreign players among them. Its membership has since changed considerably. As well as its principal conductors the orchestra also performs under several leading guest conductors, and with an international range of soloists who in the 1996-7 season will include Barbara Hendricks, Elena Bashkirova and Evelyn Glennie. In its musical programming the OBC has two main areas of emphasis: to present a full and enterprising international repertoire, and also to perform and record the range of Catalan music. Its main concert season at the Palau runs from October to May; there are concerts most Fridays (9pm) and Saturdays (7pm), and hugely popular, lower-price Sunday morning concerts at 11pm. The orchestra also perform in free concerts at the **Saló de Cent**, and many of its soloists play in chamber groups, such as the Quartet de Corda Gaudí and the Quintet de Corda de Barcelona.

Orquestra Simfònica del Gran Teatre del Liceu

Information *see* **Gran Teatre del Liceu**
This, the other full-scale orchestra resident in Barcelona after the OCB, is the permanent resident orchestra of the Liceu, formed in the early eighties as part of an attempt to give the opera house more solidity as a musical venue, creating in-

house productions rather than just relying on visiting companies, and with less of an air of an upper-class social club. Since the destruction of the Liceu the orchestra has performed at various Barcelona venues, and at major one-off events such as the Perelada festival (*see* **Festivals**).

Orquestra Simfònica del Vallès

Information *C/Narcís Giralt 40, Sabadell (727 03 00)*.
Founded in 1987, the Orquestra Simfònica del Vallès has become one of the leading symphony orchestras in Catalonia, although it is still generally considered to be at a lower level than the two Barcelona orchestras. It performs every Friday from October to June at the **Teatre Municipal La Faràndula** *C/Alfons XIII, Sabadell (725 83 16)*, and on some Saturday mornings at the Palau in Barcelona.

Venues

Barcelona had long had a shortage of music venues, but since the Liceu fire the pressure on space has been immense. The **Mercat de les Flors** and **Teatre Victòria** (*see chapter* **Theatre**) have taken some of the strain. Look out, also, for concerts in the **Conservatori Superior Municipal de Música**, at C/Bruc 112 (458 43 02).

Auditori del Centre Cultural de la Fundació 'la Caixa'

Passeig de Sant Joan 108 (458 89 07). Metro Verdaguer/bus 15, 20, 21, 45, 47, 55. **Open** *centre* 11am-8pm Tue-Sat; 11am-3pm Sun, public holidays. *box office* 11am-8pm Tue-Sat; *advance sales* box office & Servi-Caixa. **Tickets** *main concert series* 500-2,000ptas; *family concerts* 500ptas; 250ptas under-14s. **Credit** V.
The arts foundation of 'la Caixa' is the city's main patron of musical activity outside of official funding, and has a concert programme throughout the year in its main cultural centre and art gallery. Its philosophy is both to support young local musicians, and to provide Catalan audiences with opportunities to hear well-known performers from abroad. Concerts generally form short series, such as a recent one of all Beethoven's string quartets. As well as the main programme there are 'family concerts' on Saturday mornings at 12.30pm, of music selected to engage and appeal to kids, but still performed by entirely professional and often well-known musicians. For the main centre, *see chapter* **Art Galleries**; the centre also has a great, open-access music library, the **Mediateca**, for which *see chapter* **Students**.

La Casa Elizalde

C/València 302 (487 80 92). Metro Passeig de Gràcia/bus 39, 43, 44, 45. **Open** *information & box office* 10am-2pm, 5-9pm, Mon-Fri. **Tickets** 400ptas. **No credit cards**.
Casa Elizalde is a multi-purpose, city-owned cultural centre housed in a strikingly ornate Eixample building, with a beautiful courtyard that's used for some performances in summer. It runs courses on a vast array of subjects, and hosts classical concerts, usually on Saturdays at 7.30pm, and on some other nights. Most feature soloists, duets or quartets, and there are series of contemporary music concerts.

Fundació Joan Miró

Plaça Neptú, Parc de Montjuïc (329 19 08). Metro Paral.lel, then Funicular de Montjuïc/bus 61. **Open** (*see chapter* **Museums** for main museum) *box office* from 30min before performance times; *phone reservations* 9am-2pm, 3-6pm, Mon-Fri. **Tickets** 700ptas; 1,800ptas ticket for three concerts; 4,000ptas ticket for eight concerts. **Credit** AmEx, MC, V.
The Fundació Miró contains the main centre for contemporary music development in Spain. It has a main, summer concert series, *Nit de Música*, from June to September, with eight

concerts spread over that time, on Thursdays at 8pm. There are also series at other times of the year, featuring Catalan and international musicians. *See also chapter* **Museums**.

Gran Teatre del Liceu

La Rambla 61 (information 412 19 03/412 35 32). Metro Liceu/bus 14, 18, 38, 59, 64, 91. **Open** *box office* 3-7pm Mon-Fri; *advance sales* box office & Servi-Caixa. **Tickets** prices vary according to venue.
The Liceu-in-stone may be a building site, but the Liceu as an *institution* seems to have been given a new lease of life, as, freed from its cosy old edifice, it struggles to keep itself alive in public memory and satisfy the passionate audience of local opera-lovers. The phantom-Liceu seeks to present a full season, with performances in the Palau, the Teatre Victòria and the Mercat de les Flors. Opera productions are generally at the Victòria and often feature visiting European companies, or collaborative productions; concert performances are staged at the Palau. As well as locally through Servi-Caixa tickets for the Liceu season can be booked from abroad on a special 24-hour phoneline, on 343-417 00 60.

Palau de la Música Catalana

C/Sant Francesc de Paula 2 (268 10 00). Metro Urquinaona/bus 17, 19, 40, 45. **Open** *box office* 10am-9pm Mon-Fri; 3-9pm Sat; 10am-11pm Sun; *advance sales* box office and by phone. **Tickets** *main OBC concert series* 1,500-6,500ptas Fri, Sat; 900-3,900ptas. Sun. **Credit** MC, V.
The Palau remains Barcelona's main (and only substantial) concert hall. The building, one of the must-sees of the city in itself, is a delightful modernist extravaganza (*see chapter* **Sightseeing**), but it's also an ideally-sized auditorium with fine acoustics. The original stage was too small, but restoration work in the last decade has included an extension of the concert pit. Musicians love playing here. Its never-ending agenda includes concerts by a great many international orchestras, singers and soloists, in the Ibercàmera and Euroconcert seasons, as well as its weekly OBC concerts. The only concern might be that this wonderful old building could collapse under the strain now being put upon it.

Sala Cultural Caja Madrid

Plaça Catalunya 9 (301 44 94). Metro Catalunya/bus all routes to Plaça Catalunya. **Open** *information* 11am-1pm, 6-9pm, Tue-Sat; 11am-1pm Sun. **Tickets** free.
This small concert hall in Plaça Catalunya is run by a Madrid savings bank. Concerts are held every Tuesday at 7.30pm, and occasionally on other days of the week, between October and June: its programmes are varied, including piano solos, chamber music and a few orchestral works.

Saló de Cent, Ajuntament de Barcelona

Ajuntament de Barcelona, Plaça Sant Jaume (402 70 00). Metro Liceu, Jaume I/bus 17, 40, 45. **Open** *information* 8am-3pm Mon-Fri. **Performances** *Oct-June* 8pm Thur; doors open 7pm. **Tickets** free.
Every Thursday during the main music season (except public holidays), the magnificent fourteenth-century council chamber in the Ajuntament, the *Saló de Cent*, is thrown open to a free concert by musicians from the OBC. The programme is generally of fairly well-known works, and the concerts offer a matchless opportunity to admire the architecture.

Teatre Lliure

C/Montseny 47 (218 92 51). Metro Fontana/bus 22, 24, 28, 39, N4, N6. **Open** *box office* from 5pm Tue-Sat; *phone reservations* 5-8pm Tue-Sat; *advance sales* box office & Caixa de Catalunya. **Open** Mon & Thu; 10pm Sun. **Tickets** 1,600ptas. **No credit cards**.
This innovative centre is also a focus for contemporary music. Programmes, performed by its own orchestra, are exclusively twentieth-century. In 1996 it celebrated the centenary of Catalan composer Robert Gerhard with concerts of many of his works. *See also chapter* **Theatre**.

Lawrence Foster and the **OBC** *await you at the* **Palau de la Música Catalana**.

Traditional Music

Centre Artesà Tradicionàrius
Travessera de Sant Antoni 6-8 (218 44 85). Metro Fontana/bus 22, 24, 28, N4, N6. **Advance sales** Servi-Caixa. **Concerts** 10.30pm Mon, Thur. Closed July, Aug. **Tickets** free Mon; 600ptas Thur; *special concerts* 1,000-1,500ptas. **No credit cards**.

The Tradicionàrius is a centre, founded in 1993, primarily for the study, teaching and performance of all the many different varieties of Catalan traditional music, instruments and dances. It also takes an interest in traditional music and dance from every part of the world, and its twice-weekly concerts (generally the same, but free on Mondays) can feature musicians from anywhere from Andalusia to Ireland. From January to March it hosts the Tradicionàrius festival, with concerts several nights a week exclusively of Catalan music.

Festivals

The main arts festivals, the **Grec** and the **Mercè** (*see chapter* **Barcelona by Season**), feature a wide range of music, and the **Festival de la Guitarra** (*see chapter* **Music: Rock, Roots & Jazz**) brings to the city fine classical guitarists. In summer, the festivals held near the Costa Brava provide great opportunities for escaping the heat of Barcelona. For travel information, *see chapter* **Trips Out of Town: Beaches**.

Festival de Música Antiga
Information *Centre Cultural de la Fundació 'la Caixa', Passeig de Sant Joan 108 (458 89 07).* **Dates** April-May. **Tickets** prices vary according to venue.

Organised by the Fundació 'la Caixa', this well-established and very popular festival brings together fine performers and ensembles from across Europe in early, Renaissance and Baroque music. One of its greatest attractions is its venues: churches such as Sant Felip Neri, Santa Maria del Pi and Santa Maria del Mar, and the Monastery of Pedralbes.

Festival de Cadaqués
Information *Orquestra de Cadaqués, C/Arcs 8, Barcelona (302 27 22),* or during festival *Oficina de Turisme, Cadaqués (972/25 83 11).* **Dates** mid-July-mid-Aug. **Tickets** 1,000-3,500ptas.

The programme at this festival in perhaps the most chic town on the Catalan coast usually comprises a mix of the great classics, but also featured are contemporary works and music competitions.

Festival Internacional de Música Castell de Perelada
Castell de Peralada, Peralada, Girona (972/53 81 25). **Information** *Ibercàmera (301 69 43).* **Dates** mid-July-late Aug. **Box office** *from 10 June* 9am-9pm daily; *advance sales* box office & Servi-Caixa. **Tickets** 3,000-10,000ptas. **Credit** MC, V.

Held in the gardens of the castle (now also a casino) of Perelada, close to Figueres, this is a notably upmarket festival, and for many people the social outing is as important as the (excellent) music. It attracts major international names – Teresa Berganza, Mikhail Baryshnikov – and the programme is usually heavily opera-oriented.

Festival Internacional de Música Torroella de Montgrí
Information *Festival Internacional de Música, Apartat 70, Codina 28, 17257 Torroella de Montgrí (972/76 06 05).* **Dates** mid-Jul-late Aug. **Advance booking** from early June. **Tickets** 500-8,000ptas.

In Torroella, a small town north of Begur, summer concerts take place in a beautiful Gothic church, or in the main square. Recent highlights have included appearances by tenor Jaume Aragall and the English Chamber Orchestra. A course is also run for young conductors and teachers.

Music: Rock, Roots & Jazz

With jazz, pop, salsa, flamenco and a summer techno/fringe-fest, Barcelona's music scene is never routine.

Barcelona's musical scene makes up for its small size by its diversity. Most name international acts now include Barcelona on their European tours. World music, salsa and especially jazz are well represented in local venues. Even flamenco, seen for years in Catalonia as a more-or-less foreign, often incorrigibly naff cultural leftover from another era, is enjoying a healthy revival spurred on by the 'new flamenco' movement of Madrid.

Catalonia produces several varieties of home-grown music. *Rock Català* – heavy-ish rock/pop groups who sing only in Catalan – is well-supported by the local industry, but rarely lives up to the hype. Exceptions are Sau, Els Pets and the reggae-pop of Um-Pah-Pah. *Barna-pop*, Barcelona-based dance-pop, is more accessible, and more fun. Names to watch out for are Los Sencillos, Peanut Pie, the Spanish hip-hop of Misión Hispana, and 7 Notas 7 Colores. Barcelona's sizeable international population has helped make it a fine breeding ground for cross-cultural experiments. KRAB, the musical off-shoot of theatre group La Fura dels Baus (*see chapter* **Theatre**), have impressed and surprised critics with their post-industrial techno, and the soft dance-soul of the Princes of Time has a regular Monday slot at **Jamboree**.

In complete contrast there is *cançó*, Catalonia's tradition of ballad singing, often politically inspired, that was long a symbol of the country's modern identity. It has, understandably, lost its radical edge since the sixties and seventies, when the dictatorship gave it a powerful *raison d'etre*. Names still worthy of note, both very original musicians with great voices, are Lluis Llach and the Mallorcan Maria del Mar Bonet. Joan Manuel Serrat, a star throughout Spain and Latin America, sings as much in Spanish as in Catalan, which separates him from some of his former colleagues.

And then there's rumba. The rest of the world may have cottoned on to it via the French-based Gypsy Kings, but gypsy rumba – the flamenco-ish, feet-tapping, hand-clapping music that simply refuses to die – was born in Barcelona. The pattern set by Peret, the gypsy from the Raval who is the king of rumba, is now carried on by Rhumbaketumba, Ai, Ai, Ai, Sabor de Gràcia, Son como Son and any number of bands you may stumble across on the outside stages at local *festes*. And the renaissance of pure flamenco that has been underway throughout Spain has finally reached Catalonia, sustained by the children of migrants from the south. Local artists Mayte Martín, Miguel Poveda and Duquende are rated among the most accomplished *cante jondo* voices in the country, and the jazz/flamenco fusion group Jaleo have filled venues from Tibidabo to Tokyo.

OTHER STYLES

Sustained by an important international festival each October and two schools – the Taller de Músics and Aula de la Musica –, Barcelona´s jazz scene is one of the most vibrant in Europe. Most prominent and most recorded of Catalan jazz artists is without doubt the 50-year-old pianist Tete Montoliú. The list of artists with whom he's recorded is impressive: everyone from Ronald Kirk to Dexter Gordon, and his collaboration on the classic *Ben Webster Meets Don Byas in the Black Forest* reinforced his reputation as one of the greats. Singers based in Barcelona include the big bluesy sound of Big Mama and the Mouserockers, and Americans Monica Green and Deborah Carter. Lucky Guri, the Catalan singer/piano-man who's become a Barcelona institution, does everything from ragtime to be-bop in his own inimitable style.

Roots, reggae and African music have long enjoyed a following here. Local reggae/ragga outfits include the ska band Dr Calypso, the rockier Radical Style and the African-influenced Roots Generator. Ragna and the Paissas fuse reggae with Latin vocals. Internationally known African musicians regularly perform in the **Grec** and **Mercé** festivals (*see* **Music Fests**). BCN-based African performers include the Senegalese *kora*/percussion outfit Kaira, Ze Ze Lokito, who do a rumba-ish form of Zairean music, and the *soukous* of Pepe Kallé.

Finally, salsa, merengue and other Spanish-Caribbean rhythms continue to be one of the reigning forces in the music scene, helped along by Barcelona's ample Caribbean population. Top-flight

Music Fests

Fangonia get futuristic at **Sonar.**

Barcelona's musical menu is enriched every year with a varied spicing of festivals. In summer, the city's streets and squares provide perfect outdoor venues, and the sounds of rock, jazz, rumba and other musics last well into the night.

The first gathering of the year is actually outside the city in Terrassa, **Jazz-Terrassa** in March, which has featured names such as Johnny Griffin and Ray Brown (info. 733 21 61; for information on getting to Terrassa, *see chapter* **Trips Out of Town**). April sees the **Festival de Guitarra** (info. 232 67 54), in the Palau de la Música (*see chapter* **Music: Classical & Opera**) and other venues, which brings together guitar music of all kinds (except heavy rock) – from the best flamenco performers to jazz and Julian Bream.

An event that looks set to get bigger and bigger is **Sonar** (info. 442 29 72) in June, an 'advanced music meeting' that's Europe's only official electronic music and multi-media arts festival. It showcases international DJs, techno/dance and experimental groups in gigs at the CCCB, MACBA

(*see chapters* **Art Galleries** *and* **Museums**) and a giant tent in the Poble Espanyol, with all kinds of related attractions alongside.

The city Ajuntament's two major festivals either side of summer both feature musicians from flamenco and African music to James Brown and Gilberto Gil. In the **Grec**, during the balmy nights of July, concerts take place in the Plaça del Rei, Port Vell, the Cathedral steps and the Poble Espanyol. **La Mercé** in September has incorporated an 'independent' music festival, **BAM** (info. 401 97 16). Groups from all over Europe and Africa – albeit of varying quality – give free gigs across the city in a 'battle of the bands'-type scenario (for main festivals, *see chapter* **Barcelona by Season**).

Lastly, there's the long-running **Festival Internacional de Jazz** (info. 232 67 54) in October. Acts of the standing of the Jazz Crusaders and Eddie Palmieri play in the Palau de la Musica, and in jam sessions at the Harlem Jazz and Jazz Sí.

acts such as Los Van Van and NG La Banda come over regularly and play to packed houses, and local talent includes the legendary Lucrecia (who has a regular Saturday-night spot at **Luz de Gas**), the Orquesta Canaima and the addictive merengue sounds of Quisqueya Band.

VENUES & PROGRAMMES

Opportunities to hear music in Barcelona have improved apace in the last few years, with the opening of more venues and greater variety in programming. Music from pure classical to experimental also features sporadically at the **CCCB** (*see chapter* **Art Galleries**), and **L'Espai** (*see chapter* **Dance**). Many bars, such as **Laie** (*see chapters* **Cafés & Bars** *and* **Shopping**) and other venues listed in *chapter* **Nightlife** also may feature live music. Big-draw international acts often perform in one of the sports venues at Montjuïc, in descending order of size the **Estadi Olímpic**, the **Palau Sant Jordi** and the **Palau d'Esports** (*see chapter* **Sports & Fitness**). Only the likes of Madonna or Prince take on the Olympic stadium; the Palau d'Esports has the worst acoustics. Tickets for all three can be bought at the booth in Plaça Universitat (*see chapter* **Services**). A better venue for performers and audiences is **Zeleste**.

Some venues specialise in their music, but many have eclectic booking policies, and it's worth checking several to find what you want. One problem has been finding out when/where gigs were taking place – one had to rely on the dry *Guía del Ocio*, or word of mouth. Recently, new freebie magazines that can be picked up in cafés and shops have made things easier: look for *Mondo Sonoro*, *A Barna*, *Disco 2000*, *Ruta Latina* (for salsa and Latin) and *Bee-Guided* (summer only). *Barcelona en Música*, free in record shops and tourist offices, is useful, as is the *Tentaciones* supplement with Friday's *El País*.

Rock/Jazz & Musics Various

Ballet Blau

C/Junta de Comerç 23 (301 96 64). Metro Liceu/bus 14, 18, 38, 59, N4, N6. **Open** 10pm-3am Tue-Sun. **Admission** free. **No credit cards.**
A cavernous-looking cabaret with high-camp décor, run by the owners of the ever-popular Bar Marsella nearby (*see chapter* **Nightlife**), that presents an enterprising mix, with regular drag shows, cabaret and gay club sessions, and also live bands, generally on Fridays and Saturdays. The music is generally jazz, blues or acid jazz, although other styles are also heard. *See also chapter* **Gay & Lesbian Barcelona**.

Bikini

C/Déu i Mata 105 (322 08 00). Metro Les Corts/bus 15, 43, 59. **Open** (three rooms) *Cockteleria/Dry* 7pm-4.30am Mon-Wed; 7pm-5am Thur; 7pm-6am Fri, Sat; *Rock* 11.30pm-5am Mon-Wed; 11.30pm-5am Thur; 11.30pm-6am Fri-Sat; *Salsa* same hours as Rock room, Mon-Sat; 11.30pm-4.30am Sun. **Admission** 1,000ptas (Mon-Thur, Sat); 1,200ptas (Fri, Sat); if free, must have a drink. **Credit** AmEx, V.
Torn down to make way for **L'Illa** shopping mall, the

original Bikini was the stuff club legends are made of. Membership was like a passport to Barcelona chicdom. Rebuilt on the same site by the same management, it has changed in décor from tacky to well-tailored (it has been likened to a cinema foyer), but its eclectic musical policy survives. With one-off gigs and concert series featuring specific styles and countries, the new Bikini looks set to become as talked about as the old. *See also chapter* **Nightlife**.

Blue Note

Maremàgnum, Moll d'Espanya, Port Vell (225 80 92/225 80 03). Metro Barceloneta/bus 17, 39, 45, 57, 59, 64. **Open** 9pm-2am Tue-Wed; 9pm-4.30am Thur, Fri; 11am-4.30am Sat; 11am-2am Sun. **Admission** free, but you must have a drink. **Credit** V.
On the ground floor of the unmissable **Maremagnum** centre in the port (*see chapters* **Sightseeing** *and* **Shopping**), this is nevertheless a small, cosy, tastefully-decorated bar with live Brazilian music, be-bop, latin jazz and swing from duos and trios, Thur-Sun. Monday to Wednesday a resident piano-man covers the old standards. The crowd are friendly, and there's an outside terrace and snack-type food.

La Boîte

Avda Diagonal 477 (419 59 50). Bus 6., 7, 15, 27, 33, 34, 63, 67, 68, N8. **Open** 11pm-5.30am Mon-Thur, Sun; 11pm-6am Fri-Sat. **Admission** (includes one drink) 1,200-3,000ptas, depending on the band. **No credit cards.**
The dynamic brothers Mas i Mas, who began with the café named after them (*see chapter* **Cafés & Bars**), have lately built up something of a musical empire in Barcelona, taking over long-neglected venues such as the **Jamboree** and **Los Tarantos**. Nobody's complaining, as they have renovated them with taste, improved the acoustics and given a whole new energy to their concert programmes. La Boîte, a small basement club, was their first music venue. It features a menu of jazz, soul, blues and dance, and this is where you are most likely to hear rising British and international groups (especially of the acid-jazz/soul variety) without long queues. Drink prices are hefty, but all Mas venues offer discounts for advance booking, and cards for each venue offering five or six concerts for 5,000ptas. *See also chapter* **Nightlife**.

La Capsa

Centre de Cultura Contemporània del Prat, Avda Pare Andreu de la Palma 5-7, Prat de Llobregat (478 51 07). Bus 65, EA, EN from Plaça d'Espanya. **Open** 8.30am-11pm Mon-Thur; 10.30am-3am Fri, Sat; 10.30am-10pm Sun. **Admission** depends on the band. **No credit cards.**
An oddity in Barcelona´s music scene. Outside the city in El Prat, near the airport (and so best reached with your own transport), La Capsa is a civic centre with a so-far very promising music programme. There are concerts every Friday and some Saturdays (starting 10.30pm), featuring local and lesser-known international acts covering a whole musical spectrum: from punk and rap to world music.

Club Apolo

C/Nou de la Rambla 113 (441 40 01/442 51 83). Metro Paral.lel/bus 36, 57, 64, 91, N4, N6. **Open** depends on performance times; *disco* midnight-6am Thur, Fri. **Admission** *performances* depends on the band; *disco* 1,000ptas (includes one drink). **No credit cards.**
As well as being one of the best clubs in town, this ex music-hall brings in top live acts of the world music/reggae, dancier pop/rock, flamenco and salsa variety, locally-based and from further afield. There are plenty of tables, plus an upper balcony that ensures a good view even for big-name acts. You can stay on after the gig, when the crowds pour in and the music kicks on into night. *See also chapter* **Nightlife**.

Diamono Club Mestizo

C/Merce 31 (268 15 77). Metro Drassanes/bus 14, 36, 57, 59, 64, N4, N6, N9. **Open** *venue* 10am-2.30am Sat,

*The beautiful **Luz de Gas**. See page 204.*

Sun; *shop and hairdresser* 10am-2pm Mon-Sat.
Admission free. **No credit cards.**
An Afro/Hispanic club that also doubles as a hairdresser and shop selling African crafts and clothes, the tiny Mestizo is the only live venue in Barcelona devoted exclusively to African music. The mainly acoustic gigs feature Senegalese and Zairean musicians, and Saturday night's 'World Jam' session brings in a mix of resident African musicians and DJs. African tea and snacks are available, along with a 'very stimulating', secret-ingredient-laden ginger cocktail.

Garatge Club

C/Pallars 195 (309 14 38). Metro Llacuna/bus 40, 42, 141. **Open** midnight-5.30am Fri, Sat; 6pm-10.30am Sun; *mid-May-mid-Oct* outdoor terrace open from 8pm.
Admission depends on the band. **No credit cards.**
Offering from rock to punk and anything in between, Garatge Club in Poble Nou is for hard-nosed rock/indie fans who like their music on the noisy side.

Jamboree

Plaça Reial 17 (301 75 64). Metro Liceu/bus 14, 18, 38, 59, N4, N6, N9. **Open** 8.30pm-4.30am Sun-Thur; 8.30pm-5am Fri, Sat. **Admission** (most performances; one drink included) 1,200ptas; *disco* free. **No credit cards.**
Inaugurated in 1959, this Plaça Reial cellar was the first jazz 'cave'in Spain. It closed in 1968, but was re-opened by the Mas i Mas brothers (*see* **La Boîte**) in 1993. Barcelona-based

and visiting names in jazz, blues, latin jazz, funk and occasionally hip-hop all play at this enormously popular venue, with local dance band Princes of Time every Monday. A club session continues after the gigs. *See also chapter* **Nightlife**.

Jazz Sí Club/Café

C/Requesens 2 (329 00 20). Metro Sant Antoni/bus 20, 24, 41, 55, 64. **Open** 9am-11pm daily. **Admission** depends on the band (and includes one drink); or free (but you must have a drink). **No credit cards.**
Quirky club/café in a tiny street in the Raval near Ronda Sant Antoni, run by Barcelona's contemporary music school the Taller de Músics (at C/Requesens 5), whose students do a jazz-jam session there every Thursday night. The other fixed night is Saturday, when there's a rock/blues jam from local and visiting musicians. Other nights are totally spontaneous, for the management are open to anything. It's also a contact/meeting point for musicians, and very good, reasonably-priced snack food is available. Concerts start at 8.30pm.

London Bar

C/Nou de la Rambla 34 (318 52 61). Metro Drassanes/bus 14, 18, 38, 59, N4, N6, N9. **Open** 7pm-4am Tue-Sun. **Admission** free. **Credit** MC, V.
A Barcelona institution and a relic of the days when the *Barrio Chino* was at its peak, the bohemian-ish London is usually packed at weekends, mainly with young foreigners. Music tends to be on the blues/boogie/be-bop side, played by

Smoky jazz at the **Pipa Club**.

local and resident-foreign bands – great fun if you don't mind a noisy, smoky atmosphere. And although it's been thoughtlessly renovated at times, it's managed to save just a touch of its original 1910 Modernist decor. *See also* **Nightlife**.

Luz de Gas

C/Muntaner 246 (209 77 11/209 73 85). Bus 6, 7, 15, 33, 34, 58, 64, N8. **Open** 11pm-4.30/5.30am daily. **Admission** (includes one drink) approx 1,200ptas. **Credit** AmEx, DC, MC, V.

This beautiful, *Belle-Epoque* former music hall has a fixed programme of soul/jazz, salsa and a touch of country every night of the week. Monica Green has a regular Thursday spot with soul/funk and MOR standards, and Barcelona's very own Salsa queen, Lucrecia, appears on Saturdays. Unfortunately, the club tends to suffer from a sometimes snooty uptown clientèle and a stroppy management. *See also chapter* **Nightlife**.

Magic

Passeig Picasso 40 (310 72 67). Metro Barceloneta/bus 14, 39, 51. **Open** 11pm-6am Thu-Sat and eves of public holidays. **Admission** *performances* 500-1,200ptas; *disco* 1,000ptas (includes one drink). **No credit cards.**

The revival of Magic, first opened as a hippy hang-out in the seventies, must be proof that punk still lives (in Barcelona, at least). If the sound of bands such as Lord Sickness, The Pleasure Fuckers and Killer Barbies grabs you, then this is the place to be. Opposite the Ciutadella, this is the only central venue that programmes indie/rock on the hard side.

Nitsa

Plaça Joan Llongueras 1-3 (458 62 50). Bus 6, 7, 33, 34, 63, 66, 67, 68. **Open** midnight-6am Thur-Sat. **Admission** 800-1,500ptas (includes one drink). **No credit cards.**

As well as hosting the best in international techno DJs , Nitsa regularly presents local pop groups on the dancier side of things. In the top part of town near Plaça Macià, it also has kitsch seventies decor to look at. *See also chapter* **Nightlife**.

Otto Zutz Club

C/Lincoln 15 (238 07 22). FGC Gràcia/bus 16, 17, 25, 27, 127. **Open** 11pm-6am Tue-Sat. **Admission** 1,500-2,000ptas. **Credit** AmEx, DC, MC, V.

Upstairs at the Otto Zutz, one of the fixed points of the Barcelona night-time round, the 'Club' room offers regular concert series in jazz, fusion and, lately, flamenco. It's a comfortable, airy space with an ample amount of tables and chairs, and the ticket also entitles you to stay on in the main club after the show. *See also chapter* **Nightlife**.

Savannah

C/Muntanya 16 (231 38 77). Metro Clot/bus 33, 34, 35, 43, 44, 54, N7, N9. **Open** 11pm-5.30am Fri-Sat. **Admission** depends on the band. **No credit cards.**

A popular rock/blues venue out in Clot, pulling in some lesser known international (mainly American) players and bigger names from the national scene. Wednesday night is the 'Jam Session', in which visiting international artists often plays with local musos. It also sometimes presents fringe theatre.

La Tierra

C/Aribau 230 (230 35 53). FGC Provença/bus 6, 7, 15, 33, 34, 58, 64, N8. **Open** 11pm-5am daily. **Admission** 1,500ptas (includes one drink). **Credit** V.

La Tierra's music programmes are unclassifiable. The gigs, most nights of the week, run the range from rumba to funk to country, with salsa another fixture. Hugely popular with the wanna-be set at weekends, when a funk-soul club kicks off after the concerts. *See also chapter* **Nightlife**.

Zeleste
C/Almogàvers 122/Pamplona 88 (309 12 04). Metro Marina/bus 6, 40, 42, 141, N6. **Open** depends on performance times; *disco* 1-5am Sat, Sun mornings. **Admission** *performances* 1,500-3,500ptas depending on the band; *disco* 600-800ptas (includes one drink). **No credit cards.**
The best medium-sized music venue in Barcelona. If they're not big enough (or don't want) to fill a stadium, all first-rank national and international acts perform here: recent headliners include Massive Attack, both Blur and Oasis, and PJ Harvey. On the city-side of Poble Nou, it has three halls and also hosts club nights each weekend, when the late-night bar is open to all with no admission.

Flamenco

The **Otto Zutz** (*see above*) also now regularly presents flamenco performers.

La Macarena
C/Nou de Sant Francesc 5 (317 54 36). Metro Drassanes/bus 14, 18, 38, 59, 91, N4, N6, N9. **Open** 10.30pm-4.30am daily. **Admission** free (but you must have a drink). **Credit** MC, V.
With an interior like an Almodóvar film set and an owner who could easily be one of the extras, La Macarena is a once-in-a-lifetime experience. It's totally unpredictable: you could be treated to anything from a thrilling, spontaneous session from visiting flamenco artists or a cursory ten-minute spot from the regulars who hang around the bar. Whatever, you'll be expected to pay. There's no cover charge, but be warned: if they ask you after the show if you would 'like to buy a drink for the artists', it could empty your wallet. An acceptable way out is to leave a tip as you go; the amount should depend on the length and quality of the 'show'. Go late (2am on) and, if possible, with somebody who lives in the city.

El Tablao de Carmen
C/Arcs 9, Poble Espanyol (325 68 95). Bus 13, 61. **Open** approx 8pm-2am Tue-Sun; *Flamenco shows* 9.30pm, 11.30pm Tue-Thur, Sun; 9.30pm, midnight Fri, Sat. **Admission** *Poble Espanyol* 950-1,500ptas; *El Tablao de Carmen copa-espectacle* 4,000ptas (includes one drink); *sopar-espectacle* 7,000ptas (includes dinner & admission to Poble Espanyol). **Credit** AmEx, DC, JCB, MC, TC, V.
High-quality supper/flamenco show venue in the **Poble Espanyol** (*see chapter* **Sightseeing**), with a full *tablao* show of guitarists, singers and dancers. Great fun, it's frequented by locals and tourists alike. If you book in advance you don't have to pay the Poble admission fee.

Los Tarantos
Plaça Reial 17 (318 30 67). Metro Liceu/bus 14, 18, 38, 59, 91, N4, N6, N9. **Open** 10.15pm-4.30am daily; *Flamenco show (tablao)* 10.15pm-midnight Mon-Sat. **Admission** *Tablao* 3,500ptas (includes two drinks); *other performances* varies depending on the artist. **Credit** MC, V.
Since its makeover by the Mas brothers (*see* **La Boîte**), Los Tarantos, long-established as a flamenco show or *tablao* for tourist parties, has become the most important club on the new Catalan flamenco circuit. Regular local acts include the new *wunderkind* of *cante jondo*, Miguel Poveda, and accomplished Japanese flamenco dancer Junko. Concerts are normally after midnight at weekends, after the main *tablao*, and there's a midnight rumba slot on Wednesdays. After the live gigs, it becomes the world/Latin music part of the **Jamboree** next door, and the audience are welcome to stay on.

Jazz Specialists

La Cova del Drac
C/Vallmajor 33 (200 70 32). Metro Muntaner/bus 14, 58, 64, N8. **Open** 10pm-4am Mon, Thur; 6pm-4am Tue, Wed; 9pm-4am Fri, Sat. **Admission** (includes one drink) 800ptas (9pm show); 1,500-2,000ptas (midnight show). **Credit** V.
Swish uptown jazz club that now has few echoes of the days when, then located on C/Tuset, it was a bohemian/intellectual hang-out during the final years of Francoism. The current club has live acts nightly (with bigger, 'international' names at weekends) at midnight, with special 'new talent' gigs on Fridays and Saturdays from 9pm. Drinks are on the pricey side, but La Cova has a reputation for excellence.

Harlem Jazz Club
C/Comtessa de Sobradiel 8 (310 07 55). Metro Jaume I/bus 17, 40, 45. **Open** 8pm-3.30am Tue-Thur; 8pm-4.30am Fri-Sun. **Admission** free (but you must have a drink). **No credit cards.**
A great favourite with Barcelona jazz *aficionados*, an intimate Barri Gòtic club with a great atmosphere. Features local talent and jam sessions by international musicians visiting for the jazz festivals and workshops.

Pipa Club
Plaça Reial 3 (302 47 32). Metro Liceu/bus 14, 18, 38, 59, 91, N4, N6, N9. **Open** 10pm-4am daily; *concerts* midnight Thur-Sat; *jam session* 11pm Sun. **Admission** 500ptas (Thur-Sat); free (Sun). **No credit cards.**
Pipa means pipe, and 'Pipa Club' is exactly what it is during the day – a meeting-place for pipe-smokers. At night it turns into a venue for local and some foreign (mainly contemporary) jazz talent, and you might find boleros or tangos on some nights. Also worth a visit to admire the extensive collection of smoking paraphernalia that lines the walls.

Latin

Live latin music also features at **La Tierra**.

Antilla Cosmopolita
C/Muntaner 244 (200 77 14). Bus 6, 7, 15, 33, 34, 58, 64, N8. **Open** 9pm-4.30am Mon-Thur; 11pm-6am Fri, Sat, eves of public holidays; 11pm-4.30am Sun. **Admission** 1,500ptas (includes one drink); *members* free. **No credit cards.**
Great live bands get the crowd moving from Sunday to Thursday in the most popular, bouncing salsa/Latin venue in Barcelona, and on Fridays and Saturdays there's a 'salsoteca'. They also offer free dance classes from Monday to Thursday (10pm-midnight): just turn up at the door, then hang around till the concerts start at 1pm to strut your stuff. Dance fiends heading for a weekend in the Montseny might like to know they can also shake a hip at the **Antilla-La Garriga**, Avda Pau Casals 1 (871 46 62), in the attractive small town of La Garriga. *See also chapter* **Nightlife**.

Agua de Luna
C/Viladomat 211 (410 04 40). Bus 43, 44. **Open** 8pm-4am Tue-Thur, Sun; 10pm-5am Fri, Sat. **Admission** 1,000ptas. **No credit cards.**
Live acts take place spasmodically, but are generally high-quality, in this recently opened 'salsotecha'. All types of *música latina* can be heard: from *danzón, mambo, samba* and *soca* to anything in between. Sunday is tango night (with free classes, 10pm-midnight) and Thursdays are for 'hard core' salsa-lovers. Free dance classes are offered on Wednesdays and Thursdays (10pm-midnight).

Sports & Fitness

In this sports-mad town FC Barcelona takes pride of place, but there's a wealth of other facilities to let you swim, swing a club or slice a racquet.

You want scarves? you want pens? you want hats? **FC Barcelona** *has them all.*

Every day two competing papers hit the Barcelona newsstands that are devoted entirely to sports, *Sport* and *El Mundo Deportivo*, and they often outsell the more conventional press. This is only one indication of the city's passionate interest in watching, thinking about, dissecting and generally following sport. Enthusiasm has been encouraged by the recent successes of Catalan sportsmen and women – such as Arantxa Sánchez Vicario and Sergi Bruguera in tennis, or Carles Saínz in rally-driving. A near-unique feature of Barcelona, though, is the extent to which attention centres around one giant club – Fútbol Club Barcelona, *el Barça*, which extends into virtually every other team sport as well as soccer.

Opportunities actually to take part in sport were increased substantially, as one might expect, by the building programmes for the '92 Olympics. The opening up of these facilities to general use has not been without problems, but nevertheless the city can offer a number of very well-patronised, international-class public sports centres.

Spectator Sports

As with theatre tickets, a wide range of tickets can be bought by credit card through *Servi-Caixa* machines at savings banks (*see chapter* **Services**).

American Football

Barcelona Dragons
Estadi Olímpic de Montjuïc, Avda de l'Estadi (425 49 49). Metro Espanya, then escalators, or Paral.lel then Funicular de Montjuïc/bus 61. **Ticket office** *match days only* 4-8pm. **Tickets** 1,100-5,100ptas. **Credit** V.
Part of the 'World League' of American football, the Dragons have been surprisingly successful in gaining support in a city with very little experience of the game. They have the privilege of playing in the **Estadi Olímpic**, usually on Sundays from April to June at 6pm. The promotors try to make it a full day out, with bands, cheerleaders and all the usual razzle-dazzle Americana attached to the sport. Most players are American, but in accordance with a league rule there are also a few locals in the squad. Tickets can be bought on the day at the stadium, or in advance at the ticket booth at Gran Via/Plaça Universitat (who have information on forthcoming games: *see chapter* **Services**) or through the

savings bank *Servi-Caixa* machines. They rarely fill the stadium, so getting a ticket is never a problem.

Basketball

Second only to football in popularity. The season runs from September to May, and league games are usually on Sunday evenings, European and Spanish Cup matches mid-week.

FC Barcelona

Palau Blaugrana, Avda Aristides Maillol (496 36 00). Metro Maria Cristina, Collblanc/bus 15, 52, 53, 54, 56, 57, 75. **Ticket office** 10am-2pm, 4-8pm, Mon-Fri, and from two hours before match times. **Tickets** 500-2,700ptas. **No credit cards.**
The basketball arm of *Barça*, European Cup finalist in 1996, is fanatically well-supported, and it's advisable to book tickets in advance. League games are mainly on Sundays at 6/6.30pm; Cup and European games 8/8.30pm in the week. Tickets can also be bought through *Servi-Caixa*.

Joventut

Avda Alfons XIII-C/Ponent 143-161, Badalona (460 20 40). Metro Gorg/bus 44. **Ticket office** from one hour before match times. **Tickets** 1,000-3,000ptas **No credit cards.**
Badalona's standard-bearers stand head-to-head with their wealthier neighbours, and unlike them have actually won the European Basketball Cup. Sunday games are at 7.30pm, and the fans are still more passionate than at Barcelona.

Football

The city's two first division clubs are FC Barcelona and Espanyol. Such is the all-absorbing power of *Barça* that lower-division teams tend to be reduced to semi-pro status through lack of support, but football completists might check out **Sant Andreu** and **Hospitalet**, both forever trying to reach somewhere near the big league.
The season traditionally runs from the first weekend in September to May, and league games are played at 5pm on Sundays, although some are now also played (and shown live on TV) at 8.30pm on Saturdays. Midweek cup and European games are also usually at 8.30pm. In late August both main clubs have pre-season tournaments which generally involve major European and Latin American sides, with games at 7pm. For more on football, *see* **It's only a game.**

FC Barcelona

Nou Camp, Avda Aristides Maillol (496 36 00). Metro Maria Cristina, Collblanc/bus 15, 52, 53, 54, 56, 57, 75. **Ticket office** 10am-1pm, 4-8pm, Mon-Fri; *match days* 10am-1pm, and from two hours before match time. **Tickets** 2,500-12,500ptas. **Credit** MC, V.
Although the Nou Camp stadium has a capacity of nearly 120,000, tickets to see *Barça* are often hard to come by, for most are reserved for the club's 100,000-plus *socis* (members/season-ticket holders). The best way to see a game is to phone the club about two weeks in advance and ask which day and time tickets go on sale; then go to the ground about two hours beforehand and queue. Alternatively, on match days there are usually touts (scalpers) around the stadium if you want to try your luck. Important games are generally sold out entirely to *socis*. There is a wide range of ticket prices, and, since the *entrades generals* areas (available to non-members) are often not very well-placed, it's advisable to spend at least 3,500ptas to get a decent view. Barcelona also has teams in the Spanish second and third divisions and at amateur level. The second-division team, *Barça-B*, plays in the *Mini-estadi*, a fully equipped 16,000-seater ground connected to the main stadium by a tunnel and walkways. Tickets are generally about 1,000-2,000ptas, and games are at about 5pm on Saturdays; on days when the A and B teams are both at home, a joint ticket allows you to see both games.

RCD Espanyol

Avda de Sarrià 120 (203 48 00). FGC Bonanova/bus 6, 16, 33, 34, 66, 70, 74. **Ticket office** 9.30am-1.30pm, 5-8pm, Mon-Fri; *match days* from two hours before match time. **Tickets** 2,000-6,000ptas. **No credit cards.**
It is easier to see Espanyol games, although the same procedure applies for buying tickets in advance, and again it's worth spending a bit extra for a better seat. The Sarrià stadium is relatively small (42,000), and the subject of many requests by the club to alter and extend it, blocked, *Espanyolistes* believe, by the pro-*Barça* majority on the city council. Because of this, and since Espanyol qualified for the UEFA Cup in 1996-97, the club will play its European games in the **Estadi Olímpic**, as their own ground does not meet UEFA regulations. Check the press for details.

Greyhound Racing

Canódromo Pabellón

C/Llançà 2-12 (325 46 08). Metro Espanya/bus 9, 13, 51, 53, 65, 91. **Open** 11am-2pm, 5-9pm, Mon, Fri-Sun, public holidays); 5-9pm Tue-Thur. **Admission** free.
A small track overlooked by apartment balconies just off the Plaça d'Espanya. A relaxed atmosphere and small bets (winners and second place only) with odds to match are the order of the day. A great place to pop in, have a beer and a sandwich, and watch the races, which are run every 15 minutes.

Ice Hockey

FC Barcelona

FC Barcelona Pista de Gel, Avda Aristides Maillol (496 36 00). Metro Maria Cristina, Collblanc/bus 15, 52, 53, 54, 56, 57, 75. **Games** *junior* 12.30/1pm, *senior* 9.30pm, Sat. **Admission** free
Once again, it's *Barça* that sponsors the only professional ice hockey team in town. The rink, open to the public on non-match days (*see below* **Ice Skating**), is a part of the club's vast sports complex. Games are not played all year: a schedule is available at the arena or over the phone. Not the highest standard of play, but it can be exciting nonetheless.

Roller Hockey

FC Barcelona

Palau Blaugrana, Avda Aristides Maillol (496 36 00). Metro Maria Cristina, Collblanc/bus 15, 52, 53, 54, 56, 57, 75. **Ticket office** from two hours before match times. **Games** *Oct-June* 8pm Mon-Sat, noon Sun. **Tickets** 900-1,000ptas. **No credit cards.**
A sport that's almost exclusive to Spain (and especially Catalonia), and has the distinction of providing the sporting credentials of one JA Samaranch, President of the International Olympic Committee. It is played with a hard ball and field hockey sticks on regular roller skates; rules follow ice hockey regulations, with one notable exception: body-checking and most other forms of contact are prohibited, making it more like field hockey. Matches are played in the same hall as basketball, the *Palau Blaugrana* indoor arena.

Show-jumping & Polo

Reial Club de Polo

Avda Dr. Marañón 17-31 (402 93 00). Metro Zona Universitària/bus 7, 67, 68, 74, 75. **Times & tickets** vary according to competition.
The Polo Club hosts matches at various times during the spring and summer, as well as show-jumping and dressage competitions. The atmosphere is suitably élite, but it can be a pleasant place to spend an afternoon in the sunshine. Schedules of events are available from the club or by phone.

Other Events

Barcelona Marathon (Marató de Catalunya-Barcelona)

Information & entry forms *C/Jonqueres 16, 9-C, 08003 (268 01 14/fax 268 43 34).* **Date** mid-March.
The Barcelona Marathon will celebrate its twentieth anniversary in 1997. From 1992-96 the race ended in the Estadi Olímpic, which required a crippling final climb up Montjuïc. This led to very poor times and an increasing absence of international competitors, and from 1997 the organisers, recognising defeat, will again end the race on the flat in Plaça d'Espanya. It starts north of the city in Mataró, and thousands are expected to take part. The city also holds two half-marathons at different times of year, and the **Cursa de la Mercè** fun run during **La Mercè** in September (*see chapter* **Barcelona by Season**). The city sports information centre (*see below* **Participation**) has details of all events.

Motor Sports

Circuit de Catalunya *Carretera de Parets dels Vallès a Granollers, Montmeló (571 97 00). By car A7 or N152 to Parets del Vallès exit (20km).* **Times & tickets** vary according to competition.
In Montmeló, near the A7 north of Barcelona towards Granollers, this racetrack was inaugurated in 1991 and now hosts the Spanish Grand Prix (usually late May), as well as many other competitions in different classes, including motorcycle meetings. For an event calendar, call the circuit, or check with the **RACC** in Barcelona (*see chapter* **Survival**) or similar motoring organisations in other countries.

Tennis

Reial Club de Tennis Barcelona – 1899 *C/Bosch i Gimpera 5-13 (203 78 52). Bus 63, 114.* **Open** *club* (members-only except during competitions) 8am-10pm daily; *ticket office* 9am-6pm daily during competitions.
The city's most prestigious tennis club hosts one major international tournament, the 10-day **Trofeig Comte de Godó**, part of the men's ATP tour, generally in mid-April. Agassi, Sampras, Muster, and Becker have all competed in this big-money tournament, as have the best Spanish players. Tickets cost 2,400-8,000ptas; they are available through *Servi-Caixa*, and *bono* tickets are available for admission on several days.
A smaller tournament is the **Open de Catalunya**, a women's invitation event held at the **Club de Tenis Hispano-Francés** (428 12 36) in Vall d'Hebron. Usually at the end of June, it also often attracts world-ranked players.

Participation

The Ajuntament runs an extensive network of *Poliesportius* or sports centres. The activities available at each vary: some have just basic gyms and indoor sports halls suitable for basketball and five-a-side football, others a lavish range of facilities that include swimming pools and running tracks. Charges are low, and you do not need to be a resident to use them. Information on city facilities (and on sports events) can be obtained from :

Servei d'Informació Esportiva

Avda de l'Estadi 30-40 (information phoneline 402 30 00). Metro Espanya, then escalators, or Paral.lel then Funicular de Montjuïc/bus 61. **Open** 8am-2.30pm, 4-6.15pm, Mon-Fri.
The Ajuntament's official 'sports information service', in an office alongside the **Piscina Bernat Picornell** (*see below* **Swimming Pools**). They have leaflets listing district sports centres; you can also call the phoneline and ask which is your nearest. Staff may not speak English, but are very helpful.

Billiards, Snooker, Pool

Many bars have Spanish billiards tables (*carambolas*, blue and without pockets) or American pool, and a few full-size snooker tables. If you're unfamiliar with local rules, watching a few games should make everything clear. A favourite bar for *billar* is **Velódromo** (*see chapter* **Cafés & Bars**).

Club Billars Monforte

La Rambla 27 (318 10 19).Metro Drassanes/bus 14, 18, 38, 59, 64, 91. **Open** 10am-10pm daily. **Membership** 1,000ptas per month; *tables* 200ptas per hour (one person); 360ptas per hour (two people). **No credit cards**.
An old fashioned club in a room of faded glory, with men of a certain age playing cards, dominoes and billiards. Officially it's members only, but non-members are usually made welcome. Five billiards, three pool and one snooker table. You need to knock on the door after 10pm, and it doesn't hurt to phone ahead and let them know you're dropping in.

Snooker Club Barcelona

C/Roger de Llúria 42 (317 97 60). Metro Urquinaona/bus 7, 18, 39, 45, 47, 56, N1, N2, N3, N9. **Open** 6pm-3am Mon-Thur; 6pm-4am Fri, Sat; 6pm-2am Sun. **Tables** 1,000ptas per hour. **Credit** MC, V.
A stylish design-bar/billiard hall with four full-size snooker tables, Players of any age and gender are welcomed. Two tables are reserved for members; two are open. The club also has one pool table. Arrive early to be sure of getting a game. *See also chapter* **Nightlife**.

Bowling

Bowlers can also find eight fifties-style lanes in the **Boliche** bar, Avda Diagonal 510 (237 90 98; Metro Diagonal).

Bowling Barcelona

C/Sabino Arana 6 (330 50 48). Metro Maria Cristina/bus 7, 59, 67, 68, 70, 72, 74, 75. **Open** 11am-2am Mon-Thur; 11am-3am Fri; 11am-4am Sat; 11am midnight Sun. **Rates** 350ptas per game 11am-5pm Mon-Fri; 500ptas per game from 5pm Mon-Fri, 11am-5pm Sat, Sun; 660ptas per game from 5pm Sat, Sun. *Shoe hire* 150ptas. **No credit cards**.
This centre has recently added additional facilities in a bid to keep up with the nearby Pedralbes bowl. Lunch-time is a good time to go, and take advantage of the cheaper day rates.

Bowling Pedrables

Avda Dr. Marañón 11 (333 03 52). Metro Collblanc/bus 54, 75. **Open** 10am-2am Mon-Thur; 10am-4am Fri, Sat; 10am-midnight Sun. Aug open from 5pm only. **Rates** 200ptas per game 10am-5pm Mon-Fri; 350ptas per game from 5pm Mon-Fri, 10am-5pm Sat, Sun; 500ptas per game from 5pm Sat, Sun. *Shoe hire* 100ptas. **Credit** V.
A very well-equipped operation: you can hire gloves as well as shoes, and also play snooker, pool or darts. There are 14 lanes, a bar and a dining area. Best time is early afternoon, as it gets crowded with students later in the day. If it's full when you arrive, leave your name at reception and they will page you at the bar when a lane becomes free.

Cricket

Barcelona Cricket Club

Information *C/Cendra 7 baixos (tel/fax 441 43 69).*
Yes – the crack of ball on willow is available here. The club is part of a 16-team Spanish league, and currently holds the league title and the Spanish cup. They play 50-over one-day matches on Saturdays, from 11am, and friendly matches on Sundays. They are open to games from visiting teams, so any village or pub side planning a trip to Barcelona should phone or fax the club. More information can also be obtained from the club's honourary secretary, Lyn Scannel (209 06 39).

It's only a game

In November 1995 the Nou Camp stadium rang to the sound of 124,000 voices as FC Barcelona played Real Madrid. In the same year, cash registers rang up profits to the tune of £300 million. *Barça*, as it is known, is one of the leading football clubs in the world, but also the fifth most successful business in Spain.

Barcelona is arguably the richest and best-supported sports club in the world, and clever marketing is a key to its continued success. The club's emblems can be found on anything you care to name, from sweets and pens to wine, whisky and silverware (to pick up some of this stuff, and team shirts, look no further than the **Botiga del Barça** in **Maremagnum**). Due to its wealth the club can haughtily decline to have a sponsor's logo on its shirts. Its largesse, meanwhile, allows minority sports to flourish, for as well as the football squads teams in 19 other sports carry the FC Barcelona colours. Even golfers can be sponsored by *Barça*.

Behind this effort are the club's over 100,000 *socis* or members throughout Catalonia. *Barça*, remarkably, focuses the attention and emotions of almost an entire nation. From the 1920s and right through the Franco regime, the club was seen as a (sometimes the only) symbol of Catalan aspirations. This emotional identification is still there. Turn on Catalan TV and there are comedy programmes around the club's comings and goings, and endless discussions of last week's game; pick up a sports paper and the latest crisis in the club is picked over page after page. In *el Barça*, Catalans' oft-cultivated image of cool rationality seems to dissolve into melodrama.

ON THE BENCH

All this giant structure still has to revolve around the club's main activity, which, as someone once said, is just 11 men kicking a ball around a park. On 18 May 1996 front pages were cleared across Catalonia. Barcelona chairman Josep Lluís Núñez had sacked Johan Cruyff. The former Dutch superstar had consistently been one of the rudest men on the planet, especially to directors, but was also the most successful manager in the club's history.

A persistent problem of Barcelona has been that, as with other big clubs, its players have often found it hard to sustain the weight of expectation attached to them. Time and again the team would come close to the highest honours, and then fall at the last hurdle, leaving the fans in a fog of masochistic anguish. Under

Cruyff all that changed, and Barcelona established a record of consistent achievement: four league titles in a row, a European Cup in 1992, and a stylish, effective team. It's not surprising that with Cruyff's exit many felt queasily that the bad old days might be about to return.

A point often made is that, with all its resources, Barcelona should not have any problem. It can buy the best international stars – the likes of Cruyff himself, Maradona, Lineker, Romario, Koeman, Laudrup and currently Hagi and Figo – and regularly produces fine homegrown players, through the *'Masia'*, the boarding school in the vast *Barça* complex, where about 40 boys take lessons in football along with regular school work. Current players such as Guardiola, De la Peña, Sergi and Nadal have all risen through this system, and the second-division *Barça-B*, before reaching the first team.

Bringing all this to bear on the pitch, though, is another matter. After chairman Núñez had decided to show Cruyff who was calling the shots his choice as new manager was – *Bobby Robson*. Cruyff, meanwhile, adopted a King-across-the-water posture, announcing that he was going to stay in Barcelona, while some fans began anti-Núñez campaigns. Should Robson run into the mire, judgement on him, and perhaps on Núñez, will be swift. And whatever happens, it's sure to give sports hacks plenty to write about.

THE POOR RELATIONS

FC Barcelona has few rivals in the area of self-promotion, but on the pitch, everyone wants to beat them – especially their eternally smaller neighbour, **RCD Espanyol**. Their Sarrià ground is only a kick away from the Nou Camp, but they lack the cash that comes to clubs of *Barça* proportions. In recent years, however, thanks in great part to astute management by José Antonio Camacho, the Blue-and-Whites have seen a steady improvement in their fortunes, with a lively team that has qualified for Europe and beaten *Barça* itself on several occasions. It has always been said that Espanyol is the team of non-Catalans living in Catalonia, but unobtrusively, perhaps perversely, there are quite a few Catalans who follow the club.

Both clubs offer tours of their stadia, in a trip that will excite any fan of the game. And at the Nou Camp you can see the **Museu del FC Barcelona** (*see chapter* **Museums**), which, naturally, is the most-visited museum in the city.

*Perfecting the swing at **Golf Range Diagonal**.*

Cycling

Barcelona's cycle routes (*Carrils Bici*) that have appeared in the last few years are sometimes not as practical as they might be, but they still give you a good idea of how to get around the city by bike, and are very popular for recreational cycling if not for everyday transport. Information on recommended routes is available from tourist offices and the Sports Information Service; as well as routes in the city, there are some around Collserola (*see chapter* **Barcelona by Area**). For cycle hire, *see chapter* **Services**.

General Fitness

Califòrnia Look

Plaça de Ramon Berenguer el Gran 2 (319 87 25). Metro Jaume I/bus 17, 40, 45. **Open** 7am-10.30pm Mon-Fri; 10am-4pm Sat; 11am-4pm Sun; hours variable July-Aug. **Rates** 1,200-2,400ptas per day; 4,000-5,500ptas one week; 8,500-11,000ptas per month. **No credit cards**.
This well-equipped, flexible gym and fitness centre is one of few in Barcelona that caters to the short-term visitor, with day, one-week, two-week, three-week and monthly rates. For each period there are two charge rates: the basic rate give you access to all the sports facilities – gym, weights, aerobics, sauna – , the higher rate also gives you ultra-violet treatment and a range of beauty services. The weekly and monthly rates work out as very reasonable if you plan to use the centre three or more times a week.

Golf Courses

Club de Golf El Prat

El Prat de Llobregat (379 02 78). By car Carretera de l'Aeroport (21km). **Open** *Oct-April* 8am-8pm; *May-Sept* 8am-9pm, daily. **Rates** *non-members* 11,380ptas per day Mon-Fri; 22,825ptas per day Sat, Sun, public holidays. **No credit cards**.
On the coast near the airport, this is a première 36-hole course that has hosted the Spanish Open six times. Equipment is available for hire, but you must be a member of a federated club to be able to play. From October to May it is members only at weekends; at all times you're best bet is to go in the week, when the course is less crowded.

Club de Golf Sant Cugat

C/de la Vila, Sant Cugat del Vallès (674 39 58). By car Túnel de Vallvidrera (E9) to Valldoreix/by train FGC from Plaça Catalunya to Valldoreix. **Open** 7.30am-8.30pm Tue-Fri, public holidays; 7am-9pm Sat-Sun. **Rates** *non-members* 7,050 ptas per day Mon-Fri; 16,000ptas per day Sat, Sun, public holidays. **No credit cards**.
The course was built in 1919, and saw the professional debut of Seve Ballesteros. A drawback for visiting golfers is that you cannot hire clubs or trolleys. Green fees allow you access to the club bar, restaurant and swimming pool.

Golf Driving Ranges

Golf Range Diagonal

Plaça Mireia, Esplugues de Llobregat (473 96 71). By car Ronda de Dalt, exit at Junction 11 and keep left. **Open** *Sept-April* 9.30am-9pm Mon-Fri; 9.30am-7pm Sat, Sun. *May-July* 9.30am-1pm Mon-Fri; 9.30am-7pm Sat, Sun. *Aug* open Mon-Fri only. **Admission** *half-hour* 1,000ptas; *one hour* 1,500ptas. **No credit cards**.
Just outside the city in Esplugues, this is an open-air driving and practice range. It's very popular, so book. Equipment hire is included in the fee, and lessons can also be arranged. There is a bar and restaurant for lounging in between bouts.

Only Golf

C/Villarroel 253 (405 06 05). Metro Hospital Clínic/bus 14, 59, 63, 66, 67, 68. **Open** 10am-9.30pm Mon-Fri. Closed public holidays. **Admission** *non-members* 3,000ptas per hour. **Credit** V.
Indoors, and using nets and electronics, this practice set-up is easy to get to, but this somewhat restrictive high-tech system takes time to get used to. There's a bar and restaurant, and again, it's wise to book. Weekdays are less busy.

Horse Riding

Hípica Severino de Sant Cugat

C/Princep, Sant Cugat del Vallès (674 11 40). By car Carretera de l'Arrabassada (exit 5 from Ronda de Dalt). **Open** 10am-1pm, 4-07pm, daily. **Rates** from 1,600ptas per one-hour lesson. **No credit cards**.

This school takes groups on rides through the countryside around Sant Cugat and along the north side of Collserola. All-day rides include a lunch stop along the way. Weekend rides must be booked at least two days in advance.

Ice Skating

FC Barcelona Pista de Gel
Avda Aristides Maillol (496 36 00). Metro Maria Cristina, Collblanc/bus 15, 52, 53, 54, 56, 57, 75. **Open** *Sept-June* 10am-1.45pm, 4.30-7.45pm, Mon-Thur; 4.30-8.45pm Fri, Sun, public holidays. *1-20 July* 10am-1.30pm, 4-7pm, Mon-Thur; 10am-1.30pm, 4-8pm, Fri; 5-9pm Sat, Sun. Closed 21 July-Aug. **Rates** (skates included) *Mon-Fri* 1,000ptas; 850ptas under-12s. *Sat, Sun, public holidays* 1,200ptas; 975ptas under-12s. **No credit cards.**
Part of the FC Barcelona complex, this is a basic, functional skating rink with skate hire, a bar and a restaurant. Saturdays in season, it's used for ice hockey.

Skating Roger de Flor
C/Roger de Flor 168 (245 28 00). Metro Tetuan/bus 6, 19, 50, 51, 54, 55. **Open** *Sept-June* 10.30am-1.30pm Tue, Thur; 10.30am-1.30pm, 5-10pm, Wed; 10.30am-1.30pm, 5pm-1am, Fri; 10.30am-2pm, 4.30pm-1am, Sat; 10.30am-2pm, 4.30-10pm Sun, public holidays. *July-Aug* 5-10pm Mon; 10.30am-1.30pm, 5-10pm, Tue-Fri; 10.30am-2pm, 4.30pm-1am Sat; 10.30am-2pm, 4.30-10pm Sun, public holidays. **Rates** *Mon-Fri* 575ptas; *Sat, Sun, public holidays* 775ptas. *Skate hire* 425ptas; *glove hire* 100ptas. **No credit cards.**
This modern rink has all the usual bar and restaurant facilities, and offers good discounts to groups of 10 or more if you arrange your visit at least a day in advance.

Jogging & Running

The best, most easily-accessible place for jogging is along the **seafront**, from Barceloneta past the Vila Olímpica and beyond. The 5km stretch of new and reclaimed beaches allows you to try your legs to the limit, on sand or the paved promenade, and there's usually a fine fresh breeze. Away from the water, the next best spot is **Montjuïc**. You can run up from the bottom, at Plaça d'Espanya, or begin running at the top: either way you'll do some climbing, and should take this into account. Another good place to run, if out of the way, is **Tibidabo** and **Collserola**. From Plaça Dr Andreu at the top of the tram line, quiet roads lead along the hillside that are fairly level, and have great views. Within the city, street running is not usually pleasant due to the traffic.

Skiing

Ski in the city in summer – why not? A dry slope has been installed at the **Pistes d'Esquí Montjuïc** *Avda Miramar 31 (221 10 66)*, near the swimming pools on Montjuïc. You can hire all the gear and take a lesson, then enjoy a swim as *après-ski*. One catch: you must be in a group of 10, and book a week ahead (at which time you negotiate a price). For places to do real skiing, *see chapter* **Trips Out of Town: Inland**; the most economical way to get to them is with a weekend package, available from all Barcelona travel agents.

Squash

Squash Barcelona
Avda Dr Marañón 17 (334 02 58). Metro Collblanc/bus 54, 75. **Open** 9am-midnight Mon-Fri; 10am-10pm Sat; 10am-8pm Sun. *Aug* closed Sun. **Rates** from 665ptas per half-hour. **No credit cards.**
The largest squash complex in Barcelona, with 14 squash and two racquet-ball courts. There are lots of areas for watching, along with the usual bar and restaurant.

Squash 2000
C/Sant Antoni Maria Claret 84 (458 22 02). Metro Joanic/bus 15, 20, 45, 47. **Open** 7am-11.30pm Mon, Wed, Fri; 8am-11.30pm Tue, Thur; 8am-10pm Sat, Sun. **Rates** from 1,010ptas per half-hour. **No credit cards.**
Twelve squash courts, plus a sauna and well-appointed bar and restaurant areas, have made this new complex very popular: courts must be booked well in advance.

Swimming Pools

There are 27 municipal pools in Barcelona, and before the city reclaimed its beachfront it was hard to see water in the crush of bodies in summer. Nowadays they are still far from empty, but it's not quite so hectic. For a list of pools, visit or call the **Servei d'Informació Esportiva** at the Picornell (*see above*). Unfortunately, the most spectacular of the 1992 pools, the **Piscina Municipal de Montjuïc**, venue for the diving events and with a fabulous view over the city, has already closed for repairs. Hopefully, it may reopen in 1997.

Club de Natació Atlètic Barceloneta
Plaça del Mar, Passeig Marítim (221 00 10). Bus 17, 45, 57, 59, 64. **Open** 6.30am-10pm Mon-Fri; 7am-10pm Sat; *end-Sept-mid-June* 8am-5pm, *15 June-15 Sept* 8am-8pm, Sun, public holidays. **Admission** *non-members* 1,000ptas. **No credit cards.**
This Barceloneta club has three indoor pools and the usual bar and restaurant, and welcomes non-members. A good place if you're not quite ready to brave the summer sun.

Piscina Bernat Picornell
Avda de l'Estadi 30-40 (423 40 41). Metro Espanya, then escalators, or Paral.lel then Funicular de Montjuïc/bus 61. **Open** 7am-midnight Mon-Fri; 7am-9pm Sat; *end-Sept-May* 7.30am-2.30pm, *25 May-24 Sept* 7.30am-8pm, Sun, public holidays. **Admission** *Oct-April* 1,100ptas; *May-Sept* 600ptas; 400ptas under-12s. **Credit** MC, V.
Built in 1969, this pool was entirely renovated to be the main swimming venue for the 1992 games, and so gives you the chance to do your laps in an Olympic-standard pool where the world's best faced glory or defeat. Ancillary facilities are also excellent, and as in all city pools entry fees are low. Another plus is that it is now heated in spring and autumn.

Tennis

There are still not enough public courts to satisfy demand in Barcelona, so phone ahead to book or check court availability. Weekday mornings are the least crowded times.

Club Vall Parc
Carretera de l'Arrabassada 97 (212 67 89). Bus A6/By car Arrabassada then Carretera de les Aigües. **Open** 8am-midnight daily. **Rates** *tennis courts* 2,575ptas per hour. **No credit cards.**
On Tibidabo, near the Vall d'Hebron, this private club offers 14 open-air courts and two open-air swimming pools. A bar and restaurant, and pleasant surroundings, also ensure that it's a well-frequented place, and booking is a must. You can hire racquets, but must bring your own tennis balls.

Centre Municipal de Tennis Vall d'Hebron
Passeig de la Vall d'Hebron 178-196 (427 65 00). Metro Montbau/bus 27, 60, 73, 76, 85. **Open** 8am-11pm Mon-Fri; 8am-9pm Sat; *Oct-April* 8am-7pm, *May-Sept* 8am-9pm, Sun, public holidays. **Admission** 1,500-2,500ptas. **No credit cards.**
The city tennis centre purpose-built for the Olympics, some wayform from the centre of town, but very modern and efficiently run. It has 17 clay tennis courts and a full-size court for the Basque game *pelota*, as well as a bar, restaurant and lounge. You will need your own racquet and balls.

Theatre

With a visual style of its own and an all-new National Theatre due to open its doors, Barcelona's theatre scene is on a roll.

Catalan theatre has no great dramatic classics to fall back on, but modern Barcelona has made up for it with the most innovative, dynamic and varied contemporary theatre scene in Spain. Theatre attendance figures here have practically tripled in the last 10 years. During 1997, moreover, the entry of the remarkable **Teatre Nacional de Catalunya** into full functioning will provide an all-new boost to theatre in the city.

Barcelona is a bilingual city, and its theatre increasingly bridges a potentially limiting but ideally enriching gap between Catalan and Castilian. As well as home-based productions, exchange visits by major companies from Madrid and the rest of Spain are increasingly common. But, if you understand neither language, the doors of Barcelona's theatres are still not closed, for many Catalan theatre groups employ a very distinctive, highly visual style, with great use of mime, music and spectacular theatrical effects, which communicates easily with international audiences. Even more 'textual' theatre can be appreciated to a level that might surprise you, thanks to the dynamic staging of many productions.

The main theatre season runs from September to June, and during August many theatres are closed completely. Earlier in the summer, though (late June to July), is usually the best time to catch visiting international performers, famous and unfamiliar, in Barcelona, during the **Festival del Grec**, which brings in local, national and international theatre companies in over 100 different performances (*see chapter* **Barcelona by Season**).

Times & Tickets

The main performances at most theatres are usually at 9 or 10pm. Most theatres also have earlier 'matinee' performances at around 6pm, usually (but not in every case) on Thursdays and Saturdays, and all theatres are closed on Mondays. Advance bookings are best made through the ticket-sales operations of savings banks (*see chapter* **Services**). Tickets for most Barcelona theatres can be bought at branches of the **Caixa de Catalunya**, or by phone with a credit card on the same Caixa's *Tel-entrades* line (310 12 12); tickets for some others are sold through *Servi-Caixa* machines of **'la Caixa'**, or by phone on 902 33 22 11. There is no additional commission. Also, box offices often take cash sales only, but credit cards can be used at *Caixes*. Which *Caixa* handles the tickets of a particular theatre is indicated below. The best places to find details of current programmes are the *Guía del Ocio*, newspapers and, for *Tel-entrades* theatres, the *Guía de Teatre* available at all Caixa de Catalunya branches.

The suave **La Cubana**.

Major Companies

Els Comediants

Over 25 years, around the figure of director/guiding light Joan Font, Els Comediants have developed a unique style of performance based in street theatre, mime, circus, music and Mediterranean traditions of folklore, *festa* and celebration. A Comediants show, often presented in border-less, open-air venues such as parks or squares, is almost as much an event as a piece of 'theatre', with a structure but no real script, and with a constant, magical use of every kind of visual element, including (usually) fireworks. Comediants, who like several other leading companies (Els Joglars, Dagoll Dagom) arose out of the exuberant alternative/street theatre scene of the seventies, now tour the world, but usually appear in Barcelona a few times a year, and a shows is often a highlight of the **Grec** (*see chapter* **Barcelona by Season**).

Companyia T de Teatre

Created in 1991 by five young actresses, this dynamic company premiered at the Mercat de les Flors with *Petits Contes Misògins*, based on Patricia Highsmith stories. They followed this success with the scathingly funny, occasionally tender *Homes!* (*Men!*). The next offering is eagerly awaited.

La Cubana

Perhaps the most fashionable company of the moment, La Cubana thrive with a dazzling mix of satire, gaudy show-biz effects, campish music, energy and audience participation. Its productions *¡Cómeme el coco, negro!* and *Cegada de amor* were resounding successes, the latter brilliantly exploiting cinematic and theatrical conventions, *Purple Rose Of Cairo*-style, to enthrall audiences. After a year in Barcelona, *Cegada de amor* spent a further year in Madrid, and the company is slated to take it to Edinburgh in 1997.

Dagoll Dagom

This company have since the seventies refined a Catalan musical genre almost all of their own, with striking use of colour and comedy. Their productions *Mar i Cel* and *Flor de Nit* were both box-office hits, as was the more recent Dorothy Parker and Cole Porter-inspired *T'Odio, Amor Meu*. They have also created sit-coms for Catalan TV. **DD** have toured most of Europe and wowed audiences as far away as Caracas and Buenos Aires, and their performance of *The Mikado* – in Catalan – was warmly received at the Glasgow Festival, somewhat to the surprise of director Anna-Rosa Cisquella.

La Fura dels Baus.

The kings of in-yer-face theatre, who have won international notoriety with provocative productions such as *Suz-O-Suz* ('85) and *Tier Mon* ('88), in which water, fire, raw meat and flour formed part of the messy recipe, along with deafening industrial sounds, power-tools, naked men, shopping trolleys, mayhem and constant motion. It's not all macho posturing and tightly-choreographed crowd-baiting, however: they also manage to stage sequences of intense poignancy and lyricism – the re-enacted births in human fish-tanks sequence from *Suz-O-Suz* – and their musical element, KRAB, are fine industrial-techno musicians. Love them or loathe them, you will not emerge unchanged. La Fura teamed up with Welsh company Brith Gof late in '95 for a wild four-day 'happening' at the Mercat de les Flors, and a new production, *Mane*, was at time of writing being brained and brawned into fruition by the whole team.

Els Joglars

A 'company' that essentially revolves around Albert Boadella, its strong-willed founder, ideologist and leader. With sardonic humour and text as well as the customary Catalan mime and dance skills, Boadella has maintained a line of caustic satire, with creations such as *Yo Tengo un Tío en América* (*I've Got an Uncle in America*), detonating the Columbus commemorations of 1992, and, more recently *Ubu President*, a reworking of *Ubu Roi* with Catalan President Jordi Pujol unmistakably in the central role.

Teatre Lliure

The Lliure is probably Barcelona's most stable theatre company, and since 1976 has kept to a line of presenting classic, and contemporary drama by Catalan and international authors, in Catalan. Its productions are very high-quality. In 1996 they presented an original product of in-company brainstorming, called '*Lear, or an Actress's Dream*', based around *King Lear* and directed by Ariel Garcia Valdés.

El Tricicle

El Tricicle – as its name suggests – consists of three actors, a comedy team as much as a theatre group, but whose shows are interlinked pieces, not just sketches. Their latest show, *Entre Tres*, is based on the interplay between an actor, a writer and a musician. Like Dagoll Dagom and La Cubana, they have successfully transferred their live output to film and television. Since they work almost completely in mime, they're easily able to cross borders, but their most global audience must have been for their skit in the Olympic closing ceremony of 1992, which seemed to offend some among the athletic fraternity.

Main Theatres

Mercat de les Flors

Plaça Margarida Xirgu, C/Lleida 59 (426 18 75). Metro Espanya/bus 9, 13, 38, 61, 65, 91. **Box office** one hour before performance; *advance sales* Caixa de Catalunya & Centre d'Informació de la Virreina. **Tickets** prices vary according to performance. **No credit cards.**
A huge, converted flower market with three halls of different sizes, and capacity for large-scale productions. It is now the usual venue for **La Fura dels Baus'** dynamic performances, and has housed Peter Brook's *Mahabharata* and other major international visiting productions. Dance and music are features of the programme as well as theatre. Run by the Ajuntament, the Mercat is the main venue for the **Grec** summer festival, with a multi-varied range of performances (*see chapter* **Barcelona by Season**). As well as through Servi-Caixa tickets can be bought at the Virreina centre on the Rambla (*see chapter* **Essential Information**).

Teatre Arnau

Avda Paral.lel 60 (441 48 81). Metro Paral.lel/bus 36, 57, 64, N4, N6. **Box office** from 8pm Tue-Sat; from 6pm Sun; *advance sales* box office & Caixa de Catalunya. **Tickets** approx 1,500-3,000ptas. **No credit cards.**
One of the historic music-halls of the Paral.lel, the Arnau now functions more as a theatre, offering small-scale musicals and lately the *Rocky Horror Show*. One thing kept from former days is that shows are late, sometimes at midnight.

Dagoll Dagom *never fail to come up with surprises.*

Teatre Borràs

Plaça Urquinaona 9 (412 15 82). Metro Urquinaona/bus all routes to Plaça Urquinaona. **Box office** from 4.30pm Tue-Sun; *advance sales* box office & Caixa de Catalunya. **Tickets** 1,900-2,800ptas. **No credit cards.**
One of Barcelona's largest theatres. Lately it has enjoyed a huge hit with a two-year (and continuing) run of Neil Simon's *The Odd Couple*, in Spanish, with Paco Morán and Joan Pera. It is run by Focus, Spain's largest private theatre company, and usually offers comedy in Spanish. Expected (eventually) to follow are Alan Ayckbourn's *Communicating Doors* and Charo López' *Tengamos el Sexo en Paz*.

Teatre Condal

Avda Paral.lel 91 (442 31 32/85 84). Metro Paral.lel/bus 20, 36, 57, 64, N4, N6. **Box office** from 4.30pm Tue-Sun; *advance sales* box office & Caixa de Catalunya. **Tickets** approx 2,000-2,800ptas. **No credit cards.**
Another large venue, also Focus-run, the Condal is on the Paral.lel, historic heartland of the city's commercial theatres. Recently it has accommodated a Catalan version of Willy Russell's *Blood Brothers* (*Germans de Sang*) with admired all-round performer Àngels Gonyalons in the starring role, and Woody Allen's *Play It Again, Sam*, with Catalan super-model-turned-actress Elsa Anka in the Diane Keaton role. Most, but not all, productions are in Catalan.

Teatre de l'Eixample

C/Aragó 140 (451 34 62). Metro Urgell/ bus 14, 20, 59. **Box office** 11.30am-12.30pm, 5-10.30pm Tue-Sat; *phone reservations* 9.15am-2pm, 4-8pm & Caixa de Catalunya. **Tickets** 1,800-2,200ptas; discounts for students, over-65s, groups. **No credit cards.**
This theatre opened in November 1995, but quickly made an impact with a programme combining main productions (nearly always in Catalan), alternative late-night shows on some weekends, music, children's theatre and films, including a weekly *Rocky Horror Picture Show* night (*see chapter* **Film**). Despite recent doubts as to its future, it's one of the best small/mid-range venues and deserves to survive.

Teatre Lliure

C/Montseny 47 (218 92 51). Metro Fontana/bus 22, 24, 28, 39, N4, N6. **Box office** from 5pm Tue-Sun; *advance sales* 5-8pm Tue-Sat (box office) & Caixa de Catalunya. **Tickets** 1,600-2,000ptas; *early show* Thur 1,200ptas. **No credit cards.**
A theatre that's played a central role in the expansion of Catalan theatre – and in many other fields – over the last twenty years, especially for 'textual' drama. It has its own repertory company (*see* **Major Companies**) and back-up workshops. It's a charming old building in Gràcia, taken over for its present role in 1976: small but versatile, it inspires great affection, and has a good bar-restaurant. All productions are in Catalan. It also hosts dance performances, and its own chamber orchestra (*see chapter* **Music: Classical & Opera**).

Teatre Poliorama

La Rambla 115 (317 59 54/71 89). Metro Catalunya/bus all routes to Plaça Catalunya. **Box office** noon-1.30pm, 4-8pm Mon; noon-1.30pm, 4pm till performance time Tue-Sun; *advance sales* noon-1.30pm, 4-8pm, Mon, Tue, Thur-Sat & Servi-Caixa. **Tickets** 1,500-2,500ptas. discounts for students, over-65s, groups. **Credit** V.
One of two theatres run by the Catalan Government's *Centre Dramàtic de la Generalitat* (CDGC), the Poliorama was acquired in 1984 to house the **Josep Maria Flotats** company, genesis of the future Catalan National Theatre (*see* **Special Feature**). It recently offered an excellent version of Sondheim's *Sweeney Todd*. Performances are in Catalan. It will be vacated when the TNC opens, and the Focus company has announced a bid for the theatre, proposing to give it a stable company structure and to stage at least three productions a year of plays by modern Catalan writers.

Teatre Romea

C/Hospital 51 (317 71 89/301 55 04). Metro Liceu/bus 14, 18, 38, 59, 91, N4, N6. **Times & tickets** as for Teatre Poliorama.
The CGDC's other theatre, the Romea has been one of the centres of the Barcelona theatre world since the last century. It offers classical and contemporary theatre, usually in Catalan but occasionally in the play's original language with Catalan simultaneous translation through headphones.

Teatre Tívoli

C/Casp 10-12 (412 20 63) Metro Catalunya/bus all routes to Plaça Catalunya. **Box office** 11.30am-2pm, from 4.30pm, Tue-Sun; *advance sales* box office & Caixa de Catalunya. **Tickets** 2,000-4,000ptas; group discounts. **No credit cards.**
Barcelona's largest theatre, seating over 1,600, offers a mixed bag of drama, films and music. Recently it has hosted a season by Flamenco phenomenon-heart-throb Joaquín Cortés.

Teatre Victòria

Avda Paral.lel 67 (443 29 29). Metro Paral.lel/bus 36, 57, 64, N4, N6. **Box office** usually from 4/5pm Tue-Sun; *advance sales* box office & Servi-Caixa. **Tickets** approx 1,500-3,000ptas; discounts Wed, Thur. **Credit** V.
Opened in 1905, the Victòria is Barcelona's second-largest venue. It is run jointly by Dagoll Dagom, El Tricicle and the production company Anexa, and enjoyed a long run of Michael Frayn's *Noises Off*, performed in a mixture of Catalan and Spanish to mirror Barcelona's bilingual reality.

Villarroel Teatre

C/Villarroel 87 (451 12 34). Metro Urgell/bus 9, 20, 50, 56, N1. **Box office** from 7.30pm Tue-Sun; *advance sales* (box office) 7.30-9.30pm Tue-Sat; (phone) 9am-2pm, 7.30pm-performance; Caixa de Catalunya. **Tickets** 1,500-2,200ptas; discounts for under-14s, over-65s, groups. **No credit cards.**
The Villarroel stages mainly non-mainstream theatre productions, such as Marta Degracia's *El Bizco* (*The Cross-Eyed Man*) in mixed Catalan and Spanish. Its financial situation is often shaky, but it always seems to survive.

Experimental/Alternative

Artenbrut

C/Perill 9-11 (457 97 05). Metro Verdaguer/bus 20, 21, 45, 47. **Box office** 8pm till performance Tue-Sun; advance sales Caixa de Catalunya. **Tickets** 1,300ptas Tue; 1,600ptas Wed-Thur & musicals (incl one drink); 1,900ptas Fri-Sun. **No credit cards.**
This small experimental venue has great intentions and an enthusiastic staff, and houses small-scale productions such as Genet's *Les Bonnes* (*Las Criadas*), in Spanish, plus late-night music/cabaret shows (Fri, Sat), and children's theatre.

La Cuina

C/Sant Pere Més Baix 7 (268 20 78). Metro Jaume I/bus 17, 19, 40, 45. **Box office** two hours before performance time; *advance sales* Caixa de Catalunya. **Tickets** 1,800ptas; 1,300ptas students, over-65s; free Mar & May-June (student productions). **No credit cards.**
With the **Teatre Adrià Gual**, this is an outlet for the work of Barcelona's Theatre Institute school, and always offers a programme of interesting, varied (and cheap) productions.

Sala Beckett

C/Alegre de Dalt 55 bis (284 53 12). Metro Joanic/bus 21, 25, 39, N4. **Open** *box office* one hour before performance; *advance sales* 10.30am-2pm, 4-6pm Mon-Fri & Caixa de Catalunya. **Tickets** 1,700ptas; discounts for students, over-65s, groups. **No credit cards.**
Founded in 1989 by the Samuel Beckett-inspired '*Teatro*

Theatre's new temple

December 1996 marks the official opening – although full productions will not begin until mid-1997 – of one more of Barcelona's grand projects, but one that has the potential to be of much more than architectural interest: the **Teatre Nacional de Catalunya** (TNC). The project was launched in 1992 under the charismatic leadership of Josep Maria Flotats, Catalonia's finest classic actor. Like many Barcelona schemes it's ambitious on a level that can only be refreshing, for it will create a world-class theatre centre.

The building, which immediately invites comparisons with the Parthenon, is the fruit of a close collaboration between Flotats and the most internationally-famous of Catalan architects, Ricard Bofill, and is intended as a homage to Greek theatre. In an unlovely area by the Plaça de les Glòries (Metro Glòries), next to the also-new Auditorium, it has like most Bofill buildings its highs and lows; the latter include the giant glass-sheet walls between the Doric columns, which would be fine in a Nordic city but could be oven-like in Barcelona in July, and represent a problem to be solved. Inside, though, there are two wonderful, entirely-independent theatres: one a beautiful wooden amphitheatre-style structure – also with a retro-look, recalling Palladio's theatre in Vicenza – with capacity of nearly a thousand, the other a smaller 'polyvalent' theatre that can be adapted to accommodate any kind of performance, from authentic-style seventeenth-century pieces to fluid space-consuming productions such as those of groups like the Fura dels Baus. At the back of the main building there are huge, separate state-of-the-art workshops and back-up facilites – also usable as film studios – that most national theatres and opera houses would die for.

The inspiration behind the TNC, Josep Maria Flotats cut his theatrical teeth in Barcelona and Strasbourg before moving to Paris, where he achieved the rare position for a foreigner of becoming one of the lead actors at the Comédie Française. He was awarded the *Légion d'Honneur*. In 1983, he came back triumphantly to Barcelona

with the Comédie's production of Molière's *Don Juan*, and decided to return permanently to his native land (and language). With Generalitat backing he was installed with his own company at the Poliorama, opening with Rostand's *Cyrano de Bergerac* in 1985. In contrast to the mime- and dance-related work of many Catalan theatre groups, he is committed to textual theatre. His approach, though, is wholly international.

A limitation of Catalan theatre has always been the lack of a classical repertoire; Flotats and his team calmly accept this and propose that the TNC, rather than look for one, should present the full range of global theatre in Catalan, while simultaneously working to assist new writers and develop theatre skills. The theatre would also be ideal for visits by major Spanish and international companies, and Flotats has ideas for international collaborations, such as simultaneous presentations of the same production in different cities, in different languages.

The opening of the TNC will give Barcelona's theatre access to a world stage, but Flotats also takes seriously the need to develop a loyal local audience for Catalonia's public-service theatre. Artistically, he has a glut of ideas, and he's committed and experienced enough to see that some of them at least become realities. For the moment, the Catalan theatre world is holding its breath.

Fronterizo' group, this small basement theatre in Gràcia stages very varied new theatre, welcoming original productions such as Bet Escudé i Gallès' *'El Destí de les Violetes'* (The Destiny of Violets). In Catalan and Spanish.

Teatre Adrià Gual
C/Sant Pere Més Baix 7 (268 20 78). Metro Jaume I/bus 17, 19, 40, 45. **Times & tickets** as for La Cuina. The main theatre of the Institut de Teatre, but presenting both student and professional productions, and dance.

Teatre Malic
C/Fusina 3 (310 70 35). Metro Jaume I/bus 39, 51. **Box office** two hours before performance; *advance sales* 10am-2pm, 4-6pm Mon-Fri & Caixa de Catalunya. **Tickets** 1,200-2,000ptas; discounts for students, over-65s, groups. **No credit cards.**
A tiny (60-seater) fringe theatre. Productions have included *Firmen!* (*Sign!*) by J.M. Padilla (about a man who's buried, then returns to life), followed by *21 històries d'amor* by Francesc Pereira. Also occasional kids' shows at weekends.

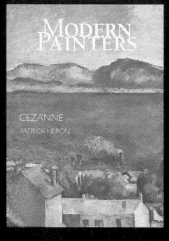

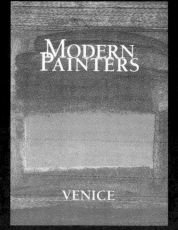

In Focus

Business

How and where to find a translator, hire a computer and negotiate local bureaucracy.

Historically, Barcelona has been Spain's most important city for international trade. Its coastal location has made it a crossroads ever since Roman times, and although Madrid, as Spain's capital, is now the number-one business centre in the country, Barcelona still runs it a very close second. Renowned as hard workers and harder negotiators, Catalans are also recognised for their creativity, and have an open-mindedness unequalled on the Iberian peninsula.

Although the nineties' recession has clearly affected the Catalan economy, the 1992 Olympics and projects associated with them have helped it avoid the full repercussions felt in the rest of Spain. A major element in the thinking behind the Games was a resolve to use them as a pretext for the renovation of Barcelona's insufficient infrastructure. Roads were built, including a ring-road and a tunnel that permits a quick exit to the motorway network and the technology parks beyond the coastal mountains. Hotels were transformed, and air-conditioning, once a luxury, became an automatic requirement in public spaces. Firms faced the challenge of providing competent services in organisation, logistics, translation and mixed-media.

However, Spain's bureaucracy has remained as intricate and cumbersome as ever, and the Generalitat, the autonomous government of Catalonia re-established in 1980, has, unfortunately, also fallen into many of the habits of its Spanish counterpart. The EU meanwhile has established its own set of rules and regulations.

It is definitely not worthwhile trying to deal with this system single-handed. A visit to the **Cambra de Comerç** (*see below*) is a must to sort out what you can do, what you have to do, and who to consult for advice and permits. Locals often make use of intermediaries such as a *Gestoria* (*see below*) rather than deal with all the formalities themselves.

Institutions & Information

Anyone working in Barcelona for more than just a passing visit will need to know about the different governing bodies and their respective areas of competence. A recommended first stop is your own consulate, which will have lists of English-speaking professionals. For consulates, and more on residency, *see chapter* **Survival**.

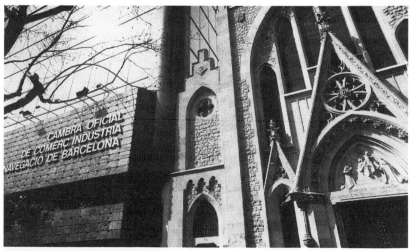

The Barcelona **Chamber of Commerce**, the city's most vital business institution.

Levels of Government

EU Office: Patronat Català Pro-Europa
*C/Bruch 50, 2º (318 26 26/fax 318 73 56). Metro
Urquinaona/bus 7, 18, 47, 50, 54, 56.* **Open** 9am-2pm
Mon, Fri; 9am-2pm, 4-6pm, Tue-Thur.
Information on EU regulations and their implications for
Spain, and on EU grants.

Central Government: Dirección General del Trabajo
*Travessera de Gràcia 303-311 (401 30 00). Metro
Joanic/bus 21, 39, 55.* **Open** 9am-2pm Mon-Fri.
Work permits for non-EU nationals. Shorter queues at 9am.

Central Government: Gobierno Civil
*Avda Marqués de l'Argentera 2 (480 03 00/482 03
11/fax 482 04 13/14). Metro Barceloneta/bus 16, 17, 36,
40, 45, 57, 59, 64.* **Open** 9am-2pm Mon-Fri.
The special foreigners' department at the Civil Government
issues residence permits for EU citizens (required to acquire
Spanish driver's licences, and to buy vehicles), and certifi-
cates of non-residence (needed for non-resident bank
accounts). Avoid queues: go on Friday. *See also chapter*
Survival.

Central Government: Delegación de Hacienda
Your business will also need a Tax Number (*Número de
Identificación Fiscal* or *NIF; NIE, Número de Identificación de
Extranjero*, for non-EU nationals), issued by the local tax
office (*Delegació d'Hisenda*, in Catalan). There are several dis-
trict offices. It is strongly advisable to obtain this via a
Gestoria (*see below*), who will almost certainly save you
money (in tax) in the process.

Catalan Government: Generalitat de Catalunya
*Plaça Antoni Lopez 5 (information 315 13 13). Metro
Jaume I/bus 14, 17, 36, 40, 45, 57, 59, 64.* **Open** 16
Sept-May 9am-7pm, *June-15 Sept* 8am-6pm, Mon-Fri.
The Generalitat provides a range of services for foreign
investors. It has offices in various parts of the city, and
English-speaking operators will direct you to the specific
address of the department you need.

City Council: Ajuntament de Barcelona
*Plaça Sant Miquel 4-5 (information 402 70 00). Metro
Jaume I/bus 17, 40, 45.* **Open** 8.30am-6pm Mon-Fri; *July,
Aug* 8.15am-2.15pm Mon-Fri.
Permits for new businesses are issued by the authorities of
each of the ten municipal districts: for details, ask for the
Ajuntament de Districte (district town hall) of the neigh-
bourhood where you will be establishing your business.

Other Official Institutions

Borsa de Valors de Barcelona (Barcelona Stock Exchange)
*Passeig de Gràcia 19 (401 35 55/fax 401 36 50). Metro
Passeig de Gràcia/bus 7, 16, 17, 22, 24, 28.* **Open** *visits*
9am-6.30pm, *library* 9am-2pm, *departments* 9am-2pm, 4-
6.30pm, Mon-Fri.

Cambra de Comerç, Indústria i Navegació de Barcelona (Chamber of Commerce)
*Avda Diagonal 452-454 (416 93 00/fax 416 93 01).
Metro Diagonal/bus 6, 7, 15, 22, 33, 34, 127.* **Open** *Oct-
May* 9am-5pm Mon-Thur; 9am-2pm Fri; *June-Sept* 8am-
3pm Mon-Fri.
Definitely the most important institution for business people,

providing a wealth of information: advice on viability of businesses; fiscal and commercial legal consultancy; market studies; databases by sectors; contacts for subcontracting;
funding, and all the steps to take when setting up a business.

PPIME: Patronal de la Petita i Mitjana Empresa de Catalunya (Catalan Small Business Association)
*C/Bruch 72-74, 6º (487 40 00/fax 487 65 20). Metro
Girona/bus 7, 47, 50, 54, 56.* **Open** 9am-9pm Mon-Fri.

Clubs & Contacts

The American Society of Barcelona
(200 37 44/fax 200 33 46). **Open** *for phone calls* 9am-
12.30pm, 3-5pm, Mon-Fri.
Meet fellow US business people, from executives to teachers, at the weekly happy hour, monthly business lunch or
one of the cultural outings. Membership 6,000ptas per year.

The British Society of Catalunya
*Via Augusta 213 (tel & fax 209 06 39). FGC Bonanova/
bus 14.* **Open** no fixed opening hours.
Keep in touch with fellow ex-pats in monthly get-togethers
and other events each year. Membership 1,500ptas a year.

Press & Publications

The main daily business publications are
Expansión and *Cinco Días*. There are also quite a
few business monthlies: *Fomento* and *Economics*
have information specific to Catalonia as well as
national and international business news. For classified advertising outlets, *see chapter* **Media**.

Banking

For everyday banking needs, *see chapter*
Essential Information.

Banc de Sabadell
*Passeig de Gràcia 36 (482 39 00/fax 488 36 92). Metro
Passeig de Gràcia/bus 7, 16, 17, 22, 24, 28.* **Open** *Oct-
May* 8.15am-4.30pm Mon-Thur; 8.15am-2pm Fri; 8.15am-
1pm Sat; *June-Sept* 8.15am-2pm Mon-Fri.
A local bank with an excellent foreign department.

Barclays Bank
*Passeig de Gràcia 45 (318 20 00). Metro Passeig de
Gràcia/bus 7, 16, 17, 22, 24, 28.* **Open** *Oct-May* 8.30am-
4.30pm Mon-Thur; 8.30am-2.30pm Fri; 8.30am-1pm Sat;
June-Sept 8.30am-2.30pm Mon-Fri.

Deutsche Bank
*Avda Diagonal 446 (404 21 02/404 21 70). Metro
Diagonal/bus 6, 15, 33, 34.* **Open** *Oct-May* 8.15am-
4.30pm Mon-Thur; 8.15am-2pm Fri; 8.15am-1pm Sat; *June-
Sept* 8.15am-2pm Mon-Fri.
New to Spain, with some of the best interest rates on loans.

Conference Venues & Services

Barcelona Convention Bureau
*C/Tarragona 149 (423 18 00/fax 423 26 49). Metro
Tarragona/bus 27, 109, 127.* **Open** 9am-2.30pm, 4-7pm,
Mon-Thur; 9am-3pm Fri.
A specialised wing of the city tourist authority, the BCB
assists organisations or individuals wishing to hold con-
ferences or similar events in the city, with full information,

publications and lists of venues and/or service companies, and facilitates contacts with them.

Centre de Relacions Empresarials
Aeroport del Prat (478 67 99/fax 478 67 05). **Open** 8.30am-8.30pm Mon-Fri.
The **Cambra de Comerç** (*see above*), provides this 'meeting point' within the airport terminals, with eight meeting rooms and access via modem to most of the information available at their main office. Information services are open to all; use of meeting rooms must be arranged through a member company of the Chamber. The Chamber can also provide conference halls, seating from 15 to 500, in the historic medieval former Stock Exchange, the **Casa Llotja** (*see chapter* **Barcelona by Area**). For information and bookings, call 416 93 30.

Fira de Barcelona
Avda Reina Maria Cristina (233 20 00/fax 233 20 01). Metro Plaça Espanya/bus 9, 13, 51, 53, 65. **Open** 9am-2pm, 4-6pm, Mon-Fri; *June-Aug* 9am-2pm Mon-Fri.
The Barcelona trade fair site is one of the largest permanent exhibition complexes in Europe. In addition to the main area at Plaça d'Espanya it also includes a state-of-the-art new site, **Montjuïc-2**, in the Zona Franca towards the airport, providing over 100,000 square metres of exhibition and convention space divided between halls of varied sizes. The Fira also administers the largest conference and convention hall in Barcelona, the **Palau de Congressos**, part of the Plaça d'Espanya site. It can be let separately (direct line 233 23 71).

Grupo Pacífico
C/Enric Granados 44 (454 54 00/fax 451 74 38). FGC Provença/bus 7, 16, 17, 20, 21, 43, 44. **Open** 9am-6pm Mon-Fri.
Provides organisational services for conferences.

Business Services
Accountants, Consultants, Legal

Arthur Andersen
Avda Diagonal 654 (280 40 40/fax 280 28 10). Bus 6, 67, 68. **Open** 8am-9pm Mon-Fri.

Gabinete Echevarría
C/Roger de Llúria 36, àtic (412 18 99/fax 302 47 44). Metro Passeig de Gràcia/bus 7, 18, 50, 54, 56. **Open** 9am-1.30pm, 4-7pm, Mon-Fri. Closed Aug.
Law practice associated with US firm Safferey Champness.

Santacana Grup
Passatge Forasté 7 (417 30 30/fax 212 18 18). FGC Av Tibidabo/bus 17. **Open** 9am-1.30pm, 3.30-7pm, Mon-Thur; 9am-1.30pm Fri. Closed Aug.
Affiliated with London accountants Moore Stephens, they provide not only standard accountancy and consultancy services but also those usually offered by *Gestorías* (*see below*).

Advertising & Corporate Image

Asterisco
C/Mendel 1-3-5, local 2 (204 12 00/fax 203 76 32). FGC Reina Elisenda/bus 22, 64, 75. **Open** 9am-1.30pm, 3-6pm, Mon-Thur; 9am-1.30pm Fri; *Aug* 9am-3pm Mon-Fri.
Advertising agency for all media.

L2M
C/Parelladas 76, 1º 2ª, Sitges (894 41 52/fax 894 45 09). Train RENFE to Sitges. **Open** 10am-1.30pm, 4.30-7pm, Mon-Fri.
Excellent designs for every aspect of corporate image, from logos and graphics to interior design and uniforms. They can accommodate every size of budget.

Gestorías – administrative services
The *Gestoría* is a distinctly Spanish institution, the main function of which is to lighten the weight of dealing with local bureaucracy by doing it for you. Combining to some degree the roles of bookkeeper, lawyer, notary and general business adviser, they can be very helpful in getting you through paperwork, sparing you the long queues in government offices, and pointing out shortcuts and money-saving strategems that foreigners are inevitably unaware of. Unfortunately, employees at local *Gestorías* rarely speak English.

Gestoría Tutzo
C/Aribau 226 (209 67 88/fax 200 41 38). Bus 6, 7, 15, 27, 33, 34, 58, 64. **Open** 8.30am-2pm, 4-7pm, Mon-Fri; *July, Aug* closed Fri afternoons.
With years of experience and very professional, Tutzo offer all the administrative services you may need – legal, international, fiscal, accounting, social security, contracts and so on – and they speak English.

Translation & Publications
BCN Consultores Lingüísticos
C/Balmes 69, 3º 2ª (454 51 12/fax 454 35 46). Metro Passeig de Gràcia/bus 7, 16, 17. **Open** 9am-7pm Mon-Fri; *Aug* 9am-3pm Mon-Fri.
Very professional translators and interpreters, although prices are a bit high: translations cost 13½ptas per word; interpreters 6,500ptas per hour.

DUUAL
C/Ciutat 7, 2º 4ª (302 29 85/fax 412 40 66). Metro Jaume I/bus 17, 40, 45. **Open** 9am-2pm, 4-7pm, Mon-Thur; 9am-2pm Fri. **Credit** V.
Net page: http://www. xs4all.nl/~jumanl/duual.html E-mail: duual@bcn.servicom.es
A sophisticated agency who were the main translators of English for the 1992 Olympics. Prices are competitive (English translations, 11ptas per word) and they have state-of-the-art DTP equipment. Also eastern European languages and others such as Chinese, Japanese, Greek and Arabic.

Traductores Jurados (Sworn Translators)
In Spain official bodies often demand that foreign documents be translated by legally-certified translators. Rates are substantially higher than for conventional translators.

Teodora Gambetta
C/Escorial 29-31, escala C, àtic, 2ª (tel & fax 219 22 25). Metro Joanic/bus 21, 39. **Open** no fixed opening hours.

Luís Pérez Pardo
C/Dr August Pi Sunyer 11, 6º 1ª (tel & fax 204 43 27). Metro Maria Cristina/bus 6, 7, 16, 33, 63, 67, 68, 70. **Open** no fixed opening hours.

Courier Services
The most economical way of sending small packages for next-day delivery within Spain is via **Postal Exprés**, available at any Post Office (*see chapter* **Survival**).

Estació d'Autobusos Barcelona-Nord

C/Ali Bei 80 (general information 265 65 08/courier service 232 43 29). Metro Arc de Triomf/bus 40, 42, 141. **Open** 7am-7.45pm Mon-Fri; 7am-12.45pm Sat. **No credit cards.**

Excellent, inexpensive service at the bus station for sending parcels on scheduled coaches to towns within mainland Spain. To send up to 10kg the same day to Madrid, for example, costs 1,700ptas, and they can also arrange pick-up and delivery in larger towns.

Eurocity

C/Milanesado 15 (203 95 04/205 45 71). FGC Tres Torres/bus 16, 70, 74, 94. **Open** 8.30am-7pm Mon-Fri. **No credit cards.**

An efficient local courier company. The basic charge to send a package by bike within Barcelona is 1,150ptas for non-account customers. Also offers national and international services.

UPS

C/Miguel Hernández, corner of C/Indústria, Polígon Industrial Zona Franca, L'Hospitalet de Llobregat (freephone 900 10 24 10/fax 263 39 09). **Open** 8am-7pm Mon-Fri. **Credit** AmEx, MC, V.

International courier company, reliable and with competitive rates. You must call by 5pm for pick-up at your door by 7pm and next-day delivery. The depot is in the Zona Franca industrial area, and if you need to drop off or collect in person it's very hard to get there except by car or cab.

Office Services
Equipment Hire

Data Rent

C/Muntaner 492, 5° 4ª (434 00 26/fax 418 78 83). Bus 16, 58, 64, 74. **Open** *Oct-May* 9am-2pm, 4-7pm, Mon-Fri; *June-Sept* 8am-3pm Mon-Fri. **No credit cards.**

IBM-compatible PCs, occasionally Macs, printers and presentation equipment for hire.

Rent

C/Numància 212 (280 21 31/fax 280 50 85). Bus 16, 34, 66, 70, 74. **Open** 10am-2pm, 4-8pm, Mon-Fri; 10am-2pm Sat. **Credit** AmEx, MC, V.

Fax machines and mobile phones for rent.

WattMac

Passeig de la Bonanova 103 (280 06 60/fax 205 34 19). FGC Sarrià/bus 22, 64, 75. **Open** 9.30am-1.30pm, 3.30-7.30pm, Mon-Fri; 10am-2pm Sat. **No credit cards.**

Macintosh computers, printers, all other Mac-compatible equipment and also slide projectors and overhead projectors, for hire for periods from three days to a month.

Business Centres

Centro de Negocios

C/Pau Claris 97, 4° 1ª (301 69 96/fax 301 69 04). Metro Passeig de Gràcia/bus 7, 18, 50, 54, 56. **Open** 8am-9pm Mon-Fri; *Aug* 9am-3pm Mon-Fri.

Very near the city centre, they offer office space, desk space in a shared office, mail box addresses, meeting rooms, secretarial services and a wide range of administrative services, for hire for variable periods.

Diagonal Business Centre

C/Sabino Arana 32 (490 01 74/fax 411 24 07). Metro Maria Cristina/bus 59, 70, 72, 75. **Open** 8am-8pm Mon-Fri.

Fully equipped offices with fax and secretarial services.

Ofitten

C/Galileu 303-305, 4° (321 08 12/fax 439 89 27). Metro Les Corts/bus 15, 43, 59. **Open** 8.30am-8.30pm Mon-Fri.

Furnished and unfurnished offices. Administrative and secretarial services also available.

On-Line Services

For quick access to cyberspace, the best places are the various Internet cafés (*see chapter* **Cafés & Bars**). Local dial-in number for CompuServe is 487 38 88; for America Online/AOL, 487 86 44.

Cinet

Passeig Lluís Companys 23 (268 26 40/e-mail cinet@cinet.fcr.es). Metro Arc de Triomf/bus 19, 39, 40, 41, 51. **Open** 9am-2pm, 4-6pm, Mon-Fri.

Cinet will connect you up to the Internet for an initial fee of 20,000ptas, directly, or 5,000ptas if via the *Infovia* system run by the Spanish phone company *Telefónica*. After that, it's 5,000ptas per month for unlimited access. Also consultancy services, and PC and modem hire.

Removals

AGS

C/Provença 288, pral (487 23 42/fax 487 96 76). Metro Diagonal/bus 22, 24, 28. **Open** 8.30am-8.30pm (varies in Aug). **No credit cards.**

International household goods movers, providing door-to-door services anywhere in the world, plus storage. Member of the British National Moving and Storage Association.

F Gil Stauffer

C/Pau Claris 176 (215 55 55/fax 215 50 16). Metro Diagonal/bus 20, 21, 39, 43, 44, 45. **Open** 9am-7.30pm Mon-Fri. **No credit cards.**

National and international movers with offices in Spain's major cities and link companies throughout the world.

Staff Hire
Business Schools

Most local business schools have a '*bolsa de trabajo*' (placement service) which can provide young, well-prepared candidates with good English.

EADA

C/Aragó 204 (323 12 08/fax 323 73 17). Metro Universitat/bus 14, 54, 58, 64, 66. **Open** 9am-1.30pm, 4-8pm, Mon-Fri; 10am-12.30pm Sat. Closed Sats in Aug, public holidays.

ESADE

Avda Pedralbes 60-62 (280 61 62/fax 204 81 05). Bus 63, 75, 114. **Open** *information* 10am-2pm, 4-7pm, Mon-Fri; *Easter* 8am-2.30pm Mon-Fri. Closed three weeks Aug.

Temp Agencies

Adia

C/Mallorca 221-223, 7° (454 38 08/fax 454 54 71). FGC Provença/bus 7, 20, 21, 43, 54, 58, 64, 66. **Open** 9am-7pm Mon-Fri.

Manpower

C/Aragó 277 (487 68 68/fax 487 98 03). Metro Passeig de Gràcia/bus 7, 16, 17, 22, 24, 28. **Open** 8am-8pm Mon-Fri.

Children

With parks and pastries, funfairs, beaches and dragons, you should have no trouble keeping the average infant amused...

Families who want to have a great time in Barcelona should think of making plenty of visits to parks, hands-on museums, pastry shops, cafés and street performances. This is how local parents keep their kids amused and cooperative. Spanish families are not nearly as large as they used to be, or as they are often thought to be – for a range of reasons the birth rate has been declining precipitately, and in Catalonia is now one of the lowest in the world – but the children they do have are adored and indulged. Parents tend to take children everywhere, including, naturally, bars and restaurants, where they participate noisily. At weekends small children can be found playing beside pavement café tables before lunch, or late at night in summer: waiters manoeuvre around them, and strangers offer smiles and sweets. Children are simply taken along, wherever they are and at any hour. Mid-week they are

less in evidence, for many are enrolled in after-school activities set up to meet child-care needs for working parents, and to supplement the school curriculum.

Despite their tolerant attitude to children, Catalans make few concessions in the form of special facilities. Children under three travel free on city public transport; for all others, fares are the same as for adults, except on the special **Bus Turístic** service (*see chapter* **Getting Around**). Don't expect child-proof environments, baby-changing rooms, smoke-free areas, pram ramps or high chairs and children's menus in restaurants. Still, you needn't be shy about asking for 'kid-style' dishes – an omelette, a smaller portion of steak or fish – even if they're not on the menu. Most restaurants will willingly oblige. For children's clothes and toy shops, *see chapter* **Shopping**.

Touristing
Sightseeing

Assuring that kids enjoy Barcelona's scenic old city can be a challenge. Street entertainers can be a great help, focussing their attention. The most kid-friendly time to visit the **Cathedral** is Sunday mornings, when local children are out in force and there's plenty going on – such as the traditional Catalan bands (*cobles*) that accompany the circles of *sardana* dancers on the square outside. Another essential part of the Cathedral tour is to visit the white geese that live in the cloister.

Another good place to head for in the Barri Gòtic is the **Plaça del Pi**. The *plaça* itself is full of activity, and more buskers and street shows, at weekends, and in the C/Petritxol which leads away from it there are several *granges*, best described as milk and coffee bars (*see chapter* **Cafés & Bars**). Open all week except for Sunday afternoons, they serve lots of hypnotic sticky treats: thick hot chocolate and cream, cakes, custards, and strawberries in season. Outside the old city is another weekend attraction, the Sunday **book and coin market** at Mercat de Sant Antoni, where collectors swap and trade stickers and other collectables (*see chapter* **Shopping**). Note that it can get very crowded.

Anyone who looks around Barcelona with kids on board will almost certainly want to make good use of the city's traditional rides, which every

L'Aquàrium de Barcelona. *See page 224.*

child who lives here has probably been on several times at least. At the bottom of the Rambla you'll find the **Golondrines**, the boats that take you on a half-hour ride through the harbour to the end of the breakwater. Boats also run to the Port Olímpic.

The other main rides all help you to get up Barcelona's two mountains of **Montjuïc** and **Tibidabo**. The **Funicular de Montjuïc** is a bit of a damp squib, underground for much of its route, but the **Teleféric** cable cars are much more exciting. At the top, kids who presumably care not a jot about its political associations are often fascinated by the **Castell de Montjuïc** (now the **Museu Militar**), with its massive walls and moat. The rest of Montjuïc is also full of interesting and surprising areas, with intertwining parks and gardens that still have an air of mystery that makes them great to explore. The trip up to Tibidabo is better, just as a ride: beginning with the clanking **Tramvia Blau**, and then continuing onto the **Funicular**, with more spectacular views, and the best view of all from the **Torre de Collserola**. For details of all rides, *see chapter* **Sightseeing**.

Parks, Playgrounds, Funfairs

Barcelona families make great use of their parks, old and new. Many contain interesting sculptures, almost all have playgrounds, and sometimes you can also find kids' entertainers.

Main city parks

For details of parks mentioned, *see chapter* **Sightseeing**. There are good playgrounds either side of the **Sagrada Família**, which can itself be a good place to visit with kids. Of the smaller parks, the **Espanya Industrial** – a place much nicer than its name suggests – has a giant dragon slide and a winding lake where you can go boating, and the **Parc Güell** has several play areas, some shady, some sunny. Like most Gaudí constructions it also provides plenty of surprises, especially in its colourful ceramic sculptures. Off the beaten track, the **Parc del Laberint** is worth a visit for its eccentric layout, ornamental pool, great views and nineteenth-century maze. Nobody gets really lost, but it's fun.

Still most convenient from the old city, though, is the city's oldest park, the **Ciutadella**, which as well as the **Zoo** has several engaging play areas and a small boating lake. This shaded garden is a good bet even in hot weather, keeping children happy and parents relaxed for hours. Just outside the park, bicycles of different sizes and skates can be rented (*see chapter* **Services**).

Montjuïc Funfair

Parc d'Atraccions de Montjuïc, Avda Miramar (441 70 24). Metro Paral.lel, then Funicular de Montjuïc/bus 61. **Open** *mid-Sept-23 June* 11.30am-9pm Sat, Sun, public holidays; *24 June-early Sept* 6pm-midnight Tue-Thur; 6pm-1am Fri, Sat; noon-11.15pm Sun. **Admission** *entrance only* 600ptas; *individual rides* approx 300ptas; *pass with unlimited number of rides* 1,800ptas; free under-3s. **No credit cards**.

Newer in origin but less recently renovated than the Tibidabo fair, this park is louder, brasher and has more straightforward rides, which is one reason why local teens often prefer it. The departure-point for the cable-car is right by the entrance to the funfair. *See also chapter* **Sightseeing**.

Parc del Castell de l'Oreneta

Camí de Can Caralleu & C/Montevideo (424 38 09). Bus 22, 64, 75. **Open** *Nov-Feb* 10am-6pm; *Mar, Oct* 10am-7pm; *April, Sept* 10am-8pm; *May-Aug* 10am-9pm, daily.
A short walk uphill from the **Monestir de Pedralbes** is a large park where, on Sunday mornings in fine weather, you can ride on a train pulled by a scale-model steam engine operated by a club of railway buffs.

Tibidabo Funfair

Parc d'Atraccions del Tibidabo, Plaça del Tibidabo 3-4 (211 79 42). FGC Av Tibidabo/bus 17, 22, 58, 73, N8; then Tramvia Blau and Funicular to park. **Open** *Oct-Mar* noon-7pm Sat, Sun, public holidays; *April, 15-30 Sept* noon-8pm Sat, Sun, public holidays; *May* noon-8pm Wed-Sun; *June, 1-14 Sept* noon-8pm Tue-Sun; *July, Aug* noon-10pm Tue-Sun. **Admission** *entrance only* 400ptas; 200ptas over-65s; free under-5s. *Individual rides* 200-400ptas. *Pass with unlimited number of rides* 1,800ptas; 400ptas under-5s. **Credit** AmEx, DC, MC, V.
An evening trip up the mountain to this recently refurbished funpark is a must in summer. Newer, more exciting rides keep teenagers interested, but the park's strongest point, apart from its 360° views, is its authentically old-fashioned-fun atmosphere, with attractions like bumper cars, roundabouts, a hall of mirrors and a breathtaking open ferris wheel. The **Museu d'Autòmates** (*see chapter* **Museums**), with antique fairground machines, is unique. And getting there, by Tram and Funicular, makes it a complete outing.

Turó Parc

Avda Pau Casals. Bus 6, 7, 14, 15, 27, 30, 33, 34, 66. **Open** *Nov-Feb* 10am-6pm; *Mar, Oct* 10am-7pm; *April, Sept* 10am-8pm; *May-Aug* 10am-9pm, daily.
This small, shady park, in the upmarket area uphill from Plaça Francesc Macià, has a mini-theatre that regularly hosts puppet shows, at noon on Sundays. There is a small fee (generally 500ptas). An attraction for older kids is its (unsupervised) cement ramps for skateboarding and roller-blading.

Zoo de Barcelona

Parc de la Ciutadella (221 25 06). Metro Barceloneta, Ciutadella/bus 14, 16, 17, 39, 40, 41, 42, 51. **Open** *Nov-Feb* 10am-5.30pm; *Mar, Oct* 9.30am-6.30pm; *April, Sept* 9.30am-7pm; *May-Aug* 9.30am-7.30pm, daily. **Admission** 1,000ptas; 500ptas over-65s; free under-3s; group discounts. **Credit** MC, V.
Barcelona's zoo is small but has been much improved lately by extensive renovation, and although many animals remain in cages clever landscaping makes the enclosures seem bigger than they are. It's enormously popular – the star attraction being the albino gorilla *Copito de Nieve* (Snowflake), in residence since the sixties. Strolls from enclosure to enclosure are short, and there are two play areas with excellent climbing frames. The children's zoo, which is full of farm animals, has equipment for younger climbers. There are also two more special areas, one the 'Jungle of Madagascar', which seeks to reproduce a complete eco-system from the island, and the **Dolphinarium** (*shows* 11.30am, 1.30pm, 4pm, Mon-Fri; noon, 1.30pm, 4pm, Sat, Sun, public holidays).

Rainy Days: Indoor Attractions

Child-friendly museums include the revamped **Museu Marítim**, which has 'experience'-type exhibits that give some of the feel of a sailing ship in a storm, or an early submarine. The all-new **Museu d'Història de Catalunya** can catch the imagination even of kids that have never heard of Catalan history with interactive exhibits such as a knight's armour that you can weigh, or a Roman crossbow. Kids into football will want to see the

Museu del FC Barcelona, especially since you also get to visit the stadium, and will probably want to buy a club shirt afterwards too. For all three, *see chapter* **Museums**. For ice rinks and bowling, *see chapter* **Sports & Fitness**.

L'Aquàrium de Barcelona

Moll d'Espanya, Port Vell (221 74 74). Metro Barceloneta/bus 14, 17, 36, 39, 40, 45, 57, 59, 64. **Open** 10am-9pm Mon-Fri; 10am-10pm Sat, Sun, public holidays. **Admission** 1,300ptas; 950ptas over-65s; free under-4s. group discounts. *Advance sales* through Caixa de Catalunya. **No credit cards.**
One of Barcelona's newest attractions is this large state-of-the-art aquarium, next to Maremagnum in the port. Great care has been taken to recreate accurately the marine environment of the Mediterranean – but your child will probably think the best feature is the 80-metre-long tunnel running through the middle of the last and largest tank, which holds some 30 sharks, along with other ocean species. Look upwards for a chilling close-up view of rows of pointy teeth.

Happy Parc

C/Comtes de Bell-lloc 74-78 (490 08 35). Metro Sants-Estació/bus 27, 43, 44, 109. **Open** 5-9pm Mon-Fri; 10am-9pm Sat, Sun, public holidays. **Rates** 500ptas per hour; 125ptas each subsequent 15min. **No credit cards.**
A private indoor funpark with running, jumping, bouncing and sliding equipment for kids from two to 12. The main branch is by Sants station. All activities are included, but note that the cost rises steeply if you stay more than an hour. **Branch**: C/Pau Claris 97 (317 86 60).

Museu de Cera (Wax Museum)

Passatge de la Banca 7 (317 26 49). Metro Drassanes/bus 14, 18, 38, 59, 64, 91. **Open** *end Sept-late June* 10am-1.30pm, 4-7.30pm, Mon-Fri; 10am-1.30pm, 4.30-8pm, Sat, Sun, public holidays. *23 June-23 Sept* 10am-8pm daily. **Admission** 800ptas; 500ptas over-65s, 5-11s; free under-5s. **No credit cards.**
Barcelona's wax museum, in a grand nineteenth-century building – formerly a bank – down an alleyway near the foot of the Rambla, is a perennial standby for a rainy day. The collection is the usual combination of world figures and other stars, with some rooms (a space capsule, a sunken ship) with trick effects that are fun for kids. In the little square outside there is an eccentric bar, **El Bosc de les Fades**, with fairy-grotto décor and waxwork figures sitting about (*see also chapter* **Cafés & Bars**).

Museu de la Ciència

C/Teodor Roviralta-C/Cister 64 (212 60 50). FGC Tibidabo, then Tramvia Blau/bus 17, 22, 73. **Open** 500ptas, *special exhibitions* 250ptas extra; 350ptas students, *special exhibitions* 200ptas extra; free under-7s, *special exhibitions* 200ptas, Clik dels Nens 300ptas. **Credit** (shop only) V.
This museum on Tibidabo has excellent interactive exhibits that teach everything from Newton's laws to cell biology and wave theory. There is also a special space, the '*Clik dels Nens*', designed by Javier Mariscal and Alfredo Arribas specially so that children aged 3-7 can experiment with objects. No parents are admitted (there are monitors), and little kids can have a great time beyond language barriers. At weekends, queues can be long. *See also chapter* **Museums**.

New Park

La Rambla 88 (412 51 78). Metro Liceu/bus 14, 18, 38, 59, 64, 91. **Open** 10am-midnight Mon-Thur; 10am-1am Fri, Sat. **No credit cards.**
You might want to keep walking past this giant new-model amusement arcade on the Rambla, but then again, you might just get dragged in. There are three floors of rides, slides, video games, virtual reality machines and so on, and a special area for young children. All attractions have to be paid for individually and cost 100-200ptas.

Splashing Around

Barcelona's new beaches in Barceloneta and Poble Nou have showers and playground equipment. For swimming pools, *see chapter* **Sports & Fitness**. A park with a lake that's good for kids is the **Creueta del Coll** (*see chapter* **Sightseeing**).

Aiguajocs

C/Comte Borrell 21-23 (443 03 35). Metro Sant Antoni/bus 20, 24, 41, 55, 64. **Open** 7am-10pm Mon-Fri; 8am-10pm Sat; 8am-3pm Sun; 9am-2pm public holidays. **Admission** (2 hours in pool) 730ptas; 487ptas over-65s, 6-15s; free under-6s. *Block ticket for 10 admissions* 5,000ptas; 3,500ptas over-65s, 6-15s. **No credit cards.**
An indoor water-park with water slides, a wave pool and so on, conveniently central close to Mercat de Sant Antoni. Kids under 18 must swim accompanied by an adult. There is also a fitness centre and sauna attached.

Illa de Fantasia

Finca Mas Brassó, Vilassar de Dalt (751 45 53). By car A19 or N11 north, left at Premià de Mar (24km). **Open** (waterpark) *May* 10am-7pm Sun; *June-11 Sept* 10am-7pm Mon-Thur, Sun; 10am-5/6am Fri, Sat; (disco) *June-11 Sept* 10pm-5/6am Fri, Sat; *11 Sept-May* 11pm-5/6am Fri, Sat. **Admission** 1,000ptas; 600ptas 3-11s; free under-3s. **No credit cards.**
The nearest full-scale waterpark to Barcelona, with a large open-air pool and slides, wave machines and play pools. After the little kids have left on summer weekends it opens up as a disco, so you can dance and fool around in the pool.

Jardí de la Torre de les Aigües

C/Roger de Llúria 56. Metro Passeig de Gràcia/bus 7, 18, 50, 54, 56. **Open** *Nov-Feb* 10am-6pm; *Mar, Oct* 10am-7pm; *April, Sept* 10am-8pm; *May-Aug* 10am-9pm, daily.
In the centre of one of few Eixample blocks not entirely built up, this unusual municipal park was once the building of a water company – hence its 1867 water tower. It also has a very pretty pond with a city-centre wading 'beach' created especially for small children.

Entertainment

Film

Children's films are rarely shown in English, but the **Verdi** and **Verdi Park** sometimes include VO versions in their children's sessions, on Saturday afternoons and Sunday mornings (*see chapter* **Film**).

Music

A high-quality programme specially designed to interest kids in music (and entertain) is that of the Saturday 'family concerts' at the **Auditori del Centre Cultural de 'la Caixa'** (*see chapter* **Music: Classical & Opera**).

Theatre

Barcelona stages some excellent children's theatre, but for most of it some understanding of Catalan is essential. A highly respected specialised children's theatre is the **Jove Teatre Regina**, C/Sèneca 22 (218 15 12); other theatres with weekend children's shows include the **Teatre de l'Eixample** and **Artenbrut** (*see chapter* **Theatre**). Puppet shows are often presented at **Teatre Malic**. The **Casa Elizalde** hosts a range of kids' entertainments on Sundays (*see chapter* **Music: Classical & Opera**). Before Christmas, there are many amateur performances all over town of *Els Pastorets* ('The Little Shepherds'), a traditional, comic Christmas play. There are various amateur productions in English around Barcelona each year, and a Christmas panto; for information, ask at **BCN Books** (*see chapter* **Shopping**).

Festivals & Seasons

Local children are able to look forward to many special events during the year. For more on all festivals, *see chapter* **Barcelona by Season**

Christmas & Three Kings

The weeks before Christmas usually mean a trip to the huge market of **Santa Llúcia** market in front of the cathedral, to buy paraphernalia for the family crib. The main event of the season for children, though, is Epiphany or the feast of the Three Kings, known here simply as **Reis**, which falls on 6 January. The night before (Twelfth Night), presents are traditionally left on balconies or inside the nearest window. Something that passes for hay must be left in an old shoe for the camels, along with a glass of brandy for one's favourite king. The fun starts on the evening of 5 January with the *Cavalcada*, the parade that follows the Three Kings' arrival in the harbour on a *Golondrina*.

February: Carnaval

The week before Lent sees children preparing for the Carnaval, when each of the city's markets organises fancy-dress contests for little children.

Easter

A main event in Easter week in Catalonia is that godparents traditionally have to buy their godchildren a *mona*, one of the elaborate sculptures in chocolate that all the *pastisseries* have produce in the preceding weeks.

May: La Tamborinada

This very popular event takes place on a Saturday in May, when for a whole day the Ciutadella is taken over by street performers, puppet shows, magicians, circus acts and other entertainers.

June: Sant Joan

The biggest festival of the summer, Midsummer Night's Eve on 23 June, when bonfires appear around the city. This can be too hectic for small kids, as the explosive celebrations carry on all night, but teenagers might relish the mayhem.

September: La Mercè

The festival theoretically celebrating the city's patron-virgin is a huge street party: every afternoon for a week, and at the weekend, public spaces fill with clowns, puppets, concerts and theatre. Young children will be thrilled – or terrified– by the dance of the giants at Plaça Sant Jaume, and older kids will get a kick out of the wild *Correfoc* with its fire-spitting dragons (suitable clothing is naturally handy).

Out of Town

An obvious place to head for is the beach. **Sitges** is, as with many things, one of the most convenient coast towns near the city, with pleasant, shallow beaches that are good for small children. If you need a more concrete activity, the **Port Aventura** theme park near the resort of Salou is a must, with some truly spectacular rides. Queues can be long in high season, so it's a good idea to get there early.

Inland, one of the places children most like is **Montserrat**, especially the means of getting there – by a dangling cable car up a sheer cliff. Close to Barcelona, one outing that's satisfying to architecturally-interested parents but also engages kids is to Gaudí's **Colònia Güell**, with its chapel resembling

a cave dug into the roots of a giant tree. For details of places mentioned, *see chapter* **Trips Out of Town**.

FGC Steam Trains

(Information & reservations 302 48 16). **Dates** Sept-June, every Sun. **Departures** from Martorell at 11.10am; arrives Monistrol at noon; departs Monistrol 12.45pm; arrives Martorell 1.30pm. **Tickets** 1,600ptas return; 1,000ptas return 3-14s; free under-3s. **No credit cards.**
The Generalitat railways have restored two fine turn of the century steam locomotives, and on Sundays except in mid-summer they take trains of period carriages on the shortish journey from Martorell to Monistrol de Montserrat, past the mountain of Montserrat. To get the train, you must first take the regular FGC service from Plaça d'Espanya to Martorell. There are hostesses on board to answer questions (who may speak some English) and at either end train buffs can fully examine the machinery. Reservations are necessary. Should you be organising a party, you can also hire the whole train.

Babysitting & Childcare

When you need time on your own, childcare can be arranged through hotels, or these agencies.

Cangur Serveis

C/Aragó 227, 1° (487 80 08/24-hour mobile 908 220 177). Metro Passeig de Gràcia/bus 7, 16, 17, 22, 24, 28. **Open** *office* 9am-7pm Mon-Fri; calls answered on mobile 24 hours daily. **No credit cards.**
A specialised childcare agency that can provide babysitters at two hours notice every day of the year. They have several English-speaking babysitters on their books, sometimes including native-speakers. Charges begin at 800ptas per hour, or 6,000ptas for a special all-night service; there are discounts for more long-term arrangements. All babysitters have relevant qualifications and references. As well as this service Cangur Serveis also offers a day crèche and other facilities at its main building, and can also organise kids' parties and provide puppeteers, clowns and other entertainers.

Cinc Serveis

C/Pelai 11, 5-C (412 56 76/24-hour mobile 908 599 700). Metro Catalunya/bus all routes to Plaça Catalunya. **Open** *office* 9.30am-1.30pm, 4.30-7.30pm, Mon-Fri; calls answered on mobile 24 hours daily. **No credit cards.**
Also a babysitting agency with a 24-hour service. All its babysitters are Spanish, but several speak good English, French or German. All are qualified and have references. The basic rate after 9pm is 1,100ptas per hour; day and longer-term rates are less. The company also has a nursing agency.

Gay & Lesbian Barcelona

Barcelona's ambiente offers a host of friendly, bustling venues, with the seaside haven of Sitges just a hop away down the coast.

As befits its image as swinging city, Barcelona boasts a flourishing gay scene, which is lively throughout the year, with the summer and the February Carnival as highlights. It also has a great added attraction thank to its proximity to the beach town of Sitges, long one of the gay meccas of the Mediterranean, which helps to ensure a steady stream of foreign visitors.

As in any big city there is a tried-and-tested nightlife circuit. Apart from the big discos, most of Barcelona's night-time venues fall into the category of *bar musical*, large bars with loud music, pricey but very large drinks, free admission and a tiny dancefloor. Also, Barcelona has many mixed venues, popular with a gay crowd rather than catering entirely for one, and cafés or bars that are gay-owned and/or have a welcoming atmosphere and a sympathetic clientèle can be just as important as exclusively-gay locales as gay meeting points. The gay scene is referred to in Spanish as the *ambiente*, which can be deliberately ambiguous as the same word is used in many other contexts just to mean atmosphere, and a bar can be *un poco de ambiente* (a bit gay), or more. There are considerably more venues for men than women, but places welcoming both sexes abound. There's a distinct lack of segregation within the scene, and dress codes are virtually non-existent.

As yet, there is no really comprehensive regular listings guide to Barcelona (for those that are available, *see chapter* **Media**), and information about what's on can be hard to find. Your best bet is to pop into **Sextienda** or **Zeus** (*see below* **Services: Shops**), where they have a free map of gay Barcelona and will answer any questions you may have. Also, look for fliers in bars, and check the local gay press (*see* **G&L Groups/Info**). Those used to countries where nightlife winds down after midnight may find that Barcelona's clubbing style takes a little getting used to. Here, the night generally starts with dinner at 10pm, coffee at 11pm and drinks at midnight, with most discos empty until around 2am. Many places don't close before 6am. Pace yourself to stay the course.

Cafés & Bars

As well as bars listed here, two other drinking holes that are not gay *per se* but nevertheless essential gay-favourites are the wonderful **Café de l'Opera** on the Rambla and the **Bar Marsella** in C/Sant Pau, gay-owned and increasingly popular. For both, *see chapter* **Cafés & Bars**. Except where stated, none of these bars take credit cards.

Ballet Blau

C/Junta de Comerç 23 (301 96 64). Metro Liceu/bus 14, 18, 38, 59, N4, N6. **Open** 10pm-3am Tue-Sun.
A large hall with a bar leading up to it, the Ballet Blau was opened by the owners of the nearby **Bar Marsella** as a venue for live shows when they could no longer have them in the bar. The décor is cherub-chic, complete with clouds and gold floor. It's popular with a mixed crowd and presents a wide mix of attractions: live music, regular drag and cabaret evenings and the women-only disco run by **FESLU** (*see* **G&L Groups/Info**) on the first Thursday of every month. *See also chapter* **Music: Rock, Roots & Jazz**.

La Bata de Boatine

C/Robador 23 (318 48 11). Metro Liceu/bus 14, 18, 38, 59, N4, N6. **Open** 10.30pm-3am Tue-Sun.
A long, narrow bar in the sleazy heart of the *Barrio Chino*, La Bata (meaning 'quilted dressing gown') was formerly an 'American bar', a prostitutes' watering hole. Now, it's an intimate, friendly place that throws occasional one-off parties hosted by '*el niño de los zancos*' ('the boy on stilts'), who, though, tends to stay on his own two feet.

Café de la Calle

C/Vic 11 (218 38 63). Metro Diagonal/bus 16, 17, 27, N4, N6. **Open** 6pm-2.30am Mon-Thur, Sun; 6pm-3am Fri, Sat.
A small, intimate affair, a bit like a combination of a café with someone's front room, with reasonably-priced drinks, good sandwiches and pleasant music that doesn't thump excessively. A good place to meet up and start the evening, popular with both gay men and lesbians.

Este Bar

C/Consell de Cent 257 (no phone). Metro Urgell/bus 14, 54, 58, 59, 64, 66, N3. **Open** 7pm-2am daily.
A staple of gay Barcelona, run by the people behind the infamous (but now defunct) Kike Bar. Quiet midweek, it's packed to the gills most weekends, and a trendy young crowd frequent it as the first stop in their (long) night out. It has bright, colourful décor, with temporary art shows around the walls, and well-chosen house music ensures a sparky atmosphere.

Heyday, *for gay men and lesbians, has added zest to the Barcelona club scene.*

New Chaps

Avda Diagonal 365 (215 53 65). Metro Diagonal/bus 6, 15, 3, 34, N4, N6. **Open** 8pm-2.30am Mon-Thur, Sun; 8pm-3am Fri, Sat. **Admission** 300ptas cover charge.
Once a cowboy hangout, complete with saloon-style swing doors, New Chaps now has chi-chi designer décor with plenty of neon lights, which are atmospherically dimmed when it starts getting full. Very cruisy and popular with an older, cloney crowd. There's a backroom, various dark corners and, for some reason, a swing (answers on a postcard, please).

Punto BCN

C/Muntaner 63-65 (453 61 23/451 91 52). Metro Universitat/bus 54, 58, 64, 66, N4. **Open** 6pm-2am daily. Closed Carnival Tue.
Prime attraction of Punto is that it opens at 6pm, and so is one of the few gay places where you can meet for an informal coffee before the rush starts. A huge, bright and friendly place, visited by a wide cross-section of the gay community, young and not-so-young alike.

Que! Te Dije

C/Riera de San Miguel 55 (no phone). Metro Diagonal/bus 7, 15, 22, 23, 33, 34, N4, N6, N8. **Open** 10.30pm-2.30am Mon-Thur, Sun; 10.30pm-3am Fri, Sat.
Welcoming little bar very popular at weekends with a mixed crowd and much favoured by the British colony. Great house music vies with '70s tack, and anywhere that calls a vodka'n'orange a 'Sharon' (in honour of a friend) must be worth a visit. A great place to start a night out.

Tèxtil Café

C/Montcada 12-14 (268 25 98). Metro Jaume I/bus 17, 40, 45. **Open** 10am-midnight Tue-Sun; *July, Aug* 10am-1am Tue-Sun. **Credit** AmEx, MC, V.
In the gorgeous courtyard of the **Museu Tèxtil** (*see chapter* **Museums**), hidden away opposite the Picasso museum on C/Montcada, this café/restaurant is gay-run, and provides good food and drink in what must be one of the most delightful spots in the city. The perfect place for that pre-lunch martini. *See also chapter* **Cafés & Bars**.

Clubs

See also chapter **Nightlife** for more venues that also draw a sizeable gay clientèle.

Capitán Banana

C/Moià 1 (202 14 30).Bus 6, 7, 15, 27, 30, 33, 34, 58, 64, N8. **Open** 12.30-5am Mon-Thur, Sun; 12.30-6am Fri, Sat. **Admission** 1,000ptas. **No credit cards.**
A disco frequented by transvestites, drag queens and those who like to look at them. It gets (extremely) lively from 3am on, before tipping its clientèle onto the streets for breakfast.

Heyday

C/Bruniquer 59-61 (no phone). Metro Joanic/bus 21, 39, 55, N4. **Open** 10.30pm-5am daily. **Admission** free, but you must buy a drink. **No credit cards.**
The latest incarnation of a gay venue that has had any number of names, an extremely popular club with a very healthy mix of lesbians and youngish gay men. The music, courtesy of Iñaki, is disco/house and keeps one of Barcelona's friendliest crowds bopping into the wee hours. They have kept the venue's strange entry system – you're not charged on entry but are given a ticket and then pay for drinks when you leave, so don't outdrink your pocket.

Martins

Passeig de Gràcia 130 (218 71 67). Metro Diagonal/bus 22, 24, 28. **Open** midnight-5am daily. **Admission** 1,000ptas (includes one drink). **No credit cards.**
On three floors, Martins is a quieter version of Metro, playing similar music. It's packed at weekends with a younger crowd, and Wednesday cabaret nights are always popular.

Metro

C/Sepúlveda 185 (323 52 27). Metro Universitat/bus 24, 41, 55, 64, 91, 141, N4, N6. **Open** midnight-5am daily. **Admission** 1,000ptas (includes one drink). **No credit cards.**
Probably the busiest of Barcelona's gay clubs. Fairly full most nights, it's jam-packed – sometimes uncomfortably

*The club may be called **Polyester**, but there's no strict dress code.*

so – at weekends, when every section of the gay male community is in evidence. Women are welcome but infrequent visitors. Extra entertainments include speciality nights (foam parties, S&M), a café, TV and backrooms; music is thumping house and occasional techno. The place is also sometimes open for Sunday afternoon matinée sessions, for a younger crowd.

Polyester
Estació de França, Avda Marqués de l'Argentera (310 51 24). **Open** 2am-6am Sat, Sun mornings. **Admission** 500-1,000ptas. **No credit cards.**
Run by legendary BCN nightowls the Mexican *Brothers on the Slide,* who have now inexplicably decided to call themselves *VOTS,* this is the favourite weekend haunt of Barcelona's trendier wild young things, very mixed but with a big gay quotient. It's in a giant basement beneath França rail station, entered through the car park, and boasts two dancefloors and a strangely-named VIP room. Sweaty and packed, with techno and house. *See also chapter* **Nightlife.**

Taller
C/Mèxic 7 (no phone). Metro Espanya/bus all routes to Plaça d'Espanya. **Open** midnight-5am Tue-Sun.
Admission 1,000ptas (incl one drink). **No credit cards.**
A dark, cavernous venue which has taken over where the renowned/notorious Distrito Distinto was forced to leave off. Empty until around 4am, it fills up with those who like to party hard. Extremely cruisy and crushed, with a large backroom upstairs. Music: house and techno.

Restaurants

Also popular and gay-run are **El Cafetí** and **Café de la Ribera** (*see chapter* **Restaurants**).

La Morera
Plaça Sant Agustí 1 (318 75 55). Metro Liceu/bus 14, 18, 38, 59, N4, N6. **Lunch served** 1-3.30pm, **dinner served** 8.30-11.45pm, Mon-Sat. **Average** 1,850ptas. **Set lunch** 925ptas. **No credit cards.**
A small restaurant in a square just off Carrer Hospital, close to the Rambla. Owner and staff are all gay, as is a large percentage of the clientèle. The food consists of better-than-average Catalan dishes, and a good range of salads. *Air-conditioning. Booking essential Fri, Sat.*

El Turia
C/Petxina 7 (317 95 09). Metro Liceu/bus 14, 18, 38, 59, N4, N6. **Lunch served** 1-4pm, **dinner served** 8-11pm, Mon-Sat. Closed Aug. **Average** 1,650ptas. **Set lunch** 1,300ptas Mon-Fri. **Set dinner** 1,500ptas Fri, Sat. **Credit** AmEx, V.
A more noticeably gay crowd than in other gay-friendly eateries; it's big, welcoming, and popular for its wonderful seafood, fresh from the Boqueria market just outside. *Air-conditioning. Booking essential.*

Gay Services
Accommodation

Hotel California
C/Rauric 14 (317 77 66/fax 317 54 74). Metro Liceu/bus 14, 18, 38, 59, N4, NS. **Rates** *single* 4,500-5,000ptas; *double* 7,000-8,000ptas. **Credit** AmEx, EC, MC, V.
The unfortunately-named California is the only hotel in Barcelona to cater for a gay (male) clientèle. It's comfortable, if not luxurious, and very central, just off the Rambla. It has 31 rooms (all with bathrooms), and although there's no bar, they can provide breakfast and drinks.

Hotel services *Air-conditioning. English & French spoken. Laundry. Safe.* **Room services** (some rooms) *Minibar. Radio. Room service (24-hour). Telephone. TV.*

Bookshop

Complices
C/Cervantes 2 (412 72 83). Metro Jaume I/bus 17, 40, 45. **Open** 10.30am-8.30pm Mon-Fri; noon-8.30pm Sat. **Credit** MC, V.
Barcelona's first gay bookshop. Run collectively by a friendly and mainly female staff, it has a wide selection of books and mags in Catalan and Spanish, as well as foreign titles.

Other Shops

Corrosiu
C/Magdalenes 14 (412 55 93). Metro Urquinaona/bus all routes to Plaça Catalunya. **Open** 5-8pm Mon; 11am-2pm, 5-8pm, Tue-Sat (may close later in summer). **No credit cards.**
Not a gay shop as such, but gay-run, Corrosiu is a second-hand clothes store that also stocks new disco-dolly wear and jewellery and an eclectic and sometimes bizarre collection of 'recycled' objects and accessories. Well worth a visit, and their 'everything-at-500ptas' weeks are not to be missed.
Branch: C/Joaquim Costa 2 (412 55 93).

Sextienda
C/Rauric 11 (318 86 76). Metro Liceu/bus 14, 18, 38, 59, N4, N6. **Open** 10am-8.30pm Mon-Sat. **Credit** MC, V.
A sex shop that hands out free gay maps of Barcelona and Sitges as well as selling mags, sex aids, condoms, poppers and videos. Friendly, helpful staff.

Zeus
C/Riera Alta 20 (442 97 95). Metro Sant Antoni/bus 24, 64. **Open** 10am-9pm Mon-Sat. **Credit** V.
Similar to Sextienda, also very friendly and also offering a free gay Barcelona/Sitges guide and information.

Zona Intima
C/Muntaner 61 (453 71 45). Metro Urgell/bus 54, 58, 64, 66, N3. **Open** 10am-2pm, 5-8.30pm, Mon-Sat. **Credit** JCB, MC, V.
Pricey designer underwear and accessories: the place to go if you can't carry on without a new pair of Calvin Kleins.

Saunas

Each centre has showers, porno lounges and cubicles. On arrival you are given a locker key, a pair of very un-chic plastic sandals and a towel. Drinks are charged to you when you leave. BYO condoms, as they can be difficult to come by inside. Most popular are the Casanova and Thermas, both when the clubs empty out and on weekend afternoons.
Sauna Casanova *C/Casanova 57 (323 78 60/318 06 38). Metro Urgell/bus 9, 50, 54, 56, 58, 64, 66, N1, N3, N8.* **Open** 11am-5.30am Mon-Thur; 11am Fri-5.30am Mon. **Admission** 1,200ptas Tue, Thur; 1,600ptas Mon, Wed, Fri-Sun. **Credit** MC, V.
Sauna Condal *C/Espolsa-Sacs 1 (301 96 80). Metro Urquinaona/bus all routes to Plaça Catalunya.* **Open** 11am-5.30am Mon-Thur; 11am Fri-5.30am Mon. **Admission** 1,200ptas Mon, Wed; 1,600ptas Tue, Thur-Sun. **Credit** MC, V.
Sauna Thermas *C/Diputació 46 (325 93 46). Metro Rocafort/bus 9, 27, 50, 56, 109, 127, N1, N2.* **Open** noon-2am Mon-Thur; noon Fri-2am Sun. **Admission** 1,500ptas. **Credit** V.

Most of the groups listed here are perhaps of most interest to the long-term visitor or resident, but all are receptive and helpful, and good places to make contacts if you're entirely a stranger in town.

Groups/Centres

Actua *C/Gomis 38, baixos (418 50 00/fax 418 89 74). Bus 22, 73, 85.* **Open** *9am-2pm, 4pm-7pm, Mon-*Fri. Modelled on Act-Up groups in the US and Britain, a thriving organisation of people living with HIV, giving counselling and information. For emergency Aids info, call their *Linia positiva* (418 18 18, 7-9pm Mon-Fri).

Ca La Dona *C/Casp 38, pral (tel/fax 412 71 61). Metro Catalunya/bus all routes to Plaça Catalunya.* **Open** *office 10am-2pm, 4-8pm Mon-Fri; closed Aug.* Barcelona's main women's centre houses several groups including a lesbian feminist outfit and *Grup d'ajuda mútua Tamaia* (412 08 83), a women's self-help group. *See also chapter* **Women's Barcelona**.

Sunny Sitges

Sitges is popular with gay men from all over the world, thanks to a combination of good beaches, a great climate, a pretty setting and an all-singing, all-dancing nightlife. It was once a sleepy fishing port, and although it has grown greatly since it became a resort, the old town at its core still retains its charm, with its church standing above the sea and the beachfront *passeig* as its backbone.

A major date in Sitges is **Carnaval** week, usually in mid-February, a main event in which is the drag parade extravaganza, when local queens emerge in all their best finery. Carnival sees the town come alive after the winter, with many bars opening up for the entire week before nodding off again until summer. A more traditionally folkloric annual highlight is the spring *Festa de Corpus Cristi*, when the town's streets are literally carpeted with flowers. It lasts just one day, a Thursday usually in May, and is genuinely spectacular.

Like swallows, the Sitges gay scene tends only really to take wing in summer. Most venues open on weekends in May; then, from the first week in June, everything opens nightly until 1 October, when **Trailer** closes its doors for the end of the season. August is the busiest month. The rest of the year is quiet, with not much going on except in the few bars that open year-round. It is, though, still a great place for a quiet day out, strolling along the beach and eating a *paella*. For more on Sitges and details of how to get there, *see chapter* **Trips Out of Town**.

Accommodation

It's easy to visit Sitges and get back to Barcelona in a day trip, but if you want to sample the late-night scene you'll need to stay over. As a resort the town naturally has any number of hotels and *hostals*, and many welcome gays, but some of the most gay-friendly are the **Hotel Romàntic**, *C/Sant Isidre 33 (894 83 75/fax 894 81 67)*, a charming little hotel in a delightful nineteenth-century villa, with friendly staff, 24-hour key access and prices (*single* 7,600ptas; *double* 10,500-11,600ptas) that include mod cons, bathroom and breakfast; the same people also run **La Renaixença**, *C/Illa de Cuba 7 (894 83 75/fax 894 81 67)*, not quite as distinctive but also a historic building. Both have attractive gardens. The **Hotel Liberty**, *C/Illa de Cuba 35 (811 08 72)*, is a less attractive but still-popular place with full modern facilities (air-conditioning, satellite TV, minibar, phone etc) and reasonable rates (*singles* 8,500ptas; *doubles* 9,500ptas). All three are very popular, so book.

Bars

Unlike those in the city, bars in Sitges tend not to be differentiated but to share roughly the same, international clientèle, mixed in style and age. None except **Trailer** have admission charges, and none accept credit cards. One place that's open year-round is **Perfil**, *C/Espalter 7 (894 44 52)*, a popular early-evening, leatherish disco bar featuring '70s tack. Usually closed up from November to Easter or May (although it can be worth checking) are the similar **Azul**, *C/Sant Bonaventura 10 (no phone)*, the mirrored, black-walled **Bourbons**, *C/Sant Bonaventura 9 (no phone)*, whose female DJ favours housey beats; leather bar **El Horno**, *C/Juan Tarrida 6 (894 09 09)*, popular with older, cloney types and with a backroom that's jammed till 1am; and music bar **Reflejos**, *C/Sant Bonaventura 19 (no phone)*, busiest midnight-3am.

Summer action, though, centres on **Mediterraneo**, *C/Sant Bonaventura 6 (no phone)*, Sitges' biggest and busiest bar, a two-floor venue with its own terrace and great music from a parade of international DJs, packed nightly from 1am and *the* place to be seen before heading off to Trailer; **Parrots Pub**, *Plaça de l'Industria (894 81 78)*, a popular, fairly cruisy outside terrace bar, much visited after a hard day on the beach; and **Trailer** itself, *C/Angel Vidal 36 (no phone)*, Sitges' only real all-gay disco, with a truly international crowd – younger and trendier on the dancefloor, older around the edges – and DJs from all over playing the latest sounds. The 1,000ptas admission includes a drink. It closes around 5am, leaving its customers to do as they will – usually on the beach, which can be as busy by night as by day.

Those after more civilised entertainment should try **Lords**, *C/Marqués de Montroig 16 (894 15 22)*, an intimate venue offering cabaret on Sunday nights; or **Mont Roig Cafè**, *C/ Marqués de Mont-roig 11-13 (894 84 39)*, open all year till 3am and with outdoor tables from Easter to October.

Restaurants

Sitges has plenty of places where you can eat in style, but gay visitors tend to favour **Casa Willy**, *C/ Parelladas 80 (894 10 71)*, a friendly place specialising in Basque cuisine, with a good lunchtime set menu; and **El Trull**, *C/Mossèn Fèlix Clarà 3 (894 57 05)*, a relaxed restaurant serving good Mediterranean fare, which also does lunches.

Casal Lambda *C/Ample 5 (412 72 72/fax 412 74 76).*
Bus 17, 40, 45. **Open** 5-9pm Mon-Thur; 5pm-midnight
Fri; noon-10pm Sat, Sun. A gay cultural organisation that
runs weekly outings and parties (open to non-members),
hosts a range of different mens' and womens' groups,
publishes leading gay monthly *Lambda* and also has an
attractive patio inside. Used more by men than women,
but the atmosphere is always welcoming and relaxed.
Coordinadora Gai-Lesbiana *C/Carolines 13, entresol
2° (902 120 140/fax 218 11 91).* *Metro Fontana/bus 22,
24, 25, 28, 31, 32, N4, N6.* **Open** 5-9pm Mon-Fri. Well-
established umbrella organisation recognised by the
Ajuntament (city council) and working with them on
issues such as AIDS. Includes a Body Positive-like self-
help group, a lesbian group, Gay Christians, a youth
group and the *Telèfon Rosa* phoneline (*see below*).
FESLU *C/Vidre 10, 2° 3ª (412 15 09).* Group of dykes
(the name stands for *festes lúdiques*, a fancy way of
saying 'Free time, party time!') who organise
'entertainment events', connected with **La Illa** (*see*
Lesbian Barcelona) and the monthly women's disco at
Ballet Blau (*see above* **Cafés & Bars**).
Front d'Alliberament Gai de Catalunya (FAG)
C/Villarroel 62, 3° 1a (454 63 98). An active group that
includes various collectives and pressure groups, and
produces the useful *Barcelona Gai* information bulletin.
Laberint *Apt de Correus 5394, 08080 Barcelona (215
63 36).* Magazine produced (sporadically) by a radical-
lesbian group, *Red de Amazonas*. In Spanish, despite the
Catalan title.

Phonelines

AIDS Information Line *(339 87 56).* **Open** 9am-
5.30pm Mon-Fri. An official Ajuntament health
information service. English speakers are available.
Telèfon Rosa *(900 601 601).* **Open** 6-10pm daily. Very
helpful service with advice on AIDS and gay rights, and
information on clubs and events. English spoken.

Lesbian Barcelona

The BCN dyke scene is small – many of the bars
are within walking distance of each other, especially the ones on or near C/Sèneca, in Gràcia –
but friendly. Lesbian culture and identity are not
particularly marked: there's less visibility, but
also less pressure to be trendy, because just
about anything goes.

It's useful to recognise a few key Castilian
phrases: to flirt is *tirar los tejos* (literally, to
throw the tiles at someone); *tener pluma* (to have
feather) is to look obviously gay; to pick up someone is *ligar* (to tie or bind!), while words for lesbian, originally derogatory but now widely
turned-around, include *bollera* (bun baker), *tor-
tillera* (omelette maker), *camionera* (lorry driver)
and *bombera* (firewoman). *Entender* (to understand) is to be gay (you understand?) and the
scene is the *ambiente*.

Gay Pride day is celebrated with a small
march and celebrations in late June, but the other
side of the liberal, laid-back attitude is a general
reluctance to be out, much less proud of it.
Rumours fly about certain unnamed prominent
singers, but only recently has the word lesbian
been used on television.

That said, Barcelona's first lesbian and gay
bookshop, **Complices** (*see page 229*), opened in
1992 and is doing booming business; lesbian
films are shown to wildly enthusiastic audiences
in the Women's Film Festival in early June (*see
chapter* **Women's Barcelona**) and there's very
little hassle on the streets. There may be no dykes
in local soap operas yet, but the scene is very
much alive.

Cafés, Bars, Restaurants, Clubs

See also the **Gay** listings (*above*) for mixed
venues where women are welcome. **Café de la
Calle** and **Heyday** are lesbian favourites, and
the monthly dyke night at **Ballet Blau** is one of
the best events on the scene. Admission is free
unless stated.

Bahia

C/Seneca 12 (no phone). *Metro Diagonal/bus 6, 7, 15,
22, 24, 27, 28, 33, 34, N4, N6.* **Open** 10pm-3am daily;
Christmas Eve 10am-midnight. **No credit cards.**
Trendy gothic bar with good music and friendly atmosphere.

Daniel's Pub

C/Santa Peronella 7-8 (209 99 78). *FGC Gràcia/bus 58,
64, N8.* **Open** 7pm-3.30am Mon-Fri, Sun; 10pm-3.30am
Sat. **No credit cards.**
Oldest lesbian bar in Spain, still run by the inimitable
Daniella. Women only, billiards and a revolving mirror ball.

La Illa

C/Reig i Bonet 3 (210 00 62). *Bus 21, 39, N4.* **Open**
7.30pm-1am Mon-Thur, Sun; 8pm-3am Fri, Sat. **No
credit cards.**
Women-only cultural association which serves as the best
lesbian sandwich bar in town and hosts a range of activities,
from *bossa nova* nights (live music on Thursdays) and dark
room discos (reggae, soul) to lesbian choir sessions (Mondays)
and great monthly theme nights.

Imagine

C/Marià Cubí 4 (no phone). *FGC Gràcia/bus 16, 17, 27.*
Open 11pm-3am Fri, Sat; 7pm-midnight Sun.
Admission free. **No credit cards.**
Another mixture of gay men and women, and a mite tacky,
with Europop music.

Members

C/Seneca 3 (237 12 04). *Metro Diagonal/bus 6, 7, 15,
22, 24, 27, 28, 33, 34, N4, N6.* **Open** 9pm-2.30am Tue-
Thur, Sun; 9pm-3am Fri, Sat. **No credit cards.**
A tiny dancefloor, but this is a standard lesbian haunt, mirrored pillars and all. Also now increasingly mixed.

La Rosa

C/Brusi 39, passatge (414 61 66). *FGC Sant
Gervasi/bus 16, 17, 27, N8.* **Open** 10pm-3am Thur-Sun,
eves of public holidays. **Admission** 350ptas. **No
credit cards.**
Late-hours at La Rosa are livened up by dykes still on the
go at 3am.

La Singular

C/Francisco Giner 50 (237 50 98). *Bus 22, 24, 28, N4,
N6.* **Meals served** 6pm-2am Tue-Fri; 1pm-2.30am Sat,
Sun. **No credit cards.**
Very friendly, dyke-run tapas bar with local home-cooked
dishes (around 600ptas) and tasty desserts (450ptas).

Students

Barcelona's colleges are energetically forging links with universities throughout Europe, and offer courses galore for foreign students.

There are currently around 162,000 students enrolled at Catalonia's eight universities. Of this total, some 120,000 attend the five universities – four public, one private – in and around Barcelona. Throughout Spain, choice at university level is limited: the British or US system whereby you can select a university on its reputation is much envied by Spanish students, who are required to attend their local university unless they are studying a course that it does not offer. Since the Barcelona universities together are some of the most comprehensive in the whole country, this means that few Catalan students study in other parts of Spain.

Moreover, a points-based entry system means that competition for places in popular subjects is intense, with those students lacking sufficient points being diverted to less competitive courses. Students shunted into courses that hold no real interest for them quickly become bored and demotivated, leading to a significant drop-out rate.

Although the universities are not considered a roaring success at home, they have been very adept in other areas, particularly in forging links with other universities in the European Union. Catalonia is ardently Europhile, even more than the rest of Spain, and its universities enthusiastically support inter-university exchange programmes. In recent years, Catalonia's universities have attracted more than 90 per cent of the 3,000 students studying in Spain under the EU's *Erasmus* scheme, and the University of Barcelona has been the biggest European provider of *Programes Interuniversitaris de Cooperació*.

The antithesis of this progressive outlook could be the students themselves. The hard-living, politically-conscious student is now a rarity here, and students appear notably conservative. Student excess and radicalism are tempered by the spectre of unemployment (particularly high among under-25s) in an increasingly competitive job market, and the sobering influence of living at home. Thanks to high property prices since Spain's boom, the proportion of students living in flats away from their parents is actually lower than in the seventies.

FUTURE PROSPECTS

The necessity to achieve academic – and subsequent job – success is one reason why even the recent ousting of the Socialists by a right-wing Partido Popular (PP) government in Madrid has scant chance of provoking student unrest here.

Barcelona's public universities are primarily administered by the Catalan government, the Generalitat, but questions of funding and basic university structures are subject to long negotiations between them and the central government.

Although a reduction in student numbers through selection has improved university conditions and morale in recent years, it is widely agreed that the degree structure and curriculum are still badly in need of modernisation. The universities, however, are clearly potential targets for PP leader and new Prime Minister Aznar's promised cost-cutting programme. In the event that cuts are proposed, their impact is likely to be softened due to the pact with Catalonia's ruling party CiU on which the PP, since it lacked a clear majority after the March 1996 elections, depended to take office.

Primary and secondary education in Spain, meanwhile, are in the throes of major changes (*la Reforma*), effective from September 1996. The general thrust of them is that all students will receive a common education up to the age of 16, when they will choose between academic (the *Batxillerat/Bachillerato*) or technical training. Generally, those studying the *Batxillerat* go on to sit university entrance exams (*Selectivitat*). Students taking the technical route generally look for work after their studies, although they can go on to university for a higher-grade technical course. Previously the academic/technical split was made at 14, a system criticised for requiring students to make an important decision too early.

DEGREES & ENROLMENT

Most Spanish degree courses now last for four years, leading to the *Llicenciatura* qualification, although some run for three years, leading to a *Diplomatura*. Students have to collect a huge number of credits to complete their courses, another area pinpointed as in need of urgent reform. The main language of teaching in Barcelona universities is now Catalan, except in certain subjects such as Spanish language and literature.

The state universities are supposedly introducing a pan-European system of credits and qualifications, and semesters instead of the previous year structure. Nevertheless, students from other EU countries still find that convalidating degrees in Spain is a bureaucratic nightmare, and nigh on impossible if their home degree does not exist here.

Study in style at **Universitat de Barcelona.**

Information & Agencies

Punt d'Informació Juvenil, Secretaria General de Joventut

C/Calabria 147-C/Rocafort 116 (483 83 84/punt d'informació juvenil 483 83 84). Metro Rocafort/bus 9, 41, 50, 56. **Open** *punt d'informació juvenil* 10am-8pm Mon-Fri; *travel agency* 10am-8pm Mon-Fri; 10am-1.30pm Sat. *Aug* (both) 10am-2pm Mon-Fri.

A 'youth information point' in the Generalitat, with information on accommodation, youth travel and other topics. A service to help young people find cheap flats is open to foreign students studying in Barcelona for a substantial period of time, if they have a letter from their university.

Universities, Public & Private

Universitat Autònoma de Barcelona

Campus de Bellaterra, 08193, Bellaterra (581 10 00). By train FGC from Plaça Catalunya to Universitat Autònoma (Sabadell line). **Open** *information: Sept-June* 9am-2pm, 3-5pm, Mon-Fri; *July, Aug* 8am-3am Mon-Fri.

Established in the 1960s, the Autonomous University occupies an unlovely, self-contained campus outside the city at Bellaterra, near Sabadell, but with frequent FGC train connections. Information on Internet is at *http://www.uab.es/*.

Universitat de Barcelona

Gran Via de les Corts Catalanes 585 (318 42 66/318 99 26). Metro Universitat/bus all routes to Plaça Universitat. **Open** *information* 9.30am-6pm Mon-Fri. Closed Aug.

Barcelona's oldest university has faculties in the main building on Plaça Universitat, the giant *Zona Universitària* on Diagonal, and scattered through other parts of the city. Its main library is housed in an attractive site on the Gran Via, and the student union and bar are in the main building. Information is also available by Internet on *http://www.ub.es/*.

Universitat Politècnica de Catalunya

Avda Dr. Marañon 42 (401 62 00/student information 401 68 44/international office 401 74 51). Metro Zona Univeristària/bus 7, 67, 68, 74, 75. **Open** varies according to department. Closed Aug.

Specialises in technical subjects such as engineering, architecture, and so on. Most of it is in the *Zona Universitària*, but it also has faculties in Terrassa and other towns. Call the student information number to find out how to contact each department. On the Internet on *http://www.upc.es/*.

Universitat Pompeu Fabra

Plaça de la Mercè 10-12 (542 20 00/information nos. 542 17 87/542 17 00). Metro Drassanes/bus 14, 18, 38, 59, 64, 91. **Open** *information* 10,30am-1.30pm, 4.30-6.30pm, Mon-Fri. Closed Aug.

The Pompeu Fabra is an economics and social-sciences-based university with faculties in central Barcelona, many in the old city. Founded only in 1991, it has tried to get away from the 'massification' of Spanish universities with smaller classes, but resources sometimes make it difficult to sustain this in practice. On the Internet at *http://www.upf.es/*.

Universitat Ramon Llull

Central office *C/Sant Joan de la Salle 8 (253 04 50). FGC Tibidabo/bus 22, 64, 75.* **Open** *information* 11am-1pm, 5-7pm, Mon-Fri.

A private university, founded to bring together a number of previously-separate institutions owned and run by the Jesuit order, although this does not mean there is a strong religious presence in teaching or their day-to-day working. Private universities are common in Spain, and popular, partly because their entry requirements are less rigorous in some areas than those of state universities. The downside is that fees are high, and so they tend to be the preserve of children of affluent parents. Internet information at *http://www.url.es/*

Studying in Barcelona

EU Programmes: Erasmus/Socrates & Lingua

The EU's **Erasmus** (to be known as **Socrates** from 1997) and **Lingua** (specifically concerned with language learning) programmes are the main student-exchange schemes that help students to move between member states. Barcelona's universities have exchange arrangements with many British colleges and universities, covering a wide range of subjects including art and design. To be eligible for any of them you must be a student at one of the local institutions. *Erasmus* is open to students from their second year onwards: prospective applicants should approach their *Erasmus* co-ordinator, who will advise with applications. Successful students receive modest supplementary grants from the European Commission. Generally, students from abroad get a better deal than home students at Catalan universities, particularly if on an exchange scheme, as home universities keep an eye on conditions and standards.

Post-Graduate Programmes

A wide range of post-graduate opportunities are open to foreign students in Barcelona. The courses listed here can be studied in English, but to successfully complete other courses you will need a decent command of Spanish or Catalan.

Estudis de Formació Continuada de la Universitat de Barcelona

Information *Palau de les Heures, recinte Llars Mundet, Passeig de la Vall d'Hebron, 08035 (428 45 85/48 35).*

The University of Barcelona runs an annual European Summer School in one of its faculties in a park in the Vall d'Hebron (Metro Montbau), with courses in areas such as management, human resources and information technology. They are aimed at graduates or professionals; most are in English, and teachers are drawn from the whole of Europe.

Winchester School of Art

Information *Park Avenue, Winchester, Hants SO23 8DL, UK (01962 842500).*

Winchester School of Art offers a one-year MA course in European Fine Art, nine months of which are spent at the School's two studios in Barcelona. The main studio is in the Barri Gòtic; the second is in Javier Mariscal's complex in Poble Nou. Classes in survival Spanish are included. Prospectuses are available from the Admissions Secretary.

MBAs

For general information on MBA courses in Europe, contact **AMBA** *15 Duncan Terrace, London N1 8BZ (0171 837 3375)*. The official *MBA Handbook* (published by AMBA in association with the *Financial Times*) is worth buying as it includes essential advice on schools and MBA programmes.

ESADE
Avda De Pedralbes 60-62 (280 61 62). Bus 63, 75, 114. **Open** *information* 10am-2pm, 4-7pm, Mon-Fri. Closed three weeks Aug.
A prestigious private business school, in Pedralbes, the city's most affluent residential area. It was set up by the Jesuits in 1958, and is now associated with the **Universitat Ramon Llull** (*see* **Universities**). The bilingual MBA programme has full- and part-time options: included are comprehensive language studies and a Spanish and International Placement Service. The first year can be studied in English or Spanish.

IESE
Avda Pearson 21 (204 40 00). Bus 63, 75, 114. **Open** *information* 9am-2pm, 3-6pm, Mon-Fri; *July, Aug* 9am-2.30pm Mon-Fri.
IESE is an offshoot of the University of Navarra, ultimately run by the other Catholic organisation heavily involved in private education in Spain, the *Opus Dei*. The university established Europe's first two-year MBA programme in 1964 and went bilingual in 1980. An intensive Spanish course is given prior to the first term and language tuition is provided throughout the year.

Music

Àrea de Música, Dept. de Cultura
Departament de Cultura, Portal de Santa Madrona 6-8 (412 56 40). Metro Drassanes/bus 14, 18, 38, 59, 64, 91. **Open** *information* 9am-2pm, 3-5.30pm, Mon-Fri; *June-15 Sept* 8am-3pm Mon-Fri.
The Generalitat Department of Culture runs a course on early music in Catalonia, usually in August, with provision for English speakers. You don't have to be a music professional to enrol, but a high level of musical proficiency is required.

Learning Catalan & Spanish

Centres de Normalització Lingüística de Barcelona
Central office & information *C/Pau Claris 162 (482 02 00). Metro Passeig de Gràcia/bus 20, 21, 39, 43, 44, 45.* **Open** 9am-2pm, 3-5.30pm, Mon-Fri.
The Generalitat's official organisation for the support of the Catalan language has centres in every municipal district of the city that provide extremely inexpensive Catalan courses from beginners' level upwards, with intensive courses in July and sometimes August. Hours vary; a list of centres is also available from the Generalitat information centre in the Palau Moja, on the corner of the Rambla and C/Portaferrisa.

Escola Oficial d'Idiomes
Avda Drassanes (329 24 58). Metro Drassanes/bus 14, 18, 38, 59, 64, 91. **Open** *offices* 9am-2pm, *student services* 10.30am-12.30pm, 4.30-5.30pm, Mon-Fri.
This 'official school' has courses at all levels in both Spanish and Catalan, as well as in several other languages for local students. They are cheap, but consequently overcrowded, and demand is such that during enrolment periods (usually, June and September) they have a ticket-and-queue system which means that you have to wait around to see if you can sit the entry test that day. Arrive early to have a chance.

International House
C/Trafalgar 14, entresol (268 45 11). Metro Urquinaona/bus 39, 41, 42, 55, 141. **Open** 8am-9pm Mon-Fri.
IH runs intensive Spanish-language courses all year round, beginning every two weeks. Courses consist of four hours' class time every weekday from 9.30am to 1.30pm.

Instituto Mangold de Idiomas
Rambla Catalunya 16 (301 25 39). Metro Catalunya/bus all routes to Plaça Catalunya. **Open** *offices* 9am-9pm Mon-Thur; 9am-8pm Fri.
A well-regarded, centrally located school that offers intensive Spanish courses from July to September. Courses last for three weeks, with classes from 9am to 2pm each day. Catalan courses are also held, but not on an intensive basis.

Universitat de Barcelona
Gran Via de les Corts Catalanes 585 (318 42 66). Metro Universitat/bus all routes to Plaça Universitat. **Open** *language course information* 9am-1pm Mon-Fri.
The university runs reasonably-priced courses for foreigners in both Catalan and Spanish, some of which also include higher-level studies in literature, culture and so on. Ask for the *Servei de Llengua Catalana* for information on Catalan courses; for *Estudios Hispánicos* for Spanish. Courses are held throughout the year, and as well as the main courses there are intensive language courses in July and September.

Libraries

Barcelona has a good network of public libraries, and a large number of specialist libraries; a full list is in the *Guia del Ciutadà*, held at the Ajuntament and city information offices. Each of the universities also has its own library, but they are normally accessible only to their own students. The following are some of the more useful, research libraries.

Ateneu Barcelonès
C/Canuda 6 (318 86 34). Metro Catalunya/bus all routes to Plaça Catalunya. **Open** 9am-10.45pm daily.
Anyone spending some time in Barcelona might consider joining this venerable cultural and philosophical society founded in 1836, which has the best private library in the city, open every day of the year, including Christmas. Initial membership costs 20,000ptas (payable in instalments), and the subsequent fee is 1,800ptas per month; there are special rates for anyone who lives more than 45km from the city. With membership you naturally also have access to its Mediterranean-gentlemen's club atmosphere and the deliciously peaceful interior garden patio and bar.

Biblioteca de Catalunya
C/Carme 47 (317 07 78). Metro Liceu/bus 14, 18, 38, 59, 64, 91. **Open** 9am-8pm Mon-Fri; 9am2pm Sat.
The largest of the city's libraries, the Catalan national collection, housed in the Medieval **Hospital de la Santa Creu** and with a wonderfully comprehensive stock reaching back several centuries. Reader's cards are required, but one-day visitors are normally allowed in on presentation of a passport, and full cards are not hard to obtain. It's not open-access, and book delivery is slow, so take this into account.

Institut Municipal d'Història/ Ca de l'Ardiaca
C/Santa Llúcia 1 (318 11 95). Metro Liceu, Jaume I/bus 17, 40, 45. **Open** 9am-8.45pm Mon-Fri; 9am-1pm Sat; *Aug* 9am-2pm.
The city newspaper archive, with an exhaustive stock of Barcelona's press, many papers from other parts of Spain,

and extensive book, map, graphics and document collections. It occupies the **Ca de l'Ardiaca** in front of the Cathedral, with one of the prettiest patios in the Barri Gòtic. A reader's card is required, for which you will need two photos.

Mediateca

Centre Cultural de la Fundació 'la Caixa', Passeig de Sant Joan 108 (458 89 07). Metro Verdaguer/bus 15, 20, 21, 45, 47, 55. **Open** 11am-8pm Tue-Fri; 11am-3pm Sat.

An extraordinarily useful facility run by the arts foundation of the omni-present 'la Caixa' savings bank, in the **Fundació la Caixa**'s main centre on Passeig de Sant Joan (*see chapter* **Art Galleries**).It's a high-tech art, music and media library that allows you to explore the latest technologies (CD-Rom, CD-I), watch satellite TV or videos, read magazines from all over the world, listen to (and borrow) records, tapes or CDs, check out a huge contemporary art slide collection, attend talks and workshops, and browse amongst a mind-boggling array of print and non-print references on contemporary art and culture. It's run mainly on a free, open-access basis, although a small fee is payable to use certain A-V materials or borrow materials (for a borrower's card, you will need your passport). A *User Guide* in English is available.

Student Life

Accommodation

Much of Barcelona's cheapest accommodation is still found centrally, in the old city. Accommodation agencies are scarce, but ads for flats to rent are often posted in shop windows and doorways. Sunday editions of local papers, especially *La Vanguardia*, and classified-ad magazines (*see chapter* **Media**) have many ads for flats for rent, although mostly at higher prices: look under *'Alquileres: Pisos'*. Under *Huéspedes* you'll find rooms to let.

If you are studying under an inter-university scheme, your home college should help you to arrange accommodation: otherwise, the public universities have accommodation offices on campus. The **Punt d'Informació Juvenil** (*see* **Information & Agencies**) is a good source of information on halls of residence and student flats, and free campus newspapers such as *Medicampus* and the *Gaceta Universitaria* contain flat-share lists. Good places to check noticeboards for flat-share ads are **International House**, the **Come In** English bookshop (*see chapter* **Shopping**), **Les Tapes** bar (*see chapter* **Cafés & Bars**), the women's bookshop **Prolèg** (*see chapter* **Women's Barcelona**), and any of the university faculties around the Zona Universitària. *See also chapter* **Survival**.

Socialising

Because so many students live with their parents in their home *barris*, and city social life in general is in any case so accessible, student life as such is fairly diffuse after classes have ended, and away from the college bars. There are a few student haunts around the campus areas, but recent student favourites have been the cheap, grungy discos in strip clubs, such as **New York, Pan-Ams** and **Starlets**, sweaty, smoky and with Britpop music. Big parties tend to be organised on-campus for ends-of-terms and Carnaval, but eternally popular for a pre-holiday blast is **La Paloma** (for all venues mentioned, *see chapter* **Nightlife**).

*If you don't want to take a book from **Biblioteca de Catalunya**, you can always paint the place.*

Women's Barcelona

Feminism-the-idea may not have a good press in Barcelona, but Catalan women know how to hold their own – and how to have fun.

The women of Barcelona consider themselves to be significantly more liberated in comparison with the rest of Spain, and the Catalan capital is in many respects a female-friendly city. A woman having a drink alone in a bar on the whole needs to watch her bag more carefully than her behind, and is unlikely to invite leery comments – which is more than can be said for the situation in comparable places in a great many countries to the north, or in North America.

Another pleasant surprise in store for any football-loving sisters from more northerly climes who turn up in this metropolis is that the heaving stands of the mighty *Barça* (Barcelona Football Club) have a seat-to-seat peanuts and soft-drink service, and contain an abundance of women of all classes and ages, whose outpourings of dramatic profanities in the face of dodgy refereeing decisions are at least equal to those of their male counterparts. Despite the time-honoured image of the macho Latin male – one that Catalans vehemently reject – aggressive sexual harassment on the streets is notable for its absence. Again, though, it's advisable to carry your essentials in your jeans pockets rather than in any casually-dangling bag.

FEMINISM, CATALAN-STYLE

1996 marked the twentieth anniversary of the appearance of a modern, overt feminist movement in Catalonia. When we asked the question, 'What is a feminist?', though, Barcelona women gave hundreds of widely-differing answers – for just two examples, 'A feminist is someone who believes profoundly that biology played a dirty trick on us, and hopes it won't last forever', and 'A feminist is a bad person, isn't she?'. Most of the women questioned felt that the greatest improvements made in the last two decades have been in terms of personal liberty, and educational opportunities.

Feminism as a concept may not be widely appreciated but, in fact, the change in the position of women may well be the most wide-reaching of all the social changes that have swept across Spain since the mid-seventies. Twenty years ago, a great many careers and areas of work were closed to women; today, – and in Catalonia more than anywhere – this applies to very few, and women can be seen driving buses, in executive positions in public bodies, in the police and running their own businesses. A no-doubt related change is the decline in the birth rate: from having the second-highest in Europe (after Ireland) in 1975, Spain as a whole now has the lowest, and it is lower in Catalonia than anywhere else in the state. The legal position of women has also changed fundamentally.

Rape, for instance, is now considered in law to be a crime against the sexual liberty of the individual rather than one 'against the honour of the father or husband of the victim', as it was under the old Spanish penal code. In 1981, divorce was finally legalised, and in 1988, after a long struggle, abortion was authorised – albeit only in special circumstances. Sexist attitudes and practices are still around, however. Despite the rapid expansion in work for women, discrimination is still rife, and it is very noticeable how few women break through the glass ceiling into directorial or managerial roles. That said, there are more women in such positions in Catalonia than in other parts of Spain. Media, politics and the arts are sectors in which women now occupy prominent positions, in Barcelona at least.

In the world of entertainment, all-women groups such as 'T de Teatre' and the recently-disbanded, international 'Stupendams', have helped the lighter side of feminism achieve an almost 'pop' status, simultaneously controlling their own management and employing women in related areas traditionally dominated by men, such as lighting and sound engineering. In the media as a whole, the image projected of women is only just beginning to change. Very occasionally a man in a pinny may appear on your television screen, busying himself around the house, but generally it is women, even when they have full-time jobs, who are expected to be the carers and homemakers, and this is reflected in 90 per cent of advertising.

THE RIGHT TO CHOOSE...

Women's health care in Barcelona gets a pretty good press, and the local health authorities are keen to show their ability to respond to specific needs with special clinics and other services. One of the greatest concerns of Catalan women's groups, however, is the ongoing battle over the abortion issue. Reform of the current abortion legislation may well take a back seat under the right-wing Partido Popular government that took power in Madrid in May 1996, or there may even be moves to return to a still more restrictive situation. Currently, abortions are not available through the Spanish national health service, and can only be obtained at private clinics at a cost of about 40,000ptas. That they can be carried out at all is considered an advance on the state of affairs before 1988, when Spanish women needing abortions had little choice but to make clandestine arrangements with underground operators using special phone codes, or scrape together the money for a quick trip to London. Catalonia has the only organisation in Spain offering financial aid – according to income – to women needing abortions, called *Salud i Família* (Health and Family). In 1995, they provided assistance for 1,700 women.

SISTERHOOD & (EXPAT) SOLIDARITY

Perhaps as a reflection of the limited interest in feminism *per se*, women-only spaces are practically non-existent in Barcelona, and paradoxically one consequence of the 'Barcelona-Beautiful' campaigns of the last ten years has been the sad demise of the unique women-only patch of Barceloneta beachfront affectionately known as 'The Cage'. There is, however, a plethora of women's organisations, in every neighbourhood or *'barri'*. A few are actively feminist in outlook, while the majority reflect the still-prevailing sense of community that exists in Catalonia, and range from immigrant pressure groups to support groups for widows and educational workshops. Non-Spanish, Arab and African immigrant women in particular, are finding a voice, and are instrumental in changing the racist attitudes of a largely-white society that tends to consider itself unbigoted, but often falls down in practice. An enormous tome listing all women's organisations in the city is available, free of charge, from Ajuntament offices (*see* **Publications**).

In the seventies, Barcelona became a language-teachers' Mecca for native English speakers. Since then, a steady stream (sometimes a raging torrent) of women has been coming into the city from all over the world to find work. The teaching boom tailed off after 1992, and many language schools closed or cut back in the subsequent recession, but, especially for women from EU countries, the range of work in other fields has widened somewhat to compensate. Expatriate women in Barcelona now work in a range of fields – as doctors, translators, artists, musicians, architects, designers.

The new man is still a twinkle in his mother's eye here. But for the independent woman – tourist or resident – this Mediterranean metropolis continues to offer a host of hassle-free opportunities and activities.

Drink a beer while you buy a book from the **Laie Llibreria Café**. *See page 238.*

Women's Organisations

Associació Catalana de la Dona

C/Providència 42, 2º 2ª (213 34 40). Metro Fontana/bus 39. **Open** by appointment.
An independent association for the promotion and defence of women's rights. It organises cultural events and also has spaces available for discussion groups and workshops.

Institut Català de la Dona

C/Viladomat 319, entresol (495 16 00). Bus 15, 27, 41, 54, 59. **Open** *16 Sept-May 9am-2pm, 3-5.30pm; June-15 Sept 8am-3pm, Mon-Fri. Centre de Documentació: 16 Sept-May 9.30am-1.30pm, 3.30-5.15pm; June-15 Sept 9.30am-2.30pm, Mon-Fri.*
The women's affairs department of the Catalan government. As well as holding an extensive resource service (the *Centre de Documentació*), it organises conferences, cultural activities, exhibitions and courses and administers the government grants available for women's projects. The main services are in C/Viladomat, but there is an information office in the city centre, in C/Portaferrisa. Some departments close in August.
Branch: C/Portaferrisa 1-3 (317 92 91).

Ca la Dona

C/Casp 38, pral (412 71 61). Metro Catalunya/bus all routes to Plaça Catalunya. **Open** *office* 10am-2pm, 4-8pm, Mon-Fri.
Defined as a meeting place for 'feminist-orientated' women, Ca la Dona acts as an umbrella for a variety of groups, houses the *Coordinadora Feminista de Catalunya*, the most important local feminist organisation, and hosts a range of activities that include video groups, an in-house magazine (*see* **Publications**) and a lesbian group. A good place to get general information.

FESLU

C/Vidre 10, 2º 3ª (412 15 09).
Formally described as 'a women's cultural activity group', FESLU roughly translated means 'Free Time, Party Time'. These women of various nationalities put together parties wherever they can, and on the proceeds run the women-only centre **La Illa** (*see chapter* **Gay & Lesbian Barcelona**).

Bookshops

Pròleg

C/Dagueria 13, baixos (319 24 25). Metro Jaume I/bus 17, 40, 45. **Open** 5-8pm Mon; 10am-2pm, 5-8pm, Tue-Fri; 11am-2pm, 5-8pm Sat. **Credit** V.
Barcelona's only feminist bookshop, Pròleg has faced the economic problems of any minority-interest bookshop, and the question of whether to remain an outlet for women's literature only. Despite these difficulties, it still has the best range of women's writing in Barcelona. Pròleg also organises poetry readings and discussions around women's issues.

Laie Llibreria Café

C/Pau Claris 85 (302 73 10).Metro Urquinaona/bus all routes to Plaça Urquinaona. **Open** *bookshop* 10am-9pm Mon-Sat; *café* 9am-1am Mon-Sat. **Credit** AmEx, DC, MC, V.
A mixed but notably women-friendly bar/restaurant/bookshop where you can browse with a book over coffee and cake, or listen to live jazz in the laidback and excellent restaurant. *See also chapters* **Cafés & Bars** *and* **Shopping**.

Health Care

Centre Jove d'Anticoncepció i Sexualitat

C/La Granja 19-21 (415 10 00). Metro Lesseps/bus 24, 31, 32, 74. **Open** *approx Oct-May* 10am-7pm Mon; noon-

7pm Tue-Thur; 10am-5pm Fri; *approx June-Sept* 10am-5pm Mon-Fri. Closed Aug.
A family planning centre specially directed at young women with a very friendly staff and a relaxed attitude towards social security status and residency papers.

Drassanes Centre de Planificació Familiar

Avda Drassanes 17-21 (329 44 95). Metro Drassanes/bus 14, 18, 38, 59, 91. **Open** 9am-2pm Mon-Fri.
This service was recently absorbed into the large social security health centre at Drassanes, but it still operates separately as a family planning clinic. The all-woman staff is friendly and relaxed, if overworked. Abortion advice is available here and they do not necessarily demand social security cards.

Publications

Like any European city, Barcelona offers a glut of conventional women-orientated magazines (*Cosmopolitan, Company* and the like) but has a distinct lack of a feminist press. There are however, three publications worth noting:

Ca La Dona

The in-house magazine of **Ca La Dona**, in Catalan, and published quarterly (300ptas). It features some world news coverage, articles on various women-related issues and information on women's events.

Guia d'Entitats i Grups de Dones de Barcelona

This large free volume lists all of the women's organisations currently operating in Barcelona, and can be obtained from the Ajuntament in the Plaça Sant Jaume.

Guia de la Dona/Guía de Mujeres

Also from the Ajuntament, this interesting 'alternative' historical guide to Barcelona by Isabel Segura takes the form of a series of itineraries around areas of interest in connection with female historical figures – and more anonymous women – from Roman times to the present day. Published in Catalan and Spanish editions, it's available from the **Llibreria de la Virreina** and other bookshops (1,800ptas).

Entertainment

As already lamented, there is a lack of women-only spaces in Barcelona, for entertainment or otherwise. Women's bars and clubs are exclusively lesbian-oriented, although heterosexual and bisexual women would almost certainly feel comfortable in any of them, except possibly for **Daniella's Pub** (*see chapter* **Gay & Lesbian Barcelona**).

Women's Film Festival

Filmoteca de la Generalitat de Catalunya, Cinema Aquitania, Avda de Sarrià 31-33 (410 75 90). Metro Hospital Clínic/bus 15, 27, 41, 54, 59, 66, N3. **Dates** first two weeks of June.
First held in 1992 and celebrated each June, this has become a highly successful event. It's organised by *'Dracmàgic'*, a company that specialises in promoting socio-cultural events, and aims to be an exhibition – not a competition – of women's cinema, past and present. Directors are invited to speak about their work, which results in some lively debates.

Trips Out of Town

Getting Started

Routes out of the city streets, by bus, car or train.

Given its small size – all its borders are within a day's reach of Barcelona by car – Catalonia is unusually varied in scenery and climate. On its northern and eastern flanks are the Pyrenees and the Mediterranean coastal mountains, while to the west it slopes into a broad plain. This means that in under a day it's possible to go from mountains where temperatures drop well below zero to places where they frequently reach 40° C.

The Catalan *'costes'* – Brava, Maresme, Garraf and Daurada – all have their share of high-throughput tourist towns. There are plenty of less well-known places, however, and as for the interior, it remains a gold-mine of beautiful towns, villages and scenery, most of it yet to be discovered by non-Catalan visitors. The Generalitat tourist office (*see chapter* **Essential Information**) and local offices stock a wealth of brochures on different areas and districts (*comarques*), national parks, and specific themes (*Modernisme*, or Roman sites). The Generalitat also publishes two comprehensive annual guides, *Hotels Catalunya* and *Catalunya Campings*, available at most bookshops.

free alternatives are indicated in the chapters that follow. The **Túnel de Vallvidrera**, the continuation of Via Augusta that leads under Collserola to Sant Cugat and Terrassa, also has a high toll.

Thanks to the *Rondes*, traffic on main roads runs fairly freely on most days, but return journeys into Barcelona on Sunday evenings are always to be avoided. For car hire, *see chapter* **Services**, and for more on driving *see chapter* **Survival**.

By Bus

Coach services around Catalonia are operated by different private companies, but are now mostly (but not entirely) concentrated at the **Estació d'Autobusos Barcelona-Nord**, C/Ali Bei 80 (Metro Arc de Triomf). General information is on 265 65 08, but each company also has its own lines. Two areas better served by buses than trains are the high Pyrenees (with the Alsina-Graells company) and the central Costa Brava (with Sarfa).

By Road

For many car-mad locals, the greatest of the 1992 additions to Barcelona has been the **Rondes**, the obstacle-free ring-road built to ease traffic into, around and out of the city. The **Ronda de Dalt** runs along the edge of Tibidabo, and the **Ronda Litoral** along the coast, meeting north and south of the city. They intersect with several motorways (*autopistes*): from the north, the A17 for Girona, and the A18 for Terrassa, Sabadell and Manresa, which run into Avda Meridiana; the A2 for Lleida and Tarragona, a continuation of Avda Diagonal; and the A16 for Sitges, reached from Gran Via. These are toll roads, however, and expensive, and it's often best to get off them once out of town. Toll-

By Train

Spanish Railways (**RENFE**) operates an extensive network within Catalonia – particularly useful for the coast, Girona, the Montseny and the Penedès. All trains stop at **Barcelona-Sants** station (Metro Sants-Estació), where tickets for regional destinations are sold at the windows labelled *Rodalies/Cercanías*. In the city centre some routes (the coast to the north, the Montseny, the Penedès) pass through **Plaça Catalunya**; others (the coast south, Girona) through **Passeig de Gràcia**.

Trains are divided into *Regulars*, which stop at every station, *Deltas*, stopping at nearly all of them, and *Catalunya Exprés*, which stop less frequently and cost a little more. Long-distance (*Largo Recorrido*) services also stop at main stations, with supplements for high-speed services. For RENFE information, call 490 02 02 (English spoken).

Some destinations (Montserrat, Igualada, Manresa) are served by Catalan Government Railways (**FGC**). It has two stations: **Plaça d'Espanya**, for Montserrat and Manresa, and **Plaça Catalunya** for the line within Barcelona and suburban line to Sant Cugat, Sabadell and Terrassa. FGC information is on 205 15 15.

Around the City

just outside Barcelona you can find a complete change of air.

Visiting Barcelona's immediate hinterland involves very little travel, yet can give the feeling that you're well away from the big city, amid pine woods or in small, quiet towns. These areas – ignored by most visitors – also contain some of the most striking creations of Catalan Modernist architecture.

The Vallès

The other side of the great ridge of Collserola from Barcelona extends the hilly plain of the Vallès. Just beyond the road and rail tunnels, **Les Planes** is a picnic area on the edge of Collserola, where an area called a *merendero* – with tables, chairs and grills – can be used by Sunday visitors who bring their own food. There are also some budget restaurants. There's an attractive walk or cycle ride from Les Planes towards **El Papiol**, a town with a medieval castle and the remains of an Iberian settlement.

A little further to the north is **La Floresta**, a leafy suburb of houses scattered between pines up and down the steep hillsides. It was originally called 'La Floresta Pearson', after the Canadian engineer who brought mains electiricity to Barcelona, in 1911, and planned the village. In the 1960s, it was known as a hippy colony, and the influence survives in the friendly 'Bar Dada' – just behind the station – a car-free zone that hosts children's theatre. La Floresta is a great place for an easy, short walk, with beautiful views.

Below Collserola, largest of a line of bucolic residential areas, stands **Sant Cugat**, a pricey town of nearly 40,000. It has a Romanesque **monastery** with twelfth-century church and cloister, and a short drive on the Arrabassada road back towards Barcelona brings you to the **Casa Lluch**, a striking 1906 Modernist creation with superb tiling.

The main centres of the Vallès are two of Catalonia's major industrial towns, Terrassa and Sabadell. **Terrassa** won a Japanese award in the 1980s as the world's ugliest city, but at its centre there are three beautiful, remarkably ancient Visigothic-Romanesque churches, **Santa Maria**, **Sant Miquel** and **Sant Pere**, with sections that date from the sixth century. The town also has a host of Modernist buildings connected with the textile industry, such as the extraordinary **Masia Freixa**, a combination of mosque and Disneyland palace, and the Aymerich i Amat factory, which now houses the **Museu de la Ciència i de la Tècnica**, a museum of science and industry (780 67 55).

The eternal rival of neighbouring Terrassa, **Sabadell** also has plenty of interesting Modernist buildings, including the unmissable covered market, the **Torre de les Aigües** (water-tower), and **Caixa d'Estalvis de Sabadell** savings bank.

Information

Getting there: Les Planes, La Floresta, Sant Cugat *By car* A7 through Túnel de Vallvidrera (exit 8 off Ronda de Dalt, 430ptas one way), or the winding but scenic Carretera de l'Arrabassada (exit 5 off Ronda de Dalt) for free. *By train* FGC from Plaça Catalunya, any train marked Terrassa or Sabadell. Journey time 15-25 min. **El Papiol** *By car* A7, then B30 from Molins de Rei. *By train* RENFE from Plaça Catalunya. **Terrassa, Sabadell** *By car* A18 or N150 (exit 1 off Ronda de Dalt). *By train* RENFE or FGC from Plaça Catalunya.
Where to eat: Les Planes is a traditional picnicking place, La Floresta has the Bar Dada. Sant Cugat has one of the best grilled-meat restaurants in the area, the reasonably-priced **Braseria La Bolera**, C/Baixada de l'Alba 20 (674 16 75). In Terrassa **Casa Toni**, Carretera de Castellar 124 (786 47 08; average 3,000ptas), has an impressive range of wines and wine-making implements on display. In Sabadell **Forrellat** C/Horta Novella 27 (725 71 51), is pricey (4,500ptas) but top-quality.

The Colònia Güell

The Colònia Güell in the small town of **Santa Coloma de Cervelló**, on the western edge of Barcelona's sprawl, was one of the most ambitious projects on which Gaudí worked for his patron Eusebi Güell. It was intended to be a model industrial village around a textile factory, with a complete range of services for the workers. Like their park in Barcelona, it was never finished.

Nevertheless, the Colònia's crypt – begun in 1898, and the only part of the church to be completed before Güell died in 1918 – is one of Gaudí's most extraordinary and architecturally experimental works. The interior combines great sobriety with a look irresistibly like a giant fairy grotto, with parabolic vaults and tree-like inclined columns that predate their use by modern architects by at least half a century. All the fittings, stained glass and pews are the originals, by Gaudí. The other buildings of the 'colony', most by Francesc Berenguer, are also interesting.

Colònia Güell

Santa Coloma de Cervelló (640 29 36). By car A2 to Sant Boi exit, then right turn to Sant Vicenç dels Horts (8km). *By train* FGC from Plaça d'Espanya to Molí Nou; the Colònia, a 10-minute walk from the station. **Open** 10am-1.15pm, 4-6pm, Mon-Wed, Fri, Sat; 10am-1.15pm Thur, Sun, public holidays. **Admission** 100ptas. **No credit cards.**

Beaches

Catalonia has some of the best-trodden beaches in the world, but it's still possible to find spots where you can rub on the oil without rubbing elbows.

Now that Barcelona has a clean and usable beach of its own and beach culture has made its way right into the city, the impulse to catch a train along the coast on a summer's day may seem less powerful. Catalonia's coastal towns, though, have many other attractions, and despite highly-developed tourism many are charming, very beautiful and surprisingly unspoilt.

South

To Sitges & Vilanova

Traditionally Barcelona's favourite, and nearest, beach has been **Castelldefels**, just 20km to the south – a dull town, to be sure, but with kilometres of windswept, undercrowded beaches and fine seafood restaurants. It's used more by locals than foreigners, and has an attractive modern marina development, **Port Ginesta**, on the western side. Only a few minutes' train ride further along is **Garraf**, a tiny village with a clean, small beach served by a couple of beach bars or *xiringuitos*, and the **Celler de Garraf**, another Modernist classic designed by Gaudí for the Güells, in 1895.

The Garraf mountains come down to the sea, and then just the other side is **Sitges**, one of Catalonia's most famous resorts. Discovered and promoted at the turn of the century by writer/artist Santiago Rusiñol – whose circle included Manuel de Falla, Ramon Casas, Nonell, Utrillo and Picasso – it was also one of the first, and has a character many others lack. Sitges attracts thousands of visitors from across Europe, especially Britain, Germany and Italy. During the fifties, the town also become a favourite resort for Barcelona gays, and gay holiday-makers from around the world now make up a good proportion of the summer crowds (for more on the Sitges gay scene, *see chapter* **Gay & Lesbian Barcelona**. Nine beaches run along the seafront. There are quieter beaches at the adjoining (and artificial) port of **Aiguadolç** – to get there, turn left out of the station. For nudist beaches in Sitges, get to the beach, turn right, and keep going till you find them.

Even when crowded, the town still has great charm, with its long promenade, the Passeig Marítim, curving along the beaches. Dominating the view at one end of the Passeig is an especially beautiful cluster of buildings around Sitges' most visible monument, the seventeenth-century church of **Sant Bartomeu i Santa Tecla**. Almost adjacent to it are the old market, the Ajuntament and, notably, the **Museu Cau Ferrat** on C/Fonollar (894 03 64), Santiago Rusiñol's old home, which he bequeathed to the town as a ready-made museum, chock-full of his own collections of paintings, archeological finds, Modernist ironwork, medieval keys, model ships, traditional ceramics and indoor fountains. Opposite is the **Palau Mar i Cel**, another delightful old residence with a finely-crafted door, an unusual interior and an eclectic collection mostly of Medieval and Baroque artwork. A third museum, the **Museu Romàntic Casa Llopis**, C/Sant Gaudenci 1 (894 29 69), has an assortment of household objects from the last century, with a valuable collection of antique dolls. A joint ticket admits you to all three museums.

Vilanova i la Geltrú, the largest port between Barcelona and Tarragona, isn't exactly a holiday resort – although it too has some good beaches – but has several museums, including the important **Biblioteca-Museu Balaguer** on Avda Víctor Balaguer (815 42 02), which contains paintings by El Greco, Catalan turn-of-the-century art, Oriental artefacts and old weapons and coins. The town also has a distinguished central square, the **Plaça de la Vila**, and is known for its Carnaval, each February, and its seafood, especially served with a spicy local variant of *romesco* sauce called *xató*.

Information

Getting there: *By car* A16 to Castelldefels, Garraf, Sitges (41km) and Vilanova, with an extra tunnel toll between Garraf and Sitges. C246 covers the same distance, but involves a slow, winding drive around the Garraf mountains. *By train* RENFE from Sants or Passeig de Gràcia to Sitges (average 30min) and Vilanova (40min). Trains approx. every 20 minutes; not all of them stop at Castelldefels and Garraf.
Tourist offices: Castelldefels *Plaça Rosa dels Vents (664 23 01);* **Sitges** *Passeig de Vilafranca (894 12 30);* **Vilanova i la Geltrú** *C/La Torre de Ribaroges/Platja. (815 45 17).*
Where to eat:
Castelldefels: There are plenty of cheap paella places near the seafront. A good more upmarket restaurant is the **Nàutic** *Passeig Marítim 374 (665 01 74).*
Sitges: Good value for money are the **Sitges** *C/Parellades 61 (894 34 93)* and **La Salseta** *C/Sant Pau 35 (811 04 19).* Slightly more expensive but worth it is **Chez Jeanette** *C/Sant Pau 23. (894 00 48),* with

Sitges, *a favourite for gays and others since the 1950s.*

seasonal Catalano-French cuisine. When the seafood gets too much, excellent grilled meat can be had at **Can Pagès** *C/Sant Pere 24-26 (894 11 95)* and **El Celler Vell** *C/Sant Bonaventura 21 (894 82 99)*. If you want to blow some money on good seafood, avoid the seafront and go straight to **La Nansa** *C/Carreta 24 (894 19 27)*. **Vilanova i la Geltrú: Avi Pep** *C/Llibertat 128 (815 17 36)* is cheap and cheerful, while the **Peixerot** *Passeig Marítim 56 (894 06 25)* gets the pick of the fish arriving daily at the town harbour.

Where to stay:
Sitges: Celimar *Passeig de la Ribera 18 (811 01 70)* is a comfortable seafront hotel charging around 11,000ptas for a double room. The quiet **Hostal Maricel** *C/Tacó 11 (894 22 99)* weighs in at 7,000ptas, and the **Parellades** *C/Parellades 11 (894 08 01)* is the cheapest at just 4,600ptas. Bookings for Sitges hotels should be made as early as possible. *See also* **Gay & Lesbian Barcelona**.

Tarragona & the Costa Daurada

About two-thirds of the way from Vilanova to Tarragona lies **Altafulla**, a small town often bypassed by the tourist trade despite having one of the best-preserved Medieval centres on the coast. The modern section is close to the seafront, where there are beaches of fine, white sand, between rocky outcrops that give shade. The old, walled town – crowned by the imposing **Castell d'Altafulla** and floodlit at night – is a 10-minute stroll inland. At **Els Munts**, about half-way

between the old and new towns, there is one of Catalonia's best-preserved Roman villas.

Tarragona, a busy provincial capital of over 100,000 people, has been mysteriously overlooked by most foreign visitors, despite the fact that as Roman *Tarraco* it was the capital of an area that covered half the Iberian peninsula, and as a result contains the largest ensemble of Roman buildings and ruins in Spain – an extraordinary architectural legacy that includes the original town walls, an amphitheatre, circus, aqueduct and forum. Much later, the Catalan colonisers who seized the area from the Moors in the early twelfth century spent 61 years constructing the **Catedral de Santa Maria**, the Romanesque-Gothic building that dominates the town, in the midst of the *ciutat antiga* or old city, comparable in beauty to the Barri Gòtic of Barcelona. Tarragona also has a breathtaking view of the sea and the city's flat hinterland, the **Camp de Tarragona**, best viewed from the long walkway called the **Passeig Arqueològic**, around the Roman walls. Below there is a busy modern boulevard, the Rambla Nova, a host of other monuments, buildings and museums from the thirteenth to the nineteenth centuries and an attractive fishermen's district with good seafood restaurants, most offering dishes with Tarragona's own characteristic *romesco* sauce.

100% fun: Port Aventura

The Port Aventura theme park near Salou – the themes being the Mediterranean, Polynesia, China, Mexico and the Wild West – received 2.7 million visitors in 1995, its first season of operation. And 94 per cent of them declared themselves 'highly satisfied' – or so said the park's own survey. The only problem detected – a catering shortage (food and drink cannot be brought into the park) – has since been rectified by tripling the number of restaurants, cafés and fast-food counters. Attractions include a ride down a waterfall, a 'typhoon' corkscrew ride, canoeing, a steam train, Chinese carousels, log-riding, virtual-reality games, and last but certainly not least, the truly stomach-crunching Dragon Khan, the largest roller-coaster in Europe, with eight 360° loops. There are also (naturally enough) special rides for little kids, and floor shows from Mariachis to Chinese acrobats.

For those who don't like this kind of thing, it should be pointed out that Port Aventura, set up jointly by the Tussauds Group, La Caixa savings bank and the Anheuser-Busch brewery, is a more authentic theme park than most: the designs of the various buildings were carefully researched, and the products on sale at the theme shops actually originate in the countries they're supposed to be from. Those who do like this kind of thing think it's great, and rate it very highly in the international theme-park league. The admission ticket entitles you to an unlimited number of rides, and on-site facilities include video and buggy hire, a purchase collecting service, wheelchair hire and special facilities for disabled people. And not a Mickey Mouse in sight.

Port Aventura

(977/77 90 90). **Open** *Mar-late June, mid-Sept-end-Oct* 10am-8pm, *late June-mid-Sept* 10am-midnight, daily. **Admission** *One day* 3,900ptas; 3,000ptas 5-12s, over-65s; free under-5s. *Two consecutive days* 5,400ptas; 4,200ptas 5-12s, over-65s; free under-5s. *Night ticket 7pm-midnight, late June-mid-Sept only* 2,300ptas; 1,700ptas 5-12s, over-65s. **Credit** AmEx, DC, JCB, MC, V.

Getting there: *By car* A2 from Barcelona, then A7 to exit 35, or N340 (108km). *By train* RENFE from Sants or Passeig de Gràcia (1hr 15min). Port Aventura has its own station; seven southbound trains a day on the Barcelona-Tarragona-Tortosa line, and ten northbound, stop there.

The beach, the pleasant **Platja del Miracle** ('Beach of the Miracle') lies just beyond the amphitheatre.

A few more kilometres west is **Salou**, largest resort of the Costa Daurada, with sand, sea, hotels, discos, bars, calamares'n'chips and sun cream all on tap. It also has some interesting Modernist buildings, and a major new attraction just outside the town, the **Port Aventura** theme park (*see* **100% fun: Port Aventura**).

Information

Getting there: *By car* A2, then A7 from Barcelona via Vilafranca (Tarragona 98km). The toll-free N340 (Molins de Rei exit from A2) follows a similar route and is also quick. *By train* RENFE from Sants or Passeig de Gràcia to Altafulla (average, by Catalunya Exprés, 55min), Tarragona (1 hr 6min) and Salou (1 hr 18min). Trains hourly approx. 6am-9.30pm.
Tourist offices: Altafulla *Plaça dels Vents. (977/65 07 52);* **Tarragona** *C/Fortuny 4 (977/23 34 15);* **Salou** *Passeig Jaume I 4 (977/35 01 02).*
Where to eat:
Altafulla: Faristol *C/Sant Martí 5 (977/65 00 77),* an eighteenth-century house converted into a bar-restaurant, is well-priced and has a pleasant outdoor terrace.
Tarragona: Bufet el Tiberi *C/Martí d'Ardenya 5 (977/23 54 03),* is a good cheap buffet restaurant. The best-known restaurant is **Sol-Ric** *Via Augusta 227 (977/23 20 32),* with a famous fish-and-shellfish *romesco* and veal with Cinzano, among other more traditional dishes, and 400 wines on its list (average 4,000ptas). **Salou:** Restaurants are pricey. **Goleta** *C/Gavina-Platja Capellans (977/38 35 66)* does good salt-baked fish.
Where to stay:
Altafulla: Yola *Via Augusta 50 (977/65 02 83),* is the only good place to stay, at around 6,000ptas a double.
Tarragona: Imperial Tarraco *Rambla Vella 2 (977/23 30 40),* is luxurious; the attractive **Forum** *Plaça de l'Ajuntament (977/23 17 18)* the cheapest *hostal* in town.
Salou: El Racó *Platja del Racó (977/37 02 16)* has doubles for 5,000 ptas. If it's full, there are 53 other places to stay in this town of just 8,000 permanent inhabitants.

North

The Costa del Maresme

The coast of the Maresme, the region immediately north of Barcelona along the shore, is close enough to the city for easy day-tripping. Two of the best places for a day out are **Caldes d'Estrac**, also known as **Caldetes**, and **Sant Pol de Mar**. Both are small towns with good beaches (some of them nudist), and plenty of tourists – local and foreign. Sant Pol has the advantage that, unlike in many places along this coast, where railway tracks run close to the beach, some of its beaches are separated from both roads and the rail line by rocky cliffs. Both villages are also worth strolling around. Caldetes has some interesting Modernist houses, a spa, and a recently restored park with a good view of the coast, and Sant Pol – which also has a striking Modernist school, from 1907 – is an unusually unspoilt, if yuppified, fishing village.

Information

Getting there: *By car* N11 from Barcelona to Caldes d'Estrac (36km) and Sant Pol (48km). *By train* RENFE from Sants or Plaça Catalunya. Trains every half-hour, journey time approx 35min.
Where to stay & eat:
Caldetes: Emma *Baixada de l'Estació 5 (791 13 05)* is one of the town's best medium-priced restaurants. If you want to stay over, the **Pinzón** *C/El Callao 4 (791 00 51),* has rooms for about 4,500ptas a night.
Sant Pol: Hostalet I *C/Manzanillo 9 (760 06 05)* and **Hostalet II** *C/Santa Clara (760 07 43)* are enjoyable hotels with doubles for around 5,000ptas. There are two or three good paella restaurants on the main street.

The Costa Brava

The Costa Brava proper lies within the *comarca* known as the **Baix Empordà**. This rocky peninsula was the original 'rugged coast' for which the name *Costa Brava* was dreamt up earlier this century by a journalist called Ferran Agulló, and is still the Costa's most unspoilt section. As there are no large sandy beaches, and access to the coast by public transport is limited, the area has largely escaped the mass tourist boom. Consequently, accommodation facilities are still limited (it is essential to book ahead in high season), as are nightlife and organised activities for children and families. This does not mean the area is undiscovered, however: it is a favourite holiday location for prosperous Catalans.

Winding roads connect the main inlets on the peninsula. The northern ones – **Sa Riera**, **Sa Tuna** and **Aiguablava** – are most accessible from Begur, while those further south – **Tamariu**, **Llafranc** and **Calella** – are best reached from Palafrugell.

Begur is an attractive old town dominated by the remains of a fourteenth-century castle. It is set just inland, high on a rocky hillside, commanding magnificent views to north and south. From there it's a steep two-mile (3km) walk down to the coast: if you're not prepared to hoof it, you'll need your own transport. A little further inland on a local road is the very carefully preserved Medieval village of **Pals**, now seemingly converted almost entirely into second homes occupied by security-obsessed people who all seem to have video-intercoms installed next to their ancient stone doorways. Pals is nonetheless a remarkable survivor, with several fine twelfth- to fifteenth-century monuments and buildings, and beautiful views over the surrounding countryside.

Sa Riera, on the little road leading directly from Pals to the coast, is the northernmost cove of the peninsula and has one of its largest sandy beaches – although still with space for only 300 bodies – and good views of the Medes islands to the north. From here, a road leads around the headland to **Sa Tuna**, a small and picturesque fishing village. There is one *hostal*-restaurant in an excellent position on the seafront, but the beach is small

Inside the hugely impressive Roman amphitheatre in **Tarragona**. *See page 243.*

and stony. From Sa Tuna, a lovely walk (about 40 minutes each way) along a well-built coastal path takes you northwards through **Aiguafreda**, a small wooded cove, to a spectacular building, once a hotel, cut into the cliff on the promontory beyond. Steps lead down to swimming pools cut into the precipitous cliff-face.

Heading south from Sa Tuna, you'll reach **Fornells** and **Aiguablava**, both in a larger bay with villas and apartment blocks dotted around the wooded hillsides. Aiguablava has a small beach with beautiful white sand, a small harbour for yachts, and the old and luxurious **Hotel Aiguablava**. **Tamariu** is a slightly larger village in a small, intimate bay, with a string of hotels and bars around the seafront which are known for their excellent seafood. There are several places nearby where you can swim from the rocks. You can also hire boats for exploring the coast or fishing (call Paco Heredia on 972/30 13 10).

Llafranc is less remote and more developed as a resort, thanks to its being connected by a main road with Palafrugell. From here you can walk to **Calella de Palafrugell**, a prettier fishing village just to the south, with another good beach. Tamariu and Llafranc are the only two places on this coastal stretch easily accessible by public transport, with regular buses from the Sarfa bus station in **Palafrugell**, the main transport centre

of the peninsula. It has a lively Sunday market, several seventeenth-century buildings, and a museum dedicated to Josep Pla, one of Catalonia's best twentieth-century writers, whose name is now inextricably linked with that of his birthplace.

It's recommendable to visit this area mid-week in summer, to avoid the weekend traffic. Essential, too, are plastic sandals or old trainers for negotiating the rocks and pebbled beaches and, more importantly, for swimming: there are a lot of spiny sea urchins in these rocky coves.

Further up the coast to the north is the small town of **Estartit**, a water-sports centre which has no great attractions but is conveniently situated opposite the **Illes Medes**, a clutch of small rocky islets that are Catalonia's only underwater nature park. Glass-bottomed boats leave every hour from Estartit (June-Sept; according to demand, April, May, October) to tour the rare coral deposits for which, as well as their bird life, the islands are renowned. The more adventurous can also go scuba-diving amongst the coral (for details, enquire at tourist office). A pleasant walk up the road from Estartit is the **Castell de Montgrí**, an unfinished but imposing twelfth-century castle with a fine view of coast and hinterland.

Information

Getting there: *By bus* Sarfa (265 11 58), nine buses daily from Estació del Nord in Barcelona to Palafrugell

To the islands

Barcelona is only a short hop from **Mallorca, Menorca, Eivissa** (aka **Ibiza**, in Spanish) and **Formentera**. Getting there is naturally easy, but note that if the Balearics are your main destination it will near-invariably be cheaper to go direct from Britain or any other northern European country than in a two-stage journey via Barcelona, given the range of offers now available to get you to Europe's number-one holiday patch.

Today synonymous with mass tourism, the islands also have a long and complex history. They were first inhabited by Megalithic peoples, whose extraordinary stone buildings – the *taliots* – still puzzle archeologists. Occupied by Moslems in the tenth century, and a favourite haunt for Arab pirates, they were conquered by the Catalan Count-Kings between 1229 and 1287. Catalan remains the principal language of the islands.

Despite being familiar to millions, all the islands have many rarely-visited, unspoilt areas, and each has a very individual character. Ibiza, centre equally of international post-hippy and club culture, is a desert island that burns yellow each summer, while small Formentera alongside it is more desertic still. Mallorca has remote, mountainous areas inland, and an attractive capital in Palma with another Catalan Gothic cathedral. Menorca, greenest of the islands, with beautiful coves around its shores, was held by Britain for 70 years in the eighteenth century, an occupation that left curious traces behind it

– door latches, sash windows, and some of the world's best gin, result of a happy encounter between Navy grog and a Mediterranean skill with herbs. The modern inhabitants of the Balearics have also produced a rich literature which – were it available in English – could provide visitors with a more complex image of the islands than the one seen just from the beach.

Information

Getting there by air: Over ten flights daily, Barcelona-Mallorca, and three daily to Ibiza and Menorca. Thanks to the recent removal of the monopoly on domestic flights three companies – Air Europa, Spanair and Iberia/Aviaco – are engaged in a price war: average cost of a return to Mallorca is currently 10,600ptas, but this may vary.

Getting there by sea: Transmediterrània, Estació Marítima de Balears, Moll de Barcelona (443 25 32), is the sole ferry operator to the islands. All ferries leave from the Estació Marítima, opposite the Drassanes at the foot of the Rambla (Metro Drassanes). There are ferries daily to Mallorca at 11pm (journey time 8hrs), plus a 1pm sailing on Sundays; ferries to Menorca or Ibiza also leave at 11-11.30pm (both 9hrs) but only on certain days of the week. Unless you sit up all night, ferries are more expensive than flying. Current mid-season (spring, summer except August, early autumn) one-way fares to Palma include 5,040ptas seat-only, or 12,600ptas per person for a cabin shared by two, with a 15% discount for return tickets. The advantages are that you can take a car or bike, there are great views on arrival, and tickets are more readily available.

Tourist offices: Mallorca: *Avda Jaime III, Palma (97171 22 16);* **Menorca:** *Plaça Esplanada 40, Mahón (971/36 37 90);* **Ibiza & Formentera:** *C/Paseo Vara del Rey 13, Ibiza (97130 19 00).*

(2hrs), some of which continue to Begur. Change in Palafrugell or Torroella for Estartit. *By car* A7 north to exit 6 onto C255; or exit 9 onto C250, C253, C255 via Palafrugell (123km). Alternatively, take the slower coastal A11, then C250, C253, C255.

Tourist offices:
Begur *Plaça de l'Església 8 (972/62 40 20);* **Pals** *C/Aniceta Figueras 6 (972/68 78 57);* **Palafrugell** *C/Carrilet 2 (972/30 02 28);* **L'Estartit** *Passeig Marítim (972/75 89 10).*

Where to eat:
Begur: Can Torrades *(972/622 28 82)*, converted from an old house, has good but pricey Catalan home cooking; **Fonda Platja** *(972/62 21 97)*, a small hotel with two bedrooms, is also expensive but serves excellent Catalan food. **La Pizzeta** *(972/622 38 83)* serves moderately-priced Italian fare. On the outskirts of Begur on the road toward Palafrugell is **Mas Comangau** *(972/62 32 10)*, a traditional restaurant popular for Sunday lunch. In **Pals,** the popular **Alfred** *C/La Font 7 (972/63 62 74)* offers good home-cooking for around 3,000ptas.

Aiguablava: Hotel Aiguablava *(see below)* has a top-class restaurant and the **Parador** at Aiguablava *(972/62 21 62)* offers panoramic views. The restaurant of **Hostal**

Sa Tuna *(see below)* is simple but has a great view. **Tamariu:** There's not much to choose between the restaurants on the sea-front. The family-run **Snack Bar Es Dofí** *(972/61 02 92)*, is the only one open all year. **Llafranc:** One of the area's best restaurants is the **Hotel Llafranc** *Passeig de Cipsela 16. (972/30 02 08).*

Where to Stay:
Begur: The **Hotel Begur** *C/de Coma i Ros 8 (972/62 22 07)* is centrally placed and open all year round (7,000ptas per double). **Pals** has the **Barris** *C/Enginyer Algarra 51 (972/63 67 02)*, for 4,500 ptas. per double. There are two **campsites** near Begur: at Sa Riera, you'll find **La Maset** *Platja de Sa Riera, (972/62 30 23)*; and on the road to Palafrugell, **Begur** *Carretera de Begur a Palafrugell (972/62 32 01).*

Sa Tuna: Hostal Sa Tuna *Platja Sa Tuna (972/262 21 98)* is perfectly located but has only eight rooms. **Aiguablava:** In the bay of Aiguablava and Fornells, the four-star **Hotel Aiguablava** *Platja de Fornells (972/62 20 58)*, is still family-run and has a swimming pool and tennis courts (11,000ptas double).

Tamariu: Hotel Hostalillo *C/Bellavista 28 (972/30 01 58)* is the largest hotel in town, with 72 rooms (11,000ptas double; open June-Sept only); the **Hostal Vora de Mar**

Passeig del Mar 6 (972/30 05 53) is the only one open all year round (5,000ptas double).

Llafranc: The **Hotel Llafranc** (*see above*) has double rooms for around 10,000ptas. Or try the two-star **Hotel Casamar** *C/Carrer de Nero 3-11 (972/30 01 04)* for 7,200ptas per double. There are two **campsites** near Calella: **La Siesta** *C/Chipitea 110-120 (972/30 02 58);* and **Moby Dick** *C/Costa Verda 16-28 (972/30 48 07).* **L'Estartit**: Santa Clara *Passeig Maritim 18 (972/75 87 67)* is pleasant, and costs 4,700 ptas.per double.

Figueres to France

The indisputable centre of the northern Costa Brava, the *comarca* of **Alt Empordà**, is the town of **Figueres**, from which it is possible to travel by car, bus and sometimes train to every other place of interest in the area. The *tramontana* wind sweeps this area at regular intervals and, according to the rest of Catalonia, leaves its inhabitants slightly touched (read, crazy), a fact apparently borne out by two of Figueres' most famous sons: Narcis Monturiol, the utopian socialist and penniless inventor of (some say) the first submarine, and Salvador Dali. One of Dali's major influences, the equally Surrealistic philosopher Francesc Pujols, was also born in the area. Another thing the Empordà is known for is its fine food, especially *mar i montanya* dishes of meat and seafood.

Figueres itself is an interesting town, not least for being the home of the **Teatre-Museu Dalí**, designed by the man himself as a kind of static spectacle complete with music, optical illusions, cars with rain inside and numerous other installations. From June to September, it stay opens later, with Dali's own choice of lighting and music as well as a free glass of *cava*. Dali's **Torre Galatea**, his egg-topped Figueres residence, is next door. Other places worth visiting are the **Museu de Juguets**, a famous toy museum, and the **Museu de l'Empordà**, for a comprehensive and well-presented overview of the district's art and history.

A straight road leads east from Figueres to **Roses**, once a major trading port and now the area's largest tourist town. It has a veritable glut of hotels, discos and overpriced restaurants, but also attractive beaches and a sixteenth-century citadel, the **Ciutadella**. To the south is the **Parc Natural dels Aiguamolls de l'Empordà**, a nature reserve in the marshlands around the mouth of the Fluvià river, famous for its vegetation and waterbirds. The park information centre at **El Cortalet**, on the road between Castelló d'Empúries and Sant Pere Pescador *(972/25 03 22)*, runs guided tours daily in July and August.

From Roses the road begins to climb in order to take you through many precipitous switchbacks with wonderful views into **Cadaqués**, at the end of the Cap de Creus peninsula. It is famous as the town whose Mayor refused to allow highrise hotels in the boom years of Costa-hotel speculation, and so has kept its little, narrow streets

and whitewashed houses. As a result, Barcelona's cultural élite made Cadaqués their favourite summer resort in the 1960s, and it's since become popular with well-heeled bohemians from all over Europe. Its cultural season includes its very own music festival each August (*see chapter* **Music: Classical & Opera**).

Consequently, Cadaqués is also relatively expensive, but is still strikingly beautiful, and all around the Cape there are any number of tiny, rocky coves offering the chance of complete relaxation. The town's native population, whose ancestors lived for centuries in total isolation from anywhere inland, are well-known for their lack of interest in outsiders.

A short walk to the next bay and you're in **Port Lligat**, a tiny fishing village where Dali built his favourite Catalan residence, now abandoned. Beyond Port Lligat a road leads to the **Cap de Creus** ('Cape of Crosses'), with a lighthouse, a nature reserve and unique, pockmarked rock formations that have led it to be used as a location in several science-fiction movies.

Port de la Selva on the north side of the Cape has never received the accolades showered on its neighbour Cadaqués, yet it is similarly unspoilt, quieter in the summer, and is closer to the magnificent monastery of **Sant Pere de Rodes**, sometimes lost in clouds up on the mountains above the town. One of the oldest and most beautiful Romanesque buildings in Catalonia, it was founded in 1022, but large sections are still intact.

A little further north again is **Llancà**, about 15 minutes' train ride from Figueres. The modern part of the village gives onto several bays and beaches, and is just a short walk from the beautiful old centre. Llancà also has good connections to the French border, for those headed in that direction.

Alternatively, if you head south from Figueres to the opposite end of the Alt Empordà you will come to the well-preserved remains of the ancient city of **Empúries**, founded in 600 BC by the Phoenicians, re-colonised by the Greeks and finally taken over by the Romans, in 2 AD. Ruins of buildings from all three periods, and the line of the original Greek harbour, are clearly visible, and it's a very attractive and atmospheric ancient site, right next to a beach. The nearest modern town is **L'Escala**, an attractive port noted for its anchovies, and birthplace of Caterina Albert, author of the classic Catalan novel *Solitud*.

Sant Pere de Rodes
Open *Oct-May* 10am-1.30pm, 3-5pm, *June-Sept* 10am-7pm, Tue-Sun. **Admission** 300ptas; 150ptas students. **No credit cards**.

The suitably surreal **Teatre-Museu Dalí**.

Rent a boat in **L'Estartit** and head up the coast. See page 247.

Teatre-Museu Dalí

Plaça Gala-Salvador Dalí 5, Figueres (972/51 19 76).
Open *Oct-June* 10.30am-5.15pm Tue-Sun; *July-Sept* 9am-
7.15pm daily. **Admission** *Oct-June* 700ptas; 400ptas
students, over-65s; *July-Sept* 1,000ptas; 700ptas students,
over-65s. **Credit** AmEx, MC, V.

Information

Getting there: *By bus* Barcelona Bus (232 04 59),
several buses daily to Figueres from Estació del Nord in
Barcelona (2hrs 30min). Sarfa (265 11 98) runs a direct
service to Roses and Cadaqués (two buses daily; 2hrs
15min). The easiest way to get to anywhere on the coast
is to take a train to Figueres, and then a Sarfa bus from
their depot next to the station. Sarfa has services to
Llança, Roses, Port de la Selva, Cadaqués and L'Escala.
By car A7 or N11 direct from Barcelona (to Figueres,
120km). From Figueres, C260 to Roses. *By train* RENFE
from Sants or Passeig de Gràcia to Figueres (1 hr
45min,Catalunya Exprés) or Llançà.
Tourist offices:
Figueres *Plaça del Sol (972/50 31 55);* **Roses** *Plaça de
les Botxes (972/25 73 31);* **Cadaqués** *C/Cotxe 2-A
(972/25 83 15);* **Llançà** *Avda d'Europa 37 (972/38 08
55);* **L'Escala** *Plaça de les Escoles 1 (972/77 06 03).*
Where to eat:
Figueres: The fast-food terraces around the Dalí
Museum are worth avoiding, as are the French-style
bars on the Rambla, the largest of which, however,
has kept its original fifties décor and is a nice place for
a drink. Most restaurants are in the old town, and
those in C/de la Jonquera have tables outside in
summer and are reasonably priced. **Presidente** *Ronda
Firal 33 (972/77 07 28)* does upmarket Catalan food
for about 3,000ptas.
Cadaqués: The best-known restaurant is **La Galiota**
C/Narcís Monturiol 9 (972/25 81 87), run by Pepita

and Núria, two of Catalonia's most famous
restaurateurs (average 5,000ptas). Also very popular is
Casa Anita *C/Miguel Roset (972/25 84 71);* and
cheap but still good is **Pizzeria Plaza** *Passeig
Marítim 10 (no phone).*
Where to Stay:
Figueres: Hotel Duran *C/Lasauca 5 (972/50 12 50)*
has doubles for 8,400ptas, while the **Hostal Bon Repòs**
C/Vilallonga 43 (972/50 92 02) is a good budget option
with doubles at 3,800ptas.
Roses: There are dozens of places in the town. **Marian**
Platja Salatar (972/25 63 00) gives onto the beach and
costs 5,500ptas. per double. **Hostal Can Salvador**
C/Puig Rom 43 (972/25 78 11) is one of the cheaper
hostals at 4,500 ptas per double.
Cadaqués: The town gets very crowded in summer, and
out of season many smaller *hostals* are closed, so it's best
to reserve ahead. The tourist office can supply a full list,
including names of families who rent out rooms. **Hostal
Marina** *C/Frederic Rahola 2 (972/25 81 99)* at 7,000ptas
per double, and the **Pension Vehí** *C/L'Església 6
(972/25 84 70)* at 5,000ptas a double, are good value.
Port de la Selva: German *C/Poeta Sagarra 11
(972/38 70 92)* is a reasonably-priced small hotel
(6,000ptas, double). **Porto Cristo** *C/Major 48 (972/38
70 62)* is the village's luxury hotel (13,000 ptas, double).
Llançà: Try the **Florida** *C/Floridablanca 16-18 (972/12
01 61)* for 4,000ptas a double, and for more comforts the
Berna *Passeig Marítim 13 (972/38 01 50)* at 7,500ptas.
Empúries: If you have a car, the best place to stay in the
area is the village of Sant Martí d'Empúries, which has
the comfortable, beautifully situated **Riomar** *Platja del
Riuet (972/77 02 07;* 7,000ptas a double), or the cheaper
Can Roura *Plaça Església 12 (972/77 03 05)* for a mere
4,500ptas per double. The **Youth Hostel** *(972/77 12 00)*
is on the beach by the ruins, but often full. An IYHF card
is required, and beds cost 1,500ptas per night.

Inland

Deep in the Catalan countryside you can come across superb scenery, tranquil monasteries, cava houses, and some wild festivals.

Of the millions who have visited the Catalan coasts over the past forty years or so only a fraction have ventured more than a short distance away from the shore. The countryside of Catalonia, though – and without over-indulging Catalan patriotism – has to be one of the most beautiful in Europe, combining Mediterranean colours and rugged hills with a lush greenness, blending into truly alpine landscapes in the Pyrenees.

In amongst the hills and valleys there are also ancient towns and villages with very distinct atmospheres, and the valleys that climb up toward the Pyrenees are one of the birthplaces of Romanesque architecture, with exquisite early-Medieval buildings in every second town and village.

Montserrat

Perched half-way up this dramatic mountain ridge (the literal translation, 'saw-tooth mountain', describes it accurately) stand the monastery and hermitages of **Montserrat**. The fortress-like atmosphere is emphasised by difficult access – the road meanders hair-raisingly and there are frequent delays. The only other way up, more spectacular still, is by cable-car.

From as early as the fifth century, hermits have been attracted to this isolated place, and a Benedictine monastery was founded here in 1025. In the twelfth century, the so-called 'Black Virgin', a small wooden statue of the Madonna and child, was installed here, although it's claimed the statue is much older. All kinds of legends and traditions have grown up around the statue over the centuries. It is the patron-virgin of Catalonia, and Montserrat is still the most common Catalan woman's name.

In the Middle Ages, the monastery became an important place of pilgrimage. Accordingly, it grew rich and powerful, its remote position helping to ensure its independence. During the Franco era, the monastery was a bastion of Catalan nationalism, and for a time the only place where mass could be celebrated in Catalan.

The **shrine of the Black Virgin** is in the sixteenth-century basilica, where it can be visited – and touched – by joining the queue to the right

of the main door and climbing up behind the altar. Two museums display gifts given to the virgin, including Old Master paintings and three works by Picasso. First-time visitors be warned, though, that the monastery itself is not especially interesting, while the cafeterias and souvenir shops tend to take the edge off the place's spirituality, although connoisseurs of religious kitsch might feel they justify the whole trip in themselves.

What are spectacular are the walks and views around the site. The whole of the mountain, 10km long, is now a nature park, and the monastery occupies only a very small part of it. Apart from the cave where the virgin was discovered – 20 minutes' walk from the monastery – there are 13 hermitages dotted around the mountain, the most accessible of which is **Sant Joan**, at the top of a funicular that runs from beside the monastery, the Funicular a St Joan. The 20-minute walk to the hermitage has superb views, and a longer, hour's walk along the ridge will take you to the hermitage of **Sant Jeroni**.

Just beyond it, it's possible to climb the **peak of Sant Jeroni**, 4,053feet (1,235m) above sea level. At foot of the mountain, the village of **Collbató** is in a beautiful location and has several illuminated caves – **les coves de Salitre** – that are open to visitors (777 03 09).

Information

Getting there: *By bus* Julià-Via from Sants bus station, at 8am (June-Sept); 9am (Oct-May). The journey takes about 80min. Julià also run guided tours to Montserrat (*see chapter* **Sightseeing**). *By car* N11 to exit at km591; or A2 to Martorell exit, then through Abrera and Monistrol (60km). The road up to the monastery is often crowded and very slow. *By train* FGC from Plaça d'Espanya, every two hours from 7.10am daily, to Aeri de Montserrat (journey time approx 1hr); then by cable car to the monastery, every 15 min. Return fare (including cable car) is around 1,700ptas.
Tourist office: Montserrat *(835 02 51)*.
Where to eat: Food at Montserrat is expensive and of indifferent quality. The restaurant at the top of the Funicular a St Joan is better and usually less crowded, but open only in summer.
Where to Stay: The two hotels run by the monks – the **Hotel Abat Cisneros** (8,360ptas double; reductions mid-Nov to mid-Mar), and **Hotel Residència Monestir** (5,100ptas.double; no singles; closed mid Mar to mid-Nov) – are both reasonable. To book at either, phone 835 02 01 or fax 828 40 06. There is a **camping site** (835 02 51) beyond St Joan funicular: look for the camping sign.

The monastery of **Santa Maria de Ripoll**, *last resting-place of Wilfred the Hairy. See page 254.*

The Royal Monasteries

Montblanc, 112km due west of Barcelona, is one of the most beautiful towns in western Catalonia, and yet all but unknown to foreign visitors. It also has around it, roughly forming a triangle, three exceptional Cistercian monasteries: **Poblet** – almost as much a national symbol as Montserrat, and a more attractive building to boot – **Santes Creus** and **Vallbona de les Monges**.

In the Middle Ages, Montblanc was an exceptionally prosperous town with an important Jewish community, a past that is reflected in the *Carrer dels Jueus* ('Jews' street'), the magnificent thirteenth-century town walls – two-thirds of which remain intact – the churches of **Santa Maria la Major**, **Sant Miquel** and **Sant Francesc**, the **Palau Reial** (Royal Palace) and the **Palau del Castlà** or castlekeeper's palace.

The great monasteries of this region were unusually grand because they enjoyed a uniquely close relationship with the Catalan-Aragonese monarchs, and were all built partly with the intention that they should house royal tombs. **Poblet**, a few kilometres west of Montblanc, was founded in 1151 by Ramon Berenguer IV, the Count-King who created the joint Catalan-Aragonese monarchy. He also seized this area from the Moslems and undertook its re-population, and to assist the process gave generous grants of land to the Cistercian order. Poblet, in particular, was a royal residence as well as a monastery, and has within it a fourteenth-century Gothic royal palace. Especially impressive are the fifteenth-century chapel of Sant Jordi and the main church with the tombs of most of the Count-Kings of Barcelona, but the entire complex is remarkable. The monastery can be seen by guided tour only, conducted by a monk.

Santes Creus, founded in 1158 and possibly still more beautiful than Poblet, was a major focus for local agriculture and building until the fourteenth century, and grew into a small village when a group of families moved into the abandoned monks' residences in 1843. Within its strongly fortified walls there are the **Palau de l'Abat** (abbot's palace), a monumental fountain, a twelfth-century church with some more royal tombs, and a superb Gothic cloister and chapterhouse.

Vallbona de les Monges, third of these Cistercian houses, is unlike the others a convent of nuns, and particularly favoured by Catalan-Aragonese Queens, especially Violant of Hungary, wife of Jaume I. She is buried here, while her husband lies at Poblet. It has a fine, part-Romanesque cloister, but is less grand than the other two. A small village was built around it in the sixteenth century when it was ordained that nuns should not live in isolated and unprotected buildings. All three monasteries still house religious communities.

Speeding towards **Montserrat**.

Monestir de Poblet

(977/87 02 54). **Open** *Mar-Sept* 10am-12.30pm, 3-6pm, daily; *Oct-Feb* closes at 5.30pm. **Admission** 400ptas; 200ptas students, over-65s.

Monestir de Santes Creus

(977/63 83 29). **Open** *Oct-May* 10am-1.10pm, 3-6pm; *June-Sept* 10am-1.10pm, 3-7pm, Tue-Sun. **Admission** 300ptas; 150ptas under-21s, over-65s.

Monestir de Santa Maria de Vallbona

(973/33 02 66). **Open** 11am-noon, 5-7pm, daily. **Admission** 200ptas; 150ptas over-65s. Hours may vary according to times of religious services.

Information

Getting there: *By bus* Hispano Igualadina (430 43 44) runs a daily service to Montblanc from C/Europa (behind the Corte Inglés on Avda Diagonal; Metro Maria Cristina). There are more services from Valls and Tarragona. *By car* A2, then A7, then again A2 direct, or N340 to El Vendrell then C246 for Valls and Montblanc. For **Poblet**, take N240 west from Montblanc and turn left in L'Espluga de Francolí. **Santes Creus** is connected by a slip road to the C246. For **Vallbona de les Monges**, take the C240 out of Montblanc towards Tàrrega and turn left at the relevant side road, which is clearly signposted. *By train* RENFE from Sants or Passeig de Gràcia to Montblanc, five trains a day (approx 2hrs).
Tourist office: Montblanc & Poblet *(977/86 00 09)*.

Where to eat: Montblanc has an inn, **Fonda Colom** C/Civaderia 3 (977/86 01 53), just behind the Plaça Major, with a five-course set meal for around 2,500ptas. You can also eat well at **Els Àngels** (see below). **Where to stay:** Highly recommended in **Montblanc** is the recently-renovated **Els Àngels** Plaça Àngels 1 (977/86 01 73), which also has a restaurant. Failing that, the **Colom** (see above) has a few rooms. **Poblet's** neighbouring village of Vimbodí has the **Fonoll** C/Ramon Berenguer IV 2 (977/87 03 33). **Santes Creus** has the equally cheap **Hostal Grau** C/Pere III 3 (977/63 83 11), and **Vallbona de les Monges** has no place to stay at all.

The Montseny to the Pyrenees

Vic & Rupit

Vic is an easy town to visit from Barcelona, and lies in the middle of the city's nearest nature reserves: the wonderful mountains of Montseny, Les Guilleries and Collsacabra, ideal for a weekend's walking (see **Walks in the Woods**). A town of 30,000 people which started life as the capital of an Iberian tribe known as the Ausetians, Vic was made a city by the Romans, and later fell briefly into the hands of the Moors. They lost it to Wilfred the Hairy (see chapter **History: The Origins**) in the late ninth century, since when it has remained an important religious, administrative and artistic centre. It has many late-Medieval houses – now mainly used as administrative and university buildings – and, in its **Plaça Major**, one of the finest and liveliest town squares in the whole of Catalonia.

In the nineteenth century, it produced one of Catalonia's greatest poets, Jacint Verdaguer, and philosopher Jaume Balmes, famous throughout Spain. Monuments worth seeing are the **Temple Romà** (Roman temple), now an art gallery, and the neo-classical **Catedral de Sant Pere**, which contains a set of sombre twentieth-century murals by painter Josep Lluís Sert, and has a perfectly-preserved eleventh-century belltower. The **Casa de la Ciutat**, in the south-east corner of the Plaça Major, dates from the fourteenth century. The square is most animated on Saturdays – market day – and during the traditional livestock market held every year during the week before Easter, the Mercat del Ram. Vic is famous for its high-quality embotits or charcuterie, and shops selling botifarres, llonganisses and other sausages can be found in almost every street.

The district of Osona, of which Vic is the capital, is unusually full of interesting villages, such as **Centelles**, **Manlleu**, and **Montesquiu**. The most rewarding route is up the main C153 road towards **Olot**, turning off to the right along local roads for **Tavertet** – a perfectly preserved seventeenth-century village with a panoramic view over the Ter valley – and **Rupit**, a village built against the side of a Medieval castle, with an old town from the sixteenth-century and an eleventh-century church,

Sant Joan de Fàbregues. From here, several impressive traditional farmhouses, such as **El Bac de Collsacabra** and **El Corriol** (which has a collection of traditional ceramics and historical artefacts), are within walking distance.

Information

Getting there: By bus Empresa Sagalès (231 27 56) from the corner of Passeig Sant Joan and C/Diputació (Metro Tetuan) to Vic. There is no direct bus to Tavertet and Rupit from Barcelona, but the best way to get there is to get a train or bus to Vic and then get one of the Pous company (850 60 63) local buses. By car For Vic, take N152 from Barcelona, direction Puigcerdà (65km). For Tavertet and Rupit, take C153 out of Vic (direction Olot). By train RENFE from Sants or Plaça Catalunya to Vic, approx two trains each hour (journey time 1hr). **Tourist office:** Vic Plaça Major 1 (886 20 91) **Where to eat:** Vic has several good medium-priced restaurants. The **Basset** C/Sant Sadurní 4 (889 02 12) does some great seafood dishes (2,000-5,000ptas). **Ca l'U** Plaça Santa Teresa 4/5 (889 03 45) is a more traditional (and cheaper) inn-style place with plenty of pork specialities: well-cooked but heavy. For something special, take the N152 toward Ripoll, and just before reaching Sant Quirze de Besora detour along a 2km-long, signposted road to the **Rectoria d'Orís** C/Rectoria (859 02 30). It's one of the best restaurants in the area – using only local produce– and has a terrific view. **Where to stay:** Vic's luxury hotel is the three-star **Ciutat de Vic** C/Jaume el Conqueridor (889 14 47), at 9,000ptas a double; whereas the **Ausa** Plaça Major 4 (885 53 11) is slightly cheaper, still comfortable and gives onto the main square. **Rupit** has a good two-star hostal, the **Estrella** Plaça Bisbe Font 1 (852 20 05).

Ripoll to the Vall de Núria

Ripoll, the next medium-sized town on the road north of Vic, grew up around the unique church and monastery of **Santa Maria de Ripoll**, known as the 'cradle of Catalonia', and with a superb twelfth-century portal that is one of the finest examples of early Romanesque stonework in Europe. This was the original fiefdom of Hairy Wilfred, Guifré el Pilós, before he became Count of Barcelona (see chapter **History: The Origins**). He is buried in Santa Maria, which he founded in 879. He also founded the monastery and town of **Sant Joan de les Abadesses**, 10km up the C151 road east, and worth a visit to see its restored Gothic bridge as well as the monastery itself, an unusually-designed twelfth-century building, constructed by masons from southern France. The monastery museum (972/72 00 13) covers a thousand years of local life.

The road from Sant Joan leads on to **Camprodon**, on the fast-flowing river Ter, which is known for a kind of crunchy biscuit called a carquinyoli, and also has a fine Romanesque church. Veering to the left from Camprodon a local road leads up the valley to the tiny mountain village of **Setcases**, a famous beauty-spot now heavily taken over by second homes, and also famous for its restaurants – locals joke that it has more of them than houses. By now you are well into the

Popping corks

Catalonia's most famous wines and all of its *cava*, or sparkling wine, come from the **Alt Penedès** west of Barcelona, one of the most respected wine-producing areas in Spain. **Vilafranca del Penedès**, the capital of the *comarca*, has a **Museu del Vi** (wine museum), with a fascinating display of wine-making equipment from across the centuries. The region's largest winemaker, **Bodegues Torres**, also offers guided tours from Monday to Saturday (890 32 26; booking essential).

Sixty per cent of the Alt Penedès is given over to vineyards. If Vilafranca is the main centre for table wine and brandies, neighbouring **Sant Sadurní d'Anoia** is the capital of the *cava* industry. **Codorníu** was the first company to begin *cava* production here, after Manuel Raventós, heir to the Codorníu estate, spent time working in the Champagne region in the 1870s, took detailed notes, and then reproduced the *méthode champenoise* in his native land. The vast cellars of the Can Codorníu building, from 1896-1906, are a beautiful example of the work of the Modernist architect Josep Puig i Cadafalch. All visits include a short film, a mini-train ride through the cellars and a *cava* tasting session. The advantage of the free weekday visits is that you see the cellar at work. At weekends, every visitor receives a free champagne glass as well as some *cava*, plus snacks.

Caves Freixenet, established in the 1920s, conducts cellar tours on weekdays only. Tours are free, and give a full run-down on their cellars and *cava* manufacturing process, as well as a tasting session. As well as these two, there are many more *caves* in Sant Sadurní that offer free tours; the tourist office has a full list. All the tours are given in English as well as several other languages.

Catalonia also has several other *denominació d'origen* wine-producing regions, such as the small **Alella**, around the town of the same name just east of Barcelona and best known for its whites, and more importantly **Priorat** and

Terra Alta, on either side of the River Ebro west of Tarragona. Falset and Gandesa, respectively, are the district capitals. The wines of both areas are heavier, stronger and less consistent than their Penedès equivalents, but can be of high quality: try the Priorat Scala Dei reds and Gandesa rosés. Local tourist offices have information on vineyard visits and tastings; in Gandesa, look out too for the **Cooperativa Agrícola**, another great Modernist contribution to the wine industry.

Caves Codorníu
Avda Codorníu, Sant Sadurní d'Anoia (818 32 32). **Open** 8am-12.30pm, 3pm-4.30 pm, Mon-Fri; 10am-1.30pm Sat, Sun. **Admission** Mon-Fri free; Sat, Sun 150ptas.

Caves Freixenet
C/Joan Sala 2, Sant Sadurní d'Anoia (818 32 00). **Tours** 9am, 10am, 11,30am, 3.30pm, 5pm, Mon-Thu; 9am, 10am, 11,30am, Fri. **Admission** free.

Museu del Vi
Plaça Jaume I 1, Vilafranca del Penedès (890 05 82). **Open** *Oct-May* 10am-2pm, 4-7pm, Tue-Sat; 10am-2pm Sun. *June-Sept* 9am-9pm Tue-Sat; 10am-2pm Sun. **Admission** 250ptas.

Wine Festivals
Most of the main wine-towns of Catalonia have festivals in autumn to celebrate the grape harvest (*verema*). In **Alella** it takes place very early, around the first weekend in September, when the year's first crushed grapes are blessed. Much larger are the events in **Vilafranca**, the first sunday in October, and **Sant Sadurní**, usually a week later. At each there are concerts, dances, exhibitions, tastings and other things going on, and in Sant Sadurní there's the crowning of the *Reina del Cava*, the Cava Queen, while most of the crowd get several free glasses of the product as well. Smaller towns have their own events; tourist offices have details.

Information
Getting there:
Alt Penedès: *By car* A2 then A7 direct to Sant Sadurní (44km) and Vilafranca del Penedès (55km), or A2 then turn onto toll-free N340 at Molins de Rei, which is much slower. *By train* RENFE from Sants or Plaça Catalunya, trains hourly 6am-10pm (45min).
Alella: *By bus* Autocars Casas (798 11 00) from corner of Gran Via and C/Roger de Flor. *By car* N11 north to Montgat, left turn to Alella (15km).
Falset & Gandesa: *By car* A2, then A7 via Vilafranca, to Reus, turn right onto N420 for Falset (143km) and Gandesa (181km). *By train* RENFE from Sants or Passeig de Gràcia to Marçà-Falset. Six trains a day; journey time approx two hours. For Gandesa, continue to Mora d'Ebre (another 20min) and catch local bus.
Tourist offices: Vilafranca del Penedès *C/Cort 14 (892 03 58)*; **Sant Sadurní d'Anoia** *Plaça de l'Ajuntament 1, baixos (891 12 12)*; **Gandesa** *Avda Catalunya (977/42 06 14)*.

Pyrenees, and the Ter valley road comes to an end at **Vallter 2000** (972/13 60 57), the easternmost ski station in the mountains, with 12 pistes and rental and sale of equipment. As with all ski resorts in the area, the best way to spend more than a day there is by booking a package, available at any travel agent in Barcelona.

Ribes de Freser, the first noteworthy town on the other main road from Ripoll, the N152 north, is an attractive place and a good base from which to travel to the picturesque-if-gentrified villages in the surrounding area, **Campelles** and especially **Queralbs**. Ribes is also the starting point for the *cremallera*, the FGC's narrow-gauge 'zipper train', which runs via Queralbs all the way up to the sanctuary of **Núria** through the valley of the same name along the Freser river. Núria itself, nestling by a lake in the middle of a plateau at over 2,000m (6,500 feet), is the home of the second-most-famous of Catalonia's patron virgins, a wooden statue of the Madonna carved in the twelfth century, and was already a refuge of hermits and place of pilgrimage long before then. The massively solid monastery around the shrine, most of it nineteenth-century, is not especially attractive, but its location is spectacular, and the zipper-train makes it an easily accessible place to try some high-mountain walking (*see* **walks in the woods**). It's also a winter-sports centre (972/73 07 13), especially suited to novice skiers.

Information

Getting there: *By bus* TEISA (972/20 48 68) from the corner of C/Pau Claris and C/Consell de Cent in Barcelona to Ripoll, Sant Joan de les Abadesses and Camprodon. *By car* N152 direct to Ripoll (104km), from Avda Meridiana. For Sant Joan de les Abadesses and Camprodon, take the C151 out of Ripoll. *By train* RENFE from Sants or Plaça Catalunya, approx two trains each hour (journey time to Ripoll approx 1hr 30min). For Queralbs and Núria change to the *cremallera* train in Ribes de Freser.
Tourist offices: Sant Joan de les Abadesses *(972/72 01 00);* **Ribes de Freser** *(972/72 71 84);* **Núria** *(972/73 07 13).*
Where to eat:
Ripoll: El Racó del Francès ('The Frenchman's Corner') *Plà d'Ordina 11 (972/70 18 94),* as its names suggests, serves French dishes(average 4,000ptas).
Sant Joan de les Abadesses:,Good, reasonably-priced local food can be found at the **Sant Pere** *C/Mestre Andreu 3 (972/72 00 77).*
Queralbs: The one good place to eat is **De La Plaça** *Plaça de la Vila 5 (972/72 70 37).*
Where to stay:
Ripoll: Good, cheap accomodation is available at **Ca la Paula** *C/Berenguer 8 (972/70 00 11)* for 3,000ptas per double (but no private bathrooms); **La Trobada** *Passeig Honorat Vilamanya 4 (972/70 23 53)* has more comfortable doubles for 7,500ptas.
Sant Joan de les Abadesses: Janpere *C/Mestre Andreu 3 (972/72 00 77)* is the best, at 6,000ptas. per double. There is very little accommodation at **Vallter**; most people stay over in towns further down the valley.
Ribes de Freser: Catalunya Park Hotel *Passeig Salvador Mauri 9 (972/72 71 98),* is very comfortable (7,000ptas per double); cheaper rooms are available at **Traces** *C/Nostra Senyora de Gràcia 1 (972/72 71 37)* for 4,000ptas per double.

Queralbs: L'Avet *C/Major (972/72 73 63)* is tiny; slightly larger is **Sierco** *C/Major 5 (972/72 73 77).* In **Núria**, there's a three-star hotel, the **Vall de Núria** *C/Santuari Mare de Déu de Núria (972/73 20 00)* for 7,500ptas a double, and a youth hostel, the **Alberg Pic de l'Aliga** *(972/73 00 48).*

Girona & Besalú

The most interesting and vibrant Catalan city after Barcelona and a virtual mini-capital in its own right, **Girona**'s origins go way back: it was one of the first Paleolithic farming communities in the region, a major trading town under the Romans, and a flourishing centre throughout the Middle Ages.

Its legacy from that time is one of the most impressive collection of Medieval buildings in Catalonia. The magnificent **Cathedral**, built from the eleventh to the fifteenth centuries, has a Romanesque cloister, a soaring Gothic nave and a five-storey tower. From the main façade, 90 steep steps lead down to the main street and the river Onyar, where the buildings packed alongside the river have been attractively renovated in varied colours.

Back at the top, just off the Cathedral square is the Carrer de la Força, leading to the uniquely atmospheric **Call**, the Medieval Jewish quarter, which has a centre for Jewish studies run by the last surviving native Jewish community on the peninsular.

Add to this the **Passeig Arqueològic**, a walk around the city's old wall; the **Banys Àrabs** – a thirteenth-century bathhouse built on the Moslem/Jewish model; seven other churches dating from between the eleventh and sixteenth centuries; an iron bridge designed by Eiffel; and the **Palau Episcopal**, with an art museum containing collections from the sixteenth to the nineteenth centuries, and you'll have a rough idea of the overall beauty of Girona. And the tradition looks set to continue: Girona today is an exceptionally active artistic and literary centre.

Banyoles, 16km north of Girona, is an attractive town divided into the **Vila Vella** or Old Town and the **Vila Nova** or New Town, both of which contain Medieval buildings. Its main attraction, though, is the nearby **Estany de Banyoles**, a natural lake in a former volcanic crater occupying over a million square metres, surrounded by several smaller lakes and containing many different types of fish. It is a very delicate environment and only eco-friendly watersports are permitted, but it hosted the rowing events in the '92 Olympics.

Besalú is a small, wonderfully peaceful Medieval town, founded in the tenth century. With hardly any modern buildings, even now, it seems suspended in time, and the whole of the town centre has been declared a monument. Of

*The remarkable twelfth-century fortified bridge of **Besalú**.*

special interest are the streets of the old Jewish *Call* and the *mikveh* (ritual Jewish baths), the two main squares and the church of **Santa Júlia**, but most eye-catching of all is the spectacular and entirely-intact twelfth-century fortified bridge over the Fluvià river.

The N260 road continues west, past extraordinary villages such as **Castellfullit de la Roca**, perched atop a precipitous crag, to **Olot**. The Medieval town was destroyed in an earthquake in 1427, but it has eighteenth-century and Modernist buildings that are unusually imposing for a town of this size. In the last century it was home to a school of landscape painters, and the local **Museu de la Garrotxa** has works by them and Casas, Rusiñol and other Modernist artists. Olot's most unusual feature, though, is that it is surrounded by some 30 long-extinct volcanoes and lava-slips, sometimes no more than green humps in the ground, which give the **Parc natural de la zona volcànica de la Garrotxa** a unique landscape.

Information

Getting there: *By bus* Take Barcelona Bus (232 04 59) to Girona from Estació del Nord; TEISA (972/20 48 68) runs to Banyoles, Besalú, Olot from the corner of C/Pau Claris and C/Consell de Cent. *By car* A7 or toll-free N11 to Girona. For Banyoles, Besalú, Olot, take the C150 from Girona (direction Besalú). *By train* RENFE from Sants or Passeig de Gràcia to Girona, trains hourly approximately 6am- 9.15pm (1hr 15min, Catalunya Exprés).

Tourist offices: Girona *Rambla Llibertat 1 (972/20 26 79;* **Banyoles** *(972/57 55 73).* **Olot** *C/Bisbe Lorenzana 15 (972/26 01 41).* These offices also have information on places to stay such as rural farmhouse lodgings in this area.

Where to eat:

Girona: **Albareda** *C/Albareda 7 (972/22 60 02),* is located in a historical building and has very high-quality fare costing around 4,000ptas. Somewhat cheaper (2,500 ptas) and certainly simpler is the very charming **Casa Marieta** *Plaça Independència 5 (972/20 10 16).*

Banyoles: **La Rectoria** *C/Espinavesa (972/55 35 51),* is a famous restaurant with a gourmet menu at 5,000ptas.

Besalú: Best restaurant is **Fonda Xiqués** *Avda Lluís Companys 6-8 (972/59 01 10)*, and cheaper food can be had at the attractive **Cúria Reial** *Plaça de la Llibertat 15 (972/59 02 63)*.
Olot: **Ramón** *Plaça Clarà 10 (972/26 10 01)* is the best value. With transport, **La Deu** *(972/26 10 04)*, on the Vic road, is well worth a visit – not least for its view.
Where to stay:
Girona: **Reyma** *C/Pujada del Rei Martí 15 (972/20 02 28)*, is a very comfortable *hostal* near the Jewish Quarter, for 6,000 ptas. a double. Rather more upmarket is the **Carlemany** *Plaça Miquel Santaló (972/21 12 12)*, a four-star hotel not far from the station, costing 13,000ptas per double room.
Banyoles: **Can Xabernet** *C/Carme 27 (972/57 02 52)* has double rooms for 7,000ptas; **L'Ast**, *Passeig Dalmau (972/54 61 54)*, has a swimming-pool and garden.
Besalú: **Venència** *C/Major 8 (972/59 12 57)* is cheap at 3,500ptas a double, or try the riverside **Siqués** above the Fonda Xiqués restaurant *(see above*
Where to eat).
Olot: The **Borrell** *C/Nònit Escubós 8 (972/26 92 75)*, with car park and wheelchair access, has doubles for 8,000ptas; the **Garrotxa** *Plaça de Móra 3 (972/26 16 12)*, is a bargain at 3,500ptas. a double.

Fire & food: country festivals

Every town and village in Catalonia has at least one major festival a year, some dating from the Middle Ages or earlier. There are literally thousands of local celebrations, at different times of the year, and for information on more of them the best place to look is in the Catalan Government's leaflets on individual *comarques* (districts).

One of the most famous is the *Patum*, held in the town of **Berga** every year at Corpus Christi, in late May or early June. They have coincided since the fourteenth century, thanks to an attempt by the Catholic Church to 'Christianise' the event, but the unique, bizarre creatures and rituals that appear in the *Patum* clearly hark back to pagan folklore. Throughout the Thursday of Corpus and the following night the streets of the old town are packed with people as, amid deafening noise, a series of strange costumed figures parade through (and often career into) the crowds, throwing out fireworks all the while – dwarfs, the Angel-knight, the dragon-like *Guites,* the magic eagle. First-time visitors should be warned that the *Patum* is a loud and rowdy, firework-based celebration at which people occasionally get injured. Many are also very drunk, but rarely ever violent.

Another melding of pagan tradition and Christian ritual, but less saturnalian, is the 500-year-old *Dansa de la Mort* ('Dance of Death'), which takes place at Easter, during the night before Good Friday, in the village of **Verges** in the Empordà. A procession of people dressed as skeletons and holding banners saying things like 'Life is short' parades through the streets in an eerie, meandering dance, to the beat of drums played by monk-figures wearing skull-masks.

More cheerful and a great deal more recent is the *Setmana Medieval* ('Medieval Week'), held in **Montblanc**. Each April 19-29, the town's inhabitants dress up in medieval outfits and set up a thirteenth-century fair, complete with tournaments, medieval theatre, all-but-forgotten crafts and a procession of flaming torches (for more information on Montblanc, *see* **The Royal Monasteries**).

The *Festa de la Calçotada* ('Feast of the Spring Onion') in the town of **Valls** is a ritual involving food and little else. Held on the last Sunday of January, this is a mass celebration of Valls' local vegetable the *calçot*, a special variety of large spring onion (scallion), which is char-grilled, peeled, dipped in a special *romesco* sauce and then tipped into the mouth (messily, but bibs are provided to protect your clothes). Although it's available in restaurants throughout Catalonia for several months of the year, the people of Valls claim that the only way to eat it is in their town, with their recipes, while looking at their scenery (*see also* chapter **Restaurants: The Catalan Menu**). Tàrrega, meanwhile, plays host each June to a three-day modern cultural festival, the **Fira del Teatre al Carrer** (Festival of Street Theatre), now an established international event.

Information

(For **Montblanc**, *see* **The Royal Monasteries**).
Getting there:
Berga: *By bus* Alsina Graells (265 68 66) from Estació del Nord, four buses daily (1hr 45min). *By car* A18 to Manresa, then C1411 to Berga (118km).
Verges: *By bus or train* To Girona (*see* **Girona & Besalú**), then Sarfa bus. *By car* A7 or N11 to Girona, C255 east, left turn to Torroella de Mongrí and Verges.
Valls: *By bus* Hispano Igualadina (430 43 44) from C/Europa, (behind the Corte Inglés on Avda Diagonal; Metro Maria Cristina). *By car* A2, then A7, then A2 to exit 11 and C246 to Valls, or N340 to Vendrell and C246 to Valls (100km). *By train* RENFE from Sants or Passeig de Gràcia, three trains each day (1hr 30min).
Tàrrega: *By bus* Alsina Graells (265 68 66) from Estació del Nord, four buses daily (journey time 1hr 55min). *By car* A2, then N11 west (97km). *By train* RENFE from Sants or Plaça Catalunya, three trains daily (3hrs 15min).
Tourist offices: **Berga** *C/dels Àngels 7 (821 03 04)*; **Torroella de Montgrí** (for Verges) *(972/75 89 10)*; **Valls** *Plaça del Blat 1 (977/60 10 43)*; **Tàrrega** *C/Agoders 16 (973/50 08 83)*.

The High Pyrenees

The *comarques* of the high Pyrenees, west of Andorra, reach altitudes of over 3,000m (9,800 feet), and contain some of the most spectacular scenery in the whole mountain range. They are also Catalonia's main districts for real mountain walking, adventure sports and skiing. Too far from Barcelona to be visitable in only a couple of days, they are great places to explore over a week or a long weekend.

The Pallars Sobirà

The Pallars Sobirà runs up to the French frontier alongside Andorra, a region of steep-sided valleys and flashing rivers, snow-covered in winter and idyllic in summer, with centuries-old villages of stone and slate that seem encrusted into the mountain sides. The capital of the *comarca* is **Sort**, the centre for organised sports in the area. There are plenty of companies in the town that organise white-water rafting and kayaking trips, bungee-jumping, caving and other adventure sports, and also hire out equipment. The tourist office has full details.

For winter, the area has two ski stations: **Super Espot**, (973/62 40 15), near the village of Espot, 24km north of Sort on a turn to the left after Llavorsi, a large, fully-equipped resort, and the newer, smaller **Port Ainé** (973/62 03 25), near the town of Rialb, just to the north of Sort. It is a much newer development, with fewer facilities. As at Vallter (*see* **Ripoll to the Vall de Núria**) they are best booked direct from Barcelona.

From spring to autumn there are different attractions. The same road that leads to Espot continues to the nature reserve of **Aigüestortes**, with a network of paths through alpine wilderness. At its centre is the **Estany de Sant Maurici**, a fabulously beautiful, crystal-clear mountain lake, but there are smaller lakes dotted all through the mountains.

In the park there are mountain shelters with full-time wardens, and given the remoteness of most areas you are advised to contact the park information centre in Espot (973/62 40 36), before embarking on any long hikes.

Information

Getting there: *By bus* Anònima Alsina Graells (265 68 66), one bus daily to Sort from Estació del Nord, leaves 7.30am and arrives 12.20pm. *By car* For Sort (approx 250km), take A18 to Manresa, C1410/C1412 to Tremp and then N260 north-east via Pobla de Segur.
Tourist office: Sort *(973/62 11 30).*
Where to eat:
Sort: There are any number of good traditional *fondes* in the old town, but **Hotel Pessets** *C/Diputació 3 (973/62 63 55)* specialises in high-quality local cuisine, wild boar stew (*civet de porc senglar*) and other specialities.
Espot: Casa Palmira *C/Únic (973/62 40 72)*, is the village's best-known restaurant.

Where to stay:
Sort: The **Ramón** *hostal, C/Major 3 (973/62 01 33)* is central and reasonably priced (3,500ptas a double), while **Pessets II** *C/Diputació 3 (973/62 00 00)* gives you a bar, swimming-pool, tennis courts, garden and restaurant for 8,000 ptas. a double.
Espot: The local luxury hotel is **Saurat** *C/Sant Martí (973/62 41 62)* costing 7,500ptas for a double room; **Sant Maurici** *C/Afores (973/62 40 40)* is a cheaper two star *hostal*.

The Val d'Aran

North of Sort, if you are travelling on the old C142 route, the road begins to wind ever more tightly up to one of the most spectacular mountain passes in Europe, the **Port de la Bonaigua** at 2,072m, which makes it very clear that the valley you are entering, the Val d'Aran, is actually on the north side of the Pyrenees, the source of the river Garonne, which meets the sea at Bordeaux. The valley is a district with an architectural style, administration and even language (Aranese, a dialect of Provençal) of its own, and that it is Spanish territory is purely an accident of history.

Vielha e Mijaran (usually just called Vielha), capital of the Val d'Aran, is a town worth visiting in its own right, for medieval houses such as **Çò de Rodés** and churches such as **Sant Pèir d'Escunhau** and **Sant Miquèu**. The valley is another great walking area, but is best known for winter sports, at its two amply-equipped ski stations: **Tuca-Malh Blanc** (973/64 10 50), south of Vielha near the village of Betren, and the giant, jet-setty **Baqueira-Beret** (973/64 44 55), patronised, among others, by the Spanish royal family.

Information

Getting there: *By bus* Anònima Alsina Graells (265 68 66), two buses daily from Estació del Nord, at 6.30am and (via Sort) 7.30am. Journey time 5hrs 45min, more if via Sort. *By car* From Sort (*see above*), C147 and C142 continue to Port de la Bonaigua (55km, but journey takes well over one hour). Most direct route from Barcelona is A18 to Manresa, C1410/C1412 to Tremp and N260 north-east from Pobla de Segur, to enter Val d'Aran by the Vielha tunnel at western end of the valley. Distance to Vielha 320km.
Tourist office: Vielha *C/Sarriulera 6 (973/64 01 10).*
Where to eat:
Vielha: Good and cheap is **Nicolàs** *C/Castèth 10 (973/64 18 20)*, while **Èra Mola** *C/Marrec 8 (973/64 24 19)* is the city's most typically Aranese restaurant.
Betren: La Borda de Betren *C/Major (973/64 00 32)*, is a rustically-decorated restaurant near Tuca-Malh Blanc
Where to stay:
Vielha: The town is rather expensive, but the **Aran** *Avda Castiero 5 (973/64 00 50)* is very reasonably priced at 9,000ptas a double in high season. Cheaper still (3,500ptas double) is the **Busquets** *C/Major 9 (973/64 02 38)*.
Baqueira: The ski resort has **Val de Ruda** *C/Carretera de la Bonaigua (973/64 58 11)*, a two star hotel dwarfed by two nearby, very expensive luxury hotels.
Betren: There is only one hotel, the **Tuca** *C/Carretera Salardú (973/64 07 00)*, complete with disco, pool and everything else for 6,900-14,300ptas per double.

Walks in the woods

Hill-walking and hiking (*excursionisme*) is one of the most popular Catalan recreations. This is hardly surprising, considering the walking opportunities provided by the area – one fifth of the country is covered by the Pyrenees, just for starters. As well as this massive range, the lesser mountains closer to Barcelona contain any number of beautiful places for less strenuous rambling.

One of the most rewarding summer walks is the 15-kilometre trip from the end of the mountain railway in **Núria** back down to **Queralbs** (or uphill in the opposite direction, to make it more difficult). The track descends past rushing streams and wild flowers through a steep gorge, and with luck you can see eagles soaring overhead. More serious hikers can continue up from Núria to the peak of **Puigmal** (2,913m), a two-and-a-half-hour walk.

Closer to Barcelona is the massif of the **Montseny**, south of Vic. A road and a rail line run right through the main valley, making access easy, and well-marked paths lead off into the pine-clad hills from right outside the two best starting points, the villages of **Aiguafreda** and **Figueró**. Two favourite walks are from Aiguafreda to the Dòlmens de la Serra de l'Arca, passing through Can Picamena (about four hours), or from Figueró to the peak of Tagamanent – at 1,056m (3,780 feet), and with a mountain chapel – and back (about four-and-a-half hours), but there are many more, and the whole area is a walkers' paradise. From further north in **Rupit**, there's a long (six hour) but beautiful walk along the cliffs of Casadavall to El Far, with superb views over the canyon-like gorge of the River Ter, and then back along the same path.

Montserrat is another place that offers a great range of walks, especially the paths that run away from the main monastery along the ridges of pointed rocks that give the place its unique silhouette. Not as spectacular but close by is the mountain of **Sant Llorenç del Munt**, between Montserrat and the Montseny. An enjoyable walk to the peak, where there is a monastery and a restaurant/bar whose supplies still arrive by donkey, starts from the village of Matadepera, north of Terrassa, and goes along the Camí dels Monjos and back down by the Camí de la Font Soleia (about three hours).

Catalonia now has an increasingly well-developed set of long-distance footpaths criss-crossing the country. Information on them and most other hiking areas is available from Generalitat tourist offices (*see chapter*

Essential Information). The best local walkers' maps are those produced by the *Editorial Alpina*, and *Edicions Proa* publishes a series of beginner's hiking manuals (*Caminant per Catalunya*), in Catalan only, but with very clear diagrams and information about public transport and other facilities. Both series and other useful publications can be found at **Llibreria Quera** and other specialised bookshops in Barcelona (*see chapter* **Shopping**). When you do make a trip into the hills, stock up on water on the way, since mountain streams can run very dry in summer, and if camping be sure to acquaint yourself with current instructions on lighting fires, as every year thousands of hectares of pines are lost to forest fires.

Information

(For **Núria**, **Rupit**, **Montserrat**, see the respective main sections).

Montseny: *By bus* Empresa Sagalés (231 27 56) from the corner of Passeig Sant Joan and C/Diputació (Metro Tetuan) to Vic stops at Figueró and Aiguafreda. *By car* N152 from Barcelona, direction Vic and Puigcerdà (approx 45km). You can also approach the Montseny from the south-east, by the A7 and C251 to Sant Celoni (60km). *By train* RENFE from Sants or Plaça Catalunya (Vic line), approx two trains hourly (journey time 50min).

Sant Llorenç del Munt: *By car* A18 or N150 (exit 1 off Ronda de Dalt) to Terrassa, then C1415 east to Matedepera. *By train & bus* RENFE or FGC from Plaça Catalunya to Terrassa, then local bus to Matedepera.

Survival

Survival

Phones, pharmacies, car parking and things lost on buses: ready solutions to life's dilemmas.

Bureaucracy/Living/Working

Although the Catalan economy is still quite healthy – and conditions are good for those in work – unemployment throughout Spain is officially around 20 per cent, and so for foreigners some kinds of jobs will not be easy to come by. Over the past ten years people from other EU countries have been able to work in an increasingly wide range of fields in Barcelona – medicine, architecture, the drinks trade, publishing – but if you've just arrived your best chances of finding work will still be in English teaching and/or translation, even though, since the city is one of the most popular destinations for EFL teachers, the market looks increasingly saturated.

If you are looking for teaching work it is very advisable to have a relevant qualification, preferably the full RSA Diploma. If you get work in a school, it will initially usually be on only a nine-month contract. There is always private teaching work available, although such are the numbers of people offering private classes in Barcelona nowadays that rates can be very low; you should try not to accept anything under 2,000ptas an hour.

To get your first classes, try putting up ads on the noticeboards at the **British Institute**, C/Amigó 83 (209 63 88), in the **Come In** bookshop (*see chapter* **Shopping**) or at the Barcelona universities, or ask around among English teachers.

If you stay and work here there are various bureaucratic hurdles you will be required to negotiate. If you come to work for a company having been contracted in your country of origin, any paperwork should be dealt with by your employer, who should also organise your tax and Social Security numbers and contributions.

Residency & related paperwork

EU citizens working for a Company/*Cuenta Ajena*

In the last few years paperwork has become at least a little easier for EU citizens working in Spain. Work permits as such no longer exist, but you must become a **resident** to work legally (you will also require a *NIE/NIF, see below* **EU citizens working freelance**).To become a resident you will need a contract or a firm offer of work (which can be for only three hours a week and with no stipulated duration, although there is no guarantee that this will be sufficient), and an application form, which is obtained from the special office for foreigners' affairs at the **Gobierno Civil** (*see below*). Note that there are different sections for *nacionales comunitarios* (EU) and *no-comunitarios*; for *comunitarios*, procedures can now be got through fairly quickly. They will also require two photocopies of the information pages of your passport and four photographs, and will ask for something in the region of 850ptas in *papel de estado*, official money vouchers, which must be purchased in *estancs*, tobacco shops. Keep photocopies yourself of all documents submitted. You may also be asked, arbitrarily, for a medical certificate and/or proof of sufficient funds. You will normally be given a Type A residency permit, valid for 12 months and not automatically renewable. This ties you to the company, region and business sector for which you have registered and, technically, you must leave the country on its expiry. Should you reapply successfully at that time, you will be issued a Type C permit, which lasts for five years and is renewable.

EU citizens working freelance/*Cuenta Própia*

To work freelance, as a *trabajador autónomo/a* or *trabajador por cuenta própia*, en essential first step is to obtain a *Número de Identificación Fiscal* or *NIF* (tax code), which as a foreigner will be the same as your *Número de Identificación de Extranjero* (*NIE*); you will find it very difficult to do any consistent business without one. You will also find it virtually indispensable to contract the services of a *Gestor* (*see chapter* **Business**) to advise you on legal procedures and tax; without one, you will waste both time and money. A *NIF/NIE* can be obtained from the Gobierno

There are many ways of supplementing your income, not all of them reliable.

Civil (*see below*), your local Tax Office (*Delegación de Hacienda*), the address of which will be in the phone book, or through your *Gestor*, which is the easiest way to do it. Once you have this number, you can open a bank account, request a telephone line, be paid by other businesses and so on. The next stop is also in the Tax Office: at the *Actividades Económicas* desk fill in form 845, specifying which sector (*Enseñanza*, for teaching) you wish to work in, and form 036, the *Declaración Censal*, and keep copies of both. Next, officially, is a visit to your local Social Security office (*Delegación de Seguridad Social*) to say you want the *alta como autónomo*; this is one point where the advice of a *Gestor* is particularly important, as the contributions you are theoretically obliged to pay can be very high (30,000ptas per month), and he/she can suggest alternatives. As an *autónomo* you will have a Social Security number, and in future will be obliged to make annual tax declarations. Once you have this initial documentation you can apply for a *Cuenta Própia* residency permit at the Gobierno Civil, with the same information (passport, proof of earnings, etc) as for the *Cuenta Ajena* permit (*see above*). If you are looking for work in areas other than teaching, with your *NIF* you can also use the efficient Generalitat employment service (*Servei Català de Col.locació*, information freephones 902 22 11 11/902 22 10 44).

Non-EU citizens

First-time applicants officially need a special visa, for which you must apply at the nearest Spanish Consulate in your home country, although you can begin the process in Spain if you don't mind making at least one trip back home. The basic documents needed are a contract or firm offer of work from a registered Spanish company, a medical certificate and a certificate of good conduct from your local police force. You must present these with various passport-style photos and translated copies of any relevant qualifications to the Consulate, who will pass them on to the Labour Ministry in Madrid. If they approve them the Consulate will then issue your special visa (this can take six months). If you apply to work freelance or to start your own business the procedures are slightly different and you will also be asked for proof of income. Once back in Spain the procedures for applying for your residency permit are similar to those for European citizens (*see above*), but you will also need a work permit,

obtainable not from the Gobierno Civil but from the **Dirección General del Trabajo** in Travessera de Gràcia (*see chapter* **Business**).

Students

Students who stay in Barcelona for over three months, including EU citizens, also officially require a residence permit, and students enrolled on full-time courses may find it creates difficulties if they do not obtain one. To do so, you will need to show the Gobierno Civil a confirmation of enrolment on a recognised course; a confirmation of income for the period of the course, currently estimated at a minimum of 740,000ptas for a 12-month period; and confirmation of health insurance status, either private or public.

Gobierno Civil

Avda Marqués de l'Argentera 2 (482 03 00/03 11/fax 482 04 13/04 14). Metro Barceloneta/bus 16, 17, 36, 40, 45, 57, 59, 64. **Open** *9am-2pm Mon-Fri.*

Renting a Flat

Since the peak of the 1992 boom passed by it has become rather easier to find vacant flats in Barcelona on reasonable terms. The best local paper for property ads is *La Vanguardia* (look under *Alquileres*), and the specialised classifieds magazines also have long lists (*see chapter* **Media**); otherwise, just look for signs headed *es lloga* (Catalan) or *se alquila* in apartment-block doorways. The fundamental element in determining your rights and obligations as a tenant is the individual rental contract (*contracte de lloguer/contrato de alquiler*) signed by you and the landlord. These contracts can vary a great deal, and before signing it's very important to be clear about the exact conditions in your contract, particularly regarding responsibility for repairs.

Contracts of over 12 months' duration are subject to an annual rental increase of not more than the official inflation rate, the *IPC* (*Indice de Precios al Consumo*, retail price index, published regularly in the press). In the current climate, though, landlords may be keen to keep good tenants, and might be willing to waive the first year's increase, or make other concessions. Note that for residents rents paid are tax deductible, provided you have all the necessary receipts. For more information on flat-sharing, *see chapter* **Students**.

Communications

For fax bureaux, *see chapter* **Services**. For courier and messenger services, *see chapter* **Business**.

Post

The central post office at the end of Via Laietana, by the port, is the main centre for all postal services. If, though, you only want to buy normal-rate stamps for postcards or letters it is much easier to do so in any *estanc* or tobacco shop (*see chapter* **Essential Information**).

Correu Central

Plaça Antoni López (318 38 31). Metro Barceloneta/bus 16, 17, 36, 40, 45, 57, 59, 64. **Open** 8am-10pm Mon-Fri; 9am-8pm Sat; 9am-1pm Sun.

In the imposing main post office the different postal services are available at separate windows around the main hall: parcel post, telegrams, telex and so on. Faxes can be sent and received at all post offices, but rates are expensive, and it's better to use private fax bureaux. There is an information desk by the main entrance. Note that within the general opening times not all services are available at all times. Letters sent Poste Restante (General Delivery) to Barcelona should be addressed to *Lista de Correos, 08070 Barcelona, Spain*. To collect them go to windows 34-36, with your passport. To send a letter by express post, say you want to send it *urgente*.

Other centrally-located post offices (open 9am-2.30pm Mon-Fri; 9.30am-1pm Sat):

Plaça Bonsuccès. Metro Catalunya/bus all routes to Plaça Catalunya.

Ronda Universitat 23. Metro Catalunya/bus all routes to Plaça Catalunya.

C/València 231. Metro Passeig de Gràcia/bus 7. 16. 17. 20, 21, 43, 44.

Postal Rates & Post Boxes

Letters and postcards weighing up to 20gm cost 19ptas within Barcelona, 30ptas to the rest of Spain, 60ptas to EU countries, 70ptas to the rest of Europe, 114ptas to the US and Canada and 160ptas to Asia and Australasia. Cards and letters to other European countries generally arrive in three to four days, and to North America in about a week. Aerogrammes (*Aerogramas*) cost 70ptas for all destinations. Normal post boxes are yellow, with two horizontal red stripes. There are also a few special red post boxes for urgent mail, with hourly collections.

Postal Exprés

Available at all post offices, this is an efficient express post system with guaranteed next-day delivery anywhere within Spain of packages weighing up to 1kg for 500ptas. It is the most convenient and reliable way of sending small packages within Spain.

Telephones

The Spanish national phone company (*Telefónica*) is a much-derided local institution. Charges are high, particularly for international calls. It is cheaper to call after 10pm and before 8am, Monday to Saturday, and all day on Sundays.

Phone Numbers

In the last year many Barcelona numbers beginning with a *2* have been changed to begin with a *4*. If you are ever given a phone number starting with a *2* and cannot get through, try redialling substituting a *4* as the first digit.

Public Phone Boxes

In older-model phones, you insert the coins into a slot or aperture at the top of the phone before dialling, and then the coins will begin to drop when the call is answered. For a local call (minimum 13ptas) you will need to insert three *duros* (five peseta coins) and you will not get change if you put in a 25 or 50ptas coin. Ever more common, though, are newer-model phones that accept coins, phonecards and credit cards, and also have a digital display with instructions in four languages including English. They will also give you credit to make further calls without having to reinsert your money, and are much more likely to work properly than the old-style call phones. Phonecards cost 1,000 or 2,000 ptas and can be bought in post offices or *estancs*. In addition, most bars and cafés have a telephone for public use. They usually accept 5 and 25ptas coins, but in some bars they are set to take only 25ptas, an illegal but not-uncommon practice.

International & Long-distance Calls

To make an international call, dial 07, wait for a loud continuous tone and then dial the country code: **Australia** 61; **Canada** 1; **Irish Republic** 353; **New Zealand** 64; **United Kingdom** 44; **USA** 1, followed by the area code (omitting the first zero in UK codes) and individual number. To call Barcelona from abroad, dial the international code (00 in the UK), then 34 for Spain and 3 for Barcelona. If you are calling a Barcelona number from anywhere else within Spain the area code is 93.

Phone Centres

At phone centres (*Locutorios*) you are allotted a booth and pay at the counter when you have finished all your calls, thus avoiding the need for pocketloads of change.

Centres: *La Rambla 88. Metro Liceu/bus 14, 18, 38, 59, 64, 59, 91.* **Open** 10am-11pm daily.

Main vestibule, Estació de Sants. **Open** 8am-10.15pm Mon-Sat; 8am-9pm Sun, public holidays.

Main vestibule, Universitat Metro, Plaça Universitat. **Open** 9am-10pm Mon-Sat; 9am-2pm Sun, public holidays.

Vestibule, Estació d'Autobusos Barcelona-Nord, C/Ali Bei 80. Metro Arc de Triomf/bus all routes to Arc de Triomf. **Open** 8am-11pm Mon-Fri.

Operator services

All services are normally in Catalan and Spanish only.

National directory enquiries 003
International directory enquiries 025
National operator 009
International operator *Europe & North Africa* 008; *Rest of World* 005
Telephone breakdowns 002
Telegrams 322 20 00.
Time 093
Weather information 094
Alarm calls 096

Once the message has finished (when it starts repeating itself), key in the number you are calling from followed by the time at which you wish to be woken, in four figures, ie. 0830 if you want to be called at 8.30am.

General information 098

A local information service provided by Telefónica, with information particularly on duty pharmacies in Barcelona. Otherwise, it is generally less reliable than the 010 line (*see chapter* **Essential Information**).

Consulates

For a full list of consulates in Barcelona look in the local phone book under *Consulats/Consulados*. Outside the office hours listed all the consulates have answerphones which will provide you with an emergency contact number. There is no longer a Canadian consulate in Barcelona; Canadian citizens in difficulties should contact the Embassy in Madrid on 91/431 43 00. For more information on what to do if you lose a passport, *see below* **Police & Security**.

American Consulate
Passeig Reina Elisenda 23 (280 22 27). FGC Reina Elisenda/bus 22, 64, 75. **Open** 9am-12.30pm, 3-5pm, Mon-Fri.

Australian Consulate
Gran Via Carles III 98 (330 94 96). Metro Maria Cristina/bus 59, 70, 72, 75. **Open** 10am-noon Mon-Fri. Closed Aug.

British Consulate
Avda Diagonal 477 (419 90 44). Bus all routes to Plaça Francesc Macià. **Open** *end Sept-mid-June* 9.30am-1.30pm, 4-5pm, Mon-Fri; *mid-June-mid-Sept* 9am-2pm Mon-Fri.

Irish Consulate
Gran Via Carles III 94 (491 50 21). Metro Maria Cristina/bus 59, 70, 72, 75. **Open** 10am-1pm Mon-Fri.

New Zealand Consulate
Travessera de Gràcia 64, 4º 2ª (209 03 99). FGC Gràcia/bus 16, 17, 27, 58, 64. **Open** 9.30am-1.30pm, 5-6.30pm, Mon-Fri.

Disabled travellers

Barcelona is one of those cities where disabled people, especially wheelchair users, can have mixed experiences. Accessible buses are in use at present on just a few routes, but are becoming more widespread, and there is a limited special taxi service (*see chapter* **Getting Around**). The main railway stations, Sants, França, Passeig de Gràcia and Plaça Catalunya, are fully accessible to wheelchairs, and this, and the existence of a special phoneline for transport information for the disabled (412 44 44) are evidence of an official desire to improve facilities as much as possible. The resources devoted to this in practice, however, remain limited. There is an ongoing programme to provide access at all Metro stations, but when it will be completed is another question; so, some stations, such as Universitat, have lavish facilities, while others have none.

Through the nineties, though, and spurred on by the experience of the Paralympic Games of 1992, there has been a visible greater awareness of the need to take disabled needs into account. The city's new museums, such as MACBA, and those that have been recently remodelled, such as the MNAC, all incorporate model facilities for full access. Older museums, though, can be much more of a problem. Thanks to the **ONCE** (Spain's lottery-funded organisation for the blind) more has traditionally been done on behalf of blind and partially-sighted people. Most street crossings in the centre have identifiable, knobbled paving and low kerbs.

Institut Municipal de Disminüits
C/Comte d'Urgell 240 (439 66 00). Metro Hospital Clínic/bus 14, 54, 59, 66. **Open** 9am-2pm Mon-Fri.
The official city organisation for the disabled collates information on changes in access and other facilities, and produces a range of leaflets on access in different fields (museums, theatres and others).

Driving in Barcelona

Driving in Barcelona can be wearing. Jams are frequent, parking space is at a premium, and tempers run short, although local 'road rage' is verbal rather than anything worse. Many local residents seem firmly wedded to the idea that the car is the best way of moving from one district to another, but one often wonders why, for within the city a private car rarely seems the quickest way of getting anywhere. It is a great asset, though, for trips outside the city (*see chapter* **Trips Out of Town**). If you do drive in or around Barcelona, some points to bear in mind are listed below. For information on car and motorcycle hire, *see chapter* **Services**.
• You can drive in Spain with a valid license from most other countries, but it is useful also to have an international driving license, available in Britain from the AA and RAC.
• Keep your driving license, vehicle documents and insurance Green Card with you at all times.
• It is obligatory to wear seat belts at all times in cities as well as on main highways, and to carry a warning triangle in your car.
• Children under 14 may not travel in the front of a car.
• Speeding fines imposed on motorways (*autopistes*) and other main highways, policed by the Guardia Civil and the Mossos d'Escuadra, are payable on the spot.
• Do not leave anything of value, including a car radio, in your car, and do not leave bags or coats in view on the seats. Take all of your luggage into your hotel when you park your car.
• In general drivers go as fast as they can irrespective of the speed limit. At traffic lights at least two cars will follow through on the amber light as it changes between green and red. Do not therefore stop sharply when you see a light begin to change, as the car behind will not be expecting this and could easily run into your back.
• When oncoming drivers flash their lights at you this means that they will *not* slow down (contrary to British practice). On main highways, the flashing of lights is usually a helpful warning that there is a speed trap up ahead.

Spanish Residents
If you become resident in Spain you must exchange your foreign licence for a Spanish one. The best way to do so is through the **RACC** (*see below*), which will take care of all the paperwork for you for about 14,000ptas. EU and US citizens do not need to take another driving test on exchanging their licences, but citizens of other countries may have to.

Breakdown Services

If you are taking a car to Spain it is advisable to join a motoring organisation such as the AA or RAC in Britain, or the AAA in the US. They have reciprocal arrangements with the local equivalent, the **RACC**, which is by far the most convenient source of assistance for drivers in distress. If you

You will be very very pleased to see this man if you break down in Barcelona.

need more than emergency repairs, main dealers for most makes of car will be found in the local yellow pages under *Automòbils/Automóviles*.

RACC (Reial Automòbil Club de Catalunya)

C/JSantaló 8 (200 33 11/24-hour breakdown assistance freephone 900 33 23 32/medical emergencies 900 36 55 05). Bus 6, 7, 14, 15, 27, 30, 33, 34, 58, 64. **Open** *Phonelines* 24 hours daily. *Office Sept-May* 9am-2pm, 4.30-7.30pm, Mon-Fri; *June-Sept* 9am-2.30pm Mon-Fri.

The RACC has English-speaking staff and will send immediate assistance if you have a breakdown. If you are outside Barcelona, you should call the emergency freephone number, but you will be referred on to another local number. Repairs are carried out on the spot where possible; if not, your vehicle will be towed to the nearest suitable garage. Members of foreign affiliated organisations are not charged for call outs. The RACC also provides a range of other services for foreign drivers at low prices, and for free or at preferential rates for members of affiliated organisations

Midas

Via Augusta 81-83 (217 81 61). FGC Gràcia/bus 16, 17, 27, 30. **Open** 8am-8pm Mon-Fri; 9am-2pm Sat. **Credit** AmEx, DC, MC, V.

An exhaust, brakes and filter repairer, offering a while-you-wait service. There are 14 more branches in Barcelona.

Neumáticos Roger de Flor SA

C/Roger de Flor 133 (231 66 16). Metro Girona/bus 6, 7, 18, 19, 50, 51, 54, 55. **Open** 7am-10pm daily. **Credit** V.

A quick-service tyre repair workshop.

Vidrauto

C/Mallorca 342 (458 36 44/459 03 64). Metro Verdaguer/bus 6, 15, 33, 34, 55. **Open** 9am-1.30pm, 3.30-8pm, Mon-Fri; 9am-1.30pm, 4-7.30pm, Sat. **Credit** AmEx, MC, V.

Vidrauto can replace all kinds of autoglass.

Parking

Parking is never easy in central Barcelona. The Municipal Police frequently give out tickets (which many people never pay), and tow cars away, which leaves you with no option. Be careful not to park in front of doorways with the sign *Gual Permanent*, indicating an entry with 24-hour right of access. In some parts of old city, notably La Ribera and the Barri Gòtic, not only parking but also entering with a car is banned to non-residents for much of the day. Large signs indicate when this is so.

Pay & Display areas (Zones Blaves)

Many streets in the central area and the Eixample are pay-and-display areas (*Zones Blaves*, Blue Zones), with parking spaces marked in blue on the street. Ticket machines will be nearby. Parking restrictions in these areas apply only 9am-2pm, Mon-Sat. During these times you are allowed to park for a maximum of two hours; the charges are 60ptas for 15min, 125ptas for 30min, 250ptas for one hour and 500ptas for two hours. If you overstay your time and are given a penalty ticket you can cancel the fine by paying an additional 500ptas. To do so, press the button *Anul.lar denúncia*, insert 500ptas and take the receipt that then comes out of the machine. The machines accept credit cards (MC, V), but do not give change.

Car Parks

Central Car Parks *C/Àngels, Plaça dels Àngels, Avda Paral.lel, Avda Francesc Cambó, Moll de la Fusta, C/Urgell, Plaça Gal.la Placídia.* **Open** 24 hours daily.

The 23 municipal underground *parkings* are indicated by a white 'P' on blue sign, with another to indicate if spaces are available: *Ple/Lleno* means full; *Lliure/Libre* means there are spaces. Rates vary: those in the centre cost 250ptas per hour, in less busy areas the rate is 150ptas per hour; at the city car parks you can also buy special payment cards, usable at all of them, valid for periods from 10 hours (1,800ptas) to 100 hours (15,000ptas), which work out more economical than paying each time. You are especially recommended to use a car park if you are driving a car with foreign plates.

Metro-Park
Plaça de les Glòries. **Open** 24 hours daily. **Credit** MC, V.
The Metro-Park is a special car park service on a similar principle to park-and-ride, and can be recommended to anyone coming to Barcelona by car from the coast for a day and so not really needing it while they are here. For 600ptas you are able to leave your car from 5am-11pm, Mon-Thur, and 5am-1am, Fri-Sat, and receive a card giving unlimited travel for one person for one day on Metro and city buses (but not the FGC). The car park is in the middle of Plaça de les Glòries, conveniently at the junction of the Diagonal, Meridiana and Gran Via, and by Glòries Metro, on line 1.

Towing Away & Car Pounds
(092). **Credit** AmEx, MC, V.
If your car has been towed away by the Municipal Police they will leave a yellow sticker on the pavement near where you left it. Call the central number (open 24 hours) and quote your car number plate to be told which of the many city car pounds your vehicle has gone to. Staff do not normally speak English. It will cost 14,000ptas to recover your vehicle during the first four hours after it was towed away, plus 240ptas for each additional hour after that, up to a maximum of 24,000ptas per 24-hour period.

Petrol

Most petrol stations (*Gasolineres*) now have unleaded fuel (*sense plom/sin plomo*) as well as regular (*super*). Diesel fuel is *gas-oil*.

24-hour petrol stations
There are several petrol stations open 24-hours throughout the year: the following are a selection in or near the central area. Petrol stations on motorways are also open 24-hours.
Raval/Poble Sec: Campsa Avda Paral.lel 37, corner of C/Palaudaries. **Credit** AmEx, MC, V.
Poble Sec/Plaça d'Espanya: Total Avda Paral.lel 150, corner of C/Rocafort. **Credit** V.
These stations also have 24-hour shops on site.
Eixample: Cepsa C/Casanova 89, corner of C/Aragó. **Credit** MC, V.
Near Plaça Francesc Macià: Cepsa C/Comte d'Urgell 230, junction with Avda Sarrià. **Credit** AmEx, MC, V.
Clot: BP C/Clot 2, junction with Avda Meridiana heading north. **Credit** MC, V.
Ronda de Dalt: BP Via Favència 133, near Parc de la Guineueta, on north side. **Credit** MC, V.

Health

All visitors can obtain emergency health care through the local national health service, the *Seguretat Social/Seguridad Social.* EU citizens are entitled to basic medical attention for free if they have an E111 form, although if you can get an E111 sent or faxed within four days you are still exempt from charges. Many medicines will be charged for. In non-emergency situations short-term visitors will find that it is usually quicker and more convenient to use private travel insurance rather than the E111 and the state system. Similarly, non-EU nationals with private medical insurance can also make use of state health services on a paying basis, but other than in emergencies it will be simpler to use a private clinic.

If you become a Spanish resident and contribute to the *Seguridad Social* you will be allocated a doctor and a local health clinic within the state system (*see above* **Bureaucracy/Living/Working**). Information on different aspects of local health services is available from the city health institute, or the **010** information line (*see chapter* **Essential Information**).

Institut Municipal d'Assistència Sanitaria/Informació Sanitària
Plaça Lesseps 1 (415 00 66). Metro Lesseps/bus 22, 24, 25, 27, 28, 30, 31, 32, 74, **Open** 8.30am-2.30pm Mon-Fri.
The city health administration office also operates as a phoneline for information on local health services or related matters.

Emergencies/Hospitals

In a medical emergency the best thing to do is to go to the Casualty (*Urgències*) department of any of the main hospitals. All are open 24 hours daily. If you are in the central area, go to the **Clínic** or the **Perecamps**. If necessary, call an ambulance on **061**.

Centre d'Urgències Perecamps
Avda Drassanes 13-15 (441 06 00). Metro Drassanes/bus 14, 18, 38, 59, N4, N6, N9.
A centrally-located specialised casualty centre, dealing only with emergencies.

Hospital Clínic
C/Casanova 143 (454 60 00). Metro Hospital Clínic/bus 14, 54, 59, 66, N3.
The main city-centre hospital, in the *Esquerra* (left side) of the Eixample.

Hospital de la Creu Roja de Barcelona
C/Dos de Maig 301 (433 15 51). Metro Hospital de Sant Pau/bus 15, 19, 20, 25, 45, 47, 50, 51, 92, N1, N5.

Hospital del Mar
Passeig Marítim 25-29 (309 21 12). Metro Ciutadella-Vila Olímpica/bus 45, 5, 71.
In the Barceloneta, near the beach. This hospital has a special clinic for infectious diseases, including AIDS.

Hospital de la Santa Creu i Sant Pau
C/Sant Antoni Maria Claret 167 (347 31 33). Metro Hospital de Sant Pau/bus 15, 19, 20, 25, 45, 47, 50, N1, N5.

Local Clinics (*Centres d'Assistència Primària*)
If you have no E111, no private insurance and are not within the local Social Security system you will still be attended at Hospital *urgències* departments. Alternatively, go to a *CAP*, lower-level local health centres where you will receive first aid and if necessary be sent on to a hospital. All are open 24 hours daily.
Central area:
Casc Antic *C/Comtal 20 (310 14 21/310 50 98).*
Drassanes *Avda Drassanes 17-21 (329 44 95/329 39 12)*
Esquerra de l'Eixample *C/Manso 19 (325 28 00).*
Raval/Plaça Universitat *C/Torres i Amat 8 (301 24 82/301 24 24).*

Private Health Care

Assistència Mèdica Integral
C/Teodora Lamadrid 42, baixos 2na (212 83 83). FGC Putxet/bus 17. **Open** 24 hours daily. **Credit** MC, V.
A comprehensive private service specialising in emergency or short-notice calls, who will make house- or hotel-calls throughout the city. Several of the doctors speak English.

Dr. Frances Lynd
C/Provença 281, baixos (215 37 93). Metro Diagonal, FGC Provença/bus 20, 21, 43, 44. **Open** 8am-8pm Mon-Fri.
Dr Lynd is a British doctor who has been practising in Barcelona for several years. She is often only at this surgery in person 3-6pm on Wednesdays; at other times, though, you can always call to make an appointment and she will ring you back.

Pharmacies

Pharmacies, *farmàcies*, are signalled by large green, usually flashing, crosses, and are plentiful throughout the city. They are normally open 9am to 1.30pm, 4.30 to 8pm, Monday to Saturday. At all other times a duty rota operates: every pharmacy has a list of *farmàcies de guàrdia* (duty pharmacies) for that day posted outside the door. Those marked in black provide a full service till 10pm, but still close for lunch; those in blue are open all day 9am-10pm, and 9am-1.30pm on Sundays. Those marked in red are on permanent emergency duty (*servei d'urgència*), from 10pm-9am and from 1.30pm on Sundays. This list is also published in local newspapers, and information is available on the *010* and *098* phonelines (recorded message, in Spanish only, between 9.30pm and 8.30am). Note that at night duty pharmacies often appear to be closed, and it's necessary to knock on the shutters to be served.

Dentists

Dentists are not covered by EU reciprocal agreements, so private rates, which can be costly, apply.

Centre Odontològic de Barcelona
C/Calàbria 251, baixos (439 45 00). Metro Entença/bus 41. **Open** 9am-8pm Mon-Fri; 9am-2pm Sat. **Credit** MC, V.
Well-equipped clinics providing a complete range of dental services. Several of the staff speak English.
Branch: Institut Odontològic de la Sagrada Família C/Sardenya 319, baixos (457 04 53). Metro Sagrada Família/bus 19, 50. **Open** 9am-8pm Mon-Fri; 9am-1pm, 3-8pm, Sat.

AIDS/HIV

There are facilities for AIDS/HIV treatment at all the main hospitals, and a special clinic at the **Hospital del Mar** (*see above* **Emergencies/ Hospitals**).

Confidential AIDS Helpline
(339 87 56). **Open** 9am-5.30pm Mon-Fri.
An official health information srvice run by the Ajuntament, with some English-speaking staff.

Contraception & Abortion

Condoms (*condons/condones* or *profilàctics/pro-filácticos*) and other forms of contraception are generally, but not always, available at pharmacies. A very few pharmacies still refuse to stock them on religious grounds. *See also chapter* **Women's Barcelona**.

Ambulatori les Drassanes/Centre de Planificació Familiar
Avda Drassanes 17-21 (329 44 95). Metro Drassanes/bus 14, 18, 38, 59, 91. **Open** 9am-2pm Mon-Fri.
A specialised family planning clinic. *See also* **Women's Barcelona**.

Complementary Medicine

Centre de Medicina Integral
Plaça Urquinaona 2, 3er 2na (318 30 50). Metro Urquinaona/bus all routes to Plaça Urquinaona. **Open** 10am-1pm, 4-8pm, Mon-Fri. **No credit cards.**
This centre provides acupuncture, homeopathy, chiropractics and virtually every other form of complementary medicine. There are some English-speaking practitioners on the staff.

Helplines

Alcoholics Anonymous
(317 77 77). **Open** 5-9pm Mon-Fri; 7-9pm Sat, Sun; answerphone at other times.
There are several English-speakers among the local AA groups.

Telèfon de l'Esperança
(418 48 48). **Open** *phoneline* 24 hours daily.
A privately-funded local helpline that caters for a wide range of needs, from psychiatric to legal. English is sometimes spoken, but it's not guaranteed.

Left Luggage

All have automatic, coin-operated luggage lockers:

Aeroport del Prat
Domestic flights terminal. **Open** 6am-midnight daily. **Rates** 600ptas per day.

Estació d'Autobusos Barcelona-Nord
C/Ali Bei 80. Metro Arc de Triomf/bus all routes to Arc de Triomf. **Open** 7am-9pm daily. **Rates** 300, 400, 600ptas per day.

Estació Marítima (Balearics Ferry Terminal)
Moll de Barcelona. Metro Drassanes/bus all routes to Passeig Colom. **Open** 8am-1am daily. **Rates** 300, 500ptas per day.

Train Stations
Open 4.30am-midnight daily. **Rates** 400, 600ptas per day.
There are lockers at Sants, Passeig de Gràcia and França, but not at any of the smaller Barcelona stations.

Lost Property

Airport & Rail stations
If you lose something land-side of check-in at **Prat Airport**, report the loss immediately to the *Aviación Civil* office in the relevant terminal, or call central airport information on 478 50 00. There is no central lost property depot for the RENFE rail network: if you think you have mislaid anything on a train, look for the *Atención al Viajero* desk or *Jefe de Estación* office at the nearest main station to where your property has gone astray, or call ahead to the destination station of the train. To get information by phone on lost property at main rail stations call their general information numbers and ask for *Objetos Perdidos*.

Pharmacies: look for the sign of the green 'X'.

Municipal Lost Property Office

Servei de Troballes *Ajuntament, C/Ciutat 9 (402 31 61). Metro Jaume I/bus 16, 17, 19, 45.* **Open** 8.30am-2.30pm Mon-Fri.

All items found on public transport and taxis in the city, or picked up by the police in the street, should eventually find their way to this office, with an entrance on the C/Ciutat side of the city hall. Within 24 hours of the loss you can also try ringing the individual services to check if anything has been found: **Buses** (441 29 99); **Metro** (456 64 00). For taxis, call the city hall office.

Police & Security

Like most European countries Spain has several police forces. In Barcelona the most important are the local *Guàrdia Urbana*, in navy and pale blue, and the *Policía Nacional*, in black and white uniforms. Each force has its own set of responsibilities, although at times they overlap. The *Urbanos* are principally concerned with traffic and parking problems and various local regulations. The force with primary responsibility for dealing with crime are the *Nacionales*. The *Guardia Civil*, in military green, are responsible for policing inter-city highways, for customs posts, and for guarding some government buildings, but are not often seen within Barcelona. The Catalan government police, the *Mossos d'Esquadra*, are taking over several of the Guardia Civil's powers outside of Barcelona.

If you are robbed or attacked you should report the incident as soon as possible to the special

tourist-attention police station or the nearest *Policía Nacional* station (*Comisaría*), which are listed in the local phone book. For police emergency phone numbers, *see* **Emergencies**.

Turisme-Atenció

La Rambla 43 (301 90 60). Metro Liceu/bus 14, 18, 38, 59, 91, N4, N6, N9. **Open** 24 hours daily.

A special station set up by the *Guàrdia Urbana*, in association with the *Policía Nacional*, to provide information assistance for foreign visitors in any kind of difficulty. Officers on duty can speak French, German, Italian and English. If you report a crime you will be asked to make an official statement (*Denuncia*), which will be typed out for you. It is of course unlikely that anything you have lost will be recovered, but you will need the *Denuncia* to make an insurance claim.

Lost Passports

The loss or theft of a passport must be reported immediately to the nearest *Comisaría*, and also to your national Consulate (*see above* **Consulates**). If you lose your passport over a weekend and have to travel on the Saturday or Sunday the consulate will charge for having to open the office specially and issue you with an emergency passport. The Spanish authorities and most airlines are often prepared to let you out of the country even without this document if you do not look suspicious and have other documents with you, including the police *Denuncia* confirming the loss of your passport, but in such cases it's advisable to be at the airport in plenty of time, and to be suitably prepared.

Public Toilets

Public toilets are not common in Barcelona. There are clean toilets with an attendant in Plaça Catalunya, in the RENFE vestibule, and at main rail stations, and there is also a toilet at the back of the Boqueria market. In many locations around the central area there are new-style cubicles of the pay-on-entry type that cost 25ptas. Apart from that, you are best advised to pop into a bar or café if in need. Major stores and fast-food restaurants are also useful stand-bys.

Religious Services

Anglican & Protestant

Saint George's Church *C/Sant Joan de la Salle 41 (418 60 78). FGC Av Tibidabo/bus 22, 64, 58, 75.* **Services** 12.30pm Wed; 11am Sun.

A British church that attracts a multi-cultural congregation.

Catholic Mass in English

Parròquia Maria Reina *Carretera d'Esplugues 103 (203 55 39). Bus 22, 60, 63, 64, 75, 114.* **English mass** 10am Sun.

Mass in English, followed by coffee and Sunday Schools for children and adults.

Jewish

Sinagoga de Barcelona *C/Avenir 24 (200 61 48). FGC Gràcia/bus 58, 64.* **Prayers** 8am, 9pm, Fri; 9am, 8.30pm, Sat; 8.30am Sun.

Moslem

Centre Islàmico *Avda Meridiana 326 (351 49 01). Metro Sagrera/bus 62.* **Prayers** 2.45pm Fri.

Further Reading

Several useful books on Barcelona are produced locally in English-language or bilingual editions, both by the city council (Ajuntament de Barcelona) and independent publishers, especially the Editorial Gustavo Gili. The best places to find most of them are the **Llibreria de la Virreina** city bookshop at La Rambla 99 (*see chapter* **Essential Information**) and the **Fundació la Caixa** in Passeig de Sant Joan.

Guides & Walks

Amelang, J, Gil, X & McDonogh, GW: *Twelve Walks through Barcelona's Past* (Aj. de Barcelona).
Well-thought out walks by historical themes ('Barcelona of the merchants', 'Bohemian Barcelona'). Original, and much better-informed than many walking guides.
García Espuche, Albert: *The Quadrat d'Or* (Aj. de Barcelona)
Building-by-building guide to the central Eixample, the 'Golden Square' of Modernist architecture.
González, A, & Lacuesta, R: *Barcelona Architecture Guide 1929-1994* (Ed. Gustavo Gili)
Thorough paperback guide to all of Barcelona's contemporary architecture.
Güell, Xavier: *Gaudí Guide* (Ed. Gustavo Gili)
Handy, with good background on all his work.
Pomés Leiz, Juliet, & Feriche, Ricardo: *Barcelona Design Guide* (Ed. Gustavo Gili)
An eccentrically wide-ranging but engaging listing of everything ever considered 'designer' in BCN.

History, Art, Architecture, Culture

Elliott, JH: *The Revolt of the Catalans*
Fascinating, highly detailed account of the *Guerra dels Segadors* and the Catalan revolt of the 1640s.
Fernández Armesto, Felipe: *Barcelona: A Thousand Years of the City's Past*
A solid, straightforward history.
Figueras, Lourdes *Domènech i Montaner*
Beautifully produced, bilingual-edition study of the classic Catalan Modernist architect.
Fraser, Ronald: *Blood of Spain*
An oral history of the Spanish Civil War and the tensions that preceded it, the most vivid account of this great conflagration: especially good on July 1936 in Barcelona.
Hughes, Robert: *Barcelona*
The most comprehensive single book on Barcelona in any language: tendentious at times, erratic, but wonderfully broad in scope and beautifully written, and covering every aspect of the city's history, legends, life and culture up to the 1900s.
Kaplan, Temma: *Red City, Blue Period – Social Movements in Picasso's Barcelona*
An interesting tracing of the interplay of avant-garde art and avant-garde politics in 1900s Barcelona.
Orwell, George: *Homage to Catalonia*
The classic account of Barcelona in revolution, by an often bewildered, always perceptive observer.
Paz, Abel: *Durruti: The People Armed*
Closer to its theme, a biography of the most legendary of Barcelona's anarchist revolutionaries.

Richardson, John: *A Life of Picasso, Vol. I, 1881-1906*
The definitive biography: volume I covers the whole of Picasso's Barcelona years among the *Modernistes*, and his later important visits to Catalonia.
Solà-Morales, Ignasi: *Fin de Siècle Architecture in Barcelona* (Ed. Gustavo Gili)
Large-scale and wide-ranging description and evaluation of the city's Modernist heritage.
Tóibín, Colm: *Homage to Barcelona*
Evocative and perceptive journey around the city: good on the booming Barcelona of the 1980s, but also excellent on Gothic architecture, Gaudí and Miró.
Vázquez Montalbán, Manuel: *Barcelonas*
Idiosyncratic but insightful reflections on the city and its history by one of its most prominent modern writers.
Zerbst, Rainer: *Antoni Gaudí*
Lavishly illustrated and comprehensive survey.

Literature

Calders, Pere: *The Virgin of the Railway and Other Stories*
Ironic, engaging, quirkily humourous stories by a Catalan writer who spent many years in exile in Mexico.
Català, Víctor: *Solitude*
The pseudonym of a woman novelist, Caterina Albert: this is her masterpiece, an intense, modernistic story from 1905 that shocked readers with its open treatment of female sexuality.
Martorell, Joanot, & Joan Martí de Gualba: *Tirant lo Blanc*
The first European prose novel, from 1490, a rambling, bawdy shaggy-dog story of travels, romances and chivalric adventures.
Mendoza, Eduardo: *City of Marvels* and *Year of the Flood*
Mendoza's sweeping, very entertaining saga of Barcelona between its great Exhibitions, 1888 and 1929, and a more recent novel of passions in the city of the 1950s.
Moncada, Jesús: *The Towpath*
A powerful contemporary novel of rural Catalonia.
Oliver, Maria Antònia: *Antipodes* and *Study in Lilac*
Two adventures of Barcelona's first feminist detective.
Rodoreda, Mercè: *The Time of the Doves* and *My Christina and Other Stories*
A translation of *La Plaça del Diamant*, most widely-read of all Catalan novels, the poignant, finely-worked story of a great survivor, Colometa, from a Gràcia shop in the thirties to the aftermath of the Civil War. Plus a collection of similarly bitter-sweet short tales by the same author.
Vázquez Montalbán, Manuel: *The Angst-Ridden Executive* and *An Olympic Death*
Two thrillers starring Vázquez Montalbán's detective and gourmet extraordinaire, Pepe Carvalho.

Food & Drink

Andrews, Colman: *Catalan Cuisine*
A mine of information on food and much else besides (but also with usable recipes). Unfortunately no longer in print in the UK, but worth looking for.
Casas, Penelope: *Food and Wines of Spain*
A useful general guide.

Index

Advertisers' Index

Maps

Welcome to New York. Now get out.

On sale in New York every Wednesday, at all airports with flights to New York and at selected newsagents and bookshops around central London.

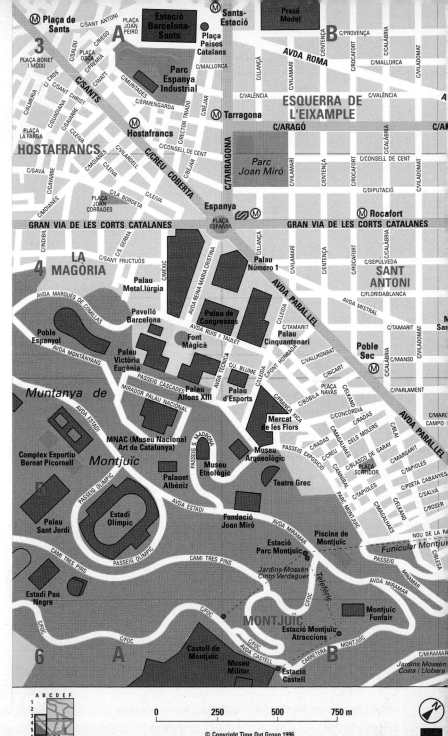

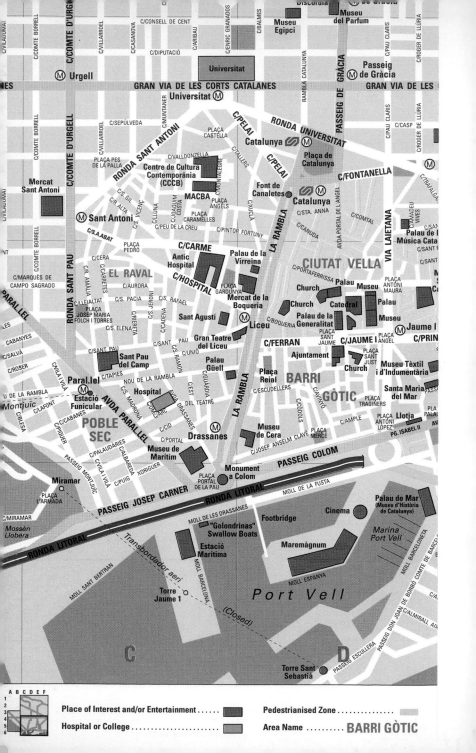

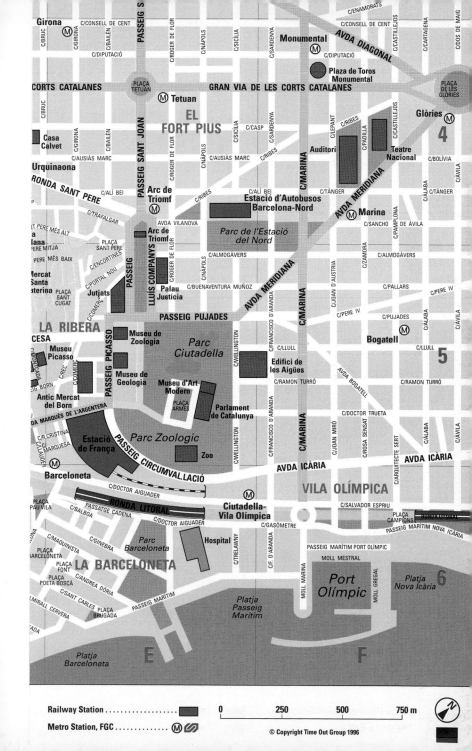

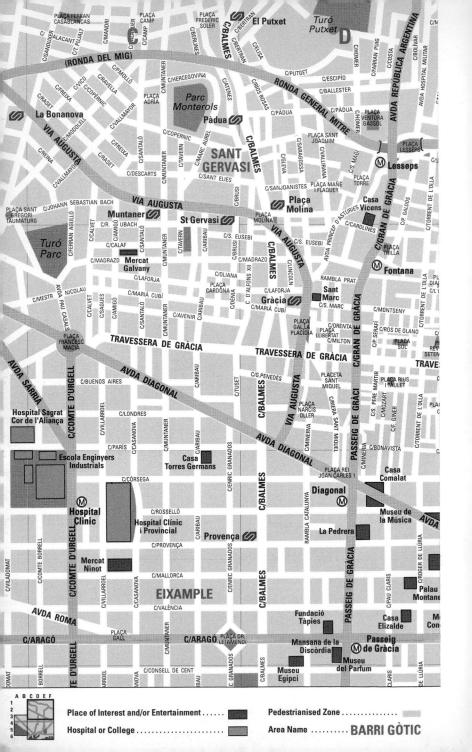

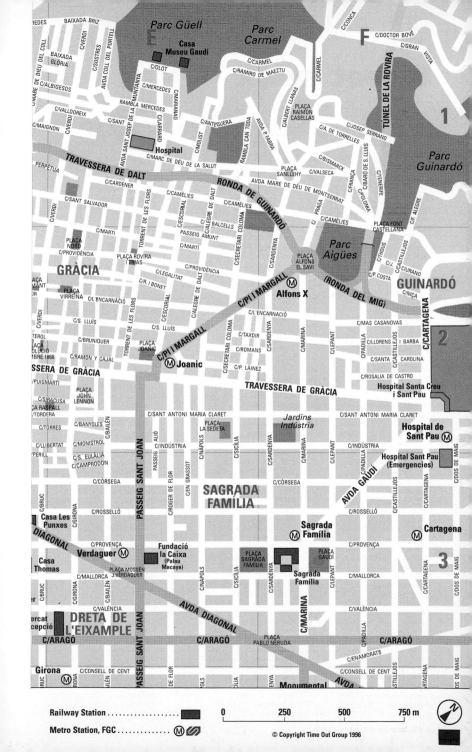

Street Index

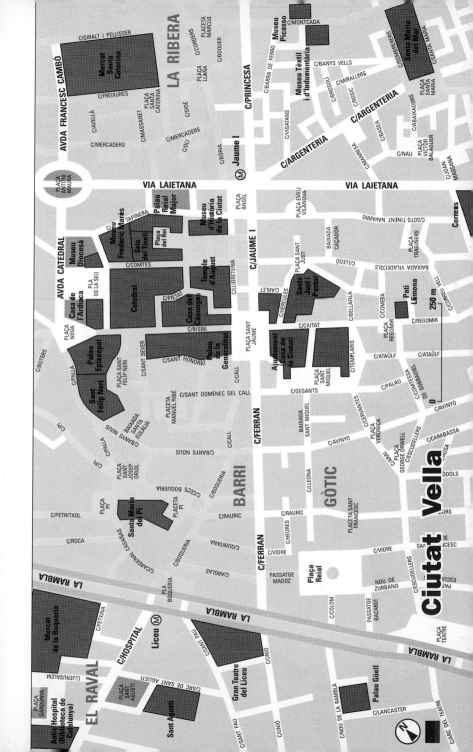

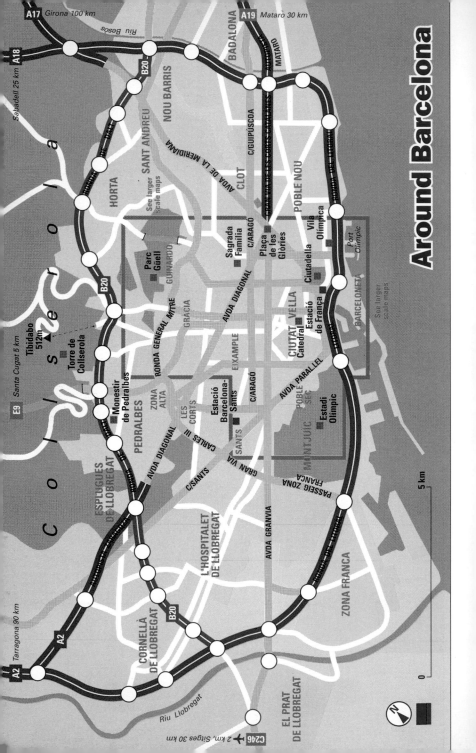

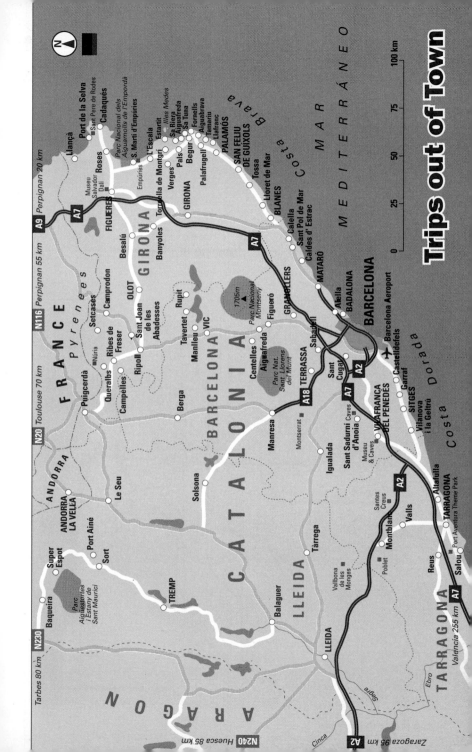

Trips out of Town

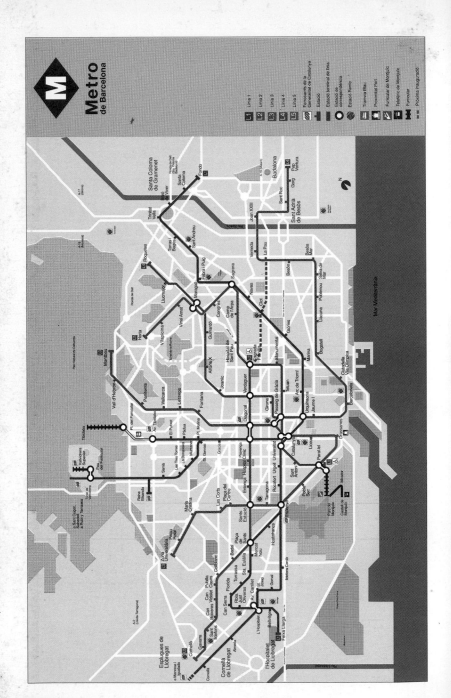